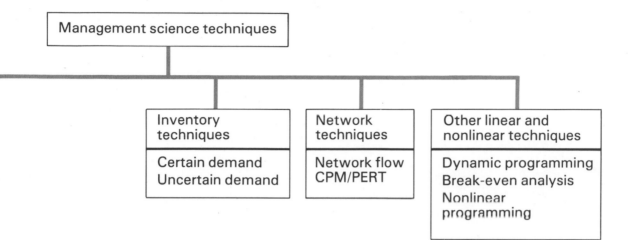

THIRD EDITION

Introduction to
Management Science

Bernard W. Taylor III

Virginia Polytechnic Institute and State University

ALLYN AND BACON Boston London Sydney Toronto

To the memory of my grandfather,

Bernard W. Taylor, Sr.

Series editor: Cary Tengler
Senior editorial assistant: Kelley Saunders-Butcher
Interior designer: Deborah Schneck
Cover administrator: Linda Dickinson
Composition buyer: Linda Cox
Manufacturing buyer: William Alberti
Editorial-production service: Lifland et al., Bookmakers

Library of Congress Cataloging-in-Publication Data

Taylor, Bernard W.
    Introduction to management science / Bernard W. Taylor III. — 3rd ed.
      p. cm.
    Includes bibliographies and index.
    ISBN 0-205-12132-2
    1. Management science. I. Title.
    T56.T38   1990   89-35521
    658 — dc20   CIP

Printed in the United States of America

10 9 8 7 6 5 4 3 2 94 93 92 91 90 89

Preface

A Note to the Student

Before writing this book I tried to recall the reasons I did not like many of the quantitatively oriented textbooks that I had used when I was a student. One prominent reason was that many of the texts consisted of long, sprawling chapters that tried to explain everything about a quantitative technique without giving very many examples. Therefore, I have written short, concise chapters centered around simple, straightforward examples that demonstrate in detail the fundamentals of the techniques. I have presented these examples so that you can easily apply the same solution steps to homework and test problems.

I have attempted to write a book that can be understood by students with limited mathematical backgrounds and by those who haven't had a math course for several quarters or semesters. Thus, when I begin to cover a particular quantitative technique, I do not automatically assume that students understand the mathematical underpinnings. This policy is followed both in chapters on relatively easy topics and in those dealing with what are often perceived as more complex management science techniques—integer programming and dynamic programming. As you read, you should find that topics you thought would be very hard are presented in such a way that they are not that difficult.

Students often have difficulty perceiving the usefulness of quantitative courses in general. When I was a student, I did not foresee how I would use such material in any position I might hold. Part of the problem is that the examples used in texts often do not appear to be realistic. However, examples must be made simple to facilitate the learning process. More realistic examples reflecting actual applications would be so complex that they would not help a student learn a technique. Let me assure you, though, that the techniques presented in this text are already being used extensively in the real world and their use is increasing rapidly. Therefore, the chances of using the techniques you learn from this text in a future course or job are very high. To demonstrate the usefulness of these techniques in the real world, I have included in many chapters an "Applications" section that documents actual applications of management science.

Even if you do not use these techniques when you get a job, the logical approach to problem solving incorporated in management science or quantitative methods is valuable for all types of jobs in all types of organizations. Management science consists of more than just a collection of techniques; it embodies a philosophy of approaching a problem in a logical manner, as does any science. Thus, this text not only teaches you specific techniques but also provides a method for approaching problems that will be very useful in your future endeavors.

A Note to the Instructor

I had two primary objectives in mind when I originally wrote this text, neither of which has been altered during the preparation of this third edition. First, I wanted the text to be comprehensive, containing all of the topics normally considered to be part of the field of management science. Second, I wanted the text to be readable.

The first objective, comprehensiveness, was attained by including twenty-four chapters that encompass the major topics in the field of management science. This format allows the book to be employed in a variety of course structures. The organization of the various techniques presented in this text is shown on the front endpaper.

The second objective, readability, was accomplished primarily by creating succinct chapters that avoid rambling discussions of the subtleties and nuances of a technique. In each chapter I have concentrated on the fundamentals of one topic or several closely related topics, rather than combining several areas of coverage in a single chapter. The techniques presented in each chapter are explained with straightforward examples that avoid lengthy written explanations. These examples are organized in a logical step-by-step solution approach that the student can subsequently apply to the problems. An attempt has been made to avoid complex mathematical notation and formulas wherever possible. These various factors help to ensure that students will assimilate the material.

To facilitate the learning process and to update the text, I have made two major additions to this edition. First, I have added an "Example Problem Solution" immediately before the problems section in most of the chapters in the text. I hope that it will help students in working the problems. Second, I have demonstrated the use of computer software packages for most of the techniques in these chapters and have increased the emphasis in the text on computerized solutions. The text now contains computer output from LINDO, QSB+, Super LINDO/PC, GINO, and Minitab. In addition to these packages, the text also demonstrates and features output from

Render and Stair's Microcomputer Software for Management Science, 2nd edition, and Lee and Shim's Micro Manager. Several software packages are available for purchase with this textbook, to provide instructors and students with an easy-to-use integrated textbook and software package.

Introduction to Management Science provides many pedagogical aids for the student. Each chapter begins with a *chapter outline* that gives a brief overview of topics covered in the chapter. *Marginal notes* help the student quickly locate specific topics, and a complete *glossary* of all the key terms is included at the end of the text. In addition, the *solutions* to all of the odd-numbered problems appear at the end of the text.

Many quantitative methods or management science texts are criticized because they contain a limited number of problems. In this third edition, the number of problems has been increased by more than 10 percent. There are now over 600 end-of-chapter problems, many with multiple parts. These problems are organized to coincide with the way the material is presented in the chapter. The problems range from very easy to very challenging. The Instructor's Manual that accompanies this text contains detailed solutions to all problems, as well as over 100 transparency masters of figures and tables from the text.

Also available is a revised Study Guide (authored by Michael Klein of Loyola University of New Orleans) that has a chapter corresponding to each chapter in the text. Each chapter consists of an outline of the text chapter, quizzes (answers are given in the back of the Study Guide), additional problems that are solved in detail, and cases whose solutions are contained in a separate Case Solutions Manual. A separate Test Bank contains over 800 short-answer questions, true/false questions, multiple-choice questions, and problems, as well as their solutions.

The text and its associated materials comprise a comprehensive package that is flexible enough to accommodate a broad range of management science course structures. The material in this package should provide the student with a thorough understanding of the individual management science techniques and an overall comprehension of the management science process.

Acknowledgments

Like any large project, the revision of a textbook is not accomplished without the help of many people. The third edition of this book is no exception, and I would like to take this opportunity to thank those who have contributed to its preparation. First, I would like to thank my friend and colleague, Larry Moore, for his help in developing the organization and approach of the original edition of this book and for his many suggestions during its revisions. We spent many hours discussing what an introductory text in management science should contain, and his ideas appear in these pages. Larry also served as a sounding board for many ideas regarding content, design, and preparation, and he read and edited many portions of the text, for which I am very grateful. I thank my colleagues at Virginia Tech, Loren Rees, Ernie Houck, and Robin Russell, for their valued assistance and many helpful suggestions. I also thank the reviewers of this third edition: William R. Brown, Towson State University; Kenneth Darby-Dowman, Polytechnic of Central London; Ed Fisher, Central Michigan State University; Ronald E. Jablonski, University of Illinois; Frank Kokotajlo, University of Nebraska, Omaha; Patrick Lee, Penn State University; and Jay Varzandeh, Arizona State University. I remain indebted to the reviewers of the first and second editions: James C. Goodwin, Jr., Richard Gunther, Robert L. Ludke, Robert D. Lynch, Mildred Massey, and Lisa Sokol. I am also very grateful to Gerry Chenault at Virginia Tech for her typing and editorial assistance. Finally, I would like to thank Kelley Saunders-Butcher and Carolyn Harris at Allyn and Bacon and Sally Lifland and Quica Ostrander at Lifland et al., whose patience and encouragement, as well as the organization they lent to the project, are greatly appreciated.

Contents

9 Goal Programming   303

10 Probability   339

11 Decision Analysis   375

12 Game Theory   427

13 Markov Analysis   457

14 Queuing Analysis   487

15 Simulation   517

16 Forecasting   565

17 Inventory Analysis with Certain Demand   603

18 Inventory Analysis with Uncertain Demand   639

19 Network Flow Models   665

20 CPM and PERT Network Analysis   699

1

Management Science

Management science is the application of a scientific approach to solving management problems in order to help managers make better decisions. As implied by this definition, management science encompasses a number of mathematically oriented techniques that have either been developed within the field of management science or been adapted from other disciplines, such as the natural sciences, mathematics, statistics, and engineering. This text provides an introduction to the techniques comprising management science and demonstrates their applications to management problems.

A scientific approach to management

Management science, although rather young, is a recognized and established discipline in the field of business administration. The applications of management science techniques are widespread, and they have been frequently credited with increasing the efficiency and productivity of business firms. In a 1975 survey responded to by 275 firms, approximately 50% indicated that they

1

used management science techniques, and 80% rated the results to be very good.[1] In a 1982 survey of corporate executives, over two-thirds of the respondents indicated that the effectiveness of management science in their firm was good or excellent, and none assigned a poor rating.[2] The increasing popularity of management science is reflected in the number of colleges and universities offering undergraduate courses and degree programs in management science. Management science (also referred to as *operations research, quantitative methods, quantitative analysis,* and *decision sciences*) is now part of the fundamental curriculum of most programs in business administration.

As you proceed through the presentations of the various management science models and techniques contained in this text, several items should be remembered. First, most of the examples presented in this text will be for business organizations, because businesses represent the main users of management science. However, management science techniques can be applied to solve problems in a variety of different types of organizations including government, military, business and industry, and health care. Second, for the mathematical techniques presented, manual solution will be emphasized, as the purpose of this text is to teach techniques and to illustrate how they are applied to problems in order to assist managers in making decisions. However, *computerized solution* is possible in every case, and when feasible and conducive to the presentation, computerized solutions will be demonstrated.

Finally, as the various management science techniques are presented, keep in mind that management science consists of more than just a collection of techniques. Management science also involves the philosophy of approaching a problem in a logical manner (i.e., a scientific approach). The logical, consistent, and systematic approach to problem solving can be as useful (and valuable) as the knowledge of the mechanics of the mathematical techniques themselves. This thought is especially important for those readers who do not always see the immediate benefit of studying mathematically oriented disciplines such as management science.

Management science can be used in a variety of organizations

Computerized solution

Management science encompasses a logical approach to problem solving

THE MANAGEMENT SCIENCE APPROACH TO PROBLEM SOLVING

As indicated in the previous section, management science encompasses a logical, systematic approach to problem solving, which

---

[1]N. Gaither, "The Adoption of Operations Research Techniques by Manufacturing Organizations," *Decision Sciences* 6, no. 4 (October 1975): 797–813.

[2]G. Forgionne, "Corporate Management Science Activities: An Update," *Interfaces* 13, no. 3 (June 1983): 20–23.

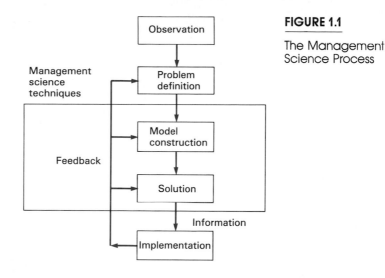

FIGURE 1.1

The Management
Science Process

closely parallels what is known as the *scientific method* for attacking problems. This approach, as shown in Figure 1.1, follows a generally recognized, ordered set of steps: (1) observation, (2) definition of the problem, (3) model construction, (4) model solution, and (5) implementation of solution results. We will analyze each of these steps individually.

The scientific method

Observation

The first step in the management science process is the identification of a problem that exists in the system (organization). The system must be continuously and closely observed so that problems can be identified as soon as they occur or are anticipated. Problems are not always the result of a crisis that must be reacted to, but instead frequently involve an anticipatory or planning situation. The person who normally identifies a problem is the manager, since the manager is the one who works in the vicinity of places where problems might occur. However, problems can often be identified by a *management scientist*, a person skilled in the techniques of management science and trained to identify problems, who has been hired specifically to solve problems using management science techniques.

Identifying the problem

The management scientist

Definition of the Problem

Once it has been determined that a problem exists, the problem must be clearly and concisely *defined*. Improperly defining a problem can easily result in no solution or an inappropriate solution. Therefore, the limits of the problem and the degree to which it pervades

Defining the objectives of the organization

other units of the organization must be included in the problem definition. Since the existence of a problem implies that the objectives of the firm are not being met in some way, the goals (or objectives) of the organization must also be clearly defined. A stated objective helps to focus attention on what the problem actually is.

Model Construction

A management science *model* is an abstract representation of an existing problem situation. It can be in the form of a graph or chart, but most frequently a management science model consists of a set of mathematical relationships. These mathematical relationships are made up of numbers and symbols.

As an example, consider a business firm that sells a product. The product costs $5 to produce and sells for $20. A model that computes the total profit that will accrue from the items sold is

$$Z = \$20x - 5x$$

Variables

In this equation x represents the number of units of the product that are sold, and Z represents the total profit that results from the sale of the product. The *symbols x* and *Z are variables*. The term *variable* is used because no set numerical value has been specified for these items. The number of units sold, x, and the profit, Z, can be any amount (within limits); they can vary. These two variables can be further distinguished. Z is a *dependent variable*, because its value is dependent on the number of units sold; x is an *independent variable*, since the number of units sold is *not* dependent on anything else (in this equation).

Dependent variable
Independent variable

Parameters

The numbers $20 and $5 in the equation are referred to as *parameters*. Parameters are constant values that are generally coefficients of the variables (symbols) in an equation. Parameters usually remain constant during the process of solving a specific problem. The parameter values are derived from *data* (i.e., pieces of information) from the problem environment. Sometimes the data are readily available and quite accurate. For example, presumably the selling price of $20 and product cost of $5 could be obtained from the firm's accounting department and would be very accurate. However, sometimes data are not as readily available to the manager or firm, and the parameters must be either estimated or based on a combination of the available data and estimates. In such cases, the model is only as accurate as the data used in constructing the model.

Data

Functional relationship

The equation as a whole is known as a *functional relationship* (also called function and relationship). The term is derived from the fact that profit, Z, is a *function* of the number of units sold, x, and the equation *relates* profit to units sold.

Since only one functional relationship exists in this example, it is also the *model*. In this case the relationship is a model of the determination of profit for the firm. However, this model does not really replicate a problem. Therefore, we will expand our example to create a problem situation.

Let us assume that the product is made from steel and that the business firm has 100 pounds of steel available. If it takes 4 pounds of steel to make each unit of the product, we can develop an additional mathematical relationship to represent steel use:

$4x = 100$ lb of steel

This equation indicates that for every unit produced, 4 of the available 100 pounds of steel will be used. Now our model consists of two relationships:

$Z = \$20x - 5x$
$4x = 100$

We say that the profit equation in this new model is an *objective function*, and the resource equation is a *constraint*. In other words, the objective of the firm is to achieve as much profit, Z, as possible, but the firm is constrained from achieving an infinite profit by the limited amount of steel available. To signify this distinction between the two relationships in this model, we will add the following notations:

maximize $Z = \$20x - 5x$
subject to
    $4x = 100$

This model now represents the manager's problem of determining the number of units to produce. You will recall that we defined the number of units to be produced as x. Thus, when we determine the value of x, it represents a potential (or recommended) *decision* for the manager. Therefore, x is also known as a *decision variable*. The next step in the management science process is to solve the model to determine the value of the decision variable.

Model Solution

Once models have been constructed in management science, they are solved using the management science techniques presented in this text. A management science solution technique usually applies to a specific type of model. Thus, the model type and solution method are both part of the management science technique. We are able to say that *a model is solved,* since the model represents a problem. When we refer to model solution we also mean problem solution.

For the example model developed in the previous section,

maximize $Z = \$20x - 5x$

subject to

$4x = 100$

the solution technique is simple algebra. Solving the constraint equation for x, we have

$4x = 100$

$x = 100/4$

$x = 25$ units

Substituting the value of 25 for x into the profit function results in the total profit:

$Z = \$20x - 5x$

$= 20(25) - 5(25)$

$= \$375$

Thus, if the manager decides to produce 25 units of the product, the business firm will receive $375 in profit. Note, however, that the value of the decision variable does not constitute an actual decision; rather, it is *information* that serves as a recommendation or guideline, helping the manager make a decision.

Some management science techniques do not generate an answer or a recommended decision. Instead, they provide *descriptive results:* results that describe the system being modeled. For example, suppose the business firm of our example desires to know the average number of units sold each month during a year. The monthly *data* (i.e., sales) for the past year are as follows:

Month	*Sales*
January	30
February	40
March	25
April	60
May	30
June	25
July	35
August	50
September	60
October	40
November	35
December	50
Total	480 units

Monthly sales average 40 units ($480 \div 12$). This result is not a decision; it is a value describing what is happening in the system. The results of the management science techniques in this text are ex-

Information to aid in making a decision

Descriptive results

amples of the two types shown in this section: (1) solutions/decisions or (2) descriptive results.

Implementation of Results

The management science technique provides information that can aid the manager in making a decision. Of course, the manager does not rigidly apply the results of a management science model solution without contemplation. In making the ultimate decision, the manager must combine the information obtained with his or her own expertise and experience. If the manager does not use the information derived from the management science technique, the results are not *implemented* (i.e., they are not put to use). If the results are not implemented, the effort and resources that went into problem definition, model construction, and solution are wasted. Thus, the last step in the management science process cannot be ignored. An effort must be made to ensure that the results will be used (assuming that the results are applicable).

Ensuring that management science results are used

Management Science as an Ongoing Process

Completion of the five steps described above does not necessarily mean that the management science process has been completed. The model results and the decisions based on the results provide *feedback* to the original model. The original management science model can then be modified to test different conditions and decisions the manager thinks might occur in the future. Or, the results may indicate that a problem exists that had not been considered previously; if so, the original model can be altered or reconstructed. Because models can be modified or reconstructed, the management science process can be continuous rather than simply providing one solution to one problem.

Model feedback

MANAGEMENT SCIENCE TECHNIQUES

This text focuses primarily on two of the five steps of the management science process: model construction and solution. These are the two steps that use the management science technique. In a textbook, it is difficult to show how an unstructured real-world problem is identified and defined, since the problems must be written out. However, once a problem statement has been given, we can show how a model is constructed and a solution is derived. The techniques presented in this text can be loosely classified into five categories, as shown in Figure 1.2.

Focusing on model construction and solution

Model classification

FIGURE 1.2

Classification of Management Science Techniques

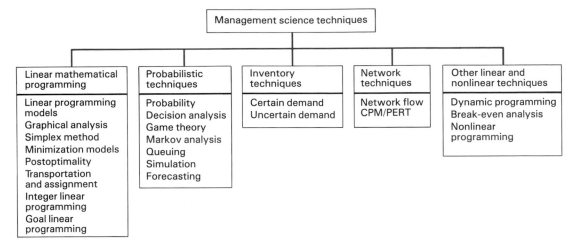

Linear Mathematical Programming Techniques

Chapters 2 through 9 present the techniques that comprise *linear mathematical programming*. (The first example used to demonstrate model construction earlier in this chapter was a very rudimentary linear programming model.) The term *programming* used to identify this technique does not refer to computer programming, but rather to a predetermined set of mathematical steps used to solve a problem. This particular class of techniques holds a predominant position in this text because it includes some of the more frequently used and popular techniques in management science.

Programming as a predetermined set of mathematical solution steps

Probabilistic Techniques

Probabilistic techniques are presented in Chapters 10 through 16. These techniques are distinguished from mathematical programming techniques in that the results are probabilistic. Mathematical programming techniques assume that all parameters in the models are known with *certainty*. Therefore, the solution results are assumed to be known with certainty, with no probability that other solutions might exist. A technique that assumes certainty in its solution is referred to as *deterministic*. In contrast, the results from a probabilistic technique *do* contain uncertainty, with some possibility that alternative solutions might exist. In the model solution presented earlier in this chapter, the result of the first example ($x = 25$ units to produce) is deterministic, whereas the result of the second example (an average of 40 units sold each month) is probabilistic.

Techniques with model parameters that are not known with certainty

Inventory Techniques

Chapters 17 and 18 present *inventory techniques*. These techniques are specifically designed for the analysis of inventory problems frequently encountered by business firms. This particular business function is singled out because it represents a significant area of cost for almost every business. Notice that this category is divided into probabilistic and deterministic techniques. Thus, at least part of this class of management science techniques could be included in the category of probabilistic techniques. That is why Figure 1.2 represents a *loose* classification of techniques. Many of the techniques cross over between classifications.

Network Techniques

Networks, the topic of Chapters 19 and 20, consist of models that are represented as diagrams rather than strictly mathematical relationships. As such, these models offer a pictorial representation of the system under analysis. These models represent either probabilistic or deterministic systems.

A pictorial representation of a system

Other Linear and Nonlinear Techniques

Chapters 21 through 23 include management science techniques that have linear and/or nonlinear components. Dynamic programming, presented in Chapter 21, is a form of mathematical programming that employs a modeling and solution logic different from that of linear programming. The models in Chapters 22 and 23 employ *calculus* as part of the solution method. Chapter 22 on break-even analysis includes calculus in its most elementary form. An extension of break-even analysis provides an excellent example of a calculus-based model, which is why it is included at this point in the text.

Calculus-based models

The final topics in this text, presented in Chapter 24, are *information and decision support systems* and *implementation*. These two topics do not actually encompass specific management science techniques. Instead, these topics characterize ways in which management science models and results interface with the manager.

Information systems
Implementation

BUSINESS USAGE OF MANAGEMENT SCIENCE TECHNIQUES

Not all management science techniques are equally useful or equally used by business firms and other organizations. Some techniques are used quite frequently by business practitioners and managers; others are rarely used. Several surveys have been conducted to deter-

Surveys of management science usage

mine the degree to which various management science techniques are used by practitioners in academia, government, and business and industry. The results of one survey, conducted in 1980 by Shannon, Long, and Buckles, are shown in Table 1.1.

These survey results indicate the percentage of survey respondents from academia, government, and industry who have used the listed management science techniques, and they provide a ranking of the techniques based on their perceived usefulness (referred to in the study as *utility*). All of the techniques listed in Table 1.1 are included in this text except replacement analysis (a financial analysis/capital budgeting procedure relating to machine replacement).

Survey of corporate executives

Another survey study of corporate executives, conducted in 1983 by Forgionne, yielded results somewhat similar to those shown in Table 1.1. The results of this survey, presented in Table 1.2, indicate the frequency of use of eight management science techniques.

The technique referred to in Table 1.2 as "statistical analysis" encompasses such topics as probability analysis, regression, hypothesis testing, exponential smoothing, and statistical sampling. Although some of these topics are reviewed in this text, they are covered more thoroughly in separate courses on statistical analysis.

The results of both surveys show that the most frequently used techniques are linear programming, simulation, and network analysis (CPM/PERT), and that some techniques, such as game theory, are used rather infrequently. An attempt has been made in this text to provide a comprehensive treatment of all the topics generally considered within the field of management science, regardless of how frequently they are used. Although some topics may have limited direct applicability, their study can reveal informative and unique

TABLE 1.1

Survey Results Indicating the Usage and Usefulness of Management Science Techniques

Technique	% Usage	Utility Rank
Linear programming	83.8%	2
Simulation	80.3	1
Network analysis	58.1	4
Queueing theory	54.7	7
Decision trees	54.7	3
Replacement analysis	38.5	5
Integer programming	38.5	6
Dynamic programming	32.5	11
Markov processes	31.6	10
Nonlinear programming	30.7	9
Goal programming	20.5	8
Game theory	13.7	12

Reprinted with permission from AIIE TRANSACTIONS, December 1980. Copyright Institute of Industrial Engineers, 25 Technology Park/Atlanta, Norcross, GA 30092.

TABLE 1.2

Survey Results Indicating Frequency of Use of
Management Science Techniques

Technique	Frequent or Moderate Use (% of Respondents)
Statistical analysis	98.4%
Computer simulation	87.1
CPM/PERT	74.2
Linear programming	74.2
Queueing theory	59.7
Nonlinear programming	46.8
Dynamic programming	38.7
Game theory	30.6

Reprinted by permission of G. Forgionne, "Corporate
Management Science Activities: An Update," in
Interfaces, 13, 3, June 1983. Copyright 1983 The Institute
of Management Sciences.

means of approaching a problem and can often enhance one's understanding of the decision-making process.

Additional results from the Forgionne survey indicate the frequency with which management science techniques are applied to
selected areas in business firms. Although these results, displayed
in Table 1.3, touch upon only some of the general areas to which
management science has been applied in business firms, they do
provide some indication of the variety and breadth of management
science applications and of the potential for applying management
science, not only in business and industry, but in government,
health care, and service organizations as well. In this text, the appli-

Areas of management science application

TABLE 1.3

Survey Results Indicating the Frequency with Which
Management Science Techniques Are Applied to
Selected Business Areas

Area	Frequent or Moderate Application (% of Respondents)
Project planning	66.2%
Capital budgeting	59.6
Production planning	56.4
Inventory analysis	51.6
Accounting	50.0
Marketing planning	46.8
Quality control	41.9
Plant location	40.3
Maintenance policy	38.7
Personnel management	32.3

Reprinted by permission of G. Forgionne, "Corporate
Management Science Activities: An Update," in *Interfaces*, 13,
3, June 1983. Copyright 1983 The Institute of Management
Sciences.

cability of management science to a variety of problem areas is demonstrated via individual chapter examples and the problems that accompany each chapter.

A small portion of the thousands of applications of management science that occur each year are recorded in various academic and professional journals. Frequently these journal articles are as complex as the applications themselves and are very difficult to read. However, one particular journal, called *Interfaces*, is devoted specifically to the application of management science and is written not just for college professors, but for business people, practitioners, and students as well. *Interfaces* is published jointly by The Institute of Management Sciences, an international professional organization whose members include college professors, business people, scientists, students, and a variety of professional people interested in the practice and application of management science, and the Operations Research Society of America.

Interfaces regularly publishes articles that report on the application of management science to a wide variety of problems. The chapters that follow will present examples from *Interfaces* of applications of management science. These examples, as presented here, do not detail the actual models and the model components. Instead, they briefly indicate the type of problem the company or organization faced, the objective of the solution approach developed to solve the problem, and the benefits derived from the model or technique (i.e., what was accomplished). The interested reader who desires more detailed information about these and other management science applications is encouraged to go to the library and peruse *Interfaces* and the many other journals that contain articles on the application of management science.

MANAGEMENT SCIENCE SOFTWARE AND COMPUTERIZED SOLUTIONS

In recent years the personal computer and accompanying software have proliferated in schools of business. The number of students and faculty who have access to personal computers has increased dramatically in just the past five years, and will undoubtedly continue to increase at a rapid rate. This development has had a significant impact on the teaching of management science. According to a survey by Render and Stair, in 1985 there were only a few management science/quantitative software packages available, but by 1986 almost 40% of the 160 schools surveyed were using management science software of some form.[3] Whereas in 1984 there were very few

---

[3]B. Render and R. Stair, "Note: A Microcomputer Revolution in the School of Business," *Interfaces* 15, no. 5 (1985): 35–38.

management science software packages, or software packages with management science capabilities, by 1988 the number of available software packages was in the hundreds.

Management science software and the personal computer have done more than serve as teaching aids. By making it much more convenient and easier to solve management science problems, they have broadened the popularity of management science in schools of business. As a result, more and more students are receiving training in management science techniques and carrying this training with them into the business world.

Correspondingly, the application of management science techniques in business has increased dramatically. One reason is simply that management science techniques are easier to apply with the personal computer and software. Another is that managers are discovering more areas in which management science techniques can be applied.

In this text the capability of various management science software packages to solve management science problems will be demonstrated. Although such software packages have many capabilities and techniques in common, they also differ in the number and types of problems they will solve. All of the management science software packages that will be demonstrated here are similar in that they are relatively inexpensive (most costing no more than a textbook), user-friendly, and easy to interpret and have accompanying documentation that is easy to read.

Summary

In the chapters that follow, the model construction and solutions that comprise each management science technique are presented in detail and illustrated with examples. In fact, the primary method of presenting the techniques will be through examples. Thus, the text offers the reader a broad spectrum of knowledge of the mechanics of management science techniques and the types of problems to which these techniques are applied. However, the ultimate test of a management scientist or a manager who uses management science techniques is the ability to transfer textbook knowledge to the business world. In such instances there is an *art* to the application of management science, but it is an art predicated on practical experience and sound textbook knowledge. Providing the first of these necessities is beyond the scope of textbooks; providing the second is the objective of this text.

Management science as an art

References

Ackoff, Russell L., and Sasieni, Maurice W. *Fundamentals of Operations Research.* New York: John Wiley and Sons, 1968.

Beer, Stafford. *Management Sciences: The Business Use of Operations Research.* New York: Doubleday, 1967.

Churchman, C. W.; Ackoff, R. L.; and Arnoff, E. L. *Introduction to Operations Research.* New York: John Wiley and Sons, 1957.

Fabrycky, W. J., and Torgersen, P. E. *Operations Economy: Industrial Applications of Operations Research.* Englewood Cliffs, N.J.: Prentice-Hall, 1966.

Forgionne, G. "Corporate Management Science Activities: An Update." *Interfaces* 13, no. 3 (June 1983): 20–23.

Gaither, N. "The Adoption of Operations Research Techniques by Manufacturing Organizations." *Decision Sciences* 6, no. 4 (October 1975): 797–813.

Hillier, F. S., and Lieberman, G. J. *Operations Research.* 4th ed. San Francisco: Holden-Day, 1987.

Lee, Sang M.; Moore, Laurence J.; and Taylor, Bernard W. *Management Science.* 3d ed. Boston: Allyn and Bacon, 1990.

Shannon, R.; Long, S.; and Buckles, B. "Operation Research Methodologies in Industrial Engineering: A Survey." *AIIE Transactions* 12, no. 4 (December 1980): 364–67.

Taha, Hamdy A. *Operations Research, An Introduction.* 4th ed. New York: Macmillan, 1987.

Teichroew, P. *An Introduction to Management Science.* New York: John Wiley and Sons, 1964.

Wagner, Harvey M. *Principles of Management Science*, Englewood Cliffs, N. J.: Prentice-Hall, 1975.

Wagner, Harvey M. *Principles of Operations Research.* 2d ed. Englewood Cliffs, N.J.: Prentice-Hall, 1975.

Problems

1. Define *management science.*

2. Discuss what the management science approach to problem solving encompasses.

3. What are the steps in the scientific method for solving problems?

4. What is a management scientist?

5. How is problem definition related to the objectives of an organization?

6. Explain what a model is and how it is used in management science.

7. Distinguish among dependent variables, independent variables, and decision variables.

8. Define a *functional relationship.*

9. What are model parameters?

10. Discuss how constraints, the objective function, and decision variables are related in a management science model.

11. Distinguish between model results that recommend a decision and model results that are descriptive.

12. A company makes wooden tables. The company sells each table for $100, and it costs $40 to make a table. The company has 500 pounds of wood, and each table requires 25 pounds of wood. The company wants to know how many tables to make. Develop a model for this problem situation and solve it to determine the number of tables to produce.

13. Why is management science an ongoing process?

14. What does implementation mean?

15. Outline the different categories of techniques presented in this chapter.

2

Introduction to Linear Programming:
Model Formulation

Many major decisions faced by a manager of a business enterprise are centered around the best way to achieve the objectives of the firm subject to the restrictions placed on the manager by the operating environment. These restrictions can take the form of limited resources, such as time, labor, energy, material, or money; or they can be in the form of restrictive guidelines, such as a recipe for making cereal or engineering specifications. In general, the most frequent objective of business firms is to gain the most profit possible, or, in other words, to *maximize* profit. The objective of individual organizational units within a firm (such as a production or packaging department) is often to *minimize* cost. When a manager attempts to solve a general type of problem by seeking an objective that is subject to restrictions, the management science technique called *linear programming* is frequently used.

There are three steps in applying the linear programming technique. First, the problem must be identified as being solvable by linear programming. Second, the unstructured problem must be formulated as a mathematical model. Third, the model must be solved using established mathematical techniques. The linear programming technique derives its name from the fact that the functional relationships in the mathematical model are *linear* and the solution technique consists of predetermined mathematical steps, i.e., a *program.* In this chapter we will concern ourselves primarily with the formulation of the mathematical model that represents the problem. In subsequent chapters the various solution techniques will be presented.

MODEL FORMULATION

A linear programming model consists of certain common components and characteristics. The model components include decision variables, an objective function, and model constraints, which consist of decision variables and parameters. *Decision variables* are mathematical symbols that represent levels of activity by the firm. For example, an electrical manufacturing firm desires to produce x_1 radios, x_2 toasters, and x_3 clocks, where x_1, x_2, and x_3 are symbols representing unknown variable quantities of each item. The final values of x_1, x_2, and x_3, as determined by the firm, constitute a *decision* (e.g., $x_1 = 10$ radios is a decision by the firm to produce 10 radios).

The *objective function* is a linear mathematical relationship that describes the objective of the firm in terms of the decision variables. The objective function always consists of either *maximizing* or *minimizing* some value (e.g., maximize the profit or minimize the cost of producing radios).

The *model constraints* are also linear relationships of the decision variables; they represent the restrictions placed on the firm by the operating environment. The restrictions can be in the form of limited resources or restrictive guidelines. For example, only 40 hours of labor may be available to produce radios during production. The actual numerical values in the objective function and the constraints, such as the 40 hours of available labor, are *parameters.*

This section presents several examples that demonstrate how a linear programming model is formulated. Although these examples are simplified, they are realistic and represent the type of problem to which linear programming can be applied. In each example the model components are distinctly identified and described. By carefully studying each of these examples, the reader can become familiar with the process of formulating linear programming models.

A PRODUCT MIX EXAMPLE

The Colonial Pottery Company produces two products daily— bowls and mugs. The company has limited amounts of two resources used in the production of these products—clay and labor. Given these limited resources, the company desires to know how many bowls and mugs to produce each day in order to maximize profit. The two products have the following resource requirements for production and profit per item produced (i.e., the model parameters).

| | Resource Requirements | | |
Product	Labor (hr/unit)	Clay (lb/unit)	Profit ($/unit)
Bowl	1	4	4
Mug	2	3	5

There are 40 hours of labor and 120 pounds of clay available each day for production. We will formulate this problem as a linear programming model by defining each component of the model separately and then combining the components into a single model.

Formulating the problem as a model

Decision Variables

The decision confronting management in this problem is how many bowls and mugs to produce. The two decision variables represent the number of bowls and mugs to be produced on a daily basis. The quantities to be produced can be represented symbolically as

x_1 = number of bowls to produce
x_2 = number of mugs to produce

The Objective Function

The objective of the company is to maximize total profit. The company's profit is the sum of the individual profits gained from each

Maximizing profit

bowl and mug. Profit derived from bowls is determined by multiplying the unit profit of each bowl, $4, by the number of bowls produced, x_1. Likewise, profit derived from mugs is the unit profit of a mug, $5, multiplied by the number of mugs produced, x_2. Thus, total profit, which we will define symbolically as Z, can be expressed mathematically as $\$4x_1 + 5x_2$. By placing the term *maximize* in front of the profit function, we express the objective of the firm—to maximize total profit:

$$\text{maximize } Z = \$4x_1 + 5x_2$$

where

$$Z = \text{total profit per day}$$
$$\$4x_1 = \text{profit from bowls}$$
$$5x_2 = \text{profit from mugs}$$

Model Constraints

Labor constraint

In this problem two resources are used for production—labor and clay—both of which are limited. Production of bowls and mugs requires both labor and clay. For each bowl produced, 1 hour of labor is required. Therefore, the labor used for the production of bowls is $1x_1$ hours. Similarly, each mug requires 2 hours of labor; thus, the labor used to produce mugs every day is $2x_2$ hours. The total labor used by the company is the sum of the individual amounts of labor used for each product,

$$1x_1 + 2x_2$$

However, the amount of labor represented by $1x_1 + 2x_2$ is limited to 40 hours per day; thus, the complete labor constraint is

$$1x_1 + 2x_2 \leq 40 \text{ hr}$$

≤ constraint

The "less than or equal to" ($\leq$) inequality is employed instead of an equality ($=$) because the 40 hours of labor is a maximum limitation that *can be used*, not an amount that *must be used*. This constraint allows the company some flexibility; the company is not restricted to using exactly 40 hours, but can use whatever amount is necessary to maximize profit, up to and including 40 hours. This means that it is possible to have idle, or excess, capacity (i.e., some of the 40 hours not used).

Material constraint

The constraint for clay is formulated in the same way as the labor constraint. Since each bowl requires 4 pounds of clay, the amount of clay used daily for the production of bowls is $4x_1$ pounds, and since each mug requires 3 pounds of clay, the amount of clay used daily for mugs is $3x_2$. Given that the amount of clay available for production each day is 120 pounds, the material constraint can be formulated as

$$4x_1 + 3x_2 \leq 120 \text{ lb}$$

A final restriction is that the number of bowls and mugs produced be either zero or a positive value, since it is impossible to produce negative items. These restrictions are referred to as *nonnegativity constraints* and are expressed mathematically as

Nonnegativity constraints

$$x_1 \geq 0, \ x_2 \geq 0$$

The complete linear programming model for this problem can now be summarized as

The formulated model

maximize $Z = \$4x_1 + 5x_2$

subject to

$$1x_1 + 2x_2 \leq 40$$
$$4x_1 + 3x_2 \leq 120$$
$$x_1, x_2 \geq 0$$

The solution of this model will result in numerical values for x_1 and x_2 that will maximize total profit, Z. As *one possible* solution, consider $x_1 = 5$ bowls and $x_2 = 10$ mugs. First we will substitute this hypothetical solution into each of the constraints in order to make sure that the solution does not require more resources than the constraints show are available.

An example solution

$$1(5) + 2(10) \leq 40$$
$$25 \leq 40$$

and

$$4(5) + 3(10) \leq 120$$
$$50 \leq 120$$

Since neither one of the constraints is violated by this hypothetical solution, we say the solution is *feasible* (i.e., it is possible). Substituting these solution values in the objective function gives $Z = 4(5) + 5(10) = \$70$. However, for the time being we do not have any way of knowing if $70 is the *maximum* profit.

A feasible solution

Now consider a solution of $x_1 = 10$ bowls and $x_2 = 20$ mugs. This solution results in a profit of

$$Z = \$4(10) + 5(20)$$
$$= 40 + 100$$
$$= \$140$$

Although this is certainly a better solution in terms of profit, it is *infeasible* (i.e., not possible) because it violates the resource constraint for labor.

An infeasible solution

$$1(10) + 2(20) \leq 40$$
$$50 \nleq 40$$

The solution to this problem must maximize profit without violating the constraints. The solution that achieves this objective is $x_1 = 24$ bowls and $x_2 = 8$ mugs, with a corresponding profit of $136. The determination of this solution is shown in Chapters 3 and 4.

AN INGREDIENTS MIXTURE EXAMPLE

A cereal company produces a cereal called Fortified Munchies, which it advertises as meeting the minimum daily requirements for vitamins A and D. The mixing department of the company uses three main ingredients in making the cereal—wheat, oats, and rice—all of which contain varying amounts of vitamins A and D. Given that each box of cereal must contain required amounts of vitamins A and D, the company has instructed the mixing department to determine how many ounces of each ingredient should go into each box of cereal in order to minimize total cost. This problem differs from the previous one in that its objective is to *minimize* cost, rather than to maximize profit. Each ingredient has the following vitamin contribution and requirement per box.

A minimization problem

| | Vitamin Contribution | | | |
| | Wheat | Oats | Rice | Milligrams |
Vitamin	(mg/oz)	(mg/oz)	(mg/oz)	Required/Box
A	10	20	8	100
D	7	14	12	70

The cost of an ounce of wheat is $.04, the cost of an ounce of oats is $.06, and the cost of an ounce of rice is $.02.

Decision Variables

Formulating the model

This problem contains three decision variables representing the number of ounces of each ingredient in a box of cereal.

x_1 = oz of wheat

x_2 = oz of oats

x_3 = oz of rice

The Objective Function

Minimizing cost

The mixing department's objective is to minimize the cost of each box of cereal. The total cost is the sum of the individual costs of each ingredient. Thus, the objective function used to minimize total cost, Z, is expressed as

minimize Z = $\$.04x_1 + .06x_2 + .02x_3$

where

Z = total cost per box

$\$.04x_1$ = cost of wheat per box

$.06x_2$ = cost of oats per box

$.02x_3$ = cost of rice per box

Model Constraints

The requirements for vitamin content of the cereal are the constraints in this problem. Each ingredient contributes a number of milligrams of each vitamin to the cereal. The constraint for vitamin A is

$10x_1 + 20x_2 + 8x_3 \geq 100$ mg

where

$10x_1$ = vitamin A contribution (in mg) of wheat

$20x_2$ = vitamin A contribution (in mg) of oats

$8x_3$ = vitamin A contribution (in mg) of rice

Rather than a $\leq$ (less than or equal to) inequality, as used in the previous example, this constraint requires a $\geq$ (greater than or equal to) inequality. This is because the vitamin content is a minimum requirement specifying that *at least* 100 milligrams of vitamin A be included in a box. If a minimum cost solution results in the inclusion of more than 100 milligrams in the cereal mix, that is acceptable; however, the amount cannot be less than 100 milligrams.

$\geq$ constraint

The constraint for vitamin D is constructed like the constraint for vitamin A.

$7x_1 + 14x_2 + 12x_3 \geq 70$ mg

As in the previous problem, there are also nonnegativity constraints in this problem, to indicate that the cereal cannot contain negative amounts of each ingredient.

$x_1, x_2, x_3 \geq 0$

In the future the nonnegativity constraints will not be specifically described but will be assumed to exist unless otherwise stated.

The linear programming model for this problem can be summarized as

The formulated model

minimize $Z = \$.04x_1 + .06x_2 + .02x_3$

subject to

$10x_1 + 20x_2 + 8x_3 \geq 100$

$7x_1 + 14x_2 + 12x_3 \geq 70$

$x_1, x_2, x_3 \geq 0$

AN INVESTMENT EXAMPLE

An individual investor has $70,000 to divide among several investments. The alternative investments are municipal bonds with an 8.5% return, certificates of deposit with a 10% return, treasury bills with a 6.5% return, and income bonds with a 13% return. The amount of time until maturity is the same for each alternative. However, each investment alternative has a different perceived risk to the investor; thus, it is advisable to diversify. The investor wants to know how much to invest in each alternative in order to maximize the return.

The following guidelines have been established for diversifying the investments and lessening the risk perceived by the investor.

1. No more than 20% of the total investment should be in income bonds.
2. The amount invested in certificates of deposit should not exceed the amount invested in the other three alternatives.
3. At least 30% of the investment should be in treasury bills and certificates of deposit.
4. The ratio of the amount invested in municipal bonds to the amount invested in treasury bills should not exceed one to three.

The investor wants to invest the entire $70,000.

Decision Variables

Formulating the model

Four decision variables represent the monetary amount invested in each investment alternative.

x_1 = amount ($) invested in municipal bonds
x_2 = amount ($) invested in certificates of deposit
x_3 = amount ($) invested in treasury bills
x_4 = amount ($) invested in income bonds

The Objective Function

Maximizing return

The objective of the investor is to maximize the total return from the investment in the four alternatives. The total return is the sum of the individual returns from each alternative. Thus, the objective function is expressed as

maximize $Z = \$.085x_1 + .100x_2 + .065x_3 + .130x_4$
where

Z = total return from all investments
$\$.085x_1$ = return from the investment in municipal bonds
$.100x_2$ = return from the investment in certificates of deposit
$.065x_3$ = return from the investment in treasury bills
$.130x_4$ = return from the investment in income bonds

Model Constraints

Formulating the investment guidelines as constraints

In this problem the constraints are the guidelines established for diversifying the total investment. Each guideline is transformed into a mathematical constraint separately.

Guideline one states that no more than 20% of the total invest-ment should be in income bonds. The total investment is $70,000; 20% of $70,000 is $14,000. Thus, this constraint is

$x_4 \leq \$14,000$

The second guideline indicates that the amount invested in cer-tificates of deposit should not exceed the amount invested in the other three alternatives. Since the investment in certificates of de-posit is x_2 and the amount invested in the other alternatives is $x_1 + x_3 + x_4$, the constraint is

$x_2 \leq x_1 + x_3 + x_4$

However, the solution technique for linear programming problems requires that constraints be in a standard form in which all decision variables are on the left side of the inequality (i.e., $\leq$) and all nu-merical values are on the right side. Thus, $x_1 + x_3 + x_4$ must be sub-tracted from both sides of the $\leq$ sign to put this constraint in proper form:

Standard constraint form

$x_2 - x_1 - x_3 - x_4 \leq 0$

The third guideline specifies that at least 30% of the investment should be in treasury bills and certificates of deposit. Since 30% of $70,000 is $21,000 and the amount invested in certificates of deposit and treasury bills is represented by $x_2 + x_3$, the constraint is

$x_2 + x_3 \geq \$21,000$

The fourth guideline states that the ratio of the amount invested in municipal bonds to the amount invested in treasury bills should not exceed one to three. This constraint is expressed as

$x_1/x_3 \leq 1/3$

This constraint is not in standard linear programming form because of the fractional relationship of the decision variables, x_1/x_3. It is con-verted as follows:

$$x_1 \leq 1x_3/3$$
$$3x_1 \leq x_3$$
$$3x_1 - x_3 \leq 0$$

Finally, the investor wants to invest the entire $70,000 in the four alternatives. Thus, the sum of all the investments in the four al-ternatives must *equal* $70,000.

An equality constraint

$x_1 + x_2 + x_3 + x_4 = \$70,000$

This last constraint differs from the $\leq$ and $\geq$ inequalities previ-ously developed in that there is a specific requirement to invest an *exact amount*. Thus, the possibility of investing more or less than $70,000 is not considered.

This problem contains all three types of constraints possible in a linear programming problem: $\leq$, $=$, and $\geq$. As this problem demonstrates, there is no restriction on mixing these types of constraints.

The complete linear programming model for this problem can be summarized as

maximize $Z = \$.085x_1 + .100x_2 + .065x_3 + .130x_4$

subject to

$$x_4 \leq 14,000$$
$$x_2 - x_1 - x_3 - x_4 \leq 0$$
$$x_2 + x_3 \geq 21,000$$
$$3x_1 - x_3 \leq 0$$
$$x_1 + x_2 + x_3 + x_4 = 70,000$$
$$x_1, x_2, x_3, x_4 \geq 0$$

A CHEMICAL MIXTURE EXAMPLE

A chemical corporation produces a chemical mixture for a customer in 1,000-pound batches. The mixture contains three ingredients— zinc, mercury, and potassium. The mixture must conform to formula specifications (i.e., a recipe) supplied by the customer. The company wants to know the amount of each ingredient to put in the mixture that will meet all the requirements of the mix and minimize total cost.

The customer has supplied the following formula specifications for each batch of mixture.

1. The mixture must contain at least 200 lb of mercury.
2. The mixture must contain at least 300 lb of zinc.
3. The mixture must contain at least 100 lb of potassium.

The cost per pound of mercury is $4; of zinc, $8; and of potassium, $9.

Decision Variables

The model for this problem contains three decision variables representing the amount of each ingredient in the mixture.

x_1 = number of lb of mercury in a batch
x_2 = number of lb of zinc in a batch
x_3 = number of lb of potassium in a batch

The Objective Function

The objective of the company is to minimize the cost of producing a batch of the chemical mixture. The total cost is the sum of the individual costs of each ingredient.

minimize $Z = \$4x_1 + 8x_2 + 9x_3$

where

Z = total cost of all ingredients

$\$4x_1$ = cost of mercury in each batch

$8x_2$ = cost of zinc in each batch

$9x_3$ = cost of potassium in each batch

Model Constraints

In this problem the constraints are derived from the chemical formula.

The first specification indicates that the mixture must contain at least 200 pounds of mercury,

$x_1 \geq 200$ lb

The second specification is that the mixture must contain at least 300 pounds of zinc,

$x_2 \geq 300$ lb

The third specification is that the mixture must contain at least 100 pounds of potassium,

$x_3 \geq 100$ lb

Finally, the sum of all ingredients must exactly equal 1,000 pounds,

$x_1 + x_2 + x_3 = 1,000$ lb

The complete linear programming model can be summarized as

minimize $Z = \$4x_1 + 8x_2 + 9x_3$

subject to

$$x_1 \geq 200$$
$$x_2 \geq 300$$
$$x_3 \geq 100$$
$$x_1 + x_2 + x_3 - 1,000$$
$$x_1, x_2, x_3 \geq 0$$

Formulating the mixture requirements

The formulated model

A MARKETING EXAMPLE

The Biggs Department Store chain has hired an advertising firm to determine the types and amount of advertising it should have for its stores. The three types of advertising available are radio and television commercials and newspaper ads. The retail chain desires to know the number of each type of advertisement it should purchase in order to maximize exposure. It is estimated that each ad or commercial will reach the following potential audience and cost the following amount.

Type of Advertisement	Exposure (people/ad or commercial)	Cost
Television commercial	20,000	$15,000
Radio commercial	12,000	6,000
Newspaper ad	9,000	4,000

The company must consider the following resource constraints.

1. The budget limit for advertising is $100,000.
2. The television station has time available for 4 commercials.
3. The radio station has time available for 10 commercials.
4. The newspaper has space available for 7 ads.
5. The advertising agency has time and staff available for producing no more than a total of 15 commercials and/or ads.

Decision Variables

Formulating the model

This model consists of three decision variables representing the number of each type of advertising produced:

x_1 = number of television commercials

x_2 = number of radio commercials

x_3 = number of newspaper ads

The Objective Function

The objective of this problem is different from the objectives in the previous examples, in which only profit was to be maximized (or cost minimized). In this problem, profit is not to be maximized; instead, audience exposure is to be maximized. Thus, this objective function demonstrates that although a linear programming model must either maximize or minimize some objective, the objective itself can be in terms of any type of activity or valuation.

Maximizing audience exposures

For this problem the objective of audience exposure is determined by summing the audience exposure gained from each type of advertising.

maximize $Z = 20{,}000x_1 + 12{,}000x_2 + 9{,}000x_3$

where

Z = total level of audience exposure

$20{,}000x_1$ = estimated number of people reached by television commercials

$12{,}000x_2$ = estimated number of people reached by radio commercials

$9{,}000x_3$ = estimated number of people reached by newspaper ads

Model Constraints

The first constraint in this model reflects the limited budget of $100,000 allocated for advertisement,

$15,000x_1 + 6,000x_2 + 4,000x_3 \leq \$100,000$

where

$\$15,000x_1$ = amount spent for television advertising
$6,000x_2$ = amount spent for radio advertising
$4,000x_3$ = amount spent for newspaper advertising

The next three constraints represent the fact that television and radio commercials are limited to 4 and 10, respectively, and newspaper ads are limited to 7.

$x_1 \leq 4$ television commercials
$x_2 \leq 10$ radio commercials
$x_3 \leq 7$ newspaper ads

The final constraint specifies that the total number of commercials and ads cannot exceed 15 because of the limitations of the advertising firm.

$x_1 + x_2 + x_3 \leq 15$ commercials and ads

The complete linear programming model for this problem is summarized as

The formulated model

maximize $Z = 20,000x_1 + 12,000x_2 + 9,000x_3$
subject to
$$\$15,000x_1 + 6,000x_2 + 4,000x_3 \leq \$100,000$$
$$x_1 \leq 4$$
$$x_2 \leq 10$$
$$x_3 \leq 7$$
$$x_1 + x_2 + x_3 \leq 15$$
$$x_1, x_2, x_3 \geq 0$$

A TRANSPORTATION EXAMPLE

The Zephyr Television Company ships televisions from three warehouses to three retail stores on a monthly basis. Each warehouse has a fixed supply per month and each store has a fixed demand per month. The manufacturer wants to know the number of television sets to ship from each warehouse to each store in order to minimize the total cost of transportation.

Each warehouse has the following supply of televisions available for shipment each month.

Warehouse	Supply (sets)	
1. Cincinnati		300
2. Atlanta	100	
3. Pittsburgh	200	
	600	

Each retail store has the following monthly demand for television sets.

Store	Demand (sets)
A. New York	150
B. Dallas	250
C. Detroit	200
	600

Costs of transporting television sets from the warehouses to the retail stores vary as a result of differences in modes of transportation and distances. The shipping cost per television set for each route is as follows.

From Warehouse	To Store		
	A	B	C
1	$6	$8	$1
2	4	2	3
3	3	5	7

Decision Variables

Formulating the model

The model for this problem consists of nine decision variables representing the number of television sets transported from each of the three warehouses to each of the three stores,

$$x_{ij} = \text{number of television sets shipped from warehouse } i \text{ to}$$
$$\text{store } j, \text{ where } i = 1, 2, 3, \text{ and } j = \text{A, B, C}$$

Double subscripted variables

The variable x_{ij} is referred to as a *double subscripted* variable. The subscript, whether double or single, simply gives a "name" to the variable (i.e., distinguishes it from other decision variables). For example, the decision variable x_{3A} represents the number of television sets shipped from warehouse 3 in Pittsburgh to store A in New York.

The Objective Function

Minimizing shipping costs

The objective function of the television manufacturer is to minimize the total transportation costs for all shipments. Thus, the objective function is the sum of the individual shipping costs from each warehouse to each store.

$$\text{minimize } Z = \$6x_{1A} + 8x_{1B} + 1x_{1C} + 4x_{2A} + 2x_{2B} + 3x_{2C} + 3x_{3A} + 5x_{3B}$$
$$+ 7x_{3C}$$

Model Constraints

The constraints in this model are the number of television sets available at each warehouse and the number of sets demanded at each store. There are six constraints — one for each warehouse's supply and one for each store's demand. For example, warehouse 1 in Cincinnati is able to supply 300 television sets to any of the three retail stores. Since the amount shipped to the three stores is the sum of x_{1A}, x_{1B}, and x_{1C}, the constraint for warehouse 1 is

$$x_{1A} + x_{1B} + x_{1C} = 300$$

This constraint is an equality for two reasons. First, no more than 300 television sets can be shipped, because that is the maximum available at the warehouse. Second, no less than 300 can be shipped, because 300 are needed to meet the total demand of 600. That is, total demand equals total supply, which equals 600. To meet the total demand at the three stores, all that can be supplied must be supplied by the three warehouses. Thus, the other two supply constraints for warehouses 2 and 3 are also equalities,

$$x_{2A} + x_{2B} + x_{2C} = 100$$
$$x_{3A} + x_{3B} + x_{3C} = 200$$

The three demand constraints are developed in the same way as the supply constraints, except that the variables summed are the number of television sets supplied from each of the three warehouses. Thus, the amount shipped to one store is the sum of the shipments from the three warehouses:

$$x_{1A} + x_{2A} + x_{3A} = 150$$
$$x_{1B} + x_{2B} + x_{3B} = 250$$
$$x_{1C} + x_{2C} + x_{3C} = 200$$

The complete linear programming model for this problem is summarized as

minimize $Z = \$6x_{1A} + 8x_{1B} + 1x_{1C} + 4x_{2A} + 2x_{2B} + 3x_{2C} + 3x_{3A} + 5x_{3B}$
$\qquad + 7x_{3C}$

subject to
$$x_{1A} + x_{1B} + x_{1C} = 300$$
$$x_{2A} + x_{2B} + x_{2C} = 100$$
$$x_{3A} + x_{3B} + x_{3C} = 200$$
$$x_{1A} + x_{2A} + x_{3A} = 150$$
$$x_{1B} + x_{2B} + x_{3B} = 250$$
$$x_{1C} + x_{2C} + x_{3C} = 200$$
$$x_{ij} \geq 0$$

CHARACTERISTICS OF LINEAR PROGRAMMING PROBLEMS

An objective function

Now that we have had the opportunity to construct several linear programming models, let's review the characteristics that identify a problem as a linear programming problem. First, the problem encompasses an objective that the decision maker wants to achieve. The most frequently encountered objective for a business firm is maximizing profit; however, the example models in this chapter have demonstrated various objectives. The first step in formulating a linear programming model from a written problem statement (such as a homework problem) is to read completely through the problem in order to identify the objective.

Decision variables

A linear programming problem requires a choice between alternative courses of action (i.e., a decision). The decision is represented in the model by decision variables. A typical choice task for a business firm is deciding how much of several different products to produce, as in the Colonial Pottery Company example presented earlier in this chapter. Identifying the choice task and defining the decision variables is usually the second step in the formulation process, since it is quite difficult to construct the objective function and constraints without first identifying the decision variables.

A third characteristic of a linear programming problem is that restrictions exist, making unlimited achievement of the objective function impossible. In a business firm these restrictions often take the form of limited resources such as labor or material; however, the example models in this chapter exhibited a variety of problem restrictions. These restrictions, as well as the objective, must be definable by mathematical functional relationships that are linear. Defining these relationships is typically the most difficult part of the formulation process.

Properties of Linear Programming Models

In addition to encompassing only linear relationships, a linear programming model also has several other implicit properties, which have been exhibited consistently throughout the examples in this chapter. The term "linear" not only means that the functions in the models are graphed as a straight line; it also means that the relationships exhibit *proportionality*. In other words, the rate of change, or slope, of the function is constant, and therefore changes of a given size in the value of a decision variable will result in exactly the same relative changes in the functional value.

Additivity

Linear programming also requires that the objective function terms and the constraint terms be *additive*. For example, in the Colonial Pottery Company model, the total profit (Z) must equal the sum of profits earned from making bowls ($4x_1$) and mugs ($5x_2$). Also, the total resources used must equal the sum of the resources used for each activity in a constraint (e.g., labor).

Another property of linear programming models is that the solution values (of the decision variables) cannot be restricted to integer values; the decision variables can take on any fractional value. Thus, the variables are said to be *continuous* or *divisible,* as opposed to *integer* or *discrete.* For example, although decision variables representing bowls or mugs or airplanes or automobiles should realistically have integer (whole number) solutions, the solution methods for linear programming will not necessarily provide such solutions. This is a property that will be discussed further as solution methods are presented in subsequent chapters.

Divisibility

The final property of linear programming models is that the values of all the model parameters are assumed to be constant and known with *certainty.* In real situations, however, model parameters are frequently uncertain, since they reflect the future as well as the present and future conditions are rarely known with certainty.

Certainty

To summarize, a linear programming model has the following general properties: linearity, proportionality, additivity, divisibility, and certainty. As various linear programming solution methods are presented throughout this book, these properties will become more obvious and their impact on problem solution will be discussed in greater detail.

Model properties

Guidelines for Model Formulation

Generally it is not feasible to attempt to "see" the whole formulation of the constraints and objective function at once, following the definition of the decision variables. A more prudent approach is to construct the objective function first (without direct concern for the constraints) and then to direct attention to each problem restriction and its corresponding model constraint. What is being suggested is a systematic approach to model formulation, in which steps are taken one at a time. In other words, do not attempt to swallow the whole problem during the first reading.

A systematic approach to model formulation

Formulating a linear programming model from a written problem statement is often difficult, but formulating a model of a "real" problem that has no written statement is even more difficult. The steps for model formulation described in this section are generally followed; however, the problem must first be defined (i.e., a problem statement or some similar descriptive apparatus must be developed). Developing such a statement can be a formidable task, requiring the assistance of many individuals and units within an organization. Developing the parameter values that are presented as givens in the written problem statements of this chapter frequently

Real problems in actual practice

requires extensive data collection efforts. The objective function and model constraints can be very complex, requiring much time and effort to develop. Simply making sure that all the model constraints have been identified and no important problem restrictions have been omitted is difficult. Finally, the problems that one confronts in actual practice are typically much larger than those presented in this chapter. It is not uncommon for linear programming models of real problems to encompass hundreds of functional relationships and decision variables. Unfortunately, it is not possible in a textbook to recreate a realistic problem environment with no written problem statement and a model of large dimensions. What is possible is to provide the fundamentals of linear programming model formulation and solution — prerequisite to solving linear programming problems in actual practice.

APPLICATIONS OF LINEAR PROGRAMMING

Straightforward and easy-to-formulate example problems were used in this chapter in order to facilitate the learning of model formulation. Applications of linear programming in practice are typically so complex that they would be of little value to the novice management scientist attempting to learn the fundamentals of linear programming model formulation. However, now that you have been introduced to linear programming, it will be interesting and beneficial to look briefly at a few examples of linear programming applications.

Examples of actual applications

Product Mix in the Wood Products Industry

Plywood Ponderosa de Mexico, S.A., based in Anahuac, Chihuahua, is the primary plywood manufacturer in Mexico, with the capacity to produce the equivalent of 85 million square feet of quarter-inch (thick) plywood annually. The company manufactures a large number of different grades and thicknesses of plywood panel, using four grades of log (classified according to quality). The plywood market in Mexico is competitive, with seasonal demand. Since the company manufactures a large variety of panel grades and thicknesses, the product mix decision was a very complex issue that had a pronounced effect on profits. The company also had a critical need to balance the available wood mix and the projected sales requirements within given production constraints. The company developed a linear programming model for determining the optimal product mix. Based on unit profits, the company had previously emphasized the production of thicker plywoods; however, the results of the lin-

Optimal product mix

ear programming model showed that thinner plywoods were, in fact, more profitable. This product mix change increased the overall profitability of the company by 20%. The model also resulted in improved use of capital equipment, raw material, and labor.[1]

Truck Fleet Management

North American Van Lines, Inc. is one of the nation's largest truck transportation companies, having a fleet of over 3,300 independently owned vehicles. The fleet administration center for this company procures new tractors from manufacturers, trades in used tractors to manufacturers, sells tractors to contract truckers, purchases used tractors from contract truckers, and recruits and trains contract workers, among other functions. Overall, the fleet administration center has primary responsibility for administering the company's fleet of tractors. The fleet administration center developed a linear programming model for generating a tractor sales mix that ultimately provides the center with sales/trade-in guidelines. The sales mix generated by the linear programming model determines the actual level of tractor sales' net contribution and provides the basis for the generation of financial planning reports for the company. The linear programming model helped North American Van Lines reduce its tractor inventory by 100 units, resulting in savings of $3 million and approximate savings in annual tractor inventory costs of $600,000.[2]

A tractor sales mix

Forest Planning

The U.S. Forest Service employs a linear programming system (FORPLAN) in almost all of its 121 national forest headquarters to conduct forest planning. The FORPLAN system resides on the USDA computer in Fort Collins, Colorado and is accessed via remote terminals at each forest headquarters. The system constructs forest models that allocate forest land according to generate management objectives, and schedules the treatment and resulting product flows. The model solutions are directed at maximizing the present net value of the forests.[3]

---

[1]A. Roy et al., "An Optimization-Based Decision Support System for a Product Mix Problem," *Interfaces* 12, no. 2 (April 1982): 26–31.

[2]D. Avramovich et al., "A Decision Support System for Fleet Management: A Linear Programming Approach," *Interfaces* 12, no. 3 (June 1982): 1–9.

[3]R. Field, "National Forest Planning Is Promoting U.S. Forest Service Acceptance of Operations Research," *Interfaces* 14, no. 5 (September-October 1984): 67–76.

Railroad Car Fleet Management

Freight car fleet mix

The Chessie System is made up of three major railroads — the Chesapeake and Ohio, Baltimore and Ohio, and Western Maryland — their subsidiaries, and a number of small railroads. In 1980 (when this application was reported) the Chessie System was the largest hauler of coal in the nation and a major transporter of merchandise freight. The Chessie System owned or leased 133,000 railroad cars, worth over $4 billion. To maintain earning capacity, the Chessie System invested large amounts of money each year in the purchase, construction, and repair of freight cars. The management science team at the Chessie System developed a linear programming model of the freight car fleet, designed to maximize long-term net discounted cash flow without exceeding the capacity of available physical facilities. The initial model consisted of 100 variables and 50 constraints; however, subsequent versions have consisted of approximately 3,500 variables and over 1,000 constraints. The first projections of the model output increased contribution to profits of the Chessie fleet by $2 million in 1978, while reducing the annual budget of the mechanical department by $6 million. The continued use of the model has resulted in a $2.5 million improvement in employee productivity, as well as a $28 million increase in car sales.[4]

Bank Financial Planning

Maximizing bank profits

In the mid-1970s the Central Carolina Bank and Trust Company became concerned with coordinating the activities of the bank in order to maximize interest rate differentials between the sources and uses of its funds. The bank had total assets of approximately $360 million, which included an investment securities portfolio of $100 million. A linear programming model was developed to maximize profits over a one-year planning horizon. The model decision variables represented dollar quantities allocated to 10 different asset categories and 11 different liability/equity categories. The asset categories included cash, treasury securities, consumer loans, commercial loans, and real estate loans. The liability/equity categories included demand deposit accounts, savings accounts, money market certificates, and certificates of deposit. Five classifications of model constraints were employed: maximum (upper bound) activity levels on various asset or liability categories, turnover constraints, policy constraints, legal/regulatory constraints, and funds flow constraints. The model generated a target balance sheet and a rank ordering of bank services.[5]

---

[4]L. Brosch et al., "Boxcars, Linear Programming, and the Sleeping Kitten," *Interfaces* 10, no. 6 (December 1980): 53–61.

[5]S. Balbirer and D. Shaw, "An Application of Linear Programming to Bank Financial Planning," *Interfaces* 11, no. 5 (October 1981): 77–83.

As an addendum to this example, it is interesting to note that a 1979 survey of 50 of the largest commercial banking companies in the country indicated that 37% used linear programming to solve bank-related problems. Also, 53% combined linear programming with some other management science technique to solve problems.[6]

Product Mix in the Steel Industry

Bethlehem Steel Company needed approximately 4,000 to 6,000 rolls of 300 different types of cast iron and steel each year to manufacture products of various sizes and shapes in its 100 mills located throughout the country. These rolls were first cast in one of two foundries and then machined in a large shop having 35 machines. Expenditures for rolls were budgeted for each plant, and the plants transmitted their orders for anticipated roll requirements to the machine shop, which decided in a short period of time which rolls it could manufacture and deliver on time during the year. Rolls that could not be made in the machine shop were purchased at a premium. However, it was almost impossible to determine how many rolls to manufacture and how many to purchase in order to assure on-time delivery throughout the year. The company developed a linear programming model (subsequently used in a larger computer system) to maximize the total tons of rolls produced during the planning period, subject to restrictions on total machine time available and demand for rolls. The computer system that incorporated the linear programming model saved the company approximately $500,000 annually in lower costs and higher profits.[7]

Steel roll production

Product Distribution in the Oil Industry

The Shell Oil Company operates an eastern and a western distribution system for its petroleum products. In the eastern system three refineries service over 100 terminal demand points via pipeline, barge, and tanker. Many of these terminals are served by more than one refinery and via different modes of transportation, with each having different costs and capacities. The distribution of Shell's petroleum products is therefore a very complex task involving large amounts of capital and operating expenditures. Approximately 10% of Shell's revenues are for transportation costs. In the early 1970s the company developed a linear programming model to determine an

[6]R. McClure and R. Miller, "The Application of Operations Research in Commercial Banking Companies," *Interfaces* 9, no. 2 (February 1979): 24–29.

[7]S. Jain et al., "Orderbook Balancing Using a Combination of Linear Programming and Heuristic Techniques," *Interfaces* 9, no. 1 (November 1978): 55–67.

optimal distribution pattern that would minimize transportation costs and satisfy terminal demands. The model contained 575 constraints reflecting restrictions on supply and demand, material balance at points where the mode of transportation of products changes, and restrictions on the transportation system. The model consisted of 1,050 variables. The company used the model to analyze the opening and closing of terminals, expansion of facilities (including refinery construction), and tanker and barge requirements, among other items.[8]

Fuel Management in the Airlines Industry

During the world oil crisis of the mid-1970s, the government limited the supply of jet fuel to the nation's airlines. As a result, fuel vendors were frequently unable to meet the airlines' demands at certain cities, resulting in canceled flights, very high prices for spot purchases of fuel, and enormous increases in operating costs. Expenditures for jet fuel became the airlines' largest single expense, accounting for 18% of total costs. To solve this problem, National Airlines developed a linear programming model to minimize the effect of price increases and fluctuating fuel allocations, and to maintain a planned flight schedule. The solution of the linear programming model resulted in optimal purchase levels from each station vendor and the amounts of fuel to be boarded on each leg of a flight sequence. During the first month the model was used, May 1974, fuel costs dropped almost $.02 per gallon, for a total savings of over $500,000, even though fuel prices increased during the month. The linear programming model consisted of approximately 800 constraints and 2,400 variables for a flight schedule of 350 flight segments, 50 station/vendor combinations, and multiple aircraft types.[9]

Chemical Production

Monsanto produces maleic anhydride (a chemical used in making plastic) at plants in St. Louis and Pensacola. The combined capacity of the two plants is more than 45% of total U.S. output of 359 million pounds per year. Capacity at both plants exceeded demand, resulting in a need to be able to assign production to each plant in an optimal manner. Three linear programming models were developed for this purpose, including a global model to determine the amount produced at each plant and individual plant models to adjust operating plans during a production period. The models, which encompassed

[8]T. Zierer et al., "Practical Applications of Linear Programming to Shell's Distribution Problems," *Interfaces* 6, no. 4 (August 1976): 13–26.

[9]D. Darnell and C. Loflin, "National Airlines Fuel Management and Allocation Model," *Interfaces* 7, no. 2 (February 1977): 1–16.

over a thousand variables and a dozen or more constraints, minimize cost subject to meeting a production target. Use of the system has resulted in estimated annual savings of between $1 and $3 million (depending on plant operating rules).[10]

Summary

The example problems in this chapter were formulated as linear programming models in order to demonstrate the modeling process. These problems were all similar in that they concerned achieving some objective subject to a set of restrictions (e.g., resource constraints, a formula for blending, investment guidelines, etc.). The linear programming models of these problems also exhibited certain common characteristics:

An objective function to be maximized or minimized
A set of constraints
Decision variables for measuring the level of activity
Linearity among all constraint relationships and the objective
function

The two chapters that follow deal with the solution of linear programming models. Although the simplex solution method, discussed in Chapter 4, is the most traditional and commonly used technique, a graphical solution approach is discussed first in Chapter 3. The graphical method has limitations (which will be discussed), but it has the advantage of representing the solution process pictorially.

Characteristics of
linear programming

References

Avramovich, D.; Cook, T.; Langston, G.; and Sutherland, F. "A Decision Support System for Fleet Management: A Linear Programming Approach." *Interfaces* 12, no. 3 (June 1982): 1–9.

Balbirer, S., and Shaw, D. "An Application of Linear Programming to Bank Financial Planning." *Interfaces* 11, no. 5 (October 1981): 77–83.

Brosch, L.; Buck, R.; Sparrow, W.; and White, J. "Boxcars, Linear Programming, and the Sleeping Kitten." *Interfaces* 10, no. 6 (December 1980): 53–61.

Charnes, A., and Cooper, W. W. *Management Models and Industrial Applications of Linear Programming.* New York: John Wiley and Sons, 1961.

Darnell, D., and Loflin, C. "National Airlines Fuel Management and Allocation Model." *Interfaces* 7, no. 2 (February 1977): 1–16.

Hadley, G. *Linear Programming.* Reading, Mass.: Addison-Wesley, 1962.

[10]R. Boykin, "Optimizing Chemical Production at Monsanto," *Interfaces* 15, no. 1 (January-February 1985): 88–95.

Hilal, S., and Erikson, W. "Matching Supplies to Save Lives: Linear Programming the Production of Heart Valves." *Interfaces* 11, no. 6 (December 1981): 48–56.

Hillier, F. S., and Lieberman, G. J. *Introduction to Operations Research.* 4th ed. San Francisco: Holden-Day, 1986.

Jain, S.; Scott, K.; and Vasold, E. "Orderbook Balancing Using a Combination of Linear Programming and Heuristic Techniques." *Interfaces* 9, no. 1 (November 1978): 55–67.

Kwak, N. K. *Mathematical Programming with Business Applications.* New York: McGraw-Hill, 1973.

Lee, Sang M.; Moore, Laurence J.; and Taylor, Bernard W. *Management Science.* 3d ed. Boston: Allyn and Bacon, 1990.

Llewellyn, R. W. *Linear Programming.* New York: Holt, Rinehart and Winston, 1964.

McClure, R., and Miller, R. "The Application of Operations Research in Commercial Banking Companies." *Interfaces* 9, no. 2 (February 1979): 24–29.

Pfaffenberger, R. C., and Walker, D. A. *Mathematical Programming for Economics and Business.* Ames, Ia.: Iowa State University Press, 1976.

Phillips, D. T.; Ravindran, A.; and Solberg, J. J. *Operations Research.* 2d ed. New York: John Wiley and Sons, 1987.

Roy, A.; Falomir, E. E.; and Lasdon, L. "An Optimization-Based Decision Support System for a Product Mix Problem." *Interfaces* 12, no. 2 (April 1982): 26–31.

Taha, H. A. *Operations Research, An Introduction.* 4th ed. New York: Macmillan, 1987.

Zierer, T.; Mitchell, W.; and White, T. "Practical Applications of Linear Programming to Shell's Distribution Problems." *Interfaces* 6, no. 4 (August 1976): 13–26.

EXAMPLE PROBLEM SOLUTION

As a prelude to the problems, this section presents an example solution to a linear programming model formulation problem.

Problem Statement

Moore's Meat Packing Company produces a hot dog mixture in 1,000-pound batches. The mixture contains three ingredients—chicken, beef, and cereal. The cost per pound of each of these ingredients is as follows.

Ingredient	Cost/lb
Chicken	$3
Beef	5
Cereal	2

Each batch must contain the following:

a. At least 200 pounds of chicken

b. At least 400 pounds of beef
c. No more than 300 pounds of cereal

The company wants to know the optimal mixture of ingredients that minimizes cost. Formulate a linear programming model for this problem.

Step 1: Identify Decision Variables

Recall that the problem should not be "swallowed whole." Identify each part of the model separately, starting with the decision variables.

x_1 = lb of chicken
x_2 = lb of beef
x_3 = lb of cereal

Step 2: Formulate the Objective Function

minimize $Z = \$3x_1 + 5x_2 + 2x_3$
where
Z = cost per 1,000-lb batch
$\$3x_1$ = cost of chicken
$5x_2$ = cost of beef
$2x_3$ = cost of cereal

Step 3: Establish Model Constraints

The constraints of this problem are embodied in the recipe restrictions and (not to be overlooked) the fact that each batch must consist of 1,000 pounds of mixture.

$x_1 + x_2 + x_3 = 1,000$ lb
$x_1 > 200$ lb of chicken
$x_2 \geq 400$ lb of beef
$x_3 \leq 300$ lb of cereal

and

$x_1, x_2, x_3 \geq 0$

The Model

minimize $Z = \$3x_1 + 5x_2 + 2x_3$
subject to
$x_1 + x_2 + x_3 = 1,000$
$x_1 \geq 200$
$x_2 \geq 400$
$x_3 \leq 300$
$x_1, x_2, x_3 \geq 0$

Problems

1. The Southern Sporting Goods Company makes basketballs and footballs. Each product is produced from two resources—rubber and leather. The resource requirements for each product and the total resources available are as follows.

	Resource Requirements per Unit	
Product	Rubber (lb)	Leather (ft²)
Basketball	3	4
Football	2	5
Total resources available	500 lb	800 ft²

Each basketball produced results in a profit of $12, and each football earns $16 in profit. Formulate a linear programming model to determine the number of basketballs and footballs to produce in order to maximize profit.

2. A company produces two products, A and B, which have profits of $9 and $7, respectively. Each unit of product must be processed on two assembly lines, where the required production times are as follows.

	Hours/Unit	
Product	Line 1	Line 2
A	12	4
B	4	8
Total hours	60	40

Formulate a linear programming model to determine the optimal product mix that will maximize profit.

3. A hospital dietitian prepares breakfast menus every morning for the hospital patients. Part of the dietitian's responsibility is to make sure that minimum daily requirements for vitamins A and B are met. At the same time, the cost of the menus must be kept as low as possible. The main breakfast staples providing vitamins A and B are eggs, bacon, and cereal. The vitamin requirements and vitamin contributions for each staple follow.

	Vitamin Contributions			Minimum Daily
Vitamin	mg/Egg	mg/Bacon Strip	mg/Cereal Cup	Requirements
A	2	4	1	16
B	3	2	1	12

An egg costs $.04, a bacon strip costs $.03, and a cup of cereal costs $.02. The dietitian wants to know how much of each staple to serve per order to meet the minimum daily vitamin requirements while minimizing total cost. Formulate a linear programming model for this problem.

4. Irwin Textile Mills produces two types of cotton cloth—denim and corduroy. Corduroy is a heavier grade of cotton cloth and, as such, requires 7.5 pounds of raw cotton per yard, whereas denim requires 5 pounds of raw cotton per yard. A yard of corduroy requires 3.2 hours of processing time; a yard of denim requires 3.0 hours. Although the demand for denim is practically unlimited, the maximum demand for corduroy is 510 yards per month. The manufacturer has 6,500 pounds of cotton and 3,000 hours of processing time available each month. The manufacturer makes a profit of $2.25 per yard of denim and $3.10 per yard of corduroy. The manufacturer wants to know how many yards of each type of cloth to produce to maximize profit. Formulate a linear programming model for this problem.

5. The Pyrotec Company produces three electrical products—clocks, radios, and toasters. These products have the following resource requirements.

| | Resource Requirements | |
Product	Cost/Unit	Labor Hours/Unit
Clock	$ 7	2
Radio	10	3
Toaster	5	2

The manufacturer has a daily production budget of $2,000 and a maximum of 660 hours of labor. Maximum daily customer demand is for 200 clocks, 300 radios, and 150 toasters. Clocks sell for $15, radios for $20, and toasters for $12. The company desires to know the optimal product mix that will maximize profit. Formulate a linear programming model for this problem.

6. Betty Malloy, owner of the Eagle Tavern in Pittsburgh, is preparing for Super Bowl Sunday, and she must determine how much beer to stock. Betty stocks three brands of beer—Yodel, Shotz, and Rainwater. The cost per gallon (to the owner) of each brand is as follows.

Brand	Cost/Gallon
Yodel	$1.50
Shotz	.90
Rainwater	.50

The tavern has a budget of $2,000 for beer for Super Bowl Sunday. Betty sells Yodel at a rate of $3.00 per gallon, Shotz at $2.50 per gallon, and Rainwater at $1.75 per gallon. Based on past football games, Betty has determined the maximum customer demand to be 400 gallons of Yodel, 500 gallons of Shotz, and 300 gallons of Rainwater. The tavern has the capacity to stock 1,000 gallons of beer; Betty wants to stock up completely. Formulate a linear programming model to determine the number of gallons of each brand of beer to order so as to maximize profit.

7. The Kalo Fertilizer Company produces two brands of lawn fertilizer—Super Two and Green Grow—at plants in Fresno, California and Dearborn, Michigan. The plant at Fresno has resources available to produce 5,000 pounds of fertilizer daily; the plant at Dearborn has enough resources to produce 6,000 pounds daily. The cost per pound of producing each brand at each plant is as follows.

	Plant	
Product	Fresno	Dearborn
Super Two	$2	$4
Green Grow	2	3

The company has a daily budget of $45,000 for both plants. Based on past sales, the company knows the maximum demand (converted to a daily basis) is 6,000 pounds for Super Two and 7,000 pounds for Green Grow. The selling price is $9 per pound for Super Two and $7 per pound for Green Grow. The company wants to know the number of pounds of each brand of fertilizer to produce at each plant in order to maximize profit. Formulate a linear programming model for this problem.

8. The United Aluminum Company of Cincinnati produces three grades (high, medium, and low) of aluminum at two mills. Each mill has a different production capacity (in tons per day) for each grade, as follows.

Aluminum	Mill	
Grade	1	2
High	6	2
Medium	2	2
Low	4	10

The company has contracted with a manufacturing firm to supply at least 12 tons of high-grade aluminum, 8 tons of medium-grade aluminum, and 5 tons of low-grade aluminum. It costs United $6,000 per day to operate mill 1 and $7,000 per day to operate mill 2. The company wants to know the number of days to operate each mill in order to meet the contract at the minimum cost. Formulate a linear programming model for this problem.

9. Fred Friendly owns an automobile dealership in Tampa, Florida. Fred is presently attempting to determine how many cars to order from the factory in Detroit. Fred has a budget of $210,000 to purchase new cars. He

stocks three different styles—the Eagle (a full-size car), the Hawk (a medium-size car), and the Sparrow (a compact). The costs to Fred of the various models are as follows.

Car	Cost
Eagle	$8,000
Hawk	5,000
Sparrow	4,500

Fred sells Eagles for $11,000, Hawks for $8,500, and Sparrows for $7,000. Based on past sales, Fred knows that the maximum demand for Eagles is 80 cars; for Hawks, 175 cars; and for Sparrows, 250 cars. Fred has 8,000 square feet of space available on his lot to store new cars. An Eagle takes up 50 square feet, a Hawk requires 35 square feet, and a Sparrow requires 25 square feet. Fred wants to know how many cars of each style he should order from the distributor in order to maximize his total profit. Formulate a linear programming model for this problem.

10. The Hickory Cabinet and Furniture Company produces sofas, tables, and chairs at its plant in Greensboro, North Carolina. The plant uses three main resources to make furniture—wood, upholstery, and labor. The resource requirements for each piece of furniture and the total resources available weekly are as follows.

Furniture Product	Resource Requirements		
	Wood (lb)	Upholstery (yd)	Labor (hr)
Sofa	7	12	6
Table	5	—	9
Chair	4	7	5
Total available resources	2,250	1,000	240

The furniture is produced on a weekly basis and stored in a warehouse until the end of the week, when it is shipped out. The warehouse has a total capacity of 650 pieces of furniture. Each sofa earns $400 in profit, each table $275, and each chair $190. The company wants to know how many pieces of each type of furniture to make per week in order to maximize profit. Formulate a linear programming model for this problem.

11. The Bradley family owns 410 acres of farmland in North Carolina on which they grow corn and tobacco. Each acre of corn costs $105 to plant, cultivate, and harvest; each acre of tobacco costs $210. The Bradleys have a budget of $52,500 for next year. The government limits the number of acres of tobacco that can be planted to 100. The profit from each acre of corn is $300; the profit from each acre of tobacco is $520. The Bradleys want to know how many acres of each crop to plant in order to maximize their profit. Formulate a linear programming model for this problem.

12. The Avalon Cosmetics Company is trying to determine the number of salespeople it should allocate to its three regions—the East, the Midwest, and the West. The company has 100 salespeople that it wants to assign to the three regions. The annual profit achieved by a salesperson in each region is as follows.

Region	Profit per Salesperson
East	$25,000
Midwest	18,000
West	31,000

Because travel distances, costs of living, and other factors vary among the three regions, the annual cost of having a salesperson is $5,000 in the East, $11,000 in the Midwest, and $7,000 in the West. The company has $700,000 budgeted for expenses. To ensure nationwide exposure for its product, the company has decided that each region must have at least ten salespeople. The company wants to know how many salespeople to allocate to each region in order to maximize profit. Formulate a linear programming model for this problem.

13. As a result of a recently passed bill, a congressman's district has been allocated $4 million for programs and projects in the district. It is up to the congressman to decide how to distribute the money. The congressman has decided to allocate the money to four ongoing programs because of their importance to his district—a job training program, a parks project, a sanitation project, and a mobile library. However, the congressman wants to distribute the money in a manner that will please the most voters, or, in other words, gain him the most votes in the upcoming election. His staff's estimates of the number of votes gained per dollar spent for the various programs are as follows.

Program	Votes per $
Job training	.02
Parks	.09
Sanitation	.06
Mobile library	.04

In order also to satisfy several local influential citizens who financed his election, he is obligated to observe the following guidelines.

a. None of the programs can receive more than 40% of the total allocation.
b. The amount allocated to parks cannot exceed the total allocated to both the sanitation project and mobile library.
c. The amount allocated to job training must at least equal the amount spent on the sanitation project.

Any money not spent in the district will be returned to the government; therefore, the congressman wants to spend it all. The congressman wants to know the amount to allocate to each program in order to maximize his votes. Formulate a linear programming model for this problem.

14. The Grady Tire Company recaps the tires of three types of vehicles—automobiles, trucks, and heavy-duty earth-moving equipment. Each type of recap requires the following amounts of labor and rubber.

Tire	Labor (hr)	Rubber (lb)
Car	1.2	23
Truck	2.3	56
Heavy-duty	4.0	250

The company has a daily supply of 2,000 pounds of rubber. The company has 6 recappers who work 8 hours per day. The demand for heavy-duty recaps averages only 5 per day. The profit gained from recapping is $8 per car tire, $23 per truck tire, and $145 per heavy-duty tire. The company wants to know how many tires of each type to recap in order to maximize profit. Formulate a linear programming model for this problem.

15. The manager of a Burger Doodle franchise wants to determine how many sausage biscuits and ham biscuits to prepare each morning for breakfast customers. Each type of biscuit requires the following resources.

Biscuit	Labor (hr)	Sausage (lb)	Ham (lb)	Flour (lb)
Sausage	.010	.10	—	.04
Ham	.024	—	.15	.04

The franchise has 6 hours of labor available each morning. The manager has a contract with a local grocer for 30 pounds of sausage and 30 pounds of ham each morning. The manager also purchases 16 pounds of flour. The profit for a sausage biscuit is $.60; the profit for a ham biscuit is $.50. The manager wants to know the number of each type of biscuit to prepare each morning in order to maximize profit. Formulate a linear programming model for this problem.

16. The Neptune Fish Market in Denver advertises fresh seafood. Its three main items are shrimp, lobster, and crabs, which it flies in from Florida, Maine, and Baltimore, respectively. The maximum amount of seafood that can be flown in per day is 200 pounds. The shipping costs per pound for shrimp, lobster, and crabs are $3, $6, and $4, respectively, and the market has $500 available for shipping each day. Once the seafood is received by the market, it must be cleaned and packaged. A pound of shrimp requires 15 minutes of preparation; a pound of lobster, 5 minutes; and a pound of crab, 4 minutes. The market has 3 hours available daily to prepare the seafood. A pound of shrimp earns the

market $9 in profit; a pound of lobster, $12; and a pound of crab, $7. The manager of the market wants to know how many pounds of each type of seafood to order each day in order to maximize profit. Formulate a linear programming model for this problem.

17. The Morris and Taylor Office Supply Company promotes its business by guaranteeing prompt delivery. Its three most demanded items are binders, file folders, and paper clips, all of which it sells by the case. The company believes it is imperative that these orders be filled immediately. In order to do so, the company estimates that it must stock 100 cases of binders, 70 cases of file folders, and 175 cases of paper clips at all times. The company does not expect to make a lot of profit from its instant delivery policy—the policy is viewed mainly as a customer service that will result in more lucrative orders. However, the company does want to at least break even, which means it must sell enough of the three items to make at least $3,500 per week. The profit per case of binders is $35; of file folders, $20; and of paper clips, $12. The cost to the company of purchasing and keeping these items in stock is $10 for binders, $16 for file folders, and $7 for paper clips. The company wants to know how many of each item to keep in stock in order to minimize cost. Formulate a linear programming model for this problem.

18. The Southfork Feed Company makes a feed mix from four ingredients—oats, corn, soybeans, and a vitamin supplement. The company has 200 pounds of oats, 300 pounds of corn, 150 pounds of soybeans, and 50 pounds of vitamin supplement available for the mix. The company has the following recipe for the mix.

    a. At least 30% of the mix must be soybeans.
    b. At least 20% of the mix must be the vitamin supplement.
    c. The ratio of corn to oats cannot exceed 2 to 1.
    d. The amount of oats cannot exceed the amount of soybeans.
    e. The mix must be at least 500 pounds.

    A pound of oats costs $.50; a pound of corn, $1.20; a pound of soybeans, $.60; and a pound of vitamin supplement, $2.00. The feed company wants to know the number of pounds of each ingredient to put in the mix in order to minimize cost. Formulate a linear programming model for this problem.

19. The United Charities annual fund-raising drive is scheduled to take place next week. Donations are collected during the day and night, by telephone and through personal contact. The average donation resulting from each type of contact is as follows.

	Phone	Personal
Day	$2	$4
Night	3	7

The charity group has enough donated gasoline and cars to make at most 300 personal contacts during one day and night. The volunteer minutes required to conduct each type of interview are as follows.

	Phone	Personal
Day	6	15
Night	5	12

The charity has 20 volunteer hours available each day and 40 volunteer hours available each night. The chairman of the fund-raising drive wants to know how many different types of contacts to schedule in a 24-hour period (i.e., one day and one night) in order to maximize total donations. Formulate a linear programming model for this problem.

20. Jean Brooks, a young attorney, has accumulated $175,000 and is seeking advice from an investment counselor on how to invest some or all of the money. With the aid of the counselor, she has decided to invest some money in each of the following alternatives — treasury bills, AAA bonds, common stock, and negotiable certificates of deposit. The counselor, after careful analysis, has determined the yield and risk rating (on a scale of 1 to 4, where 4 is the most risky) for each alternative to be as follows.

Investment Alternative	Expected Annual Yield	Risk Rating
Treasury bill	6.50	1
AAA bond	8.50	3
Common stock	12.00	4
Negotiable CD	8.00	2

Each treasury bill costs $1,000; each AAA bond costs $5,000; each stock certificate costs $200; and each certificate of deposit costs $500. Jean has determined that the average risk factor associated with her total investment should not exceed 2.5. In addition, she has decided that not more than 50% of the total investment should be in treasury bills. Jean wants to know how much to invest in each alternative in order to maximize the expected annual yield. Formulate a linear programming model for this problem.

21. Iggy Olweski, a professional football player, is retiring, and he is thinking about going into the insurance business. He plans to sell three types of policies — homeowner's insurance, auto insurance, and life insurance. The average amount of profit returned per year by each type of insurance policy is as follows.

Policy	Yearly Profit per Policy ($)
Homeowner's	$35
Auto	20
Life	58

Each homeowner's policy will cost $14 to sell and maintain; each auto policy, $12; and each life insurance policy, $35. Iggy has projected a budget of $35,000 per year. In addition, the sale of a homeowner's policy will require 6 hours of effort; the sale of an auto policy, 3 hours; and the sale of a life insurance policy, 12 hours. Based on the number of working hours he and several employees could contribute, Iggy has estimated that he would have available 20,000 hours per year. Iggy wants to know how many of each type of insurance policy he would have to sell each year in order to maximize profit. Formulate a linear programming model for this problem.

22. A publishing house publishes three weekly magazines — *Daily Life, Agriculture Today*, and *Surf's Up*. Publication of one issue of each of the magazines requires the following amounts of production time and paper.

Magazine	Production (hr)	Paper (lb)
Daily Life	.01	.2
Agriculture Today	.03	.5
Surf's Up	.02	.3

Each week the publisher has available 50 hours of production time and 3,000 pounds of paper. Total circulation for all three magazines must exceed 5,000 issues per week if the company is to keep its advertisers. The selling price per issue is $.75 for *Daily Life*, $1.50 for *Agriculture Today*, and $.40 for *Surf's Up*. Based on past sales, the publisher knows that the maximum weekly demand for *Daily Life* is 3,000 issues; for *Agriculture Today*, 2,000 issues; and for *Surf's Up*, 6,000 issues. The production manager wants to know the number of issues of each magazine to produce weekly in order to maximize total sales revenue. Formulate a linear programming model for this problem.

23. The manager of a department store in Seattle is attempting to decide on the types and amounts of advertising the store should use. He has invited representatives from the local radio station, television station, and newspaper to make presentations in which they describe their audiences.

   a. The television station representative indicates that a TV commercial, which costs $15,000, would reach 25,000 potential customers. The breakdown of the audience is as follows.

	Male	Female
Old	5,000	5,000
Young	5,000	10,000

b. The newspaper representative claims to be able to provide an audience of 10,000 potential customers at a cost of $4,000 per ad. The breakdown of the audience is as follows.

	Male	Female
Old	4,000	3,000
Young	2,000	1,000

c. The radio station representative says that the audience for one of the station's commercials, which costs $6,000, is 15,000 customers. The breakdown of the audience is as follows.

	Male	Female
Old	1,500	1,500
Young	4,500	7,500

The store has the following advertising policy:

a. Use at least twice as many radio commercials as newspaper ads.
b. Reach at least 100,000 customers.
c. Reach at least twice as many young people as old people.
d. Make sure that at least 30% of the audience is women.

Available space limits the number of newspaper ads to 7. The store wants to know the optimal number of each type of advertising to purchase to minimize total cost. Formulate a linear programming model for this problem.

24. The Rucklehouse Public Relations firm has been contracted to do a survey following a primary in New Hampshire. The firm must assign interviewers to do the survey. The interviews are conducted by telephone and in person. One person can conduct 80 telephone interviews or 40 personal interviews in a day. The following criteria have been established by the firm to ensure a representative survey:

a. At least 3,000 interviews must be conducted.
b. At least 1,000 interviews must be by telephone.
c. At least 800 interviews must be personal.

An interviewer conducts only one type of interview each day. The cost is $50 per day for a telephone interviewer and $70 per day for a personal interviewer. The firm wants to know the minimum number of interviewers to hire in order to minimize the total cost of the survey. Formulate a linear programming model for this problem.

25. The Big Pup Dog Food Company makes two brands of dog food— Chowtime and Big Pup. A batch of each brand of dog food contains two ingredients—meat and cereal fillers. The company has a maximum of 500 pounds of meat and 700 pounds of cereal. A batch of each brand is mixed according to the following specifications.

Brand	Mixing Specifications
Chowtime	At least 30% meat; not more than 40% cereal
Big Pup	At least 10% meat; not more than 60% cereal

A pound of meat costs $1, and a pound of cereal costs $.35. A pound of Chowtime sells for $4; a pound of Big Pup sells for $3. The company wants to know the number of pounds of each brand of dog food to make in order to maximize profit. Formulate a linear programming model for this problem.

26. Joe Henderson runs a small metal parts shop. The shop contains three machines—a drill press, a lathe, and a grinder. Joe has three operators, each certified to work on all three machines. However, each operator performs better on some machines than on others. The shop has contracted to do a big job that requires all three machines. The times required by the various operators to perform the required operations on each machine are summarized below.

Operator	Drill Press (min)	Lathe (min)	Grinder (min)
1	22	18	35
2	41	30	28
3	25	36	18

Joe Henderson wants to assign one operator to each machine so that the total operating time for all three operators is minimized. Formulate a linear programming model for this problem.

27. Green Valley Mills produces carpet at plants in St. Louis and Richmond. The plants ship the carpet to two outlets in Chicago and Atlanta. The cost per ton of shipping carpet from each of the two plants to the two warehouses is as follows.

	To	
From	Chicago	Atlanta
St. Louis	$40	$65
Richmond	70	30

The plant at St. Louis can supply 250 tons of carpet per week, and the plant at Richmond can supply 400 tons per week. The Chicago outlet has a demand of 300 tons per week; the outlet at Atlanta demands 350 tons per week. Company managers want to determine the number of tons of carpet to ship from each plant to each outlet in order to minimize the total shipping cost. Formulate a linear programming model for this problem.

28. The Bluegrass Distillery produces custom blended whiskey. A particular blend consists of rye and bourbon whiskey. The company has received an order for a minimum of 400 gallons of the custom blend. The customer specified that the order must contain at least 40% rye and not more than 250 gallons of bourbon. The customer also specified that the blend should be mixed in the ratio of two parts rye to one part bourbon. The distillery can produce 500 gallons per week regardless of the blend. The production manager wants to complete the order in one week. The blend is sold for $5 per gallon. The distillery company's cost per gallon is $2 for rye and $1 for bourbon. The company wants to determine the blend mix that will meet customer requirements and maximize profits. Formulate a linear programming model for this problem.

29. A manufacturer of bathroom fixtures produces fiberglass bathtubs in an assembly operation consisting of three processes—molding, smoothing, and painting. The number of units that can be put through each process in an hour is as follows.

Process	Output (units/hr)
Molding	7
Smoothing	12
Painting	10

(Note: The three processes are continuous and sequential; thus, no more units can be smoothed or painted than have been molded.) The labor costs per hour are $8 for molding, $5 for smoothing, and $6.50 for painting. The company's labor budget is $3,000 per week. A total of 120 hours of labor is available for all three processes per week. Each completed bathtub requires 90 pounds of fiberglass, and the company has a total of 10,000 pounds of fiberglass available each week. Each bathtub earns a profit of $175. The manager of the company wants to know how many hours per week to run each process in order to maximize profit. Formulate a linear programming model for this problem.

30. A manufacturing firm located in Chicago ships its product by railroad to Detroit. Several different routes are available, as shown in the following diagram, also referred to as a network.

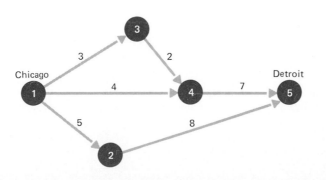

Each circle in the network represents a railroad junction. Each arrow is a railroad branch between two junctions. The number above each arrow is the number of travel hours necessary to ship 1 ton of product from junction to junction. The firm wants to ship 5 tons of its product from Chicago to Detroit in the minimum amount of time. Formulate a linear programming model for this problem.

31. Reformulate the linear programming model on page 23, assuming that the investor does not have to invest the entire $70,000 available.

32. A refinery blends four petroleum components into three grades of gasoline—regular, premium, and low lead. The maximum quantities available of each component and the cost per barrel are as follows.

Component	Maximum Barrels Available/Day	Cost (barrel)
1	5,000	$ 9.00
2	2,400	7.00
3	4,000	12.00
4	1,500	6.00

To ensure that each gasoline grade retains certain essential characteristics, the refinery has put limits on the percentages of the components in each blend. The limits as well as the selling prices for the various grades are as follows.

Grade	Component Specifications	Selling Price (barrel)
Regular	Not less than 40% of 1 Not more than 20% of 2 Not less than 30% of 3	$12.00
Premium	Not less than 40% of 3	18.00
Low Lead	Not more than 50% of 2 Not less than 10% of 1	10.00

Management wishes to determine the optimal mix of the four components that will maximize profit. Formulate a linear programming model for this problem.

33. The Cash and Carry Building Supply Company has received the following order for boards in three lengths.

Length	Order (quantity)
7 feet	700 boards
9 feet	1,200 boards
10 feet	300 boards

The company has 25-foot standard-length boards in stock. Therefore, the standard-length boards must be cut into the lengths necessary to meet order requirements. Naturally, the company wishes to minimize the number of standard-length boards used. The company must therefore determine how to cut up the 25-foot boards so as to meet the order requirements and minimize the number of standard-length boards used.

a. Formulate a linear programming model for this problem.

b. When a board is cut in a specific pattern, the amount of board left over is referred to as "trim loss." Reformulate the linear programming model for this problem, assuming that the objective is to minimize trim loss rather than to minimize the total number of boards used.

34. An investment firm has $1 million to invest in stocks, bonds, certificates of saving, and real estate. The firm wishes to determine the mix of investments that will maximize the cash value at the end of six years.

Opportunities to invest in stocks and bonds will be available at the beginning of each of the next six years. Each dollar invested in stocks will return $1.20 (a profit of $.20) two years later; the return can be immediately reinvested in any alternative. Each dollar invested in bonds will return $1.40 three years later; the return can be reinvested immediately.

Opportunities to invest in certificates of saving will be available only once, at the beginning of the second year. Each dollar invested in certificates will return $1.80 four years later. Opportunities to invest in real estate will be available at the beginning of the fifth and sixth years. Each dollar invested will return $1.10 one year later.

To minimize risk, the firm has decided to diversify its investments. The total amount invested in stocks cannot exceed 30% of total investments, and at least 25% of total investments must be in certificates of saving.

The firm's management wishes to determine the optimal mix of investments in the various alternatives that will maximize the amount of cash at the end of the sixth year. Formulate a linear programming model for this problem.

35. The Jones, Jones, Smith, and Brubaker commodities trading firm knows the prices at which it will be able to buy and sell a certain commodity during the next four months. The buying price (c_i) and selling price (p_i) for each of the given months (i) are as follows:

	Month i			
	1	2	3	4
c_i	$5	$6	$7	$8
p_i	4	8	6	7

The firm's warehouse has a maximum capacity of 10,000 bushels. At the beginning of the first month, 2,000 bushels are in the warehouse. The trading firm wants to know the amounts that should be bought and sold each month in order to maximize profit. Formulate a linear programming model for this problem. Assume that no storage costs are incurred and that sales are made at the beginning of the month, followed by purchases.

36. The production manager of Videotechnics Company is attempting to determine the upcoming five-month production schedule for video recorders. Past production records indicate that 2,000 recorders can be produced per month. An additional 600 recorders can be produced monthly on an overtime basis. Unit cost is $10 for recorders produced during regular working hours and $15 for those produced on an overtime basis. Contracted sales per month are as follows:

Month	Contracted Sales
1	$1,200
2	2,100
3	2,400
4	3,000
5	4,000

Inventory carrying costs are $2 per recorder per month. The manager does not want any inventory carried over past the fifth month. The manager wants to know the monthly production that will minimize total production and inventory costs. Formulate a linear programming model for this problem.

37. The manager of the Ewing and Barnes Department Store has four employees available to assign to three departments in the store — lamps, sporting goods, and linen. The manager wants each of these departments to have at least one employee, but not more than two. Therefore, two departments will be assigned one employee and one department will be assigned two. Each employee has different areas of expertise, which are reflected in the daily sales each employee is expected to generate in each department, shown below.

	Department		
Employee	Lamps	Sporting Goods	Linen
1	$130	$150	$ 90
2	275	300	100
3	180	225	140
4	200	120	160

The manager wishes to know which employee(s) to assign to each department in order to maximize expected sales.

a. Formulate a linear programming model for this problem.
b. Suppose that the department manager plans to assign only one employee to each department and to lay off the least productive employee. Formulate a new linear programming model that reflects this new condition.

38. Managers at the Transcontinent Shipping and Supply Company want to know the maximum tonnage of goods they can transport from city A to city F. The firm can contract for railroad cars on different rail routes linking these cities via several intermediate stations, shown in the following diagram. All railroad cars are of equal capacity.

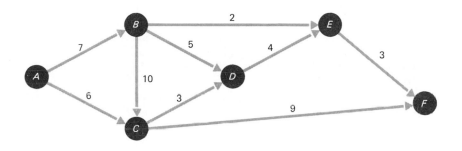

The firm can transport a maximum amount of goods from point to point, based upon the maximum number of railroad cars available on each route segment. Managers want to determine the maximum tonnage that can be shipped from city A to city F. Formulate a linear programming model for this problem.

39. Alexis Harrington received an inheritance of $95,000, and she is considering two speculative investments—the purchase of land and the purchase of cattle. Each investment would be for one year. Under the present (normal) economic conditions, each dollar invested in land will return the principal plus 20% of the principal; each dollar invested in cattle will return the principal plus 30%. However, both investments are relatively risky. If economic conditions were to deteriorate, there is an 18% chance she would lose everything she invested in land and a 30% chance she would lose everything she invested in cattle. Alexis does not want to lose more than $20,000 (on average). She wants to know how much to invest in each alternative so as to maximize the cash value of the investments at the end of one year. Formulate a linear programming model for this problem.

40. A ship has two cargo holds, one fore and one aft. The fore cargo hold has a weight capacity of 70,000 pounds and a volume capacity of 30,000 cubic feet. The aft hold has a weight capacity of 90,000 pounds and a volume capacity of 40,000 cubic feet. The shipowner has contracted to carry loads of packaged beef and grain. The total weight of the available beef is 85,000 pounds; the total weight of the available grain is 100,000 pounds. The volume per mass of the beef is .2 cubic foot

per pound, and the volume per mass of the grain is .4 cubic foot per pound. The profit for shipping beef is $.35 per pound, and the profit for shipping grain is $.12 per pound. The shipowner is free to accept all or part of the available cargo; he wants to know how much meat and grain to accept in order to maximize profit. Formulate a linear programming model for this problem.

41. The White Horse Apple Products Company purchases apples from local growers and makes applesauce and apple juice. It costs $.60 to produce a jar of applesauce and $.85 to produce a bottle of apple juice. The company has a policy that at least 30% but not more than 60% of its output must be applesauce.

    The company wants to meet but not exceed the demand for each product. The company marketing manager estimates that the demand for applesauce is a maximum of 5,000 jars, plus an additional 3 jars for each $1 spent on advertising. The maximum demand for apple juice is estimated to be 4,000 bottles, plus an additional 5 bottles for every $1 spent to promote apple juice. The company has $16,000 to spend on producing and advertising applesauce and apple juice. Applesauce sells for $1.45 per jar, and apple juice sells for $1.75 per bottle. The company wants to know how many units of each product to produce and how much to spend on advertising each product in order to maximize profit. Formulate a linear programming model for this problem.

42. Mazy's department store has decided to stay open for business on a 24-hour basis. The store manager has divided the 24-hour day into six four-hour periods and determined the following minimum personnel requirements for each period.

Time	Personnel Needed
12:00– 4:00 A.M.	90
4:00– 8:00 A.M.	215
8:00–12:00 P.M.	250
12:00– 4:00 P.M.	65
4:00– 8:00 P.M.	300
8:00–12:00 A.M.	125

Store personnel must report for work at the beginning of one of the above time periods and must work for 8 consecutive hours. The store manager wants to know the minimum number of employees to assign to each four-hour segment so as to minimize the total number of employees. Formulate a linear programming model for this problem.

43. A company that has a two-year contract to haul ore from an open-pit mine to loading docks needs 200 additional trucks. The company can purchase trucks only at the beginning of the two-year period. Alternatively, the company can lease trucks for $80,000 per year (paid at the beginning of the year). Trucks cost $140,000 each to purchase and have a useful life of two years. They have no salvage value at the end of the

two years. The mining company has $8 million cash available to lease and/or buy trucks at the beginning of year 1. In addition, the company can obtain a loan each year for as much as $20 million at 16% interest per year. The loan agreement requires that the company repay the borrowed amount plus interest at the end of the year. Each truck will earn $120,000 per year, which becomes part of the flow of cash available to the company for truck leasing and loan repayment. The company wants to minimize the total cost of expanding its fleet of trucks over a two-year period. Formulate a linear programming model for this problem.

44. The Big Country, a large amusement theme park, hires college students to work during the months of May, June, July, and August. The park needs a total of 32,000 hours of this type of labor in May, 48,000 hours in June, 64,000 hours in July, and 48,000 hours in August. Students need one month of training before they can work regularly at a job, so they must be hired at least one month before they are needed. In addition, during training, each trainee requires 50 hours of supervision by an experienced employee. The experienced employee is not available for regular work during these 50 hours. Each experienced employee can work a maximum of 160 hours per month. If more employees are available than are required, each employee works less than 160 hours; no one is laid off. Fifteen percent of all experienced employees quit each month. Employees who quit agree to work out the month in which they quit. The salary of an experienced employee is $650 per month; a trainee is paid $400 per month. Two hundred fifty experienced employees are available at the beginning of May. The personnel director at the park wants to know how many employees to hire and train through July in order to minimize cost. Formulate a linear programming model for this problem.

3

Graphical Illustration of Linear Programming

Following the formulation of a mathematical model, the next stage in the application of linear programming to a decision-making problem is to find the solution of the model. The most common solution approach is to solve algebraically the set of mathematical relationships that form the model, thus determining the values for the decision variables. However, because the relationships are *linear*, some models and solutions can be illustrated *graphically*.

The graphical method is realistically limited to models with only two decision variables, which can be represented on a graph of two dimensions. Models with three decision variables can be graphed in three dimensions, but the process is quite cumbersome, and models of four or more decision variables cannot be graphed at all.

Although the graphical method is limited as a solution approach, it is very useful at this point in our presentation of linear programming, in that it gives a "picture" of how a solution is derived. Graphs can provide a clearer understanding of how the mathematical solution approaches presented in subsequent chapters work, and thus a better understanding of the solutions.

Limitations of the graphical solution method

GRAPHICAL ILLUSTRATION OF A LINEAR PROGRAMMING MODEL

The "product mix" model developed in Chapter 2 will be used to demonstrate the graphical interpretation of a linear programming problem. Recall that the problem described the Colonial Pottery Company's attempts to decide how many bowls and mugs to produce daily, given limited amounts of labor and clay. The complete linear programming model was formulated as

maximize $Z = \$4x_1 + 5x_2$

subject to

$x_1 + 2x_2 \leq 40$ hr of labor

$4x_1 + 3x_2 \leq 120$ lb of clay

$x_1, x_2 \leq 0$

where

$x_1 =$ number of bowls produced

$x_2 =$ number of mugs produced

Further, recall that the values of \$4 and \$5 in the objective function are the profits for a bowl and mug, respectively; the values 1 and 2 in the first constraint are the hours of labor required to produce each bowl and mug, respectively; and the values 4 and 3 in the second constraint represent the pounds of clay required to produce each bowl and mug.

Figure 3.1 is a set of coordinates for the decision variables x_1 and x_2, on which the graph of our model will be drawn. Note that only the positive quadrant is drawn (i.e., the quadrant where x_1 and x_2

FIGURE 3.1

Coordinates for Graphical Analysis

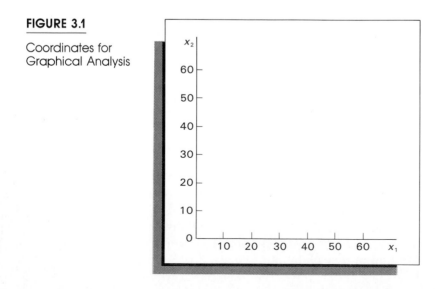

will always be positive) because of the nonnegativity constraints, $x_1 \geq 0$ and $x_2 \geq 0$.

The first step in drawing the graph of the model is to plot the constraints on the graph. This is done by treating both constraints as equations (or straight lines) and plotting each line on the graph. Consider the labor constraint line first:

$$x_1 + 2x_2 = 40$$

A simple procedure for plotting this line is to determine two points that are on the line and then draw a straight line through the points. One point can be found by letting $x_1 = 0$ and solving for x_2:

$$(0) + 2x_2 = 40$$
$$x_2 = 20$$

Thus, one point is at the coordinates $x_1 = 0$ and $x_2 = 20$. A second point can be found by letting $x_2 = 0$ and solving for x_1:

$$x_1 + 2(0) = 40$$
$$x_1 = 40$$

Now we have a second point, $x_1 = 40$, $x_2 = 0$. The line on the graph representing this equation is drawn by connecting these two points as shown in Figure 3.2. However, this is only the graph of the constraint *line* and does not reflect the entire constraint, which also includes the values that are less than or equal to ($\leq$) this line. The *area* representing the entire constraint is shown in Figure 3.3.

To test the correctness of the constraint area, check any two points — one inside the constraint area and one outside. For ex-

Plotting the constraint lines

The constraint area

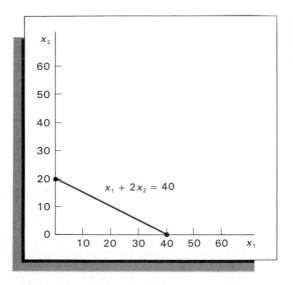

FIGURE 3.2

Graph of the Labor Constraint Line

FIGURE 3.3

The Labor
Constraint Area

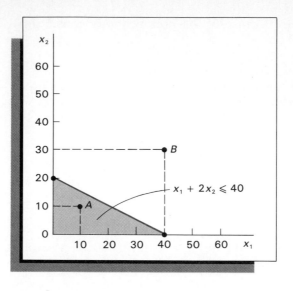

ample, check point A in Figure 3.3, which is at the intersection of $x_1 = 10$ and $x_2 = 10$. Substituting these values into the labor constraint,

$10 + 2(10) \le 40$

$30 \le 40$ hr

shows that point A is indeed within the constraint area, as these values for x_1 and x_2 yield a quantity that does not exceed the limit of 40 hours. Next, check point B at $x_1 = 40$ and $x_2 = 30$.

$40 + 2(30) \le 40$

$100 \not\le 40$ hr

Point B is obviously outside the constraint area, as the values for x_1 and x_2 yield a quantity (100) that exceeds the limit of 40 hours.

The line for the clay constraint is drawn in the same way as the one for the labor constraint — by finding two points on the constraint line and connecting them with a straight line. First, let $x_1 = 0$ and solve for x_2.

$4(0) + 3x_2 = 120$

$x_2 = 40$

This operation results in a point, $x_1 = 0$, $x_2 = 40$. Next, let $x_2 = 0$ and solve for x_1.

$4x_1 + 3(0) = 120$

$x_1 = 30$

This operation yields a second point, $x_1 = 30$, $x_2 = 0$. Plotting these points on the graph and connecting them with a line gives the constraint line and area for clay, as shown in Figure 3.4.

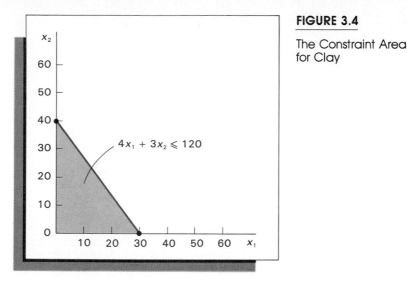

FIGURE 3.4

The Constraint Area
for Clay

Combining the two individual graphs for labor and clay (Figs. 3.3 and 3.4) produces a graph of the model constraints, as shown in Figure 3.5. The shaded area in Figure 3.5 is the area that is common to both model constraints. Therefore, this is the only area on the graph that contains points (i.e., values for x_1 and x_2) that will satisfy both constraints simultaneously. For example, consider the points R, S, and T in Figure 3.6. Point R satisfies both constraints; thus, we say it is a *feasible* solution point. Point S satisfies the clay constraint ($4x_1 + 3x_2 \leq 120$) but exceeds the labor constraint, so it is infeasible. Point T satisfies neither constraint, so it is also infeasible.

Feasible and infeasible solution points

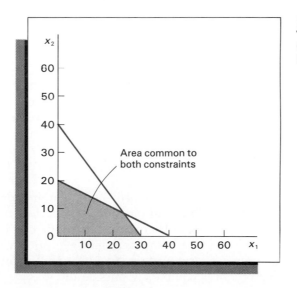

FIGURE 3.5

Graph of Both
Model Constraints

FIGURE 3.6

The Feasible
Solution Area

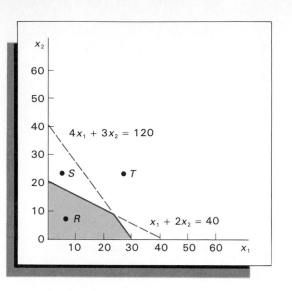

Feasible solution
area

The shaded area in Figure 3.6 is referred to as the *feasible solution area,* since all the points in this area satisfy both constraints. Some point within this feasible solution area will result in *maximum profit* for the Colonial Pottery Company. The next step in the graphical solution approach is to locate this point.

The Solution Point

Determining the
point in the feasible
solution area that
will result in
maximum profit

The second step in the graphical solution method is to locate the point in the feasible solution area that will result in the greatest total profit. To begin the solution analysis, we will first plot the objective function line for an *arbitrarily* selected level of profit. For example, if profit, Z, is $80, the objective function is

$$\$80 = 4x_1 + 5x_2$$

Plotting the
objective function
line

Plotting this line just as we plotted the constraint lines results in the graph shown in Figure 3.7. Every point on this line is in the feasible solution area and will result in a profit of $80 (i.e., every combination of x_1 and x_2 on this line will give a Z value of $80). However, let us see whether an even greater profit will still provide a feasible solution. For example, consider profits of $120 and $160, as shown in Figure 3.8.

Moving the
objective function
line through the
feasible area

A portion of the objective function line for a profit of $120 is outside the feasible solution area, but part of the line remains within the feasible area. Therefore, this profit line indicates that there are feasible solution points that give a profit greater than $80. Now let us increase profit again, to $160. This profit line, also shown in Figure 3.8, is completely outside the feasible solution area. The fact

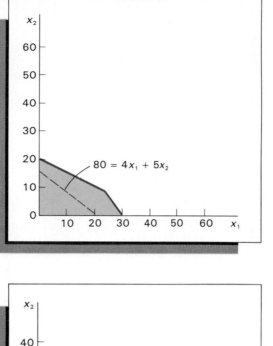

FIGURE 3.7

Objective Function
Line for $Z = \$80$

FIGURE 3.8

Alternative
Objective Function
Lines for Profits, Z,
of $80, $120, and
$160

that no points on this line are feasible indicates that a profit of $160 is not possible.

Since a profit of $160 is too great for the constraint limitations, as shown in Figure 3.8, the question of the maximum profit value remains. We can see from Figure 3.8 that profit increases as the objective function line moves away from the origin (i.e., the point $x_1 = 0$, $x_2 = 0$). Given this characteristic, the maximum profit will be attained at the point where the objective function line is farthest from the origin *and* is still touching a point in the feasible solution area. This point is shown as point B in Figure 3.9.

FIGURE 3.9

Identification of
Optimal Solution
Point

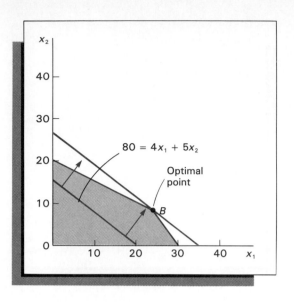

To find point B, place a straightedge parallel to the objective function line $\$80 = 4x_1 + 5x_2$ in Figure 3.8 and move it outward from the origin as far as you can without losing contact with the feasible solution area. Point B is referred to as the *optimal* (i.e., best) solution.

The optimal
solution point

The Graphical Solution

The third step in the graphical solution approach is to solve for the values of x_1 and x_2 once the optimal solution point has been found. It is possible to determine the x_1 and x_2 coordinates of point B in Figure 3.9 directly from the graph, as shown in Figure 3.10. The graphical coordinates corresponding to point B in Figure 3.10 are $x_1 = 24$ and $x_2 = 8$. This is the optimal solution for the decision variables in the problem. However, unless an absolutely accurate graph is drawn, it is frequently difficult to determine the correct solution directly from the graph. A more exact approach is to determine the solution values mathematically once the optimal point on the graph has been determined. The mathematical approach for determining the solution will be described in the following pages. First, however, we will consider a few characteristics of the solution.

Determining the
solution values
mathematically

In Figure 3.9, as the objective function was increased, the last point it touched in the feasible solution area was on the boundary of the feasible solution area. The solution point is always on this boundary, because the boundary contains the points farthest from the origin (i.e., the points corresponding to the greatest profit). This

Characteristics of
the optimal solution
point

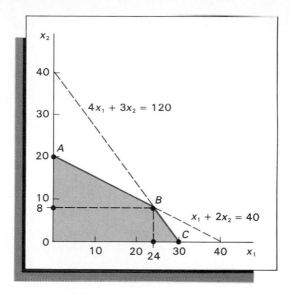

FIGURE 3.10

Optimal Solution
Coordinates

characteristic of linear programming problems reduces the number
of possible solution points considerably, from all points in the solution area to just those points on the boundary. However, the number of possible solution points is reduced even more by another
characteristic of linear programming problems.

The solution point will be on the boundary of the feasible solution area and at one of the *corners* of the boundary where two constraint lines intersect. (The graphical axes, you will recall, are also
constraints, since $x_1 \geq 0$ and $x_2 \geq 0$.) These corners (points A, B,
and C in Fig. 3.10) are protrusions, or *extremes*, in the feasible solution area; they are called *extreme points*. It has been proven mathematically that the optimal solution in a linear programming model
will always occur at an extreme point. Therefore, in our example
problem, the possible solution points are limited to the three extreme points, A, B, and C. The optimal extreme point is the extreme
point the objective function touches last as it leaves the feasible solution area, as shown in Figure 3.9.

From the graph shown in Figure 3.10, we know that the optimal
solution point is B. Since point B is formed by the intersection of two
constraint lines, these two lines are *equal* at point B. Thus, the values
of x_1 and x_2 at that intersection can be found by solving the two
equations *simultaneously*.

First, convert both equations to functions of x_1:

$x_1 + 2x_2 = 40$
$\quad\quad x_1 = 40 - 2x_2$

Extreme points

The optimal
extreme point

Solving
simultaneous
equations to
determine the
variable values at
the optimal solution
point

and

$$4x_1 + 3x_2 = 120$$
$$4x_1 = 120 - 3x_2$$
$$x_1 = 30 - 3x_2/4$$

Now let x_1 in the first equation equal x_1 in the second equation,

$$40 - 2x_2 = 30 - 3x_2/4$$

The optimal
solution values

and solve for x_2:

$$5x_2/4 = 10$$
$$x_2 = 8$$

Substituting $x_2 = 8$ into either one of the original equations gives a value for x_1:

$$x_1 = 40 - 2x_2$$
$$x_1 = 40 - 2(8)$$
$$x_1 = 24$$

Thus, the optimal solution at point B in Figure 3.10 is $x_1 = 24$ and $x_2 = 8$. Substituting these values into the objective function gives the maximum profit,

$$Z = \$4x_1 + 5x_2$$
$$Z = \$4(24) + 5(8)$$
$$Z = \$136$$

Interpreting the
solution

In terms of the original problem, the solution indicates that if the pottery company produces 24 bowls and 8 mugs, it will receive $136, the maximum daily profit possible (given the resource constraints).

An alternative way
to find the optimal
solution point

Given that the optimal solution will be at one of the extreme corner points A, B, or C, you can find the solution by testing each of the three points to see which results in the greatest profit, rather than by graphing the objective function and seeing which point it last touches as it moves out of the feasible solution area. Figure 3.11 shows the solution values for all three points, A, B, and C, and the amount of profit, Z, at each point.

As indicated in the discussion of Figure 3.9, point B is the optimal solution point because it is the last point the objective function touches before it leaves the solution area. In other words, the objective function determines which extreme point is optimal. This is because the objective function designates the profit that will accrue from each combination of x_1 and x_2 values at the extreme points. If the objective function had had different coefficients (i.e., different x_1 and x_2 profit values), one of the extreme points other than B might have been optimal.

Assume for a moment that the profit for a bowl is $7 instead of $4, and the profit for a mug is $2 instead of $5. These values result

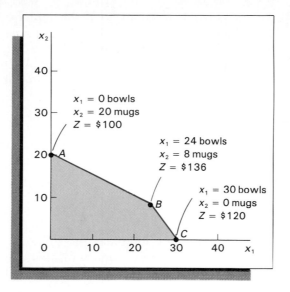

FIGURE 3.11

Solutions at All Corner Points

in a new objective function, $Z = \$7x_1 + 2x_2$. If the model constraints for labor or clay are not changed, the feasible solution area remains the same, as shown in Figure 3.12. However, the location of the objective function in Figure 3.12 is different from that of the original objective function in Figure 3.9. The reason for this change is that the new profit coefficients give the linear objective function a new *slope*.

The slope can be determined by transforming the objective function into the general equation for a straight line, $y = a + bx$, where

Changing the objective function

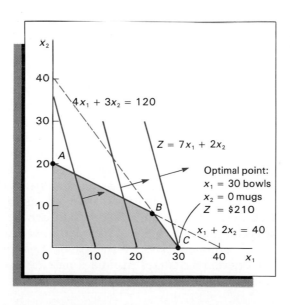

FIGURE 3.12

The Optimal Solution with $Z = 7x_1 + 2x_2$

y is the dependent variable, a is the y intercept, b is the slope, and x is the independent variable. For our example objective function, x_2 is the dependent variable corresponding to y (i.e., it is on the vertical axis), and x_1 is the independent variable. Thus, the objective function can be transformed into the general equation of a line as follows:

$$Z = 7x_1 + 2x_2$$
$$2x_2 = Z - 7x_1$$
$$x_2 = \frac{Z}{2} - \frac{7}{2}x_1$$
$$\quad \uparrow \quad \uparrow \quad \uparrow$$
$$\quad y \quad a \quad b$$

This transformation identifies the slope of the new objective function as $-7/2$ (the minus sign indicates that the line slopes downward). In contrast, the slope of the original objective function was $-4/5$.

If we move this new objective function out through the feasible solution area, the last extreme point it touches is point C. Simultaneously solving the constraint lines at point C results in the following solution:

$$x_1 = 30$$
$$4x_1 + 3x_2 = 120$$

and

$$x_2 = 40 - 4x_1/3$$
$$x_2 = 40 - 4(30)/3$$
$$x_2 = 0$$

A new solution

Thus, the optimal solution at point C in Figure 3.12 is $x_1 = 30$ bowls, $x_2 = 0$ mugs, and $Z = \$210$ profit. Altering the objective function coefficients has resulted in a new solution.

This brief example of the effects of altering the objective function highlights two useful points. First, the optimal extreme point is determined by the objective function, and an extreme point on one axis of the graph is as likely to be the optimal solution as is an extreme point on a different axis. Second, the solution is sensitive to the values of the coefficients in the objective function. If the objective function coefficients are changed, as in our example, the solution may change. This information can be of consequence to the decision maker trying to determine how much of a product to produce. *Sensitivity analysis* — the use of linear programming to evaluate the effects of changes in model parameters — will be discussed in Chapter 6.

Sensitivity analysis

It should be noted that some problems do not have a single extreme point solution. For example, when the objective function line parallels one of the constraint lines, an entire line segment is bounded by two adjacent corner points that are optimal; there is no single extreme point on the objective function line. In this situation there are *multiple optimal solutions*. This and other irregular types of solution outcomes in linear programming are discussed in Chapter 5.

Multiple optimal solutions

Summary of the Graphical Solution Steps

The steps for solving a graphical linear programming model are summarized below.

1. Plot the model constraints as equations on the graph; then, considering the inequalities of the constraints, indicate the feasible solution area.
2. Plot the objective function; then move this line out from the origin to locate the optimal solution point.
3. Solve simultaneous equations at the solution point to find the optimal solution values.

Or:

2. Solve simultaneous equations at each corner point to find the solution values at each point.
3. Substitute these values into the objective function to find the set of values that results in the maximum Z value.

GRAPHICAL SOLUTION OF A MINIMIZATION PROBLEM

The graphical solution for a minimization problem is found the same way as that for a maximization problem, except for a few minor differences. The following example problem will demonstrate the graphical solution of a minimization problem.

A farmer is preparing to plant a crop in the spring and needs to fertilize a field. There are two brands of fertilizer to choose from, Super-gro and Crop-quik. Each brand yields a specific amount of nitrogen and phosphate, as follows.

Brand	Chemical Contribution	
	Nitrogen (lb/bag)	Phosphate (lb/bag)
Super-gro	2	4
Crop-quik	4	3

The farmer's field requires at least 16 pounds of nitrogen and 24 pounds of phosphate. Super-gro costs $6 per bag, and Crop-quik costs $3. The farmer wants to know how many bags of each brand to purchase in order to minimize the total cost of fertilizing.

This problem is formulated as

minimize $Z = \$6x_1 + 3x_2$

subject to

$$2x_1 + 4x_2 \geq 16 \text{ lb of nitrogen}$$
$$4x_1 + 3x_2 \geq 24 \text{ lb of phosphate}$$
$$x_1, x_2 \geq 0$$

Graphically plotting the constraint lines

The first step is to graph the equations of the two model constraints, as shown in Figure 3.13. Next, the feasible solution area is chosen to reflect the $\geq$ inequalities in the constraints, as shown in Figure 3.14.

The feasible solution area

After the feasible solution area has been determined, the second step in the graphical solution approach is to locate the optimal point. Recall that in a maximization problem, the optimal solution is on the boundary of the feasible solution area that contains those points farthest from the origin. The optimal solution point in a minimization problem is also on the boundary of the feasible solution area; however, the boundary contains those points *closest* to the origin (0 being the lowest cost possible).

As in a maximization problem, the optimal solution is located at one of the extreme points of the boundary. In this case the corner points represent extremities in the boundary of the feasible solution

FIGURE 3.13

Constraint Lines for Fertilizer Model

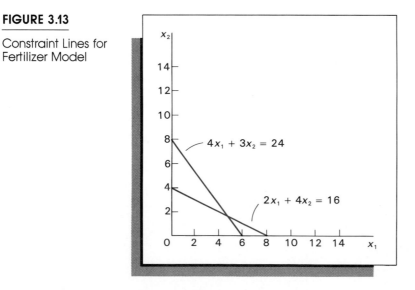

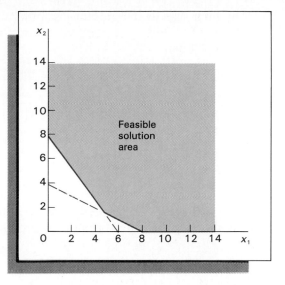

FIGURE 3.14

Feasible Solution
Area

area that are *closest* to the origin. Figure 3.15 shows the three corner points—*A, B,* and *C*—and the objective function line.

Locating the optimal solution point closest to the origin

As the objective function edges *toward* the origin, the last point it touches in the feasible solution area is *A*. In other words, point *A* is the closest the objective function can get to the origin without encompassing infeasible points. Thus it corresponds to the lowest cost that can be attained.

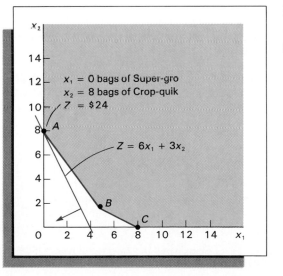

FIGURE 3.15

The Optimal
Solution Point

The final step in the graphical solution approach is to solve for the values of x_1 and x_2 at point A. Since point A is on the x_2 axis, $x_1 = 0$, and thus,

$$4(0) + 3x_2 = 24$$
$$x_2 = 8$$

The optimal solution   Given that the optimal solution is $x_1 = 0$, $x_2 = 8$, the minimum cost, Z, is

$$Z = \$6x_1 + 3x_2$$
$$Z = 6(0) + 3(8)$$
$$Z = \$24$$

This means the farmer should not purchase any Super-gro, but instead should purchase 8 bags of Crop-quik at a total cost of $24.

COMPUTERIZED GRAPHICAL SOLUTION

As noted in Chapter 1, several different computer software packages will be employed in this text to demonstrate the computerized solution of management science problems. Some of these packages have sophisticated graphic capabilities; if your personal computer is capable of producing graphic output, you can use such a package to find the graphical solution of a linear programming problem.

One very user friendly management science package that will be employed at selected points in the text is Quantitative Systems for Business Plus,[1] referred to as QSB+. QSB+ contains a linear programming module that is capable of providing a graphical solution.

Graphical Solution of the Colonial Pottery Company Example

We will use the Colonial Pottery Company example solved in the first part of this chapter to demonstrate the QSB+ software for graphically solving a linear programming model. Recall that the model in that example was as follows:

maximize $Z = \$4x_1 + 5x_2$
subject to
$$x_1 + 2x_2 \le 40 \text{ hr of labor}$$
$$4x_1 + 3x_2 \le 120 \text{ lb of clay}$$
$$x_1, x_2 \ge 0$$

---

[1]Yih-Long Chang and Robert Sullivan, *QSB+*, *Quantitative Systems for Business Plus* (Englewood Cliffs, N.J.: Prentice-Hall, 1989).

where

x_1 = number of bowls produced

x_2 = number of mugs produced

The graphical solution for this problem was shown in Figures 3.10 and 3.11.

In QSB+ all commands are made via menu displays. For this problem the first step is to input the model configuration by responding to a series of inquiries.

```
Maximize (1) or minimize (2) the objective? (Enter 1 or 2)       <1  >
Number of variables (excluding slacks/artificials):             <2  >
Number of constraints (excluding bounds):                       <2  >
Approximate percentage of non-zeros (default 5%):               <   >
Use the default variable names (X1,...,Xn) (1(Yes), 0(No)):     <1  >
Use the free format to enter data (1(Yes), 0(No)):              <0  >
Use the fixed format to enter bounds/integrality (1(Yes), 0(No)): <1  >
```

Next, in response to a menu command entered by the user, the program displays the model without the values of the parameters—for example, the values 4 and 5 in the objective function. The computer leaves blanks, which are filled by the user as follows,

```
                  Enter the Coefficients of the LP Model    Page: 1

Max   4_____X1  5_____X2
Subject to
(1)   1_____X1  2_____X2  ≤ 40_____
(2)   4_____X1  3_____X2  ≤ 120_____
```

Finally, when the user enters a menu command for "graphic solution," the following graph of the optimal solution is displayed.[2]

---

[2]Yih-Long Chang and Robert S. Sullivan, *QSB+, Quantitative Systems for Business Plus,* © 1989. Reprinted by permission of Prentice Hall, Inc., Englewood Cliffs, New Jersey.

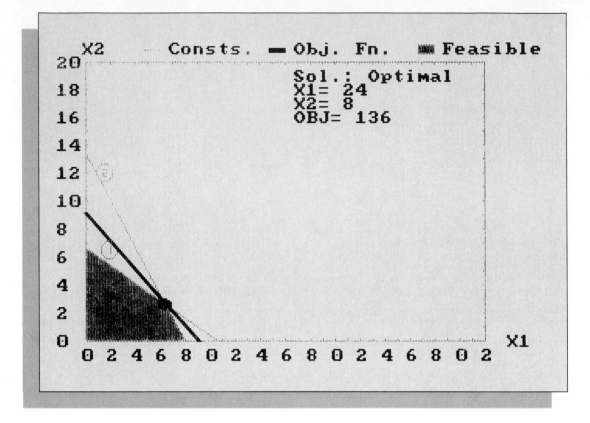

Summary

The graphical approach to the solution of linear programming problems is not a very efficient means of solving problems. For one thing, drawing accurate graphs is tedious. Moreover, the graphical approach is limited to models with only two decision variables. However, the analysis of the graphical approach provides insight into linear programming problems and their solutions that will be valuable in subsequent chapters.

In the graphical approach, once the feasible solution area and the optimal solution point have been determined from the graph, simultaneous equations are solved to determine the values of x_1 and x_2 at the solution point. The solution of simultaneous equations forms the basis of the *simplex method* for solving linear programming problems, which will be presented in the next chapter. In the simplex method, instead of determining the location of the optimal solution point graphically, we locate it mathematically through a defined set of mathematical steps.

References

Dantzig, G. B. *Linear Programming and Extensions.* Princeton, N.J.: Princeton University, 1963.

Gass, S. *Linear Programming.* 4th ed. New York: McGraw-Hill, 1975.

Gottfried, B. S., and Weisman, J. *Introduction to Optimization Theory.* Englewood Cliffs, N.J.: Prentice-Hall, 1973.

Hadley, G. *Linear Programming.* Reading, Mass.: Addison-Wesley, 1962.

Hillier, F. S., and Lieberman, G. J. *Operations Research.* 4th ed. San Francisco: Holden-Day, 1986.

Kim, C. *Introduction to Linear Programming.* New York: Holt, Rinehart and Winston, 1971.

Lee, Sang M.; Moore, Laurence J.; and Taylor, Bernard W. *Management Science.* 3d ed. Boston: Allyn and Bacon, 1990.

Moskowitz, H., and Wright, G. P. *Operations Research Techniques for Management.* Englewood Cliffs, N.J.: Prentice-Hall, 1979.

Rothenberg, R. I. *Linear Programming.* New York: Elsevier North-Holland, 1979.

Wagner, H. M. *Principles of Operations Research.* 2d ed. Englewood Cliffs, N.J.: Prentice-Hall, 1975.

EXAMPLE PROBLEM SOLUTION

As a prelude to the problems, this section will present an example of the graphical solution of a linear programming model.

Problem Statement

Solve the following linear programming model graphically:

minimize $Z = 4x_1 + 5x_2$

subject to

$$x_1 + 2x_2 \leq 10$$
$$6x_1 + 6x_2 \leq 36$$
$$x_1 \leq 4$$
$$x_1, x_2 \geq 0$$

Step 1: Plot the Constraint Lines as Equations

A simple method for plotting constraint lines is to set one of the constraint variables equal to zero and solve for the other variable, to establish a point on one of the axes. The three constraint lines are graphed in Figure 3.16.

Step 2: Determine the Feasible Solution Area

The feasible solution area is determined by identifying the space that jointly satisfies the $\leq$ conditions of all three constraints. (See Figure 3.17.)

FIGURE 3.16

The Constraint
Equations

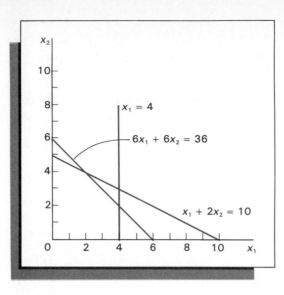

FIGURE 3.17

The Feasible
Solution Space and
Extreme Points

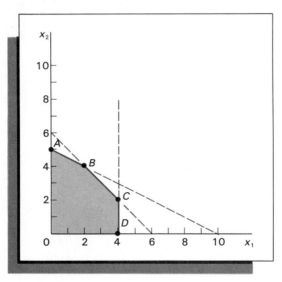

Step 3: Determine the Solution Points

The solution at point A can be determined by noting that the constraint line intersects the x_2 axis at 5; thus $x_2 = 5$, $x_1 = 0$, and $Z = 25$. The solution at point D on the other axis can be determined similarly; the constraint intersects the axis at $x_1 = 4$ and $x_2 = 0$, and $Z = 16$.

The values at points B and C must be found by solving simultaneous equations. Note that point B is formed by the intersection of the lines $x_1 + 2x_2 = 10$ and $6x_1 + 6x_2 = 36$. First convert both of these equations to functions of x_1.

$$x_1 + 2x_2 = 10$$
$$x_1 = 10 - 2x_2$$

and

$$6x_1 + 6x_2 = 36$$
$$6x_1 = 36 - 6x_2$$
$$x_1 = 6 - x_2$$

Now set the equations equal and solve for x_2.

$$10 - 2x_2 = 6 - x_2$$
$$-x_2 = -4$$
$$x_2 = 4$$

Substituting $x_2 = 4$ into either of the two equations in x_1 gives a value for x_1:

$$x_1 = 6 - x_2$$
$$x_1 = 6 - (4)$$
$$x_1 = 2$$

Thus, at point B, $x_1 = 2$, $x_2 = 4$, and $Z = 28$.

At point C, $x_1 = 4$. Substituting $x_1 - 4$ into the equation $x_1 = 6 \quad x_2$ gives a value for x_2:

$$4 = 6 - x_2$$
$$x_2 = 2$$

Thus, $x_1 = 4$, $x_2 = 2$, and $Z = 26$.

Step 4: Determine the Optimal Solution

The optimal solution is at point B, where $x_1 = 2$, $x_2 - 4$, and $Z - 28$. The optimal solution and solutions at the other extreme points are summarized in Figure 3.18.

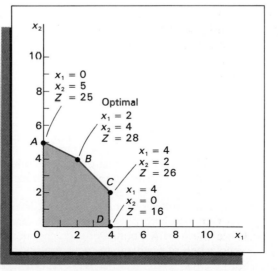

FIGURE 3.18

Optimal Solution Point

Problems

1. A company makes products 1 and 2 from two resources. The linear programming model for determining the amounts of product 1 and 2 to produce (i.e., x_1 and x_2) is

   maximize $Z = 8x_1 + 2x_2$ (profit, $)

   subject to

        $4x_1 + 5x_2 \leq 20$ (resource 1, lb)

        $2x_1 + 6x_2 \leq 18$ (resource 2, lb)

          $x_1, x_2 \geq 0$

   Solve this model graphically.

2. A company produces two products that are processed on two assembly lines. Assembly line 1 has 100 available hours, and assembly line 2 has 42 available hours. The company has formulated the following linear programming model for determining the number of each product (x_1 and x_2) to produce.

   maximize $Z = 6x_1 + 4x_2$ (profit, $)

   subject to

        $10x_1 + 10x_2 \leq 100$ (line 1, hr)

        $7x_1 + 3x_2 \leq 42$ (line 2, hr)

          $x_1, x_2 \geq 0$

   Solve this model graphically.

3. The Munchies Cereal Company makes a cereal from several ingredients. Two of the ingredients, oats and rice, provide vitamins A and B. The company wants to know how many ounces of oats and rice (x_1 and x_2) it should include in each box of cereal to meet minimum requirements for vitamins A and B while minimizing cost. The following linear programming model has been formulated for this problem.

   minimize $Z = .05x_1 + .03x_2$ (cost, $)

   subject to

        $8x_1 + 6x_2 \geq 48$ (vitamin A, mg)

        $x_1 + 2x_2 \geq 12$ (vitamin B, mg)

          $x_1, x_2 \geq 0$

   Solve this model graphically.

4. What would be the effect on the optimal solution in problem 3 if the cost of rice increased from $.03 per ounce to $.06 per ounce?

5. The Kalo Fertilizer Company makes a fertilizer using two chemicals that provide nitrogen, phosphate, and potassium. The company wants to know how many pounds of each chemical ingredient (x_1 and x_2) to put into a bag of fertilizer to meet minimum requirements for nitrogen,

phosphate, and potassium while minimizing cost. The following linear programming model has been developed.

minimize $Z = 3x_1 + 5x_2$ (cost, $)

subject to

$$10x_1 + 2x_2 \geq 20 \text{ (nitrogen, oz)}$$
$$6x_1 + 6x_2 \geq 36 \text{ (phosphate, oz)}$$
$$x_2 \geq 2 \text{ (potassium, oz)}$$
$$x_1, x_2 \geq 0$$

Solve this model graphically.

6. The Pinewood Furniture Company produces chairs and tables from two resources — labor and wood. The company has 80 hours of labor and 36 pounds of wood available each day. Demand for chairs is limited to 6 per day. The company has developed the following linear programming model for determining the number of chairs and tables (x_1 and x_2) to produce each day in order to maximize profit.

maximize $Z = 400x_1 + 100x_2$ (profit, $)

subject to

$$8x_1 + 10x_2 \leq 80 \text{ (labor, hr)}$$
$$2x_1 + 6x_2 \leq 36 \text{ (wood, lb)}$$
$$x_1 \leq 6 \text{ (demand, chairs)}$$
$$x_1, x_2 \geq 0$$

Solve this model graphically.

7. In problem 6, how much labor and wood will be unused if the optimal numbers of chairs and tables are produced?

8. The Crumb and Custard Bakery makes cakes and pies. The main ingredients are flour and sugar. The following linear programming model has been developed for determining the number of cakes and pies (x_1 and x_2) to produce each day so that profit will be maximized.

maximize $Z = x_1 + 5x_2$ (profit, $)

subject to

$$5x_1 + 5x_2 \leq 25 \text{ (flour, lb)}$$
$$2x_1 + 4x_2 \leq 16 \text{ (sugar, lb)}$$
$$x_1 \leq 5 \text{ (demand for cakes)}$$
$$x_1, x_2 \geq 0$$

Solve this model graphically.

9. In problem 8, how much flour and sugar will be left unused if the optimal numbers of cakes and pies are baked?

10. Solve the following linear programming model graphically.

maximize $Z = 3x_1 + 6x_2$
subject to
$$3x_1 + 2x_2 \leq 18$$
$$x_1 + x_2 \geq 5$$
$$x_1 \leq 4$$
$$x_1, x_2 \geq 0$$

11. Solve the following linear programming model graphically.

maximize $Z = 8x_1 + 7x_2$
subject to
$$10x_1 + 8x_2 \geq 40$$
$$6x_1 + 14x_2 \leq 48$$
$$x_2 \geq 1$$
$$x_1, x_2 \geq 0$$

12. The Elixer Drug Company produces a drug from two ingredients. Each ingredient contains the same three antibiotics in different proportions. The company has formulated the following linear programming model for determining the number of grams of each ingredient (x_1 and x_2) that must go into the drug in order to meet the antibiotic requirements at the minimum cost.

minimize $Z = 80x_1 + 50x_2$ (cost, \$)
subject to
$$3x_1 + x_2 \geq 6 \text{ (antibiotic 1, units)}$$
$$x_1 + x_2 \geq 4 \text{ (antibiotic 2, units)}$$
$$2x_1 + 6x_2 \geq 12 \text{ (antibiotic 3, units)}$$
$$x_1, x_2 \geq 0$$

Solve this model graphically.

13. A jewelry store makes necklaces and bracelets from gold and platinum. The store has developed the following linear programming model for determining the number of necklaces and bracelets (x_1 and x_2) to make in order to maximize profit.

maximize $Z = 300x_1 + 400x_2$ (profit, \$)
subject to
$$3x_1 + 2x_2 \leq 18 \text{ (gold, oz)}$$
$$2x_1 + 4x_2 \leq 20 \text{ (platinum, oz)}$$
$$x_2 \leq 4 \text{ (demand, bracelets)}$$
$$x_1, x_2 \geq 0$$

Solve this model graphically.

14. In problem 13, the maximum demand for bracelets is 4. If the store produces the optimal number of bracelets and necklaces, will the maximum demand for bracelets be met? If not, by how much will it be missed?

15. In problem 13, what profit for a necklace would result in no bracelets' being produced, and what would be the optimal solution for this profit?

16. A clothier makes coats and slacks. The two resources required are wool cloth and labor. The clothier has developed a linear programming model for determining the number of coats and pairs of slacks (x_1 and x_2) to make so that profit will be maximized.

maximize $Z = 50x_1 + 40x_2$ (profit, $)

subject to

$$3x_1 + 5x_2 \leq 150 \text{ (wool, yd}^2)$$
$$10x_1 + 4x_2 \leq 200 \text{ (labor, hr)}$$
$$x_1, x_2 \geq 0$$

Solve this model graphically.

17. In problem 16, what would be the effect on the optimal solution if the available labor were increased from 200 to 240 hours?

18. Solve the following linear programming model graphically.

maximize $Z = 1.5x_1 + x_2$

subject to

$$x_1 \leq 4$$
$$x_2 \leq 6$$
$$x_1 + x_2 \leq 5$$
$$x_1, x_2 \geq 0$$

19. Solve the following linear programming model graphically.

maximize $Z = 5x_1 + 8x_2$

subject to

$$3x_1 + 5x_2 \leq 50$$
$$2x_1 + 4x_2 \leq 40$$
$$x_1 \leq 8$$
$$x_2 \leq 10$$
$$x_1, x_2 \geq 0$$

20. Solve the following linear programming model graphically.

maximize $Z = 6.5x_1 + 10x_2$

subject to

$$2x_1 + 4x_2 \leq 40$$
$$x_1 + x_2 \leq 15$$
$$x_1 \geq 8$$
$$x_1, x_2 \geq 0$$

21. Solve the following linear programming model graphically.

maximize $Z = 5x_1 + x_2$
subject to
$$3x_1 + 4x_2 = 24$$
$$x_1 \leq 6$$
$$x_1 + 3x_2 \leq 12$$
$$x_1, x_2 \geq 0$$

22. Solve the following linear programming model graphically.

maximize $Z = 2x_1 + 5x_2$
subject to
$$7x_1 + 5x_2 \leq 70$$
$$2x_1 + 3x_2 \leq 24$$
$$x_2 \leq 5$$
$$3x_1 + 8x_2 \leq 48$$
$$x_1, x_2 \geq 0$$

23. Solve the following linear programming model graphically.

minimize $Z = 10x_1 + 20x_2$
subject to
$$x_1 + x_2 \geq 12$$
$$2x_1 + 5x_2 \geq 40$$
$$x_2 \leq 20$$
$$x_1, x_2 \geq 0$$

24. Solve the following linear programming model graphically.

minimize $Z = 8x_1 + 6x_2$
subject to
$$4x_1 + 2x_2 \geq 20$$
$$-6x_1 + 4x_2 \leq 12$$
$$x_1 + x_2 \geq 6$$
$$x_1, x_2 \geq 0$$

25. Solve the following linear programming model graphically.

maximize $Z = 4x_1 - 5x_2$
subject to
$$x_1 + 2x_2 \leq 10$$
$$6x_1 + 6x_2 \leq 36$$
$$x_1, x_2 \geq 0$$

26. Solve the following linear programming model graphically.

   maximize $Z = 3x_1 + 2x_2$
   subject to
   $$2x_1 + 4x_2 \leq 22$$
   $$-x_1 + 4x_2 \leq 10$$
   $$4x_1 - 2x_2 \leq 14$$
   $$x_1 - 3x_2 \leq 1$$
   $$x_1, x_2 \geq 0$$

27. Solve the following linear programming model graphically.

   minimize $Z = 8x_1 + 2x_2$
   subject to
   $$2x_1 - 6x_2 \leq 12$$
   $$5x_1 + 4x_2 \geq 40$$
   $$x_1 + 2x_2 \geq 12$$
   $$x_2 \leq 6$$
   $$x_1, x_2 \geq 0$$

28. A manufacturer produces both motorized and manual hand trucks. The hand trucks are assembled in shop 1, and finishing operations are done in shop 2. The manufacturer has developed the following linear programming model to determine the number of each type of hand truck to produce so that profit will be maximized.

   maximize $Z = 200x_1 + 300x_2$ (profit, $)
   subject to
   $$2x_1 + 5x_2 \leq 180 \text{ (shop 1, hr)}$$
   $$3x_1 + 3x_2 \leq 135 \text{ (shop 2, hr)}$$
   $$x_1, x_2 \geq 0$$

   Solve this model graphically.

29. Solve the following linear programming model graphically.

   minimize $Z = \$.06x_1 + .10x_2$
   subject to
   $$4x_1 + 3x_2 \geq 12$$
   $$3x_1 + 6x_2 \geq 12$$
   $$5x_1 + 2x_2 \geq 10$$
   $$x_1, x_2 \geq 0$$

30. The Copperfield Mining Company owns two mines, which produce three grades of ore—high, medium, and low. The company has a contract to supply a smelting company with 12 tons of high-grade ore,

8 tons of medium-grade ore, and 24 tons of low-grade ore. Each mine produces a certain amount of each type of ore each hour it is in operation. The company has developed the following linear programming model to determine the number of hours to operate each mine (x_1 and x_2) so that contractual obligations can be met at the lowest cost.

minimize $Z = 200x_1 + 160x_2$ (cost, \$)

subject to

$$6x_1 + 2x_2 \geq 12 \text{ (high-grade ore, tons)}$$
$$2x_1 + 2x_2 \geq 8 \text{ (medium-grade ore, tons)}$$
$$4x_1 + 12x_2 \geq 24 \text{ (low-grade ore, tons)}$$
$$x_1, x_2 \geq 0$$

Solve this model graphically.

31. A canning company produces two sizes of cans—regular and large. The cans are produced in 10,000-can lots. The cans are processed through a stamping operation and a coating operation. The company has 30 days available for both stamping and coating. In order to fulfill its obligations under a shipping contract, the company must produce at least 9 lots. The following linear programming model has been developed for determining the number of lots to produce of each size can (x_1 and x_2) in order to maximize profit.

maximize $Z = 800x_1 + 900x_2$ (profit, \$)

subject to

$$2x_1 + 4x_2 \leq 30 \text{ (stamping, days)}$$
$$4x_1 + 2x_2 \leq 30 \text{ (coating, days)}$$
$$x_1 + x_2 \geq 9 \text{ (lots)}$$
$$x_1, x_2 \geq 0$$

Solve this model graphically.

32. A manufacturing firm produces two products. Each product must go through an assembly process and a finishing process. It is then transferred to the warehouse, which has space for only a limited number of items. The following linear programming model has been developed for determining the quantity of each product to produce in order to maximize profit.

maximize $Z = 30x_1 + 70x_2$ (profit, \$)

subject to

$$4x_1 + 10x_2 \leq 80 \text{ (assembly, hr)}$$
$$14x_1 + 8x_2 \leq 112 \text{ (finishing, hr)}$$
$$x_1 + x_2 \leq 10 \text{ (inventory, units)}$$
$$x_1, x_2 \geq 0$$

Solve this model graphically.

33. Assume that the objective function in problem 32 has been changed from $Z = 30x_1 + 70x_2$ to $Z = 90x_1 + 70x_2$. Determine the slope of each objective function and discuss what effect these slopes have on the optimal solution.

34. A California grower has a 50-acre farm on which to plant strawberries and tomatoes. The grower has available 300 hours of labor and 800 tons of fertilizer and has contracted for shipping space for a maximum of 26 acres' worth of strawberries and 37 acres' worth of tomatoes. The following linear programming model has been developed for determining the number of acres of strawberries and tomatoes (x_1 and x_2) the farmer should plant in order to maximize profit.

maximize $Z = 400x_1 + 300x_2$ (profit, $)
subject to
$$x_1 + x_2 \leq 50 \text{ (available land, acres)}$$
$$10x_1 + 3x_2 \leq 300 \text{ (labor, hr)}$$
$$8x_1 + 20x_2 \leq 800 \text{ (fertilizer, tons)}$$
$$x_1 \leq 26 \text{ (shipping space, acres)}$$
$$x_2 \leq 37 \text{ (shipping space, acres)}$$
$$x_1, x_2 \geq 0$$

Solve this model graphically.

35. In problem 34, if the amount of fertilizer required for each acre of strawberries (x_1) was determined to be 20 tons instead of 8 tons, what would be the effect on the optimal solution?

36. Solve problem 1 from Chapter 2 graphically.

37. Solve problem 2 from Chapter 2 graphically.

38. Solve problem 11 from Chapter 2 graphically.

39. Solve problem 15 from Chapter 2 graphically.

40. Solve problem 24 from Chapter 2 graphically.

41. Solve problem 28 from Chapter 2 graphically.

4

The Simplex Solution Method

Chapter 3 demonstrated how a linear programming model solution can be derived from a graph of the model. Graphing can provide valuable insight into linear programming and linear programming solutions in general. However, the fact that this solution method is limited to problems with only two decision variables restricts its usefulness as a *general* solution technique. In this chapter, a mathematical approach for solving linear programming problems will be presented. This approach, called the *simplex method,* is a general solution technique. In the simplex method, the model is put into the form of a table, and then a number of mathematical steps are performed on the table. These mathematical steps in effect replicate the process of moving from one extreme point on the solution boundary to another. However, unlike the graphical method, in which we could simply search through *all* the solution points to find the best one, the simplex method moves from one *better* solution to another until the best one is found, and then it stops.

A tabular solution method with specific mathematical steps

This chapter will present the general simplex method only as it applies to a *maximization* model. The application of the simplex method to a minimization model requires a few alterations that will be covered in Chapter 5 along with several special cases including multiple optimum solutions, infeasible problems, and unbounded problems.

CONVERTING THE MODEL CONSTRAINTS

The first step in applying the simplex method is to transform the model constraints into equations—a requirement for solving simultaneous equations.

Let us return to the Colonial Pottery Company example modeled in Chapter 2 and solved graphically in Chapter 3.

maximize $Z = \$4x_1 + 5x_2$

subject to

$$x_1 + 2x_2 \leq 40 \text{ hr of labor}$$
$$4x_1 + 3x_2 \leq 120 \text{ lb of clay}$$
$$x_1, x_2 \geq 0$$

where

x_1 = number of bowls produced
x_2 = number of mugs produced

The graph of this model is shown in Figure 4.1.

FIGURE 4.1

Graph of the Pottery Company Example

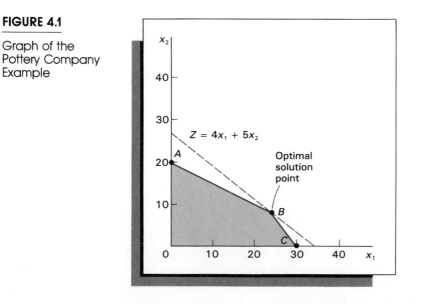

Once the optimal solution was found at point *B*, simultaneous equations were solved to determine the values of x_1 and x_2. The simplex method for solving linear programming problems is based, at least partially, on the solution of simultaneous equations. Recall that the solution occurs at an extreme point where constraint equation lines intersect with each other or with the axis. Thus, the model constraints must all be in the form of *equations* (=), rather than ≤ or ≥ inequalities.

The simplex method is based partially on the solution of simultaneous equations

The simplex method includes a standard procedure for transforming ≤ inequality constraints into equations. This transformation is achieved by adding a new variable, called a *slack variable*, to each constraint. For the pottery company example, the model constraints are

Transforming ≤ constraint inequalities into equations

$$x_1 + 2x_2 \leq 40 \text{ hr of labor}$$
$$4x_1 + 3x_2 \leq 120 \text{ lb of clay}$$

The addition of a unique slack variable (s_i) to each of these inequalities results in the following equations:

Slack variables

$$x_1 + 2x_2 + s_1 = 40 \text{ hr of labor}$$
$$4x_1 + 3x_2 + s_2 = 120 \text{ lb of clay}$$

The slack variables in these equations, s_1 and s_2, will take on any value necessary to make the left-hand side of the equation equal to the right-hand side. For example, consider a hypothetical solution of $x_1 = 5$ and $x_2 = 10$. Substituting these values into the above equations yields

$$x_1 + 2x_2 + s_1 = 40 \text{ hr of labor}$$
$$5 + 2(10) + s_1 = 40 \text{ hr of labor}$$
$$s_1 = 15 \text{ hr of labor}$$

and

$$4x_1 + 3x_2 + s_2 = 120 \text{ lb of clay}$$
$$4(5) + 3(10) + s_2 = 120 \text{ lb of clay}$$
$$s_2 = 70 \text{ lb of clay}$$

In the above example, $x_1 = 5$ bowls and $x_2 = 10$ mugs represents a solution that does not make use of the total available amount of labor and clay. For example, in the labor constraint, 5 bowls and 10 mugs require only 25 hours of labor. This leaves 15 hours that are not used. Thus, s_1 represents the amount of *unused labor*.

In the clay constraint, 5 bowls and 10 mugs require only 50 pounds of clay. This leaves 70 pounds of clay that are not used. Thus, s_2 represents the amount of *unused clay*. In general, slack variables represent the amount of *unused resources*.

A slack variable represents unused resources

The ultimate instance of unused resources occurs at the origin, where $x_1 = 0$ and $x_2 = 0$. Substituting these values into the equations yields

$$x_1 + 2x_2 + s_1 = 40$$
$$0 + 2(0) + s_1 = 40$$
$$s_1 = 40 \text{ hr of labor}$$

and

$$4x_1 + 3x_2 + s_2 = 120$$
$$4(0) + 3(0) + s_2 = 120$$
$$s_2 = 120 \text{ lb of clay}$$

Because no production takes place at the origin, all of the resources are unused; thus, the slack variables equal the total available amounts of each resource: $s_1 = 40$ hours of labor and $s_2 = 120$ pounds of clay.

Our next concern is the effect of these new slack variables on the objective function. The objective function for our example represents the profit gained from the production of bowls and mugs,

$$Z = 4x_1 + 5x_2$$

The effect of slack variables on the objective function

The coefficient, $4, is the contribution to profit of each bowl; $5 is the contribution to profit of each mug. What, then, do the slack variables s_1 and s_2 contribute? They contribute *nothing* to profit, because they represent unused resources. Profit is made only after the resources are put to use in making bowls and mugs. Using slack variables, we can write the objective function as

$$\text{maximize } Z = 4x_1 + 5x_2 + 0s_1 + 0s_2$$

As in the case of decision variables (x_1 and x_2), slack variables can have only nonnegative values, since negative resources are not possible. Therefore, for this model formulation, x_1, x_2, s_1, and $s_2 \geq 0$.

The Solution of Simultaneous Equations

Solving two equations with four unknowns

Now that both model constraints have been transformed into equations, the equations should be solved simultaneously to determine the values of the variables at every solution point. However, notice that our example problem has *two* equations and *four* unknowns (i.e., two decision variables and two slack variables), a situation that makes direct simultaneous solution impossible. The simplex method alleviates this problem by assigning some of the variables a value of zero. The number of variables assigned values of zero is $n - m$, where n equals the number of variables and m equals the number of constraints (excluding the nonnegativity constraints). For this model, $n = 4$ variables and $m = 2$ constraints; therefore, two of the variables are assigned a value of zero (i.e., $4 - 2 = 2$).

For example, letting $x_1 = 0$ and $s_1 = 0$ results in the following set of equations.

$$x_1 + 2x_2 + s_1 = 40$$
$$4x_1 + 3x_2 + s_2 = 120$$

and

$$0 + 2x_2 + 0 = 40$$
$$0 + 3x_2 + s_2 = 120$$

First solve for x_2 in the first equation:

$$2x_2 = 40$$
$$x_2 = 20$$

Then solve for s_2 in the second equation:

$$3x_2 + s_2 = 120$$
$$3(20) + s_2 = 120$$
$$s_2 = 60$$

This solution corresponds with point A in Figure 4.2. The graph in Figure 4.2 shows that at point A, $x_1 = 0$, $x_2 = 20$, $s_1 = 0$, and $s_2 = 60$, the exact solution obtained by solving simultaneous equations. This solution is referred to as a *basic feasible solution*. A feasible solution is any solution that satisfies the constraints. A *basic* feasible solution satisfies the constraints and contains as many variables with nonnegative values as there are model constraints—that is, m variables with nonnegative values and $n - m$ values set equal to zero. Typically the m variables have positive nonzero solution values;

A basic feasible solution

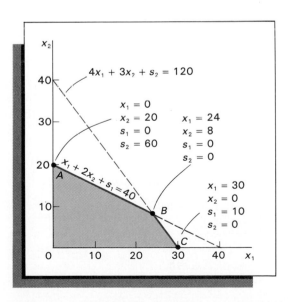

FIGURE 4.2

Solutions at Points A, B, and C

Degenerate solutions

however, when one of the m variables equals zero, the basic feasible solution is said to be *degenerate*. (The topic of *degeneracy* will be discussed in Chapter 5.)

Consider a second example where $x_2 = 0$ and $s_2 = 0$. These values result in the following set of equations.

$$x_1 + 2x_2 + s_1 = 40$$
$$4x_1 + 3x_2 + s_2 = 120$$

and

$$x_1 + 0 + s_1 = 40$$
$$4x_1 + 0 + 0 = 120$$

Solve for x_1:

$$4x_1 = 120$$
$$x_1 = 30$$

Then solve for s_1:

$$30 + s_1 = 40$$
$$s_1 = 10$$

This basic feasible solution corresponds to point C in Figure 4.2, where $x_1 = 30$, $x_2 = 0$, $s_1 = 10$, and $s_2 = 0$.

Finally, consider an example where $s_1 = 0$ and $s_2 = 0$. These values result in the following set of equations.

$$x_1 + 2x_2 + s_1 = 40$$
$$4x_1 + 3x_2 + s_2 = 120$$

and

$$x_1 + 2x_2 + 0 = 40$$
$$4x_1 + 3x_2 + 0 = 120$$

Solving a set of equations using row operations

These equations can be solved using *row operations*. In row operations, the equations can be multiplied by constant values and then added or subtracted from each other without changing the values of the decision variables. First multiply the top equation by 4 to get

$$4x_1 + 8x_2 = 160$$

and then subtract the second equation:

$$
\begin{array}{r}
4x_1 + 8x_2 = 160 \\
-4x_1 - 3x_2 = -120 \\
\hline
5x_2 = 40 \\
x_2 = 8
\end{array}
$$

Next, substitute this value of x_2 into either one of the constraints.

$$x_1 + 2(8) = 40$$
$$x_1 = 24$$

This solution corresponds to point B on the graph, where $x_1 = 24$, $x_2 = 8$, $s_1 = 0$, and $s_2 = 0$, which was previously identified in Chapter 3 as the optimal solution point.

All three of these example solutions meet our definition of *basic feasible solutions*. However, two specific questions are raised by the identification of these solutions.

1. In each example, how was it known which variables to set equal to zero?
2. How is the optimal solution identified?

The answer to both of these questions can be found by using the simplex method. The simplex method is a set of mathematical steps that determines at each step which variables should equal zero and when an optimal solution has been reached.

THE SIMPLEX METHOD

The steps of the simplex method are carried out within the framework of a table, or *tableau*. The tableau organizes the model into a form that makes applying the mathematical steps easier. The Colonial Pottery Company example will be used again to demonstrate the simplex tableau and method.

The simplex tableau

maximize $Z = \$4x_1 + 5x_2 + 0s_1 + 0s_2$
subject to
$$x_1 + 2x_2 + s_1 = 40 \text{ hr}$$
$$4x_1 + 3x_2 + s_2 = 120 \text{ lb}$$
$$x_1, x_2, s_1, s_2 \geq 0$$

The initial simplex tableau for this model, with the various column and row headings, is shown in Table 4.1.

TABLE 4.1
The Simplex Tableau

c_j						
	Basic Variables	Quantity	x_1	x_2	s_1	s_2
	z_j					
	$c_j - z_j$					

Tableau notation

The first step in filling in Table 4.1 is to record the model variables along the second row from the top. The two decision variables are listed first, in order of their subscript magnitude, followed by the slack variables, also listed in order of their subscript magnitude. This step produces the row with x_1, x_2, s_1, and s_2 in Table 4.1.

The basic feasible solution in the initial simplex tableau

The next step is to determine a basic feasible solution. In other words, which two variables will form the basic feasible solution and which will be assigned a value of zero? Instead of arbitrarily selecting a point (as we did with points A, B, and C in the previous section), the simplex method selects the origin as the initial basic feasible solution because the values of the decision variables at the origin are always known in all linear programming problems. At that point $x_1 = 0$ and $x_2 = 0$; thus the variables in the basic feasible solution are s_1 and s_2.

$$x_1 + 2x_2 + s_1 = 40$$
$$0 + 2(0) + s_1 = 40$$
$$s_1 = 40 \text{ hr}$$

and

$$4x_1 + 3x_2 + s_2 = 120$$
$$4(0) + 3(0) + s_2 = 120$$
$$s_2 = 120 \text{ lb}$$

At the initial basic feasible solution at the origin only slack variables have a numerical value other than zero

In other words, at the origin, where there is no production, all resources are slack, or unused. The variables s_1 and s_2, which form the initial basic feasible solution, are listed in Table 4.2 under the column "basic variables," and their respective values, 40 and 120, are listed under the column "quantity."

TABLE 4.2
The Basic Feasible Solution

c_j	Basic Variables	Quantity	x_1	x_2	s_1	s_2
	s_1	40				
	s_2	120				
	z_j					
	$c_j - z_j$					

The quantity column in the simplex tableau

The initial simplex tableau always begins with the solution at the origin, where x_1 and x_2 equal zero. Thus, the basic variables at the origin are the slack variables, s_1 and s_2. Since the quantity values in the initial solution always appear as the right-hand side values of the constraint equations, they can be read directly from the original constraint equations.

The top two rows and bottom two rows are standard for all tableaus; however, the number of middle rows is equivalent to the number of constraints in the model. For example, this problem has two constraints; therefore it has two middle rows corresponding to s_1 and s_2. (Recall that n variables minus m constraints equals the number of variables in the problem with values of zero. This also means that the number of basic variables with values other than zero will be equal to m constraints.)

The number of rows in a tableau

Similarly, the three columns on the left side of the tableau are standard, and the remaining columns are equivalent to the number of variables. Since there are four variables in this model, there are four columns on the right of the tableau, corresponding to x_1, x_2, s_1, and s_2.

The number of columns in a tableau

The next step is to fill in the c_j values, which are the objective function coefficients, representing the *contribution to profit* (or *cost*) for each variable x_j or s_j in the objective function. Across the top row the c_j values 4, 5, 0, and 0 are inserted for each variable in the model, as shown in Table 4.3.

The c_j values in the simplex tableau

Contribution to profit

TABLE 4.3
The Simplex Tableau with c_j Values

c_j	Basic Variables	Quantity	4 x_1	5 x_2	0 s_1	0 s_2
0	s_1	40				
0	s_2	120				
	z_j					
	$c_j - z_j$					

The values for c_j on the left side of the tableau are the contributions to profit of only those variables in the basic feasible solution, in this case s_1 and s_2. These values are inserted at this location in the tableau so that they can be used later to compute the values in the z_j row.

The columns under each variable (i.e., x_1, x_2, s_1, and s_2) are filled in with the coefficients of the decision variables and slack variables in the model constraint equations. The s_1 row represents the first model constraint; thus the coefficient for x_1 is 1, the coefficient for x_2 is 2, the coefficient for s_1 is 1, and the coefficient for s_2 is 0. The values in the s_2 row are the second constraint equation coefficients, 4, 3, 0, and 1, as shown in Table 4.4 on page 100.

Row values in the simplex tableau

This completes the process of filling in the initial simplex tableau. The remaining values in the z_j and $c_j - z_j$ rows, as well as subsequent tableau values, are computed mathematically using simplex formulas.

TABLE 4.4
The Simplex Tableau with Model Constraint Coefficients

c_j	Basic Variables	Quantity	4 x_1	5 x_2	0 s_1	0 s_2
0	s_1	40	1	2	1	0
0	s_2	120	4	3	0	1
	z_j					
	$c_j - z_j$					

The list below summarizes the steps of the simplex method (for a maximization model) that have been presented so far.

1. First, transform all inequalities to equations by adding slack variables.
2. Develop a simplex tableau with the number of columns equaling the number of variables plus three, and the number of rows equaling the number of constraints plus four.
3. Set up table headings that list the model decision variables and slack variables.
4. Insert the initial basic feasible solution — the slack variables and their quantity values.
5. Assign c_j values for the model variables in the top row and the basic feasible solution variables on the left side.
6. Insert the model constraint coefficients into the body of the table.

Computing the z_j and $c_j - z_j$ Rows

So far the simplex tableau has been set up using values taken directly from the model. From this point on the values are determined by computation.

First, the values in the z_j row are computed by multiplying each c_j *column value* (on the left side) by each variable column value (under x_1, x_2, s_1, and s_2) and then summing each of these sets of values. The z_j values are shown in Table 4.5.

Computing the z_j row values

TABLE 4.5
The Simplex Tableau with z_j Row Values

c_j	Basic Variables	Quantity	4 x_1	5 x_2	0 s_1	0 s_2
0	s_1	40	1	2	1	0
0	s_2	120	4	3	0	1
	z_j	0	0	0	0	0
	$c_j - z_j$					

For example, the value in the z_j row under the quantity column is found as follows.

c_j Quantity
$0 \times 40 = 0$
$0 \times 120 = \underline{0}$
  $z_q = 0$

The value in the z_j row under the x_1 column is found similarly.

c_j x_1
$0 \times 1 = 0$
$0 \times 4 = \underline{0}$
  $z_1 = 0$

All other z_j row values *for this tableau* will be zero when computed using this formula.

Now the $c_j - z_j$ row is computed by subtracting the z_j row values from the c_j (top) row values. For example, in the x_1 column the $c_j - z_j$ row value is computed as $4 - 0 = 4$. This value as well as other $c_j - z_j$ values are shown in Table 4.6.

Computing the c_j z_j row values

TABLE 4.6
The Complete Initial Simplex Tableau

c_j	Basic Variables	Quantity	4 x_1	5 x_2	0 s_1	0 s_2
0	s_1	40	1	2	1	0
0	s_2	120	4	3	0	1
	z_j	0	0	0	0	0
	$c_j - z_j$		4	5	0	0

Table 4.6 is the complete initial simplex tableau with all values filled in. This tableau represents the solution at the origin, where $x_1 = 0$, $x_2 = 0$, $s_1 = 40$, and $s_2 = 120$. The profit represented by this solution (i.e., the Z value) is given in the z_j row under the quantity column—0 in Table 4.6. This solution is obviously not optimal, since no profit is being made. Thus, we want to move to a solution point that will give a *better* solution. In other words, we want to produce either some bowls (x_1) or some mugs (x_2). One of the *nonbasic* variables (i.e., variables not in the present basic feasible solution) will enter the solution and become basic.

The complete initial tableau

The Entering Nonbasic Variable

As an example, suppose the pottery company decides to produce some bowls. With this decision x_1 will become a basic variable. For every unit of x_1 (i.e., each bowl) produced, profit will be increased by \$4, since that is the profit contribution of a bowl. However, when a bowl (x_1) is produced, some previously unused resources will be used. For example, if $x_1 = 1$, then

$$x_1 + 2x_2 + s_1 = 40 \text{ hr of labor}$$
$$1 + 2(0) + s_1 = 40$$
$$s_1 = 39 \text{ hr of labor}$$

and

$$4x_1 + 3x_2 + s_2 = 120 \text{ lb of clay}$$
$$4(1) + 3(0) + s_2 = 120$$
$$s_2 = 116 \text{ lb of clay}$$

In the labor constraint we see that, with the production of one bowl, the amount of slack, or unused, labor is *decreased* by *one hour*. In the clay constraint the amount of slack is *decreased* by *four pounds*. Substituting these increases (for x_1) and decreases (for slack) into the objective function gives

$$\overset{c_j}{Z = 4(1) + 5(0)} + \overset{z_j}{0(-1) + 0(-4)}$$
$$Z = 4 - 0$$
$$Z = \$4$$

The first part of this objective function relationship represents the values in the c_j row; the second part represents the values in the z_j row. The function expresses the fact that to produce some bowls we must give up some of the profit already earned from the items they replace. In this case the production of bowls replaced only slack, so no profit was lost. In general, the $c_j - z_j$ row values represent the *net increase per unit of entering a nonbasic variable into the basic solution*. Naturally, we want to make as much money as possible, since the objective is to maximize profit. Therefore, we enter the variable that will give the greatest net increase in profit per unit. From Table 4.7, we select variable x_2 as the entering basic variable because it has the greatest net increase in profit per unit, \$5—the highest positive value in the $c_j - z_j$ row.

Selecting the entering variable

TABLE 4.7
Selection of the Entering Basic Variable

c_j	Basic Variables	Quantity	4 x_1	5 x_2	0 s_1	0 s_2
0	s_1	40	1	2	1	0
0	s_2	120	4	3	0	1
	z_j	0	0	0	0	0
	$c_j - z_j$		4	5	0	0

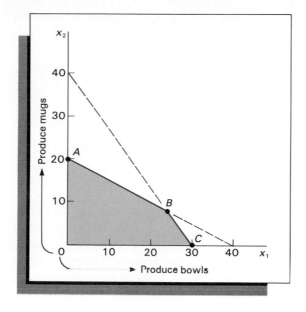

FIGURE 4.3

Selection of Which Item to Produce — the Entering Basic Variable

The x_2 column, highlighted in Table 4.7, is referred to as the *pivot column*. (The operations used to solve simultaneous equations are often referred to in mathematical terminology as "pivot operations.")

Pivot column

The selection of the entering basic variable is also demonstrated by the graph in Figure 4.3. At the origin nothing is produced. In the simplex method we move from one solution point to an *adjacent* point (i.e., *one* variable in the basic feasible solution is replaced with a variable that was previously zero). In Figure 4.3 we can move along either the x_1 axis or the x_2 axis in order to seek a better solution. Since an increase in x_2 will result in a greater profit, we choose x_2.

Moving to an adjacent solution point

The Leaving Basic Variable

Since each basic feasible solution contains only two variables with nonzero values, one of the two basic variables present, s_1 or s_2, will have to leave the solution and become zero. Since we have decided to produce mugs (x_2), we want to produce as many as possible or, in other words, as many as our resources will allow. First, in the labor constraint we will use all the labor to make mugs (since no bowls are to be produced, $x_1 = 0$; and since we will use all the labor possible and s_1 = unused labor resources, $s_1 = 0$ also).

$$1x_1 + 2x_2 + s_1 = 40 \text{ hr}$$
$$1(0) + 2x_2 + 0 = 40$$
$$x_2 = \frac{40 \text{ hr}}{2 \text{ hr/mug}}$$
$$x_2 = 20 \text{ mugs}$$

In other words, enough labor is available to produce 20 mugs. Next, perform the same analysis on the constraint for clay.

$$4x_1 + 3x_2 + s_2 = 120 \text{ lb}$$
$$4(0) + 3x_2 + 0 = 120$$
$$x_2 = \frac{120 \text{ lb}}{3 \text{ lb/mug}}$$
$$x_2 = 40 \text{ mugs}$$

This indicates that there is enough clay to produce 40 mugs. But there is enough labor to produce only 20 mugs. We are limited to the production of only 20 mugs, because we do not have enough labor to produce any more than that. This analysis is shown graphically in Figure 4.4. Since we are moving out the x_2 axis, we can move from the origin to either point A or point R. We select point A because it is the *most constrained* and thus feasible, whereas point R is infeasible.

The most constrained adjacent solution point

This analysis is performed in the simplex method by dividing the quantity values of the basic solution variables by the pivot column values. For this tableau,

Basic variables	Quantity	x_2
s_1	40	$\div 2 = 20$ the leaving basic variable
s_2	120	$\div 3 = 40$

Selecting the leaving basic variable

The leaving basic variable is the variable that corresponds to the minimum nonnegative quotient, which in this case is 20. (Note that

FIGURE 4.4

Determination of the Basic Feasible Solution Point

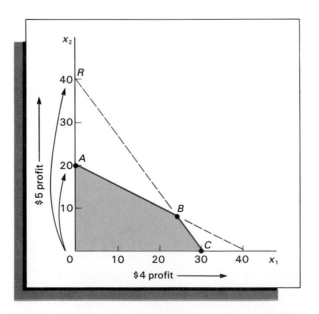

a value of zero would qualify as the minimum quotient and would be the choice for the leaving variable.) Therefore, s_1 is the leaving variable. (At point A in Figure 4.4, s_1 equals zero since all the labor is used to make the 20 mugs.) The s_1 row, highlighted in Table 4.8, is also referred to as the *pivot row*.

Pivot row

TABLE 4.8
Pivot Column, Pivot Row, and Pivot Number

c_j	Basic Variables	Quantity	4 x_1	5 x_2	0 s_1	0 s_2
0	s_1	40	1	2	1	0
0	s_2	120	4	3	0	1
	z_j	0	0	0	0	0
	$c_j - z_j$		4	5	0	0

The value of 2 at the intersection of the pivot row and the pivot column is called the *pivot number*. The pivot number, row, and column are all instrumental in developing the next tableau. We are now ready to proceed to the second simplex tableau and a *better* solution.

Pivot number

Developing a New Tableau

Table 4.9 shows the second simplex tableau with the new basic feasible solution variables of x_2 and s_2 and their corresponding c_j values.

TABLE 4.9
The Basic Variables and c_j Values for the Second Simplex Tableau

c_j	Basic Variables	Quantity	4 x_1	5 x_2	0 s_1	0 s_2
5	x_2					
0	s_2					
	z_j					
	$c_j - z_j$					

The various row values in the second tableau are computed using several simplex formulas. First, the x_2 row, called the *new tableau*

Computing the new tableau pivot row values

pivot row, is computed by dividing every value in the pivot row of the first (old) tableau by the pivot number. The formula for these computations is

$$\text{new tableau pivot row values} = \frac{\text{old tableau pivot row values}}{\text{pivot number}}$$

The new row values are shown in Table 4.10.

TABLE 4.10
Computation of the New Pivot Row Values

c_j	Basic Variables	Quantity	4 x_1	5 x_2	0 s_1	0 s_2
5	x_2	20	1/2	1	1/2	0
0	s_2					
	z_j					
	$c_j - z_j$					

Computing all remaining row values

To compute all remaining row values (in this case there is only one other row), another formula is used.

$$\begin{array}{l}\text{new tableau} \\ \text{row values}\end{array} = \begin{array}{l}\text{old tableau} \\ \text{row values}\end{array} - \left(\begin{array}{l}\text{corresponding} \\ \text{coefficients in} \\ \text{pivot column}\end{array} \times \begin{array}{l}\text{corresponding} \\ \text{new tableau} \\ \text{pivot row} \\ \text{value}\end{array}\right)$$

Thus, this formula requires the use of both the old tableau and the new one. The s_2 row values are computed in Table 4.11.

TABLE 4.11
Computation of New s_2 Row Values

Column	Old Row Value	−	(Corresponding Coefficient in Pivot Column	×	New Tableau Pivot Row Value)	=	New Tableau Row Value
quantity	120	−	(3	×	20)	=	60
x_1	4	−	(3	×	1/2)	=	5/2
x_2	3	−	(3	×	1)	=	0
s_1	0	−	(3	×	1/2)	=	−3/2
s_2	1	−	(3	×	0)	=	1

These values have been inserted in the simplex tableau in Table 4.12.

This solution corresponds to point A in the graph of this model in Figure 4.4. The solution at this point is $x_1 = 0$, $x_2 = 20$, $s_1 = 0$, $s_2 = 60$. In other words, 20 mugs are produced and 60 pounds of

TABLE 4.12
The Second Simplex Tableau with Row Values

c_j	Basic Variables	Quantity	4 x_1	5 x_2	0 s_1	0 s_2
5	x_2	20	1/2	1	1/2	0
0	s_2	60	5/2	0	−3/2	1
	z_j					
	$c_j - z_j$					

clay are left unused. No bowls are produced and no labor hours remain unused.

The second simplex tableau is completed by computing the z_j and $c_j - z_j$ row values the same way they were computed in the first tableau. The z_j rows are computed by summing the products of the c_j column and all other column values.

Column

quantity $z_q = (5)(20) + (0)(60) = 100$

x_1 $z_1 = (5)(1/2) + (0)(5/2) = 5/2$

x_2 $z_2 = (5)(1) + (0)(0) = 5$

s_1 $z_3 = (5)(1/2) + (0)(-3/2) = 5/2$

s_2 $z_4 = (5)(0) + (0)(1) = 0$

The z_j row values and the $c_j - z_j$ row values are added to the tableau to give the completed second simplex tableau shown in Table 4.13.

TABLE 4.13
The Completed Second Simplex Tableau

c_j	Basic Variables	Quantity	4 x_1	5 x_2	0 s_1	0 s_2
5	x_2	20	1/2	1	1/2	0
0	s_2	60	5/2	0	−3/2	1
	z_j	100	5/2	5	5/2	0
	$c_j - z_j$		3/2	0	−5/2	0

The value of 100 in the z_j row is the value of the objective function (profit) for this basic feasible solution.

The computational steps that we followed to derive the second tableau in effect accomplish the same thing as *row operations* in the solution of simultaneous equations. These same steps (called *iterations*) are used to derive each subsequent tableau.

Simplex iterations

The Optimal Simplex Tableau

The steps that we followed to derive the second simplex tableau are repeated to develop the third tableau. First, the pivot column or entering basic variable is determined. Since 3/2 in the $c_j - z_j$ row represents the greatest positive net increase in profit, x_1 becomes the entering nonbasic variable. Dividing the pivot column values into the values in the quantity column indicates that s_2 is the leaving basic variable *and* corresponds to the pivot row. The pivot row, pivot column, and pivot number are indicated in Table 4.14.

TABLE 4.14

The Pivot Row, Pivot Column, and Pivot Number

c_j	Basic Variables	Quantity	**4** x_1	**5** x_2	**0** s_1	**0** s_2
5	x_2	20	1/2	1	1/2	0
0	s_2	60	5/2	0	−3/2	1
	z_j	100	5/2	5	5/2	0
	$c_j - z_j$		3/2	0	−5/2	0

The net increase in profit resulting from entering a variable

At this point you might be wondering why the net increase in profit per bowl (x_1) is 3/2 (i.e., $1.50), rather than the original profit of $4. It is because the production of bowls (x_1) will require some of the resources previously used to produce mugs (x_2) only. Producing some bowls means not producing as many mugs; thus, we are giving up some of the profit gained from producing mugs in order to gain even more by producing bowls. This difference is the *net increase* of $1.50.

The new tableau pivot row (x_1) in the third simplex tableau is computed using the same formula used previously. Thus, all old pivot row values are divided through by 5/2, the pivot number. These values are shown in Table 4.16. The values for the other row (x_2) are computed as shown in Table 4.15.

TABLE 4.15

Computation of the x_2 Row for the Third Simplex Tableau

Column	Old Row Value	−	(Corresponding Coefficient in × Pivot Column	New Tableau Pivot Row Value)	=	= New Tableau Row Value
quantity	20	−	(1/2	× 24)	=	8
x_1	1/2	−	(1/2	× 1)	=	0
x_2	1	−	(1/2	× 0)	=	1
s_1	1/2	−	(1/2	× −3/5)	=	4/5
s_2	0	−	(1/2	× 2/5)	=	−1/5

These new row values, as well as the new z_j row and $c_j - z_j$ row, are shown in the completed third simplex tableau in Table 4.16.

TABLE 4.16
The Completed Third Simplex Tableau

c_j	Basic Variables	Quantity	4 x_1	5 x_2	0 s_1	0 s_2
5	x_2	8	0	1	4/5	−1/5
4	x_1	24	1	0	−3/5	2/5
	z_j	136	4	5	8/5	3/5
	$c_j - z_j$		0	0	−8/5	−3/5

Observing the $c_j - z_j$ row to determine the entering variable, we see that a nonbasic variable would not result in a positive net increase in profit, as all values in the $c_j - z_j$ row are zero or negative. This means that the optimal solution has been reached. The solution is

Determining if an optimal solution exists

$x_1 = 24$ bowls
$x_2 = 8$ mugs
$Z = \$136$ profit

which corresponds to point B in Figures 3.11 and 4.4.

An additional comment should be made regarding simplex solutions in general. Although this solution resulted in *integer* values for the variables (i.e., 24 and 8), it is possible to get a fractional solution for decision variables even though the variables reflect items that should be integers, such as airplanes, television sets, bowls, and mugs. In order to apply the simplex method, one must accept this limitation. Linear programming models can be solved using a method that ensures integer solutions; the method will be covered in Chapter 8.

Integer values are not guaranteed

COMPUTERIZED SOLUTION OF LINEAR PROGRAMMING PROBLEMS

The simplex method for solving linear programming problems can be used manually to solve relatively small problems. However, a linear programming problem with N constraints will require an average of $2N$ iterations of the simplex method. Thus, problems with only five constraints will have an average of ten iterations. Solving a problem with this many iterations can be so time consuming and subject to error that manual computation becomes impractical. For problems of a greater magnitude encompassing many iterations, manual solution becomes impossible. Dr. George Dantzig, the developer of the simplex method, recalled the first large-scale application of the simplex method to a diet problem in 1947. The linear programming model, which included 9 equations and 77 variables, was solved using hand-operated desk calculators and took 120 man-days.[1]

Computer packages

The difficulty of manually calculating the iterations of the simplex method has spurred the development of numerous computer packages (prewritten programs or codes) that replicate the process. These computer packages are usually relatively easy to use and, depending on the computer system employed, very economical.

Interactive computer programs

Linear programming problems are most frequently solved on the computer through *interactive processing*. In this mode the user carries on a "conversation" with the computer and the computer program via a remote terminal or a display terminal, or monitor, attached to a personal computer. The user inputs problem data at the terminal in response to instructions from the program that appear on the terminal screen. Usually after a few moments a solution to the problem appears on the screen, and the user is able to modify and rerun the program if desired. When the desired results are achieved, the user can then obtain a printout of the results from the computer.

The LINDO computer program

There are many linear programming software packages for solving linear programming problems. MPS and MPSX are widely used linear programming packages available on IBM systems. On a large mainframe computer, these linear programming codes can solve problems with thousands of variables and over a thousand constraints. One linear programming code that we will use to demonstrate the computerized solution of linear programming problems is called LINDO. LINDO is a powerful interactive linear programming package with (virtually identical) versions available for mainframe computers and personal computers, developed by Professor Linus Schrage at the University of Chicago.[2] The LINDO package is used widely by universities and businesses and is well suited for instructional purposes because of the easy dialogue established between the user and the computer program. Following the demonstration of LINDO, we will illustrate the use of a management science software package for the personal computer that has linear programming solution capabilities.

---

[1]G. Dantzig, "Reminiscences About the Origins of Linear Programming," *Operations Research Letters* 1, no. 2 (April 1982): 43–48.

[2]L. Schrage, *LINDO* (Palo Alto, Calif: The Scientific Press, 1981).

Solving the Colonial Pottery Company Example on the Computer

Again we will use the Colonial Pottery Company example, this time to demonstrate the computerized solution of a linear programming maximization problem using LINDO/PC. Recall the model formulation of this example:

maximize $Z = \$4x_1 + 5x_2$
subject to
$$x_1 + 2x_2 \leq 40 \text{ hr of labor}$$
$$4x_1 + 3x_2 \leq 120 \text{ lb of clay}$$
$$x_1, x_2 \geq 0$$
where
x_1 = number of bowls produced
x_2 = number of mugs produced

The LINDO/PC input instructions are straightforward, requiring that the objective function and the constraints be typed in at the terminal, just as they are shown in the model formulation. (If a linear programming package other than LINDO is used at your school, its input and output format will in all likelihood differ from the LINDO input and output format.) The LINDO/PC input for the Colonial Pottery Company example appears on the terminal exactly as shown here.

LINDO/PC input format

```
: max 4x1 + 5x2
? st
? x1 + 2x2 < 40
? 4x1 + 3x2 < 120
? end
:
```

The ? represents queries from the program for more data; the objective function, the constraints, and the terms "st" (i.e., subject to) and "end" are typed in by the user. Note that the user also types in < rather than ≤ for the constraints. Since most terminal keyboards do not have a ≤ key, the program recognizes < as ≤. The program displays the complete model formulation on the terminal in response to the command "look all":

Model formulation

```
: look all

MAX      4 X1 + 5 X2
SUBJECT TO
        2)    X1 + 2 X2 <=    40
        3)   4 X1 + 3 X2 <=    120
END
PRESS RETURN TO CONTINUE?
```

The LINDO/PC program always considers the objective function as the first model function and the first constraint as the second model function; thus, all constraints are numbered sequentially, beginning with the first constraint identified as function number 2.

Assuming that the user does not detect any errors in the model formulation, he or she commands the program to proceed to a solution. The user can ask for only the final solution or for the solution and all the simplex tableaus leading to that solution. Below, the series of tableaus leading to the optimal solution and the final solution are all shown as they appear on the terminal.

This computerized solution of the Colonial Pottery Company example mirrors the simplex solution shown earlier in this chapter. The three tableaus required for the computer solution correspond to the tableaus in Tables 4.6, 4.13, and 4.16, and the optimal solution is the same as the solution computed manually and shown in Table 4.16. However, the computerized tableaus differ slightly in format from the simplex tableaus described in this chapter.

Differences between LINDO/PC output and simplex tableaus

In the simplex tableaus in this chapter, the quantity column is the third column from the left. However, in the computerized tableau these same values appear on the far right. For example, the quantity column values 8, 24, and 136 in Table 4.16 are found on the far right side of the final computerized tableau. The z_i row does not exist at all in the computerized tableau, and instead of having a $c_i - z_i$ row as the bottom row of the simplex tableau, the computerized tableau has an equivalent $z_i - c_i$ row, labeled "ART," at the top. Also, recall that the functions in the computerized model are numbered sequentially beginning with the objective function. Thus, the slack variables for the two model constraint equations are labeled "SLK 2" and "SLK 3" (rather than s_1 and s_2 as in Table 4.16), since they correspond to functions 2 and 3 in the computerized model.

The computerized simplex method

Although these are only minor differences, the simplex method used in the LINDO/PC program and most other commercial linear programming packages is a different version from the simplex method presented in this chapter. For a maximization problem with all $\leq$ constraints, like the Colonial Pottery Company example, the differences in the tabular iterations between the computer solution and

```
: tableau

THE TABLEAU
     ROW  (BASIS)           X1        X2   SLK    2   SLK    3
        1 ART           -4.000    -5.000     .000       .000       .000
        2 SLK    2       1.000     2.000    1.000       .000    40.000
        3 SLK    3       4.000     3.000     .000      1.000   120.000
ART      ART           -4.000    -5.000     .000       .000       .000


: pivot
     X1 ENTERS AT VALUE   30.000      IN ROW    3 OBJ. VALUE=  120.00

: tableau

THE TABLEAU
     ROW  (BASIS)           X1        X2   SLK    2   SLK    3
        1 ART             .000    -2.000     .000      1.000   120.000
        2 SLK    2         .000     1.250    1.000     -.250    10.000
        3       X1        1.000      .750     .000       .250    30.000

: pivot
     X2 ENTERS AT VALUE   8.0000      IN ROW    2 OBJ. VALUE=  136.00

: tableau

THE TABLEAU
     ROW  (BASIS)           X1        X2   SLK    2   SLK    3
        1 ART             .000      .000    1.600       .600   136.000
        2       X2         .000     1.000     .800     -.200     8.000
        3       X1        1.000      .000    -.600       .400    24.000

: pivot
LP OPTIMUM FOUND  AT STEP       2

          OBJECTIVE FUNCTION VALUE

   1)         136.000000

   VARIABLE        VALUE        REDUCED COST
       X1        24.000000         .000000
       X2         8.000000         .000000


     ROW    SLACK OR SURPLUS    DUAL PRICES
      2)         .000000         1.600000
      3)         .000000          .600000

NO. ITERATIONS=        2
```

the manual solution are minor. However, for other problems such as a minimization problem the differences can be more pronounced. These differences will be discussed in greater detail in Chapter 5.

One final point regarding computerized output is that some of the final solution output has been deleted from this presentation.

These deleted parts provide information related to *duality* and *sensitivity analysis,* topics that will be covered in Chapter 6 as we expand on our discussion and demonstration of LINDO/PC.

Interactive mode

In an interactive mode, the computerized solution of a linear programming model would appear on the terminal screen just as it has been presented here. If the user so desires, the computer can provide a printout of the results. The user can solve as many problems as desired at one sitting and can have some, all, or none of the solutions printed on paper.

Personal Computer Software

Many personal computer management science software packages also include modules for solving linear programming problems, although typically these packages are not as powerful as a linear programming package like LINDO. Examples of such management science software packages include LINDO, QSB+ by Chang and Sullivan, which was introduced in Chapter 3 to solve the Colonial Pottery Company example graphically, Micro Manager by Lee and Shim,[3] and Microcomputer Software for Quantitative Analysis for Management by Render and Stair. We will use the latter package in this section. Although the linear programming component in this package is not as powerful as LINDO/PC, it can solve linear programming problems with up to 40 variables and 40 constraints, and, like LINDO/PC, it is very user friendly.

We will demonstrate Microcomputer Software using the Colonial Pottery Company example. A summary of the model and data as displayed by the computer is shown on page 115; the solution output is shown on page 116.[4]

The tableaus are straightforward and correspond closely to the simplex tableaus presented in this chapter, with one minor difference. The first two columns in the computer-generated tableau are the same as the first two columns in the chapter simplex tableaus (for example, Table 4.7). The next-to-last column, however, is labeled "Bi" in the computer tableau; it corresponds to the quantity column in the chapter tableaus.

The computerized solutions of the Colonial Pottery Company example fully demonstrate how easily and efficiently linear programming problems can be solved using a prewritten computer program such as LINDO/PC or Microcomputer Software. Thus, the

[3]S. Lee and J. Shim, *Micro Manager* (Boston: Allyn and Bacon, 1986).

[4]Barry Render and Ralph M. Stair, *Microcomputer Software for Quantitative Analysis for Management.* Copyright © 1988 by Allyn and Bacon, Inc. Reprinted with permission.

```
                        **** LINEAR PROGRAMMING ****

                          -- KEYBOARD INPUT

ENTER PROBLEM TITLE ? Colonial Pottery Co.

DO YOU WISH TO:
1 - MINIMIZE
2 - MAXIMIZE
ENTER YOUR CHOICE (1-2)

ENTER THE NUMBER OF CONSTRAINTS ? 2
ENTER THE NUMBER OF VARIABLES ? 2
ENTER THE NUMBER OF <= EQUATIONS ? 2
ENTER THE NUMBER OF = EQUATIONS ? 0
ENTER THE NUMBER OF >= EQUATIONS ? 0

    FOR OBJECTIVE FUNCTION
------------------------------------------------------------------------
ENTER COEFFICIENT # 1  OF THE OBJECTIVE FUNCTION? 4
ENTER COEFFICIENT # 2  OF THE OBJECTIVE FUNCTION? 5


        FOR (<=) CONSTRAINT #  1

ENTER THE VALUE OF COEFFICIENT  1 ? 1
ENTER THE VALUE OF COEFFICIENT  2 ? 2
ENTER THE RIGHT HAND SIDE VALUES ? 40

        FOR (<=) CONSTRAINT #  2

ENTER THE VALUE OF COEFFICIENT  1 ? 4
ENTER THE VALUE OF COEFFICIENT  2 ? 3
ENTER THE RIGHT HAND SIDE VALUES ? 120

    MAX Z = 4X1 + 5X2

    SUBJECT TO:

      1X1 + 2X2 <= 40
      4X1 + 3X2 <= 120
```

question most frequently asked is, Why learn the manual simplex method when readily available computer programs are so much easier to use? The first reason is that learning the manual simplex process increases one's overall understanding of linear programming and thus one's ability to interpret and implement solutions. Although the computer obviously facilitates solving linear programming problems, in-depth knowledge of the simplex method is a prerequisite for real expertise in the formulation and subsequent interpretation of the solution. In addition, knowledge of the manual

```
TABLEAU AFTER  0  ITERATIONS


   Cj            4.00     5.00     0.00     0.00
         Basis    x 1      x 2      s 1      s 2 :    Bi
---------------------------------------------------------------
   0.00    s 1    1.00     2.00     1.00     0.00 :   40.00
   0.00    s 2    4.00     3.00     0.00     1.00 :  120.00
---------------------------------------------------------------
         Zj       0.00     0.00     0.00     0.00     0.00
         Cj-Zj    4.00     5.00     0.00     0.00

PRESS RETURN TO CONTINUE?

TABLEAU AFTER  1  ITERATIONS


   Cj            4.00     5.00     0.00     0.00
         Basis    x 1      x 2      s 1      s 2 :    Bi
---------------------------------------------------------------
   5.00    x 2    0.50     1.00     0.50     0.00 :   20.00
   0.00    s 2    2.50     0.00    -1.50     1.00 :   60.00
---------------------------------------------------------------
         Zj       2.50     5.00     2.50     0.00    100.00
         Cj-Zj    1.50     0.00    -2.50     0.00

PRESS RETURN TO CONTINUE?

TABLEAU AFTER  2  ITERATIONS


   Cj            4.00     5.00     0.00     0.00
         Basis    x 1      x 2      s 1      s 2 :    Bi
---------------------------------------------------------------
   5.00    x 2    0.00     1.00     0.80    -0.20 :    8.00
   4.00    x 1    1.00     0.00    -0.60     0.40 :   24.00
---------------------------------------------------------------
         Zj       4.00     5.00     1.60     0.60    136.00
         Cj-Zj    0.00     0.00    -1.60    -0.60

PRESS RETURN TO CONTINUE?

AFTER 2 ITERATIONS THE FINAL OPTIMAL SOLUTION IS:
************************************************************************
                          ANSWERS
             VARIABLE              VALUE
               x 2                      8.000
               x 1                     24.000

                   OPTIMAL Z =  136
************************************************************************
```

simplex procedure is very useful in understanding the principles and applications of other topics in linear programming such as postoptimality analysis, discussed in Chapter 6.

SUMMARY OF THE SIMPLEX METHOD

The simplex method demonstrated in the previous section consists of the following steps:

1. Transform the model constraint inequalities into equations.
2. Set up the initial tableau for the basic feasible solution at the origin and compute the z_j and $c_j - z_j$ row values.
3. Determine the pivot column (entering nonbasic solution variable) by selecting the column with the highest positive value in the $c_j - z_j$ row.
4. Determine the pivot row (leaving basic solution variable) by dividing the quantity column values by the pivot column values and selecting the row with the minimum nonnegative quotient.
5. Compute the new pivot row values using the formula

$$\text{new tableau pivot row values} = \frac{\text{old tableau pivot row values}}{\text{pivot number}}$$

6. Compute all other row values using the formula

$$\begin{array}{c}\text{new tableau} \\ \text{row values}\end{array} = \begin{array}{c}\text{old row} \\ \text{values}\end{array} - \left(\begin{array}{c}\text{corresponding} \\ \text{coefficients in} \\ \text{pivot column}\end{array} \times \begin{array}{c}\text{corresponding} \\ \text{new tableau} \\ \text{pivot row} \\ \text{value}\end{array} \right)$$

7. Compute the new z_j and $c_j - z_j$ rows.
8. Determine whether the new solution is optimal by checking the $c_j - z_j$ row. If all $c_j - z_j$ row values are zero or negative, the solution is optimal. If a positive value exists, return to step 3 and repeat the simplex steps.

Summary

This chapter presented the general simplex method as it applies to a linear programming maximization model with $\leq$ constraints. Although the steps of the method are generally applicable to both maximization *and* minimization models, a minimization model requires some slight changes in the simplex tableau and in the way model constraint inequalities are converted to equations. Therefore, the application of the simplex method to a minimization problem will be considered as a separate topic in Chapter 5. The special cases of multiple optimum solutions, infeasible problems, and unbounded solutions will also be discussed in Chapter 5.

This chapter is limited to the simplex solution of maximization models

References

Dantzig, G. B. *Linear Programming and Extensions*. Princeton, N.J.: Princeton University, 1963.

Gass, S. *Linear Programming*. 4th ed. New York: McGraw-Hill, 1975.

Gottfried, B. S., and Weisman, J. *Introduction to Optimization Theory*. Englewood Cliffs, N.J.: Prentice-Hall, 1973.

Hadley, G. *Linear Programming*. Reading, Mass.: Addison-Wesley, 1962.

Hillier, F. S., and Lieberman, G. J. *Operations Research*. 4th ed. San Francisco: Holden-Day, 1986.

Kim, C. *Introduction to Linear Programming*. New York: Holt, Rinehart and Winston, 1971.

Lee, Sang M.; Moore, Laurence J.; and Taylor, Bernard W. *Management Science*. 3d ed. Boston: Allyn and Bacon, 1990.

Moskowitz, H., and Wright, G. P. *Operations Research Techniques for Management*. Englewood Cliffs, N.J.: Prentice-Hall, 1979.

Rothenberg, R. I. *Linear Programming*. New York: Elsevier North-Holland, 1979.

Wagner, H. M. *Principles of Operations Research*. 2d ed. Englewood Cliffs, N.J.: Prentice-Hall, 1975.

EXAMPLE PROBLEM SOLUTION

As a guide to the steps of the simplex method, this section presents an example of the simplex solution of a linear programming model.

The Problem Statement

Solve the following linear programming model using the simplex method.

$$\text{maximize } Z = 4x_1 + 5x_2$$
subject to
$$x_1 + 2x_2 \leq 10$$
$$6x_1 + 6x_2 \leq 36$$
$$x_1 \leq 4$$
$$x_1, x_2 \geq 0$$

Step 1: Transform the Constraints into Equations

$$\text{maximize } Z = 4x_1 + 5x_2 + 0s_1 + 0s_2 + 0s_3$$
subject to
$$x_1 + 2x_2 + s_1 = 10$$
$$6x_1 + 6x_2 + s_2 = 36$$
$$x_1 + s_3 = 4$$
$$x_1, x_2 \geq 0$$

Step 2: Set Up the Initial Tableau and Identify the Pivot Row and Pivot Column

c_j	Basic Variables	Quantity	4 x_1	5 x_2	0 s_1	0 s_2	0 s_3
0	s_1	10	1	2	1	0	0
0	s_2	36	6	6	0	1	0
0	s_3	4	1	0	0	0	1
	z_j	0	0	0	0	0	0
	$c_j - z_j$		4	5	0	0	0

x_2 is the entering variable; s_1 is the leaving variable.

Step 3: Compute the Second Iteration (Tableau)

c_j	Basic Variables	Quantity	4 x_1	5 x_2	0 s_1	0 s_2	0 s_3
5	x_2	5	1/2	1	1/2	0	0
0	s_2	6	3	0	3	1	0
0	s_3	4	1	0	0	0	1
	z_j	25	5/2	5	5/2	0	0
	$c_j - z_j$		3/2	0	−5/2	0	0

x_1 is the entering variable; s_2 is the leaving variable.

Step 4: Compute the Third Iteration

c_j	Basic Variables	Quantity	4 x_1	5 x_2	0 s_1	0 s_2	0 s_3
5	x_2	4	0	1	1	−1/6	0
4	x_1	2	1	0	−1	1/3	0
0	s_3	2	0	0	1	−1/3	1
	z_j	28	4	5	1	1/2	0
	$c_j - z_j$		0	0	−1	−1/2	0

Since all $c_j - z_j$ row values are negative or zero, the solution is optimal.

$x_1 = 2$

$x_2 = 4$

$s_3 = 2$

$Z = 28$

Computerized Solution

The computerized solution of this same example problem using Microcomputer Software is as follows:

```
                    *** LINEAR PROGRAMMING ***

                        -- DATA ENTERED --


        MAX Z = 4X1 + 5X2

        SUBJECT TO:

        1X1 + 2X2 <= 10
        6X1 + 6X2 <= 36
        1X1 + 0X2 <= 4


PRESS RETURN TO CONTINUE?




TABLEAU AFTER  0  ITERATIONS


    Cj             4.00     5.00     0.00     0.00     0.00
          Basis    x 1      x 2      s 1      s 2      s 3 :   Bi
    ------------------------------------------------------------------
    0.00    s 1    1.00     2.00     1.00     0.00     0.00 :  10.00
    0.00    s 2    6.00     6.00     0.00     1.00     0.00 :  36.00
    0.00    s 3    1.00     0.00     0.00     0.00     1.00 :   4.00
    ------------------------------------------------------------------
            Zj     0.00     0.00     0.00     0.00     0.00     0.00
            Cj-Zj  4.00     5.00     0.00     0.00     0.00

PRESS RETURN TO CONTINUE?




TABLEAU AFTER  1  ITERATIONS


    Cj             4.00     5.00     0.00     0.00     0.00
          Basis    x 1      x 2      s 1      s 2      s 3 :   Bi
    ------------------------------------------------------------------
    5.00    x 2    0.50     1.00     0.50     0.00     0.00 :   5.00
    0.00    s 2    3.00     0.00    -3.00     1.00     0.00 :   6.00
    0.00    s 3    1.00     0.00     0.00     0.00     1.00 :   4.00
    ------------------------------------------------------------------
            Zj     2.50     5.00     2.50     0.00     0.00    25.00
            Cj-Zj  1.50     0.00    -2.50     0.00     0.00

PRESS RETURN TO CONTINUE?
```

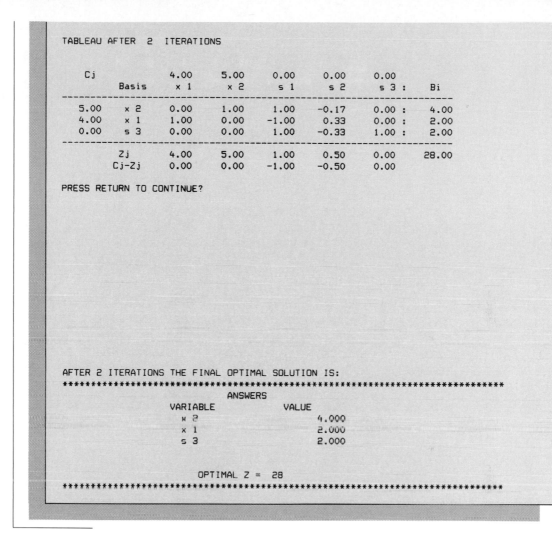

```
     TABLEAU AFTER  2  ITERATIONS


         Cj              4.00     5.00     0.00     0.00     0.00
                 Basis    x 1      x 2      s 1      s 2      s 3 :    Bi
     ---------------------------------------------------------------------
         5.00     x 2     0.00     1.00     1.00    -0.17     0.00 :   4.00
         4.00     x 1     1.00     0.00    -1.00     0.33     0.00 :   2.00
         0.00     s 3     0.00     0.00     1.00    -0.33     1.00 :   2.00
     ---------------------------------------------------------------------
                  Zj      4.00     5.00     1.00     0.50     0.00     28.00
                Cj-Zj     0.00     0.00    -1.00    -0.50     0.00

     PRESS RETURN TO CONTINUE?
```

```
     AFTER 2 ITERATIONS THE FINAL OPTIMAL SOLUTION IS:
     **************************************************************************
                              ANSWERS
                     VARIABLE                VALUE
                       x 2                    4.000
                       x 1                    2.000
                       s 3                    2.000


                     OPTIMAL Z =  28
     **************************************************************************
```

Problems

1. A manufacturer produces two products, A and B, from steel. The manufacturer has developed the following linear programming model to determine the quantity of each product (x_1 and x_2) to produce in order to maximize profit.

   maximize $Z = 5x_1 + 10x_2$ (profit, $)

   subject to

   $$4x_1 + 5x_2 \le 40 \text{ (steel, lb)}$$
   $$x_1, x_2 \ge 0$$

   a. Solve this problem graphically.
   b. Solve this problem using the simplex method.

2. Shown below is a simplex tableau for a linear programming model.

c_j	Basic Variables	Quantity	10 x_1	2 x_2	6 x_3	0 s_1	0 s_2	0 s_3
2	x_2	10	0	1	−2	1	−1/2	0
10	x_1	40	1	0	2	0	1/2	0
0	s_3	30	0	0	8	−3	3/2	1
	z_j	420	10	2	16	2	4	0
	$c_j − z_j$		0	0	−10	−2	−4	0

a. What is the solution given in this tableau?
b. Is the solution in this tableau optimal? Why?
c. What does x_3 equal in this tableau? s_2?
d. Write out the original objective function for the linear programming model, using only decision variables.
e. How many constraints are in the linear programming model?
f. Explain briefly why it would have been difficult to solve this problem graphically.

3. Chapter 3 presented the following problem (1) to be solved graphically. A company makes products 1 and 2 from two resources. The linear programming model for determining the amounts of product 1 and 2 to produce (x_1 and x_2) is

maximize $Z = 8x_1 + 2x_2$ (profit, $)
subject to
$$4x_1 + 5x_2 \leq 20 \text{ (resource 1, lb)}$$
$$2x_1 + 6x_2 \leq 18 \text{ (resource 2, lb)}$$
$$x_1, x_2 \geq 0$$

Solve this model using the simplex method.

4. Chapter 3 presented the following problem (2) to be solved graphically. A company produces two products that are processed on two assembly lines. Assembly line 1 has 100 available hours and assembly line 2 has 42 available hours. The company has formulated the following linear programming model for determining the number of each product (x_1 and x_2) to produce.

maximize $Z = 6x_1 + 4x_2$ (profit, $)
subject to
$$10x_1 + 10x_2 \leq 100 \text{ (line 1, hr)}$$
$$7x_1 + 3x_2 \leq 42 \text{ (line 2, hr)}$$
$$x_1, x_2 \geq 0$$

Solve this model using the simplex method.

5. Chapter 3 presented the following problem (6) to be solved graphically. The Pinewood Furniture Company produces chairs and tables from two resources — labor and wood. The company has 80 hours of labor and 36 pounds of wood available each day. Demand for chairs is limited to 6 per day. The company has developed the following linear programming model for determining the number of chairs and tables (x_1 and x_2) to produce each day in order to maximize profit.

maximize $Z = 400x_1 + 100x_2$ (profit, $)

subject to

$$8x_1 + 10x_2 \leq 80 \text{ (labor, hr)}$$
$$2x_1 + 6x_2 \leq 36 \text{ (wood, lb)}$$
$$x_1 \leq 6 \text{ (demand, chairs)}$$
$$x_1, x_2 \geq 0$$

Solve this model using the simplex method.

6. Chapter 3 presented the following problem (8) to be solved graphically. The Crumb and Custard Bakery makes cakes and pies from flour and sugar. The following linear programming model has been developed for determining the number of cakes and pies (x_1 and x_2) to produce each day so that profit will be maximized.

maximize $Z = x_1 + 5x_2$ (profit, $)

subject to

$$5x_1 + 5x_2 \leq 25 \text{ (flour, lb)}$$
$$2x_1 + 4x_2 < 16 \text{ (sugar, lb)}$$
$$x_1 \leq 5 \text{ (demand for cakes)}$$
$$x_1, x_2 \geq 0$$

Solve this model using the simplex method.

7. Chapter 3 presented the following problem (13) to be solved graphically. A jewelry store makes necklaces and bracelets from gold and platinum. The store has developed the following linear programming model for determining the number of necklaces and bracelets (x_1 and x_2) to make in order to maximize profit.

maximize $Z = 300x_1 + 400x_2$ (profit, $)

subject to

$$3x_1 + 2x_2 \leq 18 \text{ (gold, oz)}$$
$$2x_1 + 4x_2 \leq 20 \text{ (platinum, oz)}$$
$$x_2 \leq 4 \text{ (demand, bracelets)}$$
$$x_1, x_2 \geq 0$$

Solve this model using the simplex method.

8. A sporting goods company makes baseballs and softballs on a daily basis from leather and yarn. The company has developed the following

linear programming model for determining the number of baseballs and softballs to produce (x_1 and x_2) in order to maximize profits.

maximize $Z = 5x_1 + 4x_2$ (profit, $)

subject to

$.3x_1 + .5x_2 \leq 150$ (leather, ft^2)

$10x_1 + 4x_2 \leq 2{,}000$ (yarn, yd)

$x_1, x_2 \geq 0$

Solve this model using the simplex method.

9. A clothing shop makes suits and blazers. The three main resources used are material, rack space, and labor. The shop has developed the following linear programming model for determining the number of suits and blazers to make (x_1 and x_2) in order to maximize profits.

maximize $Z = 100x_1 + 150x_2$ (profit, $)

subject to

$10x_1 + 4x_2 \leq 160$ (material, yd^2)

$x_1 + x_2 \leq 20$ (rack space)

$10x_1 + 20x_2 \leq 300$ (labor, hr)

$x_1, x_2 \geq 0$

Solve this model using the simplex method.

10. Solve the following linear programming model using the simplex method.

maximize $Z = 100x_1 + 20x_2 + 60x_3$

subject to

$3x_1 + 5x_2 \leq 60$

$2x_1 + 2x_2 + 2x_3 \leq 100$

$x_3 \leq 40$

$x_1, x_2, x_3 \geq 0$

11. Solve the following linear programming model (a) graphically and (b) using the simplex method.

maximize $Z = 3x_1 + 4x_2$

subject to

$3x_1 + 2x_2 \leq 18$

$2x_1 + 4x_2 \leq 20$

$x_1 \leq 5$

$x_1, x_2 \geq 0$

12. The Cookie Monster Store at South Acres Mall makes three types of cookies—chocolate chip, pecan chip, and pecan sandies. The three main ingredients are chocolate chips, pecans, and sugar. The store has

120 pounds of chocolate chips, 40 pounds of pecans, and 300 pounds of sugar. The following linear programming model has been developed for determining the number of batches of chocolate chip cookies (x_1), pecan chip cookies (x_2), and pecan sandies (x_3) to make in order to maximize profit.

maximize $Z = 10x_1 + 12x_2 + 7x_3$ (profit, $)

subject to

$$20x_1 + 15x_2 + 10x_3 \leq 300 \text{ (sugar, lb)}$$
$$10x_1 + 5x_2 \leq 120 \text{ (chocolate chips, lb)}$$
$$x_1 + 2x_3 \leq 40 \text{ (pecans, lb)}$$
$$x_1, x_2, x_3 \geq 0$$

Solve this model using the simplex method.

13. The Eastern Iron and Steel Company makes nails, bolts, and washers from leftover steel and coats them with zinc. The company has 24 tons of steel and 30 tons of zinc. The following linear programming model has been developed for determining the number of batches of nails (x_1), bolts (x_2), and washers (x_3) to produce in order to maximize profit.

maximize $Z = 6x_1 + 2x_2 + 12x_3$ (profit, $1,000s)

subject to

$$4x_1 + x_2 + 3x_3 \leq 24 \text{ (steel, tons)}$$
$$2x_1 + 6x_2 + 3x_3 \leq 30 \text{ (zinc, tons)}$$
$$x_1, x_2, x_3 \geq 0$$

Solve this model using the simplex method.

14. The Valley Wine Company produces two kinds of wine — Valley Nectar and Valley Red. The wines are produced from grapes, and the company has 64 tons of grapes this season. However, production is limited by the availability of only 50 cubic yards of storage space for aging and 120 hours of processing time. The following linear programming model has been developed for determining the number of 1,000-gallon batches of Nectar (x_1) and Red (x_2) to produce in order to maximize profit.

maximize $Z = 9x_1 + 12x_2$ (profit, $1,000s)

subject to

$$4x_1 + 8x_2 \leq 64 \text{ (grapes, tons)}$$
$$5x_1 + 5x_2 \leq 50 \text{ (storage space, yd}^3)$$
$$15x_1 + 8x_2 \leq 120 \text{ (processing time, hr)}$$
$$x_1 \leq 7 \text{ (demand, Nectar)}$$
$$x_2 \leq 7 \text{ (demand, Red)}$$
$$x_1, x_2 \geq 0$$

Solve this model using the simplex method.

15. Solve the following linear programming model using the simplex method.

maximize $Z = 100x_1 + 75x_2 + 90x_3 + 95x_4$

subject to

$$3x_1 + 2x_2 \leq 40$$
$$4x_3 + x_4 \leq 25$$
$$200x_1 + 250x_3 \leq 2{,}000$$
$$100x_1 + 200x_4 \leq 2{,}200$$
$$x_1, x_2, x_3, x_4 \geq 0$$

16. Solve the following linear programming model using the simplex method.

maximize $Z = 60x_1 + 50x_2 + 45x_3 + 50x_4$

subject to

$$x_2 \leq 20$$
$$x_4 \leq 15$$
$$10x_1 + 5x_2 \leq 120$$
$$8x_3 + 6x_4 \leq 135$$
$$x_1, x_2, x_3, x_4 \geq 0$$

17. Solve the following linear programming model using the simplex method.

maximize $Z = 5x_1 + 7x_2 + 8x_3$

subject to

$$x_1 + x_2 + x_3 \leq 32$$
$$x_1 \leq 20$$
$$x_2 \leq 15$$
$$x_3 \leq 18$$
$$x_1, x_2, x_3 \geq 0$$

18. Solve the following linear programming model using the simplex method.

maximize $Z = 600x_1 + 540x_2 + 375x_3$

subject to

$$x_1 + x_2 + x_3 \leq 12$$
$$x_1 \leq 5$$
$$80x_1 + 70x_2 + 50x_3 \leq 750$$
$$x_1, x_2, x_3 \geq 0$$

19. Solve the following linear programming model using the simplex method.

maximize $Z = 9x_1 + 7x_2$

subject to

$$12x_1 + 4x_2 \leq 60$$
$$4x_1 + 8x_2 \leq 40$$
$$x_1, x_2 \geq 0$$

20. Solve the following linear programming model using the simplex method.

maximize $Z = 200x_1 + 300x_2$
subject to
$$2x_1 + 5x_2 \leq 180$$
$$3x_1 + 3x_2 \leq 135$$
$$x_1, x_2 \geq 0$$

21. Solve problem 1 from Chapter 2 using the simplex method.

22. Solve problem 5 from Chapter 2 using the simplex method.

23. Solve problem 7 from Chapter 2 using the simplex method.

24. Solve problem 10 from Chapter 2 using the simplex method.

25. Solve problem 19 from Chapter 2 using the simplex method.

26. Solve problem 4 from Chapter 2 using the simplex method.

27. Solve problem 39 from Chapter 2 using the simplex method.

5

The Minimization Problem and Irregular Types of LP Problems

In the previous chapter the simplex method for solving linear programming problems was demonstrated for a maximization problem. In general, the steps of the simplex method outlined in Chapter 4 are used for any type of linear programming problem. However, a minimization problem requires a few changes in the normal simplex process. In this chapter these changes will be discussed and demonstrated.

In addition, several exceptions to the typical linear programming problem will be presented. These include problems with mixed constraints ($=$, $\leq$, and $\geq$); problems with more than one solution, no feasible solution, or an unbounded solution; problems with a tie for the pivot column; problems with a tie for the pivot row; and problems with constraints with negative quantity values. None of these kinds of problems require changes in the simplex method. They are basically unusual results in individual simplex tableaus that the reader should know how to interpret and work with.

A MINIMIZATION PROBLEM

The following problem, first introduced as a graphical example in Chapter 3, will be used to demonstrate the application of the simplex method to a minimization problem. A farmer wants to determine how many bags of two kinds of fertilizer, Super-gro and Crop-quik, to purchase in order to meet the minimum nitrogen and phosphate requirements of a field. Each type of fertilizer provides a specific nitrogen and phosphate content. The model was formulated as

A minimization example

minimize $Z = \$6x_1 + 3x_2$
subject to
$$2x_1 + 4x_2 \geq 16 \text{ lb of nitrogen}$$
$$4x_1 + 3x_2 \geq 24 \text{ lb of phosphate}$$
$$x_1, x_2 \geq 0$$
where
$x_1 = $ bags of Super-gro fertilizer
$x_2 = $ bags of Crop-quik fertilizer
$Z = $ farmer's total cost (\$) of purchasing fertilizer

Converting $\geq$ inequality constraints into equalities

In Chapter 4 the first step of the simplex process was to convert all the model $\leq$ constraint inequalities to equations. The same general step is required for a minimization model. However, because this type of problem has $\geq$ constraints (as opposed to the $\leq$ constraints of the Colonial Pottery Company maximization example in Chapter 4), the constraints are converted to equations a little differently.

Surplus variables

Instead of adding a slack variable, with a $\geq$ constraint we start by subtracting a *surplus* variable. Whereas a slack variable is added and reflects unused resources, a surplus variable is subtracted and reflects the excess above a minimum resource requirement level. Like the slack variable, a surplus variable is represented symbolically by s_i and must be nonnegative.

For the nitrogen constraint the subtraction of a surplus variable gives

$$2x_1 + 4x_2 - s_1 = 16$$

The surplus variable s_1 transforms the nitrogen constraint into an equation.

As an example, consider the hypothetical solution $x_1 = 0$ and $x_2 = 10$. Substituting these values into the above equation yields

$$2(0) + 4(10) - s_1 = 16$$
$$-s_1 = 16 - 40$$
$$s_1 = 24 \text{ lb of nitrogen}$$

In this equation s_1 can be interpreted as the *extra* amount of nitrogen above the minimum requirement of 16 lb that would be obtained by purchasing 10 bags of Crop-quik fertilizer. However, the simplex method requires that the initial basic feasible solution be at the origin, where $x_1 = 0$ and $x_2 = 0$. Testing these solution values, we have

$$2x_1 + 4x_2 - s_1 = 16$$
$$2(0) + 4(0) - s_1 = 16$$
$$s_1 = -16$$

The idea of "negative excess pounds of nitrogen" is illogical and violates the nonnegativity restriction of linear programming. The reason the surplus variable does not work is shown in Figure 5.1. The solution at the origin is outside the feasible solution space.

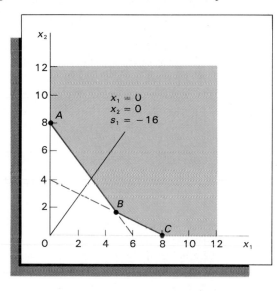

FIGURE 5.1

Graph of the
Fertilizer Example

In order to alleviate this difficulty and get a solution at the origin, we add an *artificial* variable (A_i) to the constraint equation,

Artificial variable

$$2x_1 + 4x_2 - s_1 + A_1 = 16$$

The artificial variable, A_1, does not have a meaning as a slack variable or a surplus variable does. It is inserted into the equation simply to give a positive solution at the origin; we are artificially creating a solution.

$$2x_1 + 4x_2 - s_1 + A_1 = 16$$
$$2(0) + 4(0) - 0 + A_1 = 16$$
$$A_1 = 16$$

The artificial variable is somewhat analogous to a booster rocket — its purpose is to get us off the ground, but once we get started it has no real use and thus is discarded. The artificial solution helps get the simplex process started, but we do not want it to end up in the optimal solution, since it has no real meaning.

When a surplus variable is subtracted and an artificial variable is added, the phosphate constraint becomes

$$4x_1 + 3x_2 - s_2 + A_2 = 24$$

The effect of surplus variables on the objective function

The effect of surplus and artificial variables on the objective function must now be considered. Like a slack variable, a surplus variable has no effect on the objective function in terms of increasing or decreasing cost. For example, a surplus of 24 pounds of nitrogen does not contribute to the cost of the objective function, since the cost is determined solely by the number of bags of fertilizer purchased (i.e., the values of x_1 and x_2). Thus, a coefficient of 0 is assigned to each surplus variable in the objective function.

The effect of artificial variables on the objective function

By assigning a "cost" of $0 to each surplus variable, we are not prohibiting it from being in the final optimal solution. It would be quite realistic to have a final solution that showed some surplus nitrogen or phosphate. Likewise, assigning a cost of $0 to an artificial variable in the objective function would not prohibit it from being in the final optimal solution. However, if the artificial variable appeared in the solution, it would render the final solution meaningless. Therefore, we must ensure that an artificial variable is *not* in the final solution.

As previously noted, the presence of a particular variable in the final solution is based on its relative profit or cost. For example, if a bag of Super-gro cost $600 instead of $6 and Crop-quik stayed at $3, it is doubtful that the farmer would purchase Super-gro (i.e., x_1 would not be in the solution). Thus, we can prohibit a variable from being in the final solution by assigning it a very *large cost*. Rather than assigning a dollar cost to an artificial variable, we will assign a value of M, which represents a large positive cost (say, $1,000,000). This operation produces the following objective function for our example:

$$\text{minimize } Z = 6x_1 + 3x_2 + 0s_1 + 0s_2 + MA_1 + MA_2$$

The minimization model in proper form for simplex solution

The completely transformed minimization model can now be summarized as

$$\text{minimize } Z = 6x_1 + 3x_2 + 0s_1 + 0s_2 + MA_1 + MA_2$$
$$\text{subject to}$$
$$2x_1 + 4x_2 - s_1 + A_1 = 16$$
$$4x_1 + 3x_2 - s_2 + A_2 = 24$$
$$x_1, x_2, s_1, s_2, A_1, A_2 \geq 0$$

The Simplex Tableau

The initial simplex tableau for a minimization model is developed the same way as one for a maximization model is developed, except for one small difference. Rather than computing $c_j - z_j$ in the bottom row of the tableau, we compute $z_j - c_j$, which represents the *net per unit decrease in cost*, and the largest positive value is selected as the entering variable and pivot column. (An alternative would be to leave the bottom row as $c_j - z_j$ and select the largest *negative* value as the pivot column. However, in order to maintain a consistent rule for selecting the pivot column, we will use $z_j - c_j$.)

Changing the $c_j - z_j$ row to $z_j - c_j$

The initial simplex tableau for this model is shown in Table 5.1. Notice that A_1 and A_2 form the initial solution at the origin, since that was the reason for inserting them in the first place — to get a solution at the origin. This is not a basic feasible solution, since the origin is not in the feasible solution area, as shown in Figure 5.1. As indicated previously, it is an artificially created solution. However, the simplex process will move toward feasibility in subsequent tableaus. Note that across the top the decision variables are listed first, then surplus variables, and finally artificial variables.

The initial simplex tableau with artificial variables forming the basic feasible solution

TABLE 5.1

The Initial Simplex Tableau

c_j	Basic Variables	Quantity	6 x_1	3 x_2	0 s_1	0 s_2	M A_1	M A_2
M	A_1	16	2	4	−1	0	1	0
M	A_2	24	4	3	0	−1	0	1
	z_j	40M	6M	7M	−M	−M	M	M
	$z_j - c_j$		6M − 6	7M − 3	−M	−M	0	0

In Table 5.1 the x_2 column was selected as the pivot column because $7M - 3$ is the largest positive value in the $z_j - c_j$ row. A_1 was selected as the leaving basic variable (and pivot row), since the quotient of 4 for this row was the minimum positive row value.

Selecting the pivot column

Selecting the pivot row

The second simplex tableau is developed using the simplex formulas presented in Chapter 4. It is shown in Table 5.2.

Notice that the A_1 column has been eliminated in the second simplex tableau. Once an artificial variable leaves the basic feasible solution, it will never return because of its high cost, M. Thus, like the booster rocket, it can be eliminated from the tableau. However, the artificial variable is the *only* variable that can be treated this way.

Eliminating artificial variables that leave the basic solution

The third simplex tableau, with x_1 replacing A_2, is shown in Table 5.3. Both the A_1 and A_2 columns have been eliminated, since both variables have left the solution. The x_1 row is selected as the

TABLE 5.2
The Second Simplex Tableau

c_j	Basic Variables	Quantity	6 x_1	3 x_2	0 s_1	0 s_2	M A_2
3	x_2	4	1/2	1	−1/4	0	0
M	A_2	12	5/2	0	3/4	−1	1
	z_j	12M + 12	5M/2 + 3/2	3	−3/4 + 3M/4	−M	M
	$z_j − c_j$		5M/2 − 9/2	0	−3/4 + 3M/4	−M	0

TABLE 5.3
The Third Simplex Tableau

c_j	Basic Variables	Quantity	6 x_1	3 x_2	0 s_1	0 s_2
3	x_2	8/5	0	1	−2/5	1/5
6	x_1	24/5	1	0	3/10	−2/5
	z_j	168/5	6	3	3/5	−9/5
	$z_j − c_j$		0	0	3/5	−9/5

pivot row, since it corresponds to the minimum positive ratio of 16. In selecting the pivot row, the −4 value for the x_2 row was not considered because the minimum *positive* value is selected. Selecting the x_2 row would result in a negative quantity value for s_1 in the fourth tableau, which is not feasible.

The fourth simplex tableau, with s_1 replacing x_1, is shown in Table 5.4.

TABLE 5.4
Optimal Simplex Tableau

c_j	Basic Variables	Quantity	6 x_1	3 x_2	0 s_1	0 s_2
3	x_2	8	4/3	1	0	−1/3
0	s_1	16	10/3	0	1	−4/3
	z_j	24	4	3	0	−1
	$z_j − c_j$		−2	0	0	−1

Table 5.4 is the optimal simplex tableau, since the $z_j − c_j$ row contains no positive values. The optimal solution is

    $x_1 = 0$ bags of Super-gro
    $s_1 = 16$ extra lb of nitrogen
    $x_2 = 8$ bags of Crop-quik
    $s_2 = 0$ extra lb of phosphate
    $Z = \$24$, total cost of purchasing fertilizer

To summarize, the adjustments necessary to apply the simplex method to a minimization problem are as follows:

1. Transform all $\geq$ constraints to equations by subtracting a surplus variable and adding an artificial variable.
2. Assign a c_j value of M to each artificial variable in the objective function.
3. Change the $c_j - z_j$ row to $z_j - c_j$.

Although the fertilizer example model we just used included only $\geq$ constraints, it is possible for a minimization problem to have $\leq$ and $=$ constraints in addition to $\geq$ constraints. Similarly, it is possible for a maximization problem to have $\geq$ and $=$ constraints in addition to $\leq$ constraints. Problems that contain a combination of different types of inequality constraints are referred to as *mixed constraint problems*.

A MIXED CONSTRAINT PROBLEM

So far we have discussed maximization problems with all $\leq$ constraints and minimization problems with all $\geq$ constraints. However, we have yet to solve a problem with a mixture of $\leq$, $\geq$, and $=$ constraints. Further, we have not yet looked at a maximization problem with a $\geq$ constraint. The following is a maximization problem with $\leq$, $\geq$, and $=$ constraints.

A leather shop makes custom-designed, hand-tooled briefcases and luggage. The shop makes a $400 profit from each briefcase and a $200 profit from each piece of luggage. (The profit for briefcases is higher because briefcases require more hand tooling.) The shop has a contract to provide a store with exactly 30 items per month. A tannery supplies the shop with at least 80 square yards of leather per month. The shop must use at least this amount, but can order more. Each briefcase requires 2 square yards of leather; each piece of luggage requires 8 square yards of leather. From past performance, the shop owners know they cannot make more than 20 briefcases per month. They want to know the number of briefcases and pieces of luggage to produce in order to maximize profit.

This problem is formulated as

maximize $Z = \$400x_1 + 200x_2$

subject to

$$x_1 + x_2 = 30 \text{ contracted items}$$
$$2x_1 + 8x_2 \geq 80 \text{ yd}^2 \text{ of leather}$$
$$x_1 \leq 20 \text{ briefcases}$$
$$x_1, x_2 \geq 0$$

where

$x_1 = $ briefcases
$x_2 = $ pieces of luggage

Preparing an
equality constraint
for the simplex
method

The first step in the simplex method is to transform the inequalities into equations. The first constraint for the contracted items is already an equation; therefore, it is not necessary to add a slack variable. There can be no slack in the contract with the store, since exactly 30 items must be delivered. Even though this equation already appears to be in the necessary form for simplex solution, let us test it at the origin to see if it meets the starting requirements.

$$x_1 + x_2 = 30$$
$$0 + 0 = 30$$
$$0 \neq 30$$

Since zero does not equal 30, the constraint is not feasible in this form. Recall that a $\geq$ constraint did not work at the origin either in an earlier problem. Therefore, an artificial variable was added. The same thing can be done here.

$$x_1 + x_2 + A_1 = 30$$

Now at the origin, where $x_1 = 0$ and $x_2 = 0$,

$$0 + 0 + A_1 = 30$$
$$A_1 = 30$$

The effect of an
artificial variable
on the objective
function of a
maximization
model

Any time a constraint is initially an equation, an artificial variable is added. However, the artificial variable cannot be assigned a value of M in the objective function of a maximization problem. Since the objective is to maximize profit, a positive M value would represent a large positive *profit* that would definitely end up in the final solution. As an artificial variable has no real meaning and is inserted into the model merely to create an initial solution at the origin, its existence in the final solution would render the solution meaningless. To prevent this from happening, we must give the artificial variable a large *cost* contribution, or $-M$.

The constraint for leather is a $\geq$ inequality. It is converted to equation form by subtracting a surplus variable and adding an artificial variable:

$$2x_1 + 8x_2 - s_1 + A_2 = 80$$

As in the equality constraint, the artificial variable in this constraint must be assigned an objective function coefficient of $-M$.

The final constraint is a $\leq$ inequality and is transformed by adding a slack variable:

The mixed
constraint model in
proper form for
simplex solution

$$x_1 + s_2 = 20$$

The completely transformed linear programming problem is as follows:

maximize $Z = 400x_1 + 200x_2 + 0s_1 + 0s_2 - MA_1 - MA_2$

subject to

$$x_1 + x_2 + A_1 = 30$$
$$2x_1 + 8x_2 - s_1 + A_2 = 80$$
$$x_1 + s_2 = 20$$
$$x_1, x_2, s_1, s_2, A_1, A_2 \geq 0$$

The initial simplex tableau for this model is shown in Table 5.5.

TABLE 5.5
The Initial Simplex Tableau

c_j	Basic Variables	Quantity	400 x_1	200 x_2	0 s_1	0 s_2	$-M$ A_1	$-M$ A_2
$-M$	A_1	30	1	1	0	0	1	0
$-M$	A_2	80	2	8	-1	0	0	1
0	s_2	20	1	0	0	1	0	0
	z_j	$-110M$	$-3M$	$-9M$	M	0	$-M$	$-M$
	$c_j - z_j$		$400 + 3M$	$200 + 9M$	$-M$	0	0	0

Notice in Table 5.5 that the basic solution variables are a mix of artificial and slack variables. Note also that the third row quotient for determining the pivot row $(20 \div 0)$ is an undefined value, or ∞. Therefore, this row would never be considered as a candidate for the pivot row. The second, third, and optimal tableaus for this problem are shown in Tables 5.6, 5.7, and 5.8.

The basic variables for a mixed constraint model

TABLE 5.6
The Second Simplex Tableau

c_j	Basic Variables	Quantity	400 x_1	200 x_2	0 s_1	0 s_2	$-M$ A_1
$-M$	A_1	20	3/4	0	1/8	0	1
200	x_2	10	1/4	1	$-1/8$	0	0
0	s_2	20	1	0	0	1	0
	z_j	$2,000 - 20M$	$50 - 3M/4$	200	$-25 - M/8$	0	$-M$
	$c_j - z_j$		$350 + 3M/4$	0	$25 + M/8$	0	0

TABLE 5.7
The Third Simplex Tableau

c_j	Basic Variables	Quantity	400 x_1	200 x_2	0 s_1	0 s_2	$-M$ A_1
$-M$	A_1	5	0	0	1/8	$-3/4$	1
200	x_2	5	0	1	$-1/8$	$-1/4$	0
400	x_1	20	1	0	0	1	0
	z_j	$9,000 - 5M$	400	200	$-25 - M/8$	$350 + 3M/4$	$-M$
	$c_j - z_j$		0	0	$25 + M/8$	$-350 - 3M/4$	0

The solution for the leather shop problem is

$x_1 = 20$ briefcases

$x_2 = 10$ pieces of luggage

$s_1 = 40$ extra yd^2 of leather

$Z = \$10,000$ profit per month

TABLE 5.8

The Optimal Simplex Tableau

c_j	Basic Variables	Quantity	400	200	0	0
			x_1	x_2	s_1	s_2
0	s_1	40	0	0	1	−6
200	x_2	10	0	1	0	−1
400	x_1	20	1	0	0	1
	z_j	10,000	400	200	0	200
	$c_j - z_j$		0	0	0	−200

Rules for preparing $\leq$, $=$, and $\geq$ constraints for the simplex method

It is now possible to summarize a set of rules for transforming all three types of model constraints.

		Objective Function Coefficient	
Constraint	Adjustment	Maximization	Minimization
$\leq$	Add a slack variable	0	0
$=$	Add an artificial variable	$-M$	M
$\geq$	Subtract a surplus variable and add an artificial variable	0 $-M$	0 M

IRREGULAR TYPES OF LINEAR PROGRAMMING PROBLEMS

Linear programming models for which the general rules do not always apply

The basic forms of typical maximization and minimization problems have been shown in Chapter 4 and in this chapter. However, there are several special types of atypical linear programming problems. Although these special cases do not occur frequently, they will be described so that you can recognize them when they arise. These special types include problems with more than one optimal solution, infeasible problems, problems with unbounded solutions, problems with ties for the pivot column and/or ties for the pivot row, and problems with constraints with negative quantity values.

MULTIPLE OPTIMAL SOLUTIONS

Consider the Colonial Pottery Company example with the objective function changed from $Z = 4x_1 + 5x_2$ to $Z = 4x_1 + 3x_2$.

Models with more than one unique best solution

> maximize $Z = 4x_1 + 3x_2$
> subject to
> $x_1 + 2x_2 \leq 40$ hr of labor
> $4x_1 + 3x_2 \leq 120$ lb of clay
> $x_1, x_2 \geq 0$
>
> where
> x_1 = bowls produced
> x_2 = mugs produced

The graph of this model is shown in Figure 5.2. The slight change in the objective function makes it now *parallel* to the constraint line, $4x_1 + 3x_2 = 120$. Both lines now have the same *slope* of $-4/3$. Therefore, as the objective function edge moves outward from the origin, it touches the whole line segment BC rather than a single extreme corner point before it leaves the feasible solution area. This means that every point along this line segment is optimal (i.e., each point results in the same profit of $Z - \$120$). The end points of this line segment, B and C, are typically referred to as the *alternate optimal solutions*. It is understood that these points represent the end points of a range of optimal solutions.

An objective function parallel to a constraint line

Alternate optimal solutions

The pottery company therefore has several options in deciding on the number of bowls and mugs to produce. These options give the company greater flexibility in its decision making. The optimal simplex tableau for this problem is shown in Table 5.9.

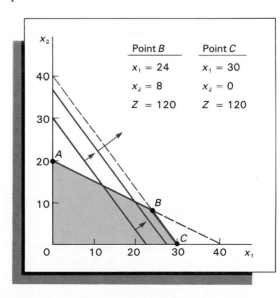

FIGURE 5.2

Graph of the Colonial Pottery Company Example with Multiple Optimal Solutions

TABLE 5.9
The Optimal Simplex Tableau

| c_j | Basic Variables | Quantity | 4 | 3 | 0 | 0 |
			x_1	x_2	s_1	s_2
0	s_1	10	0	5/4	1	−1/4
4	x_1	30	1	3/4	0	1/4
	z_j	120	4	3	0	1
	$c_j − z_j$		0	0	0	−1

Using the $c_j − z_j$ (or $z_j − c_j$) row to recognize the existence of multiple optimal solutions

Table 5.9 corresponds to point C in Figure 5.2. The fact that this problem contains multiple optimal solutions can be determined from the $c_j − z_j$ row. Recall that the $c_j − z_j$ row values are the net increases in profit per unit for the variable in each column. Thus, $c_j − z_j$ values of zero indicate no net increase in profit *and* no net loss in profit. We would expect the basic variables, s_1 and x_1, to have zero $c_j − z_j$ values because they are part of the basic feasible solution; they are already in the solution so they cannot be entered again. However, the x_2 column has a $c_j − z_j$ value of zero and it is not part of the basic feasible solution. This means that if some mugs (x_2) were produced, we would have a new product mix but the same total profit. Thus, a multiple optimal solution is indicated by a $c_j − z_j$ (or $z_j − c_j$) row value of zero for a nonbasic variable.

Determining the alternate solution

To determine the alternate end point solution, let x_2 be the entering variable (pivot column) and select the pivot row as usual. This selection results in the s_1 row being the pivot row. The alternate solution corresponding to point B in Figure 5.2 is shown in Table 5.10.

TABLE 5.10
The Alternative Optimal Tableau

	Basic Variables	Quantity	x_1	x_2	s_1	s_2
3	x_2	8	0	1	4/5	−1/5
4	x_1	24	1	0	−3/5	2/5
	z_j	120	4	3	0	1
	$c_j − z_j$		0	0	0	−1

Multiple optimal solutions provide greater flexibility to the decision maker

As noted, multiple optimal solutions can benefit the decision maker, since the number of decision options is enlarged. The multiple optimal solutions (along the line segment BC in Fig. 5.2) allow the decision maker greater flexibility. For example, in the case of the Colonial Pottery Company, it may be easier to sell bowls than mugs; thus the solution shown in Table 5.9 (where only bowls are produced) would be more desirable than the solution shown in Table 5.10 (where a mix of bowls and mugs is produced).

An Infeasible Problem

In some cases a linear programming problem has no feasible solution area; thus, there is no basic feasible solution to the problem. An example of an infeasible problem is formulated below and depicted graphically in Figure 5.3.

Problems with no solution

$$\text{maximize } Z = 5x_1 + 3x_2$$
subject to
$$4x_1 + 2x_2 \leq 8$$
$$x_1 \geq 4$$
$$x_2 \geq 6$$
$$x_1, x_2 \geq 0$$

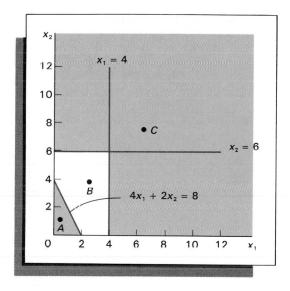

FIGURE 5.3

Graph of an Infeasible Problem

Point A in Figure 5.3 satisfies only the constraint $4x_1 + 2x_2 \leq 8$, whereas point C satisfies only the constraints $x_1 \geq 4$ and $x_2 \geq 6$. Point B satisfies none of the constraints. The three constraints do not overlap to form a feasible solution area. Since no point satisfies all three constraints simultaneously, there is no solution to the problem. The final simplex tableau for this problem is shown in Table 5.11.

The tableau in Table 5.11 has all zero or negative values in the $c_j - z_j$ row, indicating that it is optimal. However, the solution is $x_2 = 4$, $A_1 = 4$, and $A_2 = 2$. Since the existence of artificial variables in the final solution makes the solution meaningless, this is not a real solution. In general, any time the $c_j - z_j$ (or $z_j - c_j$) row indicates that the solution is optimal but there are artificial variables in the solution, the solution is infeasible. Infeasible problems do not typically occur, but when they do they are usually a result of errors

Recognizing an infeasible problem in the simplex tableau

TABLE 5.11

The Final Simplex Tableau for an Infeasible Problem

c_j	Basic Variables	Quantity	5 x_1	3 x_2	0 s_1	0 s_2	0 s_3	$-M$ A_1	$-M$ A_2
3	x_2	4	2	1	1/2	0	0	0	0
$-M$	A_1	4	1	0	0	-1	0	1	0
$-M$	A_2	2	-2	0	$-1/2$	0	-1	0	1
	z_j	$12 - 6M$	$6 + M$	3	$3/2 + M/2$	M	M	$-M$	$-M$
	$c_j - z_j$		$-1 - M$	0	$-3/2 - M/2$	$-M$	$-M$	0	0

in defining the problem or in formulating the linear programming model.

An Unbounded Problem

In some problems the feasible solution area formed by the model constraints is not closed. In these cases it is possible for the objective function to increase indefinitely without ever reaching a maximum value, since it never reaches the boundary of the feasible solution area.

Problems where the objective function increases indefinitely

An example of this type of problem is formulated below and shown graphically in Figure 5.4.

maximize $Z = 4x_1 + 2x_2$

subject to

$$x_1 \geq 4$$
$$x_2 \leq 2$$
$$x_1, x_2 \geq 0$$

FIGURE 5.4

An Unbounded Problem

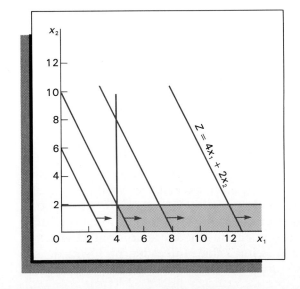

In Figure 5.4 the objective function is shown to increase without bound; thus, a solution is never reached.

A solution space that is not completely closed in

The second tableau for this problem is shown in Table 5.12. In this simplex tableau, s_1 is chosen as the entering nonbasic variable and pivot column. However, there is no pivot row or leaving basic variable. One row value is -4 and the other is undefined. This indicates that a "most constrained" point does not exist and that the solution is unbounded. In general, a solution is unbounded if the row value ratios are all negative or undefined.

Identifying an unbounded solution in the simplex tableau

TABLE 5.12
The Second Simplex Tableau

c_j	Basic Variables	Quantity	**4** x_1	**2** x_2	**0** s_1	**0** s_2	
c_j	Variables	Quantity	x_2	x_2	-4	s_2	
4	x_1	4	1	0	-1	0	$4 \div -1 = -4$
0	s_2	2	0	1	0	1	$2 \div 0 = \infty$
	z_j	16	4	0	-4	0	
	$c_j - z_j$		0	2	4	0	

Unlimited profits are not possible in the real world, and an unbounded solution, like an infeasible solution, typically reflects an error in defining the problem or in formulating the model.

Tie for the Pivot Column

Sometimes when selecting the pivot column, you may notice that the greatest positive $c_j - z_j$ (or $z_j - c_j$) row values are the same; thus there is a tie for the pivot column. When this happens, one of the two tied columns should be selected arbitrarily. Even though one choice may require fewer subsequent iterations than the other, there is no way of knowing this beforehand.

A tie for the entering nonbasic variable

Tie for the Pivot Row—Degeneracy

It is also possible to have a tie for the pivot row (i.e., two rows may have identical lowest nonnegative values). Like a tie for a pivot column, a tie for a pivot row should be broken arbitrarily. However, after the tie is broken, the basic variable that was the *other* choice for the leaving basic variable will have a quantity value of zero in the next tableau. This condition is commonly referred to as *degeneracy*, because theoretically it is possible for subsequent simplex tableau solutions to degenerate so that the objective function value never improves and optimality never results. This occurs infrequently, however.

A quantity value of zero

In general, tableaus with ties for the pivot row should be treated normally. If the simplex steps are carried out as usual, the solution will evolve normally.

The following is an example of a problem containing a tie for the pivot row.

$$\text{maximize } Z = 4x_1 + 6x_2$$

subject to

$$6x_1 + 4x_2 \leq 24$$
$$x_2 \leq 3$$
$$5x_1 + 10x_2 \leq 40$$
$$x_1, x_2 \geq 0$$

For the sake of brevity we will skip the initial simplex tableau for this problem and go directly to the second simplex tableau in Table 5.13, which shows a tie for the pivot row between the s_1 and s_3 rows.

TABLE 5.13
The Second Simplex Tableau with a Tie for the Pivot Row

c_j	Basic Variables	Quantity	**4** x_1	6 x_2	0 s_1	0 s_2	0 s_3	
0	s_1	12	6	0	1	−4	0	$12 \div 6 = 2$
6	x_2	3	0	1	0	1	0	Tie
0	s_3	10	5	0	0	−10	1	$10 \div 5 = 2$
	z_j	18	0	6	0	6	0	
	$c_j - z_j$		4	0	0	−6	0	

The s_3 row is selected arbitrarily as the pivot row, resulting in the third simplex tableau, shown in Table 5.14.

TABLE 5.14
The Third Simplex Tableau with Degeneracy

c_j	Basic Variables	Quantity	4 x_1	6 x_2	0 s_1	**0** s_2	0 s_3
0	s_1	0	0	0	1	8	−6/5
6	x_2	3	0	1	0	1	0
4	x_1	2	1	0	0	−2	1/5
	z_j	26	4	6	0	−2	4/5
	$c_j - z_j$		0	0	0	2	−4/5

Note that in Table 5.14 a quantity value of zero now appears in the s_1 row, representing the degenerate condition resulting from the

Margin notes:

An example of degeneracy

The s_1 and s_3 rows are tied for the pivot row

The basic variable s_1 equals zero

tie for the pivot row. However, the simplex process should be continued as usual: s_2 should be selected as the entering basic variable and the s_1 row should be selected as the pivot row. (Recall that the pivot row value of zero is the minimum nonnegative quotient.) The final optimal tableau is shown in Table 5.15.

TABLE 5.15
The Optimal Simplex Tableau for a Degenerate Problem

The optimal tableau

c_j	Basic Variables	Quantity	4	6	0	0	0
			x_1	x_2	s_1	s_2	s_3
0	s_2	0	0	0	1/8	1	−3/20
6	x_2	3	0	1	−1/8	0	3/20
4	x_1	2	1	0	1/4	0	−1/10
	z_j	26	4	6	1/4	0	1/2
	$c_j - z_j$		0	0	−1/4	0	−1/2

Notice that the optimal solution did not change from the third to the optimal simplex tableau. The graphical analysis of this problem shown in Figure 5.5 reveals the reason for this.

A graphical presentation of degeneracy

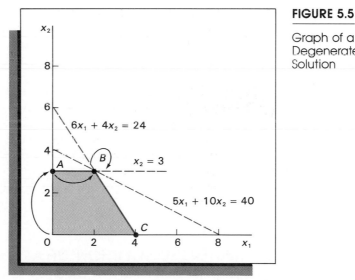

FIGURE 5.5

Graph of a Degenerate Solution

Notice that in the third tableau (Table 5.14) the simplex process went to point B, where all three constraint lines intersect. This is, in fact, what caused the tie for the pivot row and the degeneracy. Subsequently, the simplex process stayed at point B in the optimal tableau (Table 5.15). The two tableaus represent two different basic feasible solutions corresponding to two different sets of model constraint equations.

Negative Quantity Values

A negative value on the right-hand side of a model constraint

Occasionally a model constraint is formulated with a negative quantity value on the right side of the inequality sign—for example,

$$-6x_1 + 2x_2 \geq -30$$

This is an improper condition for the simplex method, because for the method to work, all quantity values must be positive or zero. This difficulty can be alleviated by multiplying the inequality by -1, which also changes the direction of the inequality.

Converting a negative quantity value to a positive value

$$(-1)(-6x_1 + 2x_2 \geq -30)$$
$$6x_1 - 2x_2 \leq 30$$

Now the model constraint is in proper form to be transformed into an equation and solved by the simplex method.

Summary of Simplex Irregularities

Multiple optimal solutions are identified by $c_j - z_j$ (or $z_j - c_j$) = 0 for a nonbasic variable. To determine the alternate solution(s), enter the nonbasic variable(s) with a $c_j - z_j$ value equal to zero.

An *infeasible problem* is identified in the simplex procedure when an optimal solution is achieved (i.e., when all $c_j - z_j \geq 0$) and one or more of the basic variables are artificial.

An *unbounded problem* is identified in the simplex procedure when it is not possible to select a pivot row—that is, when the values obtained by dividing the quantity values by the corresponding pivot column values are negative or undefined.

When a *pivot column tie* exists, select one of the columns arbitrarily.

Degeneracy occurs when there is a tie for the pivot row. A row should be chosen arbitrarily to break the tie. This step will result in a zero in the quantity column; however, the simplex procedure should be continued normally.

When *negative quantity values* appear in constraints, multiplying the constraint by -1 will make them positive and will reverse the inequality.

COMPUTERIZED SOLUTION OF A MINIMIZATION AND A MIXED CONSTRAINT PROBLEM

In Chapter 4 a software package called Microcomputer Software for Quantitative Analysis for Management, by Render and Stair, was used to solve a linear programming maximization problem. We will now use this package to solve the minimization problem and mixed constraint problem examples introduced earlier in this chapter.

First we will solve the fertilizer example of a minimization problem. You will recall that this example problem was formulated as follows.

minimize $Z = \$6x_1 + 3x_2$

subject to

$2x_1 + 4x_2 \geq 16$ lb of nitrogen

$4x_1 + 3x_2 \geq 24$ lb of phosphate

$x_1, x_2 \geq 0$

where

x_1 = bags of Super-gro fertilizer

x_2 = bags of Crop-quik fertilizer

Z = farmer's total cost (\$) of fertilizer

The problem input is as follows.   Problem input

```
                    **** LINEAR PROGRAMMING ****

                           KEYBOARD INPUT

    ENTER PROBLEM TITLE ? Fertilizer Example

    DO YOU WISH TO:
    1 - MINIMIZE
    2 - MAXIMIZE
    ENTER YOUR CHOICE (1-2)


    ENTER THE NUMBER OF CONSTRAINTS ? 2
    ENTER THE NUMBER OF VARIABLES ? 2
    ENTER THE NUMBER OF <= EQUATIONS ? 0
    ENTER THE NUMBER OF = EQUATIONS ? 0
    ENTER THE NUMBER OF >= EQUATIONS ? 2


       FOR OBJECTIVE FUNCTION
    ----------------------------------------------------------------------
    ENTER COEFFICIENT # 1  OF THE OBJECTIVE FUNCTION? 6
    ENTER COEFFICIENT # 2  OF THE OBJECTIVE FUNCTION? 3



    ENTER THE NUMBER OF CONSTRAINTS ? 2
    ENTER THE NUMBER OF VARIABLES ? 2
    ENTER THE NUMBER OF <= EQUATIONS ? 0
    ENTER THE NUMBER OF = EQUATIONS ? 0
    ENTER THE NUMBER OF >= EQUATIONS ? 2
```

```
      FOR OBJECTIVE FUNCTION
-------------------------------------------------------------------------------
ENTER COEFFICIENT # 1  OF THE OBJECTIVE FUNCTION? 6
ENTER COEFFICIENT # 2  OF THE OBJECTIVE FUNCTION? 3


        FOR (>=) CONSTRAINT #  1

ENTER THE VALUE OF COEFFICIENT  1 ? 2
ENTER THE VALUE OF COEFFICIENT  2 ? 4
ENTER THE RIGHT HAND SIDE VALUES ? 16

        FOR (>=) CONSTRAINT #  2

ENTER THE VALUE OF COEFFICIENT  1 ? 4
ENTER THE VALUE OF COEFFICIENT  2 ? 3
ENTER THE RIGHT HAND SIDE VALUES ? 24
```

The model formulation

The model formulation as it is displayed by the computer program is shown below.

```
                    -- DATA ENTERED --



    MIN Z = 6X1 + 3X2

    SUBJECT TO:

      2X1 + 4X2 >= 16
      4X1 + 3X2 >= 24
```

The computerized solution

The tableaus leading to the optimal solution and the final optimal solution are all shown here as they appear on the terminal.

TABLEAU AFTER 0 ITERATIONS

Cj	Basis	6.00 x 1	3.00 x 2	0.00 s 1	0.00 s 2	M a 1	M a 2 :	Bi
M	a 1	2.00	4.00	-1.00	0.00	1.00	0.00 :	16.00
M	a 2	4.00	3.00	0.00	-1.00	0.00	1.00 :	24.00
	Zj	6M	7M	1M	-1M	1M	1M	40M
	Cj-Zj	-6M+ 6	-7M+ 3	-1M	1M	0.00	0.00	

PRESS RETURN TO CONTINUE?

TABLEAU AFTER 1 ITERATIONS

Cj	Basis	6.00 x 1	3.00 x 2	0.00 s 1	0.00 s 2	M a 1	M a 2 :	Bi
3.00	x 2	0.50	1.00	-0.25	0.00	0.25	0.00 :	4.00
M	a 2	2.50	0.00	0.75	-1.00	-0.75	1.00 :	12.00
	Zj	2.5M+ 1.5	3.00	.7M- .8	-1M	-.8M+ .7	1M	12M+ 12
	Cj-Zj	-2.5M+ 4.5	0.00	-.8M+ .7	1M	1.7M-.8	0.00	

PRESS RETURN TO CONTINUE?

TABLEAU AFTER 2 ITERATIONS

Cj	Basis	6.00 x 1	3.00 x 2	0.00 s 1	0.00 s 2	M a 1	M a 2 :	Bi
3.00	x 2	0.00	1.00	-0.40	0.20	0.40	-0.20 :	1.60
6.00	x 1	1.00	0.00	0.30	-0.40	-0.30	0.40 :	4.80
	Zj	6.00	3.00	0.60	-1.80	-0.60	1.80	33.60
	Cj-Zj	0.00	0.00	-0.60	1.80	1M+ .6	1M-1.8	

PRESS RETURN TO CONTINUE?

TABLEAU AFTER 3 ITERATIONS

Cj	Basis	6.00 x 1	3.00 x 2	0.00 s 1	0.00 s 2	M a 1	M a 2 :	Bi
3.00	x 2	1.33	1.00	0.00	-0.33	0.00	0.33 :	8.00
0.00	s 1	3.33	0.00	1.00	-1.33	-1.00	1.33 :	16.00
	Zj	4.00	3.00	0.00	-1.00	0.00	1.00	24.00
	Cj-Zj	2.00	0.00	0.00	1.00	1M	1M-1	

PRESS RETURN TO CONTINUE?

AFTER 3 ITERATIONS THE FINAL OPTIMAL SOLUTION IS:
****

ANSWERS

VARIABLE	VALUE
x 2	8.000
s 1	16.000

OPTIMAL Z = 23.999
****

Notice that the computerized tableau iterations for this problem do not exactly replicate the simplex tableaus described in Tables 5.1 through 5.4. The primary difference is that the computerized simplex procedure does not use $z_j - c_j$. Instead, it uses $c_j - z_j$ and then selects the column with the largest *negative* value. Thus, the solution is optimal when all $c_j - z_j$ row values are positive. Also, the artificial variables are not eliminated from the tableau as they leave the basic solution.

A computer solution of a mixed constraint problem

Next, we will look at the computerized solution of the mixed constraint problem solved in Tables 5.5 through 5.8. The model formulation for this problem was as follows.

maximize $Z = \$400x_1 + 200x_2$

subject to

$$x_1 + x_2 = 30 \text{ contracted items}$$
$$2x_1 + 8x_2 \geq 80 \text{ yd}^2 \text{ of leather}$$
$$x_1 \leq 20 \text{ briefcases}$$
$$x_1, x_2 \geq 0$$

where

x_1 = briefcases

x_2 = pieces of luggage

Problem input

The problem input, tableau iterations, and final optimal solution follow.

```
                    *** LINEAR PROGRAMMING ***

                        -- DATA ENTERED --

           MAX Z = 400X1 + 200X2

           SUBJECT TO:

             1X1 + 0X2 <= 20
             1X1 + 1X2  = 30
             2X1 + 8X2 >= 80

        PRESS RETURN TO CONTINUE?
   TABLEAU AFTER  0  ITERATIONS

      Cj           400.00  200.00    0.00    0.00     -M      -M
              Basis   x 1     x 2     s 1     s 2     a 1     a 2 :    Bi
   -------------------------------------------------------------------------
      0.00    s 1    1.00    0.00    1.00    0.00    0.00    0.00 :   20.00
       -M     a 1    1.00    1.00    0.00    0.00    1.00    0.00 :   30.00
       -M     a 2    2.00    8.00    0.00   -1.00    0.00    1.00 :   80.00
   -------------------------------------------------------------------------
   -24
              Zj       -3M     -9M    0.00     1M     -1M     -1M    -110M
            Cj-Zj  3M+ 400 9M+ 200   0.00     -1M    0.00    0.00

   PRESS RETURN TO CONTINUE?
```

```
TABLEAU AFTER  1  ITERATIONS


     Cj          400.00  200.00    0.00    0.00     -M      -M
            Basis    x 1     x 2     s 1     s 2     a 1     a 2 :    Bi
    ------------------------------------------------------------------------
     0.00    s 1    1.00    0.00    1.00    0.00    0.00    0.00 :   20.00
      -M     a 1    0.75    0.00    0.00    0.13    1.00   -0.13 :   20.00
   200.00    x 2    0.25    1.00    0.00   -0.13    0.00    0.13 :   10.00
    ------------------------------------------------------------------------
    -24
            Zj   -.8M+ 50  200.00    0.00  -.2M-25    -1M  .1M+ 25-20M+ 2000
            Cj-Zj .7M+ 350   0.00    0.00  .1M+ 25    0.00 -1.2M-25

PRESS RETURN TO CONTINUE?

TABLEAU AFTER  2  ITERATIONS


     Cj          400.00  200.00    0.00    0.00     -M      -M
            Basis    x 1     x 2     s 1     s 2     a 1     a 2 :    Bi
    ------------------------------------------------------------------------
   400.00    x 1    1.00    0.00    1.00    0.00    0.00    0.00 :   20.00
      -M     a 1    0.00    0.00   -0.75    0.13    1.00   -0.13 :    5.00
   200.00    x 2    0.00    1.00   -0.25   -0.13    0.00    0.13 :    5.00
    ------------------------------------------------------------------------
    -24
            Zj   400.00  200.00 .7M+ 350  -.2M-25    -1M  .1M+ 25-5M+ 9000
            Cj-Zj   0.00    0.00 -.8M-350  .1M+ 25    0.00 -1.2M-25

PRESS RETURN TO CONTINUE?

TABLEAU AFTER  3  ITERATIONS


     Cj          400.00  200.00    0.00    0.00     -M      -M
            Basis    x 1     x 2     s 1     s 2     a 1     a 2 :    Bi
    ------------------------------------------------------------------------
   400.00    x 1    1.00    0.00    1.00    0.00    0.00    0.00 :   20.00
     0.00    s 2    0.00    0.00   -6.00    1.00    8.00   -1.00 :   40.00
   200.00    x 2    0.00    1.00   -1.00    0.00    1.00    0.00 :   10.00
    ------------------------------------------------------------------------
    -24
            Zj   400.00  200.00  200.00    0.00  200.00    0.00 10000.00
            Cj-Zj   0.00    0.00 -200.00    0.00 -1M-200     -1M

PRESS RETURN TO CONTINUE?


AFTER 3 ITERATIONS THE FINAL OPTIMAL SOLUTION IS:
****************************************************************************
                        ANSWERS
                VARIABLE           VALUE
                   x 1             20.000
                   s 2             40.000
                   x 2             10.000


                OPTIMAL Z =  10000
****************************************************************************
```

Notice that the tableau iterations in this computer solution differ slightly from the manual simplex iterations shown in Tables 5.5 through 5.8. The reason is that the Microcomputer Software package requests the data on the constraints in a different order, so the order of the rows in the computerized tableaus differs from that in Tables 5.5 to 5.8. However, all tableau values are the same.

Summary

This chapter discussed variations from the general simplex method described in Chapter 4. These variations included a minimization problem, a mixed constraint problem, problems with multiple optimum solutions, problems with no feasible solution, unbounded problems, tied pivot columns and pivot rows, and negative constraint quantities.

The discussion of these exceptional cases of linear programming problems completes the presentation of the simplex method. Over the course of these last four chapters, you have learned how to formulate the model, how to analyze the model graphically, and how to solve the model regardless of any special conditions. The next chapter focuses on ways to analyze the final simplex solution, using the theory of *duality* and *sensitivity analysis*.

References

Dantzig, G. B. *Linear Programming and Extensions.* Princeton, N.J.: Princeton University, 1963.

Gass, S. *Linear Programming.* 4th ed. New York: McGraw-Hill, 1975.

Gottfried, B. S., and Weisman, J. *Introduction to Optimization Theory.* Englewood Cliffs, N.J.: Prentice-Hall, 1973.

Hadley, G. *Linear Programming.* Reading, Mass.: Addison-Wesley, 1962.

Hillier, F. S., and Lieberman, G. J. *Operations Research.* 4th ed. San Francisco: Holden-Day, 1986.

Kim, C. *Introduction to Linear Programming.* New York: Holt, Rinehart and Winston, 1971.

Lee, Sang M.; Moore, Laurence J.; and Taylor, Bernard W. *Management Science.* 3d ed. Boston: Allyn and Bacon, 1990.

Moskowitz, H., and Wright, G. P. *Operations Research Techniques for Management.* Englewood Cliffs, N.J.: Prentice-Hall, 1979.

Rothenberg, R. I. *Linear Programming.* New York: Elsevier North-Holland, 1979.

Wagner, H. M. *Principles of Operations Research.* 2d ed. Englewood Cliffs, N.J.: Prentice-Hall, 1975.

EXAMPLE PROBLEM SOLUTION

As a prelude to the problems, this section presents an example of a mixed constraint problem solution using the simplex method.

The Problem Statement

Solve the following linear programming model using the simplex method:

maximize $Z = 20x_1 + 10x_2$
subject to
$$x_1 + x_2 = 150$$
$$-x_1 \geq -40$$
$$x_2 > 20$$
$$x_1, x_2 \geq 0$$

Step 1: Transform the Constraints to Equations

maximize $Z = 20x_1 + 10x_2 + 0s_1 + 0s_2 - MA_1 - MA_2$
subject to
$$x_1 + x_2 + A_1 = 150$$
$$x_1 + s_1 = 40$$
$$x_2 - s_2 + A_2 = 20$$
$$x_1, x_2 \geq 0$$

Step 2: Set Up the Initial Tableau and Identify the Pivot Row and Pivot Column

c_j	Basic Variables	Quantity	20 x_1	10 x_2	0 s_1	0 s_2	$-M$ A_1	$-M$ A_2
$-M$	A_1	150	1	1	0	0	1	0
0	s_1	40	1	0	1	0	0	0
$-M$	A_2	20	0	1	0	-1	0	1
	z_j	$-170M$	$-M$	$-2M$	0	M	$-M$	$-M$
	$c_j - z_j$		$20 + M$	$10 + 2M$	0	$-M$	0	0

x_2 is the entering variable; A_2 is the leaving variable.

Step 3: Compute the Second Iteration (Tableau)

c_j	Basic Variables	Quantity	20 x_1	10 x_2	0 s_1	0 s_2	$-M$ A_1
$-M$	A_1	130	1	0	0	1	1
0	s_1	40	1	0	1	0	0
10	x_2	20	0	1	0	-1	0
	z_j	$200 - 130M$	$-M$	10	0	$-10 - M$	$-M$
	$c_j - z_j$		$20 + M$	0	0	$10 + M$	0

x_1 is the entering variable; s_1 is the leaving variable.

Step 4: Compute the Third Iteration (Tableau)

c_j	Basic Variables	Quantity	20 x_1	10 x_2	0 s_1	0 s_2	$-M$ A_1
$-M$	A_1	90	0	0	-1	1	1
20	x_1	40	1	0	1	0	0
10	x_2	20	0	1	0	-1	0
	z_j	$1,000 - 90M$	20	10	$20 + M$	$-10 - M$	$-M$
	$c_j - z_j$		0	0	$-20 - M$	$10 + M$	0

s_2 is the entering variable; A_1 is the leaving variable.

Step 5: Compute the Fourth Iteration (Tableau)

c_j	Basic Variables	Quantity	20 x_1	10 x_2	0 s_1	0 s_2
0	s_2	90	0	0	-1	1
20	x_1	40	1	0	1	0
10	x_2	110	0	1	-1	0
	z_j	1,900	20	10	10	0
	$c_j - z_j$		0	0	-10	0

Since all $c_j - z_j$ row values are negative or zero, the solution is optimal.

$x_1 = 40$
$x_2 = 110$
$s_2 = 90$
$Z = 1,900$

Problems

1. A livestock feed is produced from soybeans and corn, each of which provides protein. The following linear programming model has been developed to determine how many pounds of soybeans and corn (x_1 and x_2) should be in the feed mix in order to provide a minimum protein requirement while minimizing cost.

minimize $Z = 10x_1 + 20x_2$ (cost, $\$$)
subject to
$$2x_1 + 6x_2 \geq 18 \text{ (protein, gm)}$$
$$x_1, x_2 \geq 0$$

a. Solve this model graphically.
b. Solve this model using the simplex method.

2. The following is a simplex tableau for a linear programming model.

c_j	Basic Variables	Quantity	6 x_1	20 x_2	12 x_3	0 s_1	0 s_2
6	x_1	20	1	1	0	0	0
12	x_3	10	0	1/3	1	0	−1/6
0	s_1	10	0	1/3	0	1	−1/6
	z_j	240	6	10	12	0	−2
	$z_j - c_j$		0	−10	0	0	−2

a. Is this a maximization or a minimization problem? Why?
b. What is the solution given in this tableau?
c. Is the solution given in this tableau optimal? Why?
d. Write out the original objective function for the linear programming model using only decision variables.
e. How many constraints are in the linear programming model?
f. Were any of the constraints originally equations? Why?
g. What is the value of x_2 in this tableau?

3. In Chapter 3 the following problem (3) was to be solved graphically. The Munchies Cereal Company makes a brand of cereal from several ingredients. Two of the ingredients, oats and rice, provide vitamins A and B. The company has developed the following linear programming model to determine how many ounces of oats (x_1) and rice (x_2) should be in each box of cereal to meet minimum daily requirements of vitamins A and B while minimizing cost.

minimize $Z = .05x_1 + .03x_2$ (cost, $)

subject to

$$8x_1 + 6x_2 \geq 48 \text{ (vitamin A, mg)}$$
$$x_1 + 2x_2 \geq 12 \text{ (vitamin B, mg)}$$
$$x_1, x_2 \geq 0$$

Solve this model using the simplex method.

4. In Chapter 3 the following problem (5) was to be solved graphically. The Kalo Fertilizer Company makes a fertilizer using two chemicals that provide nitrogen, phosphate, and potassium. The company wants to know how many pounds of each ingredient (x_1 and x_2) to put into a bag of fertilizer to meet minimum requirements of nitrogen, phosphate, and potassium while minimizing cost. The following linear programming model has been developed.

minimize $Z = 3x_1 + 5x_2$ (cost, $)

subject to

$$10x_1 + 2x_2 \geq 20 \text{ (nitrogen, oz)}$$
$$6x_1 + 6x_2 \geq 36 \text{ (phosphate, oz)}$$
$$x_2 \geq 2 \text{ (potassium, oz)}$$
$$x_1, x_2 \geq 0$$

Solve this model using the simplex method.

5. In Chapter 3 the following problem (26) was to be solved graphically.

minimize $Z = .06x_1 + .10x_2$

subject to

$$4x_1 + 3x_2 \geq 12$$
$$3x_1 + 6x_2 \geq 12$$
$$5x_1 + 2x_2 \geq 10$$
$$x_1, x_2 \geq 0$$

Solve this model using the simplex method.

6. In Chapter 3 the following problem (27) was to be solved graphically. The Copperfield Mining Company owns two mines, which produce three grades of ore — high, medium, and low. The company has a contract to supply a smelting company with 12 tons of high-grade ore, 8 tons of medium-grade ore, and 24 tons of low-grade ore. Each mine produces a certain amount of each type of ore each hour it is in opera-

tion. The company has developed the following linear programming model to determine the number of hours to operate each mine (x_1 and x_2) so that its contractual obligations can be met at the lowest cost.

minimize $Z = 200x_1 + 160x_2$ (cost, $)

subject to

$$6x_1 + 2x_2 \geq 12 \text{ (high-grade ore, tons)}$$
$$2x_1 + 2x_2 \geq 8 \text{ (medium-grade ore, tons)}$$
$$4x_1 + 12x_2 \geq 24 \text{ (low-grade ore, tons)}$$
$$x_1, x_2 \geq 0$$

Solve this model using the simplex method.

7. A marketing firm has contracted to do a survey on a political issue for a Spokane television station. The firm conducts interviews during the day and at night by telephone and in person. Each hour an interviewer works at each type of interview results in an average number of interviews. In order to have a representative survey, the firm has determined that there must be at least 400 day interviews, 100 personal interviews, and 1,200 interviews overall. The company has developed the following linear programming model to determine the number of hours of telephone interviews during the day (x_1), telephone interviews at night (x_2), personal interviews during the day (x_3), and personal interviews at night (x_4) that should be conducted in order to minimize cost.

minimize $Z = 2x_1 + 3x_2 + 5x_3 + 7x_4$ (cost, $)

subject to

$$10x_1 + 4x_3 \geq 400 \text{ (day interviews)}$$
$$4x_3 + 5x_4 \geq 100 \text{ (personal interviews)}$$
$$x_1 + x_2 + x_3 + x_4 \geq 1,200 \text{ (total interviews)}$$
$$x_1, x_2, x_3, x_4 \geq 0$$

Solve this model using the simplex method.

8. A wood products firm in Oregon plants three types of trees—white pines, spruce, and ponderosa pines—to produce pulp for paper products and wood for lumber. The company wants to plant enough acres of each type of tree to produce at least 27 tons of pulp and 30 tons of lumber. The company has developed the following linear programming model to determine the number of acres of white pines (x_1), spruce (x_2), and ponderosa pines (x_3) to plant in order to minimize cost.

minimize $Z = 120x_1 + 40x_2 + 240x_3$ (cost, $)

subject to

$$4x_1 + x_2 + 3x_3 \geq 27 \text{ (pulp, tons)}$$
$$2x_1 + 6x_2 + 3x_3 \geq 30 \text{ (lumber, tons)}$$
$$x_1, x_2, x_3 \geq 0$$

Solve this model using the simplex method.

9. A baby products firm produces a strained baby food containing liver and milk, which contribute protein and iron to the baby food. Each jar of baby food must have 36 milligrams of protein and 50 milligrams of iron. The company has developed the following linear programming model to determine the number of ounces of liver (x_1) and milk (x_2) to include in each jar of baby food in order to meet the requirements for protein and iron at the minimum cost.

minimize $Z = .05x_1 + .10x_2$ (cost, \$)
subject to
$$6x_1 + 2x_2 \geq 36 \text{ (protein, mg)}$$
$$5x_1 + 5x_2 \geq 50 \text{ (iron, mg)}$$
$$x_1, x_2 \geq 0$$

Solve this model using the simplex method.

10. Solve the linear programming model in problem 9 graphically and identify the points on the graph that correspond to each simplex tableau.

11. Solve the following linear programming model using the simplex method.

minimize $Z = 8x_1 + 10x_2 + 4x_3$
subject to
$$x_1 + x_2 + x_3 \geq 40$$
$$2x_1 + 6x_2 \geq 60$$
$$x_3 \geq 100$$
$$x_1, x_2, x_3 \geq 0$$

12. Solve the following linear programming model using the simplex method.

minimize $Z = 4x_1 + 6x_2$
subject to
$$x_1 + x_2 \geq 8$$
$$2x_1 + x_2 \geq 12$$
$$x_1, x_2 \geq 0$$

13. Solve the following linear programming model using the simplex method.

minimize $Z = 20x_1 + 16x_2$
subject to
$$3x_1 + x_2 \geq 6$$
$$x_1 + x_2 \geq 4$$
$$2x_1 + 6x_2 \geq 12$$
$$x_1, x_2 \geq 0$$

14. Solve the preceding linear programming model in problem 13 graphically and identify the points on the graph that correspond to each simplex tableau.

15. Transform the following linear programming model into proper form for solution by the simplex method.

maximize $Z = 8x_1 + 2x_2 + 7x_3$

subject to

$$2x_1 + 6x_2 + x_3 = 30$$
$$3x_2 + 4x_3 \geq 60$$
$$4x_1 + x_2 + 2x_3 \leq 50$$
$$x_1 + 2x_2 \geq 20$$
$$x_1, x_2, x_3 \geq 0$$

16. Transform the following linear programming model into proper form for solution by the simplex method.

minimize $Z = 40x_1 + 55x_2 + 30x_3$

subject to

$$x_1 + 2x_2 + 3x_3 \leq 60$$
$$2x_1 + x_2 + x_3 = 40$$
$$x_1 + 3x_2 + x_3 \geq 50$$
$$5x_2 + 3x_3 \geq 100$$
$$x_1, x_2, x_3 \geq 0$$

17. A manufacturing firm produces two products using labor and material. The company presently has a contract to produce 5 of product 1 and 12 of product 2. The company has developed the following linear programming model to determine the number of units of product 1 (x_1) and product 2 (x_2) to produce in order to maximize profit.

maximize $Z = 40x_1 + 60x_2$ (profit, $)

subject to

$$x_1 + 2x_2 \leq 30 \text{ (material, lb)}$$
$$4x_1 + 4x_2 \leq 72 \text{ (labor, hr)}$$
$$x_1 \geq 5 \text{ (contract, product 1)}$$
$$x_2 \geq 12 \text{ (contract, product 2)}$$
$$x_1, x_2 \geq 0$$

Solve this model using the simplex method.

18. A custom tailor makes pants and jackets from imported Irish wool. In order to get any wool at all, the tailor must purchase at least 25 square feet each week. Each pair of pants and each jacket requires 5 square feet of material. The tailor has 16 hours available each week to make pants and jackets. The demand for pants is never more than 5 pairs per week. The tailor has developed the following linear programming model to determine the number of pants (x_1) and jackets (x_2) to make each week in order to maximize profit.

maximize $Z = x_1 + 5x_2$ (profit, $100s)
subject to
$$5x_1 + 5x_2 \geq 25 \text{ (wool, ft}^2)$$
$$2x_1 + 4x_2 \leq 16 \text{ (labor, hr)}$$
$$x_1 \leq 5 \text{ (demand, pants)}$$
$$x_1, x_2 \geq 0$$

Solve this model using the simplex method.

19. A sawmill in Tennessee produces cherry and oak boards for a large furniture manufacturer. Each month the sawmill must deliver at least 5 tons of wood to the manufacturer. It takes the sawmill 3 days to produce a ton of cherry and 2 days to produce a ton of oak, and the sawmill can allocate 18 days out of a month for this contract. The sawmill can get enough cherry to make 4 tons of wood and enough oak to make 7 tons of wood. The sawmill owner has developed the following linear programming model to determine the number of tons of cherry (x_1) and oak (x_2) to produce in order to minimize cost.

minimize $Z = 3x_1 + 6x_2$ (cost, $)
subject to
$$3x_1 + 2x_2 \leq 18 \text{ (production time, days)}$$
$$x_1 + x_2 \geq 5 \text{ (contract, tons)}$$
$$x_1 \leq 4 \text{ (cherry, tons)}$$
$$x_2 \leq 7 \text{ (oak, tons)}$$
$$x_1, x_2 \geq 0$$

Solve this model using the simplex method.

20. Solve the following linear programming model using the simplex method.

maximize $Z = 4x_1 + 5x_2$
subject to
$$2x_1 + 2x_2 \geq 8$$
$$x_2 = 3$$
$$9x_1 + 3x_2 \leq 27$$
$$x_1, x_2 \geq 0$$

21. Solve the following linear programming model using the simplex method.

maximize $Z = 10x_1 + 5x_2$
subject to
$$2x_1 + x_2 \geq 10$$
$$x_2 = 4$$
$$x_1 + 4x_2 \leq 20$$
$$x_1, x_2 \geq 0$$

22. Solve the following linear programming problem using the simplex method.

maximize $Z = x_1 + 2x_2 - x_3$
subject to
$$4x_2 + x_3 \le 40$$
$$x_1 - x_2 \le 20$$
$$2x_1 + 4x_2 + 3x_3 \le 60$$
$$x_1, x_2, x_3 \ge 0$$

23. Solve the following linear programming model using the simplex method.

minimize $Z = 4x_1 + 3x_2$
subject to
$$2x_1 + x_2 \ge 10$$
$$-3x_1 + 2x_2 \le 6$$
$$x_1 + x_2 \ge 6$$
$$x_1, x_2 \ge 0$$

24. Solve the following linear programming model using the simplex method.

maximize $Z = 10x_1 + 5x_2$
subject to
$$3x_1 + 9x_2 \ge 27$$
$$8x_1 + 6x_2 \ge 48$$
$$-4x_1 + 6x_2 \le -12$$
$$8x_1 + 12x_2 = 24$$
$$x_1, x_2 \ge 0$$

25. Solve the following linear programming model using the simplex method.

minimize $Z = 6x_1 + 4x_2$
subject to
$$3x_1 + 2x_2 \ge 18$$
$$2x_1 + 4x_2 = 20$$
$$2x_2 \le 8$$
$$x_1, x_2 \ge 0$$

26. Solve the following linear programming problem using the simplex method.

maximize $Z = 2x_1 + 4x_2 - 2x_3$
subject to
$$2x_1 + x_2 - 4x_3 \le 6$$
$$-4x_1 - 2x_2 + x_3 \le 5$$
$$2x_1 + 6x_2 = 10$$
$$x_1, x_2, x_3 \ge 0$$

27. Solve the following linear programming problem using the simplex method.

maximize $Z = x_1 + 2x_2 + 2x_3$

subject to

$$x_1 + x_2 + 2x_3 \leq 12$$
$$2x_1 + x_2 + 5x_3 = 20$$
$$x_1 + x_2 - x_3 \geq 8$$
$$x_1, x_2, x_3 \geq 0$$

28. The following is a simplex tableau for a linear programming model.

c_j	Basic Variables	Quantity	1 x_1	2 x_2	−1 x_3	0 s_1	0 s_2	0 s_3
2	x_2	10	0	1	1/4	1/4	0	0
0	s_2	20	0	0	−3/4	3/4	1	−1/2
1	x_1	10	1	0	1	−1/2	0	1/2
	z_j	30	1	2	3/2	0	0	1/2
	$c_j - z_j$		0	0	−5/2	0	0	−1/2

a. Is this a maximization or a minimization problem? Why?
b. What is the solution given in this tableau?
c. Write out the original objective function for the linear programming model, using only decision variables.
d. How many constraints are in the linear programming model?
e. Were any of the constraints originally equations? Why?
f. What does s_1 equal in this tableau?
g. This solution is optimal. Are there multiple optimal solutions? Why?
h. If there are multiple optimal solutions, identify the alternate solutions.

29. A farmer has a 40-acre farm in Georgia. The farmer is trying to determine how many acres of corn, peanuts, and cotton to plant. Each crop requires labor, fertilizer, and insecticide. The farmer has developed the following linear programming model to determine the number of acres of corn (x_1), peanuts (x_2), and cotton (x_3) to plant in order to maximize profit.

maximize $Z = 400x_1 + 350x_2 + 450x_3$ (profit, $)

subject to

$$2x_1 + 3x_2 + 2x_3 \leq 120 \text{ (labor, hr)}$$
$$4x_1 + 3x_2 + x_3 \leq 160 \text{ (fertilizer, tons)}$$
$$3x_1 + 2x_2 + 4x_3 \leq 100 \text{ (insecticide, tons)}$$
$$x_1 + x_2 + x_3 \leq 40 \text{ (acres)}$$
$$x_1, x_2, x_3 \geq 0$$

Solve this model using the simplex method.

30. Solve the following linear programming model (a) graphically and (b) using the simplex method.

maximize $Z = 3x_1 + 2x_2$

subject to

$$x_1 + x_2 \leq 1$$
$$x_1 + x_2 \geq 2$$
$$x_1, x_2 \geq 0$$

31. Solve the following linear programming model (a) graphically and (b) using the simplex method.

maximize $Z = x_1 + x_2$

subject to

$$x_1 - x_2 \geq -1$$
$$-x_1 + 2x_2 \leq 4$$
$$x_1, x_2 \geq 0$$

32. Solve the following linear programming model using the simplex method.

maximize $Z = 7x_1 + 5x_2 + 5x_3$

subject to

$$x_1 + x_2 + x_3 \leq 25$$
$$2x_1 + x_2 + x_3 \leq 40$$
$$x_1 + x_2 \leq 25$$
$$x_3 \leq 6$$
$$x_1, x_2, x_3 \geq 0$$

33. Solve the following linear programming model using the simplex method.

minimize $Z = 15x_1 + 25x_2$

subject to

$$3x_1 + 4x_2 \geq 12$$
$$2x_1 + x_2 \geq 6$$
$$3x_1 + 2x_2 \leq 9$$
$$x_1, x_2 \geq 0$$

34. Solve the following linear programming model (a) graphically and (b) using the simplex method.

maximize $Z = 5x_1 + 2x_2$

subject to

$$3x_1 + 5x_2 \leq 15$$
$$10x_1 + 4x_2 \leq 20$$
$$x_1, x_2 \geq 0$$

35. Solve problem 3 from Chapter 2 using the simplex method.

36. Solve problem 4 from Chapter 2 using the simplex method.

37. Solve problem 19 from Chapter 2 using the simplex method.

38. Solve problem 21 from Chapter 2 using the simplex method.

39. Solve problem 24 from Chapter 2 using the simplex method.

40. Solve problem 27 from Chapter 2 using the simplex method.

Postoptimality Analysis

Once the solution to a linear programming problem has been determined, there may be a tendency to stop analysis of the model. However, further analysis of the final optimal solution often results in more useful information than is given by the solution. The analysis of the optimal simplex solution in order to gather such additional information is known as *postoptimality analysis*, the topic of this chapter.

The optimal solution of a linear programming model can be analyzed in two ways. First, the *dual* of the model can be formulated and interpreted. The dual is an alternative form of the model that contains useful information regarding the value of the resources that form the constraints of the model. Second, the various numerical coefficients in the model constraints and objective function can be analyzed to see what effect any changes in them might have on the optimal solution. This process is known as *sensitivity analysis*. Duality and sensitivity analysis are similar topics in that they involve an examination of the final optimal simplex solution in order to gain additional information.

Analyzing the optimal simplex tableau for information other than the solution

THE DUAL

The primal and the dual
Every linear programming model has two forms: the *primal* and the *dual*. The original form of a linear programming model is called the primal. All the examples in Chapters 2 through 5 are primal models. The dual is an alternative model form derived completely from the primal. The dual is useful because it provides the decision maker with an alternative way of looking at a problem. Whereas the primal gives solution results in terms of the amount of profit gained from producing products, the dual provides information on the *value* of the constrained resources in achieving that profit.

The value of resources

The following example will demonstrate how the dual form of a model is derived and what it means. The Hickory Furniture Company produces tables and chairs on a daily basis. Each table produced results in $160 in profit; each chair results in $200 in profit. The production of tables and chairs is dependent on the availability of limited resources—labor, wood, and storage space. The resource requirements for the production of tables and chairs and the total resources available are as follows.

	Resource Requirements		
Resource	Table	Chair	Total Available/Day
Labor	2 hr	4 hr	40 hr
Wood	18 lb	18 lb	216 lb
Storage	24 ft^2	12 ft^2	240 ft^2

The primal form of a model

The company wants to know the number of tables and chairs to produce per day in order to maximize profit. The model for this problem is formulated as follows.

maximize $Z = \$160x_1 + 200x_2$
subject to
$$2x_1 + 4x_2 \leq 40 \text{ hr of labor}$$
$$18x_1 + 18x_2 \leq 216 \text{ lb of wood}$$
$$24x_1 + 12x_2 \leq 240 \text{ ft}^2 \text{ of storage space}$$
$$x_1, x_2 \geq 0$$
where
x_1 = number of tables produced
x_2 = number of chairs produced

The dual form of a model

This model represents the primal form. For a primal maximization model, the dual form is a minimization model. The dual form of this example model is minimize $Z = 40y_1 + 216y_2 + 240y_3$

    subject to

        $2y_1 + 18y_2 + 24y_3 \geq 160$

        $4y_1 + 18y_2 + 12y_3 \geq 200$

               $y_1, y_2, y_3 \geq 0$

The specific relationships between the primal and the dual demonstrated in this example are

Relationships between primal and dual models

1. The dual variables, y_1, y_2, and y_3, correspond to the model constraints in the primal. For every constraint in the primal there will be a variable in the dual. For example, in this case the primal has *three constraints;* therefore, the dual has *three decision variables.*
2. The quantity values on the right-hand side of the primal inequality constraints are the objective function coefficients in the dual. The constraint quantity values in the primal, 40, 216, and 240, form the dual objective function: $Z = 40y_1 + 216y_2 + 240y_3$.
3. The model constraint coefficients in the primal are the decision variable coefficients in the dual. For example, the labor constraint in the primal has the coefficients 2 and 4. These values are the y_1 variable coefficients in the model constraints of the dual: $2y_1$ and $4y_1$.
4. The objective function coefficients in the primal, 160 and 200, represent the model constraint requirements (quantity values on the right-hand side of the constraint) in the dual.
5. Whereas the maximization primal model has $\leq$ constraints, the minimization dual model has $\geq$ constraints.

The primal-dual relationships can be observed by comparing the two model forms shown in Figure 6.1.

Comparing the primal and dual models

FIGURE 6.1

The Primal-Dual Relationships

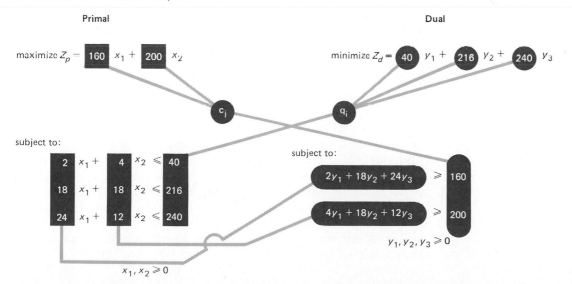

Now that we have developed the dual form of the model, the next step is determining what the dual means. In other words, what do the decision variables y_1, y_2, and y_3 mean, what do the $\geq$ model constraints mean, and what is being minimized in the dual objective function?

Interpreting the Dual Model

The dual model can be interpreted by observing the solution to the primal form of the model. The simplex solution to the primal model is shown in Table 6.1.

TABLE 6.1
The Optimal Simplex Solution for the Primal Model

c_j	Basic Variables	Quantity	160 x_1	200 x_2	0 s_1	0 s_2	0 s_3
200	x_2	8	0	1	1/2	−1/18	0
160	x_1	4	1	0	−1/2	1/9	0
0	s_3	48	0	0	6	−2	1
	z_j	2,240	160	200	20	20/3	0
	$c_j - z_j$		0	0	−20	−20/3	0

Interpreting this primal solution, we have

x_1 = 4 tables
x_2 = 8 chairs
s_3 = 48 ft^2 of storage space
Z = $2,240 profit

Interpreting the meaning of $c_j - z_j$ row values for slack variables

This optimal primal tableau also contains information about the dual. In the $c_j - z_j$ row of Table 6.1, the negative values of −20 and −20/3 under the s_1 and s_2 columns indicate that if one unit of either s_1 or s_2 were entered into the solution, profit would *decrease* by $20 or $6.67 (i.e., 20/3), respectively.

Recall that s_1 represents unused labor and s_2 represents unused wood. In the present solution, s_1 and s_2 are not basic variables, so they both equal zero. This means that all of the material and labor are being used to make tables and chairs, and there are no excess (slack) labor hours or pounds of material left over. Thus, if we enter s_1 or s_2 into the solution, then s_1 or s_2 no longer equals zero; we would be decreasing the use of labor or wood. If, for example, one unit of s_1 is entered into the solution, then one unit of labor previously used is not used, and profit is reduced by $20.

Let us assume that one unit of s_1 has been entered into the solution so that we have one hour of unused labor (s_1 = 1). Now let us remove this unused hour of labor from the solution so that all labor is again being used. We previously noted that profit was decreased by $20 by entering one hour of unused labor; thus it can be expected that if we take this hour back (and use it again), profit will be increased by $20. This is analogous to saying that if we could get one more hour of labor, we could increase profit by $20. Therefore, if we could purchase one hour of labor, we would be willing to pay up to $20 for it because that is the amount by which it would increase profit.

The negative $c_j - z_j$ row values of $20 and $6.67 are the *marginal values* of labor (s_1) and wood (s_2), respectively. These values are also often referred to as *shadow prices*, since they reflect the maximum "price" one would be willing to pay to obtain one more unit of the resource.

The marginal values of resources

Continuing this analysis, we note that the profit in the primal model was shown to be $2,240. For the furniture company, the value of the resources used to produce tables and chairs must be in terms of this profit. In other words, the value of the labor and wood resources is determined by their contribution toward the $2,240 profit. Thus, if the company wanted to assign a *value* to the resources it used, it could not assign an amount greater than the profit earned by the resources. Conversely, using the same logic, the total *value* of the resources must also be at least as much as the profit they earn. Thus, the value of all the resources must *exactly equal* the profit earned by the optimal solution.

The value of resources equals the optimal profit

The logic used to determine the marginal value of the resources in the model can also be used to analyze the model constraints. For example, the labor constraint is

Determining the total value of the resources used to get the optimal solution

$$2x_1 + 4x_2 \le 40 \text{ hr of labor}$$

Recall that the solution to the primal model (from Table 6.1) is

$x_1 = 4$ tables
$x_2 = 8$ chairs

and that the value of one hour of labor is $20.

Since one table requires 2 hours of labor and an hour of labor is worth $20, if four tables were produced we would have

($20/hr) (4 tables) (2 hr/table) = $160

as the value of the labor used to produce tables.

Looking again at the labor constraint, we see that 4 hours of labor are necessary to produce a chair. Since the value of labor is $20 per hour and 8 chairs are produced, we have

($20/hr) (8 chairs) (4 hr/chair) = $640

which is the value of the labor used to produce chairs.

Adding the value of labor used to produce tables and the value of labor used to produce chairs gives us the *total value of labor*:

$160 + $640 = $800, the value of labor

The same type of analysis can be used to determine the total value of wood in producing tables and chairs. Recall that the value of one pound of wood is $6.67, and that the model constraint for wood is

$$18x_1 + 18x_2 \leq 216 \text{ lb of wood}$$

Thus, for tables the value of wood is

($6.67/lb) (4 tables) (18 lb/table) = $480

and for chairs the value of wood is

($6.67/lb) (8 chairs) (18 lb/chair) = $960

Adding the value of wood used to produce both tables and chairs gives us the *total value of wood:*

$480 + $960 = $1,440

Now summing the total value of labor and the total value of wood yields

$800 (labor) + $1,440 (wood) = $2,240

which is also the profit, Z, shown in the optimal solution to our example.

The marginal value of a resource that is not completely used

However, what happened to the third resource, storage space? All the resource value in the model appears to have been divided between labor and wood. The answer can be seen in Table 6.1. Notice that the $c_j - z_j$ row value for s_3 (which represents unused storage space) is zero. This means that storage space has a marginal value of zero; that is, we would not be willing to pay anything for an extra foot of storage space.

The reason more storage space has no marginal value is because storage space was not a limitation in the production of tables and chairs. Table 6.1 shows that 48 square feet of storage space were left unused (i.e., $s_3 = 48$) after the 4 tables and 8 chairs were produced. Since the company already has 48 square feet of storage space left over, an extra square foot would have no additional value; the company cannot even use all of the storage space it presently has available.

Now let us look again at the dual form of the model.

minimize $Z_d = 40y_1 + 216y_2 + 240y_3$
subject to
$$2y_1 + 18y_2 + 24y_3 \geq 160$$
$$4y_1 + 18y_2 + 12y_3 \geq 200$$
$$y_1, y_2, y_3 \geq 0$$

Given the previous discussion on the value of the model resources, we can now define the decision variables of the dual, y_1, y_2, and y_3, to represent the marginal values of the resources:

Defining the dual variables

y_1 = marginal value of one hr of labor = $20
y_2 = marginal value of one lb of wood = $6.67
y_3 = marginal value of one ft^2 of storage space = $0

These solution values for the dual variables can be verified by solving the dual model using the simplex method. The optimal simplex tableau for the dual is shown in Table 6.2. Notice that (except for their signs) the $z_j - c_j$ values for the y_3, s_1, and s_2 columns are the same as the optimal quantity values in the optimal simplex tableau for the primal shown in Table 6.1.

TABLE 6.2
The Optimal Simplex Tableau for the Dual Model

c_j	Basic Variables	Quantity	40 y_1	216 y_2	240 y_3	0 s_1	0 s_2
216	y_2	6.67	0	1	2	-1/9	1/18
40	y_1	20	1	0	-6	1/2	-1/2
	z_j	2,240	40	216	192	-4	-8
	$z_j - c_j$		0	0	-48	-4	-8

Now consider the dual constraints. The first dual constraint is

Interpreting the dual constraints

$2y_1 + 18y_2 + 24y_3 \geq$ $160 profit per table

This constraint means that the value of the three resources (labor, wood, and storage space) used in producing a single table must be at least as great as the profit obtained from the table. Substituting the values of the dual variables into this constraint gives

$2y_1$ = value of labor used to produce a table
2($20) = $40

$18y_2$ = value of wood used to produce a table
18($6.67) = $120

$24y_3$ = value of storage space used for a table
24($0) = $0

Adding these individual values gives

$2y_1 + 18y_2 + 24y_3 \geq$ $160, the profit per table
2($20) + 18($6.67) + 24($0) $\geq$ $160
$40 + $120 + $0 $\geq$ $160
$160 $\geq$ $160

In other words, $160, the value of the resources used to produce a table, is at least as great as or equal to $160, the profit of a table.

The second dual constraint can be analyzed similarly.

$$4y_1 + 18y_2 + 12y_3 \geq \$200, \text{ the profit per chair}$$
$$4(\$20) + 18(\$6.67) + 12(\$0) \geq \$200$$
$$\$80 + \$120 + \$0 \geq \$200$$
$$\$200 \geq \$200$$

That is, $200, the value of the resources used to produce a chair, is at least as great as or equal to $200, the profit of a chair.

The dual objective function

Now only the objective function in the dual remains unexplained. The objective function is

$$\text{minimize } Z_d = 40y_1 + 216y_2 + 240y_3$$

Recall that the objective function coefficients represent the total resource quantities available—40 hours of labor, 216 pounds of wood, and 240 square feet of storage space. Thus, if we multiply the marginal value of one unit of resource by the total amount of that resource and add these values, we have the *total value* of the resources:

$$Z_d = (40 \text{ hr})(\$20/\text{hr}) + (216 \text{ lb})(\$6.67/\text{lb}) + (240 \text{ ft}^2)(\$0/\text{ft}^2)$$
$$Z_d = \$800 + 1{,}440 + 0$$
$$Z_d = \$2{,}240, \text{ the value of the resources}$$

In the previous discussion of the total value of the resources, Z_d, we noted that this value was also equal to the optimal Z value in the primal. Thus,

$$Z_p = \$2{,}240 = Z_d$$

As previously explained, the value of the resources cannot exceed the profit obtained through the use of those resources. Likewise, the value of the resources must be at least as much as that profit. Therefore, the total optimal value of the resources must exactly equal the total optimal profit.

The dual model has now been completely defined. Notice that the dual form of the model was developed completely from the primal model. In addition, the solution of the dual was determined completely from the primal solution—it was unnecessary to perform any further simplex operations to determine all information about the dual.

In general, the primal solution and dual solution have the following relationship:

Relationships between the primal and dual solutions

Primal	*Dual*
$c_j - z_j$ for slack variables, s_i	values for decision variables, y_i
$c_j - z_j$ for decision variables, x_i	values for slack variables, s_i
Z_p, the objective function value	Z_d, the objective function value

Additional Aspects of Formulating the Dual

The Hickory Furniture Company example, which was used to demonstrate how the primal is transformed into the dual, was a maximization problem with all $\leq$ constraints. Now let us consider a minimization primal with $\geq$ constraints. The fertilizer model first introduced in Chapter 3 will be used as an example. This model was formulated as

Formulating the dual of a minimization model

minimize $Z = 6x_1 + 3x_2$
subject to
$2x_1 + 4x_2 \geq 16$ lb of nitrogen
$4x_1 + 3x_2 \geq 24$ lb of phosphate
$x_1, x_2 \geq 0$
where
x_1 = number of bags of Super-gro fertilizer
x_2 = number of bags of Crop-quik fertilizer
Z = total cost of purchasing fertilizer

The dual of this model is formulated as follows.

The dual of the model

maximize $Z_d = 16y_1 + 24y_2$
subject to
$2y_1 + 4y_2 \leq 6$, cost of Super-gro
$4y_1 + 3y_2 \leq 3$, cost of Crop-quik
$y_1, y_2 \geq 0$
where
y_1 = marginal value of nitrogen
y_2 = marginal value of phosphate

The decision variables in the dual reflect the value of each ingredient—nitrogen and phosphate—used in achieving the minimum cost of fertilizing. The problem specifies certain requirements for nitrogen and phosphate, and these ingredients acquire a value based on the cost of meeting those requirements. The optimal simplex tableaus for the primal and dual models are presented in Tables 6.3 and 6.4, respectively.

The primal solution in Table 6.3 indicates that 8 bags of Crop-quik fertilizer and no bags of Super-gro fertilizer should be purchased at a cost of $24. The dual solution shown in Table 6.4 indicates that phosphate has a marginal value of $1 in achieving the minimum cost of fertilizer, whereas nitrogen has no marginal value since 16 extra pounds of nitrogen were available in the primal solution (i.e., $s_1 = 16$ in Table 6.3).

TABLE 6.3
The Optimal Simplex Tableau for the Primal

c_j	Basic Variables	Quantity	6 x_1	3 x_2	0 s_1	0 s_2
3	x_2	8	4/3	1	0	−1/3
0	s_1	16	10/3	0	1	−4/3
	z_j	24	4	3	0	−1
	$z_j - c_j$		−2	0	0	−1

TABLE 6.4
The Optimal Simplex Tableau for the Dual

c_j	Basic Variables	Quantity	16 y_1	24 y_2	0 s_1	0 s_2
0	s_1	2	−10/3	0	1	−4/3
24	y_2	1	4/3	1	0	1/3
	z_j	24	32	24	0	8
	$c_j - z_j$		−16	0	0	−8

A Mixed Constraint Problem

The following example will be used to demonstrate how a mixed constraint primal model is transformed into its dual form.

$$\text{maximize } Z = 10x_1 + 6x_2$$
subject to
$$x_1 + 4x_2 \leq 40$$
$$3x_1 + 2x_2 = 60$$
$$2x_1 + x_2 \geq 25$$
$$x_1, x_2 \geq 0$$

The standard form of a primal model

One of the conditions necessary for transforming a primal problem into a dual is that the primal be in a *standard form*. For a maximization primal, all model constraints must be $\leq$, and for a minimization primal, all model constraints must be $\geq$. Thus, when a maximization model includes mixed constraints, the first step is to convert all model constraints into $\leq$ form.

The first constraint,

$$x_1 + 4x_2 \leq 40$$

Converting a constraint equation into standard form

is already in proper form. The second constraint, however, is an equation,

$$3x_1 + 2x_2 = 60$$

and must be converted to a $\leq$ constraint. This equation is equivalent to the following two constraints.

$3x_1 + 2x_2 \geq 60$
$3x_1 + 2x_2 \leq 60$

In other words, if the constraint values are greater than or equal to 60 *and* less than or equal to 60, then the only quantity that satisfies both constraints is *equal to* 60.

However, this does not quite complete the conversion, since a $\geq$ constraint still exists. This constraint can be converted by multiplying the constraint by -1.

$(-1)(3x_1 + 2x_2 \geq 60)$
$\quad -3x_1 - 2x_2 \leq -60$

This new form of the constraint appears to violate the simplex restriction that all quantity values must be either zero or positive. However, the constraint is not being converted so that it can be solved with the simplex method; rather, it is being converted into the dual form. In the dual, the quantity (right-hand side) values of the primal form the coefficients of the objective function, and these can be negative.

The last model constraint is in $\geq$ form,

$2x_1 + x_2 \geq 25$

and can be converted exactly the same way as the previous constraint was, by multiplying it by -1.

$(-1)(2x_1 + x_2 \geq 25)$
$\quad -2x_1 - x_2 \leq -25$

The primal form of the model in standard form can now be summarized as

The primal in standard form

maximize $Z_P = 10x_1 + 6x_2$
subject to
$\quad\quad x_1 + 4x_2 \leq 40$
$\quad\quad 3x_1 + 2x_2 \leq 60$
$\quad -3x_1 - 2x_2 \leq -60$
$\quad -2x_1 + x_2 \leq -25$
$\quad\quad\quad x_1, x_2 \geq 0$

The dual form of this model is formulated as

minimize $Z_d = 40y_1 + 60y_2 - 60y_3 - 25y_4$
subject to
$\quad y_1 + 3y_2 - 3y_3 - 2y_4 \geq 10$
$\quad 4y_1 + 2y_2 - 2y_3 - y_4 \geq 6$
$\quad\quad\quad y_1, y_2, y_3, y_4 \geq 0$

Use of the Dual

The importance of the dual to the decision maker lies in the information it provides about the model resources. Often the manager is less concerned about profit than about the use of resources, because the manager often has more control over the use of resources than over the accumulation of profits. The dual solution informs the manager of the value of the resources, which is important in deciding whether to secure more resources and how much to pay for these additional resources.

If the manager secures more resources, the next question is, "How does this affect the original solution?" The feasible solution area is determined by the values forming the model constraints, and if those values are changed, it is possible for the feasible solution area to change. The effect on the solution of changes to the model is the subject of sensitivity analysis, the next topic to be presented in this chapter.

SENSITIVITY ANALYSIS

When linear programming models were formulated in previous chapters, it was implicitly assumed that the *parameters* of the model were known with certainty. These parameters include the objective function coefficients, such as profit per table; model constraint quantity values, such as available hours of labor; and constraint coefficients, such as pounds of wood per chair or pounds of clay per bowl. In all of the examples presented so far, the models were formulated as if these parameters were known exactly or with certainty. However, rarely does a manager know all of these parameters exactly. In reality the model parameters are simply estimates (or "best guesses") that are subject to change. For this reason it is of interest to the manager to see what effect a change in a parameter will have on the solution to the model. Changes may be either reactions to anticipated uncertainties in the parameters or reactions to information gained from the dual. The analysis of parameter changes and their effects on the model solution is known as *sensitivity analysis*.

The most obvious way to ascertain the effect of a change in the parameter of a model is to make the change in the original model, *resolve* the model, and compare the solution results with the original. However, resolving a problem can be very time consuming and, as we will demonstrate in this chapter, unnecessary. In most cases the effect of changes on the model can be determined directly from the final simplex tableau.

Changes in Objective Function Coefficients

To demonstrate sensitivity analysis for the coefficients in the objective function, we will use the Hickory Furniture Company example developed in the previous section. The model for this example was formulated as

maximize $Z = \$160x_1 + 200x_2$

subject to

$$2x_1 + 4x_2 \leq 40 \text{ hr of labor}$$
$$18x_1 + 18x_2 \leq 216 \text{ lb of wood}$$
$$24x_1 + 12x_2 \leq 240 \text{ ft}^2 \text{ of storage space}$$
$$x_1, x_2 \geq 0$$

where

x_1 = number of tables produced
x_2 = number of chairs produced

The coefficients in the objective function will be represented symbolically as c_j (the same notation used in the simplex tableau). Thus, $c_1 = 160$ and $c_2 = 200$. Now, let us consider a change in one of the c_j values by an amount Δ. For example, let us change $c_1 = 160$ by $\Delta = 90$. In other words, we are changing c_1 from \$160 to \$250. The effect of this change on the solution of this model is shown graphically in Figure 6.2.

A Δ change in an objective function coefficient

Originally the solution to this problem was located at point B in Figure 6.2, where $x_1 - 4$ and $x_2 - 8$. However, increasing c_1 from

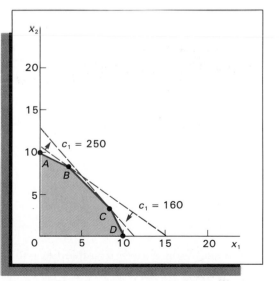

FIGURE 6.2

A Change in c_1

Determining a
range for c_j over
which the current
solution will remain
optimal

$160 to $250 shifts the slope of the objective function so that point C ($x_1 = 8$, $x_2 = 4$) becomes the optimal solution. This demonstrates that a change in one of the coefficients of the objective function can change the optimal solution. Therefore, sensitivity analysis is performed to determine the range over which c_j can be changed without altering the optimal solution.

The range of c_j that will maintain the optimal solution can be determined directly from the optimal simplex tableau. The optimal simplex tableau for our furniture company example is shown in Table 6.5.

TABLE 6.5
The Optimal Simplex Tableau

c_j	Basic Variables	Quantity	160 x_1	200 x_2	0 s_1	0 s_2	0 s_3
200	x_2	8	0	1	1/2	−1/18	0
160	x_1	4	1	0	−1/2	1/9	0
0	s_3	48	0	0	6	−2	1
	z_j	2,240	160	200	20	20/3	0
	$c_j - z_j$		0	0	−20	−20/3	0

Δ changes in the
optimal simplex
tableau

First, consider a Δ change for c_1. This will change the c_1 value from $c_1 = 160$ to $c_1 = 160 + \Delta$, as shown in Table 6.6. Notice that when c_1 is changed to $160 + \Delta$, the new value is included not only in the top c_j row, but also in the left-hand c_j column. This is because x_1 is a basic solution variable. Since $160 + \Delta$ is in the left-hand column, it becomes a multiple of the column values when the new z_j row values and the subsequent $c_j - z_j$ row values, also shown in Table 6.6, are computed.

TABLE 6.6
Optimal Simplex Tableau with $c_1 = 160 + \Delta$

c_j	Basic Variables	Quantity	160 + Δ x_1	200 x_2	0 s_1	0 s_2	0 s_3
200	x_2	8	0	1	1/2	−1/18	0
160 + Δ	x_1	4	1	0	−1/2	1/9	0
0	s_3	48	0	0	6	−2	1
	z_j	2,440 + 4Δ	160 + Δ	200	20 − Δ/2	20/3 + Δ/9	0
	$c_j - z_j$		0	0	−20 + Δ/2	−20/3 − Δ/9	0

Solving Δ
inequalities

The solution shown in Table 6.6 will remain optimal as long as the $c_j - z_j$ row values *remain negative*. (If $c_j - z_j$ becomes positive, the product mix will change, and if it becomes zero, there will be an alternative solution.) Thus, for the solution to remain uniquely optimal,

$$-20 + \Delta/2 < 0$$

and

$$-20/3 - \Delta/9 < 0$$

Both of these inequalities must be solved for Δ.

$$-20 + \Delta/2 < 0$$
$$\Delta/2 < 20$$
$$\Delta < 40$$

and

$$-20/3 - \Delta/9 < 0$$
$$-\Delta/9 < 20/3$$
$$-\Delta < 60$$
$$\Delta > -60$$

Thus, $\Delta < 40$ and $\Delta > -60$. Now recall that $c_1 = 160 + \Delta$; therefore, $\Delta = c_1 - 160$. Substituting the amount $c_1 - 160$ for Δ in these inequalities,

$$\Delta < 40$$
$$c_1 - 160 < 40$$
$$c_1 < 200$$

and

$$\Delta > -60$$
$$c_1 - 160 > -60$$
$$c_1 > 100$$

Therefore, the range of values for c_1 over which the solution basis will remain optimal (although the value of the objective function may change) is

The sensitivity range for c_1

$$100 < c_1 < 200$$

Next, consider a Δ change in c_2 so that $c_2 = 200 + \Delta$. The effect of this change in the final simplex tableau is shown in Table 6.7.

A Δ change for c_2

TABLE 6.7
Optimal Simplex Tableau with $c_2 = 200 + \Delta$

c_j	Basic Variables	Quantity	160 x_1	200 + Δ x_2	0 s_1	0 s_2	0 s_3
200 + Δ	x_2	8	0	1	1/2	-1/18	0
160	x_1	4	1	0	-1/2	1/9	0
0	s_3	48	0	0	6	-2	1
	z_j	2,240 + 8Δ	160	200 + Δ	20 + $\Delta/2$	20/3 - $\Delta/18$	0
	$c_j - z_j$		0	0	-20 - $\Delta/2$	-20/3 + $\Delta/18$	0

As before, the solution shown in Table 6.7 will remain optimal as long as the $c_j - z_j$ row values remain negative or zero. Thus, for the solution to remain optimal, we must have

$$-20 - \Delta/2 < 0$$

and

$$-20/3 + \Delta/18 < 0$$

Solving these inequalities for Δ gives

$$-20 - \Delta/2 < 0$$
$$-\Delta/2 < 20$$
$$\Delta > -40$$

and

$$-20/3 + \Delta/18 < 0$$
$$\Delta/18 < 20/3$$
$$\Delta < 120$$

Thus, $\Delta > -40$ and $\Delta < 120$. Since $c_2 = 200 + \Delta$, we have $\Delta = c_2 - 200$. Substituting this value for Δ in the inequalities yields

$$\Delta > -40$$
$$c_2 - 200 > -40$$
$$c_2 > 160$$

and

$$\Delta < 120$$
$$c_2 - 200 < 120$$
$$c_2 < 320$$

Therefore, the range of values for c_2 over which the solution will remain optimal is

$$160 < c_2 < 320$$

The ranges for both objective function coefficients are as follows:

$$100 < c_1 < 200$$
$$160 < c_2 < 320$$

Determining the c_j
sensitivity range for
a nonbasic
variable

However, these ranges reflect a possible change in either c_1 or c_2, not simultaneous changes in both c_1 and c_2. Both of the objective function coefficients in this example were for basic solution variables. Determining the c_j sensitivity range for a decision variable that is *not basic* is much simpler. Since it is not in the basic variable column, the Δ change does not become a multiple of the z_j row. Thus, the Δ change will show up in only one column in the $c_j - z_j$ row. An example of this type of Δ change when a variable is not basic is shown in the tableau in Table 6.8 for the c_1 coefficient.

TABLE 6.8
The Optimal Simplex Table When x_1 Is Not a Basic Variable

c_j	Basic Variables	Quantity	4 + Δ	10	0	0
			x_1	x_2	s_1	s_2
10	x_2	20	1/2	1	1/2	0
0	s_2	60	5/2	0	−3/2	1
	z_j	200	5	10	5	0
	$c_j - z_j$		−1 + Δ	0	−5	0

Since the solution shown in Table 6.8 will remain optimal if the $c_j - z_j$ row values remain negative or zero, there is only one inequality to solve.

$$-1 + \Delta < 0$$
$$\Delta < 1$$

Since $c_1 = 4 + \Delta$ and $\Delta = c_1 - 4$,

$$\Delta < 1$$
$$c_1 - 4 < 1$$
$$c_1 < 5$$

Thus, as long as $c_1 < 5$, the present solution will remain optimal.

Changes in Constraint Quantity Values

In order to demonstrate the effect of a change in the quantity values of the model constraints, we will again use the Hickory Furniture Company example.

maximize $Z = 160x_1 + 200x_2$
subject to
$$2x_1 + 4x_2 \leq 40 \text{ hr of labor}$$
$$18x_1 + 18x_2 \leq 216 \text{ lb of wood}$$
$$24x_1 + 12x_2 \leq 240 \text{ ft}^2 \text{ of storage space}$$
$$x_1, x_2 \geq 0$$

The quantity values 40, 216, and 240 will be represented symbolically as q_i. Thus, $q_1 = 40$, $q_2 = 216$, and $q_3 = 240$. Now consider a Δ change in q_2. For example, let us change $q_2 = 216$ by Δ = 18. In other words, q_2 is changed from 216 pounds to 234 pounds. The effect of this change is shown graphically in Figure 6.3.

In Figure 6.3 a change in q_2 is shown to have the effect of changing the feasible solution area from $0ABCD$ to $0AB'C'D$. Originally, the optimal solution point was B; however, the change in q_2 causes B' to be the new optimal solution point. Thus, a change in a q_i value

The effect of a change in a quantity value on the feasible solution area

FIGURE 6.3

A Δ Change in q_2

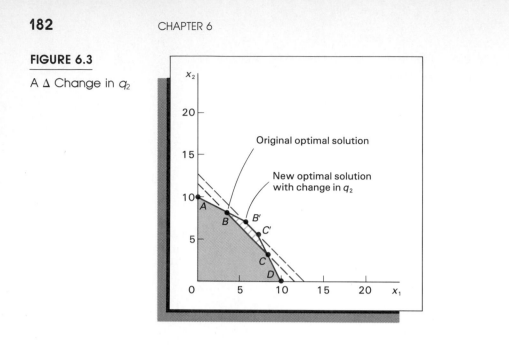

can change the feasible solution area. Therefore, the purpose of sensitivity analysis is to determine the range for q_i over which the solution basis will remain feasible.

Determining Δ changes in q_i from the optimal tableau

As in the case of the c_j values, the range for q_i can be determined directly from the optimal simplex tableau. As an example, consider a Δ increase in the number of labor hours. The model constraints become

$$2x_1 + 4x_2 \leq 40 + 1\,\Delta$$
$$18x_1 + 18x_2 \leq 216 + 0\,\Delta$$
$$24x_1 + 12x_2 \leq 240 + 0\,\Delta$$

Notice in the initial simplex tableau for our example (Table 6.9) that the changes in the quantity column are the same as the coefficients in the s_1 column.

TABLE 6.9
The Initial Simplex Tableau

c_j	Basic Variables	Quantity	160 x_1	200 x_2	0 s_1	0 s_2	0 s_3
0	s_1	$40 + 1\,\Delta$	2	4	1	0	0
0	s_2	$216 + 0\,\Delta$	18	18	0	1	0
0	s_3	$240 + 0\,\Delta$	24	12	0	0	1
	z_j	0	0	0	0	0	0
	$c_j - z_j$		160	200	0	0	0

This duplication will carry through each subsequent tableau, so the s_1 column values will duplicate the Δ changes in the quantity column in the final tableau (Table 6.10).

TABLE 6.10
The Final Simplex Tableau

c_j	Basic Variables	Quantity	160 x_1	200 x_2	0 s_1	0 s_2	0 s_3
200	x_2	$8 + \Delta/2$	0	1	1/2	−1/18	0
160	x_1	$4 - \Delta/2$	1	0	−1/2	1/9	0
0	s_3	$48 + 6\Delta$	0	0	6	−2	1
	z_j	$2,240 + 20\Delta$	160	200	20	20/3	0
	$c_j - z_j$		0	0	−20	−20/3	0

In effect, the Δ changes form a separate column identical to the s_1 column. Therefore, to determine the Δ change, we need only observe the slack (s_i) column corresponding to the model constraint quantity (q_i) being changed.

Recall that a requirement of the simplex method is that the quantity values not be negative. If any q_i value becomes negative, the solution will no longer be *feasible*. Thus, the inequalities

Solving Δ inequalities

$$8 + \Delta/2 \geq 0$$
$$4 - \Delta/2 \geq 0$$
$$48 + 6\Delta \geq 0$$

are solved for Δ:

$$8 + \Delta/2 \geq 0$$
$$\Delta/2 \geq -8$$
$$\Delta > -16$$

and

$$4 - \Delta/2 \geq 0$$
$$-\Delta/2 \geq -4$$
$$\Delta \leq 8$$

and

$$48 + 6\Delta \geq 0$$
$$6\Delta \geq -48$$
$$\Delta \geq -8$$

Since $q_1 = 40 + \Delta$, then $\Delta = q_1 - 40$. These values are substituted into the inequalities $\Delta \geq -16$, $\Delta \leq 8$, and $\Delta \geq -8$ as follows.

$$\Delta \geq -16$$
$$q_1 - 40 \geq -16$$
$$q_1 \geq 24$$

$$\Delta \leq 8$$
$$q_1 - 40 \leq 8$$
$$q_1 \leq 48$$

$$\Delta \geq -8$$
$$q_1 - 40 \geq -8$$
$$q_1 \geq 32$$

The sensitivity range for q_1

Summarizing these inequalities, we have

$$24 \leq 32 \leq q_1 \leq 48$$

The value of 24 can be eliminated, since q_1 must be greater than 32; thus,

$$32 \leq q_1 \leq 48$$

As long as q_1 remains in this range, the present basic solution variables will remain positive and feasible. However, the quantity values of those basic variables may change. In other words, although the variables in the basis remain the same, their values can change.

In order to determine the range of feasibility for q_2 (where $q_2 = 216 + \Delta$), the s_2 column values are to develop the Δ inequalities.

$$8 - \Delta/18 \geq 0$$
$$4 + \Delta/9 \geq 0$$
$$48 - 2\Delta \geq 0$$

Solving Δ inequalities

The inequalities are solved as follows.

$$8 - \Delta/18 \geq 0$$
$$-\Delta/18 \geq -8$$
$$\Delta \leq 144$$

$$4 + \Delta/9 \geq 0$$
$$\Delta/9 \geq -4$$
$$\Delta \geq -36$$

$$48 - 2\Delta \geq 0$$
$$-2\Delta \geq -48$$
$$\Delta \leq 24$$

Since $q_2 = 216 + \Delta$, we have $\Delta = q_2 - 216$. Substituting this value into the inequalities $\Delta \leq 144$, $\Delta \geq -36$, and $\Delta \leq 24$ gives a range of possible values for q_2:

$$\Delta \leq 144$$
$$q_2 - 216 \leq 144$$
$$q_2 \leq 360$$

$$\Delta \geq -36$$
$$q_2 - 216 \geq -36$$
$$q_2 \geq 180$$

$$\Delta \leq 24$$
$$q_2 - 216 \leq 24$$
$$q_2 \leq 240$$

That is,

$$180 \leq q_2 \leq 240 \leq 360$$

The value 360 can be eliminated, since q_2 cannot exceed 240. Thus, the range over which the basic solution variables will remain feasible is

The sensitivity range for q_2

$$180 \leq q_2 \leq 240$$

Sensitivity analysis of constraint quantity values can be used in conjunction with the dual solution to make decisions regarding model resources. Recall from our analysis of the dual solution of the Hickory Furniture Company example that

Using the sensitivity ranges for q_i in conjunction with the dual for decision making

$y_1 = \$20$, marginal value of labor
$y_2 = \$6.67$, marginal value of wood
$y_3 - \$0$, marginal value of storage space

Since the resource with the greatest marginal value is labor, the manager might desire to secure some additional hours of labor. How many hours should the manager get? Given that the range for q_1 is $32 \leq q_1 \leq 48$, the manager could secure up to an additional 8 hours of labor (i.e., 48 total hours) before the solution basis became infeasible. If the manager did purchase 8 more hours, the solution values could be found by observing the quantity values in Table 6.10:

$x_2 = 8 + \Delta/2$
$x_1 = 4 - \Delta/2$
$s_3 = 48 + 6\Delta$

Since $\Delta = 8$,

$x_2 = 8 + (8)/2$
$x_2 = 12$

$x_1 = 4 - (8)/2$
$x_1 = 0$

$s_3 = 48 + 6(8)$
$s_3 = 96$

Total profit will be increased by \$20 for each extra hour of labor.

$$Z = \$2,240 + 20\,\Delta$$
$$= 2,240 + 20(8)$$
$$= 2,240 + 160$$
$$= \$2,400$$

In this example for the Hickory Furniture Company, we considered only $\leq$ constraints in determining the sensitivity ranges for q_i values. To compute the q_i sensitivity range, we observed the slack column, s_i, since a Δ change in q_i was reflected in the s_i column. However, recall that with a $\geq$ constraint we subtract a surplus variable rather than adding a slack variable to form an equality (in addition to adding an artificial variable). Thus, for a $\geq$ constraint we must consider a $-\Delta$ change in q_i in order to use the s_i (surplus) column to perform sensitivity analysis. In that case sensitivity analysis would be performed exactly as shown in this example, except that the value of $q_i - \Delta$ would be used instead of $q_i + \Delta$ when computing the sensitivity range for q_i.

Additional Model Parameter Changes

Sensitivity analysis is not confined solely to determining ranges for c_j and q_i. Other model parameters can also be analyzed to determine the effect on the solution of changes in their values. These additional parameters include the constraint coefficients. For example, in our Hickory Furniture Company example, the labor constraint is

$$2x_1 + 4x_2 \leq 40 \text{ hr}$$

The x_1 coefficient 2 represents the hours required to produce a table. Changing this coefficient to 1 hour per table alters the feasible solution area shown in Figure 6.3. The feasible solution area in Figure 6.4 changes from $0ABCD$ to $0AB'CD$ as a result of the change in the x_1 coefficient in the labor constraint. The solution point also changes from point B to point B'. The determination of a sensitivity range for the model constraint coefficients from the final simplex tableau is beyond the scope of this text, however, and will not be pursued.

An Application of Sensitivity Analysis

The section titled "Applications of Linear Programming" in Chapter 2 introduced several real applications of linear programming. One such application was for fuel management at National Airlines. Because jet fuel supplies were limited during the oil crisis of the mid-1970s, fuel vendors frequently were unable to meet the airline's demand for fuel at specific cities. This resulted in canceled flights,

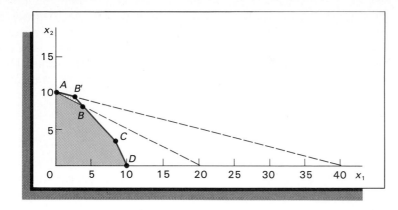

FIGURE 6.4

A Change in the Constraint Coefficient

very high prices for spot purchases of fuel, and large increases in operating costs. National Airlines developed a linear programming model to minimize the effects of price increases and fluctuating fuel allocations, and to maintain a planned flight schedule. The model solution indicated the optimal purchase levels from each station vendor and the amount of fuel to be boarded on each leg of a flight sequence. During the first month the model was implemented, total savings exceeded $500,000, even with a fuel price increase.

National Airlines also used sensitivity analysis to make additional decisions regarding fuel purchases. As noted, the model results indicated the optimal quantities to purchase from each fuel vendor at each station. However, if a vendor subsequently discovered that the indicated allotment of fuel could not be delivered, then the airline had to purchase fuel from another vendor. Since the linear programming solution was optimal, any purchase changes would increase cost. Therefore, the airline had to know how the purchase decision should be changed in order to keep the additional cost at a minimum. Sensitivity analysis assisted the airline managers in making these purchase decisions by enabling them to quickly analyze supply and price changes among the vendors.

For example, after the linear programming solution indicated an optimal purchase quantity from Shell Oil Company at a particular station, sensitivity analysis enabled the airline to determine maximum and minimum amounts that could be purchased from Shell at various stations and the changes in cost associated with these alternative purchase quantities. Purchases outside this range would result in a new decision (i.e., solution). In addition, the model provided a sensitivity range for the maximum and minimum price per gallon of fuel. As long as the price remained within that range, the optimal purchase quantity also remained the same. However, if the price exceeded these maximum and minimum limits, the fuel purchasing plan would no longer be optimal and a new solution would be required. Such information has allowed National Airlines to respond immediately to price changes. The effect of price increases has been minimized and normal scheduled operations have continued even with erratic fuel deliveries and price fluctuations. This has resulted in savings of many millions of dollars for National Airlines.[1]

POSTOPTIMALITY ANALYSIS USING THE COMPUTER

In Chapters 4 and 5 we demonstrated the use of the LINDO/PC and Microcomputer Software for Quantitative Analysis for Management computer packages to solve several linear programming problems. These packages can also generate the dual shadow prices and perform sensitivity analysis on the objective function coefficients, c_j, and the constraint quantity values, q_i. First, the LINDO/PC capabilities will be demonstrated, again using the Hickory Furniture Company example, which has the following model formulation.

maximize $Z = \$160x_1 + 200x_2$

subject to

$$2x_1 + 4x_2 \leq 40 \text{ hr of labor}$$
$$18x_1 + 18x_2 \leq 216 \text{ lb of wood}$$
$$24x_1 + 12x_2 \leq 240 \text{ ft}^2 \text{ of storage space}$$
$$x_1, x_2 \geq 0$$

where

x_1 = number of tables produced
x_2 = number of chairs produced

The LINDO/PC computer output for this example, including the shadow prices, is as follows.

```
: look all

MAX      160 X1 + 200 X2
SUBJECT TO
        2)    2 X1 + 4 X2 <=    40
        3)   18 X1 + 18 X2 <=   216
        4)   24 X1 + 12 X2 <=   240
END

: tableau

THE TABLEAU
    ROW   (BASIS)          X1          X2    SLK   2   SLK   3
      1 ART            -160.000    -200.000      .000       .000
      2 SLK    2          2.000       4.000     1.000       .000
      3 SLK    3         18.000      18.000      .000      1.000
      4 SLK    4         24.000      12.000      .000       .000
```

[1]D. Darnell and C. Loflin, "National Airlines Fuel Management and Allocation Model," *Interfaces* 7, no. 2 (February 1977): 1–16.

```
      ROW   SLK    4
       1       .000       .000
       2       .000     40.000
       3       .000    216.000
       4      1.000    240.000


: pivot
      X2 ENTERS AT VALUE    10.000      IN ROW    2 OBJ. VALUE=   2000.0

: tableau

THE TABLEAU
      ROW  (BASIS)        X1        X2 SLK    2 SLK    3
       1 ART           -60.000      .000    50.000       .000
       2       X2         .500     1.000      .250       .000
       3 SLK    3         9.000      .000    -4.500      1.000
       4 SLK    4        18.000      .000    -3.000       .000


      ROW   SLK    4
       1       .000   2000.000
       2       .000     10.000
       3       .000     36.000
       4      1.000    120.000


: pivot
      X1 ENTERS AT VALUE    4.0000      IN ROW    3 OBJ. VALUE=   2240.0

: tableau

THE TABLEAU
      ROW  (BASIS)        X1        X2 SLK    2 SLK    3
       1 ART              .000      .000    20.000      6.667
       2       X2         .000     1.000      .500      -.056
       3       X1        1.000      .000     -.500       .111
       4 SLK    4         .000      .000     6.000     -2.000


      ROW   SLK    4
       1       .000   2240.000
       2       .000      8.000
       3       .000      4.000
       4      1.000     48.000


: pivot
LP OPTIMUM FOUND  AT STEP      2

         OBJECTIVE FUNCTION VALUE

 1)          2240.00000

   VARIABLE         VALUE        REDUCED COST
         X1      4.000000           .000000
         X2      8.000000           .000000


      ROW    SLACK OR SURPLUS      DUAL PRICES
       2)          .000000         20.000000
       3)          .000000          6.666667
       4)        48.000000           .000000

NO. ITERATIONS=      2
```

Notice that the shadow prices for the example are referred to as *dual prices* in the LINDO/PC output. Recall that we previously determined the marginal value of the resources as

y_1 = marginal value of one hr of labor = \$20.00

y_2 = marginal value of one lb of wood = \$6.67

y_3 = marginal value of one ft^2 of storage space = \$0

These values, shown in the LINDO/PC output under the column "Dual Prices," correspond to the original row of the slack variable, which also represents an individual resource in the initial tableau. In other words, row 2 corresponds to the labor resource constraint to which "SLK 2" was added. Thus, the dual (shadow) prices for rows $2(y_1)$, $3(y_2)$, and $4(y_3)$ are shown as 20, 6.67, and 0, respectively.

After the problem solution has been generated by LINDO/PC, the program will always ask the user if sensitivity analysis is desired. A "yes" response will result in the following sensitivity analysis output for our example problem.

```
DO RANGE(SENSITIVITY) ANALYSIS?
? yes


RANGES IN WHICH THE BASIS IS UNCHANGED:

                          OBJ COEFFICIENT RANGES
VARIABLE          CURRENT         ALLOWABLE       ALLOWABLE
                    COEF          INCREASE        DECREASE
      X1        160.000000       40.000000       60.000000
      X2        200.000000      120.000000       40.000000

                          RIGHTHAND SIDE RANGES
    ROW           CURRENT         ALLOWABLE       ALLOWABLE
                    RHS           INCREASE        DECREASE
      2         40.000000         8.000000        8.000000
      3        216.000000        24.000000       36.000000
      4        240.000000       INFINITY         48.000000
:
```

Recall that we previously determined sensitivity ranges for the objective function coefficients,

$$100 < c_1 < 200$$
$$160 < c_2 < 320$$

and for the constraint quantity values,

$$32 \leq q_1 \leq 48$$
$$180 \leq q_2 \leq 240$$

The LINDO/PC-generated sensitivity analysis output is presented in a slightly different format. For the objective function coefficients, the LINDO/PC output indicates the original coefficient for a specific decision variable and then denotes the maximum allowable increase and decrease that can occur for that coefficient. For example, for the variable "x_1" the current coefficient is identified as 160, the maximum allowable increase is 40, and the maximum allowable decrease is 60 (when rounded). Thus, the objective function coefficient for x_1 can increase to 200 or decrease to 100 — the range we originally determined for c_1.

The sensitivity ranges for the q_i values are presented in a similar manner. For a specific row corresponding to a constraint, the original quantity value, referred to as "RHS" (which stands for the right-hand side of the constraint), is indicated, and then the maximum allowable increase and decrease are denoted. For example, for row 2, which corresponds to the first quantity value, the current q_i value is 40, the maximum allowable increase is 8, and the maximum allowable decrease is 8. Thus, the quantity value for the first constraint can increase to 48 or decrease to 32 — the range we originally determined for q_i.

The Microcomputer Software for Quantitative Analysis for Management package, by Render and Stair, provides similar results for the objective function coefficients and the quantity values (again referred to as "RHS" values), but in a slightly different, tabular format.

LINDO/PC format for sensitivity analysis

```
*******************************************************************
                      ANSWERS
          VARIABLE              VALUE
             x 2                   8.000
             x 1                   4.000
             s 3                  48.000


                SHADOW PRICES:

          CONSTRAINT #           VALUE
               1                20.000
               2                 6.667
               3                 0.000

             OPTIMAL Z =  2240
*******************************************************************
```

```
                SENSITIVITY ANALYSIS
                ********************


              RIGHTHAND SIDE RANGES

CONSTRAINT      LOWER           RHS             UPPER
  NUMBER        LIMIT           VALUE           LIMIT
==================================================================
      1         32.00           40.00           48.00
      2        180.00          216.00          240.00
      3        192.00          240.00          NO LIMIT
------------------------------------------------------------------


          OBJECTIVE FUNCTION COEFFICIENT RANGES

                LOWER           CURRENT         UPPER
VARIABLE        LIMIT           VALUE           LIMIT
==================================================================
     x 1       100.00          160.00          200.00
     x 2       160.00          200.00          320.00
------------------------------------------------------------------
```

The sensitivity ranges in these tables are more consistent with the format presented in this chapter in that the specific range values are shown, rather than only the allowable increases and decreases. However, both sets of sensitivity output are easy to obtain and interpret.

Summary

In this chapter we examined several different ways of analyzing the final simplex solution to gather additional information. First the formulation of the dual was discussed and the dual solution was interpreted. The dual solution was shown to contain useful information regarding the economic value of the model resources. Next, sensitivity analysis of various model parameters was presented. The chapter demonstrated how potential model changes can be examined within the context of the simplex tableau in order to ascertain their effect on the optimal solution.

This chapter completes the presentation of the *general* linear programming model and the simplex method, but it does not complete the presentation of linear programming. Several important variations from the basic linear programming model will be examined in subsequent chapters. The variations include transportation and assignment problems, integral programming, and goal programming.

References

Baumol, W. J. *Economic Theory and Operations Analysis.* 4th ed. Englewood Cliffs, N.J.: Prentice-Hall, 1977.

Dantzig, G. B. *Linear Programming and Extensions.* Princeton, N.J.: Princeton University Press, 1963.

Darnell, D., and Loflin, C. "National Airlines Fuel Management and Allocation Model." *Interfaces* 7, no. 2 (February 1977): 1–16.

Hadley, G. *Linear Programming.* Reading, Mass.: Addison-Wesley Publishing Co., 1962.

Lee, Sang M.; Moore, Laurence J.; and Taylor, B. W. *Management Science.* 3d ed. Boston: Allyn and Bacon, 1990.

Loomba, N. P. *Linear Programming: A Managerial Perspective.* 2d ed. New York: Macmillan Co., 1976.

Pfaffenberger, R. C., and Walker, David A. *Mathematical Programming for Economics and Business.* Ames, Ia.: Iowa State University Press, 1976.

Phillips, D. T.; Ravindran, A.; and Solberg, J. J. *Operations Research: Principles and Practice.* 2d ed. New York: John Wiley and Sons, 1987.

Spivey, W. A., and Thrall, R. M. *Linear Optimization.* New York: Holt, Rinehart, and Winston, 1970.

Taha, H. A. *Operations Research: An Introduction.* 4th ed. New York: Macmillan Co., 1987.

EXAMPLE PROBLEM SOLUTION

The following example problem will illustrate the solution steps for duality and sensitivity analysis to be used in subsequent problems in this chapter.

The Problem Statement

A company produces two products (x_1 and x_2) subject to labor, material, and storage constraints, as embodied in the following linear programming model.

maximize $Z = 400x_1 + 500x_2$ (profit, \$)

subject to

$$x_1 + 2x_2 \leq 10 \text{ hr of labor}$$
$$6x_1 + 6x_2 \leq 36 \text{ lb of material}$$
$$8x_1 + 4x_2 \leq 40 \text{ ft}^2 \text{ of storage space}$$
$$x_1, x_2 \geq 0$$

The optimal tableau for this model is as follows.

c_j	Basic Variables	Quantity	400	500	0	0	0
			x_1	x_2	s_1	s_2	s_3
500	x_2	4	0	1	1	−1/6	0
400	x_1	2	1	0	−1	1/3	0
0	s_3	8	0	0	4	−2	1
	z_j	2,800	400	500	100	50	0
	$c_j - z_j$		0	0	−100	−50	0

a. Formulate the dual of this model, define the dual variables, and indicate their values.
b. Use sensitivity analysis to determine the optimal ranges for c_1 and the feasible ranges for q_1.

Step 1: Formulate the Dual and Define the Dual Variables

$$\text{minimize } Z = 10y_1 + 36y_2 + 40y_3$$
subject to
$$y_1 + 6y_2 + 8y_3 \geq 400$$
$$2y_1 + 6y_2 + 4y_3 \geq 500$$
$$y_1, y_2, y_3 \geq 0$$
where
y_1 = marginal value of labor
y_2 = marginal value of material
y_3 = marginal value of storage space

According to the $c_j - z_j$ row of the optimal tableau, the values are as follows:

$y_1 = 100$
$y_2 = 50$
$y_3 = 0$

Step 2: Determine the Optimal Range for c_1

c_j	Basic Variables	Quantity	400 + Δ	500	0	0	0
			x_1	x_2	s_1	s_2	s_3
500	x_2	4	0	1	1	−1/6	0
400 + Δ	x_1	2	1	0	−1	1/3	0
0	s_3	8	0	0	4	−2	1
	z_j	2,800 + 2Δ	400 + Δ	500	100 − Δ	50 + Δ/3	0
	$c_j - z_j$		0	0	−100 + Δ	−50 − Δ/3	0

Solve for the $c_j - z_j$ inequalities:

$$-100 + \Delta < 0$$
$$\Delta < 100$$

and

$$-50 - \Delta/3 < 0$$
$$-\Delta/3 < 50$$
$$-\Delta < 150$$
$$\Delta > -150$$

Since $c_1 = 400 + \Delta$, we have

$$\Delta = c_1 - 400$$

Substitution yields

$$\Delta < 100$$
$$c_1 - 400 < 100$$
$$c_1 < 500$$

and

$$\Delta > -150$$
$$c_1 - 400 > -150$$
$$c_1 > 250$$

Thus, the range for c_1 is

$$250 < c_1 < 500$$

Step 3: Determine the Feasible Range for q_1

The s_1 column in the optimal tableau is used to develop the following inequalities relative to q_1.

$$4 + \Delta \geq 0$$
$$2 - \Delta \geq 0$$
$$8 + 4\Delta \geq 0$$

Solving each for Δ yields

$$4 + \Delta \geq 0$$
$$\Delta \geq -4$$

and

$$2 - \Delta \geq 0$$
$$\Delta \leq 2$$

and

$$8 + 4\Delta \geq 0$$
$$4\Delta \geq -8$$
$$\Delta \geq -2$$

Since $q_1 = 10 + \Delta$, we have $\Delta = q_1 - 10$. Substituting this value for Δ into the inequalities developed above yields

$$\Delta \geq -4$$
$$q_1 - 10 \geq -4$$
$$q_1 \geq 6$$

and

$$\Delta \leq 2$$
$$q_1 - 10 \leq 2$$
$$q_1 \leq 12$$

and

$$\Delta \geq -2$$
$$q_1 - 10 \geq -2$$
$$q_1 \geq 8$$

These results can be summarized as

$$6 \leq 8 \leq q_1 \leq 12$$

so the feasible range for q_1 is

$$8 \leq q_1 \leq 12$$

The Computerized Solution

The dual values and sensitivity ranges for all objective function coefficients and quantity values, obtained using the Microcomputer Software computer program, are as follows.

```
***********************************************************************
                         ANSWERS
            VARIABLE                VALUE
              x 2                       4.000
              x 1                       2.000
              s 3                       8.000




              SHADOW PRICES:


          CONSTRAINT #            VALUE
               1                 100.000
               2                  50.000
               3                   0.000

           OPTIMAL Z =   2800
***********************************************************************
```

```
                        SENSITIVITY ANALYSIS
                        ********************


                      RIGHTHAND SIDE RANGES

     CONSTRAINT       LOWER              RHS                 UPPER
      NUMBER          LIMIT             VALUE                LIMIT
   ============================================================
         1             8.00             10.00               12.00
         2            30.00             36.00               40.00
         3            32.00             40.00             NO LIMIT


            OBJECTIVE FUNCTION COEFFICIENT RANGES


                      LOWER             CURRENT              UPPER
     VARIABLE         LIMIT              VALUE               LIMIT
   ============================================================
       x 1           250.00            400.00              500.00
       x 2           400.00            500.00              800.00
```

Problems

1. The Old English Metal Crafters Company makes brass trays and buckets. The number of trays (x_1) and buckets (x_2) that can be produced daily is constrained by the availability of brass and labor, as reflected in the following linear programming model.

   maximize $Z = 6x_1 + 10x_2$ (profit, $)
   subject to
   $$x_1 + 4x_2 \le 90 \text{ (brass, lb)}$$
   $$2x_1 + 2x_2 \le 60 \text{ (labor, hr)}$$
   $$x_1, x_2 \ge 0$$

   The final optimal simplex tableau for this model is as follows.

c_j	Basic Variables	Quantity	6 x_1	10 x_2	0 s_1	0 s_2
10	x_2	20	0	1	1/3	−1/6
6	x_1	10	1	0	−1/3	2/3
	z_j	260	6	10	4/3	7/3
	$c_j - z_j$		0	0	−4/3	−7/3

   a. Formulate the dual of this model.
   b. Define the dual variables and explain what they mean.
   c. What do the dual variables equal?

2. The Southwest Foods Company produces two brands of chili—Razorback and Longhorn—from several ingredients, including chili beans and ground beef. The number of 100-gallon batches of Razorback chili (x_1) and Longhorn chili (x_2) that can be produced daily is constrained by the availability of chili beans and ground beef, as shown in the following linear programming model.

maximize $Z = 200x_1 + 300x_2$ (profit, $)

subject to

$$10x_1 + 50x_2 \leq 500 \text{ (chili beans, lb)}$$
$$34x_1 + 20x_2 \leq 800 \text{ (ground beef, lb)}$$
$$x_1, x_2 \geq 0$$

The final optimal simplex tableau for this model is as follows.

c_j	Basic Variables	Quantity	200 x_1	300 x_2	0 s_1	0 s_2
300	x_2	6	0	1	17/750	−1/150
200	x_1	20	1	0	−1/75	1/30
	z_j	5,800	200	300	310/75	70/15
	$c_j - z_j$		0	0	−310/75	−70/15

a. Interpret the meaning of the $c_j - z_j$ values in this tableau.
b. Formulate the dual of this model.
c. What do the dual variables equal and what do they mean?

3. The Agrimaster Company produces two kinds of fertilizer spreaders—regular and cyclone. Each spreader must go through two production processes. Letting x_1 = the number of regular spreaders produced and x_2 = the number of cyclone spreaders produced, the problem can be formulated as follows.

maximize $Z = 9x_1 + 7x_2$ (profit, $)

subject to

$$12x_1 + 4x_2 \leq 60 \text{ (process 1, production hr)}$$
$$4x_1 + 8x_2 \leq 40 \text{ (process 2, production hr)}$$
$$x_1, x_2 \geq 0$$

The final optimal simplex tableau for this problem is as follows.

c_j	Basic Variables	Quantity	9 x_1	7 x_2	0 s_1	0 s_2
9	x_1	4	1	0	1/10	−1/20
7	x_2	3	0	1	−1/20	3/20
	z_j	57	9	7	11/20	12/20
	$c_j - z_j$		0	0	−11/20	−12/20

a. Formulate the dual for this problem.
b. Define the dual variables.
c. Interpret the $c_j - z_j$ values in this tableau.
d. Allocate profit between the resources to show how much each resource contributes to total profit.

4. The Stratford House Furniture Company makes two kinds of tables — end tables (x_1) and coffee tables (x_2). The manufacturer is restricted by material and labor constraints, as shown in the following linear programming formulation.

maximize $Z = 200x_1 + 300x_2$ (profit, $)
subject to
$$2x_1 + 5x_2 \leq 180 \text{ (labor, hr)}$$
$$3x_1 + 3x_2 \leq 135 \text{ (wood, lb)}$$
$$x_1, x_2 \geq 0$$

The final optimal simplex tableau for this problem is as follows.

c_j	Basic Variables	Quantity	200 x_1	300 x_2	0 s_1	0 s_2
300	x_2	30	0	1	1/3	-2/9
200	x_1	15	1	0	-1/3	5/9
	z_j	12,000	200	300	100/3	400/9
	$c_j - z_j$		0	0	-100/3	400/9

a. Formulate the dual for this problem.
b. Define the dual variables.
c. Allocate profit between the resources to show how much each resource contributes to total profit.

5. A manufacturing firm produces electric motors for washing machines and vacuum cleaners. The firm has resource constraints for production time, steel, and wire. The linear programming model for determining the number of washing machine motors (x_1) and vacuum cleaner motors (x_2) to produce has been formulated as follows.

maximize $Z = 70x_1 + 80x_2$ (profit, $)
subject to
$$2x_1 + x_2 \leq 19 \text{ (production, hr)}$$
$$x_1 + x_2 \leq 14 \text{ (steel, lb)}$$
$$x_1 + 2x_2 \leq 20 \text{ (wire, ft)}$$
$$x_1, x_2 \geq 0$$

The final optimal simplex tableau for this model is as follows.

c_j	Basic Variables	Quantity	70 x_1	80 x_2	0 s_1	0 s_2	0 s_3
70	x_1	6	1	0	2/3	0	-1/3
0	s_2	1	0	0	-1/3	1	-1/3
80	x_2	7	0	1	-1/3	0	2/3
	z_j	980	70	80	20	0	30
	$c_j - z_j$		0	0	-20	0	-30

a. Formulate the dual for this problem.
b. What do the dual variables equal and what do they mean?
c. Allocate profit among the resources to show how much each resource contributes to total profit.

6. A manufacturer produces products 1 and 2, for which profits are $9 and $12, respectively. Each product must go through two production processes that have labor constraints. There are also material constraints and storage limitations. The linear programming model for determining the number of product 1 to produce (x_1) and the number of product 2 to produce (x_2) is given as follows.

maximize $Z = 9x_1 + 12x_2$ (profit, $)

subject to

$$4x_1 + 8x_2 \le 64 \text{ (process 1, labor hr)}$$
$$5x_1 + 5x_2 \le 50 \text{ (process 2, labor hr)}$$
$$15x_1 + 8x_2 \le 120 \text{ (material, lb)}$$
$$x_1 \le 7 \text{ (storage space, ft}^2\text{)}$$
$$x_2 \le 7 \text{ (storage space, ft}^2\text{)}$$
$$x_1, x_2 \ge 0$$

The final optimal simplex tableau for this problem is as follows.

c_j	Basic Variables	Quantity	9 x_1	12 x_2	0 s_1	0 s_2	0 s_3	0 s_4	0 s_5
9	x_1	4	1	0	-1/4	2/5	0	0	0
0	s_5	1	0	0	-1/4	1/5	0	0	1
0	s_3	12	0	0	7/4	-22/5	1	0	0
0	s_4	3	0	0	1/4	-2/5	0	1	0
12	x_2	6	0	1	1/4	-1/5	0	0	0
	z_j	108	9	12	3/4	6/5	0	0	0
	$c_j - z_j$		0	0	-3/4	-6/5	0	0	0

a. Formulate the dual for this problem.
b. What do the dual variables equal and what does this dual solution mean?
c. Allocate profit among the resources to show how much each resource contributes to total profit.

7. A manufacturer produces products 1, 2, and 3 daily. The three products are processed through three production operations that have time constraints, and the finished products are then stored. The following linear programming model has been formulated to determine the number of product 1 (x_1), product 2 (x_2), and product 3 (x_3) to produce.

maximize $Z = 40x_1 + 35x_2 + 45x_3$ (profit, \$)

subject to

$$2x_1 + 3x_2 + 2x_3 \leq 120 \text{ (operation 1, hr)}$$
$$4x_1 + 3x_2 + x_3 \leq 160 \text{ (operation 2, hr)}$$
$$3x_1 + 2x_2 + 4x_3 \leq 100 \text{ (operation 3, hr)}$$
$$x_1 + x_2 + x_3 < 40 \text{ (storage, ft}^2)$$
$$x_1, x_2, x_3 \geq 0$$

The final optimal simplex tableau for this model is as follows.

c_j	Basic Variables	Quantity	40 x_1	35 x_2	45 x_3	0 s_1	0 s_2	0 s_3	0 s_4
0	s_1	10	$-1/2$	0	0	1	0	1/2	-4
0	s_2	60	2	0	0	0	1	1	-5
45	x_3	10	1/2	0	1	0	0	1/2	-1
35	x_2	30	1/2	1	0	0	0	$-1/2$	2
	z_j	1,500	40	35	45	0	0	5	25
	$c_j - z_j$		0	0	0	0	0	-5	-25

a. Formulate the dual for this problem.
b. What do the dual variables equal and what do they mean?
c. How does the fact that this is a multiple optimum solution affect the interpretation of the dual solution values?

8. A school dietician is attempting to plan a lunch menu that will minimize cost and meet certain minimum dietary requirements. The two staples in the meal are meat and potatoes, which provide protein, iron, and carbohydrates. The following linear programming model has been formulated to determine how many ounces of meat (x_1) and ounces of potatoes (x_2) to put in a lunch.

minimize $Z = .03x_1 + .02x_2$ (cost, \$)

subject to

$$4x_1 + 5x_2 \geq 20 \text{ (protein, mg)}$$
$$12x_1 + 3x_2 \geq 30 \text{ (iron, mg)}$$
$$3x_1 + 2x_2 \geq 12 \text{ (carbohydrates, mg)}$$
$$x_1, x_2 \geq 0$$

The final optimal simplex tableau for this problem is as follows.

c_j	Basic Variables	Quantity	.03 x_1	.02 x_2	0 s_1	0 s_2	0 s_3
.02	x_2	3.6	0	1	0	.20	−.80
.03	x_1	1.6	1	0	0	−.13	.20
0	s_1	4.4	0	0	1	.47	−3.2
	z_j	.12	.03	.02	0	0	−.01
	$z_j - c_j$		0	0	0	0	−.01

a. Formulate the dual for this problem.
b. What do the dual variables equal and what do they mean?

9. Given the linear programming problem in problem 6,

   maximize $Z = 9x_1 + 12x_2$
   subject to
   $$4x_1 + 8x_2 \leq 64$$
   $$5x_1 + 5x_2 \leq 50$$
   $$15x_1 + 8x_2 \leq 120$$
   $$x_1 \leq 7$$
   $$x_2 \leq 7$$
   $$x_1, x_2 \geq 0$$

   solve the dual model using the simplex method, and compare the dual optimal tableau to the primal optimal tableau.

10. Given problem 5,

    maximize $Z = 70x_1 + 80x_2$
    subject to
    $$2x_1 + x_2 \leq 19$$
    $$x_1 + x_2 \leq 14$$
    $$x_1 + 2x_2 \leq 20$$
    $$x_1, x_2 \geq 0$$

    solve the dual model using the simplex method, and compare the dual optimal tableau with the primal optimal tableau.

11. Formulate the dual for the following linear programming model.

    maximize $Z = 10x_1 + 5x_2 + 8x_3$
    subject to
    $$6x_1 + 12x_2 + 4x_3 \leq 1,600$$
    $$x_1 + 3x_2 + 2x_3 \leq 400$$
    $$x_1 + x_2 + x_3 \leq 300$$
    $$x_1 \leq 150$$
    $$x_2 \leq 200$$
    $$x_3 \leq 100$$
    $$x_1, x_2, x_3 \geq 0$$

12. Formulate the dual for the following linear programming model.

maximize $Z = 25x_1 + 20x_2 + 10x_3 + 30x_4$
subject to
$$x_1 + x_2 \leq 400$$
$$x_3 + x_4 \leq 600$$
$$50x_1 + 45x_2 \leq 16{,}000$$
$$40x_3 + 30x_4 \leq 25{,}000$$
$$2x_1 + 3x_3 \leq 800$$
$$4x_2 + x_4 \leq 900$$
$$x_1, x_2, x_3, x_4 \geq 0$$

13. Formulate the dual for the following linear programming model.

minimize $Z = x_1 + x_2 + x_3 + x_4$
subject to
$$10x_1 + 12x_2 + 7x_3 + 8x_4 \geq 300$$
$$50x_3 + 25x_4 \geq 600$$
$$20x_2 + 30x_4 \geq 800$$
$$x_1 \geq 10$$
$$x_2 \geq 8$$
$$x_3 \geq 10$$
$$x_4 \geq 20$$
$$x_1, x_2, x_3, x_4 \geq 0$$

14. Formulate the dual for the following linear programming model.

maximize $Z = 5x_1 + x_2$
subject to
$$4x_1 + 3x_2 = 24$$
$$x_1 \leq 6$$
$$x_1 + 3x_2 \leq 12$$
$$x_1, x_2 \geq 0$$

15. Formulate the dual for the following linear programming model.

maximize $Z = 2x_1 + 2x_2 - x_3$
subject to
$$x_1 + x_2 - 2x_3 \leq 6$$
$$-2x_1 - x_2 + x_3 \leq 5$$
$$2x_1 + 6x_2 = 10$$
$$x_1, x_2, x_3 \geq 0$$

16. Formulate the dual for the following linear programming model.

maximize $Z = 4x_1 + 10x_2 + 6x_3$

subject to

$$x_1 + 3x_2 + 4x_3 \leq 40$$
$$2x_2 + x_3 \leq 20$$
$$10x_1 + 6x_2 + 20x_3 = 100$$
$$x_1 + 2x_2 = 60$$
$$x_1, x_2, x_3 \geq 0$$

17. Formulate the dual for the following linear programming model.

maximize $Z = x_1 + 2x_2 + 2x_3$

subject to

$$x_1 + x_2 + 2x_3 \leq 12$$
$$2x_1 + x_2 + 5x_3 = 20$$
$$x_1 + x_2 - x_3 \geq 8$$
$$x_1, x_2, x_3 \geq 0$$

18. Formulate the dual for the following linear programming model.

maximize $Z = 4x_1 + 2x_2$

subject to

$$x_1 + x_2 \geq 1$$
$$-4x_1 + x_2 \leq 0$$
$$-x_1 + 4x_2 \geq 0$$
$$-x_1 + x_2 \leq 1$$
$$x_1 + x_2 \leq 6$$
$$x_1 \leq 3$$
$$x_1, x_2 \geq 0$$

19. For problem 1 in this chapter, perform the following sensitivity analyses:

   a. Determine the optimal ranges for c_1 and c_2.
   b. Determine the feasible ranges for q_1 (pounds of brass) and q_2 (labor hours).

20. From problem 2 in this chapter, perform the following sensitivity analyses:

   a. Determine the optimal ranges for c_1 and c_2.
   b. Determine the feasible ranges for q_1 (pounds of beans) and q_2 (pounds of ground beef).

21. For problem 3 in this chapter, perform the following sensitivity analyses:

   a. Determine the optimal ranges for c_1 and c_2.
   b. Determine the feasible ranges for q_1 and q_2 (production hours for process 1 and 2, respectively).

22. For problem 4 in this chapter, perform the following sensitivity analyses:

   a. Determine the optimal ranges for c_1 and c_2.
   b. Determine the feasible ranges for q_1 (labor hours) and q_2 (pounds of wood).

23. For problem 5 in this chapter, perform the following sensitivity analyses:

   a. Determine the optimal ranges for c_1 and c_2.
   b. Determine the feasible ranges for q_1 (production hours), q_2 (pounds of steel), and q_3 (feet of wire).

24. For problem 6 in this chapter, perform the following sensitivity analyses:

   a. Determine the optimal range for c_1.
   b. Determine the feasible ranges for q_1 (labor hours for process 1).

25. For problem 7 in this chapter, perform the following sensitivity analyses:

   a. Determine the optimal range for c_2.
   b. Determine the feasible range for q_4 (square feet of storage space).

26. For problem 8 in this chapter, perform the following sensitivity analyses:

   a. Determine the optimal ranges for c_1 and c_2.
   b. Determine the feasible ranges for q_1, q_2, and q_3 (milligrams of protein, iron, and carbohydrates).

27. Given the linear programming model

   maximize $Z = 6x_1 + 2x_2 + 12x_3$
   subject to
   $$4x_1 + x_2 + 3x_3 \leq 24$$
   $$2x_1 + 6x_2 + 3x_3 \leq 30$$
   $$x_1, x_2, x_3 \geq 0$$

   and its optimal simplex tableau,

c_j	Basic Variables	Quantity	6 x_1	2 x_2	12 x_3	0 s_1	0 s_2
12	x_3	8	4/3	1/3	1	1/3	0
0	s_2	6	−2	5	0	−1	1
	z_j	96	16	4	12	4	0
	$c_j - z_j$		−10	−2	0	−4	0

   a. Find the ranges for all c_j values for which the present solution will remain optimal.
   b. Find the ranges for all q_i values for which the present solution will remain feasible.

28. Given the linear programming model

maximize $Z = 10x_1 + 8x_2$

subject to

$$x_1 + 3x_2 \leq 30$$
$$6x_1 + 3x_2 \leq 120$$
$$x_1, x_2 \geq 0$$

and its optimal simplex tableau,

c_j	Basic Variables	Quantity	10 x_1	8 x_2	0 s_1	0 s_2
8	x_2	4	0	1	2/5	−1/15
10	x_1	18	1	0	−1/5	1/5
	z_j	212	10	8	6/5	22/15
	$c_j - z_j$		0	0	−6/5	−22/15

a. Find the optimal ranges of all c_j values.
b. Find the feasible ranges for all q_i values.

29. Given the linear programming model

minimize $Z = 3x_1 + 5x_2 + 2x_3$

subject to

$$x_1 + x_2 - 3x_3 \geq 35$$
$$x_1 + 2x_2 \geq 50$$
$$-x_1 + x_2 \geq 25$$
$$x_1, x_2, x_3 \geq 0$$

and its optimal simplex tableau,

c_j	Basic Variables	Quantity	3 x_1	5 x_2	2 x_3	0 s_1	0 s_2	0 s_3
0	s_2	15	0	0	−4	−3/2	1	−1/2
3	x_1	5	1	0	−2	−1/2	0	1/2
5	x_2	30	0	1	−1	−1/2	0	−1/2
	z_j	165	3	5	−11	−4	0	−1
	$z_j - c_j$		0	0	−13	−4	0	−1

a. Find the optimal ranges for all c_j values.
b. Find the feasible ranges for all q_i values.

30. Given the linear programming model

maximize $Z = 5x_1 + 7x_2 + 8x_3$

subject to

$$x_1 + x_2 + x_3 \leq 32$$
$$x_1 \leq 20$$
$$x_2 \leq 15$$
$$x_3 \leq 18$$
$$x_1, x_2, x_3 \geq 0$$

and its optimal simplex tableau,

c_j	Basic Variables	Quantity	5 x_1	7 x_2	8 x_3	0 s_1	0 s_2	0 s_3	0 s_4
7	x_2	14	1	1	0	1	0	0	−1
0	s_2	20	1	0	0	0	1	0	0
0	s_3	1	1	0	0	1	0	1	1
8	x_3	18	0	0	1	0	0	0	1
	z_j	242	7	7	8	7	0	0	1
	$c_j - z_j$		−2	0	0	−7	0	0	−1

a. Find the optimal ranges for all c_j values.
b. Find the feasible ranges for all q_i values.

31. In problem 1, what is the maximum price the Old English Metal Crafters Company would be willing to pay for additional labor hours, and how many hours could be purchased at that price (from problem 19)?

32. a. In problem 2, what is the maximum price the Southwest Foods Company would be willing to pay for additional pounds of chili beans, and how many pounds could be purchased at that price (from problem 20)?

b. If the company wanted to secure additional amounts of only one of the ingredients, beans or ground beef, which should it be?

c. If the company changed the selling price of Longhorn chili so that the profit was $400 instead of $300, would the optimal solution be affected?

33. In problem 3, what is the maximum price the Agrimaster Company would be willing to pay for additional hours of process 1 production time, and how many hours could be purchased at that price (from problem 21)?

34. a. In problem 4, what is the maximum price the Stratford House Furniture Company would be willing to pay for additional wood, and how many pounds of wood could be purchased at that price (from problem 22)?

b. If the furniture company wanted to secure additional units of only one of the resources, labor or wood, which should it be?

35. Managers at the manufacturing firm in problem 5 have determined that the firm can purchase a new production machine that will increase available production time from 19 to 25 hours. Would this change affect the optimal solution (from problem 23)?

36. In problem 7, what is the maximum price the manufacturer would be willing to pay to lease additional storage space, and how many additional square feet could be leased at that price (from problem 25)?

37. In problem 8, what would it be worth for the school dietician to be able to reduce the requirement for carbohydrates, and what is the smallest number of mg of carbohydrates that would be required at that value (from problem 26)?

38. The Sunshine Food Processing Company produces three canned fruit products — mixed fruit (x_1), fruit cocktail (x_2), and fruit delight (x_3). The main ingredients in each product are pears and peaches. Each product is produced in lots and must go through three processes — mixing, canning, and packaging. The resource requirements for each product and each process are shown in the following linear programming formulation.

maximize $Z = 10x_1 + 6x_2 + 8x_3$ (profit, \$)

subject to

$$20x_1 + 10x_2 + 16x_3 \le 320 \text{ (pears, lb)}$$
$$10x_1 + 20x_2 + 16x_3 \le 400 \text{ (peaches, lb)}$$
$$x_1 + 2x_2 + 2x_3 \le 43 \text{ (mixing, hr)}$$
$$x_1 + x_2 + x_3 \le 60 \text{ (canning, hr)}$$
$$2x_1 + x_2 + x_3 \le 40 \text{ (packaging, hr)}$$
$$x_1, x_2, x_3 \ge 0$$

The optimal simplex tableau is as follows.

c_j	Basic Variables	Quantity	10 x_1	6 x_2	8 x_3	0 s_1	0 s_2	0 s_3	0 s_4	0 s_5
10	x_1	8	1	0	8/15	1/15	1/30	0	0	0
6	x_2	16	0	1	8/15	−1/30	1/15	0	0	0
0	s_3	3	0	0	2/5	0	−1/10	1	0	0
0	s_4	36	0	0	−1/15	−1/30	−1/30	0	1	0
0	s_5	8	0	0	−3/5	−1/10	0	0	0	1
	z_j	176	10	6	128/15	7/15	1/15	0	0	0
	$c_j - z_j$		0	0	−8/15	−7/15	−1/15	0	0	0

a. What is the maximum price the company would be willing to pay for additional pears? How much could be purchased at that price?

b. What is the marginal value of peaches? Over what range is this price valid?

c. The company can purchase a new mixing machine that would increase the available mixing time from 40 to 60 hours. Would this affect the optimal solution?

d. The company can also purchase a new packaging machine that would increase the available packaging time from 40 to 50 hours. Would this affect the optimal solution?

e. If the manager were to attempt to secure additional units of only one of the resources, which should it be?

39. The Evergreen Products Firm produces three types of pressed paneling from pine and spruce. The three types of paneling are Western (x_1), Old English (x_2), and Colonial (x_3). Each sheet must be cut and pressed. The resource requirements are given in the following linear programming formulation.

maximize $Z = 4x_1 + 10x_2 + 8x_3$ (profit, $)

subject to

$$5x_1 + 4x_2 + 4x_3 \leq 200 \text{ (pine, lb)}$$
$$2x_1 + 5x_2 + 2x_3 \leq 160 \text{ (spruce, lb)}$$
$$x_1 + x_2 + 2x_3 \leq 50 \text{ (cutting, hr)}$$
$$2x_1 + 4x_2 + 2x_3 \leq 80 \text{ (pressing, hr)}$$
$$x_1, x_2, x_3 \geq 0$$

The optimal simplex tableau is as follows.

c_j	Basic Variables	Quantity	4 x_1	10 x_2	8 x_3	0 s_1	0 s_2	0 s_3	0 s_4
0	s_1	80	7/3	0	0	1	0	−4/3	−2/3
0	s_2	70	−1/3	0	0	0	1	1/3	−4/3
8	x_3	20	1/3	0	1	0	0	2/3	−1/6
10	x_2	10	1/3	1	0	0	0	1/3	1/3
	z_j	260	6	10	8	0	0	2	2
	$c_j - z_j$		−2	0	0	0	0	−2	−2

a. What is the marginal value of an additional pound of spruce? Over what range is this value valid?

b. What is the marginal value of an additional hour of cutting? Over what range is this value valid?

c. Given a choice between securing more cutting hours or more pressing hours, which should management select? Why?

d. If the amount of spruce available to the firm were decreased from 160 to 100 pounds, would this reduction affect the solution?

e. What unit profit would have to be made from Western paneling before management would consider producing it?

f. Management is considering changing the profit of Colonial paneling from \$8 to \$13. Would this change affect the solution?

40. A manufacturing firm produces four products. Each product requires material and machine processing. The linear programming model formulated to determine the number of product 1 (x_1), product 2 (x_2), product 3 (x_3), and product 4 (x_4) to produce is as follows.

maximize $Z = 2x_1 + 8x_2 + 10x_3 + 6x_4$ (profit, \$)

subject to

$$2x_1 + x_2 + 4x_3 + 2x_4 \leq 200 \text{ (material, lb)}$$
$$x_1 + 2x_2 + 2x_3 + x_4 \leq 160 \text{ (machine processing, hr)}$$
$$x_1, x_2, x_3, x_4 \geq 0$$

The optimal simplex tableau is as follows.

c_j	Basic Variables	Quantity	2 x_1	8 x_2	10 x_3	6 x_4	0 s_1	0 s_2
6	x_4	80	1	0	2	1	2/3	−1/3
8	x_2	40	0	1	0	0	−1/3	2/3
	z_j	800	6	8	12	6	4/3	10/3
	$c_j - z_j$		−4	0	−2	0	−4/3	−10/3

a. What is the marginal value of an additional pound of material? Over what range is this value valid?

b. What is the marginal value of additional hours of processing time? Over what range is this value valid?

c. How much would the contribution to profit of x_1 have to increase before x_1 would be produced?

7

Transportation and Assignment Problems

In this chapter we will examine two special types of linear programming problems that can be solved by methods other than the simplex method: *transportation problems* and *assignment problems*. Both of these problem types could be solved using the simplex method, but the process would result in rather large simplex tableaus and numerous simplex iterations. Because of the unique characteristics of each problem, however, alternative solution methods requiring considerably less mathematical manipulation than the simplex method have been developed. These solution methods will be described and demonstrated in this chapter; in addition, the computerized solution of the transportation problem will be presented.

THE TRANSPORTATION MODEL

Unique
characteristics of
the transportation
model

The transportation model is formulated for a class of problems with the following unique characteristics: (1) a product is *transported* from a number of sources to a number of destinations at the minimum possible cost, and (2) each source is able to supply a fixed number of units of the product to each destination, which has a fixed demand for the product. Although the general transportation model can be applied to a wide variety of problems, it is this particular application to the transportation of goods that is most familiar and from which the problem draws its name.

A transportation
example

The following example demonstrates the formulation of the transportation model. Wheat is harvested in the Midwest and stored in grain elevators in three cities—Kansas City, Omaha, and Des Moines. These grain elevators supply three flour mills, located in Chicago, St. Louis, and Cincinnati. Grain is shipped to the mills in railroad cars, each capable of holding one ton of wheat. Each grain elevator is able to supply the following number of tons (i.e., railroad cars) of wheat to the mills on a monthly basis.

Supply at each
source

Grain Elevator	Supply
1. Kansas City	150
2. Omaha	175
3. Des Moines	275
	600 tons

Each mill demands the following number of tons of wheat per month.

Demand at each
destination

Mill	Demand
A. Chicago	200
B. St. Louis	100
C. Cincinnati	300
	600 tons

Transportation costs

The cost of transporting one ton of wheat from each grain elevator (source) to each mill (destination) differs according to the distance and rail system. These costs are shown below. For example, the cost of shipping one ton of wheat from the grain elevator at Omaha to the mill at Chicago is $7.

Grain Elevator	Chicago A	St. Louis B	Cincinnati C
Kansas City	$6	8	10
Omaha	7	11	11
Des Moines	4	5	12

The problem is to determine how many tons of wheat to transport from each grain elevator to each mill on a monthly basis in order to minimize the total cost of transportation. A diagram of

FIGURE 7.1

Network of Transportation Routes for Wheat Shipments

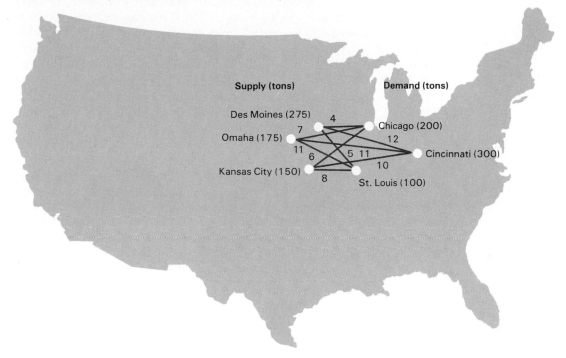

the different transportation routes with supply, demand, and cost figures is given in Figure 7.1.

The linear programming model for this problem is formulated as follows.

$$\text{minimize } Z = \$6x_{1A} + 8x_{1B} + 10x_{1C} + 7x_{2A} + 11x_{2B} + 11x_{2C} + 4x_{3A}$$
$$+ 5x_{3B} + 12x_{3C}$$

subject to

$$x_{1A} + x_{1B} + x_{1C} - 150$$
$$x_{2A} + x_{2B} + x_{2C} = 175$$
$$x_{3A} + x_{3B} + x_{3C} = 275$$
$$x_{1A} + x_{2A} + x_{3A} = 200$$
$$x_{1B} + x_{2B} + x_{3B} = 100$$
$$x_{1C} + x_{2C} + x_{3C} = 300$$
$$x_{ij} \geq 0$$

The general linear programming model of a transportation problem

In this model the decision variables, x_{ij}, represent the number of tons of wheat transported from each grain elevator, i (where $i = 1, 2, 3$), to each mill, j (where $j = A, B, C$). The objective function represents the total transportation cost for each route. Each term in the objective function reflects the cost of the tonnage transported for one route. For example, if 20 tons are transported from elevator 1 to mill A, the cost of \$6 is multiplied by x_{1A} (= 20), which equals \$120.

Definitions of variables

The objective function

The first three constraints in the linear programming model represent the supply at each elevator; the last three constraints represent the demand at each mill. As an example, consider the first supply constraint, $x_{1A} + x_{1B} + x_{1C} = 150$. This constraint represents the tons of wheat transported from Kansas City to all three mills: Chicago (x_{1A}), St. Louis (x_{1B}), and Cincinnati (x_{1C}). The amount transported from Kansas City is limited to the 150 tons available. Note that this constraint (as well as all others) is an equation (=) rather than a ≤ inequality because all of the tons of wheat available will be needed to meet the *total demand* of 600 tons. In other words, the three mills demand 600 total tons, which is the exact amount that can be supplied by the three grain elevators. Thus, all that *can* be supplied *will be*, in order to meet demand. This type of model, in which supply exactly equals demand, is referred to as a *balanced* transportation model. The balanced model will be used to demonstrate the solution of a transportation problem.

Constraint equations

A balanced transportation model

SOLUTION OF THE TRANSPORTATION MODEL

To this point, linear programming models have been solved using the simplex method. However, manual simplex solution of this transportation model would be very time consuming. Since there are nine decision variables, six constraints, and six artificial variables to be added, the resulting simplex tableau would be rather large. Fortunately, several alternative solution methods that require considerably less manual effort are available for solving transportation problems.

Transportation models are solved within the context of a *tableau*, as in the simplex method. The tableau for our wheat transportation model is shown in Table 7.1.

TABLE 7.1
The Transportation Tableau

From \ To	A	B	C	Supply
1	6	8	10	150
2	7	11	11	175
3	4	5	12	275
Demand	200	100	300	600

Each cell in the tableau represents the amount transported from one source to one destination. Thus, the amount placed in each cell is the value of a decision variable for that cell. For example, the cell at the intersection of row 1 and column A represents the decision variable x_{1A}. The smaller box within each cell contains the transportation cost for that route. For example, in cell 1A the value, $6, is the cost of transporting one ton of wheat from Kansas City to Chicago. Along the outer rim of the tableau are the supply and demand constraint quantity values, which are referred to as *rim requirements*.

The two methods for solving a transportation model are the *stepping-stone method* and the *modified distribution method* (also known as MODI). Recall that prior to applying the simplex method, an initial solution had to be established in the initial simplex tableau. This same condition must be met in solving a transportation model. However, notice that artificial variables (the initial solution variables for a problem with = constraints) are not included in Table 7.1. Thus, in a transportation model the initial solution is not at the origin, where the artificial variables would take on all quantity values. In a transportation model an initial solution can be found by several alternative methods, including the *northwest corner method*, the *minimum cell cost method*, and *Vogel's Approximation Method*.

Since transportation problems are also linear programming problems, they can be solved using the computer software packages demonstrated in Chapters 4, 5, and 6. Following the presentation of the manual solution methods for solving the transportation problem and the presentation of the assignment problem, the computerized solution of the transportation problem will be demonstrated.

The Northwest Corner Method

With the northwest corner method, an initial allocation is made to the cell in the upper left-hand corner of the tableau (i.e., the "northwest corner"). The amount allocated is the most possible, *subject to* the supply and demand constraints for that cell. In our example, we first allocate as much as possible to cell 1A (the northwest corner). This amount is 150 tons, since that is the maximum that can be supplied by grain elevator 1 at Kansas City, even though 200 tons are demanded by mill A at Chicago. This initial allocation is shown in Table 7.2.

We next allocate to a cell *adjacent* to cell 1A, in this case either cell 2A or cell 1B. However, cell 1B no longer represents a feasible allocation, since the total tonnage of wheat available at source 1 (i.e., 150 tons) has already been allocated. Thus, cell 2A represents the only feasible alternative, and as much as possible is allocated to this

Margin notes:

Tableau cells

Rim requirements

Transportation model solution methods

Methods for determining an initial basic feasible solution

Allocating to an adjacent feasible cell

TABLE 7.2

The Initial NW Corner Allocation

From \ To	A		B		C		Supply
1	150	6		8		10	150
2		7		11		11	175
3		4		5		12	275
Demand	200		100		300		600

cell. The amount allocated at 2A can be either 175 tons, the supply available from source 2 (Omaha), or 50 tons, the amount *now* demanded at destination A. (Recall that 150 of the 200 tons demanded at A have already been supplied.) Since 50 tons is the most constrained amount, it is allocated to cell 2A, as shown in Table 7.3.

TABLE 7.3

The Second NW Corner Allocation

From \ To	A		B		C		Supply
1	150	6		8		10	150
2	50	7		11		11	175
3		4		5		12	275
Demand	200		100		300		600

Notice that the shaded cells in Tables 7.2 and 7.3 are no longer feasible possibilities, and have therefore been eliminated from consideration.

The third allocation is made in the same way as the second allocation. The only feasible cell adjacent to cell 2A is cell 2B. The most that can be allocated is either 100 tons (the amount demanded at mill B) or 125 tons (175 tons minus the 50 tons allocated to cell 2A). The smaller (most constrained) amount, 100 tons, is allocated to cell 2B, as shown in Table 7.4.

Meeting all rim requirements

The fourth allocation is 25 tons to cell 2C, and the fifth allocation is 275 tons to cell 3C, both of which are shown in Table 7.5. Notice that all of the row and column allocations add up to the appropriate rim requirements.

TABLE 7.4
The Third NW Corner Allocation

From \ To	A	B	C	Supply
1	6 150	8	10	150
2	7 50	11 100	11	175
3	4	5	12	275
Demand	200	100	300	600

TABLE 7.5
The Initial Solution

From \ To	A	B	C	Supply
1	6 150	8	10	150
2	7 50	11 100	11 25	175
3	4	5	12 275	275
Demand	200	100	300	600

The transportation cost of this solution is computed by substituting the cell allocations (i.e., the amounts transported),

The initial solution from the northwest corner method

$$x_{1A} = 150 \qquad x_{2C} = 25$$
$$x_{2A} = 50 \qquad x_{3C} = 275$$
$$x_{2B} = 100$$

into the objective function.

$$Z = \$6x_{1A} + 8x_{1B} + 10x_{1C} + 7x_{2A} + 11x_{2B} + 11x_{2C} + 4x_{3A} + 5x_{3B} + 12x_{3C}$$
$$= 6(150) + 8(0) + 10(0) + 7(50) + 11(100) + 11(25) + 4(0) + 5(0)$$
$$\quad + 12(275)$$
$$= \$5,925$$

The steps of the northwest corner method are summarized below.

Steps of the northwest corner method

1. Allocate as much as possible to the cell in the upper left-hand corner, subject to the supply and demand constraints.
2. Allocate as much as possible to the next adjacent feasible cell.
3. Repeat step 2 until all rim requirements have been met.

The Minimum Cell Cost Method

Allocate as much as possible to the cell with the minimum cost

With the minimum cell cost method, the initial allocation is made to the cell having the lowest cost. In the transportation tableau for our example problem, cell 3A has the minimum cost of $4. As much as possible is allocated to this cell; the choice is either 200 tons or 275 tons. Even though 275 tons could be supplied to cell 3A, the most we can allocate is 200 tons, since only 200 tons are demanded. This allocation is shown in Table 7.6.

TABLE 7.6
The Initial Minimum Cell Cost Allocation

To From	A	B	C	Supply
1	6	8	10	150
2	7	11	11	175
3	4 200	5	12	275
Demand	200	100	300	600

Notice that all the cells in column A have now been eliminated, since all the wheat demanded at destination A, Chicago, has been supplied by source 3, Des Moines.

The next allocation is made to the cell that has the minimum cost and also is feasible. This is cell 3B with a cost of $5. The most that can be allocated is 75 tons (275 tons minus the 200 tons already supplied). This allocation is shown in Table 7.7.

TABLE 7.7
The Second Minimum Cell Cost Allocation

To From	A	B	C	Supply
1	6	8	10	150
2	7	11	11	175
3	4 200	5 75	12	275
Demand	200	100	300	600

The third allocation is made to cell 1B, which has the minimum cost of $8. (Notice that cells with lower costs, such as 1A and 2A, are not considered because they were previously ruled out as infeasible.) The amount allocated is 25 tons. The fourth allocation of 125 tons is made to cell 1C, and the last allocation of 175 tons is made to cell 2C. These allocations, which complete the initial minimum cell cost solution, are shown in Table 7.8.

TABLE 7.8
The Initial Solution

From \ To	A		B		C		Supply
1		6	25	8	125	10	150
2		7		11	175	11	175
3	200	4	75	5		12	275
Demand	200		100		300		600

The total cost of this initial solution is $4,550, as compared to a total cost of $5,925 for the initial northwest corner solution. It is not a coincidence that a lower total cost is derived using the minimum cell cost method; it is a logical occurrence. The northwest corner method does not consider cost at all in making allocations — the minimum cell cost method does. It is therefore quite natural that a lower initial cost will be attained using the latter method. Thus, the initial solution achieved by using the minimum cell cost method is usually better in that, since it has a lower cost, it is closer to the optimal solution; fewer subsequent iterations will be required to achieve the optimal solution.

A better initial solution than the one that results from the northwest corner method

The steps of the minimum cell cost method are summarized below.

Steps of the minimum cell cost method

1. Allocate as much as possible to the feasible cell with the minimum transportation cost.
2. Repeat step 1 until all rim requirements have been met.

Vogel's Approximation Method

The third method for determining an initial solution, Vogel's Approximation Method (also called VAM), is based on the concept of *penalty cost* or *regret*. If a decision maker incorrectly chooses from several alternative courses of action, a penalty may be suffered (and the decision maker may regret the decision that was made). In a transportation problem, the courses of action are the alternative routes and a wrong decision is allocating to a cell that does not contain the lowest cost.

Penalty costs

In the VAM method, the first step is to develop a penalty cost for each source and destination. For example, consider column A in

Developing penalty costs for each row and column

Table 7.9. Destination A, Chicago, can be supplied by Kansas City, Omaha, and Des Moines. The best decision would be to supply Chicago from source 3, because cell 3A has the minimum cost of $4. If a wrong decision were made and the next highest cost of $6 were selected at cell 1A, a "penalty" of $2 per ton would result (i.e., $6 − 4 = $2). This demonstrates how the penalty cost is determined for each row and column of the tableau. The general rule for computing a penalty cost is to subtract the minimum cell cost from the next highest cell cost in each row and column. The penalty costs for our example are shown at the right and at the bottom of Table 7.9.

TABLE 7.9
The VAM Penalty Costs

To From	A	B	C	Supply	
1	6	8	10	150	2
2	7	11	11	175	4
3	4	5	12	275	1
Demand	200	100	300	600	
	2	3	1		

The initial VAM allocation

The initial allocation in the VAM method is made in the row or column that has the highest penalty cost. In Table 7.9, row 2 has the highest penalty cost of $4. We allocate as much as possible to the feasible cell in this row with the minimum cost. In row 2, cell 2A has the lowest cost of $7, and the most that can be allocated to cell 2A is 175 tons. With this allocation the greatest penalty cost of $4 has been avoided, since the best course of action has been selected. The allocation is shown in Table 7.10.

TABLE 7.10
The Initial VAM Allocation

To From	A	B	C	Supply	
1	6	8	10	150	2
2	7 175	11	11	175	
3	4	5	12	275	1
Demand	200	100	300	600	
	2	3	2		

After the initial allocation is made, *all* penalty costs must be recomputed. In some cases the penalty costs will change; in other cases they will not. For example, the penalty cost for column C in Table 7.10 changed from $1 to $2 (because cell 2C is no longer considered in computing penalty cost), and the penalty cost in row 2 was eliminated altogether (since no more allocations are possible for that row).

Recomputing all penalty costs

Eliminating penalty costs

Next, we repeat the previous step and allocate to the row or column with the highest penalty cost, which is now column B with a penalty cost of $3 (see Table 7.10). The cell in column B with the lowest cost is 3B, and we allocate as much as possible to this cell, 100 tons. This allocation is shown in Table 7.11.

TABLE 7.11

The Second VAM Allocation

To From	A	B	C	Supply	
1	6	8	10	150	2
2	7 175	11	11	175	
3	4	5 100	12	275	8
Demand	200	100	300	600	
	2		2		

Note that all penalty costs have been recomputed in Table 7.11. Since the highest penalty cost is now $8 for row 3 and since cell 3A has the minimum cost of $4, we allocate 25 tons to this cell, as shown in Table 7.12.

TABLE 7.12

The Third VAM Allocation

To From	A	B	C	Supply
1	6	8	10	150
2	7 175	11	11	175
3	4 25	5 100	12	275
Demand	200	100	300	600
			2	

Table 7.12 also shows the recomputed penalty costs after the third allocation. Notice that by now only column C has a penalty

cost. Rows 1 and 3 have only one feasible cell, so a penalty does not exist for these rows. Thus, the last two allocations are made to column C. First, 150 tons are allocated to cell 1C, since it has the lowest cell cost. This leaves only cell 3C as a feasible possibility, so 150 tons are allocated to this cell. Both of these allocations are shown in Table 7.13.

TABLE 7.13
The Initial VAM Solution

From \ To	A	B	C	Supply
1	6	8	10 150	150
2	7 175	11	11	175
3	4 25	5 100	12 150	275
Demand	200	100	300	600

The VAM initial solution compared to the northwest corner and minimum cell cost initial solutions

The total cost of this initial solution is $5,125, which is not as high as the northwest corner initial solution of $5,925 or as low as the minimum cell cost solution of $4,550. Like the minimum cell cost method, VAM typically results in a lower cost for the initial solution than does the northwest corner method.

The steps of Vogel's Approximation Method can be summarized as follows:

Steps of Vogel's Approximation Method

1. Determine the penalty cost for each row and column by subtracting the lowest cell cost in the row or column from the next lowest cell cost in the same row or column.
2. Select the row or column with the highest penalty cost.
3. Allocate as much as possible to the feasible cell with the lowest transportation cost in the row or column with the highest penalty cost.
4. Repeat steps 1, 2, and 3 until all rim requirements have been met.

The Stepping-Stone Solution Method

Solution methods once an initial solution is derived

Once an initial *basic feasible solution* has been determined by any of the previous three methods, the next step is to solve the model for the optimal (i.e., minimum total cost) solution. There are two basic solution methods: the stepping-stone method and the modified distribution method (MODI). The *stepping-stone solution method* will be demonstrated first. Since the initial solution obtained by the minimum cell cost method had the lowest total cost of the three initial solutions, we will use it as the starting solution. Table 7.14 repeats the initial solution developed from the minimum cell cost method.

Using the minimum cell cost initial solution

TABLE 7.14
The Minimum Cell Cost Solution

From \ To	A	B	C	Supply
1	6	8 25	10 125	150
2	7	11	11 175	175
3	4 200	5 75	12	275
Demand	200	100	300	600

The basic solution principle in a transportation problem is to determine whether a transportation route not presently being used (i.e., an empty cell) would result in a lower total cost if it were used. For example, Table 7.14 shows four empty cells (1A, 2A, 2B, 3C) representing unused routes. Our first step in the stepping-stone method is to evaluate these empty cells to see whether the use of any of them would reduce total cost. If we find such a route, then we will allocate as much as possible to it.

Determining if there is an unused route that would lower costs if used

First, let us consider allocating one ton of wheat to cell 1A. If one ton is allocated to cell 1A, cost will be increased by $6 — the transportation cost for cell 1A. However, by allocating one ton to cell 1A we increase the supply in row 1 to 151 tons, as shown in Table 7.15.

Allocating one ton to cell 1A

TABLE 7.15
The Allocation of One Ton to Cell 1A

From \ To	A	B	C	Supply	
1	+1 6	8 25	10 125	150	151
2	7	11	11 175	175	
3	4 200	5 75	12	275	
Demand	200	100	300	600	

The constraints of the problem cannot be violated and feasibility must be maintained. If we add one ton to cell 1A, we must subtract one ton from another allocation along that row. Cell 1B is a logical

Maintaining the rim requirements

candidate, since it contains 25 tons. By subtracting one ton from cell 1B, we now have 150 tons in row 1, and we have satisfied the supply constraint again. At the same time, subtracting one ton from cell 1B has reduced total cost by $8.

However, by subtracting one ton from cell 1B, we now have only 99 tons allocated to column B, where 100 tons are demanded, as shown in Table 7.16. In order to compensate for this constraint violation, one ton must be added *to a cell that already has an allocation.* Since cell 3B has 75 tons, we will add one ton to this cell, which again satisfies the demand constraint of 100 tons.

TABLE 7.16
The Subtraction of One Ton from Cell 1B

From \ To	A	B	C	Supply
1	+1 · 6	−1 · 8 / 25	10 / 125	150
2	7	11	11 / 175	175
3	4 / 200	5 / 75	12	275
Demand	200	100 / 99	300	600

A requirement of this solution method is that units can only be added to and subtracted from cells that already have allocations. That is why one ton was added to cell 3B and not to cell 2B. It is from this requirement that the method derives its name. The process of adding and subtracting units from allocated cells is analogous to crossing a pond by stepping on stones (i.e., only allocated-to cells).

By allocating one extra ton to cell 3B we have increased cost by $5, the transportation cost for that cell. However, we have also increased the supply in row 3 to 276 tons, a violation of the supply constraint for this source. As before, this violation can be remedied by subtracting one ton from cell 3A, which contains an allocation of 200 tons. This satisfies the supply constraint again for row 3, and it also reduces the total cost by $4, the transportation cost for cell 3A. These allocations and deletions are shown in Table 7.17.

Notice in Table 7.17 that by subtracting one ton from cell 3A we did not violate the demand constraint for column A, since we previously added one ton to cell 1A.

Now let us review the increases and reductions in costs resulting from this process. We initially increased cost by $6 at cell 1A, then reduced cost by $8 at cell 1B, then increased cost by $5 at cell 3B, and, finally, reduced cost by $4 at cell 3A.

$$1A \rightarrow 1B \rightarrow 3B \rightarrow 3A$$
$$+\$6 - 8 + 5 - 4 = -\$1$$

Stepping on stones (i.e., allocated-to cells)

The net cost change from allocating to cell 1A

TABLE 7.17

The Addition of One Ton to Cell 3B and the Subtraction of One Ton from Cell 3A

From \ To	A	B	C	Supply
1	+1 ——— 6	−1 8 25	10 125	150
2	7	11	11 175	175
3	−1 ←— 4 +1 200	5 75	12	275
Demand	200	100	300	600

In other words, for each ton allocated to cell 1A (a route presently not used), total cost will be reduced by $1. This indicates that the initial solution is not optimal, since a lower cost can be achieved by allocating additional tons of wheat to cell 1A. Therefore, cell 1A represents a possible choice for the *entering nonbasic variable* for this tableau (that is, cell 1A is analogous to a pivot column in the simplex method). However, another variable (empty cell) may result in an even greater decrease in cost than cell 1A. If such a cell exists, it will be selected as the entering variable; if not, cell 1A will be selected. In order to identify the appropriate entering variable, the remaining empty cells must be tested as cell 1A was.

The entering nonbasic variable

Before testing the remaining empty cells, let us identify a few of the general characteristics of the stepping-stone process. First, we always start with an empty cell and form a *closed path* of cells that presently have allocations. In developing the path, it is possible to skip over both unused and used cells. In any row or column there must be *exactly one* addition and *one* subtraction. (For example, in row 1, wheat is added at cell 1A and is subtracted at cell 1B.)

A closed path

Let us test cell 2A to see if it results in a cost reduction. The stepping-stone closed path for cell 2A is shown in Table 7.18. Notice that the path for cell 2A is slightly more complex than the path for cell 1A. Notice also that the path crosses itself at one point, which is perfectly acceptable. An allocation to cell 2A will reduce cost by $1, as shown in the computation in Table 7.18. Thus, we have located another possible entering variable, although it is no better than cell 1A.

The remaining stepping-stone paths and the resulting computations for cells 2B and 3C are shown in Tables 7.19 and 7.20, respectively.

Notice that after all four unused routes are evaluated, there is a tie for the entering variable between cells 1A and 2A. Both show a reduction in cost of $1 per ton allocated to that route. The tie can be broken arbitrarily, just as we broke a tie between tied pivot columns

Selecting the cell to allocate to — the entering nonbasic variable

TABLE 7.18

The Stepping-Stone Path for Cell 2A

From \ To	A	B	C	Supply
1	6	8 / 25	10 / 125	150
2	7	11	11 / 175	175
3	4 / 200	5 / 75	12	275
Demand	200	100	300	600

2A → 2C → 1C → 1B → 3B → 3A

+ $7 − 11 + 10 − 8 + 5 − 4 = −$1

TABLE 7.19

The Stepping-Stone Path for Cell 2B

From \ To	A	B	C	Supply
1	6	8 / 25	10 / 125	150
2	7	11	11 / 175	175
3	4 / 200	5 / 75	12	275
Demand	200	100	300	600

2B → 2C → 1C → 1B

+ $11 − 11 + 10 − 8 = +$2

TABLE 7.20

The Stepping-Stone Path for Cell 3C

From \ To	A	B	C	Supply
1	6	8 / 25	10 / 125	150
2	7	11	11 / 175	175
3	4 / 200	5 / 75	12	275
Demand	200	100	300	600

3C → 1C → 1B → 3B

+ $12 − 10 + 8 − 5 = +$5

in the simplex method. We will select cell 1A (i.e., x_{1A}) to enter the solution basis.

Since the total cost of the model will be reduced by $1 for each ton we can reallocate to cell 1A, we naturally want to reallocate as much as possible. In order to determine how much to allocate, we need to look at the path for cell 1A again, as shown in Table 7.21.

TABLE 7.21
The Stepping-Stone Path for Cell 1A

From \ To	A	B	C	Supply
1	+ [6]	− [8] 25	[10] 125	150
2	[7]	[11]	[11] 175	175
3	− [4] 200	+ [5] 75	[12]	275
Demand	200	100	300	600

The stepping-stone path in Table 7.21 shows that tons of wheat must be subtracted at cells 1B and 3A in order to meet the rim requirements and thus satisfy the model constraints. Since we cannot subtract more than is available in a cell, we are limited by the 25 tons in cell 1B. In other words, if we allocate more than 25 tons to cell 1A, we must subtract more than 25 tons from 1B, which is impossible since only 25 tons are available. Therefore, 25 tons is the amount we reallocate to cell 1A according to our path. That is, 25 tons are added to 1A, subtracted from 1B, added to 3B, and subtracted from 3A. This reallocation is shown in Table 7.22.

Reallocating units to the selected cell

TABLE 7.22
The Second Iteration of the Stepping-Stone Method

From \ To	A	B	C	Supply
1	[6] 25	[8]	[10] 125	150
2	[7]	[11]	[11] 175	175
3	[4] 175	[5] 100	[12]	2/5
Demand	200	100	300	600

The process culminating in Table 7.22 represents one *iteration* of the stepping-stone method. The process has been very similar to the simplex method. We selected x_{1A} as the entering variable, and it turned out that x_{1B} was the leaving variable (since it now has a value of zero in Table 7.22). Thus, at each iteration one variable enters and one leaves, just as in the simplex method.

An iteration of the stepping-stone method

Now we must check to see whether the solution shown in Table 7.22 is, in fact, optimal. We do this by plotting the paths for

Repeating the stepping-stone process

the unused routes (i.e., empty cells 2A, 1B, 2B, and 3C) shown in Table 7.22. These paths are shown in Tables 7.23 through 7.26.

TABLE 7.23
The Stepping-Stone Path for Cell 2A

From \ To	A	B	C	Supply
1	6 25	8	10 125	150
2	7	11	11 175	175
3	4 175	5 100	12	275
Demand	200	100	300	600

2A → 2C → 1C → 1A

+ $7 − 11 + 10 − 6 = $0

TABLE 7.24
The Stepping-Stone Path for Cell 1B

From \ To	A	B	C	Supply
1	6 25	8	10 125	150
2	7	11	11 175	175
3	4 175	5 100	12	275
Demand	200	100	300	600

1B → 3B → 3A → 1A

+ $8 − 5 + 4 − 6 = +$1

TABLE 7.25
The Stepping-Stone Path for Cell 2B

From \ To	A	B	C	Supply
1	6 25	8	10 125	150
2	7	11	11 175	175
3	4 175	5 100	12	275
Demand	200	100	300	600

2B → 3B → 3A → 1A → 1C → 2C

+ $11 − 5 + 4 − 6 + 10 − 11 = +$3

TABLE 7.26
The Stepping-Stone Path for Cell 3C

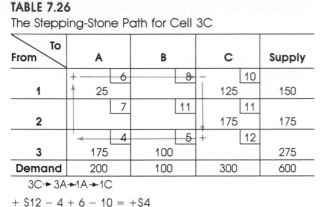

From \ To	A	B	C	Supply
1	25 (6) +	(8) −	125 (10)	150
2	(7)	(11)	175 (11)	175
3	175 (4)	100 (5) +	(12)	275
Demand	200	100	300	600

3C → 3A → 1A → 1C

+ \$12 − 4 + 6 − 10 = +\$4

Our evaluation of the four paths indicates no cost reductions; therefore, the solution shown in Table 7.22 is optimal. The solution and total minimum cost are

$$x_{1A} = 25 \text{ tons} \qquad x_{3A} = 175 \text{ tons}$$
$$x_{1C} = 125 \text{ tons} \qquad x_{3B} = 100 \text{ tons}$$
$$x_{2C} = 175 \text{ tons}$$
$$Z = \$6(25) + 8(0) + 10(125) + 7(0) + 11(0) + 11(175) + 4(175) + 5(100)$$
$$+ \: 12(0)$$
$$= \$4,525$$

However, notice in Table 7.23 that the path for cell 2A resulted in a cost change of \$0. In other words, allocating to this cell would neither increase nor decrease total cost. This situation indicates that the problem has *multiple optimal solutions* (a topic first discussed in Chapter 5). Thus, x_{2A} could be entered into the solution and there would not be a change in the total minimum cost of \$4,525. To identify the alternative solution, we would allocate as much as possible to cell 2A, which in this case is 25 tons of wheat. The alternative solution is shown in Table 7.27.

TABLE 7.27
The Alternative Optimal Solution

From \ To	A	B	C	Supply
1	(6)	(8)	150 (10)	150
2	25 (7)	(11)	150 (11)	175
3	175 (4)	100 (5)	(12)	275
Demand	200	100	300	600

The solution in Table 7.27 also results in a total minimum cost of $4,525.

The steps of the stepping-stone method are summarized below.

1. Determine the stepping-stone paths and cost changes for each empty cell in the tableau.
2. Allocate as much as possible to the empty cell with the greatest net decrease in cost.
3. Repeat steps 1 and 2 until all empty cells have positive cost changes that indicate an optimal solution.

The Modified Distribution Method

The *modified distribution method* (MODI) is basically a modified version of the stepping-stone method. However, in the MODI method, the individual cell cost changes are determined mathematically, without identifying all of the stepping-stone paths for the empty cells.

In order to demonstrate MODI, we will again use the initial solution obtained by the minimum cell cost method. The tableau for the initial solution with the modifications required by MODI are shown in Table 7.28.

TABLE 7.28
The Minimum Cell Cost Initial Solution

v_j		$v_A =$	$v_B =$	$v_C =$	
u_i	To From	A	B	C	Supply
$u_1 =$	1	6	25 8	125 10	150
$u_2 =$	2	7	11	175 11	175
$u_3 =$	3	200 4	75 5	12	275
	Demand	200	100	300	600

The extra left-hand column with the u_i symbols and the extra top row with the v_j symbols represent column and row values that must be computed in MODI. These values are computed for all *cells* with allocations by using the following formula.

$$u_i + v_j = c_{ij}$$

The value c_{ij} is the transportation cost for cell *ij*. For example, the formula for cell 1B is

$$u_1 + v_B = c_{1B}$$

and, since $c_{1B} = 8$,

$u_1 + v_B = 8$

The formulas for the remaining cells that presently contain allocations are shown below.

x_{1C}: $u_1 + v_C = 10$
x_{2C}: $u_2 + v_C = 11$
x_{3A}: $u_3 + v_A = 4$
x_{3B}: $u_3 + v_B = 5$

Now there are five equations with six unknowns. To solve these equations, it is necessary to assign only one of the unknowns a value of zero. Thus, if we let $u_1 = 0$, we can solve for all remaining u_i and v_j values.

x_{1B}: $u_1 + v_B = 8$
      $0 + v_B = 8$
          $v_B = 8$
x_{1C}: $u_1 + v_C = 10$
      $0 + v_C = 10$
          $v_C = 10$
x_{2C}: $u_2 + v_C = 11$
      $u_2 + 10 = 11$
          $u_2 = 1$
x_{3B}: $u_3 + v_B = 5$
      $u_3 + 8 = 5$
          $u_3 = -3$
x_{3A}: $u_3 + v_A = 4$
      $3 + v_A = 4$
          $v_A = 7$

Notice that the equation for cell 3B had to be solved before the cell 3A equation could be solved. Now all the u_i and v_j values can be substituted into the tableau, as shown in Table 7.29.

Next, we use the following formula to evaluate all *empty cells*:

$c_{ij} - u_i - v_j = k_{ij}$

> Computing the cost change for each unused route

where k_{ij} equals the cost increase or decrease that would occur by allocating to a cell.

For the empty cells in Table 7.29, the formula yields the following values:

x_{1A}: $k_{1A} = c_{1A} - u_1 - v_A = 6 - 0 - 7 = -1$
x_{2A}: $k_{2A} = c_{2A} - u_2 - v_A = 7 - 1 - 7 = -1$
x_{2B}: $k_{2B} = c_{2B} - u_2 - v_B = 11 - 1 - 8 = +2$
x_{3C}: $k_{3C} = c_{3C} - u_3 - v_C = 12 - (-3) - 10 = +5$

TABLE 7.29
The Initial Solution with All u_i and v_j Values

u_i	v_j / From \ To	$v_A = 7$ / A	$v_B = 8$ / B	$v_C = 10$ / C	Supply
$u_1 = 0$	1	6	8 25	10 125	150
$u_2 = 1$	2	7	11	11 175	175
$u_3 = -3$	3	4 200	5 75	12	275
	Demand	200	100	300	600

These calculations indicate that either cell 1A or cell 2A will decrease cost by \$1 per allocated ton. Notice that those are exactly the same cost changes for all four empty cells as were computed in the stepping-stone method. That is, the same information is obtained by evaluating the paths in the stepping-stone method and by using the mathematical formulas of the MODI.

We can select either cell 1A or 2A to allocate to, since they are tied at -1. If cell 1A is selected as the entering nonbasic variable, then the stepping-stone path for that cell must be determined so that we know how much to reallocate. This is the same path previously identified in Table 7.21. Reallocating along this path results in the tableau shown in Table 7.30 (and previously shown in Table 7.22).

The second iteration of the MODI method

TABLE 7.30
The Second Iteration of the MODI Solution Method

u_i	v_j / From \ To	$v_A =$ / A	$v_B =$ / B	$v_C =$ / C	Supply
$u_1 =$	1	6 25	8	10 125	150
$u_2 =$	2	7	11	11 175	175
$u_3 =$	3	4 175	5 100	12	275
	Demand	200	100	300	600

Recomputing u_i and v_j

The u_i and v_j values for Table 7.30 must now be recomputed using our formula for the allocated-to cells.

$$x_{1A}: \quad u_1 + v_A = 6$$
$$0 + v_A = 6$$
$$v_A = 6$$

$$x_{1C}:\ u_1 + v_C = 10$$
$$0 + v_C = 10$$
$$v_C = 10$$
$$x_{2C}:\ u_2 + v_C = 11$$
$$u_2 + 10 = 11$$
$$u_2 = 1$$
$$x_{3A}:\ u_3 + v_A = 4$$
$$u_3 + 6 = 4$$
$$u_3 = -2$$
$$x_{3B}:\ u_3 + v_B = 5$$
$$-2 + v_B = 5$$
$$v_B = 7$$

These new u_i and v_j values are shown in Table 7.31.

TABLE 7.31
The New u_i and v_j Values for the Second Iteration

u_i	From \ To	v_j	$v_A = 6$ A	$v_B = 7$ B	$v_C = 10$ C	Supply
$u_1 = 0$	1		25 [6]	[8]	125 [10]	150
$u_2 = 1$	2		[7]	[11]	175 [11]	175
$u_3 = -2$	3		175 [4]	100 [5]	[12]	275
	Demand		200	100	300	600

The cost changes for the empty cells are now computed using the formula $c_{ij} - u_i - v_j = k_{ij}$.

$$x_{1B}:\ k_{1B} = c_{1B} - u_1 - v_B = 8 - 0 - 7 = +1$$
$$x_{2A}:\ k_{2A} = c_{2A} - u_2 - v_A = 7 - 1 - 6 = 0$$
$$x_{2B}:\ k_{2B} = c_{2B} - u_2 - v_B = 11 - 1 - 7 = +3$$
$$x_{3C}:\ k_{3C} = c_{3C} - u_3 - v_C = 12 - (-2) - 10 = +4$$

Computing the cost change for each unused route

Since none of these values is negative, the solution shown in Table 7.31 is optimal. However, as in the stepping-stone method, cell 2A with a zero cost change indicates a multiple optimal solution.

The steps of the modified distribution method can be summarized as follows.

Steps of MODI

1. Develop an initial solution using one of the three methods available.
2. Compute u_i and v_j values for each row and column by applying the formula $u_i + v_j = c_{ij}$ to each cell that has an allocation.

3. Compute the cost change, k_{ij}, for each empty cell using the formula $c_{ij} - u_i - v_j = k_{ij}$.
4. Allocate as much as possible to the empty cell that will result in the greatest net decrease in cost $(-k_{ij})$. Allocate according to the stepping-stone path for the selected cell.
5. Repeat steps 2 through 4 until all k_{ij} values are positive or zero.

The Unbalanced Transportation Model

Thus far, the methods for determining an initial solution and an optimal solution have been demonstrated within the context of a balanced transportation model. Realistically, however, an *unbalanced problem* is a more likely occurrence. Consider our example of transporting wheat. By changing the demand at Cincinnati to 350 tons, we create a situation in which total demand is 650 tons and total supply is 600 tons.

Demand exceeds supply

Inserting a dummy row

In order to compensate for this difference in the transportation tableau, a "dummy" row is added to the tableau, as shown in Table 7.32.

TABLE 7.32
An Unbalanced Model (Demand > Supply)

To From	A	B	C	Supply
1	6	8	10	150
2	7	11	11	175
3	4	5	12	275
Dummy	0	0	0	50
Demand	200	100	350	650

The dummy row is assigned a supply of 50 tons to balance the model. The additional 50 tons demanded, which cannot be supplied, will be allocated to a cell in the dummy row. The transportation costs for the cells in the dummy row are zero, since the tons allocated to these cells are not amounts really transported, but the amounts by which demand was not met. These dummy cells are, in effect, *slack variables*.

Supply exceeds demand

Inserting a dummy column

Now consider our example with the supply at Des Moines increased to 375 tons. This increases total supply to 700 tons, while total demand remains at 600 tons. To compensate for this imbalance, we add a dummy column instead of a dummy row, as shown in Table 7.33.

TABLE 7.33
An Unbalanced Model (Supply > Demand)

From \ To	A	B	C	Dummy	Supply
1	6	8	10	0	150
2	7	11	11	0	175
3	4	5	12	0	375
Demand	200	100	300	100	700

The addition of a dummy row or a dummy column has no effect on the initial solution methods or on the methods for determining an optimal solution. The dummy row or column cells are treated the same as any other tableau cell. For example, in the minimum cell cost method, three cells would be tied for the minimum cost cell, each with a cost of zero. In this case (or any time there is a tie between cells) the tie would be broken arbitrarily.

Degeneracy

In all the tableaus showing a solution to the wheat transportation problem, the following condition was met.

m rows $+ n$ columns $- 1 =$ the number of cells with allocations

For example, in any of the balanced tableaus for wheat transportation, the number of rows was 3 (i.e., $m = 3$) and the number of columns was 3 (i.e., $n = 3$); thus,

$3 + 3 - 1 = 5$ cells with allocations

These tableaus always had five cells with allocations; thus, our condition for normal solution was met. When this condition is not met and fewer than $m + n - 1$ cells have allocations, the tableau is said to be *degenerate*.

Violation of the $m + n - 1$ condition

Consider the wheat transportation example with the supply values changed to the amounts shown in Table 7.34. The initial solution shown in this tableau was developed using the minimum cell cost method.

The tableau shown in Table 7.34 does not meet the condition

$m + n - 1 =$ the number of cells with allocations
$3 + 3 - 1 = 5$ cells

since there are only four cells with allocations. The difficulty resulting from a degenerate basic feasible solution is that neither the stepping-stone method nor MODI will work unless the above condi-

The difficulties resulting from a degenerate solution

TABLE 7.34
The Minimum Cell Cost Initial Solution

From \ To	A	B	C	Supply
1	6	8 100	10 50	150
2	7	11	11 250	250
3	4 200	5	12	200
Demand	200	100	300	600

tion is met (there is an appropriate number of cells with allocations). When the tableau is degenerate, a closed path cannot be completed for all cells in the stepping-stone method, *and* all the $u_i + v_j = c_{ij}$ computations cannot be completed in MODI. For example, a closed path cannot be determined for cell 1A in Table 7.34.

Artificially creating an allocated-to cell

To create a closed path, one of the empty cells must be artificially designated as a cell with an allocation. Cell 1A in Table 7.35 is designated arbitrarily as a cell with an artificial allocation of "0". This indicates that this cell will be treated as a cell with an allocation in determining stepping-stone paths or MODI formulas, although there is no real allocation in this cell. Notice that the location of 0 was *arbitrary*, since there is no general rule for allocating the artificial cell. Allocating 0 to a cell does not guarantee that all of the stepping-stone paths can be determined. For example, if 0 had been allocated to cell 2B instead of to cell 1A, none of the stepping-stone paths could have been determined, even though technically the tableau would no longer be degenerate. In such a case, the 0 must be reallocated to another cell and all paths determined again. This process must be repeated until an artificial allocation has been made that will enable the determination of all paths. In most cases, however, there is more than one possible cell to which such an allocation can be made.

TABLE 7.35
The Initial Solution

From \ To	A	B	C	Supply
1	6 0	8 100	10 50	150
2	7	11	11 250	250
3	4 200	5	12	200
Demand	200	100	300	600

The stepping-stone paths and cost changes for this tableau are shown below.

$$2A \quad 2C \quad 1C \quad 1A$$
$$x_{2A}: 7 - 11 + 10 - 6 = 0$$
$$2B \quad 2C \quad 1C \quad 1B$$
$$x_{2B}: 11 - 11 + 10 - 8 = +2$$
$$3B \quad 1B \quad 1A \quad 3A$$
$$x_{3B}: 5 - 8 + 6 - 4 = -1$$
$$3C \quad 1C \quad 1A \quad 3A$$
$$x_{3C}: 12 - 10 + 6 - 4 = +4$$

Since cell 3B shows a $1 decrease in cost for every ton of wheat allocated to it, we will allocate 100 tons to cell 3B. This results in the tableau shown in Table 7.36.

TABLE 7.36
The Second Stepping-Stone Iteration

From \ To	A		B		C		Supply
1	100	6		8	50	10	150
2		7		11	250	11	250
3	100	4	100	5		12	200
Demand	200		100		300		600

Notice that the solution in Table 7.36 now meets the condition $m + n - 1 = 5$. Thus, in applying the stepping-stone method (or MODI) to this tableau, it is not necessary to make an artificial allocation to an empty cell. It is quite possible to begin the solution process with a normal tableau and have it become degenerate or begin with a degenerate tableau and have it become normal. If it had been indicated that the cell with the 0 should have units subtracted from it, no actual units could have been subtracted. In that case the 0 would have been moved to the cell that represents the entering variable. (The solution shown in Table 7.36 is optimal; however, a multiple optimal solution exists at cell 2A.)

Prohibited Routes

Sometimes one or more of the routes in the transportation model are *prohibited*. That is, units cannot be transported from a particular source to a particular destination. When this situation occurs, we must make sure that no units in the optimal solution are allocated to

Routes over which units cannot be transported

the cell representing this route. In our study of the simplex tableau, we learned that assigning a large coefficient of M to an artificial variable would keep it out of the final solution. This same principle can be used in a transportation model for a prohibited route. A value of M is assigned as the transportation cost for a cell that represents a prohibited route. Thus, when the prohibited cell is evaluated, it will always contain a large positive cost change of M, which will keep it from being selected as an entering variable.

COMPUTERIZED SOLUTION OF A TRANSPORTATION PROBLEM

Since the transportation model is a linear programming model, it can be solved using the LINDO/PC computer package introduced in Chapter 4. The LINDO/PC solution of a transportation problem will be demonstrated using the wheat shipping problem solved earlier in this chapter with the stepping-stone and MODI methods. We will employ both LINDO/PC and the QSB+ software package (employed in Chapter 3) to demonstrate the computerized solution of a transportation problem. LINDO/PC solves the transportation model as a linear programming model whereas QSB+ solves the model in the same format followed in this chapter, i.e., the transportation tableau, minimum cell cost initial solution and MODI solution. The two computer approaches demonstrate how different packages can be used depending on availability, as well as indicating the advantages and disadvantages of each type of computerized approach.

The LINDO/PC input and output for this problem follow.

```
: look all

MIN      6 X1A + 8 X1B + 10 X1C + 7 X2A + 11 X2B + 11 X2C + 4 X3A + 5 X3B
       + 12 X3C
SUBJECT TO
       2)    X1A + X1B + X1C =      150
       3)    X2A + X2B + X2C =      175
       4)    X3A + X3B + X3C =      275
       5)    X1A + X2A + X3A =      200
       6)    X1B + X2B + X3B =      100
       7)    X1C + X2C + X3C =      300
END

:
```

```
           OBJECTIVE FUNCTION VALUE

   1)          4525.00000

      VARIABLE         VALUE          REDUCED COST
         X1A         25.000000           .000000
         X1B           .000000          1.000000
         X1C        125.000000           .000000
         X2A           .000000           .000000
         X2B           .000000          3.000000
         X2C        175.000000           .000000
         X3A        175.000000           .000000
         X3B        100.000000           .000000
         X3C           .000000          4.000000


         ROW    SLACK OR SURPLUS      DUAL PRICES
          2)          .000000        -10.000000
          3)          .000000        -11.000000
          4)          .000000         -8.000000
          5)          .000000          4.000000
          6)          .000000          3.000000
          7)          .000000           .000000

      NO. ITERATIONS=       5
```

The optimal solution

Notice that the optimal solution generated by the LINDO/PC program is identical to the solution shown in Table 7.27 and identified as the alternative optimal solution.

Next we will solve the same problem using the QSB+ software package introduced in Chapter 3. The solution output is in a tableau form very similar to that used in this chapter. The initial solution is obtained using the minimum cell cost method (which is referred to by the software as "MM," for minimum matrix) and the MODI solution approach. The solution iterations very closely follow Tables 7.28 through 7.31 in this chapter. Although this output is visually preferable to that of LINDO/PC, the software is limited in displaying tableaus to problems in which the number of sources is less than five and the number of destinations less than six. For a problem of greater dimensions, only the final solution is provided.

Initial solution by MM

SN \ DN	A		B		C		Supplies	U(i)
1	+6.000		+8.000		+10.00		+150.0	+125.0
				+25.00		+125.0		
2	+7.000		+11.00		+11.00		+175.0	0
						+175.0		
3	+4.000		+5.000		+12.00		+275.0	+75.00
	+200.0		+75.00					
Demands	+200.0		+100.0		+300.0			
V(j)	+200.0		+25.00		+175.0			

Minimum Value of OBJ = 4550

Iteration 1

SN \ DN	A		B		C		Supplies	U(i)
1	+6.000		+8.000		+10.00		+150.0	0
	**		+25.00		+125.0			
2	+7.000		+11.00		+11.00		+175.0	+1.000
						+175.0		
3	+4.000		+5.000		+12.00		+275.0	-3.000
	+200.0		+75.00					
Demands	+200.0		+100.0		+300.0			
V(j)	+7.000		+8.000		+10.00			

Current Minimum Value of OBJ = 4550 with e(1, 1) =-1

Final tableau (Total iterations = 1)

SN \ DN	A		B		C		Supplies	U(i)
1	+6.000		+8.000		+10.00		+150.0	0
	+25.00				+125.0			
2	+7.000		+11.00		+11.00		+175.0	+1.000
						+175.0		
3	+4.000		+5.000		+12.00		+275.0	-2.000
	+175.0		+100.0					
Demands	+200.0		+100.0		+300.0			
V(j)	+6.000		+7.000		+10.00			

Minimum Value of OBJ = 4525 with multiple optimals.

```
        The optimal solution has been found. Press any key to continue.


    |                Summary of Results for Wheat Shipments     Page : 1      |
    |------------------------------------------------------------------------|
    |From |To   |Shipment|@ cost |Opp.Ct.||From |To   |Shipment|@ cost |Opp.Ct.|
    |------------------------------------------------------------------------|
    |1    |A    |+25.000 |+6.0000|      0||2    |C    |+175.00 |+11.000|      0|
    |1    |B    |      0 |+8.0000|+1.0000||3    |A    |+175.00 |+4.0000|      0|
    |1    |C    |+125.00 |+10.000|      0||3    |B    |+100.00 |+5.0000|      0|
    |2    |A    |      0 |+7.0000|      0||3    |C    |      0 |+12.000|+4.0000|
    |2    |B    |      0 |+11.000|+3.0000||     |     |        |       |       |
    |------------------------------------------------------------------------|
    |     Minimum value of OBJ =   4525 (multiple sols.)  Iterations = 1      |
```

THE ASSIGNMENT MODEL

The assignment model is a special form of a linear programming model that is similar to the transportation model. In the assignment model, however, the supply at each source and the demand at each destination are each limited to one unit.

A transportation model in which the supply at each source and demand at each destination are one

The following example will be used to demonstrate the assignment model and its special solution method. The Atlantic Coast Conference has four basketball games on a particular night. The conference office wants to assign four teams of officials to the four games in a way that will minimize the total distance traveled by the officials. The distances in miles for each team of officials to each game location are shown in Table 7.37.

An assignment model example

TABLE 7.37
The Travel Distances to Each Game for Each Team of Officials

Officials	Game Sites			
	Raleigh	Atlanta	Durham	Clemson
A	210	90	180	160
B	100	70	130	200
C	175	105	140	170
D	80	65	105	120

The supply is always one team of officials, and the demand is for only one team of officials at each game. Table 7.37 is already in the proper form for the assignment tableau. Since supply and demand are always one, it is not necessary to include supply and demand rows in the tableau.

Developing an opportunity cost table

Row reductions

The first step in the assignment method of solution is to develop an *opportunity cost table*. We accomplish this by first subtracting the minimum value in each row from every other value in the row. These computations are referred to as *row reductions*. We applied a similar principle in the VAM method when we determined penalty costs. In other words, the best course of action is determined for each row, and the penalty or "lost opportunity" is developed for all other row values. The row reductions for this example are shown in Table 7.38.

TABLE 7.38
The Assignment Tableau with Row Reductions

Officials	Game Sites			
	Raleigh	Atlanta	Durham	Clemson
A	120	0	90	70
B	30	0	60	130
C	70	0	35	65
D	15	0	40	55

Column reductions

Next, the minimum value in each column is subtracted from all other column values. These computations are called *column reductions* and are shown in Table 7.39.

TABLE 7.39
The Tableau with Column Reductions

Officials	Game Sites			
	Raleigh	Atlanta	Durham	Clemson
A	105	0	55	15
B	15	0	25	75
C	55	0	0	10
D	0	0	5	0

Unique assignments reflect an optimal solution

Table 7.39 represents the completed opportunity cost table for our example. Assignments can be made in this table wherever a zero is present. For example, team A can be assigned to Atlanta. An *optimal solution* results when each of the four teams can be uniquely assigned to a different game.

Notice in Table 7.39 that the assignment of team A to Atlanta means that no other team can be assigned to that game. Once this assignment is made, the zero in row B is infeasible, which indicates that there is not a unique optimal assignment for team B. Therefore, Table 7.39 does not contain an optimal solution.

A test to determine if four unique assignments exist in Table 7.39 is to draw the minimum number of horizontal or vertical lines necessary to cross out all zeros through the rows and columns of the table. For example, Table 7.40 shows that three lines are required to cross out all zeros.

The line test for determining the number of unique assignments available

TABLE 7.40

The Opportunity Cost Table with the Line Test

Officials	Raleigh	Game Sites Atlanta	Durham	Clemson
A	105	0	55	15
B	15	0	25	75
C	55	0	0	10
D	0	0	5	0

The three lines indicate that there are only three unique assignments, whereas four are required for an optimal solution. (Note that even if the three lines could have been drawn differently, the subsequent solution method would not be affected.) Next, subtract the minimum value that is not crossed out from all other values not crossed out. Then add this minimum value to those cells where two lines intersect. The minimum value not crossed out in Table 7.40 is 15. The second iteration for this model with the appropriate changes is shown in Table 7.41.

An assignment model iteration

TABLE 7.41

The Second Iteration

Officials	Raleigh	Game Sites Atlanta	Durham	Clemson
A	90	0	40	0
B	0	0	10	60
C	55	15	0	10
D	0	15	5	0

No matter how the lines are drawn in Table 7.41, at least four are required to cross out all the zeros. This indicates that four unique assignments can be made and that an optimal solution has been reached. Now let us make the assignments from Table 7.41.

First, team A can be assigned to either the Atlanta game or the Clemson game. We will assign team A to Atlanta first. This means

The optimal solution

that team A cannot be assigned to any other game, and no other team can be assigned to Atlanta. Therefore, row A and the Atlanta column can be eliminated. Next, team B is assigned to Raleigh. (Team B cannot be assigned to Atlanta, which has already been eliminated.) The third assignment is of team C to the Durham game. This leaves team D for the Clemson game. These assignments and their respective distances (from Table 7.37) are summarized as follows.

	Distance
Team A → Atlanta	90
Team B → Raleigh	100
Team C → Durham	140
Team D → Clemson	120
	450 miles

An alternative optimal solution

Now let us go back and make the initial assignment of team A to Clemson (the alternative assignment we did not initially make). This will result in the following set of assignments.

	Distance
Team A → Clemson	160
Team B → Atlanta	70
Team C → Durham	140
Team D → Raleigh	80
	450 miles

These two assignments represent *multiple optimal solutions* for our example problem. Both assignments will result in the officials' traveling a minimum total distance of 450 miles.

An unbalanced assignment problem

Adding a dummy column

Like a transportation problem, an assignment model can be unbalanced when supply exceeds demand or demand exceeds supply. For example, assume that instead of four teams of officials, there are five teams, to be assigned to the four games. In this case a *dummy column* is added to the assignment tableau to balance the model, as shown in Table 7.42.

TABLE 7.42
An Unbalanced Assignment Tableau with a Dummy Column

Officials	Game Sites				
	Raleigh	Atlanta	Durham	Clemson	Dummy
A	210	90	180	160	0
B	100	70	130	200	0
C	175	105	140	170	0
D	80	65	105	120	0
E	95	115	120	100	0

In solving this model, one team of officials would be assigned to the dummy column. If there were five games and only four teams of officials, a *dummy row* would be added instead of a dummy column. The addition of a dummy row or column does not affect the solution method.

Adding a dummy row

Prohibited assignments are also possible in an assignment problem, just as prohibited routes can occur in a transportation model. In the transportation model, an M value was assigned as the cost for the cell representing the prohibited route. This same method is used for a prohibited assignment. A value of M is placed in the cell that represents the prohibited assignment.

The steps of the assignment solution method are summarized below.

Steps of the assignment solution method

1. Perform row reductions by subtracting the minimum value in each row from all other row values.
2. Perform column reductions by subtracting the minimum value in each column from all other column values.
3. In the completed opportunity cost table, cross out all zeros using the minimum number of horizontal and/or vertical lines.
4. If fewer than m lines are required (where m = the number of rows or columns), subtract the minimum uncrossed value from all other uncrossed values, and add this same minimum value to all cells where two lines intersect. Leave all other values unchanged, and repeat step 3.
5. If m lines are required, the tableau contains the optimal solution and m unique assignments can be made. If fewer than m lines are required, repeat step 4.

COMPUTERIZED SOLUTION OF AN ASSIGNMENT PROBLEM

Both the LINDO/PC and QSB+ computer software packages can be used to solve assignment problems just as the transportation problem was solved. The QSB+ solution output for our example of assigning ACC officials to game sites, which appears on page 246, is almost identical to the solution format shown in Tables 7.37 through 7.41. (The notation "Cov.Ln" refers to the covering lines across the row and column zeros.)

On page 247 is the LINDO/PC computer solution for the same example. The problem is solved as a linear programming model, and for this reason the model input process is somewhat more tedious than with QSB+. The solution required 11 simplex iterations, so only the model and final solution are shown.

Initial tableau

Ob\Tk	Ral	Atl	Dur	Clem	Cov.Ln
A	+210.0	+90.00	+180.0	+160.0	
B	+100.0	+70.00	+130.0	+200.0	
C	+175.0	+105.0	+140.0	+170.0	
D	+80.00	+65.00	+105.0	+120.0	
Cov.Ln					

Iteration 1

Ob\Tk	Ral	Atl	Dur	Clem	Cov.Ln
A	+105.0	0	+55.00	+15.00	
B	+15.00	0	+25.00	+75.00	
C	+55.00	0	0	+10.00	<--
D	0	0	+5.000	0	<--
Cov.Ln		∧			

Iteration 2

Ob\Tk	Ral	Atl	Dur	Clem	Cov.Ln
A	+90.00	0	+40.00	0	
B	0	0	+10.00	+60.00	
C	+55.00	+15.00	0	+10.00	<--
D	0	+15.00	+5.000	0	
Cov.Ln	∧	∧		∧	

Summary of Assignments for ACC Officials Page: 1					
Object	Task	Cost/Prof.	Object	Task	Cost/Prof.
A	Clem	+160.0	C	Dur	+140.0
B	Atl	+70.00	D	Ral	+80.00
Minimum value of OBJ = 450 Total iterations = 2					

```
MIN      210 XAR + 90 XAA + 180 XAD + 160 XAC + 100 XBR + 70 XBA
         + 130 XBD + 200 XBC + 175 XCR + 105 XCA + 140 XCD + 170 XCC + 80 XDR
         + 65 XDA + 105 XDD + 120 XDC
SUBJECT TO
        2)    XAR + XAA + XAD + XAC =      1
        3)    XBR + XBA + XBD + XBC =      1
        4)    XCR + XCA + XCD + XCC =      1
        5)    XDR + XDA + XDD + XDC =      1
        6)    XAR + XBR + XCR + WDR =      1
        7)    XAA + XBA + XCA + XDA =      1
        8)    XAD + XBD + XCD + XDD =      1
        9)    XAC + XBC + XCC + XDC =      1
END

:


              OBJECTIVE FUNCTION VALUE

   1)         450.000000


       VARIABLE           VALUE
          XAR            .000000
          XAA            .000000
          XAD            .000000
          XAC           1.000000
          XBR            .000000
          XBA           1.000000
          XBD            .000000
          XBC            .000000
          XCR            .000000
          XCA            .000000
          XCD           1.000000
          XCC            .000000
          XDR           1.000000
          XDA            .000000
          XDD            .000000
          XDC            .000000
```

APPLICATION OF A TRANSPORTATION MODEL

A Transportation Model for Transporting Military Inductees

Thailand inducts men into its compulsory military service four times per year. Men living in the coastal provinces are inducted into the Navy. When drafted, they first report to one of 36 draft centers and then are transported to one of four branch bases; subsequently they are shipped to the main base at Sattahep. This process presents two problems. First, how many men from each draft center should be transported to each branch base, so that transportation costs will be minimized? Second, given a fleet of ships at the main base, which ships should be used and how should they be routed to transport men from the branch bases to the main base? The first problem is a straightforward transportation problem, with the drafting centers as sources and the branch bases as destinations. The optimal results of the first problem (i.e., the numbers of men assigned to each base) are subsequently used as input to the second problem, referred to as a vehicle-routing problem, which is solved using an integer programming formulation.[1]

Summary

In this chapter two special types of linear programming problems were presented: the transportation problem and the assignment problem. The various solution methods for each type of problem were demonstrated using examples. A unique characteristic of the solutions to these problems is that they contain *integer* values rather than fractional values. The solution methods for these problems ensure integer solutions. Linear programming problems other than transportation problems often require integer solutions. Since the general simplex solution method does not ensure integer solutions, other approaches have been developed for generating integer solutions for problems requiring them. These integer solution approaches are the subject of Chapter 8.

Integer solution values

References

Ackoff, R. L., and Sasieni, M. W. *Fundamentals of Operations Research*. New York: John Wiley and Sons, 1968.

Charnes, A., and Cooper, W. W. *Management Models and Industrial Applications of Linear Programming*. New York: John Wiley and Sons, 1961.

Churchman, C. W.; Ackoff, R. L.; and Arnoff, E. L. *Introduction to Operations Research*. New York: John Wiley and Sons, 1957.

Hillier, F. S., and Lieberman, G. J. *Introduction to Operations Research*. 4th ed. San Francisco: Holden-Day, 1986.

Hitchcock, F. L. "The Distribution of a Product from Several Sources to Numerous Localities." *Journal of Mathematics and Physics* 20 (1941): 224, 230.

Hoffmann, T. R. *Production: Management and Manufacturing Systems*. Belmont, Calif.: Wadsworth, 1967.

Koopmans, T. C., ed. *Activity Analysis of Production and Allocation*. Cowles Commission Monograph No. 13. New York: John Wiley and Sons, 1951.

Kwak, N. K. *Mathematical Programming with Business Applications*. New York: McGraw-Hill, 1973.

[1]P. Choypeng, P. Puakpong, and R. Rosenthal, "Optimal Ship Routing and Personnel Assignment for Naval Recruitment in Thailand," *Interfaces* 16, no. 4 (July-August 1986): 47–52.

Lee, Sang M.; Moore, Laurence J.; and Taylor, Bernard W. *Management Science*. 3d ed. Boston: Allyn and Bacon, 1990.

Levin, R. I., and Lamone, R. *Linear Programming for Management Decisions.* Homewood, Ill.: Irwin, 1969.

Llewellyn, R. W. *Linear Programming.* New York: Holt, Rinehart and Winston, 1964.

Orchard-Hays, W. *Advanced Linear Programming Computing Techniques.* New York: McGraw-Hill, 1968.

Taha, H. A. *Operations Research.* 4th ed. New York: Macmillan Co., 1987.

EXAMPLE PROBLEM SOLUTION

This example will demonstrate the procedure for solving a transportation problem.

Problem Statement

A concrete company transports concrete from three plants to three construction sites. The supply capacities of the three plants, the demand requirements at the three sites, and the transportation costs per ton are as follows:

Plant	Construction Site			Supply (tons)
	A	B	C	
1	$ 8	5	6	120
2	15	10	12	80
3	3	9	10	80
Demand (tons)	150	70	60	280

Determine the initial solution to this problem using the minimum cell cost method, and solve the problem using the stepping-stone method.

Step 1: The Initial Solution

The initial solution, obtained using the minimum cell cost method, is shown below.

From \ To	A	B	C	Supply
1	8	5 70	6 50	120
2	15 70	10	12 10	80
3	3 80	9	10	80
Demand	150	70	60	280

Step 2: Solve Using the Stepping-Stone Method

From \ To	A	B	C	Supply
1	−1 [8]	[5] 70	[6] 50	120
2	[15] 70	−1 [10]	[12] 10	80
3	[3] 80	+10 [9]	+10 [10]	80
Demand	150	70	60	280

Allocate 50 tons to cell 1A.

From \ To	A	B	C	Supply
1	[8] 50	[5] 70	+1 [6]	120
2	[15] 20	−2 [10]	[12] 60	80
3	[3] 80	+9 [9]	+10 [10]	80
Demand	150	70	60	280

Allocate 20 tons to cell 2B.

From \ To	A	B	C	Supply
1	[8] 70	[5] 50	−1 [6]	120
2	+2 [15]	[10] 20	[12] 60	80
3	[3] 80	+9 [9]	+8 [10]	80
Demand	150	70	60	280

Allocate 50 tons to cell 1C.

From \ To	A	B	C	Supply
1	[8] +1	[5] 70	[6] 50	120
2	+1 [15]	[10] 70	[12] 10	80
3	[3] 80	+10 [9]	+9 [10]	80
Demand	150	70	60	280

The solution shown above is optimal:

$$x_{1A} = 70 \qquad x_{2B} = 70 \qquad x_{3A} = 80$$
$$x_{1C} = 50 \qquad x_{2C} = 10$$
$$Z = \$1,920$$

Problems

1. Given the following transportation tableau, determine the initial solution using the northwest corner method, the minimum cell cost method, and Vogels Approximation Method (VAM), and compute the total cost for each.

From \ To	A	B	C	Supply
1	10	9	5	60
2	6	8	7	30
3	4	3	2	60
Demand	40	40	70	150

2. Given the following transportation tableau and solution, determine the optimal solution using the stepping-stone method.

From \ To	A	B	C	Supply
1	7	5 / 30	9 / 120	150
2	10 / 100	12	10 / 100	200
3	6	3 / 50	14	50
Demand	100	80	220	400

3. Green Valley Mills produces carpet at plants in St. Louis and Richmond. The carpet is then shipped to two outlets located in Chicago and Atlanta. The cost per ton of shipping carpet from each of the two plants to the two warehouses is as follows.

From	To Chicago	Atlanta
St. Louis	$40	65
Richmond	70	30

The plant at St. Louis can supply 250 tons of carpet per week; the plant at Richmond can supply 400 tons per week. The Chicago outlet has a demand of 300 tons per week, and the outlet at Atlanta demands 350 tons per week. The company wants to know the number of tons of carpet to ship from each plant to each outlet in order to minimize the total shipping cost. Solve this transportation problem.

4. Solve the following transportation problem.

From \ To	1	2	3	Supply
A	7	10	9	35
B	12	5	4	20
C	8	3	11	60
Demand	40	45	30	115

5. A transportation problem involves the following costs, supply, and demand.

From	To 1	2	3	4	Supply
1	$ 7	6	2	12	70
2	3	9	8	7	40
3	10	4	11	5	100
Demand	30	60	90	30	

a. Find the initial solution using the northwest corner method, the minimum cell cost method, and Vogel's Approximation Method. Compute total cost for each.
b. Using the VAM initial solution, find the optimal solution using the stepping-stone method. Compute total minimum cost for the solution.

6. A transportation problem involves the following costs, supply, and demand.

From	To 1	2	3	4	Supply
1	$500	750	300	450	12
2	650	800	400	600	17
3	400	700	500	550	11
Demand	10	10	10	10	

a. Find the initial solution using the northwest corner method, the minimum cell cost method, and Vogel's Approximation Method. Compute total cost for each.
b. Using the VAM initial solution, find the optimal solution using the modified distribution method (MODI).

7. Consider the following transportation tableau and solution.

From \ To	A		B		C		Supply
1		12		10	600	6	600
2	400	4		15		3	400
3	300	9		7		M	300
4		11	500	8	300	6	800
Dummy	200	0		0		0	200
Demand	900		500		900		2300

a. Is this a balanced or an unbalanced transportation problem? Explain.
b. Is this solution degenerate? Explain. If it is degenerate, show how it would be put into proper form.
c. Is there a prohibited route in this problem?
d. Compute the total cost of this solution.
e. What is the value of x_{2B} in this solution?

8. Solve the following transportation problem.

From	To 1	2	3	Supply
1	$ 40	10	20	800
2	15	20	10	500
3	20	25	30	600
Demand	1050	500	650	

9. Given a transportation problem with the following costs, supply, and demand, find the initial solution using the minimum cell cost method and Vogel's Approximation Method. Is the VAM solution optimal?

From	To 1	2	3	Supply
A	$ 6	7	4	100
B	5	3	6	180
C	8	5	7	200
Demand	135	175	170	

10. Consider the following transportation problem.

From	To 1	2	3	Supply
A	$ 6	9	M	130
B	12	3	5	70
C	4	8	11	100
Demand	80	110	60	

a. Find the initial solution using VAM and solve using the stepping-stone method.
b. Formulate this problem as a general linear programming model.

11. Solve the following linear programming problem.

minimize
$$Z = 3x_{11} + 12x_{12} + 8x_{13} + 10x_{21} + 5x_{22} + 6x_{23} + 6x_{31} + 7x_{32} + 10x_{33}$$
subject to
$$x_{11} + x_{12} + x_{13} = 90$$
$$x_{21} + x_{22} + x_{23} = 30$$
$$x_{31} + x_{32} + x_{33} = 100$$
$$x_{11} + x_{21} + x_{31} \leq 70$$
$$x_{12} + x_{22} + x_{32} \leq 110$$
$$x_{13} + x_{23} + x_{33} \leq 80$$
$$x_{ij} \geq 0$$

12. Consider the following transportation problem.

From	To A	B	C	D	Supply
1	$ 5	12	7	10	50
2	4	6	7	6	50
3	2	8	5	3	60
Demand	40	20	30	70	

a. Find the initial solution using the northwest corner method, the minimum cell cost method, and VAM. Compute the cost for each method.

b. Solve using the VAM initial solution and MODI.

13. Consider the following transportation problem.

From	To 1	To 2	To 3	Supply
A	$ 6	9	7	130
B	12	3	5	70
C	4	8	11	100
Demand	80	110	60	

a. Find the initial solution using the minimum cell cost method.
b. Solve using the stepping-stone method.

14. Steel mills in three cities produce the following amounts of steel:

Location	Weekly Production (tons)
A. Bethlehem	150
B. Birmingham	210
C. Gary	320
	680

These mills supply steel to four cities where manufacturing plants have the following demand.

Location	Weekly Demand (tons)
1. Detroit	130
2. St. Louis	70
3. Chicago	180
4. Norfolk	240
	620

Shipping costs per ton of steel are as follows.

From	To 1	To 2	To 3	To 4
A	$14	9	16	18
B	11	8	7	16
C	16	12	10	22

Because of a truckers' strike, shipments are presently prohibited from Birmingham to Chicago.

a. Set up a transportation tableau for this problem and determine the initial solution. Identify the method used to find the initial solution.
b. Solve this problem using MODI.

c. Are there multiple optimum solutions? Explain. If so, identify them.

d. Formulate this problem as a general linear programming model.

15. Tobacco is stored in warehouses in four cities at the end of each growing season.

Location	Capacity (tons)
A. Charlotte	90
B. Raleigh	50
C. Lexington	80
D. Danville	60
	280

These warehouses supply the following amounts of tobacco to cigarette companies in three cities.

Plant	Demand (tons)
1. Richmond	120
2. Winston-Salem	100
3. Durham	110
	330

The railroad shipping costs per ton of tobacco are shown below.

From	To 1	2	3
A	$ 7	10	5
B	12	9	4
C	7	3	11
D	9	5	7

Because of railroad construction, shipments are presently prohibited from Charlotte to Richmond.

a. Set up the transportation tableau for this problem and determine the initial solution using VAM and compute total cost.

b. Solve using MODI.

c. Are there multiple optimal solutions? Explain. If there are alternative solutions, identify them.

d. Formulate this problem as a linear programming model.

16. Below is a linear programming problem.

minimize
$$Z = 17x_{11} + 10x_{12} + 15x_{13} + 11x_{21} + 14x_{22} + 10x_{23} + 9x_{31} + 13x_{32} + 11x_{33} + 19x_{41} + 8x_{42} + 12x_{43}$$

subject to

$$x_{11} + x_{12} + x_{13} = 120$$
$$x_{21} + x_{22} + x_{23} = 70$$
$$x_{31} + x_{32} + x_{33} = 180$$
$$x_{41} + x_{42} + x_{43} = 30$$
$$x_{11} + x_{21} + x_{31} + x_{41} = 200$$
$$x_{12} + x_{22} + x_{32} + x_{42} = 120$$
$$x_{13} + x_{23} + x_{33} + x_{43} = 80$$
$$x_{ij} \geq 0$$

a. Set up the transportation tableau for this problem and determine the initial solution using VAM.
b. Solve using the stepping-stone method.

17. Oranges are grown, picked, and then stored in warehouses in Tampa, Miami, and Fresno. These warehouses supply oranges to markets in New York, Philadelphia, Chicago, and Boston. The following table shows the shipping costs per truckload ($100s), supply, and demand.

From	To New York	Philadelphia	Chicago	Boston	Supply
Tampa	$ 9	14	12	17	200
Miami	11	10	6	10	200
Fresno	12	8	15	7	200
Demand	130	170	100	150	

Because of an agreement between distributors, shipments are prohibited from Miami to Chicago.

a. Set up the transportation tableau for this problem and determine the initial solution using the minimum cell cost method.
b. Solve using MODI.
c. Are there multiple optimum solutions? Explain. If so, identify them.
d. Formulate this problem as a linear programming model.

18. A transportation problem involves the following supply, demand, and costs.

From	To A	B	C	Supply
1	$ 7	10	6	300
2	4	9	8	150
3	5	7	5	400
Demand	200	400	350	

a. Set up the transportation tableau for this problem and find the initial solution by the northwest corner method, the minimum cell cost method, and VAM. Compute the cost for each method.
b. Using the VAM initial solution, solve the problem using the stepping-stone method.

19. A manufacturing firm produces diesel engines in four cities — Phoenix, Seattle, St. Louis, and Detroit. The company is able to produce the following numbers of engines per month.

Plant	Production
1. Phoenix	5
2. Seattle	25
3. St. Louis	20
4. Detroit	25

Three trucking firms purchase the following numbers of engines for their plants in three cities.

Firm	Demand
A. Greensboro	10
B. Charlotte	20
C. Louisville	15

The transportation costs per engine ($100s) from sources to destinations are shown below.

	To		
From	A	B	C
1	$ 7	8	5
2	6	10	6
3	10	4	5
4	3	9	11

However, the Charlotte firm will not accept engines made in Seattle, and the Louisville firm will not accept engines from Detroit; therefore, these routes are prohibited.

a. Set up the transportation tableau for this problem. Find the initial solution using VAM.
b. Solve for the optimal solution using the stepping-stone method. Compute the total minimum cost.
c. Formulate this problem as a linear programming model.

20. Consider the following transportation problem.

From	To A	B	C	D	Supply
1	$12	10	9	15	36
2	10	8	2	10	25
3	9	5	13	8	30
Demand	26	40	25	30	

a. Find the initial solution using the northwest corner method.
b. Solve using the stepping-stone method.

21. The Interstate Truck Rental firm has accumulated extra trucks at three of its truck leasing outlets, as shown below.

Leasing Outlet	Extra Trucks
1. Atlanta	70
2. St. Louis	115
3. Greensboro	60
	245

The firm also has four outlets with shortages of rental trucks, as follows.

Leasing Outlet	Truck Shortage
A. New Orleans	80
B. Cincinnati	50
C. Louisville	90
D. Pittsburgh	25
	245

The firm wants to transfer trucks from those outlets with extras to those with shortages at the minimum total cost. The following costs of transporting these trucks from city to city have been determined.

From	To A	B	C	D
1	$ 70	80	45	90
2	120	40	30	75
3	110	60	70	80

a. Find the initial solution using the minimum cell cost method.
b. Solve using the stepping-stone method.

22. The Shotz Beer Company has breweries in two cities; the breweries can supply the following numbers of barrels of draft beer to the company's distributors each month.

Brewery	Monthly Supply (barrels)
A. Tampa	3,500
B. St. Louis	5,000
	8,500

The distributors, spread throughout six states, have the following total monthly demand:

Distributor	Monthly Demand (barrels)
1. Tennessee	1,600
2. Georgia	1,800
3. North Carolina	1,500
4. South Carolina	950
5. Kentucky	1,250
6. Virginia	1,400
	8,500

The company must pay the following shipping costs per barrel:

From	To					
	1	2	3	4	5	6
A	$.50	.35	.60	.45	.80	.75
B	.25	.65	.40	.55	.20	.65

a. Find the initial solution using VAM.
b. Solve using the stepping-stone method.

23. Computers Unlimited sells microcomputers to universities and colleges on the east coast, and ships them from three distribution warehouses. The firm is able to supply the following numbers of microcomputers to the universities by the beginning of the academic year:

Distribution Warehouse	Supply (microcomputers)
1. Richmond	420
2. Atlanta	610
3. Washington, D.C.	340
	1,370

Four universities have ordered microcomputers that must be delivered and installed by the beginning of the academic year:

University	Demand (microcomputers)
A. Tech	520
B. A and M	250
C. State	400
D. Central	380
	1,550

The shipping and installation costs per microcomputer from each distributor to each university are as follows:

From	To A	B	C	D
1	$22	17	30	18
2	15	35	20	25
3	28	21	16	14

a. Find the initial solution using VAM.
b. Solve using MODI.

24. A large manufacturing company is closing three of its existing plants and intends to transfer some of its more skilled employees to three plants that will remain open. The number of employees available for transfer from each closing plant is as follows:

Closing Plant	Transferable Employees
1	60
2	105
3	70
	235

The following number of employees can be accommodated at the three plants remaining open:

Open Plants	Employees Demanded
A	45
B	90
C	35
	170

Each transferred employee will increase product output per day at each plant as follows:

From	To A	B	C
1	5	8	6
2	10	9	12
3	7	6	8

The company wants to transfer employees so as to ensure the maximum increase in product output.

a. Find the initial solution using VAM.
b. Solve using MODI.

25. A metal parts shop has three operators and three machines: a drill press, a lathe, and a grinder. Each operator is qualified to operate each machine. The following table shows the time (in minutes) required by each operator to produce a part on each machine.

	Machine		
Operator	Press	Lathe	Grinder
1	22	18	35
2	41	30	28
3	25	36	18

Determine the optimal assignment that will minimize the total machine time.

26. A plant has four operators to be assigned to four machines. The time (minutes) required by each worker to produce a product on each machine is shown below.

	Machine			
Operator	A	B	C	D
1	10	12	9	11
2	5	10	7	8
3	12	14	13	11
4	8	15	11	9

Determine the optimal assignment and compute total minimum time.

27. A shop has four machinists to be assigned to four machines. The hourly cost of having each machine operated by each machinist is as follows.

Machinist	Machine A	B	C	D
1	$12	11	8	14
2	10	9	10	8
3	14	8	7	11
4	6	8	10	9

However, because he does not have enough experience, machinist 3 cannot operate machine B.

a. Determine the optimal assignment and compute total minimum cost.
b. Formulate this problem as a general linear programming model.

28. The Omega pharmaceutical firm has five salespersons, whom the firm wants to assign to five sales regions. Given their various previous contacts, the salespersons are able to cover the regions in different amounts of time. The amount of time (days) required by each salesperson to cover each city is shown below.

Salesperson	Region A	B	C	D	E
1	17	10	15	16	20
2	12	9	16	9	14
3	11	16	14	15	12
4	14	10	10	18	17
5	13	12	9	15	11

Which salesperson should be assigned to each region in order to minimize total time? Identify the optimal assignments and compute total minimum time.

29. The Bunker Manufacturing firm has five employees and six machines, and wants to assign the employees to the machines so as to minimize cost. A cost table showing the cost incurred by each employee on each machine is given below.

Employee	Machine A	B	C	D	E	F
1	$12	7	20	14	8	10
2	10	14	13	20	9	11
3	5	3	6	9	7	10
4	9	11	7	16	9	10
5	10	6	14	8	10	12

Because of union rules regarding departmental transfers, employee 3 cannot be assigned to machine E and employee 4 cannot be assigned to machine B. Solve this problem, indicate the optimal assignment, and compute total minimum cost.

30. Given the following cost table for an assignment problem, determine the optimal assignment and compute total minimum cost. Identify all alternative solutions if there are multiple optimal solutions.

Operator	Machine A	B	C	D
1	$10	2	8	6
2	9	5	11	9
3	12	7	14	14
4	3	1	4	2

31. An electronics firm produces electronic components, which it supplies to various electrical manufacturers. Quality control records indicate that different employees produce different numbers of defective items. The average number of defects produced by each employee for each of six components is given in the following table.

Employee	Component A	B	C	D	E	F
1	30	24	16	26	30	22
2	22	28	14	30	20	13
3	18	16	25	14	12	22
4	14	22	18	23	21	30
5	25	18	14	16	16	28
6	32	14	10	14	18	20

Determine the optimal assignment that will minimize the total average number of defects per month.

32. A dispatcher for the Citywide Taxi Company presently has six taxicabs at different locations and five customers who have called for service. The mileage from each taxi's present location to each customer is shown below.

Cab	Customer 1	2	3	4	5
A	7	2	4	10	7
B	5	1	5	6	6
C	8	7	6	5	5
D	2	5	2	4	5
E	3	3	5	8	4
F	6	2	4	3	4

Determine the optimal assignment(s) that will minimize the total mileage traveled.

8

Integer Programming

In the linear programming models formulated and solved in the previous chapters, the implicit assumption was that solutions could be fractional (i.e., noninteger). Although the Colonial Pottery Company model in Chapter 4 generated an integer solution of 24 bowls and 8 mugs (Table 4.16), an integer solution is not generally guaranteed by the simplex method. If a noninteger solution, such as 23.73 bowls and 8.51 mugs, had resulted, it would have been difficult to implement the solution by producing 73 percent of a bowl and 51 percent of a mug.

When applications of the simplex method result in noninteger values, it is sometimes assumed that the solution values can be "rounded off" to the nearest feasible integer values. This method would cause little concern if, for example, $x_1 = 8,000.4$ nails were rounded off to 8,000 nails, since nails cost only a few cents apiece.

Problems that require integer solution values

The limitation of rounding off noninteger solutions

However, if we are considering the production of jet aircraft and $x_1 = 7.4$ jet airliners, rounding off could affect profit (or cost) by millions of dollars. In this case we need to solve the problem so that an *optimal integer solution* is guaranteed. In this chapter, the different forms of integer linear programming models are presented, and several solution approaches that generate optimal integer solutions are demonstrated.

INTEGER PROGRAMMING MODELS

Three basic types of integer programming models

There are three basic types of integer linear programming models: a total integer model, a 0–1 integer model, and a mixed integer model. In a *total integer* model all of the decision variables are required to have integer solution values. In a *0–1 integer* model all of the decision variables have integer values of zero or one. Finally, in a *mixed integer* model some of the decision variables (but not all) are required to have integer solutions. The following three examples demonstrate each of these types of integer programming models.

A Total Integer Model Example

A model in which all decision variables must have integer solution values

The owner of a machine shop is planning to expand by purchasing some new machines — presses and lathes. The owner has estimated that each press purchased will increase profit by $100 per day and each lathe will increase profit by $150 daily. The number of machines the owner can purchase is limited by the cost of the machines and the available floor space in the shop. The machine purchase prices and space requirements are as follows:

Machine	Required Floor Space (ft^2)	Purchase Price
Press	15	$8,000
Lathe	30	4,000

The owner has a budget of $40,000 for purchasing machines and 200 square feet of available floor space. The owner wants to know how many of each type of machine to purchase in order to maximize the daily increase in profit.

The linear programming model for an integer programming problem is formulated in exactly the same way as the linear programming examples in Chapters 2 through 7. The only difference is that in this problem, the decision variables are restricted to integer values, since the owner cannot purchase a fraction, or portion, of a machine. The linear programming model is shown below.

maximize $Z = \$100x_1 + 150x_2$

subject to

$$8,000x_1 + 4,000x_2 \leq \$40,000$$
$$15x_1 + 30x_2 \leq 200 \text{ ft}^2$$
$$x_1, x_2 \geq 0 \text{ and integer}$$

where

x_1 = number of presses

x_2 = number of lathes

The decision variables in this model are restricted to whole machines. The fact that *both* decision variables, x_1 and x_2, can assume any integer value greater than or equal to zero is what gives this model its designation as a total integer model.

A 0–1 Integer Model Example

A community council must decide which recreation facilities to construct in its community. Four new recreation facilities have been proposed—a swimming pool, a tennis center, an athletic field, and a gymnasium. The council wants to construct facilities that will maximize the expected daily usage by the residents of the community subject to land and cost limitations. The expected daily usage and cost and land requirements for each facility are shown below.

A model in which all decision variables must have solution values of either zero or one

Recreation Facility	Expected Usage (people/day)	Cost ($)	Land Requirements (acres)
Swimming pool	300	$35,000	4
Tennis center	90	10,000	2
Athletic field	400	25,000	7
Gymnasium	150	90,000	3

The community has a $120,000 construction budget and 12 acres of land. Because the land for the swimming pool and tennis center are in the same area of the community, however, only one of these two facilities can be constructed. The council wants to know which of the recreation facilities to construct in order to maximize the expected daily usage.

The model for this problem is formulated as follows.

maximize $Z = 300x_1 + 90x_2 + 400x_3 + 150x_4$

subject to

$$\$35,000x_1 + 10,000x_2 + 25,000x_3 + 90,000x_4 \leq \$120,000$$
$$4x_1 + 2x_2 + 7x_3 + 3x_4 \leq 12 \text{ acres}$$
$$x_1 + x_2 \leq 1 \text{ facility}$$
$$x_1, x_2, x_3, x_4 = 0 \text{ or } 1$$

where

x_1 = construction of a swimming pool
x_2 = construction of a tennis center
x_3 = construction of an athletic field
x_4 = construction of a gymnasium

In this model, the decision variables can have a solution value of either *zero* or *one*. If a facility is not selected for construction, the decision variable representing it will have a value of zero. If a facility is selected, its decision variable will have a value of one.

The last constraint, $x_1 + x_2 \leq 1$, reflects the *contingency* that either the swimming pool (x_1) or the tennis center (x_2) can be constructed, but not both. In order for the sum of x_1 and x_2 to be less than or equal to one, either of the variables can have a value of one, or both variables can equal zero.

A Mixed Integer Model Example

A model in which some decision variables must have integer solution values and other values can be noninteger

Nancy Smith has $250,000 to invest in three alternative investments—condominiums, land, and municipal bonds. She wants to invest in the alternatives that will result in the greatest return on investment after one year.

Each condominium costs $50,000 and will return a profit of $9,000 if sold at the end of one year; each acre of land costs $12,000 and will return a profit of $1,500 at the end of one year; and each municipal bond costs $8,000 and will result in a return of $1,000 if sold at the end of one year. In addition, there are only 4 condominiums, 15 acres of land, and 20 municipal bonds available for purchase.

The linear programming model for this problem is formulated as follows.

$$\text{maximize } Z = \$9,000x_1 + 1,500x_2 + 1,000x_3$$
$$\text{subject to}$$
$$50,000x_1 + 12,000x_2 + 8,000x_3 \leq \$250,000$$
$$x_1 \leq 4 \text{ condominiums}$$
$$x_2 \leq 15 \text{ acres}$$
$$x_3 \leq 20 \text{ bonds}$$
$$x_2 \geq 0$$
$$x_1, x_3 \geq 0 \text{ and integer}$$

where

x_1 = condominiums purchased
x_2 = acres of land purchased
x_3 = bonds purchased

Notice that in this model the solution values for condominiums (x_1) and municipal bonds (x_3) must be integers. It is not possible to invest in a fraction of a condominium or to purchase part of a bond. However, it is possible to purchase less than an acre of land (i.e., a portion of an acre). Thus, two of the decision variables (x_1 and x_3) are restricted to integer values, whereas the other variable (x_2) can take on any real value greater than or equal to zero.

INTEGER PROGRAMMING MODEL SOLUTION

There are several methods for solving integer programming models like the examples formulated in the previous section. A frequently suggested and easy solution method is to *round off* fractional solution values to integer values. As an example, consider the total integer model for the machine shop, formulated in the previous section.

Rounding off fractional solution values

maximize $Z = 100x_1 + 150x_2$

subject to

$$8{,}000x_1 + 4{,}000x_2 \leq 40{,}000$$
$$15x_1 + 30x_2 \leq 200$$
$$x_1, x_2 \geq 0 \text{ and integer}$$

Solving this model using the simplex method results in the solution shown in Table 8.1.

TABLE 8.1
The Optimal Simplex Solution

c_j	Basic Variables	Quantity	100 x_1	150 x_2	0 s_1	0 s_2
100	x_1	2.22	1	0	.00016	−.022
150	x_2	5.55	0	1	−.00008	.044
	z_j	1,054.5	100	150	.004	4.4
	$c_j - z_j$		0	0	−.004	−4.4

Notice that this model results in a noninteger solution of 2.22 presses and 5.55 lathes. Since the solution values must be integers, let us first round off these two values to the *closest integer values*, which would be $x_1 = 2$ and $x_2 = 6$. However, if we substitute these values into the second model constraint, we find that this integer solution violates the constraint and thus is infeasible.

$$15x_1 + 30x_2 \leq 200$$
$$15(2) + 30(6) \leq 200$$
$$210 \neq 200$$

In a model where the constraints are all $\leq$ (and the constraint coefficients are positive), a feasible solution is always ensured by *rounding down*. Thus, a feasible integer solution for this problem is

$x_1 = 2$
$x_2 = 5$
$Z = \$950$

However, one of the difficulties of simply rounding down non-integer values is that another integer solution may result in a higher profit (i.e., in this problem there may be an integer solution that will result in a profit higher than \$950). In order to determine *if* a better integer solution exists, let us analyze the graph of this model, which is shown in Figure 8.1.

FIGURE 8.1

Feasible Solution
Space with Integer
Solution Points

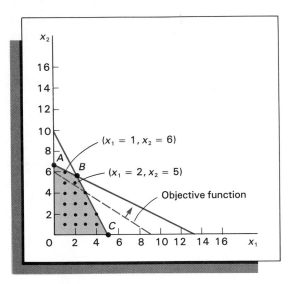

In Figure 8.1 the dots indicate integer solution points, and the point $x_1 = 2$, $x_2 = 5$ is the rounded-off solution. Notice that as the objective function edge moves outward through the feasible solution space, there is an *integer* solution point that yields a greater profit than the rounded-off solution. This solution point is $x_1 = 1$, $x_2 = 6$. At this point, $Z = \$1,000$, which is \$50 more profit per day for the machine shop than is realized by the rounded-down integer solution.

This graphical analysis explicitly demonstrates the error that can result from solving an integer programming problem by simply rounding down. In the machine shop example, the optimal integer solution is $x_1 = 1$, $x_2 = 6$, instead of the rounded-down solution, $x_1 = 2$, $x_2 = 5$ (which is often called the *suboptimal* solution or result). Because erroneous results are caused by rounding down regular simplex solutions, a more direct approach for solving integer

A suboptimal
solution

problems is required. The branch and bound method is the most popular general solution approach for integer programming problems.

The Branch and Bound Method

The *branch and bound method* is not a solution technique specifically limited to integer programming problems. It is a *solution approach* that can be applied to a number of different types of problems. The branch and bound approach is based on the principle that the total set of feasible solutions (such as the feasible area in Fig. 8.1) can be partitioned into smaller subsets of solutions. These smaller subsets can then be evaluated systematically until the best solution is found. When the branch and bound approach is applied to an integer programming problem, it is used in conjunction with the normal simplex method.

A solution approach

Partitioning the feasible solution space into smaller subsets

The machine shop example, previously used in our graphical analysis, will be used to demonstrate the branch and bound approach. We begin the branch and bound method by first solving the problem as a regular linear programming model without integer restrictions (i.e., the integer restrictions are *relaxed*). The linear programming model for the problem and the optimal relaxed solution obtained by the simplex method are repeated below.

Relaxing the integer restrictions

$$\text{maximize } Z = \$100x_1 + 150x_2$$
$$\text{subject to}$$
$$8,000x_1 + 4,000x_2 \leq \$40,000$$
$$15x_1 + 30x_2 \leq 200 \text{ ft}^2$$
$$x_1, x_2 \geq 0 \text{ and integer}$$

TABLE 8.2
The Optimal "Relaxed" Simplex Solution

c_j	Basic Variables	Quantity	100 x_1	150 x_2	0 s_1	0 s_2
100	x_1	2.22	1	0	.00016	−.022
150	x_2	5.55	0	1	−.00008	.044
	z_j	1,054.5	100	150	.004	4.4
	$c_j - z_j$		0	0	−.004	−4.4

The branch and bound method employs a diagram consisting of *nodes* and *branches* as a framework for the solution process. The first node of the branch and bound diagram, shown in Figure 8.2, contains the relaxed linear programming solution shown in Table 8.2 *and* the rounded-down solution.

A diagram of nodes and branches

FIGURE 8.2

The Initial Node in
the Branch and
Bound Diagram

UB = 1,054.50 (x_1 = 2.22, x_2 = 5.55)
LB = 950 (x_1 = 2, x_2 = 5)

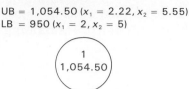

The upper bound
and lower bound
at each node

Notice that this node has two designated bounds: an upper bound (UB) of $1,054.50 and a lower bound (LB) of $950. The lower bound is the Z value for the rounded-down solution, $x_1 = 2$ and $x_2 = 5$; the upper bound is the Z value for the relaxed simplex solution, $x_1 = 2.22$ and $x_2 = 5.55$. The *optimal integer solution* will be between these two bounds.

Recall that in the graphical analysis (Fig. 8.1) our concern was that rounding down would result in a suboptimal solution. In other words, we were hoping that a Z value greater than $950 might be possible. We were not concerned that a value *lower than* $950 might be available. Thus, $950 represents a *lower bound* for our solution. Alternatively, since $Z = $1,054.50 reflects an optimal solution point *on the solution space boundary*, a greater Z value cannot possibly be attained. Point B in Figure 8.1, which corresponds to the Table 8.2 solution, is the last point the objective function edge touches in the solution space. Hence, $Z = $1,054.50 is the *upper bound* of our solution.

Partitioning the
present relaxed
solution

Now that the possible feasible solutions have been narrowed to values between the upper and lower bounds, we must test the solutions within these bounds to determine the best one. The first step in the branch and bound method is to create *two* solution subsets from the present relaxed solution. This is accomplished by observing the relaxed solution value for each variable,

$$x_1 = 2.22$$
$$x_2 = 5.55$$

Selecting the
variable with the
greatest fractional
part to branch on

and seeing which one is the farthest from being an integer value (i.e., which variable has the greatest fractional part). The .55 portion of 5.55 is the greatest fractional part; thus x_2 will be the variable that we will "branch" on.

Developing two
additional
constraints

Since x_2 must be an integer value in the optimal solution, the following constraints can be developed.

$$x_2 \leq 5$$
$$x_2 \geq 6$$

In other words, x_2 can be 0, 1, 2, 3, 4, 5, or 6, 7, 8, etc., but it cannot be a value between 5 and 6, such as 5.55. These two new constraints represent the two solution subsets for our solution approach. Each of these constraints will be added to our linear programming model, which will then be solved by the simplex

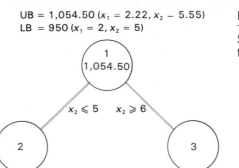

FIGURE 8.3

Solution Subsets for x_2

method to determine a relaxed solution. This sequence of events is shown on the branch and bound diagram in Figure 8.3. The solutions at nodes 2 and 3 will be the relaxed solutions obtained by solving our example model with the appropriate constraints added.

First, the solution at node 2 is found by solving the following model with the constraint $x_2 \leq 5$ added.

The node 2 model with one of the branch constraints added

$$\text{maximize } Z = \$100x_1 + 150x_2$$

subject to

$$8{,}000x_1 + 4{,}000x_2 \leq 40{,}000$$
$$15x_1 + 30x_2 \leq 200$$
$$x_2 \leq 5$$
$$x_1, x_2 \geq 0$$

The optimal simplex solution for this model with integer restrictions relaxed is shown in Table 8.3.

TABLE 8.3
The Optimal "Relaxed" Solution at Node 2

c_j	Basic Variables	Quantity	100 x_1	150 x_2	0 s_1	0 s_2	0 s_3
100	x_1	2.5	1	0	.000125	0	−0.5
0	s_2	12.5	0	0	.001875	1	−22.5
150	x_2	5	0	1	0	0	1
	z_j	1,000	100	150	.0125	0	100
	$c_j - z_j$		0	0	−.0125	0	−100

Next, the solution at node 3 is found by solving the model with $x_2 \geq 6$ added.

The node 3 model with the second branch constraint added

$$\text{maximize } Z = \$100x_1 + 150x_2$$

subject to

$$8{,}000x_1 + 4{,}000x_2 \leq 40{,}000$$
$$15x_1 + 30x_2 \leq 200$$
$$x_2 \geq 6$$
$$x_1, x_2 \geq 0$$

The optimal simplex solution for this model with integer restrictions relaxed is shown in Table 8.4.

TABLE 8.4

The Optimal "Relaxed" Solution at Node 3

c_j	Basic Variables	Quantity	100 x_1	150 x_2	0 s_1	0 s_2	0 s_3
0	s_1	5,352	0	0	1	−533.3	266.6
100	x_1	1.33	1	0	0	.067	2
150	x_2	6.00	0	1	0	0	−1
	z_j	1,033	100	150	0	6.7	50
	$c_j - z_j$		0	0	0	−6.7	−50

The solutions in Tables 8.3 and 8.4 reflect the partitioning of the original relaxed model into two subsets formed by the addition of the two constraints. The resulting solution sets are shown in the graphs in Figure 8.4.

Determining the new upper and lower bounds

Notice that in the node 2 graph in Figure 8.4, the solution point $x_1 = 2.5$, $x_2 = 5$ results in a maximum Z value of $1,000, which is the upper bound for this node. Next, notice that in the node 3 graph, the solution point $x_1 = 1.33$, $x_2 = 6$ results in a maximum Z value of $1,033. Thus, $1,033 is the upper bound for node 3. The lower bound at each of these nodes is the maximum *integer* solution. Since neither of these relaxed solutions is totally integer, the lower bound remains $950, the integer solution value already obtained at node 1 for the rounded-down integer solution. The diagram in Figure 8.5 reflects the addition of the upper and lower bounds at each node.

FIGURE 8.4

Feasible Solution Spaces for Nodes 2 and 3

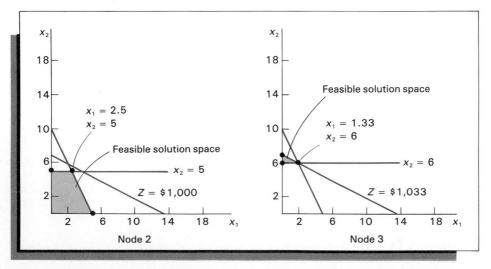

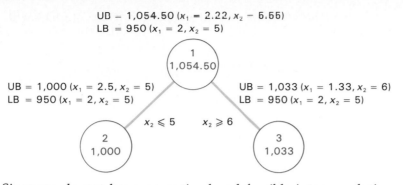

FIGURE 8.5

Branch and Bound
Diagram with
Upper and Lower
Bounds at Nodes 2
and 3

Since we do not have an optimal and feasible integer solution yet, we must continue to branch (i.e., partition) the model, from either node 2 or node 3. A look at Figure 8.5 reveals that if we branch from node 2, the maximum value that can possibly be achieved is $1,000 (the upper bound). However, if we branch from node 3, a higher maximum value of $1,033 is possible. Thus, we will branch from node 3. In general, *always branch from the node with the maximum upper bound*.

Determining the
node to branch
from

Now the steps for branching previously followed at node 1 are repeated at node 3. First, the variable that has the value with the greatest fractional part is selected. Since x_2 has an integer value, x_1, with a fractional part of .33, is the only variable we can select. Thus, two new constraints are developed from x_1,

Partitioning the
solution at node 3

$$x_1 \leq 1$$
$$x_1 \geq 2$$

This process creates the new branch and bound diagram shown in Figure 8.6.

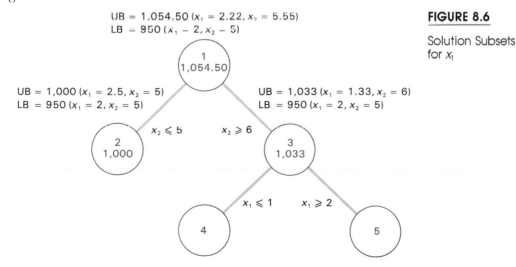

FIGURE 8.6

Solution Subsets
for x_1

Next, the relaxed linear programming model with the new constraints added must be solved at nodes 4 and 5. (However, do not

The node 4 model

forget that the model is not the original, but the original with the constraint previously added, $x_2 \geq 6$.) Consider the node 4 model first.

maximum $Z = 100x_1 + 150x_2$

subject to

$$8,000x_1 + 4,000x_2 \leq 40,000$$
$$15x_1 + 30x_2 \leq 200$$
$$x_2 \geq 6$$
$$x_1 \leq 1$$
$$x_1, x_2 \geq 0$$

The optimal simplex solution for this model with integer restrictions relaxed is shown in Table 8.5

TABLE 8.5
The Optimal "Relaxed" Solution at Node 4

c_j	Basic Variables	Quantity	100 x_1	150 x_2	0 s_1	0 s_2	0 s_3	0 s_4
0	s_1	7,333.33	0	0	1	−133.3	0	−6,000
0	s_3	.17	0	0	0	.033	1	−.50
150	x_2	6.17	0	1	0	.033	0	−.50
100	x_1	1	1	0	0	0	0	1
	z_j	1,025.5	100	150	0	5	0	25
	$c_j - z_j$		0	0	0	−5	0	−25

The node 5 model

Next consider the node 5 model.

maximize $Z = 100x_1 + 150x_2$

subject to

$$8,000x_1 + 4,000x_2 \leq 40,000$$
$$15x_1 + 30x_2 \leq 200$$
$$x_2 \geq 6$$
$$x_1 \geq 2$$
$$x_1, x_2 \geq 0$$

The optimal simplex solution for this model is shown in Table 8.6.

TABLE 8.6
The Optimal "Relaxed" Solution at Node 5

c_j	Basic Variables	Quantity	100 x_1	150 x_2	0 s_1	0 s_2	0 s_3	0 s_4	−M A_2
0	s_1	5,360	0	0	1	−8,000	−4,000	0	0
100	x_1	1.33	1	0	0	1	2	0	0
150	x_2	6	0	1	0	0	−1	0	0
−M	A_2	.77	0	0	0	−1	−2	−1	1
	z_j	900 − .77M	100	150	0	100 + M	50 + 2M	M	−M
	$c_j - z_j$		0	0	0	−100 − M	−50 − 2M	−M	0

Because the solution shown in Table 8.6 contains an artificial variable, it is *infeasible*. Therefore, no solution exists at node 5, and we have only to evaluate the solution at node 4. The branch and bound diagram reflecting these results is shown in Figure 8.7.

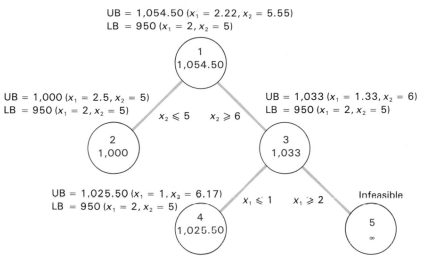

UB = 1,054.50 (x_1 = 2.22, x_2 = 5.55)
LB = 950 (x_1 = 2, x_2 = 5)

1
1,054.50

UB = 1,000 (x_1 = 2.5, x_2 = 5)
LB = 950 (x_1 = 2, x_2 = 5)

$x_2 \leqslant 5$ $x_2 \geqslant 6$

UB = 1,033 (x_1 = 1.33, x_2 = 6)
LB = 950 (x_1 = 2, x_2 = 5)

2
1,000

3
1,033

UB = 1,025.50 (x_1 = 1, x_2 = 6.17)
LB = 950 (x_1 = 2, x_2 = 5)

$x_1 \leqslant 1$ $x_1 \geqslant 2$ Infeasible

4
1,025.50

5
∞

FIGURE 8.7

Branch and Bound Diagram with Upper and Lower Bounds at Nodes 4 and 5

The branch and bound diagram in Figure 8.7 indicates that we still have not reached an optimal integer solution; thus, we must repeat the branching steps followed earlier. Since a solution does not exist at node 5, there is no comparison between the upper bounds at nodes 4 and 5. We must branch from node 4. Next, since x_1 has an integer value, x_2, with a fractional part of .17, is selected by default. The two new constraints developed from x_2 are

$$x_2 \leq 6$$
$$x_2 \geq 7$$

This creates the new branch and bound diagram in Figure 8.8.

The relaxed linear programming model with the new constraints added must be solved at nodes 6 and 7. Consider the node 6 model first.

Partitioning the solution at node 4

The node 6 model

maximize $Z = 100x_1 + 150x_2$
subject to
$$8,000x_1 + 4,000x_2 \leq 40,000$$
$$15x_1 + 30x_2 \leq 200$$
$$x_2 \geq 6$$
$$x_1 \leq 1$$
$$x_2 \leq 6$$
$$x_1, x_2 \geq 0$$

FIGURE 8.8

Solution Subsets
for x_2

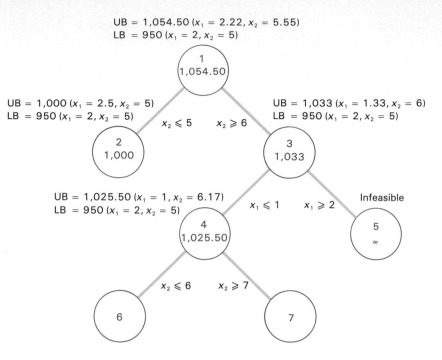

The optimal simplex solution for this relaxed linear programming model is shown in Table 8.7.

TABLE 8.7
The Optimal "Relaxed" Solution at Node 6

c_j	Basic Variables	Quantity	100	150	0	0	0	0	0
			x_1	x_2	s_1	s_2	s_3	s_4	s_5
0	s_1	8,000	0	0	1	0	0	−8,000	−4,000
0	s_2	5	0	0	0	1	0	−15	−30
150	x_2	6	0	1	0	0	0	0	1
100	x_1	1	1	0	0	0	0	1	0
0	s_3	0	0	0	0	0	1	0	1
	z_j	1,000	100	150	0	0	0	100	150
	$c_j - z_j$		0	0	0	0	0	−100	−150

The node 7 model

Next, consider the node 7 model.

maximize $Z = 100x_1 + 150x_2$
subject to
$$8,000x_1 + 4,000x_2 \leq 40,000$$
$$15x_1 + 30x_2 \leq 200$$
$$x_2 \geq 6$$
$$x_1 \leq 1$$
$$x_1 \geq 7$$
$$x_1, x_2 \geq 0$$

The optimal simplex tableau for this model is shown in Table 8.8.

TABLE 8.8
The Optimal "Relaxed" Solution at Node 7

c_j	Basic Variables	Quantity	100 x_1	150 x_2	0 s_1	0 s_2	0 s_3	0 s_4	0 s_5	$-M$ A_2
0	s_1	13,333	6,000	0	1	-133.3	0	0	0	0
0	s_3	.67	.50	0	0	.033	1	0	0	0
150	x_2	6.67	.50	1	0	.033	0	0	0	0
0	s_4	1	1	0	0	0	0	1	0	0
$-M$	A_2	.33	$-.50$	0	0	$-.033$	0	0	-1	1
	z_j	$1,000.5 - .33M$	$75 + .5M$	150	0	$49.5 + .033M$	0	0	M	$-M$
	$c_j - z_j$		$25 - .5M$	0	0	$-49.5 - .033M$	0	0	$-M$	0

However, Table 8.8 contains an artificial variable in the solution; thus, the solution is infeasible and no solution exists at node 7. The branch and bound diagram reflecting these results is shown in Figure 8.9.

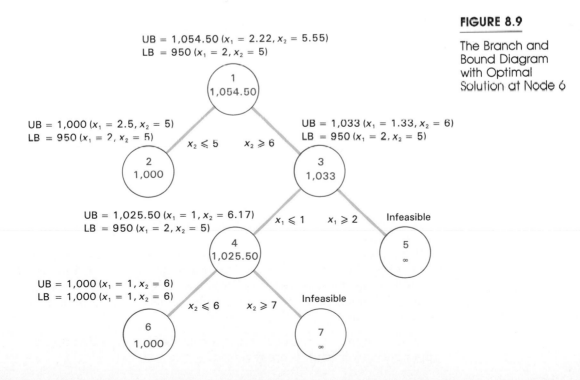

FIGURE 8.9

The Branch and Bound Diagram with Optimal Solution at Node 6

UB = 1,054.50 (x_1 = 2.22, x_2 = 5.55)
LB = 950 (x_1 = 2, x_2 = 5)

1
1,054.50

UB = 1,000 (x_1 = 2.5, x_2 = 5)
LB = 950 (x_1 = 2, x_2 = 5)

$x_2 \leq 5$ $x_2 \geq 6$

2
1,000

UB = 1,033 (x_1 = 1.33, x_2 = 6)
LB = 950 (x_1 = 2, x_2 = 5)

3
1,033

UB = 1,025.50 (x_1 = 1, x_2 = 6.17)
LB = 950 (x_1 = 2, x_2 = 5)

$x_1 \leq 1$ $x_1 \geq 2$ Infeasible

4
1,025.50

5
∞

UB = 1,000 (x_1 = 1, x_2 = 6)
LB = 1,000 (x_1 = 1, x_2 = 6)

$x_2 \leq 6$ $x_2 \geq 7$ Infeasible

6
1,000

7
∞

The version of the branch and bound diagram in Figure 8.9 indicates that the optimal integer solution, $x_1 = 1$, $x_2 = 6$, has been
reached at node 6. The value of 1,000 at node 6 is the maximum, or
upper bound, integer value that can be obtained. It is also the recomputed lower bound, since it is the maximum integer solution
achieved to this point. Thus, it is not possible to achieve any higher
value by further branching from node 6. A comparison of the node 6
solution with those at nodes 2, 5, and 7 shows that a better solution
is not possible. The upper bound at node 2 is 1,000, which is the
same as that obtained at node 6; thus node 2 can result in no improvement. The solutions at nodes 5 and 7 are infeasible (and thus
further branching will result in only infeasible solutions). By the process of elimination, the integer solution at node 6 is optimal.

In general, the optimal integer solution is reached when a feasible integer solution is generated at a node and the upper bound at
that node is greater than or equal to the upper bound at any other
ending node (i.e., a node at the end of a branch).

In the context of the original example, this solution indicates
that if the machine shop owner purchases one press and six lathes, a
daily increase in profit of $1,000 will result. Notice that this solution
is the same integer solution achieved graphically in Figure 8.1.

The steps of the branch and bound method for determining an
optimal integer solution for a maximization model can be summarized as follows.

1. Find the optimal simplex solution to the linear programming
   model with the integer restrictions relaxed.
2. At node 1 let the relaxed simplex solution be the upper bound
   and the *rounded-down* integer solution be the lower bound.
3. Select the variable with the greatest fractional part for branching.
   Create two new constraints for this variable reflecting the partitioned integer values. The result will be a new $\leq$ constraint and a
   new $\geq$ constraint.
4. Create two new nodes; one for the $\geq$ constraint and one for the $\leq$
   constraint.
5. Solve the *relaxed* linear programming model with the new constraint added at each of these nodes.
6. The relaxed simplex solution is the upper bound at each node,
   and the *existing* maximum integer solution (at any node) is the
   lower bound.
7. If the process produces a feasible integer solution with the greatest upper bound value of any ending node, the optimal integer
   solution has been reached. If a feasible integer solution does not
   emerge, branch from the node with the greatest upper bound.
8. Return to step 3.

For a minimization model, relaxed solutions are rounded up and
upper and lower bounds are reversed.

Solution of the Mixed Integer Model

Mixed integer linear programming problems can also be solved using the branch and bound method. The same basic steps that were applied to the total integer model in the previous section are used for a mixed integer model with only a few differences.

Applying the branch and bound method to mixed integer models

First, at node 1 only those variables with integer restrictions are rounded down to achieve the *lower bound*. Second, in determining which variable to branch from, we select the greatest fractional part from among only those variables that must be integer. All other steps remain the same. The optimal solution is reached when a feasible solution is generated at a node that has integer values for those variables requiring integers and that has reached the maximum upper bound of all ending nodes.

Solution of the 0–1 Integer Model

The 0–1 integer model can also be solved using the branch and bound method with a few minor changes. First, the 0–1 restrictions for variables must be reflected as model constraints, $x_j \leq 1$. As an example, consider the 0–1 integer model for selecting recreational facilities formulated earlier in this chapter.

Applying the branch and bound method to 0–1 integer models

maximize $Z = 300x_1 + 90x_2 + 400x_3 + 150x_4$
subject to
$$\$35{,}000x_1 + 10{,}000x_2 + 25{,}000x_3 + 90{,}000x_4 \leq \$120{,}000$$
$$4x_1 + 2x_2 + 7x_3 + 3x_4 \leq 12 \text{ acres}$$
$$x_1 + x_2 \leq 1 \text{ facility}$$
$$x_1, x_2, x_3, x_4 = 0 \text{ or } 1$$

In order to apply the branch and bound method, the following four constraints have to be added to the model in place of the single restriction $x_1, x_2, x_3, x_4 = 0$ or 1.

$x_1 \leq 1$
$x_2 \leq 1$
$x_3 \leq 1$
$x_4 \leq 1$

The only other change in the normal branch and bound method is at step 3. Once the variable, x_j, with the greatest fractional part has been determined, the two new constraints developed from this variable are $x_j = 0$ and $x_j = 1$. These two new constraints will form the two branches at each node.

Another method for solving 0–1 integer problems is *implicit enumeration*. In implicit enumeration, obviously infeasible solutions are eliminated and the remaining solutions are evaluated (i.e., enumer-

Implicit enumeration

ated) to see which is the best. This approach will be demonstrated using our original 0–1 example model for selecting a recreational facility (i.e., without the $x_j \leq 1$ constraints).

Complete enumeration

The *complete enumeration* (i.e., the list of all possible solution sets) for this model is as follows.

Solution	x_1	x_2	x_3	x_4	Feasibility	Z Value
1	0	0	0	0	Feasible	0
2	1	0	0	0	Feasible	300
3	0	1	0	0	Feasible	90
4	0	0	1	0	Feasible	400
5	0	0	0	1	Feasible	150
6	1	1	0	0	Infeasible	∞
7	1	0	1	0	Feasible	700
8	1	0	0	1	Infeasible	∞
9	0	1	1	0	Feasible	490
10	0	1	0	1	Feasible	240
11	0	0	1	1	Feasible	550
12	1	1	1	0	Infeasible	∞
13	1	0	1	1	Infeasible	∞
14	1	1	0	1	Infeasible	∞
15	0	1	1	1	Infeasible	∞
16	1	1	1	1	Infeasible	∞

Eliminating infeasible solutions

Solutions 6, 12, 14, and 16 can be immediately eliminated, because they violate the third constraint, $x_1 + x_2 \leq 1$. Solutions 8, 13, and 15 can also be eliminated, because they violate the other two constraints. This leaves eight possible solution sets (assuming that solution 1—i.e., choosing none of the recreational facilities—can be eliminated) for consideration. After evaluating the objective function value of these eight solutions, we find the best solution to be 7, with

The optimal solution

$x_1 = 1$, $x_2 = 0$, $x_3 = 1$, $x_4 = 0$. Within the context of the example, this solution indicates that a swimming pool (x_1) and an athletic field (x_3) should be constructed and that these facilities will generate an expected usage of 700 people per day.

The process of eliminating infeasible solutions and then evaluating the feasible solutions to see which is best is the basic principle behind implicit enumeration. However, implicit enumeration is usually done more systematically, by evaluating solutions with branching diagrams like those used in the branch and bound method, rather than by sorting through a complete enumeration as in the previous example.

COMPUTERIZED SOLUTION OF INTEGER PROGRAMMING PROBLEMS

LINDO/PC computer solution

The LINDO/PC computer package demonstrated in Chapters 4 and 7 for solving linear programming problems and in Chapter 6 for performing postoptimality analysis has the capability to solve 0–1 integer programming problems but not regular and mixed integer programming problems. However, there is a more powerful version of LINDO/PC called Super LINDO/PC,[1] available from LINDO Systems, Inc., which has the capability to solve regular and mixed integer programming problems. This section will demonstrate the computerized solution of a 0–1 integer programming problem using LINDO/PC and the solution of regular and mixed integer programming problems with Super LINDO/PC.

The 0–1 Integer Programming Problem Solution

The solution of 0–1 integer programming problems with the LINDO/PC package will be demonstrated using the model for selecting recreational facilities formulated earlier in this chapter and solved through a complete enumeration in the previous section.

maximize $Z = 300x_1 + 90x_2 + 400x_3 + 150x_4$

subject to

$$\$35,000x_1 + 10,000x_2 + 25,000x_3 + 90,000x_4 \leq \$120,000$$
$$4x_1 + 2x_2 + 7x_3 + 3x_4 < 12 \text{ acres}$$
$$x_1 + x_2 \leq 1 \text{ facility}$$
$$x_1, x_2, x_3, x_4 \geq 0$$

where

$x_1 =$ construction of a swimming pool

$x_2 =$ construction of a tennis center

$x_3 =$ construction of an athletic field

$x_4 =$ construction of a gymnasium

$Z =$ total expected usage (people) per day

The LINDO/PC computer input and output follow. Notice that the only difference between the LINDO/PC input for the 0–1 integer programming capability and regular LINDO/PC input is that with the 0–1 input, each decision variable is indicated as being an integer after the model has been input.

LINDO/PC computer input

```
: max 300x1 + 90x2 + 400x3 + 150x4
? st
? 35000x1 + 10000x2 + 25000x3 + 90000x4 < 120000
? 4x1 + 2x2 + 7x3 + 3x4 < 12
? x1 + x2 < 1
? end
: integer x1
: integer x2
: integer x3
: integer x4
```

[1] L. Schrage, *Super LINDO/PC* (Redwood City, Calif.: The Scientific Press, 1985).

The optimal solution generated by LINDO/PC is shown below.

```
MAX     300 X1 + 90 X2 + 400 X3 + 150 X4
SUBJECT TO
      2)   35000 X1 + 10000 X2 + 25000 X3 + 90000 X4 <=     120000
      3)   4 X1 + 2 X2 + 7 X3 + 3 X4 <=    12
      4)   X1 + X2 <=    1
END
INTEGER-VARIABLES=        4
```

The optimal
solution

```
                    OBJECTIVE FUNCTION VALUE

      1)          700.000000

      VARIABLE          VALUE         REDUCED COST
          X1          1.000000        -210.000000
          X2           .000000            .000000
          X3          1.000000        -400.000000
          X4           .000000        -150.000000


         ROW    SLACK OR SURPLUS      DUAL PRICES
          2)        60000.000000          .000000
          3)            1.000000          .000000
          4)             .000000        90.000000

     NO. ITERATIONS=        13
     BRANCHES=    1 DETERM=   1.000E  0
     BOUND ON OPTIMUM:   700.0000
     DELETE        X4 AT LEVEL        1
     ENUMERATION COMPLETE. BRANCHES=        1   PIVOTS=    13

     LAST INTEGER SOLUTION IS THE BEST FOUND
```

The solution shown in the LINDO/PC output above is the same as that determined by complete enumeration in the previous section.

$x_1 = 1$ swimming pool

$x_2 = 0$ tennis center

$x_3 = 1$ athletic field

$x_4 = 0$ gymnasium

$Z = 700$ people per day, expected usage

The Total Integer Programming Problem Solution

The solution of a total integer programming problem with the Super LINDO/PC package will be demonstrated using the model for purchasing new machinery formulated in the first part of this chapter and solved with the branch and bound method.

maximize $Z = \$100x_1 + 150x_2$

subject to

$8,000x_1 + 4,000x_2 \leq \$40,000$

$15x_1 + 30x_2 \leq 200 \text{ ft}^2$

$x_1, x_2 \geq 0$ and integer

where

x_1 = number of presses

x_2 = number of lathes

```
: max 100x1 + 150x2
? st
? 8000x1 + 4000x2 < 40000
? 15x1 + 30x2 < 200
? end

: gin x1
: gin x2
:

: look all

MAX      100 X1 + 150 X2
SUBJECT TO
        2)   8000 X1 + 4000 X2 <=    40000
        3)     15 X1 +   30 X2 <=      200
END
GIN       2

:

        OBJECTIVE FUNCTION VALUE

     1)     1000.00000

  VARIABLE        VALUE          REDUCED COST
        X1         1.000000      -100.000000
        X2         6.000000      -150.000000

        ROW    SLACK OR SURPLUS     DUAL PRICES
        2)         8000.000000          .000000
        3)            5.000000          .000000

NO. ITERATIONS=       8
BRANCHES=    3 DETERM.=   1.000E  0
:
```

The optimal solution

The input and output, shown on page 287, are very similar to those for regular LINDO and a 0–1 integer problem, except that the fact that the variables x_1 and x_2 are restricted to integer values is indicated by the designations "gin x1" and "gin x2" after the model has been input.

The Mixed Integer Programming Problem Solution

The solution of a mixed integer problem with Super LINDO/PC will be demonstrated using the mixed integer model example for investments formulated earlier in this chapter.

maximize $Z = \$9,000x_1 + 1,500x_2 + 1,000x_3$

subject to

$$50,000x_1 + 12,000x_2 + 8,000x_3 \leq \$250,000$$
$$x_1 \leq 4 \text{ condominiums}$$
$$x_2 \leq 15 \text{ acres}$$
$$x_3 \leq 20 \text{ bonds}$$
$$x_2 \geq 0$$
$$x_1, x_3 \geq 0 \text{ and integer}$$

where

x_1 = condominiums purchased
x_2 = acres of land purchased
x_3 = bonds purchased

The computerized solution to this example is as follows.

```
: solu

        OBJECTIVE FUNCTION VALUE

      1)     42250.0000

  VARIABLE          VALUE          REDUCED COST
       X1         4.000000        -2750.000000
       X3          .000000            .000000
       X2         4.166667            .000000


      ROW    SLACK OR SURPLUS     DUAL PRICES
       2)            .000000         .125000
       3)            .000000         .000000
       4)          10.833330         .000000
       5)          20.000000         .000000

 NO. ITERATIONS=        5
 BRANCHES=      0 DETERM.=  1.200E  4
 :
```

APPLICATIONS OF INTEGER PROGRAMMING

Energy Optimization at an Oil Refinery

At Exxon's refinery and chemical plant complex in Baton Rouge, Louisiana, a mixed integer linear programming model was developed to evaluate and select energy improvement projects. Over 10% of all energy consumed in the industrial sector is used by the refining business, and in many refineries, over half of the operating costs are for energy, which is used primarily in the form of heat for processing. Exxon concentrated on energy efficiency at its major facilities, and most particularly at its Baton Rouge facility, which accounts for approximately 31% of Exxon's total refining capacity. At the Baton Rouge facility several strategic options for more efficient use of energy were identified. Each of these options consisted of hundreds of discrete energy improvement projects.

Selecting energy improvement projects

The objective of the company was to perform an economic assessment of these energy improvement projects and optimize the group as a package. A multiple time period, mixed integer programming model was developed for this problem. The objective function of the model was to maximize the net present value of total energy savings less the capital investment and expenses associated with the projects. The model constraints included utility balances and project selection limitations. The optimal solution provided the best selection of projects from an economic perspective. Over 900 discrete (i.e., integer) projects were screened, from which approximately 200 were selected.

The solution approach enabled the company to identify approximately a 10% savings in energy. It is estimated that the incremental benefits at the Baton Rouge facility will be on the order of $100 million to be realized between 1985 and the year 2000. The model was subsequently applied to other Exxon facilities with similar success.[2]

Government Crude Oil Sales

Another application of integer programming in the energy industry relates to the sale of crude oil from reserves controlled by the federal government. In 1976, full production at the Elk Hills Naval Petroleum Reserve in California was authorized by law for a period of six

---

[2]W. McMahan and P. Roach, "Site Energy Optimization, A Math Programming Approach," *Interfaces* 12, no. 6 (December 1982): 66–82.

Awarding oil
contracts to
bidders

years. A major difficulty at the Elk Hills reserve was the structuring and awarding of contracts to private companies to move the oil into the marketplace. By law the secretary of energy was required to sell oil to the highest qualified bidder while limiting the quantity of oil sold to any single purchaser. A mixed integer programming model was developed that awarded contracts to bidders while maximizing total revenue.

Bidders responded to offerings by indicating a bid price and the maximum and minimum quantity desired from a specific shipping point. The mixed integer programming model determined whether the government should accept or reject a bid from a bidder (a 0 or 1 integer decision representing rejection or acceptance, respectively) and the quantity of oil to be awarded to the bidder. The model was used in the crude oil sale conducted at Elk Hills in December 1978. Twenty-one companies made a total of 62 bids, which represented a 300% oversubscription to the sale. Although it is impossible to totally evaluate the effect of the model, because of the number of external (world) forces that affect oil prices, sales based on the bids selected by using the integer programming model resulted in an increase in revenue of over $7 million during the sale period.[3]

Sales Region Configuration

In 1982, the Variable Annuity Life Insurance Company (VALIC) was motivated to determine how to organize its sales force of 336 individuals across regions in order to achieve the lowest cost solution in terms of number of regions and geographic configurations. As constraints the company specified that the number of regions should not go below the existing 16; that the number of regions could at most double; and that disproportions in market potential should not be exacerbated. A branch and bound mixed integer program model was developed, with an objective function that minimized the sum of variable costs (i.e., operating expenses and the cost of forgone sales, based on the distance of a salesperson from a customer) and fixed costs, which would increase directly with the number of regions. The model solution specified an increase in sales regions from 16 to 25 and the geographic customer base to be served by each region, and savings were estimated to be in excess of $8.8 million.[4]

[3]B. Jackson and J. Brown, "Using LP for Crude Oil Sales at Elk Hills: A Case Study," *Interfaces* 10, no. 3 (June 1980): 65–69.

[4]B. Gelb and B. Khumawala, "Reconfiguration of an Insurance Company's Sales Regions," *Interfaces* 14, no. 6 (November-December 1984): 87–94.

Optimal Assignment of Gymnasts to Events

An integer programming model was developed to assign members of a women's gymnastics team to the four events conducted at a typical NCAA meet: vault, uneven bars, balance beam, and floor exercises. Each team can enter up to six gymnasts in each event, and the top five scores among these entrants contribute to the team score. At least four of the entrants must participate in all four events. These conditions formed the model constraints; the objective was to maximize the team's overall expected score. The model was tested at Utah State University, and made it possible to analyze the effects of changing conditions, such as improved performance or injuries, on the team score; to indicate to a team member why she was not selected for a particular event; and to eliminate the time the coach spent manually evaluating different team combinations.[5]

Summary

In this chapter we found that simply rounding off noninteger simplex solution values for models requiring integer solutions is not always appropriate. Rounding can often lead to suboptimal results. Therefore, general solution approaches are needed to solve the three forms of linear integer programming models—total integer models, mixed integer models, and 0–1 integer models. The most frequently used solution approach, the branch and bound method, was demonstrated as a general solution approach.

Having analyzed integer problems and the techniques for solving them, we have now covered most of the basic forms of linear programming models and solution techniques. One exception is a problem that contains more than one objective. The topic of goal programming, presented in the next chapter, encompasses this type of problem.

References

Baumol, W. J. *Economic Theory and Operations Analysis.* 4th ed. Englewood Cliffs, N.J.: Prentice-Hall, 1977.

[5]P. Ellis and R. Corn, "Using Bivalent Integer Programming to Select Teams for Intercollegiate Women's Gymnastics Competition," *Interfaces* 14, no. 3 (May-June 1984): 41–46.

Budnick, F. S.; Mojena, R.; and Vollman, T. E. *Principles of Operations Research for Management.* Homewood, Ill.: Richard D. Irwin, 1977.

Dantzig, G. B. "On the Significance of Solving Linear Programming Problems with Some Integer Variables." *Econometrica* 28 (1960): 30–44.

Gomory, R. E. "An Algorithm for Integer Solutions to Linear Programs." In *Recent Advances in Mathematical Programming,* edited by R. L. Graves and P. Wolfe. New York: McGraw-Hill, 1963.

Hartley, R. V. *Operations Research: A Managerial Emphasis.* Pacific Palisades, Calif.: Goodyear Publishing Co., 1976.

Jackson, B., and Brown, J. "Using LP for Crude Oil Sales at Elk Hills: A Case Study." *Interfaces* 10, no. 3 (June 1980): 65–69.

Kwak, N. K. *Mathematical Programming with Business Applications.* New York: McGraw-Hill, 1973.

Lawler, E. L., and Wood, D. W. "Branch and Bound Methods — A Survey." *Operations Research* 14 (1966): 699–719.

Little, J. D. C., et al. "An Algorithm for the Traveling Salesman Problem." *Operations Research* 11 (1963): 972–89.

McMahan, W., and Roach, P. "Site Energy Optimization, A Math Programming Approach." *Interfaces* 12, no. 6 (December 1982): 66–82.

McMillan, C., Jr. *Mathematical Programming.* New York: John Wiley and Sons, 1970.

Mitten, L. G. "Branch-and-Bound Methods: General Formulation and Properties." *Operations Research* 18 (1970): 24–34.

Plane, D. R., and McMillan, C., Jr. *Discrete Optimization.* Englewood Cliffs, N.J.: Prentice-Hall, 1971.

Wagner, H. M. *Principles of Operations Research.* 2d ed. Englewood Cliffs, N.J.: Prentice-Hall, 1975.

EXAMPLE PROBLEM SOLUTION

The following example problem demonstrates the branch and bound solution process for a total integer programming problem.

Problem Statement

A textbook publishing company has developed two new sales regions and is planning to transfer some of its existing sales force into these regions. The company has 10 salespeople available for transfer. Because of different geographic configurations and the location of schools in each region, the average annual expenses for a salesperson differ in the two regions; the average is $10,000 per salesperson in region 1 and $7,000 per salesperson in region 2. The total annual expense budget for the new region is $72,000. It is estimated that a salesperson in region 1 will generate an average of $85,000 in sales each year and a salesperson in region 2 will generate $60,000 annually.

Solve this problem using the branch and bound method.

Step 1: Formulate the Integer Programming Model

maximize $Z = \$85,000x_1 + 60,000x_2$

subject to

$$x_1 + x_2 \leq 10 \text{ salespeople}$$
$$\$10,000x_1 + 7,000x_2 \leq \$72,000 \text{ expense budget}$$
$$x_1, x_2 \geq 0 \text{ and integer}$$

Step 2: Compute the "Relaxed" Simplex Solution

c_j	Basic Variables	Quantity	85,000 x_1	60,000 x_2	0 s_1	0 s_2
60,000	x_2	9.333	0	1	3.33	0
85,000	x_1	0.667	1	0	−2.33	.0001
	z_j	616,666.7	0	0	1,667	8.50
	$c_j - z_j$		0	0	−1,667	−8.50

Step 3: Set the Initial Node and the Upper and Lower Bounds

UB = 616,666.7 (x_1 = 0.667, x_2 = 9.333)
LB = 540,000 (x_1 = 0, x_2 = 9)

(1)

Step 4: Branch on x_1 ($x_1 \leq 0$, $x_1 \geq 1$)

UB − 616,666.7 (x_1 = 0.667, x_2 = 9.33)
LB = 540,000 (x_1 = 0, x_2 = 9)

(1)

UB = 600,000 (x_1 = 0, x_2 = 10) $x_1 \leq 0$ $x_1 \geq 1$ UB = 616,428.6 (x_1 = 1, x_2 = 8.857)
LB = 540,000 (x_1 = 0, x_2 = 9)   LB = 540,000 (x_1 = 0, x_2 = 9)

(2)   (3)

Step 5: Branch on x_2 ($x_2 \leq 8$, $x_2 \geq 9$)

Step 6: Branch on x_1 ($x_1 \leq 1$, $x_1 \geq 2$)

Step 7: Branch on x_2 ($x_2 \leq 7$, $x_2 \geq 8$)

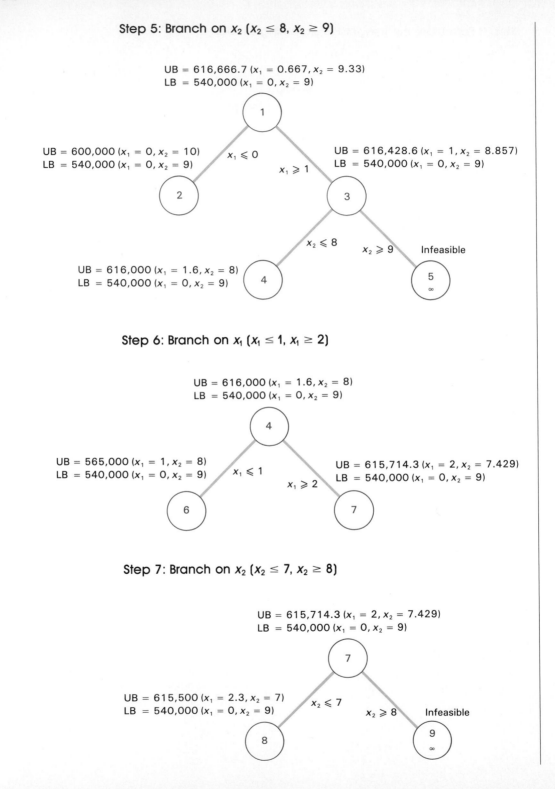

Step 8: Branch on x_1 ($x_1 \leq 2$, $x_1 \geq 3$)

UB = 615,500 (x_1 = 2.3, x_2 = 7)
LB = 540,000 (x_1 = 0, x_2 = 9)

UB = 590,000 (x_1 = 2, x_2 = 7)
LB = 540,000 (x_1 = 0, x_2 = 9)

$x_1 \leq 2$ $x_1 \geq 3$

UB = 615,000 (x_1 = 3, x_2 = 6)
LB = 540,000 (x_1 = 0, x_2 = 9)

(8)
(10)   (11)

Since all nodes either have reached an integer solution or are infeasible, the branch and bound process is complete. The optimal solution was reached at node 11:

$x_1 = 3$

$x_2 = 6$

$Z = \$615,000$

In other words, the optimal use of the company's sales force is to assign 3 salespeople to region 1 and 6 salespeople to region 2, which will generate an average of $615,000 in sales annually. The computerized solution for this problem can also be obtained using Super LINDO/PC, as shown previously in this chapter.

```
: look all

MAX       85000 X1 + 60000 X2
SUBJECT TO
        2)    X1 + X2 <=    10
        3)    10000 X1 + 7000 X2 <=    72000
END
GIN       2

:

: solu

        OBJECTIVE FUNCTION VALUE

        1)    615000.000

    VARIABLE         VALUE          REDUCED COST
        X1          3.000000        -85000.000000
        X2          6.000000        -60000.000000

        ROW    SLACK OR SURPLUS      DUAL PRICES
        2)          1.000000            .000000
        3)           .000000            .000000

NO. ITERATIONS=        17
BRANCHES=       5 DETERM.=   1.000E   0
:
```

Problems

1. Consider the following linear programming model.

   maximize $Z = 5x_1 + 4x_2$
   subject to
   $$3x_1 + 4x_2 \leq 10$$
   $$x_1, x_2 \geq 0 \text{ and integer}$$

   a. Solve this model using the branch and bound method.
   b. Demonstrate the solution partitioning graphically.

2. Solve the following linear programming model using the branch and bound method.

   minimize $Z = 3x_1 + 6x_2$
   subject to
   $$7x_1 + 3x_2 \geq 40$$
   $$x_1, x_2 \geq 0 \text{ and integer}$$

3. The following problem (16) was presented in Chapter 3. A clothier makes coats and slacks from wool cloth and labor. The clothier has developed the following linear programming model for determining the number of coats and pairs of slacks (x_1 and x_2) to make in order to maximize profit.

   maximize $Z = 50x_1 + 40x_2$ (profit, \$)
   subject to
   $$3x_1 + 5x_2 \leq 150 \text{ (wood, yd}^2\text{)}$$
   $$10x_1 + 4x_2 \leq 200 \text{ (labor, hr)}$$
   $$x_1, x_2 \geq 0$$

   Although originally there were no integer restrictions placed on this model, realistically there should be, since the clothier would not make a partial coat or pair of slacks. Therefore, solve this model with the added restriction that x_1 and x_2 must be integers, using the branch and bound method.

4. The following problem (6) was presented in Chapter 3. The Pinewood Furniture Company produces chairs and tables from labor and wood. The following linear programming model has been developed for determining the number of chairs (x_1) and tables (x_2) to produce daily in order to maximize profit.

   maximize $Z = 400x_1 + 100x_2$ (profit, \$)
   subject to
   $$8x_1 + 10x_2 \leq 80 \text{ (labor, hr)}$$
   $$2x_1 + 6x_2 \leq 36 \text{ (wood, lb)}$$
   $$x_1 \leq 6 \text{ (demand, chairs)}$$
   $$x_1, x_2 \geq 0$$

Although originally there were no integer restrictions placed on this model, realistically there should be, since the furniture manufacturer would not make a partial table or chair. Therefore, solve this model with the added restriction that x_1 and x_2 must be integers, using the branch and bound method.

5. A glass blower makes glass decanters and glass trays on a weekly basis. Each item requires 1 pound of glass, and the glass blower has 15 pounds of glass available every week. A glass decanter requires 4 hours of labor, a glass tray requires only 1 hour of labor, and the glass blower works 25 hours a week. The profit from a decanter is $50, and the profit from a tray is $10. The following linear programming model has been developed for determining the number of decanters (x_1) and trays (x_2) to produce in order to maximize profit.

maximize $Z = 50x_1 + 10x_2$

subject to

$$x_1 + x_2 \leq 15$$
$$4x_1 + x_2 \leq 25$$
$$x_1, x_2 \geq 0 \text{ and integer}$$

The relaxed optimal solution to this model is shown below.

c_j	Basic Variables	Quantity	50 x_1	10 x_2	0 s_1	0 s_2
0	s_1	8.75	0	$-1/4$	1	$-1/4$
50	x_1	6.25	1	$1/4$	0	$1/4$
	z_j	312.50	50	$25/2$	0	$25/2$
	$c_j \quad z_j$		0	$-5/2$	0	$-25/2$

a. Determine the integer solution to this model using the branch and bound method.

b. Demonstrate the solution partitioning graphically.

6. The Livewright Medical Supplies Company has a total of 12 salespeople it wants to assign to three regions—the South, the East, and the Midwest. A salesperson in the South earns $600 in profit per month for the company, a salesperson in the East earns $540, and a salesperson in the Midwest earns $375. The southern region can have a maximum assignment of 5 salespeople. The company has a total of $750 per day available for expenses for all 12 salespeople. The company has developed the following linear programming model for determining the number of salespeople to assign to the South (x_1), the East (x_2), and the Midwest (x_3) in order to maximize profit.

$$\text{maximize } Z = 600x_1 + 540x_2 + 375x_3$$

subject to

$$x_1 + x_2 + x_3 \leq 12$$
$$x_1 \leq 5$$
$$80x_1 + 70x_2 + 50x_3 \leq 750$$
$$x_1, x_2, x_3 \geq 0 \text{ and integer}$$

Solve this model using the branch and bound method.

7. The Audiocorp Company makes stereos and televisions. The company has enough material to produce 9 units daily, and 25 hours of labor are available each day. The company has developed the following linear programming model for determining the number of stereos (x_1) and televisions (x_2) to produce each day in order to maximize profit.

$$\text{maximize } Z = 300x_1 + 400x_2 \text{ (profit, \$)}$$

subject to

$$x_1 + x_2 \leq 9 \text{ (material, units)}$$
$$2x_1 + 5x_2 \leq 25 \text{ (labor, hr)}$$
$$x_1, x_2 \geq 0 \text{ and integer}$$

Solve this model using the branch and bound method.

8. The Ambrose Bennett Jewelry Store makes custom jewelry to sell at Christmas every year. The store uses gold and labor to make necklaces and bracelets, which generate profits of $500 and $400, respectively. The store has developed the following linear programming model for determining the number of bracelets (x_1) and necklaces (x_2) to make in order to maximize profit.

$$\text{maximize } Z = 500x_1 + 400x_2$$

subject to

$$2x_1 + 5x_2 \leq 35$$
$$3x_1 + 2x_2 \leq 20$$
$$x_1, x_2 \geq 0 \text{ and integer}$$

The relaxed optimal simplex solution for this model is shown below.

c_j	Basic Variables	Quantity	500 x_1	400 x_2	0 s_1	0 s_2
400	x_2	5.91	0	1	3/11	−2/11
500	x_1	2.73	1	0	−2/11	5/11
	z_j	3,729	500	400	200/11	1700/11
	$c_j - z_j$		0	0	−200/11	−1700/11

Solve this problem using the branch and bound method.

9. Larry Fitzgerald has $500,000 to invest in condominium units and land. He has developed the following mixed integer linear programming model for determining how many condominium units (x_1) and acres (x_2) to purchase in order to maximize the return on the investment.

maximize $Z = 800x_1 + 600x_2$ (annual return, $)
subject to
$$70x_1 + 30x_2 \leq 500 \text{ (capital outlay, \$1,000s)}$$
$$x_1 + 2x_2 \leq 14 \text{ (annual maintenance budget, \$1,000s)}$$
$$x_1 \geq 0 \text{ and integer}$$
$$x_2 \geq 0$$

Solve this model using the branch and bound method.

10. The owner of the Consolidated Machine Shop has $10,000 available to purchase a lathe, a press, a grinder, or some combination thereof. The following 0–1 integer linear programming model has been developed for determining which of the three machines (lathe, x_1; press, x_2; or grinder, x_3) should be purchased in order to maximize annual profit.

maximize $Z = 1,000x_1 + 700x_2 + 800x_3$ (profit, $)
subject to
$$5,000x_1 + 6,000x_2 + 4,000x_3 \leq 10,000 \text{ (cost, \$)}$$
$$x_1, x_2, x_3 = 0 \text{ or } 1$$

Solve this model using the branch and bound method.

11. Solve the following mixed integer linear programming model using the branch and bound method.

maximize $Z = 5x_1 + 6x_2 + 4x_3$
subject to
$$5x_1 + 3x_2 + 6x_3 \leq 20$$
$$x_1 + 3x_2 \leq 12$$
$$x_1, x_3 \geq 0$$
$$x_2 \geq 0 \text{ and integer}$$

12. Solve problem 10 using the implicit enumeration method.

13. A multimillionaire from the Middle East wants to invest $15 million by purchasing some or all of the following properties: a shopping center that costs $9 million, a professional basketball franchise that costs $5 million, and a 20-story office building that costs $10 million. The annual return from the shopping center is $1 million; from the basketball franchise, $400,000; and from the office building, $1.2 million. The investor has hired a manager who works 50 hours per week. The time required by the manager to oversee operations of the shopping center is 30 hours; the basketball franchise, 10 hours; and the office building, 20 hours. Because of potential problems due to traffic conditions at the

shopping center and fan reaction to the basketball team, the investor will purchase only one or the other. The investor wants to know which properties to purchase in order to maximize the return. Formulate a linear programming model for this problem and solve it using the most convenient method.

14. Consider the following linear programming model.

maximize $Z = 20x_1 + 30x_2 + 10x_3 + 40x_4$

subject to

$$2x_1 + 4x_2 + 3x_3 + 7x_4 \leq 10$$
$$10x_1 + 7x_2 + 20x_3 + 15x_4 \leq 40$$
$$x_1 + 10x_2 + x_3 \leq 10$$
$$x_1, x_2, x_3, x_4 = 0 \text{ or } 1$$

a. Solve this problem using the implicit enumeration method.
b. What difficulties would be encountered with the implicit enumeration method if this problem were expanded to contain five or more variables and more constraints?

15. In the Example Problem Solution for this chapter, a textbook company was attempting to determine how many sales representatives to assign to each of two new regions. The company has now decided that if any sales representatives are assigned to region 1, a sales office must be established at an annual cost of $18,000. This altered problem is an example of a type of integer programming problem known as a "fixed charge" problem.

a. Reformulate the integer programming model to reflect this new condition.
b. Solve this new problem. (Computerized solution is required.)

16. The Texas Consolidated Electronics Company is contemplating a research and development program encompassing eight research projects. The company is constrained from embarking on all projects by the number of available management scientists (40) and the budget available for R&D projects ($300,000). Further, if project 2 is selected, project 5 must also be selected (but not vice versa). Following are the resource requirements and the estimated profit for each project.

Project	Expense (thousands of dollars)	Management Scientists Required	Estimated Profit (millions of dollars)
1	60	7	$.36
2	110	9	.82
3	53	8	.29
4	47	4	.16
5	92	7	.56
6	85	6	.61
7	73	8	.48
8	65	5	.41

a. Formulate the integer programming model for this problem.

b. Solve this problem. (Computerized solution is required.)

17. Problem 42 in Chapter 2 described Mazey's department store, which operates on a 24-hour basis and is attempting to determine the minimum number of employees to assign to each work shift in order to minimize the total number of employees. This problem is an example of a class of integer problems known as "set covering" problems. Formulate and solve this problem. (Computerized solution is required.)

18. Vladimir Pushkin, a Russian athlete who visits the United States and Europe frequently, is allowed to return with a limited number of consumer items not generally available in the Soviet Union. The items, which are carried in a duffel bag, cannot exceed a weight of 5 pounds. Once Vladimir is in Russia, he sells the items on the black market at highly inflated prices. The three most popular items in the Soviet Union are denim jeans, radio/cassette players, and tapes of U.S. rock groups. The black market profit (in U.S. dollars) and weight of each item are as follows.

Item	Weight (lb)	Profit ($)
1. Denim jeans	2	$ 90
2. Radio/cassette players	3	150
3. Tapes	1	30

Vladimir wants to determine the combination of items he should pack in his duffel bag that will maximize his black market profit. This problem is an example of a type of integer programming problem known as a "knapsack" problem. Formulate and solve this problem.

Goal Programming

In all of the linear programming models presented in Chapters 2 through 8, a single objective was either maximized or minimized. However, an organization often has more than one objective, some of which may relate to something other than profit or cost. For example, one objective of a business firm might be to maximize profit, but other objectives might be to minimize labor layoffs and pollution. If a strike is imminent or the firm is about to be fined for pollution, these objectives may be more important than maximizing profit.

Organizations with more than one objective

For solving problems in an organizational environment in which there is more than one objective, *goal programming* is an appropriate technique. Goal programming is very similar to regular linear programming as presented in Chapters 2 through 7, except that it includes more than one objective. Like linear programming models, goal programming models consist entirely of linear functions.

Developing a goal programming model is similar to developing a linear programming model. Like linear programming, goal program-

Similarities to linear programming

ming can be illustrated using a graphical approach. The solution approach for goal programming consists of a modified version of the simplex method presented in Chapters 4 and 5. Because of the similarities, some of the material presented in this chapter will seem very familiar, although it relates to the new topic of goal programming.

MODEL FORMULATION

A goal program-ming example

The Colonial Pottery Company example will be employed again to illustrate the way a goal programming model is formulated and the differences between a linear programming model and a goal programming model. Recall that this model was originally formulated in Chapter 2 as follows.

maximize $Z = \$4x_1 + 5x_2$

subject to

$$x_1 + 2x_2 \leq 40 \text{ hr of labor}$$
$$4x_1 + 3x_2 \leq 120 \text{ lb of clay}$$
$$x_1, x_2 \geq 0$$

where

x_1 = number of bowls produced

x_2 = number of mugs produced

The objective function, Z, represents the total profit to be made from bowls and mugs, given that $4 is the profit per bowl and $5 is the profit per mug. The first constraint is for available labor. It shows that a bowl requires 1 hour of labor and a mug requires 2 hours, and 40 hours of labor are available daily. The second constraint is for clay, and it shows that each bowl requires 4 pounds of clay and each mug requires 3 pounds, and the daily limit of clay is 120 pounds.

This is a standard linear programming model, and as such it has a single objective function for profit. However, let us suppose that instead of one objective, the pottery company has several objectives that are listed here *in order of importance*.

Multiple objectives

1. To avoid layoffs, the company does not want to use fewer than 40 hours of labor per day.
2. The company would like to achieve a *satisfactory* profit level of $160 per day.
3. Since the clay must be stored in a special place so that it does not dry out, the company prefers not to keep more than 120 pounds on hand each day.
4. Because high overhead costs result when the plant is kept open past normal hours, the company would like to minimize the amount of overtime.

These different objectives of the company are referred to as *goals* Goals
in the context of the goal programming technique. The company
would, naturally, like to come as close as possible to achieving each
of these goals. Since the regular form of the linear programming
model presented in previous chapters only considers one objective,
we must develop an alternative form of the model to reflect these
multiple goals. Our first step in formulating a goal programming
model is to transform the linear programming model constraints into
goals.

Labor Goal

The first goal of the pottery company is to avoid *underutilization* of Goal constraint
labor—that is, using fewer than 40 hours of labor each day. To represent the possibility of underutilizing labor, the linear programming
constraint for labor, $x_1 + 2x_2 \leq 40$ hours of labor, is reformulated as

$$x_1 + 2x_2 + d_1^- - d_1^+ = 40 \text{ hr}$$

This reformulated equation is referred to as a *goal constraint*. The
two new variables d_1^- and d_1^+, are called *deviational variables*. They Deviational
variables
represent the amount of labor hours (d_1^-) and the amount of labor
hours exceeding 40 (d_1^+). More specifically, d_1^- represents labor underutilization and d_1^+ represents *overtime*. For example, if $x_1 =$
5 bowls and $x_2 = 10$ mugs, then a total of 25 hours of labor have
been expended. Substituting these values into our goal constraint
gives

$$(5) + 2(10) + d_1^- - d_1^+ = 40$$
$$25 + d_1^- - d_1^+ = 40$$

Since only 25 hours were used in production, labor was under-
utilized by 15 hours ($40 - 25 = 15$). Thus, if we let $d_1^- = 15$ hours
and $d_1^+ = 0$ (since there is obviously no overtime), we have

$$25 + d_1^- - d_1^+ = 40$$
$$25 + 15 - 0 = 40$$
$$40 = 40$$

Now consider the case where $x_1 = 10$ bowls and $x_2 = 20$ mugs.
This means that a total of 50 hours have been used for production,
or 10 hours above the goal level of 40 hours. This extra 10 hours is
overtime. Thus, $d_1^- = 0$ (since there is no underutilization) and
$d_1^+ = 10$ hours.

In each of these two brief examples, at least one of the devia- At least one
deviational
variable in a goal
constraint must
equal zero
tional variables equaled zero. In the first example, $d_1^+ = 0$, and in
the second example, $d_1^- = 0$. This is because it is impossible to use
fewer than 40 hours of labor and more than 40 hours of labor *at the
same time*. Of course, both deviational variables, d_1^- and d_1^+, could

have equaled zero if exactly 40 hours were used in production. The examples illustrate one of the fundamental characteristics of goal programming, which is that *at least one or both of the deviational variables in a goal constraint must equal zero.*

The next step in formulating our goal programming model is to represent the goal of not using fewer than 40 hours of labor. We do this by creating a new form of objective function,

$$\text{minimize } P_1 d_1^-$$

The objective function in all goal programming models is to *minimize* deviation from the goal constraint levels. In this objective function the goal is to minimize d_1^-, the underutilization of labor. If d_1^- equaled zero, then we would not be using fewer than 40 hours of labor. Thus, it is our objective to make d_1^- equal zero or the minimum amount possible. The symbol P_1 in the objective function designates the minimization of d_1^- as the *priority one* goal. This means

that when this model is solved, the first step will be to minimize the value of d_1^- before any other goal is addressed.

The fourth priority goal in this problem is also associated with the labor constraint. The fourth goal, P_4, reflects a desire to minimize overtime. Recall that hours of overtime are represented by d_1^+; the objective function therefore becomes

$$\text{minimize } P_1 d_1^-, \quad P_4 d_1^+$$

As before, the objective is to minimize the deviational variable, in this case d_1^+. In other words, if d_1^+ equaled zero, there would be no overtime at all. In solving this model, the achievement of this fourth ranked goal will not be attempted until goals one, two, and three have been considered.

Profit Goal

The second goal in our goal programming model is to achieve a profit of $160. Recall that the original linear programming objective function was

$$Z = 4x_1 + 5x_2$$

Now we reformulate this objective function as a goal constraint with the following goal level.

$$4x_1 + 5x_2 + d_2^- - d_2^+ = \$160$$

The deviational variables d_2^- and d_2^+ represent the amount of profit less than $160 ($d_2^-$) and the amount of profit exceeding $160 ($d_2^+$). The pottery company's goal of achieving $160 in profit is represented in the objective function as

$$\text{minimize } P_1 d_1^-, \quad P_2 d_2^-, \quad P_4 d_1^+$$

Notice that only d_2^- is being minimized, and not d_2^+, since it is logical to assume that the pottery company would be willing to accept all profits in excess of $160 (i.e., it does not desire to minimize d_2^+, excess profit). By minimizing d_2^- at the second priority level, the pottery company hopes that d_2^- will equal zero, which will result in at least $160 in profit.

Material Goal

The third goal of the company is to avoid keeping more than 120 pounds of clay on hand each day. The goal constraint is

$$4x_1 + 3x_2 + d_3^- - d_3^+ = 120 \text{ lb}$$

Since the deviational variable d_3^- represents the amount of clay less than 120 pounds and d_3^+ represents the amount in excess of 120 pounds, this goal can be reflected in the objective function as

$$\text{minimize } P_1 d_1^-, \quad P_2 d_2^-, \quad P_3 d_3^+, \quad P_4 d_1^+$$

The term $P_3 d_3^+$ represents the company's desire to minimize d_3^+, the amount of clay in excess of 120 pounds. The P_3 designation indicates that it is the pottery company's third most important goal.

The complete goal programming model can now be summarized as follows.

$$\text{minimize } P_1 d_1^-, \ P_2 d_2^-, \ P_3 d_3^+, \ P_4 d_1^+$$

subject to

$$\begin{aligned}
x_1 + 2x_2 + d_1^- - d_1^+ &= 40 \\
4x_1 + 5x_2 + d_2^- - d_2^+ &= 160 \\
4x_1 + 3x_2 + d_3^- - d_3^+ &= 120 \\
x_1, x_2, d_1^-, d_1^+, d_2^-, d_2^+, d_3^-, d_3^+ &\geq 0
\end{aligned}$$

The complete goal programming model

The one basic difference between this model and the standard linear programming model is that the objective function terms *are not summed* to equal a total value, Z. This is because the deviational variables in the objective function represent different units of measure. For example, d_1^- and d_1^+ represent hours of labor, d_2^- represents dollars, and d_3^+ represents pounds of clay. It would be illogical to sum hours, dollars, and pounds. The objective function in a goal programming model specifies only that the deviations from the goals represented in the objective function be minimized *individually* in order of their priority.

Terms are not summed in the objective function

Alternative Forms of Goal Constraints

Let us now alter the above goal programming model so that our fourth priority goal limits overtime to 10 hours, instead of minimizing overtime. Recall that the goal constraint for labor is

$$x_1 + 2x_2 + d_1^- - d_1^+ = 40$$

In this goal constraint, d_1^+ represents overtime. Since the new fourth priority goal is to limit overtime to 10 hours, the following goal constraint is developed.

A goal constraint
with all deviational
variables

$$d_1^+ + d_4^- - d_4^+ = 10$$

Although this goal constraint looks unusual, it is acceptable in goal programming to have an equation with *all deviational variables*. In this equation, d_4^- represents the amount of overtime less than 10 hours, and d_4^+ the amount of overtime greater than 10 hours. Since the company desires to *limit overtime* to 10 hours, d_4^+ is minimized in the objective function.

$$\text{minimize } P_1d_1^-, \quad P_2d_2^-, \quad P_3d_3^+, \quad \boxed{P_4d_4^+}$$

Now let us consider the addition of a fifth priority goal to this example. Assume that the pottery company has limited warehouse space, so it can produce no more than 30 bowls and 20 mugs daily. If possible, the company would like to produce these amounts. However, because the profit for mugs is greater than the profit for bowls (i.e., $5 rather than $4), it is more important to achieve the goal for mugs. This fifth goal requires that two new goal constraints be formulated, as follows:

$$x_1 + d_5^- = 30 \text{ bowls}$$
$$x_2 + d_6^- = 20 \text{ mugs}$$

Notice that the positive deviational variables d_5^+ and d_6^+ have been deleted from these goal constraints. This is because the statement of the fifth goal specifies that "no more than 30 bowls and 20 mugs" can be produced. In other words, positive deviation, or overproduction, is not possible.

Weighting goals at the same priority level

Since the actual goal of the company is to achieve the levels of production shown in these two goal constraints, the negative deviational variables d_5^- and d_6^- are minimized in the objective function. However, recall that it is *more important* to the company to achieve the goal for mugs, since mugs generate greater profit. This condition is reflected in the objective function, as follows.

$$\text{minimize } P_1d_1^-, \quad P_2d_2^-, \quad P_3d_3^+, \quad P_4d_4^+, \quad \boxed{4P_5d_5^- + 5P_5d_6^-}$$

Since the goal for mugs is more important than the goal for bowls, the *degree of importance* should be in proportion to the amount of profit (i.e., $5 for each mug and $4 for each bowl). Thus, the goal for mugs is more important than the goal for bowls by a ratio of 5 to 4.

Weights

The coefficients of 5 for $P_5d_6^-$ and 4 for $P_5d_5^-$ are referred to as *weights*. In other words, the minimization of d_6^- is "weighted" higher than the minimization of d_5^- at the fifth priority level. When this model is solved, the achievement of the goal for minimizing d_6^- (mugs) will be attempted before the achievement of the goal for minimizing d_5^- (bowls), even though both goals are at the same priority level.

Notice, however, that these two weighted goals have been summed because they are at the same priority level. Their sum represents achievement of the desired goal at this particular priority level. The complete goal programming model with the new goals for both overtime and production is

minimize $P_1d_1^-$, $P_2d_2^-$, $P_3d_3^+$, $P_4d_4^+$, $4P_5d_5^- + 5P_5d_6^-$
subject to

$$x_1 + 2x_2 + d_1^- - d_1^+ = 40$$
$$4x_1 + 5x_2 + d_2^- - d_2^+ = 160$$
$$4x_1 + 3x_2 + d_3^- - d_3^+ = 120$$
$$d_1^+ + d_4^- - d_4^+ = 10$$
$$x_1 + d_5^- = 30$$
$$x_2 + d_6^- = 20$$
$$x_1, x_2, d_1^-, d_1^+, d_2^-, d_2^+, d_3^-, d_3^+, d_4^-, d_4^+, d_5^-, d_6^- \geq 0$$

GRAPHICAL INTERPRETATION OF GOAL PROGRAMMING

In Chapter 3, the solution of linear programming models was analyzed using graphical analysis. Since goal programming models are linear, they can also be analyzed graphically. The original goal programming model for the Colonial Pottery Company, formulated at the beginning of this chapter, will be used as an example.

minimize $P_1d_1^-$, $P_2d_2^-$, $P_3d_3^+$, $P_4d_1^+$
subject to

$$x_1 + 2x_2 + d_1^- - d_1^+ = 40$$
$$4x_1 + 5x_2 + d_2^- - d_2^+ = 160$$
$$4x_1 + 3x_2 + d_3^- - d_3^+ = 120$$
$$x_1, x_2, d_1^-, d_1^+, d_2^-, d_2^+, d_3^-, d_3^+ \geq 0$$

In order to graph this model, the deviational variables in each goal constraint are set equal to zero, and we graph each subsequent equation on a set of coordinates just as in Chapter 3. Figure 9.1 on page 310 is a graph of the three goal constraints for this model.

Notice that in Figure 9.1 there is no feasible solution space indicated as in a regular linear programming model. This is because all three goal constraints are *equations;* thus all solution points are on the constraint lines.

The solution logic in a goal programming model is to attempt to achieve the goals in the objective function in order of their priorities. As a goal is achieved, the next highest ranked goal is then considered. However, a higher-ranked goal that has been achieved is never given up in order to achieve a lower-ranked goal.

Graphing the goal constraints

The goal programming solution logic

FIGURE 9.1

Goal Constraints

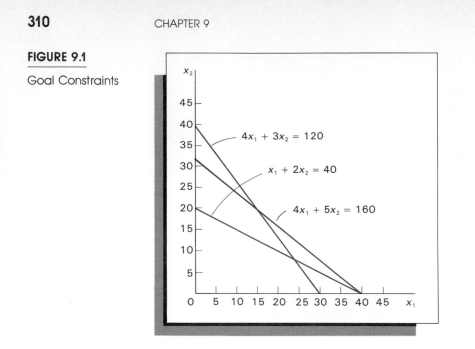

Achieving the
priority one goal

In this example we first consider the priority one goal of mini-mizing d_1^-. The relationship of d_1^- and d_1^+ to the goal constraint is shown in Figure 9.2. The area below the goal constraint line $x_1 + 2x_2 = 40$ represents possible values for d_1^-, and the area above the line represents values for d_1^+. In order to achieve the goal of mini-

FIGURE 9.2

The First Priority
Goal: Minimize d_1^-

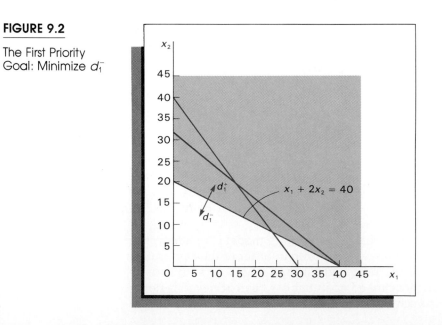

mizing d_1^-, the area below the constraint line corresponding to d_1^- is eliminated, leaving the shaded area as a possible solution area.

Next, we consider the second priority goal of minimizing d_2^-. In Figure 9.3, the area below the constraint line $4x_1 + 5x_2 = 160$ represents the values for d_2^-, and the area above the line represents the values for d_2^+. In order to minimize d_2^-, the area below the constraint line corresponding to d_2^- is eliminated. Notice that by eliminating the area for d_2^-, we do not affect the priority one goal of minimizing d_1^-.

Achieving the priority two goal

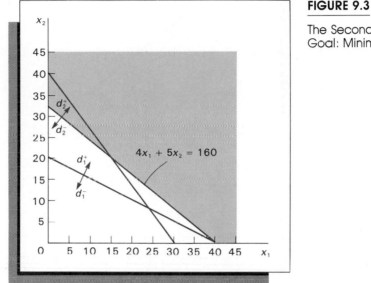

FIGURE 9.3

The Second Priority Goal: Minimize d_2^-

Next, the priority three goal of minimizing d_3^+ is considered. Figure 9.4 on page 312 shows the areas corresponding to d_3^- and d_3^+. In order to minimize d_3^+, the area above the constraint line $4x_1 + 3x_2 = 120$ is eliminated. After considering the first three goals, we are left with the area between the line segments AC and BC, which contains possible solution points that satisfy the first three goals.

Finally, we must consider the fourth priority goal of minimizing d_1^+. In order to achieve this final goal, the area above the constraint line $x_1 + 2x_2 = 40$ must be eliminated. However, if we eliminate this area, then both d_2^- and d_3^- must take on values. In other words, we cannot minimize d_1^+ totally without violating the priority one and two goals. Therefore, we want to find a solution point that satisfies the first three goals, but achieves as much of the fourth priority goal as possible.

Not completely achieving the priority four goal

Point C in Figure 9.5 on page 312 is a solution that *satisfies* these conditions. Notice that if we move down the goal constraint line $4x_1 + 3x_2 = 120$ toward point D, d_1^+ is further minimized; however,

FIGURE 9.4

The Third Priority
Goal: Minimize d_3^+

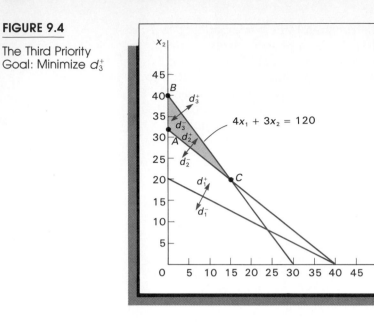

FIGURE 9.5

The Fourth Priority
Goal (Minimize d_1^+)
and the Solution

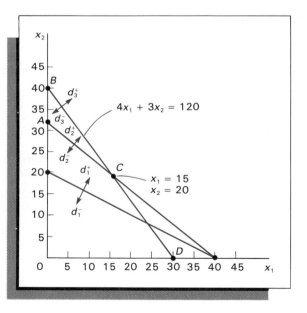

d_2^- takes on a value as we move past point C. Thus, the minimization of d_1^+ would be accomplished only at the expense of a higher ranked goal.

The goal programming solution

The solution at point C is determined by simultaneously solving the two equations that intersect at this point. Doing so results in the following solution.

$$x_1 = 15 \text{ bowls}$$
$$x_2 = 20 \text{ mugs}$$
$$d_1^+ = 15 \text{ hours}$$

Since the deviational variables d_1^-, d_2^-, and d_3^+ all equal zero, they have been minimized and the first three goals have been achieved. Since $d_1^+ = 15$ hours of overtime, the fourth priority goal has not been achieved. The solution to a goal programming model such as this one is referred to as the *most satisfactory* solution rather than the optimal solution, since it satisfies the specified goals as well as possible.

As a solution approach, the graphical method suffers from the same limitations for a goal programming model as for a regular linear programming model (i.e., it is limited to two dimensions). A more general solution approach consists of a modified version of the simplex method, which was first presented in Chapter 4.

The most satisfactory solution rather than the optimal solution

THE MODIFIED SIMPLEX METHOD

In demonstrating the *modified simplex method* for solving a goal programming model, the Colonial Pottery Company example used in the graphical analysis in the previous section will again be used.

minimize $P_1 d_1^-, P_2 d_2^-, P_3 d_3^+, P_4 d_1^+$
subject to
$$x_1 + 2x_2 + d_1^- - d_1^+ = 40$$
$$4x_1 + 5x_2 + d_2^- - d_2^+ = 160$$
$$4x_1 + 3x_2 + d_3^- - d_3^+ = 120$$
$$x_1, x_2, d_1^-, d_1^+, d_2^-, d_2^+, d_3^-, d_3^+ \geq 0$$

The simplex tableau presented in Chapter 4 must be modified slightly for a goal programming model. The initial modified simplex tableau for this example is shown in Table 9.1.

TABLE 9.1
The Initial Modified Simplex Tableau

P_j	Basic Variables	Quantity	x_1	x_2	P_1 d_1^-	P_2 d_2^-	d_3^-	P_4 d_1^+	d_2^+	P_3 d_3^+
P_1	d_1^-	40	1	2	1	0	0	−1	0	0
P_2	d_2^-	160	4	5	0	1	0	0	−1	0
	d_3^-	120	4	3	0	0	1	0	0	−1
	P_4	0	0	0	0	0	0	$-P_4$	0	0
	P_3	0	0	0	0	0	0	0	0	$-P_3$
$z_j - P_j$	P_2	$160P_2$	$4P_2$	$5P_2$	0	0	0	0	$-P_2$	0
	P_1	$40P_1$	P_1	$2P_1$	0	0	0	$-P_1$	0	0

In the simplex tableau modified for goal programming, the model variables are listed across the top, with decision variables first, then negative deviational variables, and then positive deviational variables. Rather than assigning the c_j value to each variable across the top row, we assign the priority level P_j.

The initial basic feasible solution variables are always the negative deviational variables for each constraint. The negative deviational variables are analogous to slack variables in a regular linear programming model, and you will recall that slack variables (when present) always form the initial solution in the simplex method. For this example, d_1^-, d_2^-, and d_3^- are the initial basic variables. The priority level, P_j, for each of these deviational variables is assigned in the left-hand column. In this case minimizing d_1^- is the priority one goal, P_1; minimizing d_2^- is the priority two goal, P_2.

The row values within the body of the tableau are the values corresponding to the goal constraints and are assigned exactly the same way as in the regular simplex method. Notice that the z_j and $z_j - c_j$ rows of the regular simplex method are replaced by four $z_j - P_j$ rows corresponding to the four priority levels. The $z_j - P_j$ rows are computed exactly the same way as in the simplex method, except that computations must be done for each priority level. Although the z_j rows must be computed, they are deleted from the tableau, since their inclusion would make the tableau very large and cumbersome.

For example, consider the x_1 column. Multiplying the x_1 column values by the P_j column values results in

$$\begin{aligned}
P_j \quad & x_1 \\
P_1 \times 1 &= P_1 \\
P_2 \times 4 &= 4P_2 \\
0 \times 4 &= 0
\end{aligned}$$

Since P_j equals zero for x_1, the $z_j - P_j$ values are

$$\begin{aligned}
z_j &- P_j \\
P_1 - 0 &= P_1 \\
4P_2 - 0 &= 4P_2 \\
0 - 0 &= 0
\end{aligned}$$

Instead of being listed all on one row, these values are assigned according to priority. In the $z_j - P_j$ rows in Table 9.1, priority one values are listed across the bottom row, priority two values are listed across the row next to the bottom, and so forth. For example, the $z_j - P_j$ value of P_1 is listed in the bottom row (under the x_1 column), and $4P_2$ is listed in the x_1 column in the next to the bottom row. All other $z_j - P_j$ values are computed the same way.

The next step in the simplex process is to select the *pivot column*. In the modified tableau, the pivot column is determined by choosing the column *in the priority one row* with the maximum positive $z_j - P_j$ value (just as in the regular simplex method). In other words, we seek to satisfy the priority one goal first. If there is no positive value in the priority one row, we go to the next priority row. In Table 9.1, the maximum positive value in the priority one row is $2P_1$; thus the x_2 column is the pivot column and x_2 is the entering nonbasic variable.

The entering nonbasic variable

The *pivot row* is determined by dividing the quantity values by the x_2 column values and selecting the minimum positive value (as in the simplex method). This results in the selection of the d_1^- row as the pivot row.

The second modified simplex tableau is shown in Table 9.2.

TABLE 9.2
The Second Modified Simplex Tableau

P_j	Basic Variables	Quantity	x_1	x_2	P_1 d_1^-	P_2 d_2^-	d_3^-	P_4 d_1^+	d_2^+	P_3 d_3^+
P_2	x_2	20	1/2	1	1/2	0	0	−1/2	0	0
	d_2^-	60	3/2	0	−5/2	1	0	5/2	−1	0
	d_3^-	60	5/2	0	−3/2	0	1	3/2	0	−1
	P_4	0	0	0	0	0	0	−P_4	0	0
	P_3	0	0	0	0	0	0	0	0	−P_3
$z_j - P_j$	P_2	$60P_2$	$3P_2/2$	0	$-5P_2/2$	0	0	$5P_2/2$	−P_2	0
	P_1	0	0	0	−P_1	0	0	0	0	0

In Table 9.2 the new pivot row values (for the x_2 row) are computed the same way as in the simplex method, by using the formula

Computing the new tableau row values

$$\text{new tableau pivot row values} = \frac{\text{old pivot row values}}{\text{pivot number}}$$

All other row values (i.e., d_2^- and d_3^- rows) are also computed the same way as in the simplex method, by using the formula

$$\begin{matrix}\text{new tableau} \\ \text{row value}\end{matrix} = \begin{matrix}\text{old tableau} \\ \text{row value}\end{matrix} - \left(\begin{matrix}\text{corresponding} \\ \text{coefficients in} \\ \text{pivot column}\end{matrix} \times \begin{matrix}\text{corresponding} \\ \text{new tableau} \\ \text{pivot row} \\ \text{value}\end{matrix}\right)$$

Table 9.2 does not show any positive values in the priority one $z_j - P_j$ row, which means that the priority one goal has been satisfied. Next, in the priority two row we see several positive values, the largest of which is $5P_2/2$ in the d_1^+ column. Therefore, the d_1^+ column is the pivot column and d_1^+ is the entering nonbasic variable. The d_2^- row is selected as the pivot row.

The third modified simplex tableau is shown in Table 9.3.

TABLE 9.3
The Third Modified Simplex Tableau

P_j	Basic Variables	Quantity			P_1	P_2		P_4		P_3
			x_1	x_2	d_1^-	d_2^-	d_3^-	d_1^+	d_2^+	d_3^+
P_4	x_2	32	4/5	1	0	1/5	0	0	−1/5	0
	d_1^+	24	3/5	0	−1	2/5	0	1	−2/5	0
	d_3^-	24	8/5	0	0	−3/5	1	0	3/5	−1
	P_4	$24P_4$	$3P_4/5$	0	$-P_4$	$2P_4/5$	0	0	$-2P_4/5$	0
	P_3	0	0	0	0	0	0	0	0	$-P_3$
$z_j - P_j$	P_2	0	0	0	0	$-P_2$	0	0	0	0
	P_1	0	0	0	$-P_1$	0	0	0	0	0

In Table 9.3, there are no positive values in the priority one, two, or three $z_j - P_j$ rows, which means the goals at these first three priority levels have been satisfied. However, the priority four row has several positive values, the largest of which is $3P_4/5$ in the x_1 column. Thus, the x_1 column is the pivot column and the d_3^- row is the pivot row.

The fourth modified simplex tableau is shown in Table 9.4.

TABLE 9.4
The Optimal Modified Simplex Tableau

P_j	Basic Variables	Quantity			P_1	P_2		P_4		P_3
			x_1	x_2	d_1^-	d_2^-	d_3^-	d_1^+	d_2^+	d_3^+
P_4	x_2	20	0	1	0	1/2	−1/2	0	−1/2	1/2
	d_1^+	15	0	0	−1	5/8	−3/8	1	−5/8	3/8
	x_1	15	1	0	0	−3/8	5/8	0	3/8	−5/8
	P_4	$15P_4$	0	0	$-P_4$	$5P_4/8$	$-3P_4/8$	0	$-5P_4/8$	$3P_4/8$
	P_3	0	0	0	0	0	0	0	0	$-P_3$
$z_j - P_j$	P_2	0	0	0	0	$-P_2$	0	0	0	0
	P_1	0	0	0	$-P_1$	0	0	0	0	0

Determining when the most satisfactory solution exists

Observing the $z_j - P_j$ rows in Table 9.4, we see no positive values in the priority one, two, or three rows; therefore, the goals at these priority levels remain satisfied. Looking at the priority four row, we see positive values in the d_2^- and d_3^+ columns. However, notice the negative values in these columns at higher priority levels. For example, in the d_2^- column, a positive value of $5P_4/8$ appears at the priority four level, but a negative value of $-P_2$ appears at the priority two level. This means that if we enter the deviational variable d_2^- into the solution (by selecting this column as the pivot column), we will be giving up the priority two goal that has already been satisfied in order to satisfy a priority four goal. We have already stated that a higher priority goal is never sacrificed for the sake of achieving a lower-ranked goal. Given this condition, the solution shown in Table 9.4 is the *most satisfactory* solution. For this goal programming model, The most satisfactory solution

$x_1 = 15$ bowls

$x_2 = 20$ mugs

$d_1^+ = 15$ hr of overtime

Notice that this is the same solution we achieved using graphical analysis.

Summary of the Steps of the Modified Simplex Method

1. Set up the initial tableau using negative deviational variables for the initial basic feasible solution. Compute the $z_j - P_j$ rows.
2. Determine the pivot column (entering nonbasic variable) by selecting the column with the maximum positive value at the highest priority level that has not been completely attained.
3. Determine the pivot row (leaving solution variable) by dividing the quantity column values by the pivot column values and selecting the row with either the minimum positive value or zero.
4. Compute the new pivot row values using the formula

$$\text{new tableau pivot row value} = \frac{\text{old pivot row value}}{\text{pivot number}}$$

5. Compute all other row values using the formula

$$\begin{array}{c}\text{new tableau} \\ \text{row value}\end{array} = \begin{array}{c}\text{old tableau} \\ \text{row value}\end{array} - \left(\begin{array}{c}\text{corresponding} \\ \text{coefficients in} \\ \text{pivot column}\end{array} \times \begin{array}{c}\text{corresponding} \\ \text{new tableau} \\ \text{pivot row} \\ \text{value}\end{array}\right)$$

6. Compute the new $z_j - P_j$ row.
7. Determine whether the new solution is the most satisfactory by checking the $z_j - P_j$ rows. If no positive values appear at any priority level or if there is a positive value with a corresponding negative value at a higher priority, the solution has been reached. If this condition is not met, return to step 2 and repeat the modified simplex steps.

COMPUTERIZED SOLUTION OF GOAL PROGRAMMING PROBLEMS

Goal programming capabilities are not generally available in most management science personal computer software packages, and mainframe programs are even more scarce. However, Micro Manager, by Lee and Shim, is one PC software package that does have a goal programming capability. The Micro Manager goal programming solution output for the revised Colonial Pottery Company example presented at the beginning of this chapter is shown below.

```
PROGRAM: Goal Programming

***** INPUT DATA ENTERED *****

Min  Z = P 1 dn 1  + P 2 dn 2  + P 3 dp 3  + P 4 dp 1

Subject to:

C 1     1 x 1 + 2 x 2 + dn 1 - dp 1  =   40
C 2     4 x 1 + 5 x 2 + dn 2 - dp 2  =  160
C 3     4 x 1 + 3 x 2 + dn 3 - dp 3  =  120



*****   PROGRAM OUTPUT   *****

Analysis of decision variables

     Variable        Solution value
        x 2              20.00
        x 1              15.00

Analysis of the objective function

     Priority       Nonachievement
        P 1              0.00
        P 2              0.00
        P 3              0.00
        P 4             15.00
```

The model data are easily input into the Micro Manager program, and the output is straightforward and self-explanatory. However, as noted, Micro Manager is one of the few packages that include goal programming capabilities, whereas virtually all management science software packages include linear programming capabilities. Therefore, the solution of a goal programming problem using a sequential linear programming approach will now be demonstrated. We will use the Colonial Pottery Company example and the LINDO/PC software package we have used in previous chapters.

In this sequential procedure, we create a new problem for each priority in the objective function, beginning with the first priority. For our example, our first problem is as follows.

minimize d_1^-

subject to

$$x_1 + 2x_2 + d_1^- - d_1^+ = 40$$
$$4x_1 + 5x_2 + d_2^- - d_2^+ = 160$$
$$4x_1 + 3x_2 + d_3^- - d_3^+ = 120$$

Solving this problem will give us the achievement for d_1^-, and we will subsequently add this achievement to our next linear programming model with a new objective function representing the second priority (P_2) goal. The LINDO/PC solution to this initial problem is as follows.

```
: min d1n
? st
? x1 + 2x2 + d1n - d1p = 40
? 4x1 + 5x2 + d2n - d2p = 160
? 4x1 + 3x2 + d3n - d3p - 120
? end
:



          OBJECTIVE FUNCTION VALUE

   1)            .000000000

   VARIABLE         VALUE          REDUCED COST
      D1N           .000000          1.000000
       X1         24.000000           .000000
       X2          8.000000           .000000
      D1P           .000000           .000000
      D2N         24.000000           .000000
      D2P           .000000           .000000
      D3N           .000000           .000000
      D3P           .000000           .000000


       ROW     SLACK OR SURPLUS     DUAL PRICES
        2)           .000000           .000000
        3)           .000000           .000000
        4)           .000000           .000000

   NO. ITERATIONS=        3
```

Notice that the objective function value is zero. Hence $d_1^- = 0$ (i.e., D1N = 0) and the first priority goal has been completely achieved. Next, we add $d_1^- = 0$ to our model as a fourth constraint and set as our new objective function the minimization of d_2^-, which is the second priority goal.

minimize d_2^-

subject to

$$x_1 + 2x_2 + d_1^- - d_1^+ = 40$$
$$4x_1 + 5x_2 + d_2^- - d_2^+ = 160$$
$$4x_1 + 3x_2 + d_3^- - d_3^+ = 120$$
$$d_1^- = 0$$

LINDO/PC produces the following solution for this model.

```
: alt
ROW:
1
VAR:
d2n
VARIABLE NOT IN THIS ROW.  WANT IT INCLUDED?
? y
NEW COEFFICIENT:
? 1
: look all

MIN      D2N
SUBJECT TO
        2)   D1N + X1 + 2 X2 - D1P =    40
        3)   4 X1 + 5 X2 + D2N - D2P =     160
        4)   4 X1 + 3 X2 + D3N - D3P =     120
        5)   D1N =    0
END

:

            OBJECTIVE FUNCTION VALUE

    1)       .000000000

    VARIABLE        VALUE         REDUCED COST
        D1N          .000000          .000000
        X1         15.000000          .000000
        X2         20.000000          .000000
        D1P        15.000000          .000000
        D2N          .000000         1.000000
        D2P          .000000          .000000
        D3N          .000000          .000000
        D3P          .000000          .000000


    ROW    SLACK OR SURPLUS     DUAL PRICES
        2)          .000000          .000000
        3)          .000000          .000000
        4)          .000000          .000000
        5)          .000000          .000000

NO. ITERATIONS=         1
```

The objective function value of zero indicates that the second goal has been completely achieved and $d_2^- = 0$ (i.e., D2N = 0). Next we add this goal achievement to our model as a constraint; the new objective function is to minimize d_3^+, the third priority goal. This new LINDO/PC formulation and the solution output are as follows.

```
: alt
ROW:
1
VAR:
d2n
NEW COEFFICIENT:
? 0
: alt
ROW:
1
VAR:
d3p
VARIABLE NOT IN THIS ROW.  WANT IT INCLUDED?
? y
NEW COEFFICIENT:
? 1

: ext
BEGIN EXTEND WITH ROW    6
? d2n = 0
? end
: look all

MIN      D3P
SUBJECT TO
        2)    D1N + X1 + 2 X2 - D1P =      40
        3)    4 X1 + 5 X2 + D2N - D2P =      160
        4)    4 X1 + 3 X2 + D3N - D3P =      120
        5)    D1N =    0
        6)    D2N =    0
END

:
            OBJECTIVE FUNCTION VALUE
    1)         .000000000

VARIABLE          VALUE         REDUCED COST
    D1N           .000000           .000000
     X1         15.000000           .000000
     X2         20.000000           .000000
    D1P         15.000000           .000000
    D2N           .000000           .000000
    D2P           .000000           .000000
    D3N           .000000           .000000
    D3P           .000000          1.000000

    ROW    SLACK OR SURPLUS     DUAL PRICES
    2)           .000000           .000000
    3)           .000000           .000000
    4)           .000000           .000000
    5)           .000000           .000000
    6)           .000000           .000000

NO. ITERATIONS=        0
```

The third priority goal has also been achieved ($d_3^+ = 0$). We add this achievement as a constraint and create a new objective function to minimize d_1^+ (the fourth priority goal). The LINDO/PC formulation of this fourth model in our sequence of linear programming models is shown below, along with the solution output.

```
: alt
ROW:
1
VAR:
d3p
NEW COEFFICIENT:
? 0
: alt
ROW:
1
VAR:
d1p
VARIABLE NOT IN THIS ROW.  WANT IT INCLUDED?
? y
NEW COEFFICIENT:
? 1
: ext
BEGIN EXTEND WITH ROW   7
? d3p = 0
? end

: look all

MIN      D1P
SUBJECT TO
        2)    D1N + X1 + 2 X2 - D1P =      40
        3)    4 X1 + 5 X2 + D2N - D2P =     160
        4)    4 X1 + 3 X2 + D3N - D3P =     120
        5)    D1N =     0
        6)    D2N =     0
        7)    D3P =     0
END

:


            OBJECTIVE FUNCTION VALUE

   1)         15.0000000

   VARIABLE          VALUE          REDUCED COST
        D1N          .000000          1.000000
         X1        15.000000           .000000
         X2        20.000000           .000000
        D1P        15.000000           .000000
        D2N          .000000           .000000
        D2P          .000000           .625000
        D3N          .000000           .375000
        D3P          .000000           .000000
```

```
       ROW   SLACK OR SURPLUS    DUAL PRICES
        2)           .000000       1.000000
        3)           .000000       -.625000
        4)           .000000        .375000
        5)           .000000        .000000
        6)           .000000        .625000
        7)           .000000        .375000

   NO. ITERATIONS=        2
```

Since this last model is the last in our sequence, all four priorities have been examined and the final and most satisfactory solution is

x_1 = 15 bowls

x_2 = 20 mugs

d_1^+ = 15 hr of labor

Of course, such a solution procedure would not be worthwhile without the capability to solve each new model in the sequence with the computer. However, such a process is quite easily carried out with a package like LINDO/PC. At each step, one can simply use LINDO/PC commands to modify the previous model by adding a constraint and changing the objective function, rather than re-entering the whole model each time.

This sequential solution procedure is a very intuitive and logical approach to solving a goal programming model. You can see that this sequential computerized solution process exactly duplicates the steps in the graphical solution approach encompassed in Figures 9.2 to 9.5.

APPLICATIONS OF GOAL PROGRAMMING

In this chapter we have considered only one example of goal programming, and it was for a business enterprise (the Colonial Pottery Company). However, goal programming is an especially useful technique for organizations such as government agencies, hospitals, schools, and charitable organizations. Such organizations typically have a variety of goals other than earning a profit. For example, a space agency such as NASA is concerned not with profit, but with several objectives related to space exploration and the research and development of new technology. Although NASA would have a goal related to cost minimization, that goal probably would not be the agency's most important objective. Similarly, the objectives of a school relate to quality of education, the number of students it can educate, meeting local or state guidelines, and, to a lesser extent,

Organizations with several goals other than profit maximization

minimizing the cost of running the school. Goal programming is much more applicable to the resource allocation problems of these types of organizations than is regular linear programming.

Although goal programming is a relatively new management science technique (it was first described in 1961 by Charnes and Cooper), it has been widely applied in practice. A textbook by Milan Zeleny, *Multiple Criteria Decision Making,* provides an extensive bibliography of books and articles related to goal programming, many of which document applications in business, government, the military, and health care.

A bibliography on goal programming applications

In addition, the journal *Interfaces,* referred to in previous chapters on linear programming, has reported several applications of goal programming during the past few years. Following are brief summaries of three of these applications.

Human Resource Allocation in Schools

The St. Louis Division of the Blue Hills Home Corporation employs 22 teachers who provide remedial educational services for 22 private schools in the St. Louis metropolitan area. Under the old teacher assignment system, a teacher attended two schools each day, one in the morning and one in the afternoon, for an entire year. Assignments were based primarily on the distance teachers traveled to their two schools. However, frequently school administrators and teachers expressed pleasure or displeasure with individual assignments. Teachers had assignment preferences based on, for example, supervisory personnel and working environment, and administrators had preferences for individual teachers based on job performance, skills, productivity, and so forth. All of these factors complicated the teacher assignment process. A goal programming model that reflected these different assignment factors was developed.

Assigning teachers to schools

The goal programming model included 462 decision variables representing alternative assignments of two schools for each of the 22 teachers. The first priority goal encompassed 44 goal constraints representing the assignment of teachers to schools. The second priority goal consisted of three sets of goal constraints reflecting the preferences of supervisors, teachers, and school administrators. The third priority goal involved a single constraint for travel costs. The model solution was in the form of 0–1 values representing no assignment and assignment for a particular teacher–school combination, respectively.

The model was used to make the yearly assignment of teachers in St. Louis. The fact that the preferences of teachers, administrators, and supervisors were reflected in the model significantly enhanced acceptance of the solution assignments. In addition, the average travel distance was decreased by approximately 15%, resulting in approximately 15% savings in transportation costs.[1]

Trucking Terminal Site Location

The liquid foods division of the Truck Transport Corporation of East St. Louis, Illinois, consists of a network of five terminals. For a number of reasons, the company wanted to relocate its East St. Louis terminal. The company's East St. Louis terminal was served by as many as 30 independent truck drivers, most of whom lived within a 100-mile radius of the terminal. Moving the terminal outside the radius could result in a significant loss of drivers due to the increased transportation cost (which the driver would absorb) from each driver's home to the new terminal site. The potential loss of these independent drivers represented a serious threat to the survival of the company's liquid foods division. In addition, the customers' preference for the terminal site was an important factor, since service was perceived as a function of distance from the terminal.

The company developed a goal programming model consisting of five priority levels. The decision variables for the model represented the trips from each terminal site (i.e., the company's present terminals and one new site) to each customer and each truck driver's home. The first priority goal constraints reflected the transportation requirements that the terminals supply the average number of trips required by the major customers, and that the terminals supply the truck drivers with their requested average number of trips. The second priority goal constraints reflected potential driver dissatisfaction with particular terminal managers, as determined through a driver survey. The third priority goal constraints attempted to minimize potential customer dissatisfaction with new terminal managers. These constraints were constructed using a customer survey. The fourth and fifth priority goal constraints sought to minimize the cost of transportation between the drivers' homes and the terminals, and between the terminals and the customers, respectively. The goal programming model consisted of 170 decision variables and 65 goal constraints. The model was reconstructed and solved for each of five potential site locations.

The terminal site was relocated as a result of the model analysis. Six months following the move, the company had experienced no more than the normal expected attrition of drivers and no turnover

[1]S. Lee and M. Schniederjans, "A Multicriteria Assignment Problem: A Goal Programming Approach," *Interfaces* 13, no. 4 (August 1983): 75–81.

in customers, and drivers had experienced no significant increases in the costs of traveling from their homes to the new terminal site.[2]

Armed Services Recruitment

At present, approximately 80% of all enlistees into the armed services use a recruiting mechanism called the Delayed Entry Program (DEP), which allows a recruit to delay reporting to boot camp for up to a year. This procedure, besides being a powerful inducement to enlist, improves planning and forecasting and reduces attrition once recruits are actually inducted. However, it also has several disadvantages: it can reduce productivity (when recruiters feel they can "live off their DEP pipeline" to meet accession quotas); it may be difficult to reverse (if accession goals are suddenly reduced); and attrition can be high among recruits during the year in DEP. The Navy developed a system encompassing a goal programming model wherein the DEP is considered as a scarce resource to be allocated such that the overall productivity of the recruiting force is maximized. The system varies accession quotas across geographic areas and reflects differences between areas in terms of population size and mix, unemployment rates, number of recruiters, and the like. The model is solved monthly using recent data on the number of contracts obtained in the previous period, changes in the area's DEP pools, changes in the number of recruiters, and changes in the Navy's recruiting goals. In one year the system resulted in approximately a 50% reduction in DEP/recruiter imbalances.[3]

Summary

This chapter presented a variation of linear programming for problems in which there is more than one objective. Goal programming is especially useful for organizations that do not have a single, clearly defined objective, such as profit maximization or cost minimization. Goal programming is often applicable to decision-making problems in public or governmental organizations where

---

[2]M. Schniederjans et al., "An Application of Goal Programming to Resolve a Site Location Problem," *Interfaces* 12, no. 3 (June 1982): 65–72.

[3]R. Morey, "Managing the Armed Services' Delayed Entry Pools to Improve Productivity in Recruiting," *Interfaces* 15, no. 5 (September-October 1985): 81–90.

levels of service or efficiency in carrying out numerous goals are more important than profit or cost.

The presentation of goal programming completes the coverage of linear programming. One of the implicit assumptions of linear programming has been that all parameters and values in the model were known with certainty. Upcoming chapters will consider techniques that are probabilistic, used when a situation includes uncertainty.

Conclusion of linear programming coverage

References

Charnes, A., and Cooper, W. W. *Management Models and Industrial Applications of Linear Programming*. New York: John Wiley and Sons, 1961.

Dyer, J. S. "Interactive Goal Programming." *Management Science* 19, no. 1 (1972): 62–70.

Ignizio, J. P. *Goal Programming and Extensions*. Lexington, Mass.: Lexington Books, 1976.

Ijiri, Y. *Management Goals and Accounting for Control*. Chicago: Rand McNally, 1965.

Kornbluth, J. S. H. "A Survey of Goal Programming." *Omega* 1, no. 2 (1973).

Lee, S. M. *Goal Programming for Decision Analysis*. Philadelphia: Auerbach Publishers, 1972.

Lee, S. M., and Clayton, E. R. "A Goal Programming Model for Academic Resource Allocation." *Management Science* 18, no. 8 (1972): 395–408.

Lee, S. M., and Schniederjans, M. "A Multicriteria Assignment Problem: A Goal Programming Approach." *Interfaces* 13, no. 4 (August 1983): 75–81.

Schniederjans, M.; Kwak, N.; and Helmer, M. "An Application of Goal Programming to Resolve a Site Location Problem." *Interfaces* 12, no. 3 (June 1982). 65–72.

Zeleny, M. *Multiple Criteria Decision Making*. New York: McGraw-Hill, 1982.

EXAMPLE PROBLEM SOLUTION

As a prelude to the Problems section, the following example demonstrates the formulation and solution of a goal programming problem.

Problem Statement

The Rucklehouse Public Relations firm has been contracted to do a survey following a primary in New Hampshire. The firm must assign interviewers to carry out the survey. The interviews are conducted by telephone and in person. One person can conduct 80 telephone interviews or 40 personal interviews in a day. It costs $50 per day for a telephone interviewer and $70 per day for a personal interviewer. The following goals, in priority order, have been established by the firm to ensure a representative survey.

a. At least 3,000 total interviews should be conducted.
b. An interviewer should conduct only one type of interview each day. The firm wants to maintain its daily budget of $2,500.
c. At least 1,000 interviews should be by telephone.

Formulate a goal programming model to determine the number of interviewers to hire in order to satisfy these goals, and solve the model using the modified simplex method.

Step 1: Model Formulation

minimize $P_1 d_1^-, P_2 d_2^+, P_3 d_3^-$

subject to

$$80x_1 + 40x_2 + d_1^- - d_1^+ = 3{,}000 \text{ interviews}$$
$$50x_1 + 70x_2 + d_2^- - d_2^+ = \$2{,}500 \text{ budget}$$
$$80x_1 + d_3^- - d_3^+ = 1{,}000 \text{ telephone interviews}$$

where

$x_1 =$ number of telephone interviewers
$x_2 =$ number of personal interviewers

Step 2: The Modified Simplex Solution, Initial Tableau

P_j	Basic Variables	Quantity	x_1	x_2	P_1 d_1^-	P_3 d_2^-	d_3^-	d_1^+	P_2 d_2^+	d_3^+
P_1	d_1^-	3,000	80	40	1	0	0	−1	0	0
	d_2^-	2,500	50	70	0	1	0	0	−1	0
P_3	d_3^-	1,000	80	0	0	0	1	0	0	−1
	P_3	$1{,}000P_3$	$80P_3$	0	0	0	0	0	0	$-P_3$
$z_j - P_j$	P_2	0	0	0	0	0	0	0	0	0
	P_1	$3{,}000P_1$	$80P_1$	$40P_1$	0	0	0	$-P_1$	0	0

Step 3: The Second Tableau (x_1 enters, d_3^- leaves)

P_j	Basic Variables	Quantity	x_1	x_2	P_1 d_1^-	d_2^-	P_3 d_3^-	d_1^+	P_2 d_2^+	d_3^+
P_1	d_1^-	2,000	0	40	1	0	−1	−1	0	1
	d_2^-	1,875	0	70	0	1	−5/8	0	−1	5/8
	x_1	12.5	1	0	0	0	1/80	0	0	−1/80
	P_3	0	0	0	0	0	$-P_3$	0	0	0
$z_j - P_j$	P_2	0	0	0	0	0	0	0	$-P_2$	0
	P_1	$2{,}000P_1$	0	$40P_1$	0	0	$-P_1$	$-P_1$	0	P_1

Step 4: The Third Tableau (x_2 enters, d_2^- leaves)

P_j	Basic Variables	Quantity	x_1	x_2	P_1 d_1^-	d_2^-	P_3 d_3^-	d_1^+	P_2 d_2^+	d_3^+
P_1	d_1^-	928.8	0	0	1	$-4/7$	$-9/14$	-1	$4/7$	$9/14$
0	x_2	26.78	0	1	0	$1/70$	$-5/560$	0	$-1/70$	$5/560$
0	x_1	12.50	1	0	0	0	$1/80$	0	0	$-1/80$
	P_3	0	0	0	0	0	$-P_3$	0	0	0
$z_j - P_j$	P_2	0	0	0	0	0	0	0	$-P_2$	0
	P_1	$928P_1$	0	0	0	$-4P_1/7$	$-5P_1/7$	$-P_1$	$4P_1/7$	0

Step 5: The Fourth Tableau (d_2^+ enters, d_1^- leaves)

P_j	Basic Variables	Quantity	x_1	x_2	P_1 d_1^-	d_2^-	P_3 d_3^-	d_1^+	P_2 d_2^+	d_3^+
P_2	d_2^+	1,625.4	0	0	$7/4$	-1	$-9/8$	$-7/4$	1	$9/8$
0	x_2	50	0	1	$1/40$	0	$-1/40$	$-1/40$	0	$1/40$
0	x_1	12.5	1	0	0	0	$1/80$	0	0	$-1/80$
	P_3	0	0	0	0	0	$-P_3$	0	0	0
$z_j - P_j$	P_2	$1,625.4P_2$	0	0	$7P_2/4$	$-P_2$	$-5P_2/4$	$-7P_2/4$	0	$9P_2/8$
	P_1	0	0	0	$-P_1$	0	0	0	0	0

Step 6: The Fifth Tableau (d_3^+ enters, d_2^+ leaves)

P_j	Basic Variables	Quantity	x_1	x_2	P_1 d_1^-	d_2^-	P_3 d_3^-	d_1^+	P_2 d_2^+	d_3^+
0	d_3^+	1,444.50	0	0	$14/9$	$-8/9$	-1	$-14/9$	$8/9$	1
0	x_2	13.88	0	1	$-1/72$	$1/45$	0	$1/72$	$-1/45$	0
0	x_1	30.56	1	0	$7/360$	$-1/90$	0	$-7/360$	$1/90$	0
	P_3	0	0	0	0	0	$-P_3$	0	0	0
$z_j - P_j$	P_2	0	0	0	0	0	0	0	$-P_2$	0
	P_1	0	0	0	$-P_1$	0	0	0	0	0

The solution is

$x_1 = 30.56$

$x_2 = 13.88$

$d_3^+ = 1,444.50$

Problems

1. A manufacturing company produces products 1, 2, and 3. The three products have the following resource requirements and produce the following profit.

Product	Labor (hr/unit)	Material (lb/unit)	Profit ($/unit)
1	5	4	3
2	2	6	5
3	4	3	2

At present the firm has a daily labor capacity of 240 available hours and a daily supply of 400 pounds of material. The general linear programming formulation for this problem is as follows.

maximize $Z = 3x_1 + 5x_2 + 2x_3$

subject to

$$5x_1 + 2x_2 + 4x_3 \leq 240$$
$$4x_1 + 6x_2 + 3x_3 \leq 400$$
$$x_1, x_2, x_3 \geq 0$$

Management has developed the following set of goals, arranged in order of their importance to the firm.

(1) Because of recent labor relations difficulties, management wants to avoid underutilization of normal production capacity.
(2) Management has established a satisfactory profit level of $500 per day.
(3) Overtime is to be minimized as much as possible.
(4) Management wants to minimize the purchase of additional materials so as to avoid handling and storage problems.

Formulate a goal programming model to determine the number of each product to produce so as to best satisfy the goals.

2. The Homesaver Appliance Company produces washing machines and dryers. Manufacturing either product requires one hour of production time. The plant has a normal production capacity of 40 hours per week. The maximum number of washers that can be stored per week is 24; 30 dryers can be stored per week. The profit for a washer is $80, and the profit for a dryer is $40. The manager of the company has established the following goals, arranged in order of their importance:

(1) Minimization of underutilization of normal production capacity
(2) Production of as many washers and dryers as possible. However, since the profit for a washer is twice that for a dryer, the manager has twice as much desire to produce washers as to produce dryers.
(3) Minimization of overtime

    a. Formulate a goal programming model for determining the number of washers and dryers to produce in order to satisfy the goals in the best way.

    b. Reformulate the goal programming model from part (a) to include a fourth priority goal of limiting overtime to ten hours per week (if possible).

3. The Bay City Parks and Recreation Department has received a federal grant of $600,000 to expand its public recreation facilities. City council representatives have demanded four different types of facilities — gymnasiums, athletic fields, tennis courts, and swimming pools. In fact, the demand by various communities in the city has been for 7 gyms, 10 athletic fields, 8 tennis courts, and 12 swimming pools. Each facility costs a certain amount, requires a certain number of acres, and is expected to be used a certain amount, as follows:

Facility	Cost ($)	Required Acres	Expected Usage (people/week)
Gymnasium	$80,000	4	1,500
Athletic field	24,000	8	3,000
Tennis court	15,000	3	500
Swimming pool	40,000	5	1,000

The Parks and Recreation Department has located 50 acres of land for construction (although more land could be located if necessary). The department has established the following goals, listed in order of their priority:

(1) The department wants to spend the total grant, because any amount not spent must be returned to the government.

(2) The department wants the facilities to be used by a total of at least 20,000 people each week.

(3) The department wants to avoid having to secure more than the 50 acres of land already located.

(4) The department would like to meet the demands of the city council for new facilities. However, this goal should be weighted according to the number of people expected to use each facility.

(5) If the department must secure more land, it wants to limit the amount to 10 acres.

Formulate a goal programming model for determining how many of each type of facility should be constructed to best achieve the city's goals.

4. A farmer in the Midwest has 1,000 acres of land on which he intends to plant corn, wheat, and soybeans. Each acre of corn costs $100 for preparation, requires 7 worker days of labor, and yields a profit of $30. An acre of wheat costs $120 to prepare, requires 10 worker days of labor, and yields $40 profit. An acre of soybeans costs $70 to prepare, requires 8 worker days, and yields $20 profit. The farmer has taken out a loan of

$80,000 for crop preparation and has contracted with a union for 6,000 worker days of labor. A Midwestern granary has agreed to purchase 200 acres of corn, 500 acres of wheat, and 300 acres of soybeans. The farmer has established the following goals, in order of their importance.

(1) In order to maintain good relations with the union, the labor contract must be honored; that is, the full 6,000 worker days of labor contracted for must be used.
(2) Preparation costs should not exceed the loan amount so that additional loans will not have to be secured.
(3) The farmer desires a profit of at least $105,000 in order to remain in good financial condition.
(4) Contracting for excess labor should be avoided.
(5) The farmer would like to use as much of the available acreage as possible.
(6) The farmer would like to meet the sales agreement with the granary. However, the goal should be weighted according to the profit returned by each crop.

Formulate a goal programming model for determining the number of acres of each crop the farmer should plant in order to satisfy the goals in the best possible way.

5. The Growall Fertilizer Company produces three types of fertilizer — Supergro, Dynaplant, and Soilsaver. The company has the capacity to produce a maximum of 2,000 tons of fertilizer in a week. It costs $800 to produce a ton of Supergro, $1,500 for Dynaplant, and $500 for Soilsaver. The production process requires 10 hours of labor for a ton of Supergro, 12 hours for a ton of Dynaplant, and 18 hours for a ton of Soilsaver. The company has 800 hours of normal production labor available each week. Each week the company can expect a demand for 800 tons of Supergro, 900 tons of Dynaplant, and 1,100 tons of Soilsaver. The company has established the following goals, in order of their priority.

(1) The company does not want to spend over $20,000 per week on production if possible.
(2) The company would like to limit overtime to 100 hours per week.
(3) The company wants to meet demand for all three fertilizers; however, it is twice as important to meet the demand for Supergro as it is to meet the demand for Dynaplant, and it is twice as important to meet the demand for Dynaplant as it is to meet the demand for Soilsaver.
(4) It is desirable to avoid producing under capacity, if possible.
(5) Because of union agreements, the company wants to avoid under-utilization of labor.

Formulate a goal programming model for determining the number of tons of each brand of fertilizer to produce in order to satisfy the goals.

6. The Barrett Textile Mill was checked by inspectors enforcing the Occupational Safety and Health Act (OSHA). The inspectors found violations

in four categories: hazardous materials, fire protection, hand-powered tools, and machine guarding. In each category the mill was not in 100% compliance. Each percentage point of increase in the compliance level in each category will reduce the frequency of accidents, decrease the accident cost per worker, and constitute progress toward satisfying the OSHA compliance level. However, achieving compliance does cost the mill money. The following table shows the benefits (in accident frequency and accident cost per worker) and the costs of a percentage-point increase in compliance in each category.

Category	Accident Frequency Reduction (accidents/ 10^5 hr of exposure)	Accident Cost/ Worker Reduction	Cost/ Percentage Point Compliance
1. Hazardous materials	.18	$1.21	$135
2. Fire protection	.11	.48	87
3. Hand-powered tools	.17	.54	58
4. Machine guarding	.21	1.04	160

To achieve 100% compliance in all four categories, the mill would have to increase compliance in hazardous materials by 60 percentage points (i.e., it is presently at 40% compliance), in fire protection by 28 percentage points, in hand-powered tools by 35 percentage points, and in machine guarding by 17 percentage points. However, the management of the mill faces a dilemma, in that only $52,000 is available to spend on safety. Any larger expenditure could jeopardize the financial standing of the mill. Thus, management hopes to achieve a level of accident reduction and compliance that is within the company's budget limitation and that will satisfy OSHA authorities enough to temporarily delay punitive action. Therefore, management has established four goals, which are listed in order of importance.

(1) Do not exceed the budget constraint of $52,000.
(2) Achieve the percentage increases in compliance necessary to achieve 100% compliance in each category.
(3) Achieve total accident frequency reduction of 20 accidents/10^5 hours of exposure. (This goal denotes management's desire to minimize the frequency of accidents even if 100% compliance cannot be achieved in all categories.)
(4) Reduce the total accident cost/worker to $115.

Formulate a goal programming model for determining the percentage points of compliance needed in each category to satisfy the goals.

7. Consider the following modified simplex tableau.

P_j	Basic Variables	Quantity	0 x_1	0 x_2	0 d_1^-	P_1 d_2^-	0 d_3^-	P_2 d_1^+	0 d_2^+	P_3 d_3^+
P_3	d_3^+	48	0	$-4/5$	$-3/5$	4	-1	0	-4	1
P_2	d_1^+	40	0	-12	-4	20	0	1	-20	0
0	x_1	88	1	$-4/15$	$-3/5$	4	0	0	-4	0
P_3		$48P_3$	0	$4P_3/5$	$-3P_3/5$	$4P_3$	$-P_3$	0	$-4P_3$	0
P_2		$40P_2$	0	$-12P_2$	$-4P_2$	$20P_2$	0	0	$-20P_2$	0
P_1		0	0	0	0	$-P_1$	0	0	0	0

a. Determine how many goal constraints there are in this goal programming model.

b. Write out the original objective function.

c. Write out the solution shown in this tableau.

d. Determine whether this solution is the most satisfactory one that can be achieved. Explain.

e. Determine whether any of the goals were not achieved in this solution. Explain.

8. Solve the following goal programming model (a) using the modified simplex method and (b) graphically.

minimize $P_1 d_1^+, P_2 d_2^-, P_3 d_3^-$

subject to

$$4x_1 + 2x_2 + d_1^- - d_1^+ = 80$$
$$x_1 + d_2^- - d_2^+ = 30$$
$$x_2 + d_3^- - d_3^+ = 50$$
$$x_j, d_i^-, d_i^+ \geq 0$$

9. Solve the following goal programming model (a) using the modified simplex method and (b) graphically.

minimize $P_1 d_1^- + P_1 d_1^+, P_2 d_2^-, P_3 d_3^-, 3P_4 d_2^+ + 5P_4 d_3^+$

subject to

$$x_1 + x_2 + d_1^- - d_1^+ = 800$$
$$5x_1 + d_2^- - d_2^+ = 2{,}500$$
$$3x_2 + d_3^- - d_3^+ = 1{,}400$$
$$x_j, d_i^-, d_i^+ \geq 0$$

10. Solve the following goal programming model using the modified simplex method.

minimize $P_1 d_3^+, P_2 d_1^-, P_3 d_2^-, P_4 d_1^+$

subject to

$$x_1 + 2x_2 + d_1^- - d_1^+ = 20$$
$$x_2 + d_2^- = 12$$
$$d_1^+ + d_3^- - d_3^+ = 6$$
$$x_j, d_i^-, d_i^+ \geq 0$$

11. Solve the following goal programming model using the modified simplex method.

minimize $P_1 d_2^+, P_2 d_1^-, P_3 d_4^+, P_4 d_1^+$

subject to

$$2x_1 + 3x_2 + x_3 + d_1^- - d_1^+ = 300$$
$$5x_2 + 4x_3 + d_2^- - d_2^+ = 400$$
$$x_1 + x_2 + x_3 + d_3^- - d_3^+ = 200$$
$$d_3^+ + d_4^- - d_4^+ = 50$$
$$x_j, d_i^-, d_i^+ \geq 0$$

12. A manufacturer produces products A and B on two production lines. The following goal programming model has been developed for determining the number of product A (x_1) and product B (x_2) needed to meet the manufacturer's goals.

minimize $P_1 d_1^-, P_2 d_4^+, 4P_3 d_2^- + 3P_3 d_3^-, 3P_4 d_2^+ + 4P_4 d_3^+$

subject to

$$2x_1 + 1.5x_2 + d_1^- - d_1^+ = 180 \text{ (material, lb)}$$
$$x_1 + d_2^- - d_2^+ = 40 \text{ (line 1 capacity, hr)}$$
$$x_2 + d_3^- - d_3^+ = 40 \text{ (line 2 capacity, hr)}$$
$$d_2^+ + d_4^- - d_4^+ = 10 \text{ (overtime, hr)}$$
$$x_j, d_i^-, d_i^+ \geq 0$$

Solve this goal programming model using the modified simplex method.

13. Solve the following goal programming model using the modified simplex method.

minimize $P_1 d_4^+, P_2 d_2^-, P_3 d_1^-, P_4 d_3^+$

subject to

$$x_1 + d_1^- - d_1^+ = 4$$
$$x_2 + d_2^- - d_2^+ = 6$$
$$3x_1 + 2x_2 + d_3^- - d_3^+ = 18$$
$$d_3^+ + d_4^- - d_4^+ = 3$$
$$x_j, d_i^-, d_i^+ \geq 0$$

14. Solve the following goal programming model using the modified simplex method.

minimize $P_1 d_3^-, P_2 d_2^-, P_3 d_1^+, P_4 d_2^+$

subject to

$$4x_1 + 6x_2 + d_1^- - d_1^+ = 48$$
$$2x_1 + x_2 + d_2^- - d_2^+ = 20$$
$$d_2^+ + d_3^- - d_3^+ = 10$$
$$x_2 + d_4^- = 6$$
$$x_j, d_i^-, d_i^+ \geq 0$$

15. The Wearever Carpet Company produces two brands of carpet — shag and sculptured. The following goal programming model has been developed for determining the number of yards of shag (x_1, in 100-yard lots) and sculptured (x_2, in 100-yard lots) to produce daily in order to meet goals for production capacity, daily sales demand, and overtime.

minimize $P_1 d_1^-, 5P_2 d_2^-, 2P_2 d_3^-, P_3 d_4^+$

subject to

$$8x_1 + 6x_2 + d_1^- - d_1^+ = 480 \text{ (production capacity, hr)}$$
$$x_1 + d_2^- = 40 \text{ (demand, 100 yd)}$$
$$x_2 + d_3^- = 50 \text{ (demand, 100 yd)}$$
$$d_1^+ + d_4^- - d_4^- = 20 \text{ (overtime, hr)}$$
$$x_j, d_i^-, d_i^+ \geq 0$$

Solve this goal programming model using the modified simplex method.

16. The East Midvale Textile Company produces denim and brushed cotton cloth. The average production rate for both types of cloth is 1,000 yards per hour, and the normal weekly production capacity (running two shifts) is 80 hours. The marketing department estimates that the maximum weekly demand is for 60,000 yards of denim and 35,000 yards of brushed cotton. The profit is $3.00 per yard for denim and $2.00 per yard for brushed cotton. The following four goals, listed in order of importance, have been established by the company.

(1) Eliminate underutilization of production capacity in order to maintain stable employment levels.
(2) Limit overtime to 10 hours.
(3) Do not exceed demand for denim and brushed cotton.
(4) Minimize overtime as much as possible.

a. Formulate a goal programming model for determining the number of yards (in 1,000-yard lots) to produce in order to satisfy the goals.
b. Solve this model using the modified simplex method.

17. The Oregon Atlantic Company produces two kinds of paper — newsprint and white wrapping paper (butcher paper). It requires 5 minutes to produce a yard of newsprint and 8 minutes to produce a yard of wrapping paper. The company has 4,800 minutes of normal production capacity available each week. The profit is $0.20 for a yard of newsprint and $0.25 for a yard of wrapping paper. The weekly demand is for 500 yards of newsprint and 400 yards of wrapping paper. The company has established the following goals, in order of priority.

(1) Limit overtime to 480 minutes.
(2) Achieve a profit of $300 each week.
(3) Fulfill the demand for the products in order of magnitude of their profits.
(4) Avoid underutilization of production capacity.

   a. Formulate a goal programming model for determining the number of yards of each type of paper to produce weekly in order to satisfy the various goals.

   b. Solve the goal programming model using the modified simplex method.

18. a. Describe the steps required to solve problem 8 on the computer using the sequential linear programming approach, and relate this description to the graphical solution of this problem.

   b. If you have access to a linear programming software package and computer, solve problem 8 using the sequential linear programming approach.

19. A rural clinic hires its staff from nearby cities and towns on a part-time basis. The clinic attempts to have a general practitioner (GP), a nurse, and an internist on duty during at least a portion of each week. The clinic has a weekly budget of $1,200. A GP charges the clinic $40 per hour, a nurse charges $20 per hour, and an internist charges $150 per hour. The clinic has established the following goals in order of priority.

(1) A nurse should be available at least 30 hours per week.
(2) The weekly budget of $1,200 should not be exceeded.
(3) A GP or internist should be available at least 20 hours per week.
(4) An internist should be available at least 6 hours per week.

Formulate a goal programming model for determining the number of hours to hire each staff member in order to satisfy the various goals, and solve the model.

10

Probability

The techniques presented in Chapters 2 through 9 are typically thought of as *deterministic*; that is, they are not subject to uncertainty or variation. With deterministic techniques, the assumption is that conditions of complete certainty and perfect knowledge of the future exist. In the linear programming models presented in previous chapters, the various parameters of the models and the model results were assumed to be known with certainty. In the model constraints we did not say that a bowl would require 4 pounds of clay "70% of the time." We specifically stated that each bowl would require exactly 4 pounds of clay (i.e., there was no uncertainty in our problem statement). Similarly, the solutions we derived for the linear programming models contained no variation or uncertainty. It was assumed that the results of the model would occur in the future, without any degree of doubt or chance.

Deterministic techniques

In contrast, many of the techniques in management science do reflect *uncertain* information and result in *uncertain* solutions. These techniques are said to be *probabilistic*. This means that there can be more than one outcome or result to a model and that there is some doubt about which outcome will occur. The solutions generated by

Uncertainty in management science techniques

339

these techniques have a probability of occurrence. They may be in the form of *averages*; the actual values that occur will vary over time.

Many of the upcoming chapters in this text present probabilistic techniques. The presentation of these techniques requires that the reader have a fundamental understanding of probability. Thus, the purpose of this chapter is to provide an overview of the fundamentals, properties, and terminology of probability.

TYPES OF PROBABILITY

Two types of
probability

Two basic types of probability can be defined: *objective probability* and *subjective probability*. First, we will consider what constitutes an objective probability.

Objective Probability

Consider a referee's flipping a coin before a football game to determine which team will kick off and which team will receive. Before the referee tosses the coin, both team captains know that they have a .50 (or 50%) chance (or probability) of winning the toss. None of the onlookers in the stands or anywhere else would argue that the probability of a head or a tail was not .50. In this example, the probability of .50 that either a head or a tail will occur when a coin is tossed is called an *objective probability*. More specifically, it is referred to as a *classical* or *a priori* (prior to the occurrence) probability, one of the two types of objective probabilities.

Classical or a priori
probability

A classical, or a priori, probability can be defined as follows. Given a set of outcomes for an activity (such as a head or a tail when a coin is tossed), the probability of a specific (desired) outcome (such as a head) is the ratio of the number of specific outcomes to the total number of outcomes. For example, in our coin-tossing example the probability of a head is the ratio of the number of specific outcomes (a head) to the total number of outcomes (a head and a tail), or 1/2. Similarly, the probability of drawing an ace from a deck of 52 cards would be found by dividing 4 (the number of aces) by 52 (the total number of cards in a deck) to get 1/13. If we spin a roulette wheel with 50 red numbers and 50 black numbers, the probability of the wheel's landing on a red number is 50 divided by 100, or 1/2.

These examples are referred to as a priori probabilities because we can state the probabilities *prior to* the actual occurrence of the activity (i.e., ahead of time). This is because we know (or assume we know) the number of specific outcomes and total outcomes prior to the occurrence of the activity. For example, we know that a deck of cards consists of 4 aces and 52 total cards before we draw a card from the deck, and that a coin contains one head and one tail before we toss it. These probabilities are also known as classical probabilities because some of the earliest references in history to probabilities were related to games of chance, to which (as the examples above show) these probabilities readily apply.

The second type of objective probability is referred to as the *relative frequency* probability. This type of objective probability indicates the relative frequency with which a specific outcome has been observed to occur in the long run. It is based on the observation of past occurrences. For example, suppose that over the past four years 3,000 business students have taken the introductory management science course at State University and 300 of them have made an A in the course. The relative frequency probability of making an A in management science would be 300/3,000, or .10. Whereas in the case of a classical probability we indicate a probability before an activity (such as tossing a coin) takes place, in the case of a relative frequency we determine the probability after observing what 3,000 students have done in the past.

The relative frequency definition of probability is more general and widely accepted than the classical definition. Actually, the relative frequency definition can encompass the classical case. For example, if we flip a coin many times, in the long run the relative frequency of a head's occurring will be .50. If, however, you tossed a coin ten times, it is conceivable that you would get 10 consecutive heads. Thus, the relative frequency (probability) of a head would be 1.0. This illustrates one of the key characteristics of a relative frequency probability: the relative frequency probability becomes more accurate as the total number of observations of the activity increases. If a coin were tossed 10,000 times, the relative frequency would approach 1/2 (assuming a fair coin).

Relative frequency probability

Relative frequency is the more widely used definition of objective probability

Subjective Probability

When relative frequencies are not available, a probability is often determined anyway. In these cases a person must rely on personal belief, experience, and knowledge of the situation to develop a probability estimate. A probability estimate that is not based on prior or past evidence is a *subjective probability*. For example, when a meteorologist forecasts a "60% chance of rain tomorrow," the .60 probability is usually based on the meteorologist's experience and expert analysis of the weather conditions. In other words, the meteorologist is not saying that these exact weather conditions have occurred 1,000 times in the past and on 600 occasions it has rained, thus there is a 60% probability of rain. Likewise, when a sportswriter says that a football team has an 80% chance of winning, it is usually not because the team has won 8 of its 10 previous games. The prediction is judgmental, based on the sportswriter's knowledge of the teams in-

A probability estimate based on personal belief, experience, and knowledge of the situation

volved, the playing conditions, and so forth. If the sportswriter had based the probability estimate solely on the team's relative frequency of winning, then it would have been an objective probability. However, once the relative frequency probability becomes colored by personal belief, it is subjective.

Subjective probability estimates are frequently used in making business decisions. For example, suppose the manager of Colonial Pottery Company (referred to in previous chapters) is thinking about producing plates in addition to the bowls and mugs already being produced. In making the decision as to whether to produce plates, the manager will determine the chances of the new product's being successful and returning a profit. Although the manager can use personal knowledge of the market and judgment to determine a *probability of success,* direct relative frequency evidence is not generally available. The manager cannot observe the frequency with which the introduction of this new product was successful in the past. Thus, the manager must make a subjective probability estimate.

This type of subjective probability analysis is common in the business world. Decision makers frequently must consider their chances for success or failure, the probability of achieving a certain market share or profit, the probability of a level of demand, and the like without the benefit of relative frequency probabilities based on past observations. Although there may not be a consensus as to the accuracy of a subjective estimate, as there is with an objective probability (e.g., everyone is sure there is a .50 probability of getting a head when a coin is tossed), subjective probability analysis is often the only means available for making probabilistic estimates and it is a method frequently used.

A brief note of caution must be made regarding the use of subjective probabilities. Different people will often arrive at different subjective probabilities, whereas everyone should arrive at the same objective probability, given the same numbers and correct calculations. Therefore, when a probabilistic analysis is to be made of a situation, the use of objective probability will provide more consistent results. In the material on probability in the remainder of this chapter, we will be using objective probabilities unless the text indicates otherwise.

FUNDAMENTALS OF PROBABILITY

An experiment

Let us return to our example of a referee's tossing a coin prior to a football game. In the terminology of probability, the coin toss is referred to as an *experiment.* An experiment is an activity (such as tossing a coin) that results in one of the several possible outcomes. Our coin-tossing experiment can result in either one of two outcomes, which are referred to as *events*: a head or a tail. The probabilities associated with each event in our experiment are shown below.

Event	*Probability*
Head	.50
Tail	.50
	1.00

This simple example highlights two of the fundamental characteristics of probability. First, *the probability of an event is always greater than or equal to zero and less than or equal to one* (i.e., $0 \le P$ (event) $\le$ 1.0). In our coin-tossing example, each event has a probability of .50, which is in the range of 0 to 1.0. Second, *the probabilities of all the events included in an experiment must sum to one*. Notice in our example that the probability of each of the two events is .50 and the sum of these two probabilities is 1.0.

The specific example of tossing a coin also exhibits a third characteristic: the events (in a set of events) are *mutually exclusive*. The events in an experiment are mutually exclusive if only one of them can occur at a time. In the context of our experiment, the term *mutually exclusive* means that any time the coin is tossed *only one* of the two events can take place—either a head or a tail can occur, but not both. Consider a customer who goes into a store to shop for shoes. The store manager estimates that there is a .60 probability that the customer will buy a pair of shoes and a .40 probability that the customer will not buy a pair of shoes. These two events are mutually exclusive, since it is impossible to buy shoes and not buy shoes at the same time. In general, events are mutually exclusive if only one of the events can occur, but not both.

Since the events in our example of obtaining a head or tail are mutually exclusive, we can infer that the probabilities of mutually exclusive events *sum to 1.0*. Also, the probabilities of mutually exclusive events can be added. The following example will demonstrate these fundamental characteristics of probability.

The staff of the dean of the business school at State University has analyzed the records of the 3,000 students who received a grade in management science during the past four years. The dean wants to know the number of students who made each grade (A, B, C, D, or F) in the course. The dean's staff has developed the following table of information:

Event Grade	Number of Students	Relative Frequency	Probability
A	300	300/3,000	.10
B	600	600/3,000	.20
C	1,500	1,500/3,000	.50
D	450	450/3,000	.15
F	150	150/3,000	.05
	3,000		1.00

This example demonstrates several of the characteristics of probability. First, the *data* (numerical information) in the second column show how the students are distributed across the different grades (events). The third column shows the relative frequency with which each event occurred for the 3,000 observations. In other words, the relative frequency of a student's making a C is 1,500/3,000, which also means that the probability of selecting a student who had obtained a C at random from those students who took management science in the past four years is .50.

This information, organized according to the events in the experiment, is called a *frequency distribution*. The list of the corresponding probabilities for each event in the last column is referred to as a *probability distribution*.

All of the events in this example are mutually exclusive; it is not possible for two or more of these events to occur at the same time. A student can make only one grade in the course, not two or more grades. As indicated previously, mutually exclusive probabilities of an experiment can be summed to equal one. There are five mutually exclusive events in this experiment, the probabilities of which (.10, .20, .50, .15, and .05) sum to one.

This example exhibits another characteristic of probability. Since the five events in the example are all that can occur (i.e., no other grade in the course is possible), the experiment is said to be *collectively exhaustive*. Likewise, the coin-tossing experiment is collectively exhaustive, since the only two events that can occur are a head and a tail. In general, when a *set of events* includes all the events that can possibly occur, the set is said to be collectively exhaustive.

Marginal
probability

The probability of a single event's occurring, such as a student's receiving an A in a course, is represented symbolically as $P(A)$. This probability is called the *marginal probability* in the terminology of probability. For our example, the marginal probability of a student's getting an A in management science is

$$P(A) = .10$$

For mutually exclusive events, it is possible to determine the probability that one or the other of several events will occur. This is done by summing the individual marginal probabilities of the events. For example, the probability of a student's receiving an A or a B is determined as follows.

$$P(A \text{ or } B) = P(A) + P(B)$$
$$= .10 + .20$$
$$= .30$$

In other words, 300 students received an A and 600 students received a B; thus the number of students who received an A or a B is 900. Dividing 900 students who received an A or a B by the total number of students, 3,000, yields the probability of a student's receiving an A or B (i.e., $P(A \text{ or } B) = .30$).

Mutually exclusive events can be shown pictorally with a *Venn diagram*. Figure 10.1 shows a Venn diagram for the mutually exclusive events A and B in our example.

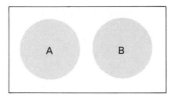

A Venn diagram

FIGURE 10.1

Venn Diagram for Mutually Exclusive Events

Now let us consider a case in which two events are *not* mutually exclusive. In this case the probability that A or B or *both* will occur is expressed as

$$P(A \text{ or } B) = P(A) + P(B) - P(AB)$$

where the term $P(AB)$, referred to as the *joint probability* of A and B, is the probability that *both* A and B will occur. For mutually exclusive events, this term would have to equal zero, since both events cannot occur together. Thus, for mutually exclusive events our formula would become

$$\begin{aligned} P(A \text{ or } B) &= P(A) + P(B) - P(AB) \\ &= P(A) + P(B) - 0 \\ &= P(A) + P(B) \end{aligned}$$

which is the same formula we developed previously for mutually exclusive events.

The following example will illustrate the case in which two events are *not* mutually exclusive. Suppose it has been determined that 40% of all students in the school of business are presently taking management and 30% of all the students are taking finance. Also, it has been determined that 10% take both subjects. Thus our probabilities are

$$P(M) = .40$$
$$P(F) = .30$$
$$P(MF) = .10$$

The probability of a student's taking one or the other or both of the courses is determined as follows.

$$\begin{aligned} P(M \text{ or } F) &= P(M) + P(F) - P(MF) \\ &= .40 + .30 - .10 \\ &= .60 \end{aligned}$$

Observing this formulation closely, we can see why the joint probability, $P(MF)$, was subtracted out. The 40% of the students

Events that are not mutually exclusive

Joint probability

who were taking management also included those students taking both courses. Likewise, the 30% of the students taking finance also included those students taking both courses. Thus, if we add the two marginal probabilities we are *double counting* the percentage of students taking both courses. By subtracting out one of these probabilities (that we added in twice), we derive the correct probability.

Figure 10.2 contains a Venn diagram that shows the two events M and F that are not mutually exclusive, and the joint event MF.

A Venn diagram of events that are not mutually exclusive

FIGURE 10.2

Venn Diagram for Non–Mutually Exclusive Events and the Joint Event

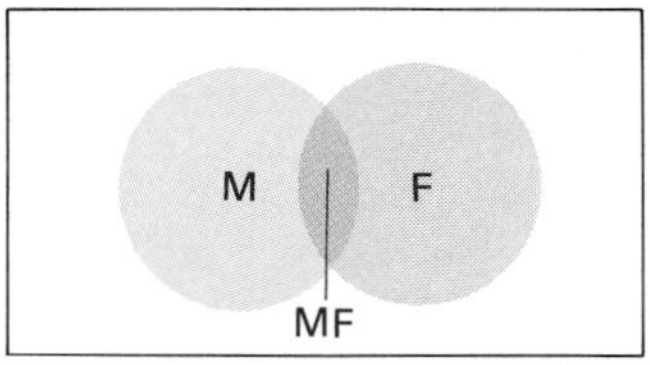

An alternative way to construct a probability distribution is to add the probability of an event to the sum of all previously listed probabilities in a probability distribution. Such a list is referred to as a *cumulative probability distribution*. The cumulative probability distribution for our management science grade example is shown below.

Event Grade	Probability	Cumulative Probability
A	.10	.10
B	.20	.30
C	.50	.80
D	.15	.95
F	.05	1.00
	1.00	

The value of a cumulative probability distribution is that it organizes the event probabilities in a way that it makes it easier to answer certain questions about the probabilities. For example, if we want to know the probability that a student will get a grade of C *or higher*, we can add the probabilities of the mutually exclusive events A, B, and C.

$$P(A \text{ or } B \text{ or } C) = P(A) + P(B) + P(C)$$
$$= .10 + .20 + .50$$
$$= .80$$

Or, we can look directly at the cumulative probability distribution and see that the probability of a C and the events preceding it in the distribution (A and B) equals .80. Alternatively, if we want to know the probability of a grade lower than C, we can subtract the cumulative probability of a C from 1.00 (i.e., $1.00 - .80 = .20$).

STATISTICAL INDEPENDENCE AND DEPENDENCE

Statistically, events are either independent or dependent. If the occurrence of one event does not affect the probability of the occurrence of another event, the events are *independent*. Conversely, if the occurrence of one event affects the probability of the occurrence of another event, the events are *dependent*. We will first turn our attention to a discussion of independent events.

Independent Events

When we toss a coin, the two events—getting a head and getting a tail—are independent. If we get a head on the first toss, this result has absolutely no effect on the probability of getting a head or a tail on the next toss. The probability of getting either a head or a tail will still be .50, regardless of the outcomes of previous tosses. In other words, the two events are independent.

A succession of events that do not affect each other

When events are independent, it is possible to determine the probability of both events' occurring in succession by multiplying the probabilities of each event. For example, what is the probability of getting a head on the first toss and a tail on the second toss? The answer is

The probability of independent events' occurring in succession

$$P(HT) = P(H) \cdot P(T)$$

where

$$P(H) = \text{probability of a head}$$
$$P(T) = \text{probability of a tail}$$
$$P(HT) = \text{joint probability of a head and a tail}$$

Therefore,

$$P(HT) = P(H) \cdot P(T)$$
$$P(HT) = (.5)(.5)$$
$$P(HT) = .25$$

As we indicated previously, the probability of both events' occurring, $P(HT)$, is referred to as the *joint probability*.

Another property of independent events relates to *conditional probabilities*. A conditional probability is the probability that event A will occur given that event B has already occurred. This relationship is expressed symbolically as

Conditional probabilities

$$P(A/B)$$

The term in parentheses "A slash B," means "A *given* the occurrence of B." Thus, the entire term $P(A/B)$ is interpreted as the probability that A will occur *given* that B has already occurred. If A and B are independent events, then

$$P(A/B) = P(A)$$

In words, this result says that if A and B are independent, then the probability of A, given the occurrence of event B, is simply equal to the probability of A. Since the events are independent of each other, the occurrence of event B will have no effect on the occurrence of A. Therefore, the probability of A is in no way dependent on the occurrence of B.

In summary, if events A and B are independent, the following two properties hold.

1. $P(AB) = P(A) \cdot P(B)$
2. $P(A/B) = P(A)$

Probability Trees

Illustrating the probability of successive independent events

Consider an example in which a coin is tossed three consecutive times. The possible outcomes of this example can be illustrated using a *probability tree*, as shown in Figure 10.3.

FIGURE 10.3

Probability Tree for Coin-Tossing Example

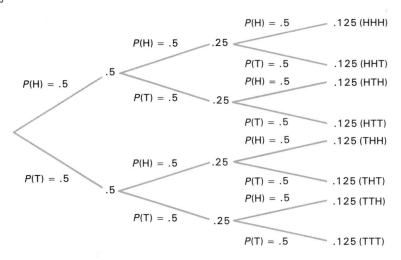

The probability tree in Figure 10.3 demonstrates the probabilities of the various occurrences given three tosses of a coin. Notice that at each toss the probability of either event's occurring remains the same, or $P(H) = P(T) = .5$. Thus, the events are independent. Next, the joint probabilities of events' occurring in succession are computed by multiplying the probabilities of each event. For example, the probability of getting a head on the first toss, a tail on the second, and a tail on the third is .125.

$$P(HTT) = P(H) \cdot P(T) \cdot P(T)$$
$$= (.5)(.5)(.5)$$
$$= .125$$

However, do not confuse the results in the probability tree with conditional probabilities. The probability of a head and then two tails' occurring on three consecutive tosses is computed prior to any tosses' taking place. If the first two tosses have already occurred, the probability of getting a tail on the third toss is still .5.

$$P(T/HT) = P(T)$$
$$= .5$$

The Binomial Distribution

Some additional information can be drawn from the probability tree of our example. For instance, what is the probability of achieving exactly two tails on three tosses? The answer can be found by observing the instances where two tails occurred. It can be seen that two tails in three tosses occurred three times, each time with a probability of .125. Thus, the probability of getting exactly two tails in three tosses is the sum of these three probabilities, or .375. The use of a probability tree can become very cumbersome, especially if we are considering an example with twenty tosses. However, the example of tossing a coin exhibits certain properties that enable us to define it as a *Bernoulli process*. The properties of a Bernoulli process are listed below.

A Bernoulli process

1. There are two possible outcomes for each trial (i.e., each toss of the coin). Outcomes could be success or failure, yes or no, heads or tails, good or bad, and so on.
2. The probability of the outcomes remains constant over time. In other words, the probability of getting a head on a coin toss remains the same regardless of the number of tosses.
3. The outcomes of the trials are independent. The fact that we get a head on the first toss does not affect the probabilities on subsequent tosses.
4. The number of trials is *discrete* and integer. The term *discrete* indicates values that are *countable*, and thus usually integer — for example, 1 car or 2 people rather than 1.34 cars or 2.51 people. There are 1, 2, 3, 4, 5, . . . tosses of the coin and not 3.36 tosses.

Properties of a Bernoulli process

Discrete trials

Given the properties of a Bernoulli process, a *binomial probability distribution function* can be used to determine the probability of a number of successes in *n* trials. The binomial distribution is an ex-

Discrete probability distribution

ample of a *discrete probability distribution*, since the value of the distribution (the number of successes) is discrete, as is the number of trials. The formula for the binomial distribution is

The binomial distribution formula

$$P(r) = \frac{n!}{r!\,(n - r)!} p^r q^{n-r}$$

where

p = probability of a success

$q = 1 - p$ = probability of a failure

n = number of trials

r = number of successes in n trials

Factorials

The terms $n!$, $(n - r)!$, and $r!$ are called *factorials*. Factorials are computed using the formula

$$m! = m(m - 1)\,(m - 2)\,(m - 3) \cdots (2)\,(1)$$

$0!$ always equals one.

The binomial distribution formula may look complicated, but using it is not difficult. For example, suppose we want to determine the probability of getting exactly 2 tails in 3 tosses of a coin. For this example, getting a tail is a success, since it is the object of the analysis. The probability of a tail, p, equals .5; therefore, $q = 1 - .5 = .5$. The number of tosses, n, is 3, and the number of tails, r, is 2. Substituting these values into the binomial formula will result in the probability of 2 tails in 3 coin tosses.

$$P(2 \text{ tails}) = P(r = 2)\frac{3!}{2!\,(3 - 2)!}(.5)^2(.5)^{3-2}$$

$$= \frac{(3 \cdot 2 \cdot 1)}{(2 \cdot 1)\,(1)}(.25)\,(.5)$$

$$= \frac{6}{2}(.125)$$

$$P(r = 2) = .375$$

Notice that this is the same result achieved by using a probability tree in the previous section.

A binomial distribution example

Now let us consider an example of more practical interest. An electrical manufacturer produces transistors. The transistors are inspected at the end of the production process at a quality control station. Out of every batch of transistors, 4 are randomly selected and tested for defects. Given that 20% of all transistors are defective, what is the probability that each batch of transistors will contain exactly 2 defective transistors?

The two possible outcomes in this example are a good transistor and a defective transistor. Since defective transistors are the object of our analysis, a defective item is a success. The probability of a success is the probability of a defective transistor, or $p = .2$. The number of trials, n, equals 4. Now let us substitute these values into the binomial formula.

$$P(r = 2 \text{ defectives}) = \frac{4!}{2!\,(4-2)!}(.2)^2(.8)^2$$

$$= \frac{(4 \cdot 3 \cdot 2 \cdot 1)}{(2 \cdot 1)(2 \cdot 1)}(.04)(.64)$$

$$= \frac{24}{4}(.0256)$$

$$= .1536$$

Thus, the probability of getting exactly 2 defective items out of 4 transistors is .1536.

Now, let us alter this problem to make it even more realistic. The manager has determined that 4 transistors from every large batch should be tested for quality. If *2 or more* defective transistors are found, the whole batch will be rejected. The manager wants to know the probability of rejecting an entire batch of transistors, if, in fact, the batch has 20% defective items.

A more realistic example

From our previous use of the binomial distribution, we know that it gives us the probability of *an exact* number of *integer* successes. Thus, if we want the probability of 2 or more defective items, it is necessary to compute the probability of 2, 3, and 4 defective items. That is,

$$P(r \geq 2) = P(r = 2) + P(r = 3) + P(r = 4)$$

Substituting the values $p = .2$, $n = 4$, $q = .8$, and $r = 2$, 3, and 4 into the binomial distribution results in the probability of 2 or more defective items:

$$P(r \geq 2) = \frac{4!}{2!\,(4-2)!}(.2)^2(.8)^2 + \frac{4!}{3!\,(4-3)!}(.2)^3(.8)^1 + \frac{4!}{4!\,(4-4)!}(.2)^4(.8)^0$$

$$= .1536 + .0256 + .0016$$

$$= .1808$$

Thus, the probability that a batch of transistors will be rejected for poor quality is .1808.

Notice that the *collectively exhaustive* set of events for this example is 0, 1, 2, 3, and 4 defective transistors. Since the sum of the probabilities of a collectively exhaustive set of events equals 1.0,

$$P(r = 0, 1, 2, 3, 4) = P(r = 0) + P(r = 1) + P(r = 2) + P(r = 3)$$
$$+ P(r = 4) = 1.0$$

Recall that the results of the immediately preceding example show that

$$P(r = 2) + P(r = 3) + P(r = 4) = .1808$$

Given this result, we can compute the probability of "less than 2 defectives" as follows.

$$P(r < 2) = P(r = 0) + P(r = 1)$$
$$= 1.0 - [P(r = 2) + P(r = 3) + P(r = 4)]$$
$$= 1.0 - .1808$$
$$= .8192$$

It should be apparent at this point that our examples included very small values for n and r. This enabled us to work out the examples by hand. Problems containing larger values for n and r can be solved using Table A.2 in Appendix A. For example, from the table we can find that $P(r \geq 2)$ is .1808, as follows.

$$P(r \geq 2) = P(r = 2) + P(r = 3) + P(r = 4)$$
$$= .1536 + .0256 + .0016$$
$$= .1808$$

Dependent Events

As stated earlier, if the occurrence of one event affects the probability of the occurrence of another event, the events are *dependent*. The following example illustrates dependent events.

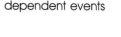

Two buckets each contain a number of colored balls. Bucket 1 contains 2 red balls and 4 white balls, and bucket 2 contains 1 blue ball and 5 red balls. A coin is tossed. If a head results, a ball is drawn out of bucket 1. If a tail results, a ball is drawn from bucket 2. These events are illustrated in Figure 10.4.

FIGURE 10.4

Dependent Events

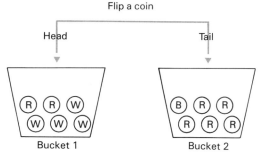

In this example the probability of drawing a *blue* ball is clearly dependent on whether a head or a tail occurs on the coin toss. If a tail occurs, there is a 1/6 chance of drawing a blue ball from bucket 2. However, if a head results, there is no possibility of drawing a blue ball from bucket 1. In other words, the probability of the event "drawing a blue ball" is dependent on the event "flipping a coin."

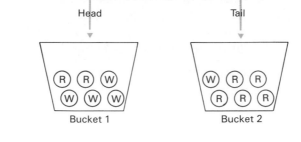

FIGURE 10.5

Another Set of
Dependent Events

Like statistically independent events, dependent events exhibit certain defining properties. In order to describe these properties, we will alter our previous example slightly, so that bucket 2 contains 1 white ball and 5 red balls. Our new example is shown in Figure 10.5. The outcomes that can result from the events illustrated in Figure 10.5 are shown in Figure 10.6. When the coin is flipped, one of two outcomes is possible, a head or a tail. The probability of getting a head is .50, and the probability of getting a tail is .50:

Properties of
dependent events

$$P(H) = .50$$
$$P(T) = .50$$

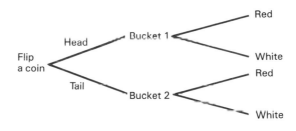

FIGURE 10.6

Probability Tree for
Dependent Events

As indicated previously, these probabilities are referred to as *marginal* probabilities. They are also *unconditional* probabilities because they are the probabilities of the occurrence of a single event and are not conditional on the occurrence of any other event(s). They are the same as the probabilities of independent events defined earlier, and like those of independent events, the marginal probabilities of a collectively exhaustive set of events *sum to one*.

Once the coin has been tossed and a head or tail has resulted, a ball is drawn from one of the buckets. If a head results, a ball is drawn from bucket 1; there is a 2/6, or .33, probability of drawing a red ball and a 4/6, or .67, probability of drawing a white ball. If a tail resulted, a ball is drawn from bucket 2; there is a 5/6, or .83, probability of drawing a red ball and a 1/6, or .17, probability of drawing a white ball. These probabilities of drawing red or white balls are called *conditional* probabilities, since they are conditional on the outcome of the event of tossing a coin. Symbolically, these conditional probabilities are expressed as follows.

$$P(R/H) = .33$$
$$P(W/H) = .67$$
$$P(R/T) = .83$$
$$P(W/T) = .17$$

The first term, which can be expressed verbally as "the probability of drawing a red ball given that a head results from the coin toss," equals .33. The other conditional probabilities are expressed similarly.

Conditional probabilities can also be defined by the following mathematical relationship. Given two dependent events A and B,

$$P(A/B) = \frac{P(AB)}{P(B)}$$

The term $P(AB)$ is the joint probability of the two events, as noted previously. This relationship can be manipulated by multiplying both sides by $P(B)$, to yield

$$P(A/B) \cdot P(B) = P(AB)$$

Thus, the joint probability can be determined by multiplying the conditional probability of A by the marginal probability of B.

Recall from our previous discussion of independent events that

$$P(AB) = P(A) \cdot P(B)$$

Substituting this result into the relationship for a conditional probability yields

$$P(A/B) = \frac{P(A) \cdot P(B)}{P(B)}$$
$$= P(A)$$

which is consistent with the property for independent events.

Returning to our example, the joint events are the occurrence of a head and a red ball, a head and a white ball, a tail and a red ball, and a tail and a white ball. The probabilities of these joint events are as follows.

$$P(RH) = P(RH) \cdot P(H)$$
$$= (.33)(.5)$$
$$= .165$$
$$P(WH) = P(W/H) \cdot P(H)$$
$$= (.67)(.5)$$
$$= .335$$

$$P(RT) - P(R/T) \cdot P(T)$$
$$= (.83)(.5)$$
$$= .415$$
$$P(WT) = P(W/T) \cdot P(T)$$
$$= (.17)(.5)$$
$$= .085$$

The marginal, conditional, and joint probabilities for this example are summarized in Figure 10.7. Table 10.1 is a *joint probability table*, which summarizes the joint probabilities for the example.

Joint probability table

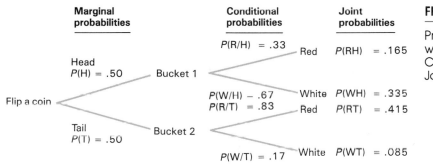

Marginal probabilities		Conditional probabilities		Joint probabilities

FIGURE 10.7

Probability Tree with Marginal, Conditional, and Joint Probabilities

TABLE 10.1
Joint Probability Table

Flip a Coin	Draw a Ball		Marginal Probabilities
	Red	White	
Head	$P(RH) = .165$	$P(WH) = .335$	$P(H) = .50$
Tail	$P(RT) - .415$	$P(WT) - .085$	$P(T) - .50$
Marginal Probabilities	$P(R) = .580$	$P(W) = .420$	1.00

Bayesian Analysis

The concept of conditional probability given statistical dependence forms the necessary foundation for an area of probability known as *Bayesian analysis*. The technique is named after Thomas Bayes, an eighteenth-century clergyman who pioneered this area of analysis.

The basic principle of Bayesian analysis is that additional information (if available) can sometimes enable one to alter (improve) the marginal probabilities of the occurrence of an event. The altered probabilities are referred to as *revised* or *posterior* probabilities.

The concept of posterior probabilities will be illustrated using the following example. A production manager for a manufacturing

Improving marginal probabilities with additional information

Revised or posterior probabilities

An example of Bayesian analysis

firm is supervising the machine setup for the production of a product. The machine operator sets up the machine. If the machine is set up correctly, there is a 10% chance that an item produced on the machine will be defective; if the machine is set up incorrectly, there is a 40% chance that an item will be defective. The production manager knows from past experience that there is a .50 probability that a machine will be set up correctly or incorrectly by an operator. In order to reduce the chance that an item produced on the machine will be defective, the manager has decided that the operator should produce a sample item. The manager wants to know the probability that the machine has been set up incorrectly if the sample item turns out to be defective.

The probabilities given in this problem statement can be summarized as follows.

$$P(C) = .50 \qquad P(D/C) = .10$$
$$P(IC) = .50 \qquad P(D/IC) = .40$$

where

$$C = \text{correct}$$
$$IC = \text{incorrect}$$
$$D = \text{defective}$$

The posterior probability

The *posterior probability* for our example is the conditional probability that the machine has been set up incorrectly, given that the sample item proves to be defective, or $P(IC/D)$. In Bayesian analysis, once we are given the initial marginal and conditional probabilities, we can compute the posterior probability using *Bayes's rule*, as follows.

Bayes's rule

$$P(IC/D) = \frac{P(D/IC)P(IC)}{P(D/IC)P(IC) + P(D/C)P(C)}$$
$$= \frac{(.40)(.50)}{(.40)(.50) + (.10)(.50)}$$
$$= .80$$

Previously the manager knew that there was a 50% chance that the machine was set up incorrectly. Now, after producing and testing a sample item, the manager knows that if it is defective there is a .80 probability that the machine was set up incorrectly. Thus, by gathering some additional information, the manager can revise the estimate of the probability that the machine was set up correctly. This will obviously improve decision making by allowing the manager to make a more informed decision as to whether to have the machine set up again.

In general, given two events, A and B, and a third event, C, that is conditionally dependent on A and B, Bayes's rule can be written as

$$P(A/C) = \frac{P(C/A)P(A)}{P(C/A)P(A) + P(C/B)P(B)}$$

EXPECTED VALUE

It is often possible to assign numerical values to the various outcomes that can result from an experiment. When the values of the variables occur in no particular order or sequence, the variables are referred to as *random variables*. Every possible value of a variable has a probability of occurrence associated with it. For example, if a coin is tossed three times, the number of heads obtained is a random variable. The possible values of the random variable are 0, 1, 2, and 3 heads. The values of the variable are random because there is no way of predicting which value (0, 1, 2, or 3) will result when the coin is tossed three times. If three tosses are made several times, the values (i.e., numbers of heads) that will result will have no sequence or pattern; they will be random.

Random variables

Like the variables defined in previous chapters in this text, random variables are typically represented symbolically by a letter, such as x, y, or z. Consider a vendor who sells hot dogs outside a building every day. If the number of hot dogs the vendor sells is defined as the random variable x, then x will equal 0, 1, 2, 3, 4 . . . hot dogs sold daily.

Although the exact values of the random variables in the examples above are not known prior to the event, it is possible to assign a probability to the occurrence of the possible values that can result. Consider a production operation in which a machine breaks down periodically. From experience it has been determined that the machine will break down 0, 1, 2, 3, or 4 times per month. Although managers do not know the exact number of breakdowns that will occur each month, they can determine the relative frequency probability of each number of breakdowns. These probabilities are shown below.

Assigning probabilities to the possible values of a random variable

An example of expected value

Random Variable x (number of breakdowns)	P(x)
0	.10
1	.20
2	.30
3	.25
4	.15
	1.00

These probability values taken together form a *probability distribution*. That is, the probabilities are distributed over the range of possible values of the random variable x.

A probability distribution

The *expected value* of the random variable (number of breakdowns in any given month) is computed by multiplying each value of the random variable by its probability. The expected value of a random variable x, written symbolically as $E(x)$, is computed as follows.

Computing the expected value

$$E(x) = \sum_{i=1}^{n} x_i P(x_i)$$

where

n = number of values of the random variable x

For our example, the expected number of breakdowns per month is computed as follows.

$$E(x) = (0)(.10) + (1)(.20) + (2)(.30) + (3)(.25) + (4)(.15)$$
$$= 0 + .20 + .60 + .75 + .60$$
$$= 2.15 \text{ breakdowns}$$

This means that, on the average, management can expect 2.15 breakdowns every month.

Mean of a probability distribution

The expected value is often referred to as the weighted average or *mean* of the probability distribution and is a measure of central tendency of the distribution. In addition to knowing the mean, it is often desirable to know how the values are dispersed (or scattered) around the mean. A measure of dispersion is the *variance*, which is computed as follows.

Dispersion around the mean: variance

1. Square the difference between each value and the expected value.
2. Multiply these resulting amounts by the probability of each value.
3. Sum the values compiled in step 2.

The general formula for computing the variance, which we will designate as σ^2, is

$$\sigma^2 = \sum_{i=1}^{n} [x_i - E(x_i)]^2 P(x_i)$$

The formula for computing variance

The variance (σ^2) for the machine breakdown example is computed as follows:

x_i	$P(x_i)$	$x_i - E(x)$	$[x_i - E(x)]^2$	$[x_i - E(x)]^2 \cdot P(x_i)$
0	.10	−2.15	4.62	.462
1	.20	−1.15	1.32	.264
2	.30	−0.15	.02	.006
3	.25	0.85	.72	.180
4	.15	1.85	3.42	.513
	1.00			1.425

$\sigma^2 = 1.425$ breakdowns per month

Standard deviation

The *standard deviation* is another widely recognized measure of dispersion. It is designated symbolically as σ and is computed by taking the square root of the variance,

$$\sigma = \sqrt{1.425} = 1.19 \text{ breakdowns per month}$$

A small standard deviation or variance, relative to the expected value, or mean, indicates that most of the values of the random variable distribution are bunched close to the expected value. Conversely, a large relative value for the measures of dispersion indicates that the values of the random variable are widely dispersed from the expected value.

THE NORMAL DISTRIBUTION

Previously a *discrete* value was defined as a value that is countable (and usually integer). A random variable is discrete if the values it can equal are finite and countable. The probability distributions we have encountered thus far have been discrete distributions. In other words, the values of the random variables that made up these discrete distributions were always finite (for example, in the preceding example there were five possible values of the random variable, breakdowns per month). Since every value of the random variable had a unique probability of occurrence, the discrete probability distribution consisted of all the (finite) values of a random variable and their associated probabilities.

A discrete random variable

In contrast, a *continuous random variable* can take on an infinite number of values within some interval. This is because continuous random variables have values that are not specifically countable and are often fractional. The distinction between discrete and continuous random variables is sometimes made by saying that discrete relates to things that can be counted and continuous relates to things that are measured. For example, a load of oil being transported by tanker may consist of *not* 1 or 2 million barrels, but 1.35 million barrels. If the range of the random variable is between 1 and 2 million barrels, then there are an infinite number of possible (fractional) values between 1 and 2 million barrels, even though the value 1.35 million corresponds to a discrete value of 1,350,000 barrels of oil. No matter how small an interval exists between two values in the distribution, there is always at least one value and, in fact, an infinite number of values, between the two values.

A continuous random variable

Since a continuous random variable can take on an extremely large or infinite number of values, assigning a unique probability to every value of the random variable would require an infinite (or very large) number of probabilities, each of which would be infinitely small. Therefore, we cannot assign a unique probability to each value of the continuous random variable, as we did in a discrete probability distribution. In a *continuous probability distribution*, we can only refer to the probability that a value of the random variable is within some *range*. For example, we can determine the probability that between 1.35 and 1.40 million barrels of oil are transported, or the probability that fewer than or more than 1.35 million barrels are shipped, but we cannot determine the probability that exactly 1.35 million barrels of oil are transported.

Continuous probability distribution

The normal distribution

One of the most frequently used continuous probability distributions is the *normal distribution,* which is a continuous curve in the shape of a bell (i.e., it is symmetrical). The normal distribution is a popular continuous distribution because it has certain mathematical properties that make it easy to work with and it is a reasonable approximation of the continuous probability distributions of a number of natural phenomena. Figure 10.8 is an illustration of the normal distribution.

FIGURE 10.8

The Normal Curve

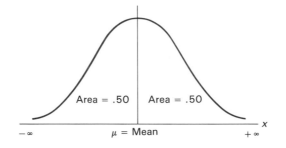

A bell-shaped curve

The mean of a normal distribution

Tails of the normal distribution

The fact that the normal distribution is a continuous curve reflects the fact that it consists of an infinite or extremely large number of points (on the curve). The bell-shaped curve can be flatter or taller, depending on the degree to which the values of the random variable are dispersed from the center of the distribution. The center of the normal distribution is referred to as the *mean* (μ), and it is analogous to the average of the distribution.

Notice that the two ends (or tails) of the distribution in Figure 10.8 extend from $-\infty$ to $+\infty$. In reality, random variables do not often take on values over an infinite range. Therefore, when the normal distribution is applied, it is actually approximating the distribution of a random variable with finite limits. The *area* under the

Area under the normal curve represents probability

normal curve represents *probability.* The entire area under the curve equals 1.0, since the sum of the probabilities of all values of a random variable in a probability distribution must equal 1.0. Fifty percent of the curve lies to the right of the mean, and 50% lies to the left. Thus, the probability that a random variable x will have a value greater (or less) than the mean is .50.

An example of a normal distribution

As an example of the application of the normal distribution, consider the Armor Carpet Store, which sells Super Shag carpet. From several years of sales records, the store management has determined that the mean number of yards of Super Shag demanded by customers during a week is 4,200 yards, and the standard deviation is 1,400 yards. It is necessary to know both the mean and the standard deviation in order to perform a probabilistic analysis using the normal distribution. The store management assumes that the continuous random variable, yards of carpet demanded per week, is normally distributed (i.e., the values of the random variable have approximately the shape of the normal curve). The mean of the normal distribution is represented by the symbol μ, and the standard deviation is represented by the symbol σ:

The mean and standard deviation

$\mu = 4,200$ yd

$\sigma = 1,400$ yd

The store manager wants to know the probability that the demand for Super Shag in the upcoming week will exceed 6,000 yards. The normal curve for this example is shown in Figure 10.9. The probability that x (the number of yards of carpet) will be equal to or greater than 6,000 is expressed as

$P(x \geq 6,000)$

which corresponds to the area under the normal curve to the right of the value 6,000, since the area under the curve (in Fig. 10.9) represents probability. In a normal distribution, area or probability is measured by determining the *number of standard deviations the value of the random variable x is from the mean*. The number of standard deviations a value is from the mean is represented by Z and is computed using the formula

Area measured by determining the number of standard deviations

$$Z = \frac{x - \mu}{\sigma}$$

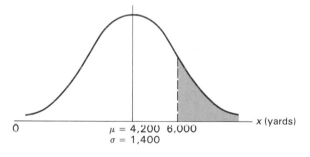

FIGURE 10.9

The Normal Distribution for Carpet Demand

$\mu = 4,200 \quad 6,000$
$\sigma = 1,400$

x (yards)

The number of standard deviations a value is from the mean gives us a consistent *standard* of measure for all normal distributions. In our example, the units of measure are yards; in other problems the units of measure may be pounds, hours, feet, or tons. By converting these various units of measure into a common measure (number of standard deviations), we create a standard that is the same for all normal distributions.

A standard of measure

Actually, the standard form of the normal distribution has a mean of zero ($\mu = 0$) and a standard deviation of one ($\sigma = 1$). The value of Z enables us to convert this scale of measure into whatever scale our problem requires.

The standard normal distribution

Figure 10.10 shows the *standard normal distribution* with our example distribution of carpet demand above it. This illustrates the conversion of the scale of measure along the horizontal axis from yards to number of standard deviations.

FIGURE 10.10

The Standard Normal Distribution

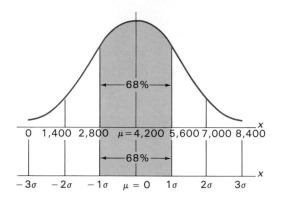

Converting units of measure to the standard normal distribution

The horizontal axis along the bottom of Figure 10.10 corresponds to the standard normal distribution. Notice that the area under the normal curve between -1σ and 1σ represents 68% of the total area under the normal curve, or a probability of .68. Now look at the horizontal axis corresponding to yards in our example. Given that the standard deviation is 1,400 yards, the area between -1σ (2,800 yards) and 1σ (5,600 yards) is also 68% of the total area under the curve. Thus, if we measure distance along the horizontal axis in terms of the number of standard deviations, we will determine the same probability no matter what the units of measure are. The formula for Z makes this conversion for us.

Returning to our example, recall that the manager of the carpet store wants to know the probability that the demand for Super Shag in the upcoming week will be 6,000 yards or more. Substituting the values $x = 6,000$, $\mu = 4,200$, and $\sigma = 1,400$ yards into our formula for Z, we can determine the number of standard deviations the value 6,000 is from the mean.

$$Z = \frac{x - \mu}{\sigma}$$
$$= \frac{6,000 - 4,200}{1,400}$$
$$= 1.29 \text{ standard deviations}$$

The value $x = 6,000$ is 1.29 standard deviations from the mean, as shown in Figure 10.11.

Normal tables

The area under the standard normal curve for values of Z has been computed and is displayed in easily accessible *normal tables*. Table A.1 in Appendix A is such a table. It shows that $Z = 1.29$ stan-

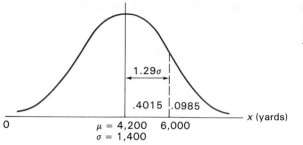

FIGURE 10.11

Determination of
the z Value

dard deviations corresponds to an area, or probability, of .4015.
However, this is the area between $\mu = 4,200$ and $x = 6,000$, since
what was measured was the area within 1.29 standard deviations of
the mean. Recall, though, that 50% of the area under the curve lies
to the right of the mean. Thus, we can subtract .4015 from .5000 to
get the area to the right of $x = 6,000$:

$$P(x \geq 6,000) = .5000 - .4015$$
$$= .0985$$

This means that there is a .0985 (or 9.85%) probability that the demand for carpet next week will be 6,000 yards or more.

Now suppose that the carpet store manager wishes to consider
two additional questions: (1) What is the probability that demand for
carpet will be 5,000 yards or less? (2) What is the probability that the
demand for carpet will be between 3,000 yards and 5,000 yards? We
will consider each of these questions separately.

Examples using
normal tables

First, we want to determine $P(x \leq 5,000)$. The area representing
this probability is shown in Figure 10.12. The area to the left of the
mean in Figure 10.12 equals .50. That leaves only the area between

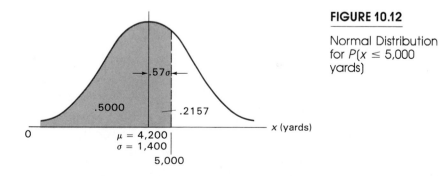

FIGURE 10.12

Normal Distribution
for $P(x \leq 5,000$
yards)

$\mu = 4{,}200$ and $x = 5{,}000$ to be determined. The number of standard deviations $x = 5{,}000$ is from the mean is

$$Z = \frac{x - \mu}{\sigma}$$

$$= \frac{5{,}000 - 4{,}200}{1{,}400}$$

$$= \frac{800}{1{,}400}$$

$$= .57 \text{ standard deviation}$$

The value $Z = .57$ corresponds to a probability of .2157 in Table A.1 in Appendix A. Thus, the area between 4,200 and 5,000 in Figure 10.12 is .2157. To find our desired probability, we simply add this amount to .5000,

$$P(x \leq 5{,}000) = .5000 + .2157$$

$$= .7157$$

Next, we want to determine $P(3{,}000 \leq x \leq 5{,}000)$. The area representing this probability is shown in Figure 10.13. The shaded area in Figure 10.13 is computed by finding two areas — the area between $x = 3{,}000$ and $\mu = 4{,}200$ and the area between $\mu = 4{,}200$ and $x = 5{,}000$ — and summing them. We already computed the area between 4,200 and 5,000 in the previous example and found it to be .2157.

FIGURE 10.13

Normal Distribution with $P(3{,}000$ yards $\leq x \leq 5{,}000$ yards)

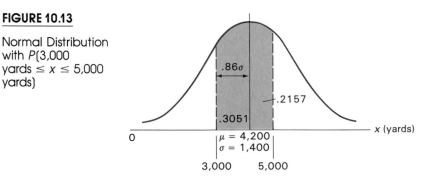

The area between $x = 3{,}000$ and $\mu = 4{,}200$ is found by determining how many standard deviations $x = 3{,}000$ is from the mean:

$$Z = \frac{3{,}000 - 4{,}200}{1{,}400}$$

$$= \frac{-1{,}200}{1{,}400}$$

$$= -.86$$

The minus sign is ignored as we find the area corresponding to the Z value of .86 in Table A.1. This value is .3051. Thus, our probability is found by summing .2157 and .3051.

$$P(3,000 \leq x \leq 5,000) = .2157 + .3051$$
$$= .5208$$

The normal distribution, although applied frequently in probability analysis, is just one of a number of continuous probability distributions. In subsequent chapters, other continuous distributions will be identified. An acquaintance with the normal distribution will make the use of these other distributions much easier.

Summary

The field of probability and statistics is quite large and complex and contains much more than has been presented in this chapter. This chapter presented the basic principles and fundamentals of probability. The primary purpose of this brief overview was to prepare the reader for the material that follows. The topics of decision analysis (Chapter 11), game theory (Chapter 12), Markov analysis (Chapter 13), probabilistic inventory models (Chapter 17), and, to a certain extent, CPM/PERT (Chapter 19) are probabilistic in nature and require an understanding of the fundamentals of probability.

References

Chou, Ya-lun. *Statistical Analysis.* 2d ed. New York: Holt, Rinehart and Winston, 1975.

Cramer, H. *The Elements of Probability Theory and Some of Its Applications.* 2d ed. New York: John Wiley and Sons, 1973.

Dixon, W. J., and Massey, F. J. *Introduction to Statistical Analysis.* 4th ed. New York: McGraw-Hill, 1983.

Hays, W. L., and Winkler, R. L. *Statistics: Probability, Inference, and Decision.* 2d ed. New York: Holt, Rinehart and Winston, 1975.

Mendenhall, W.; Reinmuth, J. E.; Beaver, R.; and Duhan, D. *Statistics for Management and Economics.* 5th ed. North Scituate, Mass.: Duxbury Press, 1986.

Neter, J.; Wasserman, W.; and Whitmore, G. A. *Applied Statistics.* 3d ed. Boston: Allyn and Bacon, 1988.

Sasaki, K. *Statistics for Modern Business Decision Making.* Belmont, Calif.: Wadsworth Publishing Co., 1969.

Spurr, W. A., and Bonini, C. P. *Statistical Analysis for Business Decisions.* Homewood, Ill.: Richard D. Irwin, 1973.

EXAMPLE PROBLEM SOLUTION

The following example will illustrate the solution of a problem involving a normal probability.

Problem Statement

The Radcliffe Chemical Company and Arsenal produces explosives for the U.S. Army. Because of the nature of its products, the company devotes strict attention to safety, which is also scrutinized by the federal government. Historical records show that the annual number of property damage and/or personal injury accidents is normally distributed with a mean of 8.3 accidents and a standard deviation of 1.8 accidents.

a. What is the probability that the company will have fewer than 5 accidents next year? More than 10?
b. The government will fine the company $200,000 if the number of accidents exceeds 12 in a one-year period. What average annual fine can the company expect?

Step 1: Set Up the Normal Distribution

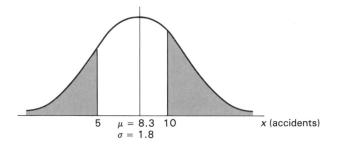

Step 2: Solve Part a

$P(x \le 5 \text{ accidents})$

$$Z = \frac{x - \mu}{\sigma}$$

$$Z = \frac{5 - 8.3}{1.8} = -1.83$$

From Table A.1 in Appendix A we see that $Z = -1.83$ corresponds to a probability of .4664; thus,

$$P(x \le 5) = .5000 - .4664$$
$$= .0336$$

$P(x \geq 10 \text{ accidents})$

$$Z = \frac{x - \mu}{\sigma}$$

$$Z = \frac{10 - 8.3}{1.8} = 0.94$$

From Table A.1 in Appendix A we find that $Z = 0.94$ corresponds to a probability of .3264; thus,

$$P(x \geq 10) = .5000 - .3264$$
$$= .1736$$

Step 3: Solve Part b

$P(x \geq 12 \text{ accidents})$

$$Z = \frac{x - \mu}{\sigma}$$

$$Z = \frac{12 - 8.3}{1.8} = 2.06$$

From Table A.1 in Appendix A we know that $Z = 2.06$ corresponds to a probability of .4803; thus,

$$P(x \geq 12) = .5000 - .4803$$
$$= .0197$$

Therefore, the company's expected annual fine is

$$\$200,000 \cdot P(x \geq 12) = (\$200,000)(.0197)$$
$$= \$3,940$$

Problems

1. Distinguish between *deterministic* and *probabilistic* management science techniques.

2. Indicate which of the following probabilities are objective and which are subjective. (Note that in some cases the probabilities may not be entirely one or the other.)

   a. The probability of snow tomorrow
   b. The probability of catching a fish
   c. The probability of the prime interest rate's rising in the coming year
   d. The probability that the Cincinnati Reds will win the World Series
   e. The probability that demand for a product will be a specific amount next month

f. The probability that a political candidate will win an election
g. The probability that a machine will break down
h. The probability of being dealt four aces in a poker hand

3. A gambler in Las Vegas is cutting a deck of cards for $1,000. What is the probability that the card that comes up for the gambler will be (a) a face card, (b) a queen, (c) a spade, or (d) a jack of spades?

4. Another gambler in Las Vegas is rolling the dice at the crap table. Define (a) the experiment and (b) the possible events.

5. The Downhill Ski Resort in Colorado has accumulated information from records of the last 30 winters regarding the measurable snowfall. This information is shown below.

Snowfall (inches)	Frequency
0–19	2
20–29	7
30–39	8
40–49	8
50+	5
	30

a. Determine the probability of each event in this frequency distribution.
b. Are all of the events in this distribution mutually exclusive? Explain.

6. Employees in the textile industry can be segmented as follows:

Employees	Number
Female and union	12,000
Female and nonunion	25,000
Male and union	21,000
Male and nonunion	42,000

a. Determine the probability of each event in this distribution.
b. Are the events in this distribution mutually exclusive? Explain.
c. What is the probability that an employee is male?
d. Is this experiment collectively exhaustive? Explain.

7. The quality control process at a manufacturing plant requires that each lot of finished units be sampled for defective items. Twenty units from each lot are inspected. If 5 or more defective units are found, the lot is rejected. If a lot is known to contain 10% defective items, what is the probability that the lot will be rejected? accepted?

8. A manufacturing company has 10 machines in continuous operation during a work day. The probability that an individual machine will break down during the day is .10. Determine the probability that during any given day 3 machines will break down.

9. A polling firm is taking a survey regarding a proposed new law. Of the voters polled, 30% are in favor of the law. If 10 people are surveyed, what is the probability that 4 will indicate that they are opposed to the passage of the new law?

10. Two law firms in a community handle all the cases dealing with consumer suits against companies in the area. The Abercrombie firm takes 40% of all suits, and the Olson firm handles the other 60%. The Abercrombie firm wins 70% of its cases, and the Olson firm wins 60% of its cases.

   a. Develop a probability tree showing all marginal, conditional, and joint probabilities.

   b. Develop a joint probability table.

   c. Using Bayes's rule, determine the probability that the Olson firm handled a particular case, given that the case has been won.

11. The Senate consists of 100 senators, of whom 34 are Republicans and 66 are Democrats. A bill to increase defense appropriations is before the Senate. Thirty-five percent of the Democrats and 70% of the Republicans favor the bill. The bill needs a simple majority to pass. Using a probability tree, determine the probability that the bill will pass.

12. A retail outlet receives radios from three electrical appliance companies. The outlet receives 20% of its radios from A, 40% from B, and 40% from C. The probability of receiving a defective radio from A is .01; from B, .02; and from C, .08.

   a. Develop a probability tree showing all marginal, conditional, and joint probabilities.

   b. Develop a joint probability table.

   c. What is the probability that a defective radio returned to the retail store came from company B?

13. A metropolitan school system consists of three districts—north, south, and central. The north district contains 25% of all students, the south district contains 40%, and the central district contains 35%. A minimum competency test was given to all students; 10% of the north district students failed, 15% of the south district students failed, and 5% of the central district students failed.

   a. Develop a probability tree showing all marginal, conditional, and joint probabilities.

   b. Develop a joint probability table.

   c. What is the probability that a student selected at random failed the test?

14. A service station owner sells Goodroad tires, which are ordered from a local tire distributor. The distributor receives tires from two plants, A and B. When the owner of the service station receives an order from the

distributor, there is a .50 probability the order consists of tires from plant A or plant B. However, the distributor will not tell the owner which plant the tires come from. The owner knows that 20% of all tires produced at plant A are defective, whereas only 10% of the tires produced at plant B are defective. When an order arrives at the station, the owner is allowed to inspect it briefly. The owner takes this opportunity to inspect one tire to see if it is defective. If the owner believes the tire came from plant A, the order will be sent back. Using Bayes's rule, determine the posterior probability that a tire is from plant A, given that the owner finds that it is defective.

15. A metropolitan school system consists of two districts, east and west. The east district contains 35% of all students, and the west district contains the other 65%. A vocational aptitude test was given to all students; 10% of the east district students failed, and 25% of the west district students failed. Given that a student failed the test, what is the posterior probability that the student came from the east district?

16. The Ramshead Pub sells a large quantity of beer every Saturday. From past sales records the pub has determined the following probabilities for sales.

Barrels	Probability
6	.10
7	.20
8	.40
9	.25
10	.05
	1.00

Compute the expected number of barrels that will be sold on Saturday.

17. The following probabilities for grades in Management Science I have been determined based on past records.

Grade	Probability
A	.10
B	.30
C	.40
D	.10
F	.10

The grades are assigned on a 4.0 scale, where an A is a 4.0, a B a 3.0, and so on. Determine the expected grade and variance for the course.

18. A market in Boston orders oranges from Florida. The oranges are shipped to Boston from Florida by either railroad, truck, or airplane; therefore, an order can take 1, 2, 3, or 4 days to arrive in Boston once it is placed. The following probabilities have been assigned to the number

of days it takes to receive an order once it is placed (referred to as lead time).

Lead Time	Probability
1	.20
2	.50
3	.20
4	.10
	1.00

Compute the expected number of days it takes to receive an order and the standard deviation.

19. An investment firm is considering two alternative investments, A and B, under two possible future sets of economic conditions, good and poor. There is a .60 probability of good economic conditions' occurring and a .40 probability of poor economic conditions' occurring. The expected gains and losses under each economic condition are as follows.

	Economic Conditions	
Investment	Good	Poor
A	$900,000	−$800,000
B	120,000	70,000

Using the expected value of each investment alternative, determine which should be selected.

20. An investor is considering two investments, an office building and bonds. The possible returns from each investment and their probabilities are as follows.

Office Building		Bonds	
Returns	Probabilities	Returns	Probabilities
$50,000	.30	$30,000	.60
60,000	.20	40,000	.40
80,000	.10		1.00
10,000	.30		
0	.10		
	1.00		

Using expected value and standard deviation as a basis for comparison, discuss which of the two investments should be selected.

21. The Jefferson High School Band Boosters Club has organized a raffle. The prize is a $6,000 car. Two thousand tickets to the raffle are to be sold at $1 apiece. If a person purchases 4 tickets, what will be the expected value of the tickets?

22. The time interval between machine breakdowns in a manufacturing firm is defined according to the following probability distribution:

Time Interval (hr)	Probability
1	.15
2	.20
3	.40
4	.25
	1.00

Determine the cumulative probability distribution and compute the expected time between machine breakdowns.

23. The life of an electronic transistor is normally distributed with a mean of 500 hours and a standard deviation of 80 hours. Determine the probability that a transistor will last for more than 400 hours.

24. The grade point average of students at a university is normally distributed with a mean of 2.6 and a standard deviation of 0.6. A recruiter for a company is interviewing students for summer employment. What percentage of the students will have a grade point average of 3.5 or greater?

25. The weight of bags of fertilizers is normally distributed with a mean of 50 pounds and a standard deviation of 6 pounds. What is the probability that a bag of fertilizer will weigh between 45 and 55 pounds?

26. The monthly demand for a product is normally distributed with a mean of 700 units and a standard deviation of 200 units. What is the probability that demand will be greater than 900 units in a given month?

27. The Polo Development Firm is building a shopping center. It has informed renters that their rental spaces will be ready for occupancy in 19 months. If the expected time until the shopping center is completed is estimated to be 14 months with a standard deviation of 4 months, what is the probability that the renters will not be able to move in in 19 months?

28. A warehouse distributor of carpet keeps 6,000 yards of deluxe shag carpet in stock during a month. The average demand for carpet from the stores that purchase from the distributor is 4,500 yards per month with a deviation of 900 yards. What is the probability that a customer's order will not be met during a month? (This situation is referred to as a stockout.)

29. The manager of the local National Video Store sells video cassette recorders at discount prices. If the store does not have a video recorder in stock when a customer wants to buy one, it will lose the sale, because the customer will purchase a recorder from one of the many local competitors. The problem is that the cost of renting warehouse space to keep

enough recorders in inventory to meet all demand is excessively high. The manager has determined that if 90% of customer demand for recorders can be met, then the combined cost of lost sales and inventory will be minimized. The manager has estimated that monthly demand for recorders is normally distributed with a mean of 180 recorders and a standard deviation of 60. Determine the number of recorders the manager should order each month in order to meet 90% of customer demand.

30. The owner of the Western Clothing Company has determined that the company must sell 670 pairs of denim jeans each month to break even (i.e., to reach the point where total revenue equals total cost). The company's marketing department has estimated that monthly demand is normally distributed with a mean of 805 pairs of jeans and a standard deviation of 207 pairs. What is the probability that the company will make a profit each month?

11

Decision Analysis

In the previous chapters dealing with linear programming, models were formulated and solved in order to aid the manager in making a decision. The solutions to the models were represented by values for *decision* variables. However, these linear programming models were all formulated under the assumption that certainty existed. In other words, it was assumed that all of the model coefficients, constraint values, and solution values were known with certainty and did not vary.

In actual practice, however, many decision-making situations occur under conditions of *uncertainty*. For example, the demand for a product may be not 100 units next week, but 50 or 200 units, depending on the state of the market (which is uncertain). Several decision-making techniques are available to aid the decision maker in dealing with this type of decision situation in which there is uncertainty.

Decision situations can be categorized into two classes: situations where probabilities *cannot* be assigned to future occurrences and situations where probabilities *can* be assigned. In this chapter we will discuss each of these classes of decision situations separately and demonstrate the decision-making criterion most commonly associated with each.

DECISION MAKING WITHOUT PROBABILITIES

Decision making is required in situations in which there are several alternatives from which the decision maker can choose. It is often possible to assign probabilities to these decision choices that aid the decision maker in selecting the one that has the best outcome. However, in some cases the decision maker is not able to assign probabilities, and it is this type of decision-making situation that we will address first.

A decision-making situation includes several components — the decisions themselves *and* the actual events that may occur in the future, known as *states of nature*. At the time the decision is made, the decision maker is uncertain which state of nature will occur in the future, and has no control over them.

Suppose a distribution company is considering purchasing a computer, in order to increase the number of orders it can process and thus increase its business. If economic conditions remain good, the company will realize a large increase in profit; however, if the economy takes a downturn, the company will lose money. In this decision situation the possible decisions are to purchase the computer and to not purchase the computer. The states of nature are *good* economic conditions and *bad* economic conditions. The state of nature that occurs will determine the outcome of the decision, and it is obvious that the decision maker has no control over which state will occur.

As another example, consider a concessions vendor who must decide whether to stock coffee for the concession stands at a football game in November. If the weather is cold, most of the coffee will be sold, but if the weather is warm, very little coffee will be sold. The decision is to order or to not order coffee, and the states of nature are warm and cold weather.

To facilitate the analysis of these types of decision situations so that the best decisions result, they are organized into *payoff tables*. In general, a payoff table is a means of organizing and illustrating the payoffs from the different decisions, given the various states of nature in a decision problem. A payoff table is constructed as shown in Table 11.1.

Payoff tables

TABLE 11.1
Payoff Table

| Decision | States of Nature | |
	a	b
1	payoff 1a	payoff 1b
2	payoff 2a	payoff 2b

Each decision, 1 or 2, in Table 11.1 will result in an outcome, or *payoff*, for the particular state of nature that will occur in the future. Payoffs are typically expressed in terms of profit revenues, or cost (although they can be expressed in terms of a variety of quantities). For example, if decision 1 is to purchase a computer and state of nature a is good economic conditions, payoff 1a could be $100,000 in profit.

Decision outcomes

The following example will illustrate the development of a payoff table. An investor is going to purchase one of three types of real estate. The investor must decide among an apartment building, an office building, and a warehouse. The future states of nature that will determine how much profit the investor will make are good economic conditions and poor economic conditions. The profits that will result from each decision in the event of each state of nature are shown in Table 11.2.

TABLE 11.2
Payoff Table for the Real Estate Investments

| Decision (Purchase) | States of Nature | |
	Good Economic Conditions	Poor Economic Conditions
Apartment building	$ 50,000	$ 30,000
Office building	100,000	−40,000
Warehouse	30,000	10,000

Decision-Making Criteria

Once the decision situation has been organized into a payoff table, several criteria are available for making the actual decision. These decision criteria, which will be presented in this section, include maximax, maximin, minimax regret, Hurwicz, and equal likelihood. On occasion these criteria will result in the same decision; however, often they will yield different decisions. The decision maker must select the criterion or combination of criteria that suits his or her needs best.

The Maximax Criterion

A decision that will result in the maximum of the maximum payoffs

With the *maximax criterion*, the decision maker selects the decision that will result in the maximum of the maximum payoffs. (In fact, this is how this criterion derives its name—a maximum of a maximum.) The maximax criterion is very optimistic. The decision maker assumes that the most favorable state of nature for each decision alternative will occur. Thus, for example, using this criterion the investor would optimistically assume that good economic conditions will prevail in the future.

A maximax example

The maximax criterion is applied in Table 11.3. The decision maker first selects the maximum payoff for each decision. Notice that all three maximum payoffs occur under good economic conditions. Of the three maximum payoffs—$50,000, $100,000, and $30,000—the maximum is $100,000; thus, the corresponding decision is to purchase the office building.

The maximax decision

TABLE 11.3

Payoff Table Illustrating a Maximax Decision

Decision (Purchase)	States of Nature	
	Good Economic Conditions	Poor Economic Conditions
Apartment building	$ 50,000	$ 30,000
Office building	100,000	−40,000
Warehouse	30,000	10,000

↑
Maximum payoff

Although the decision to purchase an office building will result in the largest payoff of $100,000, such a decision completely ignores the possibility of a potential loss of $40,000. The decision maker who uses the maximax criterion assumes a very optimistic future with respect to the states of nature.

Decision making using cost instead of profit

Before the next criterion is presented, it should be pointed out that the maximax decision rule as presented above deals with *profit*. However, if the payoff table consisted of costs, the opposite selection would be indicated: the minimum of the minimum costs. For the subsequent decision criteria we encounter, the same logic in the case of costs can be used.

The Maximin Criterion

In contrast to the maximax criterion, which is very optimistic, the *maximin criterion* is pessimistic. With the maximin criterion, the decision maker selects the decision that will reflect the *maximum* of the *minimum* payoffs. For each decision alternative, the decision maker assumes that the minimum payoff will occur. Of these minimum payoffs, the maximum is selected. The maximin criterion for our investment example is demonstrated in Table 11.4.

A decision that will result in the maximum of the minimum payoffs

TABLE 11.4
Payoff Table Illustrating a Maximin Decision

Decision (Purchase)	States of Nature	
	Good Economic Conditions	Poor Economic Conditions
Apartment building	$ 50,000	$ 30,000 ⟵ Maximum
Office building	100,000	−40,000 payoff
Warehouse	30,000	10,000

The minimum payoffs for our example are $30,000, −$40,000, and $10,000. The maximum of these three payoffs is $30,000; thus the decision arrived at using the maximin criterion would be to purchase the apartment building. This decision is relatively conservative, since the alternatives considered included only the worst outcomes that could occur. The decision to purchase the office building as determined by the maximax criterion included the possibility of a large loss (−$40,000). The worst that can occur from the decision to purchase the apartment building, however, is *a gain of $30,000*. On the other hand, the largest possible gain from purchasing the apartment building is much less than that of purchasing an office building (i.e., $50,000 versus $100,000).

A maximin example

If Table 11.4 contained costs instead of profits as the payoffs, the conservative approach would be to select the maximum cost for each decision. Then the decision that resulted in the minimum of these costs would be selected.

The Minimax Regret Criterion

In our example, suppose the investor decided to purchase the warehouse, only to discover that economic conditions in the future were better than expected. Naturally, the investor would be disappointed that the office building had not been purchased, since it would have resulted in the largest payoff ($100,000) under good economic conditions. In fact, the investor would *regret* the decision to purchase the warehouse and the *degree of regret would be $70,000*, the difference between the investor's choice and the best choice.

Regret resulting from a wrong decision

A decision that
avoids the greatest
regret

A minimax regret
example

    This brief example demonstrates the principle underlying the decision criterion known as *minimax regret* or the *regret criterion*. With this decision criterion, the decision maker attempts to avoid regret by selecting the decision alternative that minimizes the maximum regret.

    To use the minimax regret criterion, a decision maker first selects the maximum payoff under each state of nature. For our example, the maximum payoff under good economic conditions is $100,000, and the maximum payoff under poor economic conditions is $30,000. All other payoffs under the respective states of nature are subtracted from these amounts, as shown below.

Good Economic Conditions	*Poor Economic Conditions*
$100,000 − 50,000 = $50,000	$30,000 − 30,000 = $0
$100,000 − 100,000 = $0	$30,000 − (−40,000) = $70,000
$100,000 − 30,000 = $70,000	$30,000 − 10,000 = $20,000

A regret table

Opportunity loss

    These values represent the regret that would be experienced by the decision maker if a decision were made that resulted in less than the maximum payoff. The values are summarized in a modifed version of the payoff table known as a *regret table*, shown in Table 11.5. (Such a table is sometimes referred to as an opportunity loss table, in which case the term *opportunity loss* is synonymous with regret.)

TABLE 11.5
The Regret Table

Decision (Purchase)	States of Nature	
	Good Economic Conditions	Poor Economic Conditions
Apartment building	$ 50,000	$ 0
Office building	0	70,000
Warehouse	70,000	20,000

The minimax regret
decision

    In order to make the decision according to the minimax regret criterion, the maximum regret for *each decision* must be determined. The decision corresponding to the minimum of these regret values is then selected. This process is illustrated in Table 11.6.

TABLE 11.6
Regret Table Illustrating the Minimax Regret Decision

Decision (Purchase)	States of Nature	
	Good Economic Conditions	Poor Economic Conditions
Apartment building	$ 50,000	$ 0
Office building	0	70,000
Warehouse	70,000	20,000

The minimum
regret value

According to the minimax regret criterion, the decision should be to purchase the apartment building rather than the office building or the warehouse. This particular decision is based on the philosophy that the investor will experience the least amount of regret by purchasing the apartment building. In other words, if the investor purchased either the office building or the warehouse, $70,000 worth of regret could result; however, the purchase of the apartment building will result in, at most, $50,000 in regret.

The minimax regret logic

The Hurwicz Criterion

The Hurwicz criterion strikes a compromise between the maximax and maximin criteria. The principle underlying this decision criterion is that the decision maker is neither totally optimistic (as the maximax criterion assumes) nor totally pessimistic (as the maximin criterion assumes). With the Hurwicz criterion, the decision payoffs are weighted by a *coefficient of optimism*, a measure of the decision maker's optimism. The coefficient of optimism, which we will define as α, is between zero and one (i.e., $0 \le \alpha \le 1.0$). If $\alpha = 1.0$, then the decision maker is said to be completely optimistic, and if $\alpha = 0$, then the decision maker is completely pessimistic. (Given this definition, if α is the coefficient of optimism, $1 - \alpha$ is the *coefficient of pessimism*.)

A compromise between the maximax and maximin criteria

Coefficient of optimism, α

Coefficient of pessimism, $1 - \alpha$

The Hurwicz criterion requires that for each decision alternative, the maximum payoff be multiplied by α and the minimum payoff be multiplied by $1 - \alpha$. For our investment example, if α equals 0.4 (i.e., the investor is slightly pessimistic), $1 - \alpha = 0.6$ and the following values will result.

Decision

Apartment building:	$\$50,000(0.4) + 30,000(0.6) = \$38,000$
Office building:	$\$100,000(0.4) - 40,000(0.6) - \$16,000$
Warehouse:	$\$30,000(0.4) + 10,000(0.6) = \$18,000$

The Hurwicz criterion specifies selection of the decision alternative corresponding to the maximum weighted value, which is $38,000 for this example. Thus, the decision would be to purchase the apartment building.

It should be pointed out that when $\alpha = 0$, the Hurwicz criterion is actually the maximin criterion, and when $\alpha = 1.0$, it is the maximax criterion. A limitation of the Hurwicz criterion is the fact that α must be determined by the decision maker. It can be quite difficult for a decision maker to accurately determine his or her degree of optimism. Regardless of how the decision maker determines α, it is still a completely *subjective* measure of the decision maker's degree of optimism. Therefore the Hurwicz criterion is a completely subjective decision-making criterion.

Determining α

The Equal Likelihood Criterion

When the maximax criterion is applied to a decision situation, the decision maker implicitly assumes that the most favorable state of nature for each decision will occur. Alternatively, when the maximin criterion is applied, the least favorable states of nature are assumed. The *equal likelihood* (or LaPlace) *criterion* weights each state of nature equally, thus assuming that the states of nature are equally likely to occur.

Since there are two states of nature in our example, we assign a weight of .50 to each one. Next, we multiply these weights by each payoff for each decision.

Decision

Apartment building: $\$ 50,000(.50) + 30,000(.50) = \$40,000$

Office building: $\$100,000(.50) - 40,000(.50) = \$30,000$

Warehouse: $\$ 30,000(.50) + 10,000(.50) = \$20,000$

As with the Hurwicz criterion, we select the decision that has the maximum of these weighted values. Since $40,000 is the highest weighted value, the investor's decision would be to purchase the apartment building.

In applying the equal likelihood criterion, we are assuming a 50% chance, or .50 *probability*, that either state of nature will occur. Using this same basic logic, it is possible to weight the states of nature differently (i.e., unequally) in many decision problems. In other words, different probabilities can be assigned to each state of nature, indicating that one state is more likely than another to occur. The application of different probabilities to the states of nature is the principle behind the decision criteria to be presented in the next section.

Summary of Criteria Results

The decisions indicated by the decision criteria examined so far can be summarized as follows.

Criterion	*Decision (Purchase)*
Maximax	Office building
Maximin	Apartment building
Minimax regret	Apartment building
Hurwicz	Apartment building
Equal likelihood	Apartment building

The decision to purchase the apartment building was designated most often by the various decision criteria. Notice that the decision to purchase the warehouse was never indicated by any criterion. This is because the payoffs for an apartment building, under either set of future economic conditions, are always better than the payoffs for a warehouse. Thus, given any situation with these two alternatives (and any other choice, such as purchasing the office building), the decision to purchase an apartment will always be made over the decision to purchase a warehouse. In fact, the warehouse decision alternative could have been eliminated from consideration under each of our criteria. The alternative of purchasing a warehouse is said to be *dominated* by the alternative of purchasing an apartment building. In general, dominated decision alternatives can be removed from the payoff table and not considered when the various decision-making criteria are applied. This reduces the complexity of the decision analysis somewhat. However, in our discussions throughout this chapter of the application of decision criteria, we will leave the dominated alternative in the payoff table for demonstration purposes.

Dominant decision alternatives

The use of several decision criteria often results in a mix of decisions, with no one decision being selected more than the others. The criterion or collection of criteria used and the resulting decision depend on the characteristics and philosophy of the decision maker. For example, the extremely optimistic decision maker might eschew the majority of the results above and make the decision to purchase the office building because the maximax criterion most closely reflects his or her personal decision-making philosophy.

The appropriate criterion is dependent on the personality and philosophy of the decision maker

Computerized Solution of Decision-Making Problems Without Probabilities

Several management science software packages for the personal computer include programs to solve decision analysis problems. The Micro Manager PC package that we have employed previously is one such package.

The Micro Manager package will be used to illustrate the use of the maximax, maximin, minimax regret, equal likelihood (LaPlace), and Hurwicz criteria for the real estate problem considered in this section. The problem information is input very easily. A summary of the input and solution output is shown below.

```
PROGRAM: Decision Making Under Uncertainty

***** INPUT DATA ENTERED *****

-------------------------------------------
                      Events
                -------------------------
Alternative         1            2
-------------------------------------------
     1           50000.00     30000.00
     2          100000.00    -40000.00
     3           30000.00     10000.00
-------------------------------------------
Coefficient of optimism:    .4
```

```
*****   PROGRAM OUTPUT   *****

-----------------------------------------------
Decision Criterion          Optimum Alternative
-----------------------------------------------
     Laplace                        1
     Maximin                        1
     Maximax                        2
     Hurwicz (alpha = .4 )          1
     Minimax                        1
-----------------------------------------------
```

In this output "1" represents the first alternative, purchasing the apartment building, and "2" represents purchasing the office building.

DECISION MAKING WITH PROBABILITIES

The decision-making criteria just presented were based on the assumption that no information regarding the likelihood of the states of nature was available. Thus, no *probabilities of occurrence* were assigned to the states of nature, except in the case of the equal likelihood criterion. In that case, by assuming that each state of nature was equally likely and assigning a weight of .50 to each state of nature in our example, we were implicitly assigning a probability of .50 to the occurrence of each state of nature.

Probabilities can be assigned to the occurrence of states of nature

It is often possible for the decision maker to know enough about the future states of nature to assign probabilities to their occurrence. Given that probabilities can be assigned, several decision criteria are available to aid the decision maker. We will consider two of these criteria: *expected monetary value* and *expected opportunity loss* (although several others, including the *maximum likelihood criterion*, are available).

Expected Value

In order to apply the concept of expected value as a decision-making criterion, the decision maker must first estimate the probability of occurrence of each state of nature. Once these estimates have been made, the *expected value* for each decision alternative can be computed. Recall that expected value is computed by multiplying each outcome (of a decision) by the probability of its occurrence and then summing these products (see Chap. 10).

An expected value example

Using our real estate investment example, let us suppose that, based on several economic forecasts, the investor is able to estimate a .60 probability that good economic conditions will prevail and a .40 probability that poor economic conditions will prevail. This new information is shown in Table 11.7.

TABLE 11.7
Payoff Table with Probabilities for States of Nature

Decision (Purchase)	States of Nature	
	Good Economic Conditions .60	Poor Economic Conditions .40
Apartment building	$ 50,000	$ 30,000
Office building	100,000	−40,000
Warehouse	30,000	10,000

The expected value for each decision is computed as follows.

Expected value computations

EV(Apartment) = $ 50,000(.60) + 30,000(.40) = $42,000

EV(Office) = $100,000(.60) − 40,000(.40) = $44,000

EV(Warehouse) = $ 30,000(.60) + 10,000(.40) = $22,000

The best decision is the one with the greatest expected value. Since the greatest expected value is $44,000, the best decision is to purchase the office building. This does not mean that $44,000 will result if the investor purchases an office building; rather, it is assumed that one of the payoff values will result (either $100,000 or −$40,000). The expected value means that if this decision situation occurred a large number of times, an *average* payoff of $44,000 would result.

The decision with the greatest expected value

An average payoff

Expected Opportunity Loss

A decision criterion closely related to expected value is *expected opportunity loss*. To use this criterion, we multiply the probabilities by the regret (i.e., opportunity loss) for each decision outcome, rather than multiplying the decision outcomes by the probabilities of their occurrence, as we did for expected monetary value.

The concept of regret was introduced in our discussion of the minimax regret criterion. The regret values for each decision outcome in our example were shown in Table 11.6. These values are repeated in Table 11.8, with the addition of the probabilities of occurrence for each state of nature.

The regret table

The expected opportunity loss for each decision is computed as follows.

Computations of expected opportunity loss

EOL(Apartment) = $50,000(.60) + 0(.40) = $30,000

EOL(Office) = $0(.60) + 70,000(.40) = $28,000

EOL(Warehouse) = $70,000(.60) + 20,000(.40) = $50,000

TABLE 11.8

Regret (Opportunity Loss) Table with Probabilities for States of Nature

	States of Nature	
Decision (Purchase)	Good Economic Conditions .60	Poor Economic Conditions .40
Apartment building	$ 50,000	$ 0
Office building	0	70,000
Warehouse	70,000	20,000

As with the minimax regret criterion, the best decision results from minimizing the regret, or, in this case, minimizing the *expected* regret or opportunity loss. Since $28,000 is the minimum expected regret, the decision is to purchase the office building.

Notice that the decisions recommended by the expected value and expected opportunity loss criteria were the same—to purchase the office building. This is not a coincidence, as these two methods always result in the same decision. Thus, it is repetitious to apply both methods to a decision situation when one of the two will suffice.

In addition, note that the decisions from the expected value and expected opportunity loss criteria are totally dependent on the probability estimates determined by the decision maker. Thus, if inaccurate probabilities are used, erroneous decisions will result. It is therefore important that the decision maker be as accurate as possible in determining the probabilities of each state of nature.

> The expected value and expected opportunity loss criteria result in the same decision

> The necessity of accurate probability estimates

Computerized Solution Using Expected Value

The Micro Manager software package for the personal computer, discussed earlier in this chapter, not only solves decision analysis problems without probabilities, but also has the capability to solve problems using the expected value criterion. A summary of the input data and the solution output for our real estate example appears below.

```
PROGRAM: Decision Making Under Risk

***** INPUT DATA ENTERED *****

-----------------------------------
                  Events
            -------------------
               1         2
Alternative  p = 0.60 p = 0.40
-----------------------------------
    1        50000.00 30000.00
    2       100000.00-40000.00
    3        30000.00 10000.00
-----------------------------------
```

```
*****   PROGRAM OUTPUT   *****

-----------------------------------
  Alternative    Expected Value
-----------------------------------
       1            42000.00
       2            44000.00 *
       3            22000.00
-----------------------------------

* indicates optimal solution
```

Expected Value of Perfect Information

It is often possible to purchase additional information regarding future events, and thus make a better decision. For example, a real estate investor could hire an economic forecaster to perform an analysis of the economy in order to more accurately determine which economic condition will occur in the future. However, the investor (or any decision maker) would be foolish to pay more for this information than he or she stands to gain in extra profit from having the information. That is, the information has some maximum value that represents the limit of what the decision maker would be willing to spend. This value of information can be computed as an expected value—hence its name, the *expected value of perfect information* (also referred to as EVPI).

In order to compute the expected value of perfect information, we first look at the decisions under each state of nature. If we could obtain information that assured us which state of nature was going to occur (i.e., perfect information), we could select the best decision for that state of nature. For example, in our real estate investment example, if we know for sure that good economic conditions will prevail, then we will decide to purchase the office building. Similarly, if we know for sure that poor economic conditions will occur, then we will decide to purchase the apartment building. These hypothetical "perfect" decisions are summarized in Table 11.9.

Purchasing additional information to aid the decision maker

The maximum amount a decision maker would pay for additional information

The best decision under each state of nature

TABLE 11.9
Payoff Table with Decisions Given Perfect Information

| Decision (Purchase) | States of Nature | |
	Good Economic Conditions .60	Poor Economic Conditions .40
Apartment building	$ 50,000	$ 30,000
Office building	100,000	−40,000
Warehouse	30,000	10,000

The probabilities of each state of nature (i.e., .60 and .40) tell us that good economic conditions will prevail 60% of the time and poor economic conditions will prevail 40% of the time (if this decision situation is repeated many times). In other words, even though perfect information enables the investor to make the right decision, each state of nature will occur only a certain portion of the time. Thus, each of the decision outcomes obtained using perfect information must be weighted by its respective probability.

$$\$100,000(.60) + 30,000(.40) = \$72,000$$

The amount $72,000 is the expected value of the decision *given* perfect information, not the expected value *of* perfect information. The expected value of perfect information is the maximum amount that would be paid to gain information that would result in a decision better than the one made *without perfect information*. Recall that the expected value decision without perfect information was to purchase an office building, and the expected value was computed as

$$\text{EV(Office)} = \$100,000(.60) - 40,000(.40) = \$44,000$$

The expected value of perfect information is computed by subtracting the expected value without perfect information ($44,000) from the expected value given perfect information ($72,000):

$$\text{EVPI} = \$72,000 - 44,000 = \$28,000$$

The expected value of perfect information, $28,000, is the maximum amount that the investor would pay to purchase perfect information from some other source, such as an economic forecaster. Of course, perfect information is rare and usually unobtainable. Typically, the decision maker would be willing to pay some amount less than $28,000, depending on how accurate (i.e., close to perfection) the decision maker believes the information is.

It is interesting to notice that the expected value of perfect information, $28,000 for our example, is the same as the *expected opportunity loss* for the decision selected using this latter criterion:

$$\text{EOL(Office)} = \$0(.60) + 70,000(.40) = \$28,000$$

This will always be the case, and logically so, since regret reflects *the difference between the best decision under a state of nature and the decision actually made*. This is actually the same thing determined by the expected value of perfect information.

Decision Trees

Another useful technique for analyzing a decision situation is a *decision tree*. A decision tree, like the probability tree shown in Chapter 10 (Fig. 10.3), is a graphical diagram consisting of nodes and

---

The expected value given perfect information

The expected value without perfect information

The expected value of perfect information

The EVPI equals the expected opportunity loss

A graphical diagram used for making decisions

branches. However, rather than determining the probability of each branch (i.e., outcome) as in a probability tree, in a decision tree the user computes the expected value of each outcome and makes a decision based on these expected values. The primary benefit of a decision tree is that it provides an illustration (or picture) of the decision-making process. This makes it easier to correctly compute the necessary expected values and to understand the process of making the decision.

A decision tree example

Our example of the real estate investor will be used to demonstrate the fundamentals of decision tree analysis. The various decisions, probabilities, and outcomes of this example, initially presented in Table 11.7, are repeated in Table 11.10. The decision tree for this example is shown in Figure 11.1.

TABLE 11.10

Payoff Table for Real Estate Investment Example

Decision (Purchase)	States of Nature	
	Good Economic Conditions .60	Poor Economic Conditions .40
Apartment building	$ 50,000	$ 30,000
Office building	100,000	−40,000
Warehouse	30,000	10,000

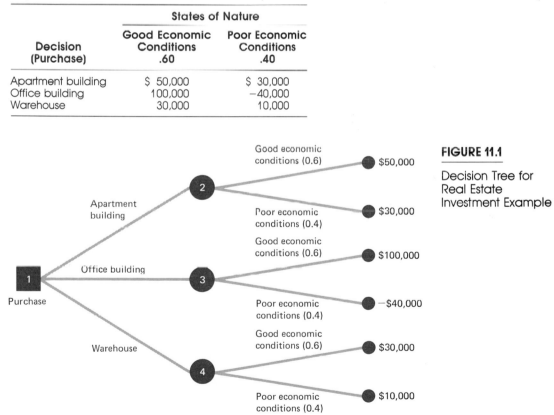

FIGURE 11.1

Decision Tree for Real Estate Investment Example

The circles (○) and squares (□) in Figure 11.1 are referred to as *nodes*. The squares are decision nodes, and the *branches* emanating from a decision node reflect the alternative decisions possible at that

Decision nodes

point. For example, in Figure 11.1, node 1 signifies a decision to purchase an apartment building, office building, or warehouse. The circles are probability nodes, and the branches emanating from them indicate the states of nature that can occur: good economic conditions or poor economic conditions.

The decision tree represents the sequence of events in a decision situation. First, one of the three decision choices is selected at node 1. Depending on the branch selected, the decision maker arrives at probability node 2, 3, or 4, where one of the states of nature will prevail, resulting in one of six possible payoffs.

Determining the best decision using a decision tree involves computing the expected value at each probability node. This is accomplished by starting with the final outcomes (payoffs) and working backward through the decision tree toward node 1. First, the expected value of the payoffs is computed at each probability node.

$$EV(\text{node } 2) = .60(\$\ 50,000) + .40(\$\ 30,000) = \$42,000$$
$$EV(\text{node } 3) = .60(\$100,000) + .40(\$-40,000) = \$44,000$$
$$EV(\text{node } 4) = .60(\$\ 30,000) + .40(\$\ 10,000) = \$22,000$$

These values are now shown as the *expected* payoffs from each of the three branches emanating from node 1 in Figure 11.2. Each of these three expected values at nodes 2, 3, and 4 is the outcome of a possible decision that can occur at node 1. Moving toward node 1, we select the branch that comes from the probability node with the highest expected payoff. In Figure 11.2, the branch corresponding to the highest payoff, $44,000, is from node 1 to node 3. This branch represents the decision to purchase the office building. The decision

Probability nodes

The sequence of events in a decision situation

Computing the expected value at each probability node

Selecting the branch with the greatest expected value

FIGURE 11.2

Decision Tree with Expected Values at Probability Nodes

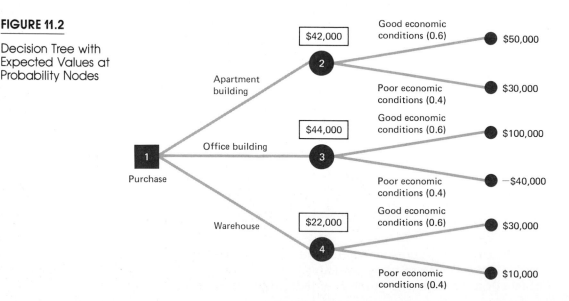

to purchase the office building, with an expected payoff of $44,000, is the same result we achieved earlier using the expected value criterion. In fact, when only one decision is to be made (i.e., there is not a series of decisions), the decision tree will always yield the same decision and expected payoff as the expected value criterion. As a result, in these decision situations the decision tree is not very useful. However, when a sequence or series of decisions is required, the decision tree can be very useful.

Sequential Decision Trees

As noted above, when a decision situation requires only a single decision, an expected value payoff table will yield the same result as a decision tree. However, a payoff table is usually *limited to* a single decision situation like our real estate investment example. If a decision situation requires a series of decisions, then a payoff table cannot be created and a decision tree becomes the best method for decision analysis.

A decision situation requiring a series of decisions

In order to demonstrate the use of a decision tree for a sequence of decisions, we will alter our real estate investment example to encompass a ten-year period during which several decisions must be made. In this new example, the *first decision* facing the investor is whether to purchase an apartment building or land. If the investor purchases the apartment building, two states of nature are possible. Either the population of the town will grow (with a probability of .60), or the population will not grow (with a probability of .40). Either state of nature will result in a payoff. On the other hand, if the investor chooses to purchase land, three years in the future another decision will have to be made regarding the development of the land. The decision tree for this example, shown in Figure 11.3 on page 392, contains all the pertinent data, including decisions, states of nature, probabilities, and payoffs.

A sequential decision tree example

At decision node 1 in Figure 11.3, the decision choices are to purchase an apartment building and to purchase land. Notice that the cost of each venture ($800,000 and $200,000, respectively) is shown in parentheses. If the apartment building is purchased, two states of nature are possible at probability node 2. The town may exhibit population growth, with a probability of .60, or there may be no population growth or a decline, with a probability of .40. If the population grows, the investor will achieve a payoff of $2,000,000 over a ten-year period. (Note that this whole decision situation encompasses a ten-year time span.) However, if no population growth occurs, a payoff of only $225,000 will result.

Decision node 1

Probability node 2

If the decision is to purchase land, two states of nature are possible at probability node 3. These two states of nature and their probabilities are identical to those at node 2; however, the payoffs

Probability node 3

Decision node 4

Decision node 5

are different. If population growth occurs *for a three-year period*, no payoff will occur, but the investor will make another decision at node 4 regarding development of the land. At that point either apartments will be built at a cost of $800,000 or the land will be sold with a payoff of $450,000. Notice that the decision situation at node 4 can occur only if population growth occurs first. If no population growth occurs at node 3, there is no payoff and another decision situation becomes necessary at node 5: the land can be developed commercially at a cost of $600,000 or the land can be sold for $210,000. (Notice that the sale of the land results in less profit if there is no population growth than if there is population growth.)

If the decision at decision node 4 is to build apartments, two states of nature are possible. The population may grow, with a conditional probability of .80, or there may be no population growth, with a conditional probability of .20. The probability of population growth is higher (and the probability of no growth is lower) than before because there has already been population growth for the first three years, as shown by the branch from node 3 to node 4. The payoffs for these two states of nature at the end of the ten-year period are $3,000,000 and $700,000, respectively, as shown in Figure 11.3.

If the investor decides to develop the land commercially at node 5, then two states of nature can occur. Population growth can occur, with a probability of .30 and an eventual payoff of $2,300,000, or no population growth can occur, with a probability of .70 and a

FIGURE 11.3

Sequential Decision Tree

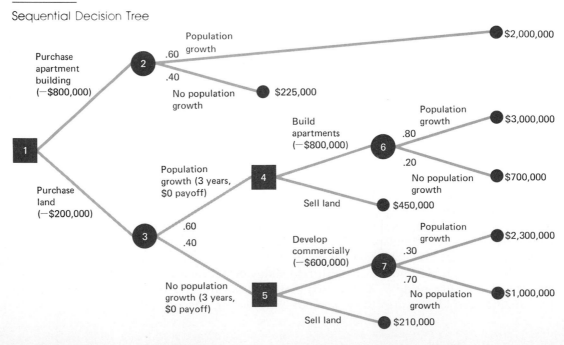

payoff of $1,000,000. The probability of population growth is low (i.e., .30) because there has already been no population growth, as shown by the branch from node 3 to node 5.

This decision situation encompasses several sequential decisions that can be analyzed using the decision tree approach outlined in our earlier (simpler) example. As before, we start at the end of the decision tree and work backward toward a decision at node 1.

First we must compute the expected values at nodes 6 and 7.

EV(node 6) = .80($3,000,000) + .20($ 700,000) = $2,540,000

EV(node 7) = .30($2,300,000) + .70($1,000,000) = $1,390,000

Both of these expected values (as well as all other nodal values) are shown in boxes in Figure 11.4.

At decision nodes 4 and 5, we must make a decision. As with a normal payoff table, we make the decision that results in the greatest expected value. At node 4 we have a choice between two values: $1,740,000, the value derived by subtracting the cost of building an apartment building ($800,000) from the expected payoff of $2,540,000, or $450,000, the expected value of selling the land computed with a probability of 1.0. The decision is to build the apartment building, and the value at node 4 is $1,740,000.

This same process is repeated at node 5. The decisions at node 5 result in payoffs of $790,000 (i.e., $1,390,000 − 600,000 = $790,000) and $210,000. Since the value $790,000 is higher, the decision is to develop the land commercially.

Expected values at nodes 6 and 7

FIGURE 11.4

Sequential Decision Tree with Nodal Expected Values

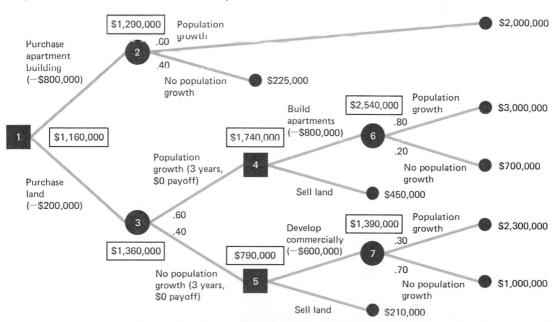

Expected values at
nodes 2 and 3

Next we must compute the expected values at nodes 2 and 3.

$$EV(\text{node 2}) = .60(\$2,000,000) + .40(\$225,000) = \$1,290,000$$
$$EV(\text{node 3}) = .60(\$1,740,000) + .40(\$790,000) = \$1,360,000$$

(Note that the expected value for node 3 is computed from the decision values previously determined at nodes 4 and 5.)

The final decision
at node 1

Now we must make the final decision for node 1. As before, we
select the decision with the greatest expected value *after the cost of
each decision is subtracted out.*

$$\text{Apartment building: } \$1,290,000 - 800,000 = \$\ \ 490,000$$
$$\text{Land: } \$1,360,000 - 200,000 = \$1,160,000$$

Since the highest *net* expected value is $1,160,000, the decision is to
purchase land and the payoff of the decision is $1,160,000.

A picture of the
decision process

This example demonstrates the usefulness of decision trees for
decision analysis. The decision tree allows the decision maker to see
the logic of decision making, because it provides a picture of the decision process. Decision trees can be used for decision problems
more complex than the example above without too much difficulty.

Computerized Decision Tree Analysis

The QSB+ software package for the personal computer, which has
been demonstrated in previous chapters, has the capability to perform decision tree analysis. For the sequential decision tree example
described in the preceding section and illustrated in Figures 11.3 and
11.4, the program input and solution output appear as follows.

```
              Input Data of the Decision Tree Page 1

Branch    Branch      Start   End     Start node   Probability    Payoff/cost
number    name        node    node      type
   1     <building>   <1 >    <2 >     <1    >     <      0>      < -800000>
   2     <land    >   <1 >    <3 >     <1    >     <      0>      < -200000>
   3     <growth  >   <2 >    <8 >     <2    >     <+.600000>     <+2000000>
   4     <nogrow  >   <2 >    <9 >     <2    >     <+.400000>     < +225000>
   5     <growth  >   <3 >    <4 >     <2    >     <+.600000>     <      0>
   6     <nogrow  >   <3 >    <5 >     <2    >     <+.400000>     <      0>
   7     <building>   <4 >    <6 >     <1    >     <      0>      < -800000>
   8     <sell    >   <4 >    <10 >    <1    >     <      0>      < +450000>
   9     <develop >   <5 >    <7 >     <1    >     <      0>      < -600000>
  10     <sell    >   <5 >    <11 >    <1    >     <      0>      < +210000>
  11     <growth  >   <6 >    <12 >    <2    >     <+.800000>     <+3000000>
  12     <nogrow  >   <6 >    <13 >    <2    >     <+.200000>     < +700000>
  13     <growth  >   <7 >    <14 >    <2    >     <+.300000>     <+2300000>
  14     <nogrow  >   <7 >    <15 >    <2    >     <+.700000>     <+1000000>
```

Given the conditional probabilities, the prior probabilities can be revised to form *posterior probabilities* by means of Bayes's rule (as shown in Chap. 10). If we know the conditional probability that a positive report was presented given that good economic conditions prevail, $P(P/g)$, the posterior probability of good economic conditions given a positive report, $P(g/P)$, can be determined using Bayes's rule, as follows.

Posterior probabilities— revised prior probabilities

Bayes's rule

$$P(g/P) = \frac{P(P/g)P(g)}{P(P/g)P(g) + P(P/p)P(p)}$$

$$= \frac{(.80)(.60)}{(.80)(.60) + (.10)(.40)}$$

$$= .923$$

The prior probability that good economic conditions will occur in the future is .60. However, by obtaining the additional information of a positive report from the analyst, the investor can revise the prior probability of good conditions to a .923 probability that good economic conditions will occur. The remaining posterior (revised) probabilities are

$P(g/N) = .250$

$P(p/P) = .077$

$P(p/N) = .750$

Computerized Bayesian Analysis

The QSB+ software package for the personal computer can also provide Bayesian analysis. The QSB+ program input and solution output for Bayesian analysis of the real estate example are as follows.

```
              Bayesian Analysis--Prior Probabilities for States of Nature

    S1:   <+.600000> S2:   <+.400000>


                 Bayesian Analysis--Conditional Probabilities

    State     Experiment Outcomes (Indicators)
    S1        I1:  +.800000 I2:  +.200000
    S2        I1:  +.100000 I2:  +.900000




              Bayesian Analysis--Posterior/Revised Probabilities

    State     Experiment Outcomes (Indicators)
    S1        I1:  +.923077 I2:  +.250000
    S2        I1:  +.076923 I2:  +.750000
```

Note that these posterior probabilities correspond to those obtained in the preceding section.

Now that the investor has the revised probabilities of future economic conditions given each report outcome, how can this probabilistic information be used in the decision-making process? The answer can best be determined within the framework of a decision tree.

Decision Trees with Posterior Probabilities

The original decision tree analysis of the real estate investment example is shown in Figures 11.1 and 11.2. Using these decision trees, we determined that the appropriate decision was the purchase of an office building, with an expected value of $44,000. However, if the investor hires an economic analyst, the decision regarding which piece of real estate to invest in will not be made until after the analyst presents the report. This creates an additional stage in the decision-making process, which is shown in the decision tree in Figure 11.5.

A decision tree with two new branches

The decision tree shown in Figure 11.5 differs in two respects from the decision trees in Figures 11.1 and 11.2. The first difference is that there are two new branches at the beginning of the decision tree that represent the two report outcomes. Notice, however, that given either report outcome, the decision alternatives, the possible states of nature, and the payoffs are the same as those in Figures 11.1 and 11.2.

Using posterior probabilities in the decision tree

The second difference is that the probabilities of each state of nature are no longer the prior probabilities given in Figure 11.1; instead they are the revised posterior probabilities computed in the previous section using Bayes's rule. If the economic analyst issues a positive report, then the upper branch in Figure 11.5 (from node 1 to node 2) will be taken. If an apartment building is purchased (the branch from node 2 to node 4), the probability of good economic conditions is .923, whereas the probability of poor conditions is .077. These are the revised posterior probabilities of the economic conditions given a positive report. However, before we can perform an expected value analysis using this decision tree, one more piece of probabilistic information must be determined—the initial branch probabilities of a positive and a negative economic report.

Initial branch probabilities

The probability of a positive report, $P(P)$, and of a negative report, $P(N)$, can be determined according to the following logic. Recall from Chapter 10 that the probability that two dependent events, A and B, will both occur is

$$P(AB) = P(A/B)P(B)$$

FIGURE 11.5

Decision Tree with Posterior Probabilities

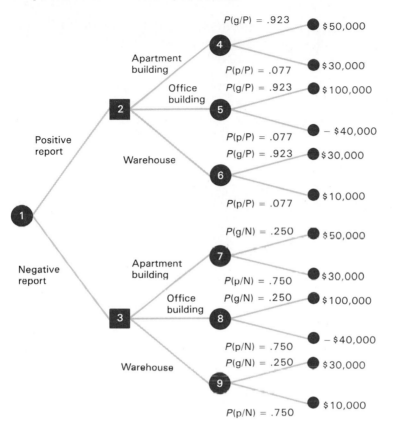

If event A is a positive report and event B is good economic conditions, then according to the above formula,

$$P(Pg) = P(P/g)P(g)$$

We can also determine the probability of a positive report and poor economic conditions the same way.

$$P(Pp) = P(P/p)P(p)$$

Next consider the two probabilities $P(Pg)$ and $P(Pp)$. These are, respectively, the probability of a positive report and good economic conditions and the probability of a positive report and poor economic conditions. These two sets of occurrences are *mutually exclusive*, since both good and poor economic conditions cannot occur simultaneously in the immediate future. Conditions will be either good or poor, but not both. To determine the *probability of a positive report*, we add the mutually exclusive probabilities of a positive report with good economic conditions and a positive report with poor economic conditions, as follows.

$$P(P) = P(Pg) + P(Pp)$$

Now, if we substitute into this formula the relationships for $P(Pg)$ and $P(Pp)$ determined earlier, we have

$$P(P) = P(P/g)P(g) + P(P/p)P(p)$$

The denominator of the Bayesian formula

You might notice that the right-hand side of this equation is the denominator of the Bayesian formula we used to compute $P(g/P)$ in the previous section. Using the conditional and prior probabilities that have already been established, we can determine that the probability of a positive report is

$$P(P) = P(P/g)P(g) + P(P/p)P(p)$$
$$= (.80)(.60) + (.10)(.40)$$
$$= .52$$

Similarly, the probability of a negative report is

$$P(N) = P(N/g)P(g) + P(N/p)P(p)$$
$$= (.20)(.60) + (.90)(.40)$$
$$= .48$$

Now we have all the information needed to perform a decision tree analysis. The decision tree analysis for our example is shown in Figure 11.6. To see how the decision tree analysis is conducted, consider the result at node 4 first. The value $48,460 is the expected value of the purchase of an apartment building given both states of nature. This expected value is computed as follows.

$$EV(\text{Apartment building}) = \$50,000(.923) + 30,000(.077)$$
$$= \$48,460$$

The expected values at nodes 5, 6, 7, 8, and 9 are computed similarly.

The investor will actually make the decision as to which investment to make at nodes 2 and 3. It is assumed that the investor will make the best decision in each case. Thus, the decision at node 2 will be to purchase an office building, with an expected value of $89,212; the decision at node 3 will be to purchase an apartment building, with an expected value of $35,000. These two results at **Decision strategies** nodes 2 and 3 are referred to as *decision strategies*. They represent *a plan* of decisions to be made given either a positive or a negative report from the economic analyst.

Expected value of a decision strategy given additional information

The final step in the decision tree analysis is to compute the expected value of the decision strategy given that an economic analysis is performed. This expected value, shown as $63,190 at node 1 in Figure 11.6, is computed as follows.

$$EV(\text{strategy}) = \$89,212(.52) + 35,000(.48)$$
$$= \$63,190$$

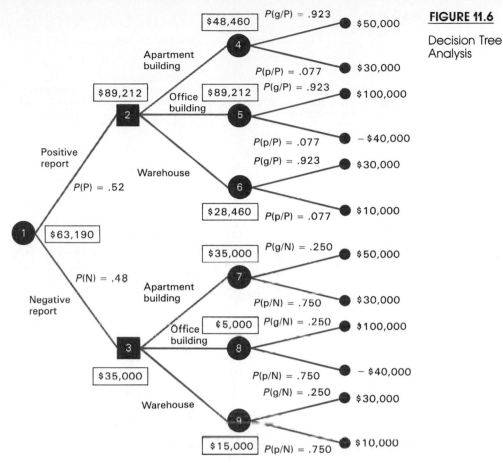

FIGURE 11.6

Decision Tree
Analysis

This amount, $63,190, is the expected value of the investor's decision strategy given that a report forecasting future economic condition is generated by the economic analyst.

Computing Posterior Probabilities with Tables

One of the difficulties that can occur with this type of decision analysis with additional information is that as the size of the problem increases (i.e., as we add more decision alternatives and states of nature) the application of Bayes's rule to compute the posterior probabilities becomes more complex. In such cases, the posterior probabilities can be computed using tables. This tabular approach will be demonstrated with our real estate investment example. The table for computing posterior probabilities for a positive report and $P(P)$ is initially set up as shown in Table 11.12.

The posterior probabilities for either state of nature (good or poor economic conditions) given a negative report are computed similarly.

Using Bayes's rule for large decision problems

Computing posterior probabilities using a table

TABLE 11.12
Computation of Posterior Probabilities

(1) States of Nature	(2) Prior Probabilities	(3) Conditional Probabilities	(4) Prior Probability × Conditional Probability: (2) × (3)	(5) Posterior Probabilities: (4) ÷ Σ(4)
Good conditions	$P(g) = .6$	$P(P/g) = .80$	$P(Pg) = .48$	$P(g/P) = \dfrac{.48}{.52} = .923$
Poor conditions	$P(p) = .4$	$P(P/p) = .10$	$P(Pp) = .04$ $\Sigma = P(P) = .52$	$P(p/P) = \dfrac{.04}{.52} = .077$

No matter how large the decision analysis, the steps of this tabular approach can be followed the same way as in this relatively small problem. This approach is more systematic than the direct application of Bayes's rule, making it easier to compute the posterior probabilities for larger problems.

The Expected Value of Sample Information

Recall that we computed the expected value of our real estate investment example to be $44,000 when we did not have any additional information. After obtaining the additional information provided by the economic analyst, we computed an expected value of $63,190 using the decision tree in Figure 11.6. The difference between these two expected values is called the *expected value of sample information* (EVSI), and it is computed as follows.

Computing the expected value of sample information

$$\text{EVSI} = \text{EV}_{\text{with information}} - \text{EV}_{\text{without information}}$$

For our example, the expected value of sample information is

$$\text{EVSI} = \$63,190 - 44,000$$
$$= \$19,190$$

This means that the real estate investor would be willing to pay the economic analyst up to $19,190 for an economic report that forecasted future economic conditions.

After we computed the expected value of the investment without additional information, we computed the *expected value of perfect information*, which equaled $28,000. However, the expected value of the sample information was only $19,190. This is a logical result, since it is rare that absolutely perfect information can be determined. Since the additional information that is obtained is less than perfect, it will be worth less to the decision maker. We can determine how

Less than perfect information

close to perfect our sample information is by computing the *efficiency of sample information* as follows.

$$\text{Efficiency} = \frac{\text{EVSI}}{\text{EVPI}}$$

$$= \frac{\$19,190}{28,000}$$

$$= .68$$

Thus, the analyst's economic report is viewed by the investor to be 68% as efficient as perfect information. In general, a high efficiency rating indicates that the information is very good, or close to being perfect information, and a low rating indicates that the additional information is not very good. For our example, the efficiency of .68 is relatively high; thus it is doubtful that the investor would seek additional information from an alternative source. (However, this is usually dependent on how much money the decision maker has available to purchase information.) If the efficiency had been lower, however, the investor might seek additional information elsewhere.

UTILITY

All of the decision-making criteria presented so far in this chapter have been based on monetary value. In other words, decisions were based on the potential dollar payoffs of the alternatives. However, there are certain decision situations in which individuals *do not* make decisions based on the expected dollar gain or loss.

Decisions not
based on dollar
gains or losses

For example, consider the individual who purchases automobile insurance. The decisions are to purchase and to not purchase, and the states of nature are *an accident* and *no accident*. The payoff table for this decision situation, including probabilities, is shown in Table 11.13.

TABLE 11.13

Payoff Table for Auto Insurance Example

	States of Nature	
Decision	No Accident .992	Accident .008
Purchase insurance	$500	$ 500
Do not purchase insurance	0	10,000

The dollar outcomes in Table 11.13 are the *costs* associated with each outcome. The insurance costs $500 whether there is an accident or no accident. If the insurance is not purchased and there is no accident, then there is no cost at all. However, if an accident does occur, then the individual will incur a cost of $10,000.

The expected cost (EC) for each decision is

$$EC(\text{Insurance}) = .992(\$500) + .008(\$\ 500) = \$500$$
$$EC(\text{No Insurance}) = .992(\$\ \ 0) + .008(\$10,000) = \$\ 80$$

Since the *lowest* expected cost is $80, the decision *should be* to not purchase insurance. However, people almost always purchase insurance (even when they are not legally required to do so). This is true of all types of insurance, such as accident, life, or fire.

Why do people shun the greater *expected* dollar outcome in this type of situation? The answer is that people want to avoid a ruinous or painful situation. When faced with a relatively small dollar cost versus a disaster, people typically pay the small cost to avert the disaster. People who display this characteristic are referred to as *risk averters* because they avoid risky situations.

Alternatively, people who go to the track to wager on horse-races, travel to Atlantic City to play roulette, or speculate in the commodities market decide to take risks even though the greatest *expected value* would occur if they simply held on to the money. These people shun the greater expected value accruing from a sure thing (keeping their money) in order to take a chance on receiving a "bonanza." Such people are referred to as *risk takers*.

For both risk averters and risk takers (as well as those who are indifferent to risk), the decision criterion is something other than the expected dollar outcome. This alternative criterion is known as *utility*. Utility is a measure of the satisfaction derived from money. In our examples of risk averters and risk takers presented above, the utility derived from their decisions *exceeded* the expected dollar value. For example, the utility to the average decision maker of having insurance is much greater than the utility of not having insurance.

As another example, consider two people, each of whom is offered $100,000 to perform some particularly difficult and strenuous task. One individual has an annual income of $10,000; the other individual is a multimillionaire. It is reasonable to assume that the average person with an annual income of only $10,000 would leap at the opportunity to earn $100,000, whereas the multimillionaire would reject the offer. Obviously, $100,000 has more *utility* (i.e., value) for one individual than for the other.

In general, the same incremental amount of money does not have the same intrinsic value to every person. For individuals with a great deal of wealth, more money does not usually have as much intrinsic value as it does for the individual who has little money. In other words, although the dollar value is the same, the value as measured by utility is different, depending on how much wealth a person presently has. Thus, utility in this case is a measure of the pleasure or satisfaction an individual would receive from an incremental increase in wealth.

In some decision situations an attempt is made to assign a subjective value to utility to a decision maker. This value is typically measured in terms of units called *utiles*. For example, the $100,000 offered to the two individuals may have a utility value of 100 utiles to the person with a low income and 0 utiles to the multimillionaire.

Measuring utility

Utiles

In our automobile insurance example, the *expected utility* of purchasing insurance could be 1,000 utiles, and the expected utility of not purchasing insurance only 1 utile. These utility values are completely reversed from the expected *monetary* values computed from Table 11.13, which explains the decision to purchase insurance.

As might be expected, it is usually very difficult to measure utility and the number of utiles derived from a decision outcome. The process is a very subjective one in which the decision maker's psychological preferences must be determined. Thus, although the concept of utility is realistic and often portrays actual decision-making criteria more accurately than does expected monetary value, its application is difficult and, as such, somewhat limited.

Measuring utility is a subjective process

APPLICATIONS OF DECISION ANALYSIS

Bidding on the Purchase of a Ship

In April 1981, a British ship named the S. S. *Kuniang* ran aground off the coast of Florida and was declared a total loss by the owners. The owners subsequently offered to sell the salvage rights in a sealed bid auction. The New England Electrical System—a public utility serving over one million customers in Massachusetts, Rhode Island, and New Hampshire—was attempting to decide whether to bid for the ship and use it to haul coal from Virginia to its power stations. The bidding process was complicated by the fact that because of a sixty-year-old protectionist act of Congress, U.S.-built ships received docking priority at port facilities. Since coal loading at ports like Newport News and Norfolk in Virginia can sometimes take as long as forty-five days, this restriction could be devastating. However, the law did not cover a foreign-built ship that had been declared a total loss (as the *Kuniang* had been) and for which the cost of repairs was at least three times the salvage value. It was estimated that the repairs to the ship would cost around $15 million. Further, it was feared that the repair costs might be viewed as an indication of the ship's salvage value. Thus, it might be necessary to increase the ship's repair costs to a value that would be at least three times the bid price in order to gain the docking priority of a U.S.-built ship.

Determining a bid using decision tree analysis

New England Electric identified four alternatives related to this decision situation. They could purchase a new ship from General Dynamics (from whom they had recently purchased one new ship); they could charter a tug and barge combination to haul coal; they could use the *Kuniang;* or they could use the *Kuniang* with a self-unloader that would decrease unloading time and increase the repair cost (but reduce carrying capacity).

The company used decision tree analysis to determine an appropriate bid for the *Kuniang* that would maximize its expected net present value. Probabilities of event outcomes were assessed subjectively by the company. Based on the decision analysis, the company bid $6.7 million for the *Kuniang* and came in second to a winning bid of $10 million. Although the company was not successful in its bid, it was extremely pleased with the decision analysis approach. They believe their failure was due to the fact that they neglected to perform a decision analysis of their competitor's position in order to obtain a better assessment of their own probability of winning with any given bid. They felt that decision analysis provided a structure for the problem, insight into the relevant information to collect, and a rationale for the eventual decision.[1]

Selecting Air Quality Control Equipment

Choosing pollution control equipment

The W. H. Sammis generating plant, located on the Ohio River in eastern Ohio, is operated by the Ohio Edison Company. The plant consists of seven coal-fired generating units. During 1979, Ohio Edison was negotiating with the U.S. Environmental Protection Agency over meeting standards on particulate matter released from the power plant as set by the Clean Air Act. Compliance could be obtained by installing either fabric filters (i.e., thousands of fiberglass bags that collect particulate matter, much as a vacuum cleaner bag collects dust) or electrostatic precipitators (mechanisms that use electric fields to impact positive charges to particles and remove them). The decision problem was further complicated by the need to comply with sulfur dioxide limits.

Decision analysis was used in the selection process to determine the choice of particulate control equipment. The decision measure used to evaluate the alternatives was the levelized revenue requirements for the remaining twenty-year life of the power generating units. Levelized revenue requirements are the annual funds (leveled according to net present value) that must be collected from customers to cover the cost of installing and operating the new equipment. A decision tree was constructed to assist in the decision

[1]D. Bell, "Bidding for the S. S. Kuniang," *Interfaces* 14, no. 2 (March–April 1984): 17–23.

analysis process. The results of the decision analysis indicated that electrostatic precipitators would result in lower expected revenue requirements and lower risk. The company selected electrostatic precipitators as a result of the decision analysis and used decision analysis to evaluate and select the vendor to install the new equipment.[2]

Prescribed Fire to Manage Forests

Prescribed burning is a tool used in forest management to achieve certain objectives such as reducing fire hazards, enhancing wildlife habitats, facilitating site preparation, and controlling insects. However, uncertainties inherent in the use of fire create difficulties in the planning and decision-making process. Decision analysis has been employed by forest managers to incorporate uncertainties into the decision process. Decisions can be grouped into three categories: treatment selection decisions, planning decisions (such as what is to be burned, how the fire should behave, what the environmental conditions should be, how the fire should be ignited, when it should be scheduled, what crew and equipment will be needed), and executive decisions (such as what resources should be committed, whether tests should be conducted, whether the fire should be started, whether the fire should be discontinued once started, and how long patrolling is required after the fire). The decision analysis model encompasses a decision tree to reflect the sequence of decisions and uncertainties, a structural model showing the decision interactions, and a value model incorporating trade-offs between objectives. The model was used in three instances at Tahoe National Forest, Prescott National Forest, and Gifford Pinchot National Forest to determine the best decision in a complex situation.[3]

Choosing forest management tactics

Mortgage Selection

Decision analysis with a decision tree can be used in a straightforward and practical way by a condominium or home buyer to determine which of three types of mortgage to select: a three-year adjustable rate mortgage, a five-year adjustable rate mortgage, or a conventional fixed rate mortgage. Each type of mortgage includes a progressively higher interest rate as part of the terms. A model for solving this type of problem was developed by Luna and Reid. The

Selecting mortgage options

---

[2]T. Madden et al., "Decision Analysis Used to Evaluate Air Quality Control Equipment for Ohio Edison Company," *Interfaces* 13, no. 1 (February 1983): 66–75.

[3]D. Cohan, S. Haas, D. Radloff, and R. Yanick, "Using Fire in Forest Management: Decision Making Under Uncertainty," *Interfaces* 14, no. 5 (September–October 1984): 8–19.

model was based on an examination of data on three- and five-year treasury bills for the past 30 years. Four decision criteria were used to evaluate the three mortgage alternatives: minimax, minimin, minimax regret, and minimizing expected mortgage costs. The first three criteria reflect different decision-making attitudes; the last criterion is based on the probability of different future interest rates. Using this last criterion, the five-year adjustable rate mortgage was selected as the recommended alternative.[4]

Summary

The purpose of this chapter was to demonstrate the concepts and fundamentals of decision making when uncertainty exists. Within this context, several decision-making criteria were presented. The maximax, maximin, minimax regret, equal likelihood, and Hurwicz decision criteria were demonstrated for cases in which probabilities could not be attached to the occurrence of outcomes. The expected value criterion and decision trees were discussed for cases in which probabilities could be assigned to the states of nature of a decision situation.

All of the decision criteria presented in this chapter were demonstrated via rather simplified examples; actual decision-making situations are usually more complex. Nevertheless, the *process* of analyzing decisions presented in this chapter is the logical method that most decision makers follow in order to make a decision.

In the examples presented in this chapter, the decision situations included only one decision maker. However, many decisions are made in competitive situations where the decision of an antagonist will affect one's own decision. This type of competitive decision situation is the subject of *game theory*, the topic of the next chapter.

Decision analysis illustrates the logical process of decision making

References

Baumol, W. J. *Economic Theory and Operations Analysis.* 4th ed. Englewood Cliffs, N.J.: Prentice-Hall, 1977.

Bell, D. "Bidding for the S. S. Kuniang." *Interfaces* 14, no. 2 (March–April 1984): 17–23.

Dorfman, R.; Samuelson, P. A.; and Solow, R. M. *Linear Programming and Economic Analysis.* New York: McGraw-Hill, 1958.

[4]R. Luna and R. Reid, "Mortgage Selection Using a Decision Tree Approach," *Interfaces* 16, no. 3 (May–June 1986): 73–81.

Holloway, C. A. *Decision Making Under Uncertainty.* Englewood Cliffs, N.J.: Prentice-Hall, 1979.

Howard, R. A. "An Assessment of Decision Analysis." *Operations Research* 28, no. 1 (January–February 1980): 4–27.

Keeney, R. L. "Decision Analysis: An Overview." *Operations Research* 30, no. 5 (September–October 1982): 803–38.

Kwak, N. K. *Mathematical Programming with Business Applications.* New York: McGraw–Hill, 1973.

Luce, R. D., and Raiffa, H. *Games and Decisions.* New York: John Wiley and Sons, 1957.

Madden, T.; Hyrnick, M.; and Hodde, J. "Decision Analysis Used to Evaluate Air Quality Control Equipment for Ohio Edison Company." *Interfaces* 13, no. 1 (February 1983): 66–75.

Von Neumann, J., and Morgenstern, O. *Theory of Games and Economic Behavior.* 3d ed. Princeton, N.J.: Princeton University Press, 1953.

Williams, J. D. *The Compleat Strategyst,* rev. ed. New York: McGraw-Hill, 1966.

EXAMPLE PROBLEM SOLUTION

The following example will illustrate the solution procedure for a decision analysis problem.

Problem Statement

T. Bone Puckett, a corporate raider, has acquired a textile company and is contemplating the future of one of its major plants located in South Carolina. Three alternative decisions are being considered: (1) expand the plant and produce lightweight, durable materials for possible sales to the military, a market with little foreign competition; (2) maintain the status quo at the plant, continuing production of textile goods that are subject to heavy foreign competition; or (3) sell the plant now. If one of the first two alternatives is chosen, the plant will still be sold at the end of a year. The amount of profit that could be earned by selling the plant in a year depends on foreign market conditions, including the status of a trade embargo bill in Congress. The following payoff table describes this decision situation.

| | States of Nature | |
Decision	Good Foreign Competitive Conditions	Poor Foreign Competitive Conditions
Expand	$ 800,000	$ 500,000
Maintain status quo	1,300,000	−150,000
Sell now	320,000	320,000

a. Determine the best decision using the following decision criteria.
   1. Maximax
   2. Maximin

3. Minimax regret
4. Hurwicz ($\alpha = 0.3$)
5. Equal likelihood

b. Assume that it is now possible to estimate a probability of .70 that good foreign competitive conditions will exist and a probability of .30 that poor conditions will exist. Determine the best decision using expected value and expected opportunity loss.

c. Compute the expected value of perfect information.

d. Develop a decision tree for this decision situation, with expected values at the probability nodes.

e. T. Bone Puckett has hired a consulting firm to provide a report on the political and market situation in the future. The report will be either positive (P) or negative (N), indicating either a good (g) or poor (p) future foreign competitive situation. The conditional probability of each report outcome given each state of nature is as follows.

$P(P/g) = .70$
$P(N/g) = .30$
$P(P/p) = .20$
$P(N/p) = .80$

Determine the posterior probabilities using Bayes's rule.

f. Perform a decision tree analysis using the posterior probability obtained in part e.

Step 1 (part a): Determine Decisions Without Probabilities

Maximax:

Maximum payoffs

Expand	$ 800,000	
Status quo	1,300,000	← maximum
Sell	320,000	

Decision: Maintain status quo

Maximin:

Minimum payoffs

Expand	$ 500,000	← maximum
Status quo	−150,000	
Sell	320,000	

Decision: Expand

Minimax Regret:

Maximum regrets

Expand	$500,000	← minimum
Status quo	650,000	
Sell	980,000	

Decision: Expand

Hurwicz ($\alpha = 0.3$):

Expand	$\$\;\;800,000(0.3) + 500,000(0.7) = \$590,000$
Status quo	$\$1,300,000(0.3) - 150,000(0.7) = \$285,000$
Sell	$\$\;\;320,000(0.3) + 320,000(0.7) = \$320,000$

Decision: Expand

Equal Likelihood:

Expand	$\$\;\;800,000(.50) + 500,000(.50) = \$650,000$
Status quo	$\$1,300,000(.50) - 150,000(.50) = \$575,000$
Sell	$\$\;\;320,000(.50) + 320,000(.50) = \$320,000$

Decision: Expand

Step 2 (part b): Determine Decisions with EV and EOL

Expected Value:

Expand	$\$\;\;800,000(.70) + 500,000(.30) = \$710,000$
Status quo	$\$1,300,000(.70) - 150,000(.30) = \$865,000$
Sell	$\$\;\;320,000(.70) + 320,000(.30) = \$320,000$

Decision: Maintain status quo

Expected Opportunity Loss:

Expand	$\$500,000(.70) + \;\;\;\;\;\;\;\;0(.30) = \$350,000$
Status quo	$\$0(.70) \;\;\;\;\;\;+ 650,000(.30) = \$195,000$
Sell	$\$980,000(.70) + 180,000(.30) = \$740,000$

Decision: Maintain status quo

Step 3 (part c): Compute EVPI

Expected value given perfect information
$$= \$1,300,000(.70) + 500,000(.30) = \$1,060,000$$

Expected value without perfect information
$$= \$1,300,000(.70) - 150,000(.30) = \$865,000$$

EVPI = $\$1,060,000 - 865,000 = \$195,000$

Step 4 (part d): Develop a Decision Tree

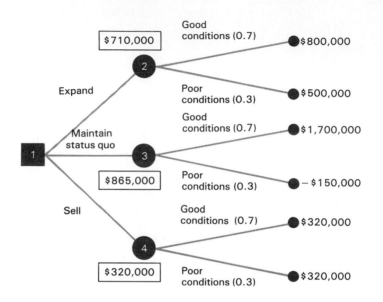

Step 5 (part e): Determine Posterior Probabilities

$$P(g/P) = \frac{P(P/g)P(g)}{P(P/g)P(g) + P(P/p)P(p)}$$

$$= \frac{(.70)(.70)}{(.70)(.70) + (.20)(.30)}$$

$$= .891$$

$$P(p/P) = .109$$

$$P(g/N) = \frac{P(N/g)P(g)}{P(N/g)P(g) + P(N/p)P(p)}$$

$$= \frac{(.30)(.70)}{(.30)(.70) + (.80)(.30)}$$

$$= .467$$

$$P(p/N) = .533$$

Step 6 (part f): Perform Decision Tree Analysis with Posterior Probabilities

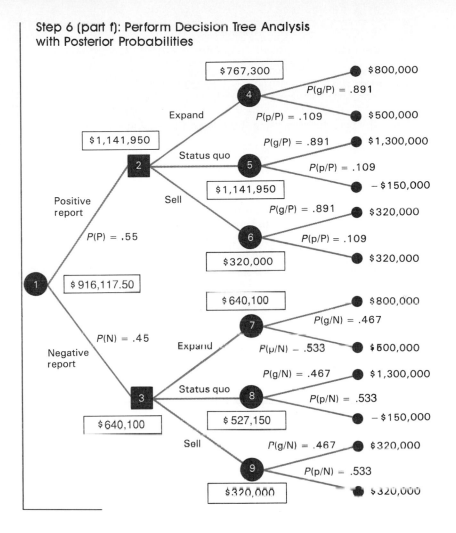

Problems

1. A farmer in Iowa is considering either leasing some extra land or investing in savings certificates at the local bank. If weather conditions are good next year, the extra land will allow the farmer to have an excellent harvest. However, if weather conditions are bad, the farmer will lose money. The savings certificates will result in the same return regardless of the weather conditions. The return for each investment given each type of weather condition is shown in the following payoff table.

	Weather	
Decision	Good	Bad
Lease land	$90,000	$−40,000
Buy savings certificate	10,000	10,000

Select the best decision using the following decision criteria.

a. Maximax
b. Maximin

2. The owner of the Burger Doodle Restaurant is considering two ways to expand operations: opening a drive-up window or serving breakfast. The increase in profits resulting from these proposed expansions depends on whether a competitor opens a franchise down the street. The possible profits from each expansion in operations given both future competitive situations are shown in the following payoff table.

	Competitor	
Decision	Open	Not Open
Drive-up window	$−6,000	$20,000
Breakfast	4,000	8,000

Select the best decision using the following decision criteria.

a. Maximax
b. Maximin

3. Stevie Stone, a bellhop at the Royal Sundown Hotel in Atlanta, has been offered a management position. Although accepting the offer would assure him a job if there were a recession, if good economic conditions prevailed he would actually make less money as a manager than as a bellhop (because of the large tips he gets as a bellhop). His salary during the next five years for each job given each future economic condition is shown in the following payoff table.

	Economic Conditions	
Decision	Good	Recession
Bellhop	$120,000	$60,000
Manager	85,000	85,000

Select the best decision using the following decision criteria.

a. Minimax regret
b. Hurwicz ($\alpha = 0.4$)
c. Equal likelihood

4. Consider the following payoff table for three alternative investments, A, B, and C, under two future states of the economy, good and bad.

	Economic Conditions	
Investment	Good	Bad
A	$ 70,000	$ 25,000
B	120,000	−60,000
C	40,000	40,000

Determine the best decision using the following decision criteria.

a. Maximax
b. Maximin
c. Minimax regret
d. Hurwicz ($\alpha = 0.3$)
e. Equal likelihood

5. Brooke Bentley, a student in business administration, is trying to decide which management science course to take next quarter —I, II, or III. "Steamboat" Fulton, "Death" Ray, and "Sadistic" Scott are the three management science professors who teach the courses. Brooke does not know who will teach what course. Brooke can expect a different grade in each of the courses depending on who teaches it next quarter, as shown in the following payoff table.

	Professor		
Course	Fulton	Ray	Scott
I	B	D	D
II	C	B	F
III	F	A	C

Determine the best course to take next quarter using the following criteria.

a. Maximax
b. Maximin

6. A farmer in Georgia must decide which crop to plant next year on his land: corn, peanuts, or soybeans. The return from each crop will be determined by whether a new trade bill with the U.S.S.R. passes the Senate. The profit the farmer will realize from each crop given the two possible results on the trade bill is shown in the following payoff table.

	Trade Bill	
Crop	Pass	Fail
Corn	$35,000	$ 8,000
Peanuts	18,000	12,000
Soybeans	22,000	20,000

Determine the best crop to plant using the following decision criteria.

a. Maximax
b. Maximin
c. Minimax regret
d. Hurwicz ($\alpha = 0.3$)
e. Equal likelihood

7. A company must decide now which of three products to make next year so as to plan and order proper materials. The cost per unit of producing each product will be determined by whether a new union labor contract passes or fails. The cost per unit for each product given each contract result is shown in the following payoff table.

| | Contract Outcome | |
Product	Pass	Fail
1	$7.50	$6.00
2	4.00	7.00
3	6.50	3.00

Determine which product should be produced using the following decision criteria.

a. Maximax
b. Maximin

8. The owner of the Columbia Construction Company must decide among building a housing development, constructing a shopping center, or leasing all the company's equipment to another company. The profit that will result from each alternative will be determined by whether material costs remain stable or increase. The profit from each alternative given the two possibilities for material costs is shown in the following payoff table.

| | Material Costs | |
Decision	Stable	Increase
Houses	$ 70,000	$30,000
Shopping Center	105,000	20,000
Leasing	40,000	40,000

Determine the best decision using the following decision criteria.

a. Maximax
b. Maximin
c. Minimax regret
d. Hurwicz ($\alpha = 0.2$)
e. Equal likelihood

9. An investor is considering investing in stocks, real estate, or bonds under uncertain economic conditions. The payoff table of returns for the investor's decision situation is shown below.

| | Economic Conditions | | |
Investment	Good	Stable	Poor
Stocks	$ 5,000	$ 7,000	$3,000
Real estate	−2,000	10,000	6,000
Bonds	4,000	4,000	4,000

Determine the best investment using the following decision criteria.

a. Equal likelihood
b. Maximin
c. Maximax
d. Hurwicz ($\alpha = 0.3$)
e. Minimax regret

10. A local real estate investor in Orlando is considering three alternative investments: a motel, a theater, or a restaurant. Profits from the motel or restaurant will be affected by the availability of gasoline and the number of tourists; profits from the theater will be relatively stable under any conditions. The following payoff table shows the profit or loss that could result from each investment.

| | Gasoline Availability | | |
Investment	Shortage	Stable Supply	Surplus
Motel	$ 8,000	$15,000	$20,000
Restaurant	2,000	8,000	6,000
Theater	6,000	6,000	5,000

Determine the best investment using the following decision criteria.

a. Maximax
b. Maximin
c. Minimax regret
d. Hurwicz ($\alpha = 0.4$)
e. Equal likelihood

11. A television network is attempting to decide during the summer which of the following three football games to televise on the Saturday following Thanksgiving Day: Alabama vs. Auburn, Georgia vs. Georgia Tech, or Army vs. Navy. The estimated viewer ratings (millions of homes) for the games depend on the win-loss records of the six teams, as shown in the following payoff table.

Game	Numbers of Viewers (millions)		
	Both Teams Have Winning Records	One Team Has Winning Record, One Team Has Losing Record	Both Teams Have Losing Records
Alabama vs. Auburn	10.2	7.3	5.4
Georgia vs. Georgia Tech	9.6	8.1	4.8
Army vs. Navy	12.5	6.5	3.2

Determine the best game to televise using the following decision criteria.

a. Equal likelihood
b. Maximin
c. Maximax

12. A manufacturer is considering three capital investments. The manufacturer can expand the physical plant, maintain it at the present size, or sell part of the physical plant. The success of each decision depends on the future demand for the manufacturer's product. The profit or loss to be realized from each decision is given in the following payoff table.

Decision	Product Demand		
	Increasing	Stable	Decreasing
Expand	$ 20,000	$ 4,000	$−10,000
Maintain status quo	11,000	8,000	−2,000
Sell	−5,000	−2,000	15,000

Determine the best decision for the manufacturer using any decision criterion you like. Explain why you preferred the decision criterion you selected.

13. An investor is considering purchasing some municipal bonds, whose return will be determined by future economic conditions. The return under each condition and the associated probabilities are shown below.

Economic Conditions		
Good .20	Fair .70	Poor .10
$10,000	$20,000	$−7,000

Compute the expected value of the investment.

14. A machine shop owner is attempting to decide whether to purchase a new drill press, a lathe, or a grinder. The return from each will be determined by whether the company succeeds in getting a government mili-

tary contract. The profit or loss from each purchase and the probabilities associated with each contract outcome are shown in the following pay-off table.

	Contract .40	No Contract .60
Purchase		
Drill press	$40,000	$−8,000
Lathe	20,000	4,000
Grinder	12,000	10,000

Compute the expected value for each purchase and select the best one.

15. A concessions manager at the Tech vs. A&M football game must decide whether to have the vendors sell sun visors or umbrellas. There is a 30% chance of rain, a 15% chance of overcast skies, and a 55% chance of sunshine, according to the weather forecast in College Junction, where the game is to be held. The manager estimates the following profits will result from each decision given each set of weather conditions.

	Weather Conditions		
Decision	Rain .30	Overcast .15	Sunshine .55
Sun visors	$−500	$−200	$1,500
Umbrellas	2,000	0	−900

a. Compute the expected value for each decision and select the best one.
b. Develop the opportunity loss table and compute the expected opportunity loss for each decision.

16. Consider the following payoff table for three alternative investments (A, B, and C) and three states of the economy.

	Economic Conditions		
Decision	1 0.3	2 0.5	3 0.2
A	$1,000	$2,000	$500
B	800	1,200	900
C	700	700	700

a. Compute the expected value for each decision and select the best one.
b. Develop the opportunity loss table and compute the expected opportunity loss for each decision.
c. Determine the expected value of perfect information (EVPI).

17. The Miramar Company is going to introduce one of three new products: a widget, a hummer, or a nimnot. The market conditions (favorable, stable, or unfavorable) will determine the profit or loss the company realizes, as shown in the following payoff table.

	Market Conditions		
Product	Favorable 0.2	Stable 0.7	Unfavorable 0.1
Widget	$120,000	$70,000	$−30,000
Hummer	60,000	40,000	20,000
Nimnot	35,000	30,000	30,000

a. Compute the expected value for each decision and select the best one.
b. Develop the opportunity loss table and compute the expected opportunity loss for each product.
c. Determine how much the firm would be willing to pay to a market research firm to gain better information about future market conditions.

18. The financial success of the Downhill Ski Resort in the Blue Ridge Mountains is dependent on the amount of snowfall during the winter months. If the snowfall averages more than 40 inches, the resort will be successful; if the snowfall is between 20 and 40 inches, the resort will receive a moderate financial return; and if snowfall averages less than 20 inches, the resort will suffer a financial loss. The financial return given each level of snowfall is shown below.

	Snowfall	
>40 inches 0.4	20 to 40 inches 0.2	<20 inches 0.4
$120,000	$40,000	$−40,000

A large hotel chain has offered to lease the resort for the winter for $40,000. Compute the expected value to determine whether the resort should operate or lease. Explain your answer.

19. An investor must decide between two alternative investments—stocks and bonds. The return for each investment given two future economic conditions is shown in the following payoff table.

	Economic Conditions	
Investment	Good	Bad
Stocks	$10,000	$−4,000
Bonds	7,000	2,000

What probability for each economic condition would make the investor indifferent to the choice between stocks and bonds?

20. Fenton and Farrah Friendly, husband and wife car dealers, are going to open a new dealership. They have offers from a foreign compact car company, a U.S. producer of full-sized cars, and a truck company. The success of each type of dealership will depend on how much gasoline is available during the next few years. The profit from each type of dealership given the availability of gas is shown in the following payoff table.

	Gasoline Availability	
Dealership	Shortage 0.6	Surplus 0.4
Compact cars	$ 300,000	$150,000
Full-sized cars	−100,000	600,000
Trucks	120,000	170,000

Determine which type of dealership the couple should purchase.

21. The Blitzkrieg Banking House in Berlin speculates in the money market. The status of the U.S. dollar determines the return from investments in other currencies. The banking house will invest in the dollar, the yen, or the mark. The return from each is shown in the following payoff table.

	Value of the Dollar		
Currency	Increases .30	Remains stable .50	Declines .20
Dollar	$210,000	$ 0	$−170,000
Yen	−10,000	20,000	80,000
Mark	−40,000	35,000	150,000

Determine the best currency to invest in and the expected value of perfect information.

22. The Steak and Chop Butcher Shop purchases steak from a local meat packing house. The meat is purchased on Monday at $2.00 per pound, and the shop sells the steak for $3.00 per pound. Any steak left over at the end of the week is sold to a local zoo for $0.50 per pound. The possible demands for steak and the probability of each are as follows.

Demand (lb)	Probability
20	.10
21	.20
22	.30
23	.30
24	.10
	1.00

The shop must decide how much steak to order in a week. Construct a payoff table for this decision situation and determine the amount of steak that should be ordered using expected value.

23. The Loebuck Grocery must decide how many cases of milk to stock each week in order to meet demand. The probability distribution of demand during a week is shown below.

Demand (cases)	Probability
15	.20
16	.25
17	.40
18	.15
	1.00

Each case costs the grocer $10 and sells for $12. Unsold cases are sold to a local farmer (who mixes the milk with feed for livestock) for $2 per case. If there is a shortage, the grocer considers the cost of customer ill will and lost profit to be $4 per case. The grocer must decide how many cases of milk to order each week.

a. Construct the payoff table for this decision situation.
b. Compute the expected value of each alternative amount of milk that could be stocked and select the best decision.
c. Construct the opportunity loss table and determine the best decision.
d. Compute the expected value of perfect information.

24. The manager of the greeting card section of Mazey's department store is considering her order for a particular line of Christmas cards. The cost of each box of cards is $3; each box will be sold for $5 during the Christmas season. After Christmas, the cards will be sold for $2 a box. The card section manager believes that all leftover cards can be sold at that price. The estimated demand during the Christmas season for the line of Christmas cards, with associated probabilities, is as follows:

Demand (boxes)	Probability
25	.10
26	.15
27	.30
28	.20
29	.15
30	.10

a. Develop the payoff table for this decision situation.
b. Compute the expected value for each alternative and identify the best decision.
c. Compute the expected value of perfect information.

25. The Palm Garden Greenhouse specializes in raising carnations that are sold to florists. Carnations are sold for $3.00 per dozen; the cost of growing the carnations and distributing them to the florists is $2.00 per dozen. Any carnations left at the end of the day are sold to local restaurants and hotels for $0.75 per dozen. The estimated cost of customer ill

will if demand is not met is $1.00 per dozen. The expected daily demand for the carnations is shown below.

Daily Demand	Probability
20	.05
22	.10
24	.25
26	.30
28	.20
30	.10
	1.00

a. Develop the payoff table for this decision situation.
b. Compute the expected value of each alternative number of carnations that could be stocked and select the best decision.
c. Construct the opportunity loss table and determine the best decision.
d. Compute the expected value of perfect information.

26. Assume that the probabilities of demand in problem 24 are no longer valid; the decision situation is now one without probabilities. Determine the best number of cards to stock using the following decision criteria.

a. Maximin
b. Maximax
c. Hurwicz ($\alpha = 0.4$)
d. Minimax regret

27. Construct a decision tree for the decision situation described in problem 16 and indicate the best decision.

28. Construct a decision tree for the decision situation described in problem 20 and indicate the best decision.

29. Given the following sequential decision tree, determine which is the optimal investment, A or B.

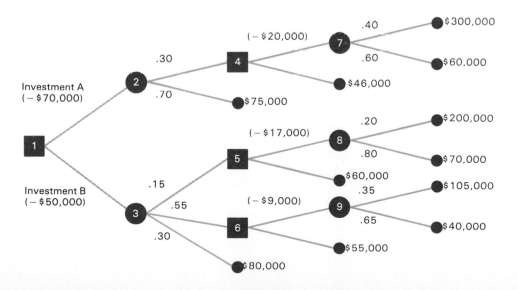

30. The Americo Oil Company is considering making a bid for a shale oil development contract to be awarded by the federal government. The company has decided to bid $110 million. The company estimates that it has a 60% chance of winning the contract with this bid. If the firm wins the contract, it can choose one of three methods for getting the oil from the shale. It can develop a new method for oil extraction, use an existing (inefficient) process, or subcontract the processing out to a number of smaller companies once the shale has been excavated. The results from these alternatives are given as follows.

Develop New Process

Outcomes	Probability	Profit (millions)
Great Success	.30	$ 600
Moderate Success	.60	300
Failure	.10	−100

Use Present Process

Outcomes	Probability	Profit (millions)
Great Success	.50	$ 300
Moderate Success	.30	200
Failure	.20	−40

Subcontract

Outcome	Probability	Profit (millions)
Moderate Success	1.00	$250

The cost of preparing the contract proposal is $2,000,000. If the company does not make a bid, it will invest in an alternative venture with a guaranteed profit of $30 million. Construct a sequential decision tree for this decision situation and determine whether the company should make a bid.

31. The machine shop owner in problem 14 is considering hiring a military consultant to ascertain whether the shop will get the government contract. The consultant is a former military officer who uses various personal contacts to find out such information. By talking to other shop owners who have hired the consultant, the owner has estimated a .70 probability that the consultant would present a favorable report given that the contract is awarded to the shop, and a .80 probability that the consultant would present an unfavorable report given that the contract is not awarded. Using decision tree analysis, determine the decision strategy the owner should follow, the expected value of this strategy, and the maximum fee the owner should pay the consultant.

32. The Miramar Company in problem 17 is considering contracting with a market research firm to do a survey to determine future market conditions. The results of the survey will indicate either positive or negative market conditions. There is a .60 probability of a positive report given favorable conditions, a .30 probability of a positive report given stable conditions, and a .10 probability of a positive report given unfavorable conditions. There is a .90 probability of a negative report given unfavor-

able conditions, a .70 probability given stable conditions, and a .40 probability given favorable conditions. Using decision tree analysis *and* posterior probability tables, determine the decision strategy the company should follow, the expected value of the strategy, and the maximum amount the company should pay the market research firm for the survey results.

33. The Friendlys in problem 20 are considering hiring a petroleum analyst to determine the future availability of gasoline. The analyst will report that either a shortage or a surplus will occur. The probability that the analyst will indicate a shortage given that a shortage actually occurs is .90; the probability that the analyst will indicate a surplus given that a surplus actually occurs is .70. Determine the decision strategy the Friendlys should follow, the expected value of this strategy, and the maximum amount the Friendlys should pay for the analyst's services.

34. Compute the efficiency of the sample information in problem 33 for the Friendly car dealership.

35. A young married couple has $5,000 to invest in either savings bonds or a real estate deal. The expected return on each investment given good and bad economic conditions is shown in the following payoff table.

| | Economic Conditions | |
Investment	Good 0.6	Bad 0.4
Savings bonds	$ 1,000	$ 1,000
Real estate	10,000	−2,000

The expected value of investing in savings bonds is $1,000, and the expected value of the real estate investment is $5,200. However, the couple decides to invest in savings bonds. Explain the couple's decision in terms of the utility they might associate with each investment.

36. The purchase of all types of insurance by individuals is an example of a case in which utility rather than expected dollar value is the decision criterion. Explain the concept of utility in terms of the purchase of insurance.

37. Many types of government expenditures reflect the concept of utility. Give three examples of such government expenditures and explain how they illustrate the concept of utility.

38. Discuss the concept of utility and risk taking as it relates to a gambler who wagers $10,000 on a 50 to 1 long shot in the Kentucky Derby.

12

Game Theory

In the previous chapter on decision analysis, we discussed methods to aid the *individual* decision maker in making decisions. All of the decision situations analyzed in Chapter 11 involved one decision maker. There were no *competitors* whose decisions might alter the decision maker's analysis of a decision situation. However, many situations do, in fact, involve several decision makers who compete with one another to arrive at the best outcome. These types of competitive decision-making situations are the subject of *game theory.* Although the topic of game theory encompasses a different type of decision situation than does decision analysis, many of the fundamental principles and techniques of decision making are the same. Thus, game theory is, in effect, an extension of decision analysis rather than an entirely new topic area.

Anyone who has played such games as card games or board games is familiar with situations in which competing participants develop plans of action in order to win. Game theory encompasses similar situations in which competing decision makers develop plans of action in order to win. In addition, game theory consists of several mathematical techniques to aid the decision maker in selecting

Competitive
decision makers

427

the plan of action that will result in the best outcome. In this chapter, we will discuss some of these techniques.

TYPES OF GAME SITUATIONS

Competitive game situations can be subdivided into several categories. One classification is based on the number of competitive decision makers, called *players*, involved in the game. A game situation consisting of two players is referred to as a *two-person game*. When there are more than two players, the game situation is known as an *n-person game*.

Games are also classified according to their outcomes in terms of each player's gains and losses. If the sum of the players' gains and losses equals zero, the game is referred to as a *zero-sum game*. In a two-person game, one player's gains represent another's losses. For example, if one player wins $100, then the other player loses $100; the two values sum to zero (i.e., +$100 and −$100). Alternatively, if the sum of the players' gains and losses does not equal zero, the game is known as a *non-zero-sum game*.

The *two-person, zero-sum game* is the one most frequently used to demonstrate the principles of game theory because it is the simplest mathematically. Thus, we will confine our discussion of game theory to this form of game situation. The complexity of the *n-person* game situation not only prohibits us from demonstrating it, but also restricts its application in real-world situations.

The Two-Person, Zero-Sum Game

Examples of competitive situations that can be organized into two-person, zero-sum games include (1) a union negotiating a new contract with management; (2) two armies participating in a war game; (3) two politicians in conflict over a proposed legislative bill, one attempting to secure its passage and the other attempting to defeat it; (4) a retail firm trying to increase its market share with a new product and a competitor attempting to minimize the firm's gains; and (5) a contractor negotiating with a government agent for a contract on a project.

The following example will demonstrate a two-person, zero-sum game. A professional athlete, Biff Rhino, and his agent, Jim Fence, are renegotiating Biff's contract with the Texas Buffaloes' general manager, Harry Sligo. The various outcomes of this game situation can be organized into a payoff table similar to the payoff tables used for decision analysis in Chapter 11. The payoff table for this example is shown in Table 12.1.

The payoff table for a two-person game is organized so that the player who is trying to maximize the outcome of the game is on

TABLE 12.1
Payoff Table for Two-Person,
Zero-Sum Game

Athlete/Agent Strategies	General Manager Strategies		
	A	**B**	**C**
1	$50,000	35,000	30,000
2	60,000	40,000	20,000

the left and the player who is trying to minimize the outcome is on the top. In Table 12.1, the athlete and agent want to maximize the athlete's contract and the general manager hopes to minimize the athlete's contract. In a sense, the athlete is an offensive player in the game and the general manager is a defensive player. In game theory it is assumed that the payoff table is known to both the offensive and the defensive player—an assumption that is often unrealistic in real-world situations and thus restricts the actual applications of this technique.

Offensive and defensive strategies

A *strategy* is a plan of action to be followed by a player. Each player in a game has two or more strategies, only one of which is selected for each playing of a game. In Table 12.1, the athlete and his agent have two strategies available, 1 and 2, and the general manager has three strategies, A, B, and C. The values in the table are the payoffs or outcomes associated with each player's strategies.

Game strategies

For our example, the athlete's strategies involve different types of contracts and the threat of a holdout and/or of becoming a free agent. The general manager's strategies are alternative contract proposals that vary with regard to such items as length of contract, residual payments, no cut/no trade clauses, and off-season promotional work. The outcomes are in terms of dollar value. If the athlete selects strategy 2 and the general manager selects strategy C, the outcome is a $20,000 gain for the athlete and a $20,000 loss for the general manager. This outcome results in a zero sum for the game (i.e., +$20,000 − 20,000 = 0). The amount, $20,000, is known as the *value of the game*.

Value of the game

The purpose of the game for each player is to select the strategy that will result in the best possible payoff or outcome regardless of what the opponent does. The best strategy for each player is known as the *optimal strategy*. Next we will discuss the methods for determining the strategies of the game.

Developing an optimal strategy

A PURE STRATEGY

When each player in the game adopts a single strategy as an optimal strategy, then the game is a *pure strategy* game. The value of a pure strategy game is the same for both the offensive player and the de-

Each player adopts a single strategy

A mixed strategy

The minimax
decision criterion
The offensive
player's strategy
The defensive
player's strategy

Decisions are
made
simultaneously
A pure strategy
example

fensive player. In contrast, in a *mixed strategy* game, the players adopt a mixture of strategies if the game is played many times.

A pure strategy game can be solved according to the *minimax decision criterion*. According to this principle, each player plays the game in order to minimize the maximum possible losses. The offensive player will select the strategy with the largest of the minimum payoffs (called the *maximin* strategy), and the defensive player will select the strategy with the smallest of the maximum payoffs (called the *minimax* strategy). In our example involving the athlete's contract negotiation process, the athlete will select the maximin strategy from strategies 1 and 2, and the general manager will select the minimax strategy from strategies A, B, and C. We will first discuss the athlete's decision, although in game theory the decisions are actually made *simultaneously*.

In order to determine the maximin strategy, the athlete first selects the minimum payoff for strategies 1 and 2, as shown in Table 12.2. The maximum of these minimum values indicates the optimal strategy and the value of the game for the athlete.

TABLE 12.2
Payoff Table with Maximin Strategy

| Athlete/Agent | General Manager Strategies | | |
Strategies	A	B	C
1	$50,000	35,000	30,000 ⟵ Maximum of
2	60,000	40,000	20,000	minimum payoffs

The athlete's
strategy

The value, $30,000, is the maximum of the minimum values for each of the athlete's strategies. Thus, the optimal strategy for the athlete is strategy 1. The logic behind this decision is as follows. If the athlete selected strategy 1, the general manager could be expected to select strategy C, which would minimize the possible loss (i.e., a $30,000 contract is better *for the manager* than a $50,000 or $35,000 contract). Alternatively, if the athlete selected strategy 2, the general manager could be expected to select strategy C for the same reason (i.e., a $20,000 contract is better for the manager than a $60,000 or $40,000 contract). Now since the athlete has anticipated how the general manager will respond to each strategy, he realizes that he can negotiate either a $30,000 or a $20,000 contract. The athlete selects strategy 1 in order to get the larger possible contract of $30,000, given the actions of the general manager.

The general
manager's strategy

Simultaneously, the general manager applies the minimax decision criterion to strategies A, B, and C. First, the general manager selects the maximum payoff for each strategy, as shown in Table 12.3. The minimum of these maximum values determines the optimal strategy and the value of the game for the general manager.

TABLE 12.3
Payoff Table with Minimax Strategy

Athlete/Agent Strategies	General Manager Strategies		
	A	B	C
1	$50,000	35,000	30,000 ← Minimum of maximum values
2	60,000	40,000	20,000

The value, $30,000, is the minimum of the maximum values for each of the general manager's strategies. Thus, the optimal strategy for the general manager is C. The logic of this decision is similar to that of the athlete's decision. If the general manager selected strategy A, the athlete could be expected to select strategy 2 with a payoff of $60,000 (i.e., the athlete will choose the better of the $50,000 and $60,000 contracts). If the general manager selected strategy B, then the athlete could be expected to select strategy 2 for a payoff of $40,000. Finally, if the general manager selected strategy C, then the athlete could be expected to select strategy 1 for a payoff of $30,000. Since the general manager has anticipated how the athlete will respond to each strategy, he realizes that either a $60,000, $40,000, or $30,000 contract could possibly be awarded. Thus, the general manager selects strategy C, which will result in the minimum contract of $30,000. In general, the manager considers the worst outcome that could result if a particular strategy were followed. Under the minimax criterion the general manager will select the strategy that ensures that he loses only the minimum of the maximum amounts that could be lost.

Dominant Strategies

We could have reduced the choices of the general manager if we had noticed that strategy C *dominates* strategies A and B. Dominance occurs when all the payoffs for one strategy are better than the corresponding payoffs for another strategy. In Table 12.3 the values $30,000 and $20,000 are both lower than the corresponding payoffs of $50,000 and $60,000 for strategy A and the corresponding payoffs of $35,000 and $40,000 for strategy B. Since strategy C dominates A and B, these two latter strategies can be eliminated from consideration altogether, as shown in Table 12.4. If this had been done, strategy C could have been selected automatically without applying the minimax criterion. Thus, the most efficient approach is to first examine the payoff table for dominance in order to possibly reduce its size.

The fact that the optimal strategy for each player in this game resulted in the *same payoff* game value of $30,000 is what classifies it as a pure strategy game. In other words, since strategy 1 is optimal for

All payoffs for one strategy are better than all payoffs for an alternative strategy

Dominated strategies can be eliminated

TABLE 12.4
Payoff Table with Dominated Strategies
Eliminated

Athlete/Agent Strategies	General Manager Strategies		
	A	B	C
1	$50,000	35,000	30,000
2	60,000	40,000	20,000

An equilibrium
point

the athlete and strategy C is optimal for the general manager, a contract for $30,000 will be awarded to the athlete. Since the outcome of $30,000 results from a pure strategy, it is referred to as an *equilibrium point* (or sometimes as a *saddle point*). A point of equilibrium is a value that is simultaneously the *minimum of a row* and the *maximum of a column*, as is the payoff of $30,000 in Table 12.3.

The minimax
criterion will result in
the optimal
strategies only if
both players use it

It is important to realize that the minimax criterion results in the optimal strategy for each player as long as each player uses this criterion. If one of the players does not use this criterion, the solution of the game will not be optimal. If we assume that both players are logical and rational, however, then we can assume that this criterion will be employed.

If an equilibrium point exists, it makes the determination of optimal strategies relatively easy, as no complex mathematical calculations are necessary. However, as we mentioned earlier, if a game does not involve a pure strategy, then it is a mixed strategy game. We will discuss a mixed strategy game next.

A MIXED STRATEGY

Optimal strategy
decisions that do
not result in an
equilibrium point

A mixed strategy game occurs when each player selects an optimal strategy and they *do not result in an equilibrium point* (i.e., the same outcome) when the maximin and minimax decision criteria are applied.

A mixed strategy
example

The following example will demonstrate a mixed strategy game. The Coloroid Camera Company (which we will refer to as Company I) is going to introduce a new instant camera into its product line and hopes to capture as large an increase in its market share as possible. In contrast, the Camco Camera Company (which we will refer to as Company II) hopes to minimize Coloroid's market share increase. Coloroid and Camco dominate the camera market, and any gain in market share for Coloroid will result in a subsequent identical loss in market share for Camco. The strategies for each company are based on their promotional campaigns, packaging, and cosmetic differences between the products. The payoff table, which includes the strategies and outcomes for each company (I = Coloroid and II = Camco), is shown in Table 12.5.

TABLE 12.5
Payoff Table for Camera Companies

Camera Company I Strategies	Camera Company II Strategies		
	A	B	C
1	9	7	2
2	11	8	4
3	4	1	7

The values in Table 12.5 are the *percentage* increases or decreases in market share for Company I.

The first step is to check the payoff table for any dominant strategies. Doing so, we find that strategy 2 dominates strategy 1, and strategy B dominates strategy A. Thus, strategies 1 and A can be eliminated from the payoff table, as shown in Table 12.6.

Eliminating dominated strategies

TABLE 12.6
Payoff Table with Strategies 1
and A Eliminated

Company I Strategies	Company II Strategies	
	B	C
2	8	4
3	1	7

Next, we apply the maximin decision criterion to the strategies for Company I, as shown in Table 12.7. The minimum value for strategy 2 is 4%, and the minimum value for strategy 3 is 1%. The maximum of these two minimum values is 4%; thus, strategy 2 is optimal for Company I.

The maximin criterion for the offensive player

TABLE 12.7
Payoff Table with Maximin
Criterion

Company I Strategies	Company II Strategies		
	B	C	
2	8	4	← Maximum of the minimum values
3	1	7	

Now the minimax decision criterion is applied to the strategies for Company II in Table 12.8. The maximum value for strategy B is 8%, and the maximum value for strategy C is 7%. Of these two maximum values, 7% is the minimum; thus, the optimal strategy for Company II is C.

The minimax criterion for the defensive player

TABLE 12.8
Payoff Table with Minimax Criterion

Company I Strategies	Company II Strategies	
	B	**C**
2	⑧	4
3	1	⑦

Minimum of maximum values

The combined strategies

Table 12.9 combines the results of the application of the maximin and minimax criteria by the companies.

TABLE 12.9
Company I and II Combined Strategies

Company I Strategies	Company II Strategies	
	B	**C**
2	8	☐4
3	1	⑦

No equilibrium point

Switching strategies

A closed loop

From Table 12.9 we can see that the strategies selected by the companies do not result in an equilibrium point. Therefore this is not a pure strategy game. In fact, this condition will not result in any strategy for either firm. Company I maximizes its market share percentage increase by selecting strategy 2. Company II selects strategy C in order to minimize Company I's market share. However, as soon as Company I noticed that Company II was using strategy C, it would switch to strategy 3 to increase its market share to 7%. This move would not go unnoticed by Company II, which would immediately switch to strategy B to reduce I's market share to 1%. This action by Company II would cause Company I immediately to switch to strategy 2 to maximize its market share increase to 8%. Given the action of Company I, Company II would switch to strategy C to minimize Company I's market share increase to 4%. Now you will notice that the two companies are right back where they started. They have completed a closed loop, as shown in Table 12.10, which could continue indefinitely if the two companies persisted.

TABLE 12.10
Payoff Table with Closed Loop

Company I Strategies	Company II Strategies	
	B	**C**
2	8	4
3	1	7

Several other methods are available for solving mixed strategy games. We will look at two of them, both of which are analytical — *the expected gain and loss method* and *linear programming*.

Methods for solving mixed strategy games

Expected Gain and Loss Method

The *expected gain and loss method* is based on the principle that in a mixed strategy game, a plan of strategies can be developed by each player so that the *expected gain* of the maximizing player or the *expected loss* of the minimizing player will be the same, regardless of what the opponent does. In other words, a player develops a plan of mixed strategies that will be employed regardless of what the opposing player does (i.e., the player is indifferent to the opponent's actions). As might be expected from its name, this method is based on the concept of expected values.

Expected gains of one player equal the expected losses of the other

The mixed strategy game for the two camera companies, described in the previous section, will be used to demonstrate this method. First, we will compute the *expected gain* for Company I. Company I arbitrarily assumes that Company II will select strategy B. Given this condition, there is a probability of p that Company I will select strategy 2 and a probability of $1 - p$ that Company I will select strategy 3. Thus, if Company II selects B, the expected gain for Company I is

Computing the expected gain for Company I

The expected gain if Company II selects strategy B

$$8p + 1(1 - p) = 1 + 7p$$

Next, Company I assumes that Company II will select strategy C. Given strategy C, there is a probability of p that Company I will select strategy 2 and a probability of $1 - p$ that Company I will select strategy 3. Thus, the expected gain for Company I given strategy C is

The expected gain if Company II selects strategy C

$$4p + 7(1 - p) = 7 - 3p$$

Previously we noted that this method was based on the idea that Company I would develop a plan that would result in the same expected gain, regardless of the strategy that Company II selected. Thus, if Company I is indifferent to whether Company II selects strategy B or C, we can simply equate the expected gain from each of these strategies:

Equating expected gains

$$1 + 7p = 7 - 3p$$

and

$$10p = 6$$
$$p = \frac{6}{10} = .60$$

The percentage of time each strategy is used by Company I

Recall that p is the probability of using strategy 2, or the *percentage of time* strategy 2 would be employed. Thus, Company I's plan is to use strategy 2 for 60% of the time, and to use strategy 3 the remaining 40% of the time. The expected gain (i.e., market share increase for Company I) can be computed using the payoff of either strategy B or C, since the gain will be the same regardless. Using the payoffs from strategy B,

The expected gain for Company I

$$EG(\text{Company I}) = .60(8) + .40(1)$$
$$= 5.2\% \text{ market share increase}$$

In order to check this result, we will compute the expected gain if strategy C is used by Company II.

$$EG(\text{Company I}) = .60(4) + .40(7)$$
$$= 5.2\% \text{ market share increase}$$

Computing the expected loss for Company II

Now we must repeat this process for *Company II* to develop its mixed strategy — except that what was Company I's expected *gain* is now Company II's expected *loss*. First, we assume that Company I will select strategy 2. Thus, Company II will employ strategy B for p percent of the time and C the remaining $1 - p$ percent of the time.

The expected loss if Company I selects strategy 2

The expected *loss* for Company II given strategy 2 is

$$8p + 4(1 - p) = 4 + 4p$$

The expected loss if Company I selects strategy 3

Next, we compute the expected loss for Company II given that Company I selects strategy 3:

$$1p + 7(1 - p) = 7 - 6p$$

Equating expected losses

Equating these two expected losses for strategies 2 and 3 will result in values for p and $1 - p$.

$$4 + 4p = 7 - 6p$$
$$10p = 3$$
$$p = \frac{3}{10} = .30$$

and

$$1 - p = .70$$

The percentage of time each strategy is used by Company II

Since p is the probability of employing strategy B, Company II will employ strategy B 30% of the time, and thus strategy C will be used 70% of the time. The actual expected loss given strategy 2 (which is the same as that for strategy 3) is computed as

The expected loss for Company II

$$EL(\text{Company II}) = .30(8) + .70(4)$$
$$= 5.2\% \text{ market share loss}$$

The mixed strategies for each company are summarized below.

Summary of mixed strategies for each company

Company I

Strategy 2: 60% of the time
Strategy 3: 40% of the time

Company II

Strategy B: 30% of the time
Strategy C: 70% of the time

The expected gain for Company I is a 5.2% increase in market share, and the expected loss for Company II is also a 5.2% market share. Thus, the mixed strategies for each company have resulted in an equilibrium point such that a 5.2% *expected* gain for Company I results in a simultaneous 5.2% *expected* loss for Company II.

An equilibrium point

It is also interesting to note that each company has improved its position over the one arrived at using the maximin and minimax strategies. Recall from Table 12.9 that the payoff for Company I was only a 4% increase in market share, whereas the mixed strategy yields an expected gain of 5.2%. The outcome for Company II from the minimax strategy was a 7% loss; however, the mixed strategies show a loss of only 5.2%. Thus, each company puts itself in a better situation by using the mixed strategy approach.

Each company improved its position by mixing strategies

This approach assumes that the game is repetitive and will be played over a period of time so that a strategy can be employed a certain percentage of that time. For our example, it can be logically assumed that the marketing of the new camera by Company I will require a lengthy time frame. Thus, each company could employ its mixed strategy.

This approach assumes that the game is repetitive

Computerized Solution of Game Theory Problems

Most management science software packages do not have the capability to solve game theory problems. Microcomputer Software for Quantitative Analysis for Management, which we have used previously in this text, is an exception. This package includes a game theory program that solves pure and mixed strategy games.

Following is the program input and solution output for the mixed strategy game of the two camera companies illustrated in the immediately preceding section. Note that Microcomputer Software requires that dominated strategies be eliminated by the user prior to input. Note also that Company I in our example is identified in the output as "X" and Company II as "Y."

```
DO YOU WANT STRATEGIES FOR X, FOR Y, OR FOR BOTH (TYPE X OR Y OR B) ? B
ENTER THE NUMBER OF POSSIBLE STRATEGIES FOR PLAYER Y (<=20) ? 2
ENTER THE NUMBER OF POSSIBLE STRATEGIES FOR PLAYER X (<=20) ? 2


DO YOU WANT TO CORRECT THE DATA ENTERED (YES OR NO) ? N


        FOR Y STRATEGY #  1

ENTER THE GAME OUTCOME VALUE FOR Y 1 ,X 1  ? 8
ENTER THE GAME OUTCOME VALUE FOR Y 1 ,X 2  ? 1

        FOR Y STRATEGY #  2

ENTER THE GAME OUTCOME VALUE FOR Y 2 ,X 1  ? 4
ENTER THE GAME OUTCOME VALUE FOR Y 2 ,X 2  ? 7


DO YOU WANT TO CORRECT GAME VALUES ENTERED (YES OR NO) ? N



                    *** GAME THEORY - MIXED STRATEGIES ***


    -- DATA ENTERED --
    PROBLEM TITLE                 = Camera Companies
    OPTIMAL STRATEGIES FOR PLAYERS X & Y
    NUMBER OF STRATEGIES FOR PLAYER Y:    2
    NUMBER OF STRATEGIES FOR PLAYER X:    2
    GAME OUTCOMES:


                    Y 1        Y 2
              --------------------
        X 1 I      8          4
        X 2 I      1          7



        ********** TWO-PERSON GAME THEORY--MIXED STRATEGIES *********

    ************************************************************************
                            ANSWERS

            X'S STRATEGY         PROPORTION OF TIME TO PLAY
                 1                         0.600
                 2                         0.400


                 VALUE OF THE GAME=   5.200
    ************************************************************************


PRESS ENTER TO CONTINUE?



        ********** TWO-PERSON GAME THEORY--MIXED STRATEGIES *********
```

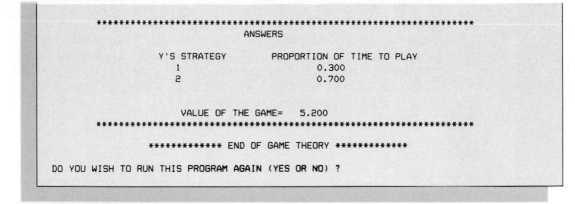

```
*******************************************************************
                            ANSWERS

        Y'S STRATEGY           PROPORTION OF TIME TO PLAY
             1                           0.300
             2                           0.700



               VALUE OF THE GAME=   5.200
*******************************************************************

          ************ END OF GAME THEORY ************

DO YOU WISH TO RUN THIS PROGRAM AGAIN (YES OR NO) ?
```

LINEAR PROGRAMMING

The determination of mixed strategies using the expected gain and loss method presented in the previous section becomes more difficult as the size of the game increases beyond two strategies per player. In other words, we cannot simply multiply one outcome under a strategy by p and the other by $1 - p$ if there are more than two outcomes per strategy. Given games of larger magnitude, *linear programming* is an alternative method for determining the mixed strategy probabilities and the value of the game. However, the formulation of the linear programming model for a game is slightly more complex than that of the models presented in Chapters 2 through 5 and, as such, must be described in detail.

The best way to present the linear programming approach to games is by example; thus, we will again use the example of the camera companies described in the previous section. The reduced payoff table for this game situation first shown in Table 12.6 is shown in Table 12.11. Although this payoff table contains only two strategies per player, it will still serve to demonstrate how linear programming can be applied to games of any size. In addition, by using this example, which we have already analyzed using the expected gain and loss method, we have the advantage of knowing the solution and understanding the logic of that solution in advance.

The expected gain and loss method is limited to two strategies per player

Linear programming is used when a game involves more than two strategies

A linear programming example for a mixed strategy game

TABLE 12.11

Payoff Table for Camera Companies Example

Company I Strategies	Company II Strategies	
	B	C
2	8	4
3	1	7

This payoff table contains enough information for two linear programming models; one for Company I and one for Company II. The purpose of each model is to determine the mixed strategies for the respective companies, which you will recall are expressed in terms of probabilities of occurrence of each strategy. Thus, for the Company I model, the decision variables can be defined as the probabilities of the occurrence of strategies 2 and 3.

p_1 = probability of the occurrence of strategy 2

p_2 = probability of the occurrence of strategy 3

Given these decision variables, we can now formulate several constraints based on the values of the outcomes in Table 12.11. Recall that when we computed the expected gain for Company I previously, we multiplied the outcomes for strategies 2 and 3 by p and $1 - p$. In this case, since p_1 and p_2 are synonymous with p and $1 - p$, we can formulate a constraint for each strategy as follows.

$$8p_1 + 1p_2 \geq v$$
$$4p_1 + 7p_2 \geq v$$

In these two constraints the symbol v represents the *value of the game*. Recall that the value of the game is the average gain for the offensive player and the identical average loss for the defensive player. We have used $\geq$ inequalities for these constraints because Company I is the maximizing (or offensive) player. In other words, Company I wants to maximize its expected gain and receive as high a value of v as possible, if Company II selects a less than optimal strategy.

We can also develop one additional constraint to reflect the fact that the sum of the probabilities equals 1.0.

$$p_1 + p_2 = 1.0$$

The model constraints in their present form can be simplified (for solution purposes) by dividing each coefficient in the constraints and the quantity values by v, as follows.

$$\frac{8p_1}{v} + \frac{1p_2}{v} \geq 1$$

$$\frac{4p_1}{v} + \frac{7p_2}{v} \geq 1$$

$$\frac{p_1}{v} + \frac{p_2}{v} = \frac{1}{v}$$

In order to further simplify the model and eliminate the v symbols, we can redefine the model decision variables.

$$x_1 = \frac{p_1}{v}$$

$$x_2 = \frac{p_2}{v}$$

Substituting these new variables into the model constraints results in the following constraints.

$$8x_1 + 1x_2 \geq 1$$
$$4x_1 + 7x_2 \geq 1$$
$$x_1 + x_2 = \frac{1}{v}$$

Now recall that this model reflects the actions of Company I, the maximizing player. The *objective* of Company I is to *maximize* the value of the game, v. However, if we maximize v, we also minimize $1/v$. For example, if $v = 10$, then $1/v = 1/10$. If v is increased to 100 (i.e., it is maximized), then $1/v = 1/100$ (i.e., it is minimized). Thus, the objective of Company I is to

Developing the objective function

$$\text{maximize } Z = v$$

We can also say

$$\text{minimize } Z = \frac{1}{v}$$

Since $x_1 + x_2 = 1/v$, this objective function is equivalent to

$$\text{minimize } Z = x_1 + x_2$$

We can now summarize the linear programming model for Company I as follows:

The linear programming model for Company I

$$\text{minimize } Z = x_1 + x_2$$
subject to
$$8x_1 + 1x_2 \geq 1$$
$$4x_1 + 7x_2 \geq 1$$
$$x_1, x_2 \geq 0$$

The solution of this model will yield values for x_1 and x_2, which we must convert back to their original form,

$$x_1 = \frac{p_1}{v}$$

$$x_2 = \frac{p_2}{v}$$

in order to determine the mixed strategy for Company I.

A model can be developed for the mixed strategy of Company II in the same way as the above model was developed for Company I. The decision variables are defined as

Developing a model for Company II

q_1 = probability of the occurrence of strategy B
q_2 = probability of the occurrence of strategy C

Decision variables

The model constraints from Table 12.11 are

Model constraints

$$8q_1 + 4q_2 \leq v$$
$$1q_1 + 7q_2 \leq v$$
$$q_1 + q_2 = 1.0$$

≤ inequalities

These constraints are ≤ inequalities, since Company II is the minimizing (or defensive) player and wants to achieve a value of the game less than v if possible.

Simplifying the model constraints

As before, if we divide these constraints by v, we can simplify them:

$$\frac{8q_1}{v} + \frac{4q_2}{v} \leq 1$$

$$\frac{1q_1}{v} + \frac{7q_2}{v} \leq 1$$

$$\frac{q_1}{v} + \frac{q_2}{v} = \frac{1}{v}$$

Redefining the decision variables

Next we redefine the model decision variables,

$$y_1 = \frac{q_1}{v}$$

$$y_2 = \frac{q_2}{v}$$

such that the model constraints are now

$$8y_1 + 4y_2 \leq 1$$
$$1y_1 + 7y_2 \leq 1$$
$$y_1 + y_2 = \frac{1}{v}$$

Developing the objective function

Since the objective of Company II is to minimize the value of the game, v, we can also maximize $1/v$. Thus, the objective function can be defined as

$$\text{maximize } Z = \frac{1}{v}$$

Since $1/v = y_1 + y_2$, the objective function can also be defined as

$$\text{maximize } Z = y_1 + y_2$$

Summary of the Company I and Company II models

The linear programming models for both companies are summarized below.

Company I	*Company II*
minimize $Z = x_1 + x_2$	maximize $Z = y_1 + y_2$
subject to	subject to
$8x_1 + 1x_2 \geq 1$	$8y_1 + 4y_2 \leq 1$
$4x_1 + 7x_2 \geq 1$	$1y_1 + 7y_2 \leq 1$
$x_1, x_2 \geq 0$	$y_1, y_2 \geq 0$

Primal and dual models

Inspecting each of these models closely, we can see that the Company I model is the *primal* form of the linear programming model and the Company II model is the *dual* form. As noted in Chapter 6, "Postoptimality Analysis," the solution to the primal provides complete information about the dual solution, so it is necessary to solve only one of the models in order to determine the mixed strategy for each company.

Solving the Company I model by the simplex method results in the optimal tableau shown in Table 12.12.

The optimal simplex solution of the Company I model

TABLE 12.12
Simplex Solution of the Company I Model

c_j	Basic Variables	Quantity	1 x_1	1 x_2	0 s_1	0 s_2
1	x_1	3/26	1	0	$-7/52$	1/52
1	x_2	2/26	0	1	2/26	$-2/13$
	z_j	5/26	1	1	$-3/52$	$-7/52$
	$z_j - c_j$		0	0	$-3/52$	$-7/52$

In order to determine the mixed strategy for Company I, we must convert the solution back to its original form. Recall that

Converting the solution into the original model form

$$\frac{p_1}{v} = x_1$$

$$\frac{p_2}{v} = x_2$$

$$\frac{1}{v} = Z$$

Since $Z = 5/26$,

$$Z = \frac{1}{v} = \frac{5}{26}$$

and

$$v = \frac{26}{5} = 5.2$$

Next, since $x_1 = 3/26$ and $x_2 = 2/26$,

$$\frac{p_1}{v} = x_1$$

$$\frac{p_1}{26/5} = \frac{3}{26}$$

$$p_1 = .60$$

and

$$\frac{p_2}{v} = x_2$$

$$\frac{p_2}{26/5} = \frac{2}{26}$$

$$p_2 = .40$$

The mixed strategy
for Company I

Thus, the mixed strategy for Company I is

$$p_1 = .60 = \text{percent of time strategy 2 should be used}$$
$$p_2 = .40 = \text{percent of time strategy 3 should be used}$$
$$v = 5.2 = \text{expected gain in percentage market share for Company I}$$

The dual solution

As noted earlier, since the Company II model is the dual form, the mixed strategy for Company II can also be determined from the simplex solution of the primal shown in Table 12.12. Observing the $z_j - c_j$ row, we can see that the dual solution values for y_1 and y_2 are

$$y_1 = \frac{3}{52}$$

$$y_2 = \frac{7}{52}$$

and

$$Z = \frac{5}{26}$$

Converting the
solution into the
original model form

Substituting these values into our original model terms will result in the mixed strategy solution. For the value of the game, v,

$$\frac{1}{v} = Z$$

$$v = \frac{26}{5}$$

For the values of q_1 and q_2,

$$\frac{q_1}{v} = y_1$$

$$\frac{q_1}{26/5} = \frac{3}{52}$$

$$q_1 = \frac{3}{10} = .30$$

and

$$\frac{q_2}{v} = y_2$$

$$\frac{q_2}{26/5} = \frac{7}{52}$$

$$q_2 = \frac{7}{10} = .70$$

The mixed strategy
for Company II

Thus, the mixed strategy for Company II is

$$q_1 = .30 = \text{percent of time strategy B should be used}$$
$$q_2 = .70 = \text{percent of time strategy C should be used}$$
$$v = 5.2 = \text{expected loss in percentage market share for Company II}$$

Note that these mixed strategies for Companies I and II are identical to those determined by the expected gain and loss method in the previous section. The linear programming method is valuable for games of *greater magnitude than two strategies per player.* For the camera company example, the expected gain and loss method is more appropriate; however, linear programming is generally the preferred approach for larger games.

Computerized LP Solution

The linear programming method may seem somewhat more laborious than the expected gain and loss method because of the effort required to convert the problem to a linear programming model. However, once formulated, the model can be solved using a computer software package such as LINDO/PC, as demonstrated in Chapters 4 and 6.

LINDO/PC computer solution

What follows is the LINDO/PC solution output for the Company I and Company II linear programming models developed in the preceding section. Note that the Company I model solution is identical to the simplex solution shown in Table 12.12. As with the simplex solution, these model results must be converted back into the original game theory form (i.e., the values of p_1, p_2, and v).

```
: look all

MIN     X1 + X2
SUBJECT TO
       2)    8 X1 + X2 >=    1
       3)    4 X1 + 7 X2 >=    1
END


: go
LP OPTIMUM FOUND  AT STEP     2

           OBJECTIVE FUNCTION VALUE

    1)          .192307700

    VARIABLE         VALUE          REDUCED COST
          X1          .115385           .000000
          X2          .076923           .000000


         ROW    SLACK OR SURPLUS     DUAL PRICES
          2)          .000000          -.057692
          3)          .000000          -.134615

    NO. ITERATIONS=        2
```

AN APPLICATION OF GAME THEORY

Armed Forces Helicopter Procurement

In 1975, the United States Navy proposed that the Marines purchase a medium lift helicopter called the HXM, which would be specially modified for Marine missions. At that time the Marine Corps was almost committed to purchasing a new small helicopter called the UH-1 for its missions. In addition, the HXM proposal placed in jeopardy another program for a medium lift helicopter (the CH-46). Faced with these alternative proposals, the Marine Commandant decided to examine the role of all Marine helicopters, both large and small. An ad hoc team was assembled and given one month to recommend decisions for current and future helicopter procurement.

The ad hoc evaluation team employed a game theory approach to the problem. A two-person zero-sum game was developed wherein player 1 selects a particular aircraft and player 2 (the enemy) selects an environment in which the aircraft must operate. Helicopter performance specifications were converted to relative indices reflecting payload and cost effectiveness, which served as the payoff measure. This approach was used to evaluate all of the helicopters in the different possible environments to which they would be subjected. The games were solved using linear programming. The game theory analysis resulted in decisions to cancel the UH-1 helicopter program and to drop all plans for procuring the new HXM helicopter. The existing CH-46 program was continued. Without the analysis, the UH-1 and HXM programs would have been continued and the CH-46 canceled erroneously, with unnecessary expenses resulting. It was estimated that these decisions would permit a savings of approximately $800 million during a fifteen-year period.[1]

Summary

Game theory provides a convenient framework for analyzing decision making by individuals in competitive situations. The analysis of two-person games in this chapter illustrated the logic of decision making among competing parties as encompassed in their choices of pure and mixed strategies. However, applications of game theory in the real world are rare.

In this chapter, the presentation of game theory was limited to two-person games. Unfortunately, there is no convenient and

Real-world applications of game theory are rare

[1] R. Thomson and C. Tiplitz, "Helicopter Fleet Mix," *Interfaces* 9, no. 2, part 2 (February 1979): 39–49.

easy means of analyzing games with more than two competing parties. For games with more than two players, the methods of analysis become quite complex and thus difficult for the manager/decision maker to apply.

However, game theory is valuable because it promotes an understanding of the logic of decision making between competing individuals. The principles and fundamentals of game theory presented in this chapter provide valuable insight into the basics of strategic planning. Although one could not expect to apply game theory often, it does provide an awareness of the mechanics of decision making.

Game theory valuable for illuminating decision-making logic of competing individuals

References

Baumol, W. J. *Economic Theory and Operations Analysis.* 4th ed. Englewood Cliffs, N.J.: Prentice-Hall, 1977.

Dorfman, R.; Samuelson, P. A.; and Solow, R. M. *Linear Programming and Economic Analysis.* New York: McGraw-Hill, 1958.

Holloway, C. A. *Decision Making Under Uncertainty.* Englewood Cliffs, N.J.: Prentice-Hall, 1979.

Kwak, N. K. *Mathematical Programming with Business Applications.* New York: McGraw-Hill, 1973.

Luce, R. D., and Raiffa, H. *Games and Decisions.* New York: John Wiley and Sons, 1957.

Thomson, R., and Tiplitz, C. "Helicopter Fleet Mix." *Interfaces* 9, no. 2, part 2 (February 1979): 39–49.

Von Neumann, J., and Morgenstern, O. *Theory of Games and Economic Behavior.* 3d ed. Princeton, N.J.: Princeton University Press, 1953.

Williams, J. D. *The Compleat Strategyst.* Rev. ed. New York: McGraw-Hill, 1966.

EXAMPLE PROBLEM SOLUTION

Two fast food chains, MacBurger and Burger Doodle, dominate the fast food market. MacBurger is currently the market leader, and Burger Doodle has developed three marketing strategies, encompassing advertising and new product lines, to gain a percentage of the market now belonging to MacBurger. The following payoff table shows the gains for Burger Doodle and the losses for MacBurger given the strategies of each company.

Burger Doodle Strategies	MacBurger Strategies		
	A	B	C
1	4	3	6
2	−2	5	1
3	3	2	4

Determine the mixed strategy for each company and the expected market share gains for Burger Doodle and losses for MacBurger, and formulate a linear programming model for this situation.

Step 1: Check for Dominance

Strategy 1 dominates 3, and strategy A dominates C; thus, the payoff table can be reduced to the following:

Burger Doodle Strategies	MacBurger Strategies	
	A	B
1	4	3
2	-2	5

Step 2: The Expected Gain and Loss Method

Burger Doodle

$$\text{Strategy A: } 4p + (-2)(1 - p) = 6p - 2$$
$$\text{Strategy B: } \quad 3p + 5(1 - p) = 5 - 2p$$
$$6p - 2 = 5 - 2p$$
$$8p = 7$$
$$p = .875 = \text{probability that strategy A}$$
$$\text{will be used}$$
$$1 - p = .125 = \text{probability that strategy B}$$
$$\text{will be used}$$
$$\text{EG (Burger Doodle)} = 4(.875) - 2(.125)$$
$$= 3.25\% \text{ market share increase}$$

MacBurger

$$\text{Strategy 1: } \quad 4p + 3(1 - p) = 3 + p$$
$$\text{Strategy 2: } -2p + 5(1 - p) = 5 - 7p$$
$$3 + p = 5 - 7p$$
$$8p = 2$$
$$p = .250$$
$$1 - p = .750$$
$$\text{EL (MacBurger)} = 4(.250) + 3(.750)$$
$$= 3.25\% \text{ market share loss}$$

Step 3: The Linear Programming Model

Burger Doodle

minimize $Z = x_1 + x_2$
subject to
$$4x_1 - 2x_2 \geq 1$$
$$3x_1 + 5x_2 \geq 1$$
$$x_1, x_2 \geq 0$$

where

$$x_1 = \frac{p_1}{v}$$

$$x_2 = \frac{p_2}{v}$$

$$Z = \frac{1}{v}$$

MacBurger

maximize $Z = y_1 + y_2$
subject to
$$4y_1 + 3y_2 \le 1$$
$$-2y_1 + 5y_2 \le 1$$
where

$$x_1 = \frac{p_1}{v}$$

$$x_2 = \frac{p_2}{v}$$

$$Z = \frac{1}{v}$$

The LINDO/PC software package provides the solution output for these models shown on page 450.

Using the results of the first (i.e., Burger Doodle) model, we can convert the linear programming solution back to the original form to get the following solution.

$$Z = \frac{1}{v} = .3077$$

and

$$v = 3.25\%$$

$$x_1 = \frac{p_1}{v}$$

$$.2692 = \frac{p_1}{3.25}$$

$$p_1 = .875$$

$$p_2 = 1 - p_1 = .125$$

These are the same results achieved using the expected gain and loss method.

```
: look all

MIN    X1 + X2
SUBJECT TO
       2)   4 X1 - 2 X2 >=   1
       3)   3 X1 + 5 X2 >=   1
END




: go
LP OPTIMUM FOUND   AT STEP     2

           OBJECTIVE FUNCTION VALUE

  1)        .307692300

   VARIABLE         VALUE          REDUCED COST
      X1          .269231            .000000
      X2          .038462            .000000


      ROW    SLACK OR SURPLUS     DUAL PRICES
       2)          .000000          -.076923
       3)          .000000          -.230769

NO. ITERATIONS=          2




 : look all

 MAX    Y1 + Y2
SUBJECT TO
       2)   4 Y1 + 3 Y2 <=   1
       3) - 2 Y1 + 5 Y2 <=   1
END




: go
LP OPTIMUM FOUND   AT STEP     2

           OBJECTIVE FUNCTION VALUE

  1)        .307692300

   VARIABLE         VALUE          REDUCED COST
      Y1          .076923            .000000
      Y2          .230769            .000000


      ROW    SLACK OR SURPLUS     DUAL PRICES
       2)          .000000           .269231
       3)          .000000           .038462

NO. ITERATIONS=          2
```

Problems

1. Below is the payoff table for two individuals competing in a game situation.

Individual I Strategies	Individual II Strategies	
	A	B
1	100	80
2	60	70

  a. Determine the optimal strategy for each player.
  b. Is this a pure or mixed strategy game? Explain.

2. Below is the payoff table for two individuals competing in a game situation.

Individual I Strategies	Individual II Strategies	
	A	B
1	50	40
2	30	60

  Is this a pure or a mixed strategy game? Explain.

3. Are there any dominant strategies in problems 1 and 2? Explain.

4. The management of the Millstone Bread Company is involved in labor negotiations with the local bakers' union. The union has three alternative contracts reflecting its strategies in the labor negotiations; the company has two contract proposals reflecting its strategies. The following payoff table shows the dollar value of each alternative contract proposal.

Union Strategies	Management Strategies	
	A	B
1	$200,000	$170,000
2	300,000	220,000
3	160,000	180,000

  a. Are there any dominant strategies in the payoff table?
  b. Determine the optimal pure strategy for both game players and the equilibrium point.
  c. Why is this a pure strategy game instead of a mixed strategy game?

5. The Army is conducting war games in Europe. One simulated encounter is between the Blue and Red Divisions. The Blue Division is on the offensive; the Red Division holds a defensive position. The results of the war game are measured in terms of troop losses. The following payoff table shows Red Division troop losses for each battle strategy available to each division.

Blue Division Strategies	Red Division Strategies		
	A	B	C
1	1,800	2,000	1,700
2	2,300	900	1,600

Determine the optimal strategy for both divisions and the number of troop losses the Red Division can expect to suffer.

6. Consider the following payoff table for two game players.

Player I Strategies	Player II Strategies		
	A	B	C
1	−250	−50	350
2	50	0	100
3	250	−100	−350

a. Determine the initial single strategy for each player.
b. Show the closed loop that will result as the players change strategies.

7. The Baseball Players Association has voted to go on strike if a settlement is not reached with the owners within the next month. The players' representative, Melvin Mulehead, has two strategies (containing different free agent rules, pension formulas, etc.); the owners' representative, Roy Stonewall, has three counterproposals. The financial gains in millions of dollars from each player strategy given each owner strategy are shown in the following payoff table.

Player Strategies	Owner Strategies		
	A	B	C
1	15	9	11
2	7	20	12

a. Determine the initial strategy for the players and for the owners.
b. Is this a pure or a mixed strategy game? Explain.

8. Consider the following mixed strategy game for two players.

Player I Strategies	Player II Strategies	
	A	B
1	8	15
2	30	12

a. Determine the initial strategy for each player.
b. Using the expected gain and loss method, determine the mixed strategies for each player.

9. Mary Washington is the incumbent Congresswoman for a district in New Mexico, and Franklin Truman is her opponent in the upcoming election. Since Truman is seeking to unseat Washington, he is on the offensive, and she hopes to minimize his gains in the polls. The following payoff table shows the possible percentage point gains for Truman given the political strategies available to each politician.

Franklin Truman Strategies	Mary Washington Strategies	
	A	B
1	7	3
2	6	10

Determine the optimal political strategy for each politician and the percentage gain in the polls Franklin Truman can expect.

10. Edgar Allan Melville is a successful novelist who is negotiating a contract for a new novel with his publisher, Potboiler Books, Inc. The novelist's contract strategies encompass various proposals for royalties, movie rights, advances, and the like. The following payoff table shows the financial gains for the novelist from each contract strategy.

Novelist Strategies	Publisher Strategies		
	A	B	C
1	$ 80,000	$120,000	$ 90,000
2	130,000	90,000	80,000
3	110,000	140,000	100,000

a. Does this payoff table contain any dominant strategies?
b. Determine the strategy for the novelist and the publisher and the gains and losses for each.

11. Consider the following payoff table for a mixed strategy game between two players.

Player I Strategies	Player II Strategies		
	A	B	C
1	50	60	30
2	10	32	25
3	20	55	45

a. Show why pure strategies do not exist.
b. Identify the closed loop that will result as the players change strategies.
c. Using dominance, reduce the payoff matrix to two strategies per player.
d. Determine the mixed strategy for each player and the expected gains and losses that result.

12. The United Dynamics Corporation is a military contractor. The company is negotiating with the military to supply an electronic range finder for tanks. The corporation is attempting to gain the maximum selling price for the range finder and has developed strategies to do so. The selling prices are shown in the following table.

United Dynamics Strategies	Military Strategies	
	A	B
1	$60,000	$100,000
2	80,000	40,000

Determine the optimal strategy and the gains and losses for each party.

13. Given the following payoff table for a mixed strategy game between two players, determine the strategy and the gains and losses for each player.

Player I Strategies	Player II Strategies			
	A	B	C	D
1	40	30	20	80
2	90	50	60	65
3	80	75	52	90
4	60	40	35	50

14. Two major soft drink companies are located in the Southeast — the Cooler Cola Company and Smoothie Soft Drinks, Inc. Cooler Cola is presently the market leader, and Smoothie has developed several mar-

keting strategies to gain a percentage of the market now belonging to Cooler Cola. The following payoff table shows the gains for Smoothie and the losses for Cooler given the strategies of each company.

Smoothie Strategies	Cooler Cola Strategies		
	A	B	C
1	10	9	3
2	4	7	5
3	6	8	−4

Determine the mixed strategy for each company and the expected market share gains for Smoothie and losses for Cooler Cola.

15. Tech is playing State in a basketball game. Tech employs two basic offenses — the shuffle and the overload; State uses three defenses — the zone, the man-to-man, and a combination zone and man-to-man. The points Tech expects to score (estimated from past games) using each offense against each State defense are given in the following payoff table.

Tech Offenses	State Defenses		
	Zone	Man-to-Man	Combination
Shuffle	72	60	83
Overload	58	91	72

Determine the mixed strategy for each team and the points Tech can expect to score. Interpret the strategy probabilities.

16. Consider the following payoff table for two game players.

Player I Strategies	Player II Strategies			
	A	B	C	D
1	6	25	18	10
2	12	14	19	11
3	20	15	7	9
4	15	30	21	16

A pure strategy is not possible for this game. Determine whether a mixed strategy is possible using the expected gain and loss method. If it is not, explain why and identify an alternative solution approach.

17. Formulate a linear programming model for the mixed strategy game in problem 7.

18. Given the following mixed strategy game, fomulate a linear programming model and solve it using the simplex method to determine the mixed strategies. Compare these results with those resulting from the expected gain and loss method.

Player I Strategies	Player II Strategies	
	A	B
1	6	10
2	8	4

19. Formulate a linear programming model for the mixed strategy game in problem 16 and determine the mixed strategies using the simplex method.

13

Markov Analysis

Markov analysis, like decision analysis (presented in Chapter 11), is a probabilistic technique. However, Markov analysis is different in that it does not provide a recommended decision. Instead, Markov analysis provides probabilistic information about a decision situation that can aid the decision maker in making a decision. In other words, Markov analysis is not an optimization technique; it is a *descriptive* technique that results in probabilistic information.

Markov analysis is specifically applicable to systems that exhibit probabilistic movement from one state (or condition) to another, over time. For example, Markov analysis can be used to determine the probability that a machine will be running one day and broken down the next, or that a customer will change brands of cereal from one month to the next. This latter type of example—referred to as the "brand switching" problem—will be used to demonstrate the principles of Markov analysis in the following discussion.

A descriptive technique

Systems that exhibit probabilistic movement from one state to another

THE CHARACTERISTICS OF MARKOV ANALYSIS

Markov analysis can be used to analyze a number of different decision situations; however, one of its more popular applications has been the analysis of customer brand switching. This is basically a marketing application that focuses on the loyalty of customers to a particular product brand, store, or supplier. Markov analysis provides information on the probability of customers' switching from one brand to one or more other brands. An example of the brand switching problem will be used to demonstrate Markov analysis.

A small community has two gasoline service stations, Petroco and National. The residents of the community purchase gasoline at the two stations on a monthly basis. The marketing department of the Petroco company surveyed a number of residents and found that the customers were not totally loyal to either brand of gasoline. Customers would change service stations as a result of advertising, service, and other factors. The marketing department found that if a customer bought gasoline from Petroco in any given month, there was only a .60 probability that the customer would buy from Petroco the next month and a .40 probability that the customer would buy from National the next month. Likewise, if a customer traded with National in a given month, there was an .80 probability that the customer would purchase gasoline from National in the next month and a .20 probability that the customer would purchase gasoline from Petroco. These probabilities are summarized in Table 13.1.

TABLE 13.1
Probabilities of Customer Movement per Month

| This Month | Next Month | |
	Petroco	National
Petroco	.60	.40
National	.20	.80

This example contains several important assumptions. *First,* notice that in Table 13.1 the probabilities in each row sum to 1.0. This means that if a customer trades with Petroco one month, the customer *must* trade with either Petroco or National the next month (i.e., the customer will not give up buying gasoline, nor will the customer trade with both in one month). *Second,* the probabilities in Table 13.1 apply to every customer who purchases gasoline. *Third,* the probabilities in Table 13.1 will not change over time. In other words, regardless of when the customer buys gasoline, the probabilities of trading with one of the service stations the next month will be the values in Table 13.1. The probabilities in Table 13.1 will not change in the future if conditions remain the same. *Finally,* the events (i.e., trading with either station) are independent over time. Where a customer buys gasoline during one month does not affect where the customer will buy during a future month.

It is these properties that make this example a Markov process. In Markov terminology, the service station a customer trades at in a given month is referred to as a *state of the system* (similar to states of nature in a decision analysis problem in Chap. 11). Thus, this example contains two states of the system—a customer will purchase gasoline at either Petroco or National in any given month. The probabilities of the various states in Table 13.1 are known as *transition* probabilities. In other words, they are the probabilities of a customer's making the transition from one state to another during one time period. Table 13.1 contains four transition probabilities.

The properties for the service station example described above define a Markov process. They are summarized in Markov terminology as follows.

Property 1: The transition probabilities for a given beginning state of the system sum to 1.0.
Property 2: The probabilities apply to all participants in the system.
Property 3: The transition probabilities are constant over time.
Property 4: The states are independent over time.

Markov Analysis Information

Now that we have defined a Markov process and determined that our example exhibits the Markov properties, the next question is "What information will Markov analysis provide?" The most obvious information available from Markov analysis is the probability of being in a state at some future time period, which is also the sort of information we can gain from a *decision tree.*

For example, suppose the service stations wanted to know the probability that a customer would trade with them in month 3 given that the customer trades with them this month (1). This analysis can be performed for each service station using decision trees, as shown in Figures 13.1 and 13.2. (Recall from Chap. 10 that the ending branch probabilities for independent events are obtained by multiplying the probabilities of the events.)

In order to determine the probability of a customer's trading with Petroco in month 3 given that the customer initially traded with Petroco in month 1, we must add the two branch probabilities in Figure 13.1 associated with Petroco.

$.36 + .08 = .44$, the probability of a customer's
trading with Petroco in month 3

FIGURE 13.1

Probabilities of
Future States Given
That a Customer
Trades with Petroco
This Month

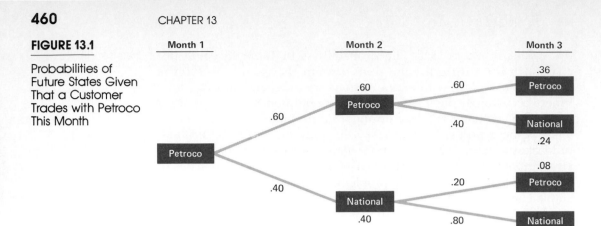

Likewise, in order to determine the probability of a customer's purchasing gasoline from National in month 3, we add the two branch probabilities in Figure 13.1 associated with National.

.24 + .32 = .56, the probability of a customer's
trading with National in month 3

This same type of analysis can be performed under the condition that a customer initially purchased gasoline from National, as shown in Figure 13.2. Given that National is the starting state in month 1, the probability of a customer's purchasing gasoline from National in month 3 is

.08 + .64 = .72

and the probability of a customer's trading with Petroco in month 3 is

.12 + .16 = .28

FIGURE 13.2

Probabilities of
Future States Given
That a Customer
Trades with
National This Month

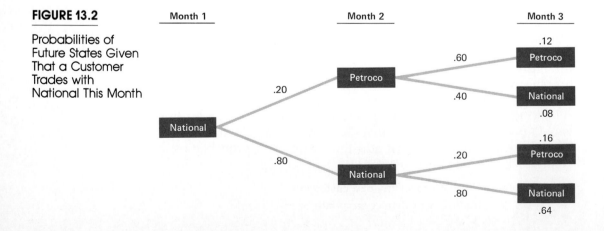

Notice that for each starting state, Petroco and National, the probabilities of ending up in either state in month 3 sum to 1.0.

| | Probability of Trade in Month 3 | | |
Starting State	Petroco	National	Sum
Petroco	.44	.56	1.00
National	.28	.72	1.00

Although the use of decision trees is perfectly logical for this type of analysis, it is time consuming and cumbersome. For example, if Petroco wanted to know the probability that a customer who trades with them in month 1 will trade with them in month 10, a rather large decision tree would have to be constructed. Alternatively, the same analysis performed above using decision trees can be done using *matrix algebra* techniques.

THE TRANSITION MATRIX

The probabilities of a customer's moving from service station to service station within a one-month period, presented in tabular form in Table 13.1, can also be presented in the form of a rectangular array of numbers called a *matrix*, as shown below.

$$T = \begin{array}{cc} & \begin{array}{cc} \text{First Month} & \text{Next Month} \\ & \text{Petroco} \quad \text{National} \end{array} \\ \begin{array}{c} \text{Petroco} \\ \text{National} \end{array} & \begin{bmatrix} .60 & .40 \\ .20 & .80 \end{bmatrix} \end{array}$$

Since we previously defined these probabilities as transition probabilities, we will refer to the above matrix, T, as a *transition matrix*. The present states of the system are listed on the left of the transition matrix, and the future states in the next time period are listed across the top. For example, there is a .60 probability that a customer who traded with Petroco in month 1 will trade with Petroco in month 2.

Several new symbols will be needed for Markov analysis using matrix algebra. We will define the probability of a customer's trading with Petroco in period i, given that the customer initially traded with Petroco, as

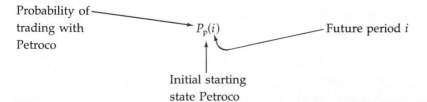

Similarly, the probability of a customer's trading with National in period i, given that a customer initially traded with Petroco, is

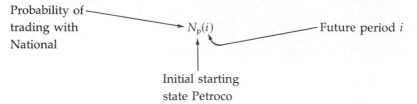

For example, the probability of a customer's trading at National in month 2, given that the customer initially traded with Petroco, is

$$N_p(2)$$

The probabilities of a customer's trading with Petroco and National in a future period i, given that the customer traded initially with National, are defined as

$$P_n(i) \quad \text{and} \quad N_n(i)$$

(When interpreting these symbols, always recall that the subscript refers to the starting state.)

Petroco as the initial starting state

If a customer is presently trading with Petroco (month 1), the following probabilities exist.

$$P_p(1) = 1.0$$
$$N_p(1) = 0.0$$

In other words, the probability of a customer's trading at Petroco in month 1, given that the customer trades at Petroco, is 1.0.

Probabilities arranged in matrix form

These probabilities can also be arranged in matrix form as follows.

$$[P_p(1) \quad N_p(1)] = [1.0 \quad 0.0]$$

System starting conditions

This matrix defines the starting conditions of our example system, given that a customer initially trades at Petroco, as in the decision tree in Figure 13.1. In other words, a customer is originally trading with Petroco in month 1. We can determine the subsequent probabilities of a customer's trading at Petroco or National in month 2 by multiplying the matrix above by the transition matrix, as follows.

Computing probabilities of a customer trading at either station in future months using matrix multiplication

$$\text{Month 2: } [P_p(2) \quad N_p(2)] = [1.0 \quad 0.0]\begin{bmatrix} .60 & .40 \\ .20 & .80 \end{bmatrix}$$
$$= [.60 \quad .40]$$

(For those who are not familiar with matrix multiplication or who would like to refresh their memories, Appendix B explains matrix multiplication in detail.)

These probabilities of .60 for a customer's trading at Petroco and .40 for a customer's trading at National are the same as those computed in the decision tree in Figure 13.1. We use the same procedure for determining the month 3 probabilities, except we now multiply the transition matrix by the month 2 matrix.

$$\text{Month 3: } [P_p(3) \quad N_p(3)] = [.60 \quad .40] \begin{bmatrix} .60 & .40 \\ .20 & .80 \end{bmatrix}$$
$$= [.44 \quad .56]$$

These are the same probabilities we computed using the decision tree analysis in Figure 13.1. However, whereas it would be cumbersome to determine additional values using the decision tree analysis, we can continue to use the matrix approach as we have above.

$$\text{Month 4: } [P_p(4) \quad N_p(4)] = [.44 \quad .56] \begin{bmatrix} .60 & .40 \\ .20 & .80 \end{bmatrix}$$
$$= [.38 \quad .62]$$

The state probabilities for several subsequent months are as follows.

Month 5: $[P_p(5) \quad N_p(5)] = [.35 \quad .65]$
Month 6: $[P_p(6) \quad N_p(6)] = [.34 \quad .66]$
Month 7: $[P_p(7) \quad N_p(7)] = [.34 \quad .66]$
Month 8: $[P_p(8) \quad N_p(8)] = [.33 \quad .67]$
Month 9: $[P_p(9) \quad N_p(9)] = [.33 \quad .67]$

Notice that as we go further and further into the future, the changes in the state probabilities become smaller and smaller until eventually there are no changes at all. At that point every month in the future will have the same probabilities. For this example, the state probabilities that result after some future month i are

In future months the state probabilities begin to show no change

$$[P_p(i) \quad N_p(i)] = [.33 \quad .67]$$

This characteristic of the state probabilities' approaching a constant value after a number of time periods is shown for $P_p(i)$ in Figure 13.3.

$N_p(i)$ exhibits this same characteristic as it approaches a value of .67. This is a potentially valuable result for the decision maker. In other words, the service station owner can now conclude that after a certain number of months in the future, there is a .33 probability that the customer will trade with Petroco if the customer initially traded with Petroco.

This same type of analysis can be performed given the starting condition in which a customer initially trades with National in month 1. This analysis, shown below, corresponds to the decision tree in Figure 13.2.

Computing future state probabilities when the initial starting state is National

Given that a customer initially trades at the National station, then

$$[P_n(1) \quad N_n(1)] = [0.0 \quad 1.0]$$

FIGURE 13.3

The Probability $P_p(i)$ for Future Values of i

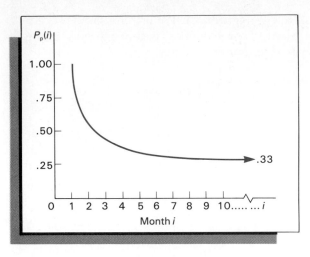

Using these initial starting-state probabilities, we can compute future state probabilities as follows.

$$\text{Month 2: } [P_n(2) \quad N_n(2)] = [0.0 \quad 1.0] \begin{bmatrix} .60 & .40 \\ .20 & .80 \end{bmatrix}$$

$$= [.20 \quad .80]$$

$$\text{Month 3: } [P_n(3) \quad N_n(3)] = [.20 \quad .80] \begin{bmatrix} .60 & .40 \\ .20 & .80 \end{bmatrix}$$

$$= [.28 \quad .72]$$

These are the same values obtained using the decision tree analysis in Figure 13.2. Subsequent state probabilities, computed similarly, are shown below.

Summary of future state probabilities for National starting state

Month 4: $[P_n(4) \quad N_n(4)] = [.31 \quad .69]$
Month 5: $[P_n(5) \quad N_n(5)] = [.32 \quad .68]$
Month 6: $[P_n(6) \quad N_n(6)] = [.33 \quad .67]$
Month 7: $[P_n(7) \quad N_n(7)] = [.33 \quad .67]$
Month 8: $[P_n(8) \quad N_n(8)] = [.33 \quad .67]$
Month 9: $[P_n(9) \quad N_n(9)] = [.33 \quad .67]$

The probability of ending up in a state in the future is independent of the starting state

As in the previous case in which Petroco was the starting state, these state probabilities also become constant after several periods. However, notice that the eventual state probabilities (i.e., .33 and .67) achieved when National is the starting state *are exactly the same* as the previous state probabilities achieved when Petroco was the starting state. In other words, the probability of ending up in a particular state in the future is not dependent on the starting state.

STEADY-STATE PROBABILITIES

The probabilities of .33 and .67 in our example are referred to as *steady-state probabilities*. The steady-state probabilities are average probabilities that the system will be in a certain state after a large number of transition periods. This does not mean the system stays in one state. The system will continue to move from state to state in future time periods; however, the average *probabilities* of moving from state to state for all periods will remain constant in the long run. In a Markov process after a number of periods have passed, the probabilities will approach steady state.

Average probabilities that the system will be in a state in the future

For our service station example, the steady-state probabilities are

Steady-state probabilities

.33 = probability of a customer's trading at Petroco after a number of months in the future, regardless of where the customer traded in month 1

.67 = probability of a customer's trading at National after a number of months in the future, regardless of where the customer traded in month 1

Notice that in the determination of the steady-state probabilities above, we considered each starting state separately. First we assumed a customer was initially trading at Petroco, and the steady-state probabilities were computed given this starting condition. Then we determined that the steady-state probabilities were the same regardless of the starting condition. However, it was not necessary to perform these matrix operations separately. We could have simply combined the operations into one matrix as follows,

Combining state probabilities into one matrix

Month 2:
$$\begin{bmatrix} P_p(2) & N_p(2) \\ P_n(2) & N_n(2) \end{bmatrix} = \begin{bmatrix} 1 & 0 \\ 0 & 1 \end{bmatrix} \begin{bmatrix} .60 & .40 \\ .20 & .80 \end{bmatrix}$$

$$= \begin{bmatrix} .60 & .40 \\ .20 & .80 \end{bmatrix}$$

Month 3:
$$\begin{bmatrix} P_p(3) & N_p(3) \\ P_n(3) & N_n(3) \end{bmatrix} = \begin{bmatrix} .60 & .40 \\ .20 & .80 \end{bmatrix} \begin{bmatrix} .60 & .40 \\ .20 & .80 \end{bmatrix}$$

$$= \begin{bmatrix} .44 & .56 \\ .28 & .72 \end{bmatrix}$$

Month 4:
$$\begin{bmatrix} P_p(4) & N_p(4) \\ P_n(4) & N_n(4) \end{bmatrix} = \begin{bmatrix} .44 & .56 \\ .28 & .72 \end{bmatrix} \begin{bmatrix} .60 & .40 \\ .20 & .80 \end{bmatrix}$$

$$= \begin{bmatrix} .38 & .62 \\ .31 & .69 \end{bmatrix}$$

until eventually we arrived at the steady-state probabilities

Month 9:
$$\begin{bmatrix} P_p(9) & N_p(9) \\ P_n(9) & N_n(9) \end{bmatrix} = \begin{bmatrix} .33 & .67 \\ .33 & .67 \end{bmatrix}$$

Direct Algebraic Determination of Steady-State Probabilities

In the previous section, we computed the state probabilities for approximately eight periods (i.e., months) before the steady-state probabilities were reached for both states. This required quite a few matrix computations. Alternatively, it is possible to solve for the steady-state probabilities directly without going through all of these matrix operations.

At some point in the future, the state probabilities remain constant from period to period

Notice that after eight periods in our previous analysis, the state probabilities did not change from period to period (i.e., from month to month). For example,

Month 8: $[P_p(8) \quad N_p(8)] = [.33 \quad .67]$
Month 9: $[P_p(9) \quad N_p(9)] = [.33 \quad .67]$

The state probabilities in periods i and $i + 1$ are equal

Thus, we can also say that after a number of periods in the future (in this case, eight), the state probabilities in period i equal the state probabilities in period $i + 1$. For our example, this means that

$$[P_p(8) \quad N_p(8)] = [P_p(9) \quad N_p(9)]$$

Deleting the period designation

In fact, it is not necessary to designate which period in the future is actually occurring. That is,

$$[P_p \quad N_p] = [P_p \quad N_p]$$

given steady-state conditions.

Determining the state probabilities for period $i + 1$

These probabilities are for some period i in the future once a steady state has already been reached. To determine the state probabilities for period $i + 1$, we would normally do the following computation.

$$[P_p(i + 1) \quad N_p(i + 1)] = [P_p(i) \quad N_p(i)]\begin{bmatrix} .60 & .40 \\ .20 & .80 \end{bmatrix}$$

However, we have already stated that once a steady state has been reached, then

$$[P_p(i + 1) \quad N_p(i + 1)] = [P_p(i) \quad N_p(i)]$$

and it is not necessary to designate the period. Thus our computation can be rewritten as

$$[P_p \quad N_p] = [P_p \quad N_p]\begin{bmatrix} .60 & .40 \\ .20 & .80 \end{bmatrix}$$

Developing a set of equations from the matrix operations

Performing matrix operations results in the following set of equations.

$$P_p = .6P_p + .2N_p$$
$$N_p = .4P_p + .8N_p$$

Recall that the transition probabilities for a row in the transition matrix (i.e., the state probabilities) must sum to 1.0.

$$P_p + N_p = 1.0$$

which can also be written as

$$N_p = 1.0 - P_p$$

Substituting this value into our first equation above ($P_p = .6P_p + .2N_p$) results in the following.

Solving simultaneous equations

$$P_p = .6P_p + .2(1.0 - P_p)$$
$$P_p = .6P_p + .2 - .2P_p$$
$$P_p = .2 + .4P_p$$
$$.6P_p = .2$$
$$P_p = .2/.6 = .33$$

and

$$N_p = 1.0 - P_p$$
$$N_p = 1.0 - .33$$
$$N_p = .67$$

These are the steady-state probabilities we computed in our previous analysis:

Steady-state probabilities using algebraic computations

$$[P_p \quad N_p] = [.33 \quad .67]$$

Application of the Steady-State Probabilities

The steady-state probabilities indicate not only the probability of a customer's trading at a particular service station in the long-term future, but also the *percentage of customers* who will trade at a service station during any given month in the long run. For example, if there are 3,000 customers in the community who purchase gasoline, then in the long run the following *expected* number will purchase gasoline at each station on a monthly basis.

Determining the number of customers that will trade at each station in future months

Petroco: $P_p(3,000) = .33(3,000)$
                            = 990 customers
National: $N_p(3,000) = .67(3,000)$
                            = 2,010 customers

Now suppose that Petroco has decided it is getting less than a reasonable share of the market and would like to increase its market share. In order to accomplish this objective, Petroco has improved

Altering the transition probabilities

its service substantially, and a survey indicates that the transition probabilities have changed to those shown below.

$$T = \begin{array}{c} \\ \text{Petroco} \\ \text{National} \end{array} \begin{array}{cc} \text{Petroco} & \text{National} \\ \begin{bmatrix} .70 & .30 \\ .20 & .80 \end{bmatrix} \end{array}$$

In other words, the improved service has resulted in a smaller probability (.30) that customers who traded initially at Petroco will switch to National the next month.

Recomputing the steady-state probabilities

Now we will recompute the steady-state probabilities based on this new transition matrix.

$$[P_p \quad N_p] = [P_p \quad N_p]\begin{bmatrix} .70 & .30 \\ .20 & .80 \end{bmatrix}$$
$$P_p = .7P_p + .2N_p$$
$$N_p = .3P_p + .8N_p$$

Solving simultaneous equations

Using the first equation and the fact that $N_p = 1.0 - P_p$, we have

$$P_p = .7P_p + .2(1.0 - P_p)$$
$$P_p = .7P_p + .2 - .2P_p$$
$$.5P_p = .2$$
$$P_p = .2/.5 = .4$$

and thus,

$$N_p = 1 - P_p$$
$$N_p = 1 - .4$$
$$N_p = .6$$

This means that out of the 3,000 customers, Petroco will now get 1,200 customers (i.e., $.40 \times 3,000$) in any given month in the long run. Thus, improvement in service will result in an increase of 210 customers per month (if the new transition probabilities remain constant for a long period of time in the future). In this situation Petroco must evaluate the trade-off between the cost of the improved service and the increase in profit from the additional 210 customers. For example, if the improved service costs $1,000 per month, then the extra 210 customers must generate an increase in profit greater than $1,000 to justify the decision to improve service.

A trade-off between costs of improved service and profit from more customers

Markov analysis results in information, not decisions

This brief example demonstrates the usefulness of Markov analysis for decision making. Although Markov analysis will not yield a recommended decision (i.e., a solution), it will provide information that will help the decision maker to make the decision.

Computerized Determination of Steady States

A number of management science software packages, including Micro Manager, QSB+ (see Chap. 3), and Microcomputer Software for

Quantitative Analysis for Management (see Chap. 4), are capable of performing Markov analysis on a personal computer. Such software and computing capabilities are extremely beneficial when the dimensions of the transition matrix exceed two states. The algebraic computations required to determine steady-state probabilities for a transition matrix with even three states are lengthy; for a matrix with more than three states, computing capabilities are a necessity. Markov analysis on the computer will be demonstrated using the service station example in this section and the Microcomputer Software package.

The following computer output generated by Microcomputer Software shows the data entered and the ultimate steady-state probabilities, referred to as "equilibrium states," for our example ("state 1" refers to Petroco and "state 2" is National).

```
                       *** MARKET SHARE ANALYSIS ***

                          -- PROGRAM OUTPUT --

      DATA ENTERED:

      PROBLEM TITLE            =  Gasoline Service Stations
      NUMBER OF STATES         =  2
      EARLIEST DESIRED PERIOD  =  1
      LATEST DESIRED PERIOD    =  20
      STATE # 1 INITIAL SHARE  =0.3
      STATE # 2 INITIAL SHARE  =0.7

      TRANSITION MATRIX VALUES:
      ----------------------------------
      STATES:    TO      1          2
      FROM  1  |       0.60       0.40
            2  |       0.20       0.80
      ----------------------------------

      EQUILIBRIUM STATES:


               EQUILIBRIUM
      STATE    MARKET SHARE
      ---------------------
        1         0.333
        2         0.667
      ---------------------
               ***** END OF MARKET SHARE ANALYSIS *****

               ***** END OF MARKOV ANALYSIS *****
```

ADDITIONAL EXAMPLES OF MARKOV ANALYSIS

Although analyzing brand switching is probably the most popular example of Markov analysis, this technique does have other appli-

A machine
breakdown
example

cations. One prominent application relates to the breakdown of a machine or system (such as a computer system, a production operation, or an electrical system). For example, a particular production machine could be assigned the states "operating" and "breakdown." The transition probabilities could then reflect the probability of a machine's either breaking down or operating in the next time period (i.e., month, day, or year).

As an example, consider a machine having the following daily transition matrix.

$$
\begin{array}{cc}
& \textbf{Day 1} \qquad\qquad \textbf{Day 2} \\
& \text{Operate} \quad \text{Breakdown} \\
T = \begin{array}{c} \text{Operate} \\ \text{Breakdown} \end{array} & \begin{bmatrix} .90 & .10 \\ .70 & .30 \end{bmatrix}
\end{array}
$$

Steady-state probabilities for the breakdown example

The steady-state probabilities for this example are

.88 = steady-state probability of the machine's operating
.12 = steady-state probability of the machine's breaking down

The cost of increased maintenance vs. profit from increased output

Now if management decide that the long-run probability of .12 for a breakdown is excessive, they might consider increasing preventive maintenance, which would change the transition matrix for this example. The decision to increase maintenance would be based on the cost of the increase versus the value of the increased production output gained from having fewer breakdowns.

An example with three states

Thus far in our discussion of Markov analysis, we have considered only examples that consisted of two states. This was partially a matter of convenience, since 2 × 2 matrices are easier to work with than matrices of a higher magnitude. However, examples that contain a larger number of states are analyzed in the same way as our previous examples. For example, consider the Carry-All Rental Truck Firm, which serves three states—Virginia, North Carolina, and Maryland. Trucks are rented on a daily basis and can be rented and returned in any of the three states. The transition matrix for this example is

$$
\begin{array}{cc}
& \textbf{Rented} \qquad\qquad\qquad \textbf{Returned} \\
& \text{Virginia} \quad \text{Maryland} \quad \text{North Carolina} \\
T = \begin{array}{c} \text{Virginia} \\ \text{Maryland} \\ \text{North Carolina} \end{array} & \begin{bmatrix} .60 & .20 & .20 \\ .30 & .50 & .20 \\ .40 & .10 & .50 \end{bmatrix}
\end{array}
$$

The steady-state probabilities for this example are determined using the same approach presented earlier, although the mathematical steps are more lengthy and complex.

The steady-state probabilities for this example are

$$
\begin{array}{ccc}
\text{Virginia} & \text{Maryland} & \text{North Carolina} \\
[.471 & .244 & .285]
\end{array}
$$

Thus, in the long run, these percentages of Carry-All trucks will end up in the three states. If the company had 200 trucks, then it could expect to have the following number of trucks available in each state at any time in the future.

Virginia	Maryland	North Carolina
[94	49	57]

SPECIAL TYPES OF TRANSITION MATRICES

In some cases the transition matrix derived from a Markov problem is not in the same form as those in the examples shown in this chapter. Some matrices have certain characteristics that alter the normal methods of Markov analysis. Although a detailed analysis of these special cases is beyond the scope of this chapter, we will give examples of them so that they can be easily recognized.

In the transition matrix

$$
T = \begin{array}{c c} & \begin{array}{c c c} 1 & 2 & 3 \end{array} \\ \begin{array}{c} 1 \\ 2 \\ 3 \end{array} & \begin{bmatrix} .40 & .60 & 0 \\ .30 & .70 & 0 \\ 1.0 & 0 & 0 \end{bmatrix} \end{array}
$$

state 3 is a *transient* state. Once state 3 is achieved, the system will never return to that state. Both states 1 and 2 contain a 0.0 probability of going to state 3. The system will move out of state 3 to state 1 (with a 1.0 probability), but will never return to state 3.

A transient state

The following transition matrix is referred to as *cyclic*.

A cyclic transition matrix

$$
T = \begin{array}{c c} & \begin{array}{c c} 1 & 2 \end{array} \\ \begin{array}{c} 1 \\ 2 \end{array} & \begin{bmatrix} 0 & 1.0 \\ 1.0 & 0 \end{bmatrix} \end{array}
$$

The system will simply cycle back and forth between states 1 and 2 without ever moving out of the cycle.

Finally, consider the following transition matrix for states 1, 2, and 3.

$$
T = \begin{array}{c c} & \begin{array}{c c c} 1 & 2 & 3 \end{array} \\ \begin{array}{c} 1 \\ 2 \\ 3 \end{array} & \begin{bmatrix} .30 & .60 & .10 \\ .40 & .40 & .20 \\ 0.0 & 0 & 1.0 \end{bmatrix} \end{array}
$$

State 3 in this transition matrix is referred to as an *absorbing* or trapping state. Once state 3 is achieved, there is a 1.0 probability that it will be achieved in succeeding time periods. Thus, the system in effect ends once state 3 is achieved. There is no movement from an absorbing state; the item is trapped in that state.

An absorbing state

The Debt Example

The bad debt example

A unique and popular application of an absorbing state matrix is the bad debt example. In this example, the states are the months during which a customer carries a debt. The customer may pay the debt (i.e., a bill) at any time and thus achieve an absorbing state for payment. However, if the customer carries the debt longer than a specified number of periods (say, two months), the debt will be labeled "bad" and will be transferred to a bill collector. The state "bad debt" is also an absorbing state. Through various matrix manipulations, the portion of accounts receivable that will be paid and the portion that will become bad debts can be determined. (Because of these matrix manipulations, the debt example is somewhat more complex than the Markov examples presented previously.)

The debt example will be demonstrated using the following transition matrix, which describes the accounts receivable for the A to Z Office Supply Company.

$$
T = \begin{array}{c} \\ p \\ 1 \\ 2 \\ b \end{array}
\begin{array}{c} \begin{array}{cccc} p & 1 & 2 & b \end{array} \\
\left[\begin{array}{cccc}
1 & 0 & 0 & 0 \\
.70 & 0 & .30 & 0 \\
.50 & 0 & 0 & .50 \\
0 & 0 & 0 & 1
\end{array} \right] \end{array}
$$

An absorbing state matrix

In this absorbing state transition matrix, state p indicates that a debt is paid, states 1 and 2 indicate that a debt is one or two months old, respectively, and state b indicates that a debt becomes bad. Notice that once a debt is paid (i.e., once the item enters state p), then the probability of moving to state 1, 2, or b is zero. If the debt is one month old, there is a .70 probability that it will be paid in the next month and a .30 probability that it will go to month 2 unpaid. If the debt is in month 2, there is a .50 probability that it will be paid and a .50 probability that it will become a bad debt in the next time period. Finally, if the debt is bad, there is a zero probability that it will return to any previous state.

Subdividing the matrix

The next step in analyzing this Markov problem is to rearrange the transition matrix into the following form.

$$
T = \begin{array}{c} \\ p \\ b \\ 1 \\ 2 \end{array}
\begin{array}{c} \begin{array}{cccc} p & b & 1 & 2 \end{array} \\
\left[\begin{array}{cc|cc}
1 & 0 & 0 & 0 \\
0 & 1 & 0 & 0 \\ \hline
.70 & 0 & 0 & .30 \\
.50 & .50 & 0 & 0
\end{array} \right] \end{array}
$$

We have now divided the transition matrix into four parts, or submatrices, which we will label as follows.

$$
T = \left[\begin{array}{c|c} I & 0 \\ \hline R & Q \end{array} \right]
$$

where

$$I = \begin{matrix} P \\ b \end{matrix} \overset{p \quad b}{\begin{bmatrix} 1 & 0 \\ 0 & 1 \end{bmatrix}} = \text{an identity matrix}$$

$$0 = \begin{matrix} P \\ b \end{matrix} \overset{1 \quad 2}{\begin{bmatrix} 0 & 0 \\ 0 & 0 \end{bmatrix}} = \text{a matrix of zeros}$$

$$R = \begin{matrix} 1 \\ 2 \end{matrix} \overset{p \quad b}{\begin{bmatrix} .70 & 0 \\ .50 & .50 \end{bmatrix}} = \begin{array}{l} \text{a matrix containing the transition} \\ \text{probabilities of the debt's being absorbed in the} \\ \text{next period} \end{array}$$

$$Q = \begin{matrix} 1 \\ 2 \end{matrix} \overset{1 \quad 2}{\begin{bmatrix} 0 & .30 \\ 0 & 0 \end{bmatrix}} = \begin{array}{l} \text{a matrix containing the transition} \\ \text{probabilities for movement between both} \\ \text{nonabsorbing states} \end{array}$$

The matrix labeled I is an *identity matrix,* so called because it has ones along the diagonal and zeros elsewhere in the matrix.

    The first matrix operation to be performed determines the *fundamental matrix* Γ, as follows.

$$F = (I - Q)^{-1}$$

The notation to raise the $(I - Q)$ matrix to the -1 power indicates what is referred to as the *inverse* of a matrix. The fundamental matrix is computed by taking the inverse of the difference between the identity matrix, I, and Q. (The computation for taking the inverse of a 2 × 2 matrix is described in Appendix B.) For our example, the fundamental matrix is computed as follows.

$$F = \left(\begin{bmatrix} 1 & 0 \\ 0 & 1 \end{bmatrix} - \begin{bmatrix} 0 & .30 \\ 0 & 0 \end{bmatrix} \right)^{-1}$$

$$F = \begin{bmatrix} 1 & -.30 \\ 0 & 1 \end{bmatrix}^{-1}$$

$$F = \begin{matrix} 1 \\ 2 \end{matrix} \overset{1 \quad 2}{\begin{bmatrix} 1 & .30 \\ 0 & 1 \end{bmatrix}}$$

    The fundamental matrix indicates the expected number of times the system will be in any of the nonabsorbing states before absorption occurs (for our example, before a debt becomes bad or is paid). Thus, according to F, if the customer is in state 1 (one month late in paying the debt), the expected number of times the customer would be two months late would be .30 before the debt is paid or becomes bad.

The identity matrix

The fundamental matrix

The inverse of a matrix

Next we will multiply the fundamental matrix by the R matrix created when the original transition matrix was partitioned.

$$
F \cdot R = \begin{array}{c} \\ 1 \\ 2 \end{array}\begin{array}{cc} 1 & 2 \\ \begin{bmatrix} 1 & .30 \\ 0 & 1 \end{bmatrix} \end{array} \cdot \begin{array}{c} \\ 1 \\ 2 \end{array}\begin{array}{cc} p & b \\ \begin{bmatrix} .70 & 0 \\ .50 & .50 \end{bmatrix} \end{array}
$$

$$
F \cdot R = \begin{array}{c} \\ 1 \\ 2 \end{array}\begin{array}{cc} p & b \\ \begin{bmatrix} .85 & .15 \\ .50 & .50 \end{bmatrix} \end{array}
$$

The probability a debt will be absorbed given any starting state

The $F \cdot R$ matrix reflects the probability that the debt will eventually be absorbed given any starting state. For example, if the debt is presently in the first month, there is an .85 probability that it will eventually be paid and a .15 probability that it will result in a bad debt.

Now, suppose the A to Z Office Supply Company has accounts receivable of $4,000 in month 1 and $6,000 in month 2. To determine what portion of these funds will be collected and what portion will result in bad debts, we multiply a matrix of these dollar amounts by the $F \cdot R$ matrix.

Accounts receivable

$$
\text{Determination of accounts} = \begin{bmatrix} 4,000 & 6,000 \end{bmatrix} \cdot \begin{array}{c} \\ 1 \\ 2 \end{array}\begin{array}{cc} p & b \\ \begin{bmatrix} .85 & .15 \\ .50 & .50 \end{bmatrix} \end{array}
$$

$$
= \begin{array}{cc} p & b \\ \begin{bmatrix} 6,400 & 3,600 \end{bmatrix} \end{array}
$$

Thus, of the total $10,000 owed, the office supply company can expect to receive $6,400, and $3,600 will become bad debts. The debt example can be analyzed even further than we have done here, although the mathematics become increasingly difficult. Several of the references listed at the end of this chapter contain extensive examples of the debt problem.

APPLICATIONS OF MARKOV ANALYSIS

A Highway Pavement System

The Highway Division of the Arizona Department of Transportation has responsibility for the maintenance of a highway network 7,400 miles long. In the mid 1970s, maintenance costs increased dramatically because of the rising costs of petroleum-based road surfacing materials. In 1975, $25 million was allocated for pavement preservation, and by 1979 allocations for this purpose had increased to $52 million. Because of the limited sources of highway maintenance funds, the Department of Transportation became increasingly concerned about the inflation of road maintenance costs. It had become imperative that a decision-making technique be developed to assist the Department in maintaining the roads in the most desirable condition possible with its allocated budget.

A Markov-based decision model was developed to solve this problem. The states of the Markov model were defined as a combination of the variables relevant to evaluating pavement condition and the maintenance that could be performed given these conditions. For example, a Markov state might indicate a level of pavement roughness and cracking for one mile of road, and the preservation action might be to resurface with a certain number of inches of asphalt. The transition probabilities specified the probability that one mile of pavement would move from one state to another in one year (the frequency of inspection) if a particular preservation action were taken at the present time. Developing a preservation policy for the entire highway network required the determination of an action for each state in each time period.

During the first year of implementation, the Markov-based system saved $14 million in preservation funds. (These large savings were achieved because the model enabled the highway division to apply preventive measures rather than concentrate on corrective measures as it had done in the past, and because the corrective measures that were applied tended to be more appropriate to a particular problem than uniformly applied corrective measures had been.) Using the model, the Highway Division further estimated that a surplus of $75.8 million would be achieved between 1982 and 1987 that could be applied to other highway construction projects. The model also enabled the Department of Transportation to reorganize and formalize its decision-making process for pavement management.[1]

Graduate Student Admissions

The Department of Educational Administration at the University of Texas at Austin admitted students to its doctoral program without any enrollment limitations or policy. Enrollment was primarily a function of recruiting success and funds available to support graduate students. However, enrollment trends changed when the department expanded to encompass two new programs and acquired a major foundation grant. In addition, the public school work force appeared to be changing, a factor that could affect student recruiting and shift students away from jobs in public schools and into doctoral programs. Because of these changes, the department wanted to

---

[1]K. Golabi et al., "A Statewide Pavement Management System," *Interfaces* 12, no. 6 (December 1982): 5–21.

know if the number of students admitted would create an undesirable dissertation load for supervising professors in the future.

A Markov model was developed to help determine the answer to this question. The model consisted of five states, including one absorbing state for graduation. (An absorbing state for forced withdrawal and no return was not included, since historical data showed a low incidence of this occurrence.) The remaining four states were "enrolled," "withdrawn," "advanced to doctoral candidacy," and "not advanced." Transition probabilities defined the probability of a student's moving from state to state during a semester. The Markov analysis indicated the mean number of semesters that a student in the doctoral program would be in a given state prior to graduation. It was determined that a small increase in student enrollment (i.e., two students) had a significant impact on faculty loads at the dissertation stage. However, the lead time provided by the analysis enabled the department to control the effects of adding students. The analysis further led to a set of decision rules that specified the maximum average number of dissertations per faculty member; the faculty positions required before new programs could be accepted; and the amount of time it would take for imbalances in dissertation load to develop if the number of faculty members decreased.[2]

Forecasting Kidney Dialysis Treatment

The alternative treatments for irreversible kidney malfunction are dialysis and transplantation, with dialysis being the more costly of the treatments. A crucial planning problem associated with kidney disease is to ensure that enough dialysis facilities are available to meet demand without overcommitting resources. The primary means of controlling the supply and distribution of dialysis treatment is the Determination of Need Program (DON), mandated by Congress to contain rising health care costs. In order to implement this program, the Massachusetts Department of Health developed a Markov-based forecasting model for determining the location and number of treatment resources needed in the future. A five-state, one-year transition model was developed, with states being ongoing dialysis treatment, three categories of kidney transplant, and death. A two-year cost savings in excess of $5.1 million was achieved when the model was implemented.[3] A subsequent study validated the model's accuracy.[4]

---

[2]E. Bessent and A. Bessent, "Student Flow in a University Department: Results of a Markov Analysis," *Interfaces* 10, no. 2 (April 1980): 52–59.

[3]J. Pliskin and E. Tell, "Using a Dialysis Need-Protection Model for Health Planning in Massachusetts," *Interfaces* 11, no. 6 (December 1981): 84–100.

[4]J. Pliskin and E. Tell, "Health Planning in Massachusetts: Revisited After Four Years," *Interfaces* 16, no. 2 (March–April 1986): 72–74.

Summary

This chapter presented an overview of an interesting and some-times useful *probabilistic* technique, Markov analysis. It demonstrated one of the most popular applications of Markov analysis, brand switching, and indicated other potential areas of application. However, realistic applications of Markov analysis have been somewhat limited. This is due in large part to the difficulty of finding decision problems that meet all the properties necessary for Markov analysis, especially the requirement for transition probabilities that are constant over time.

Markov analysis is useful for our purposes because it demonstrates a technique that does not result in a recommended decision in the form of an optimal solution. Instead, the analysis results in descriptive information that can help a decision maker make a decision. This same characteristic is exhibited by the topics presented in the next two chapters on queuing and simulation.

References

Bessent, E., and Bessent, A. "Student Flow in a University Department: Results of a Markov Analysis." *Interfaces* 10, no. 2 (April 1980): 52–59.

Feller, W. *An Introduction to Probability Theory and Its Applications.* Vol. I. 3d ed. New York: John Wiley and Sons, 1968.

Golabi, K.; Kulkarni, R.; and Way, G. "A State Pavement Management System." *Interfaces* 12, no. 6 (December 1982): 5–21.

Howard, R. A. *Dynamic Programming and Markov Processes.* Cambridge, Mass.: M.I.T. Press, 1960.

Kemeny, J. G., and Snell, J. L. *Finite Markov Chains.* Princeton, N.J.: D. Van Nostrand Company, 1960.

Parzen, E. *Stochastic Processes.* San Francisco: Holden-Day, 1962.

Searle, S. R., and Hausman, W. H. *Matrix Algebra for Business and Economics.* New York: John Wiley and Sons, 1970.

EXAMPLE PROBLEM SOLUTION

The following example problem will illustrate Markov analysis as a prelude to the problems in the next section.

Problem Statement

Westvale is a small rural community in Maine. Because it is far away from any other town, Westvale's 7,000 bank patrons do virtually all of their banking and financial business at the two banks in the town, the American National Bank and the Bank of Westvale. The Bank of Westvale is considering a marketing campaign centered around the addition of several new services and the payment of higher interest rates for savings accounts. In preparation for this campaign, the bank's marketing department performed a survey and found that if a customer traded with the Bank of Westvale in any given month there was a .70 probability that the customer would trade with that bank the next month, and a .30 probability that the customer would trade with American National the next month. Also, if a customer traded with American National in a given month, there was an .85 probability that the customer would trade with American National in the next month and a .15 probability that the customer would move to the Bank of Westvale.

Set up the transition probability matrix for this problem, determine the steady-state probabilities, and indicate the number of customers that each bank can anticipate in the long run.

Step 1: Set Up the Transition Matrix

$$T = \begin{matrix} & & \textbf{Next Month} & \\ \textbf{First Month} & \text{American National} & \text{Bank of Westvale} \\ \text{American National} & .85 & .15 \\ \text{Bank of Westvale} & .30 & .70 \end{matrix}$$

Step 2: Determine the Steady-State Probabilities

$$A = \text{American National Bank}$$
$$B = \text{Bank of Westvale}$$

$$[A \quad B] = [A \quad B]\begin{bmatrix} .85 & .15 \\ .30 & .70 \end{bmatrix}$$

The matrix operations are as follows:

$$A = .85A + .30B$$
$$B = .15A + .70B$$

and

$$A + B = 1.0$$

or

$$B = 1.0 - A$$

Substitution yields

$$\begin{aligned} A &= .85A + .30(1.0 - A) \\ &= .85A + .30 - .30A \\ &= .30 + .55A \\ &= .667 \end{aligned}$$

and

$$\begin{aligned} B &= 1.0 - A \\ &= .333 \end{aligned}$$

Thus, the steady-state probabilities are

$$[A \quad B] = [.667 \quad .333]$$

Step 3: Determine the Number of Customers for Each Bank

American National Bank: $A(7,000) = (.667)(7,000)$
$$= 4,669 \text{ customers}$$
Bank of Westvale: $B(7,000) = (.333)(7,000)$
$$= 2,331 \text{ customers}$$

Problems

1. Given two products, A and B, the following table describes the probabilities of a customer's changing products or purchasing the same product in a future period.

	Next Period	
This Period	**A**	**B**
A	.5	.5
B	.6	.4

   Using decision trees, determine the probabilities that a customer will purchase product A or B in period 3 in the future, given that the customer purchased A or B in the present period. Summarize the resulting probabilities in a table.

2. Given the transition matrix

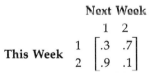

   use decision trees to determine the probabilities of being in each state in week 3 in the future, given each starting state. Summarize the resulting probabilities in a table.

3. A town has three gasoline stations, Petroco, National, and Gascorp. The residents purchase gasoline on a monthly basis. The following transition matrix contains the probabilities of the customers' purchasing a given brand of gasoline next month.

		Next Month		
		Petroco	National	Gascorp
	Petroco	.5	.3	.2
This Month	National	.1	.7	.2
	Gascorp	.1	.1	.8

Using a decision tree, determine the probabilities of a customer's purchasing each brand of gasoline in month 3, given that the customer purchases National in the present month. Summarize the resulting probabilities in a table.

4. Discuss the properties that must exist for the transition matrix in problem 3 to be considered a Markov process.

5. The only grocery store in a community stocks milk from two dairies—Creamwood and Cheesedale. The following transition matrix shows the probabilities of a customer's purchasing each brand of milk next week given that she purchased a particular brand this week.

Next Week

		Creamwood	Cheesedale
This Week	Creamwood	.7	.3
	Cheesedale	.4	.6

Given that a customer purchases Creamwood milk this week, use a decision tree to determine the probability that she will purchase Cheesedale milk in week 4.

6. Determine the state probabilities for period 3 in problem 1 using matrix multiplication methods.

7. Determine the state probabilities for week 3 in problem 2 using matrix multiplication methods.

8. Given the transition matrix in problem 3, use matrix multiplication methods to determine the state probabilities for month 3, given that a customer initially purchases Petroco gasoline.

9. Determine the state probabilities in problem 5 using matrix multiplication methods.

10. A manufacturing firm has developed a transition matrix containing the probabilities that a particular machine will operate or break down in the following week, given its operating condition in the present week.

Next Week

		Operate	Breakdown
This Week	Operate	.4	.6
	Breakdown	.8	.2

a. Assuming that the machine is operating in week 1, determine the probabilities that the machine will operate or break down in week 2, week 3, week 4, week 5, and week 6.
b. Determine the steady-state probabilities for this transition matrix algebraically, and indicate the percentage of future weeks in which the machine will break down.

11. A city is served by two newspapers—the *Tribune* and the *Daily News*. Each Sunday reader purchases one of the newspapers at a stand. The following transition matrix contains the probabilities of a customer's buying a particular newspaper in a week, given the newspaper purchased the previous Sunday.

Next Sunday

		Tribune	Daily News
This Sunday	Tribune	.65	.35
	Daily News	.45	.55

Determine the steady-state probabilities for this transition matrix algebraically and explain what they mean.

12. The Hergeshiemer Department Store wants to analyze the payment behavior of customers who have outstanding accounts. The store's credit department has determined the following bill payment pattern for credit customers from historical records.

Next Month

		Pay	Not Pay
Present Month	Pay	.9	.1
	Not Pay	.8	.2

a. If a customer did not pay his bill in the present month, what is the probability that the bill will not be paid in any of the next three months?

b. Determine the steady state probabilities for this transition matrix and explain what they mean.

13. Define what a "steady state" means in a Markov process.

14. Discuss how Markov analysis can be used for decision making, since it is not considered an optimization technique.

15. A rural community has two television stations, and each Wednesday night the local viewers watch either the "Wednesday Movie" or a show called "Western Times." The following transition matrix contains the probabilities of a viewer's watching one of the shows in a week, given that she had watched a particular show the preceding week.

Next Week

		Movie	Western
This Week	Movie	.75	.25
	Western	.45	.55

a. Determine the steady-state probabilities for this transition matrix algebraically.

b. If the community contains 1,200 television sets, how many will be tuned to each show in the long run?

c. If a prospective local sponsor wanted to pay for commercial time on one of the shows, which show would more likely be selected?

16. In problem 5, assume that 600 gallons of milk are sold weekly, regardless of the brand purchased.

   a. How many gallons of each brand of milk will be purchased in any given week in the long run?
   b. The Cheesedale dairy is considering paying $500 per week for a new advertising campaign that would alter the brand switching probabilities as follows.

		Next Week	
		Creamwood	Cheesedale
This Week	Creamwood	.6	.4
	Cheesedale	.2	.8

   If each gallon of milk sold results in $1.00 in profit for Cheesedale, should the dairy institute the advertising campaign?

17. The manufacturing company in problem 10 is considering a preventive maintenance program that would change the operating probabilities as follows.

		Next Week	
		Operate	Breakdown
This Week	Operate	.7	.3
	Breakdown	.9	.1

The machine earns the company $1,000 in profit each week it operates. The preventive maintenance program would cost $8,000 per year. Should the company institute the preventive maintenance program?

18. In problem 11, assume that 20,000 newspapers are sold each Sunday regardless of the publisher.

   a. How many copies of the *Tribune* and the *Daily News* will be purchased in a given week in the long run?
   b. The *Daily News* is considering a promotional campaign estimated to change the weekly reader probabilities as follows.

		Next Week	
		Tribune	Daily News
This Week	*Tribune*	.5	.5
	Daily News	.3	.7

   The promotional campaign will cost $150 per week. Each newspaper sold earns the *Daily News* $.05 in profit. Should the paper adopt the promotional campaign?

19. Explain the difference between an *absorbing* state and a *transient* state.

20. Determine the steady-state probabilities for the transition matrix in problem 3.

21. The following transition matrix describes the accounts receivable process for the Ewing-Barnes Department Store.

$$
T = \begin{array}{c}
 \\ p \\ 1 \\ 2 \\ b
\end{array}
\begin{array}{cccc}
p & 1 & 2 & b \\
\left[\begin{array}{cccc}
1 & 0 & 0 & 0 \\
.80 & 0 & .20 & 0 \\
.40 & 0 & 0 & .60 \\
0 & 0 & 0 & 0
\end{array}\right]
\end{array}
$$

The states p and b represent an account that is paid and a bad account, respectively. The numbers 1 and 2 represent the fact that an account is either one or two months overdue. After an account has been overdue for two months, it becomes a bad account and is transferred to the store's overdue accounts section for collection. The company has sales of $210,000 each month. Determine how much the company will be paid and how many of the debts will become bad debts in a two month period.

22. The department store in problem 21 will never be able to collect 20% of the bad accounts, and it costs the store an additional $.10 per dollar collected to collect the remaining bad accounts. The store management is contemplating a new more restrictive credit plan that would reduce sales to an estimated $195,000 per month. However, the tougher credit plan would result in the following transition matrix for accounts receivable.

$$
T = \begin{array}{c}
 \\ p \\ 1 \\ 2 \\ b
\end{array}
\begin{array}{cccc}
p & 1 & 2 & b \\
\left[\begin{array}{cccc}
1 & 0 & 0 & 0 \\
.90 & 0 & .10 & 0 \\
.70 & 0 & 0 & .30 \\
0 & 0 & 0 & 1
\end{array}\right]
\end{array}
$$

Determine whether the store should adopt the more restrictive credit plan or keep the existing one.

The following problems encompass transition matrices with three states, and should only be attempted if you have access to a software package that has the capability to perform Markov analysis.

23. In Westvale, a small rural town in Maine, virtually all shopping and business is done in the town. The town has one farm and garden center that sells fertilizer to the local farmers and gardeners. The center carries three brands of fertilizer—Plant Plus, Crop Extra, and Gro-fast—so every person in the town who uses fertilizer uses one of the three brands. The garden center has 9,000 customers for fertilizer each spring. An extensive market research study has determined that customers switch brands of fertilizer according to the following probability transition matrix.

Next Spring

		Plant Plus	Crop Extra	Gro-fast
	Plant Plus	.4	.3	.3
This Spring	Crop Extra	.5	.1	.4
	Gro-fast	.4	.2	.4

The number of customers presently using each brand of fertilizer is shown below.

Fertilizer Brand	Customers
Plant Plus	3,000
Crop Extra	4,000
Gro-fast	2,000

a. Determine the steady-state probabilities for the fertilizer brands.
b. Forecast the customer demand for each brand of fertilizer in the long run and the changes in customer demand.

24. Alter the scenario of the "Example Problem" so that there is now a third bank in Westvale, the Commerce Union Bank, and a new transition matrix, as follows:

Next Month

		A	B	C
	A	.80	.10	.10
Present Month	B	.10	.70	.20
	C	.10	.30	.60

Determine the steady-state probabilities and the number of customers expected to trade at each bank in the long run.

25. Students switch among the various colleges of a university according to the following probability transition matrix.

Next Fall

		Engineering	Liberal Arts	Business
	Engineering	.50	.30	.20
This Fall	Liberal Arts	.10	.70	.20
	Business	.10	.10	.80

Assume that the number of students in each college of the university at the beginning of the fall quarter is as follows:

Engineering	3,000
Liberal Arts	5,000
Business	2,000

a. Forecast the number of students in each college after the end of the third quarter, based on a four-quarter system.
b. Determine the steady-state conditions for the university.

26. The Hartz rental firm in the Southeast serves three states—Virginia, North Carolina, and Maryland. The firm has 700 trucks that are rented on a weekly basis and can be rented in any of the three states. The transition matrix for the movement of rental trucks from state to state is as follows:

Week $n + 1$

		Virginia	North Carolina	Maryland
	Virginia	.30	.50	.20
Week n	North Carolina	.60	.20	.20
	Maryland	.40	.10	.50

Determine the steady-state probabilities and the number of trucks in each state in the long run.

27. Klecko's Copy Center uses several copy machines that deteriorate rather rapidly in terms of the quality of copies produced as the volume of copies increases. Each machine is examined at the end of each day to determine the quality of the copies being produced, and the results of that inspection are classified as follows:

Classification	Copy Quality	Maintenance Cost per Day
1	Excellent	$ 0
2	Acceptable	100
3	Marginal	400
4	Unacceptable	800

The costs associated with each classification are for maintenance and repair and redoing unacceptable copies. When a machine reaches classification 4 and copies are unacceptable, major maintenance is required (resulting in downtime), after which the machine resumes making excellent copies. The transition matrix showing the probabilities of a machine's being in a particular classification state after inspection is as follows:

Day Two

		1	2	3	4
	1	0	.8	.1	.1
Day One	2	0	.6	.2	.2
	3	0	0	.5	.5
	4	1	0	0	0

Determine the expected daily cost of machine maintenance.

14

Queuing Analysis

Waiting in queues—waiting lines—is one of the most common occurrences in everyone's life. Anyone who has gone shopping or to a movie has experienced the inconvenience of waiting in line to make purchases or buy a ticket. Not only do people spend a significant portion of their time waiting in lines, but products queue up in production plants, machinery waits in line to be serviced, and so on. Since time is a valuable resource, the reduction of waiting time is an important topic of analysis.

Waiting lines

Like decision analysis and Markov analysis, queuing analysis is a probabilistic form of analysis, not a deterministic technique. Thus the results of queuing analysis, referred to as "operating characteristics," are probabilistic. These operating statistics (such as the average time a person must wait in line to be served) are used by the manager of the operation containing the queue to make decisions.

A probabilistic form of analysis

A number of different queuing models exist to deal with different queuing systems. We will eventually discuss many of these queuing variations, but we will concentrate on two of the most common types of systems—the single-server system and the multiple-server system.

THE SINGLE-SERVER WAITING LINE SYSTEM

The single server with a single waiting line is the simplest form of queuing system. As such, it will be used to demonstrate the fundamentals of a queuing system. As an example of this kind of system, consider the Fast Shop Drive-In Market.

A queuing example

Server

Queue

The Fast Shop Market has one checkout counter and one employee who operates the cash register at the checkout counter. The combination of the cash register and the operator is the *server* (or service facility) in this queuing system; the customers who line up at the counter to pay for their selections form the *waiting line,* or *queue.* The configuration of this example queuing system is shown in Figure 14.1.

FIGURE 14.1

The Fast Shop Market Queuing System

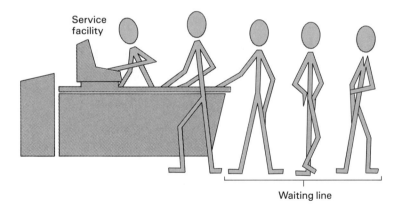

The most important factors to consider in analyzing a queuing system such as the one in Figure 14.1 are

1. The queue discipline (in what order customers are served)
2. The nature of the calling population (where customers come from)
3. The arrival rate (how often customers arrive at the queue)
4. The service rate (how fast customers are served)

We will discuss each of these items as it relates to our example.

The Queue Discipline

The *queue discipline* is the order in which waiting customers are served. Customers at the Fast Shop Market are served on a "first come, first served" basis. That is, the first person in line at the checkout counter is served first. This is the most common type of queue discipline. However, other disciplines are possible. For example, a machine operator might stack in-process parts beside a machine so that the last part is on top of the stack and will be selected first. This queue discipline would be referred to as "last in, first out." Or, the machine operator might simply reach into a box full of parts and select one at random. In this case the queue discipline is random. Often customers are scheduled for service according to a predetermined appointment, such as patients at a doctor's or dentist's office or diners at a restaurant where reservations are required. In this case the customers are taken according to a prearranged schedule regardless of when they arrive at the facility. One final example of the many types of queue disciplines is when customers are processed alphabetically according to their last names, such as at school registration or at job interviews.

The order in which customers are served

The Calling Population

The *calling population* is the source of the customers to the market, which in this case is assumed to be infinite. In other words, there is such a large number of possible customers in the area where the store is located that the number of potential customers is assumed to be infinite. Some queuing systems have finite calling populations. For example, the repair garage of a trucking firm that has 20 trucks has a finite calling population. The queue is the number of trucks waiting to be repaired, and the finite calling population is 20 trucks. However, queuing systems that have an assumed infinite calling population are more frequent.

Source of arrivals to the queuing system

The Arrival Rate

The *arrival rate* is the rate at which customers arrive at the service facility during a specified period of time. This rate can be estimated from empirical data derived from studying the system or a similar system, or it can be an average of these empirical data. For example, if 100 customers arrive at the store checkout counter during a 10-hour day, we could say the arrival rate averages 10 customers per hour. However, although we might be able to determine a rate for arrivals by counting the number of paying customers at the market during a 10-hour day, we would not know exactly when these customers would

The number of arrivals during a time period

arrive on the premises. In other words, it might be that no customers would arrive during one hour and 20 customers would arrive during another hour. In general, these arrivals are assumed to be independent of each other and to vary randomly over time.

Given these assumptions, it is further assumed that arrivals at a service facility conform to some probability distribution. Although arrivals could be described by any distribution, it has been determined (through years of research and the practical experience of people in the field of queuing) that the number of arrivals per unit of time at a service facility can frequently be defined by a *Poisson distribution*. (Appendix C at the end of this text contains a more detailed presentation of the Poisson distribution.)

Arrivals conform to a Poisson probability distribution

The Service Rate

The average number served during a time period

The *service rate* is the average number of customers who can be served during a specified period of time. For our Fast Shop Market example, 30 customers can be checked out (served) in one hour. A service rate is similar to an arrival rate in that it is a random variable. In other words, such factors as different sizes of customer purchases, the amount of change the cashier must count out, and different forms of payment alter the number of persons who can be served over time. Again, it is possible that only 10 customers might be checked out during one hour and 40 customers might be checked out during the following hour.

Service defined by an exponential probability distribution

The description of arrivals in terms of a *rate* and of service in terms of *time* is a convention that has developed in queuing theory. Like arrival rate, service time is assumed to be defined by a probability distribution. It has been determined by researchers in the field of queuing that service times can frequently be defined by an *exponential probability* distribution. (Appendix C at the end of this text contains a more detailed presentation of the exponential distribution.) However, in order to analyze a queuing system, both arrivals and service must be in compatible units of measure. Thus, service time must be expressed as a service rate to correspond with an arrival rate.

The Single-Server Model

Characteristics of the single-server queuing system

The Fast Shop Market checkout counter is an example of a single-server queuing system with the following characteristics.

1. An infinite calling population
2. A first come, first served queue discipline
3. Poisson arrival rate
4. Exponential service times

These assumptions have been used to develop a model of a single-server queuing system. However, the analytical derivation of even this simplest queuing model is relatively complex and lengthy. Thus, we will refrain from deriving the model in detail and will consider only the resulting queuing formulas. The reader must keep in mind, however, that these formulas are applicable only to queuing systems having the above conditions.

Given that

λ = the arrival rate (average number of arrivals per time period)
μ = the service rate (average number served per time period)

and that $\lambda < \mu$ (customers are served at a faster rate than they arrive), we can state the following formulas for the operating characteristics of a single-server model.

> The service rate exceeds the arrival rate

The probability that no customers are in the queuing system (either in the queue or being served) is

> Queuing formulas for the single-server model

$$P_0 = \left(1 - \frac{\lambda}{\mu}\right)$$

The probability that n customers are in the queuing system is

$$P_n = \left(\frac{\lambda}{\mu}\right)^n \cdot P_0$$

$$= \left(\frac{\lambda}{\mu}\right)^n \left(1 - \frac{\lambda}{\mu}\right)$$

The average number of customers in the queuing system (i.e., the customers being serviced and in the waiting line) is

$$L = \frac{\lambda}{\mu - \lambda}$$

The average number of customers in the waiting line is

$$L_q = \frac{\lambda^2}{\mu(\mu - \lambda)}$$

The average time a customer spends in the total queuing system (i.e., waiting and being served) is

$$W = \frac{1}{\mu - \lambda}$$

$$= \frac{L}{\lambda}$$

The average time a customer spends waiting in the queue to be served is

$$W_q = \frac{\lambda}{\mu(\mu - \lambda)}$$

The probability that the server is busy (i.e., the probability that a customer has to wait), known as the *utilization factor*, is

$$U = \frac{\lambda}{\mu}$$

The probability that the server is idle (i.e., the probability that a customer can be served) is

$$I = 1 - U$$
$$= 1 - \frac{\lambda}{\mu}$$

This last term, $1 - (\lambda/\mu)$, is also equal to P_0. The probability of no customers in the queuing system is the same as the probability that the server is idle.

These various operating characteristics can be computed for the Fast Shop Market by simply substituting the average arrival and service rates into the above formulas. For example, if

λ = 24 customers per hour arrive at checkout counter

μ = 30 customers per hour can be checked out

then

$$P_0 = \left(1 - \frac{\lambda}{\mu}\right)$$
$$= (1 - 24/30)$$
$$= .20 \text{ probability of no customers in the system}$$

$$L = \frac{\lambda}{\mu - \lambda}$$
$$= \frac{24}{30 - 24}$$
$$= 4 \text{ customers on the average in the queuing system}$$

$$L_q = \frac{\lambda^2}{\mu(\mu - \lambda)}$$
$$= \frac{(24)^2}{30(30 - 24)}$$
$$= 3.2 \text{ customers on the average in the waiting line}$$

Computing the operating statistics for the queuing example

$$W = \frac{1}{\mu - \lambda}$$

$$= \frac{1}{30 - 24}$$

$= .167$ hour (10 minutes) average time in the system per customer

$$W_q = \frac{\lambda}{\mu(\mu - \lambda)}$$

$$= \frac{24}{30(30 - 24)}$$

$= .133$ hour (8 minutes) average time in the waiting line per customer

$$U = \frac{\lambda}{\mu}$$

$$= \frac{24}{30}$$

$= .80$ probability that the server will be busy and the customer must wait

$$I - 1 - U$$

$$= 1 - .80$$

$= .20$ probability that the server will be idle and a customer can be served

Several important aspects of both the general model and this particular example will now be discussed in greater detail.

First, recall that the operating characteristics are averages. Also, they are assumed to be *steady-state* averages. The discussion of Markov analysis (see Chap. 13) indicated that the steady state was a constant average level that a system realized after a period of time. For a queuing system, the steady state is represented by the average operating statistics, also determined over a period of time.

Related to this condition is the fact that the utilization factor, U, must be less than 1.0:

$$U < 1$$

or

$$\frac{\lambda}{\mu} < 1.0$$

and

$$\lambda < \mu$$

In other words, the ratio of the arrival rate to the service rate must be less than one, which also means *the service rate must be*

Steady-state results

The utilization factor must be less than one

greater than the arrival rate if this model is to be used. The server must be able to serve customers faster than they come into the store, or the waiting line will grow to an infinite size and the system will never reach a steady state.

The Effect of Operating Characteristics on Managerial Decisions

Now let us consider the operating characteristics of our example as they relate to management decisions. The arrival rate of 24 customers per hour means that, on the average, a customer arrives every 2.5 minutes (i.e., $1/24 \times 60$ minutes). This indicates that the store is very busy. Because of the nature of the store, customers purchase few items and expect quick service. Customers expect to spend a relatively large amount of time in a supermarket, since typically they make larger purchases. But customers who shop at a drive-in market do so, at least in part, because it is quicker than a supermarket.

Alternatives for reducing customer waiting time

Given customers' expectations, the store's manager believes that it is unacceptable for a customer to wait 8 minutes and spend a total of 10 minutes in the queuing system (not including the actual shopping time). The manager wants to test several alternatives for reducing customer waiting time: (1) the addition of another employee to pack up the purchases and (2) the addition of an additional checkout counter.

Alternative I: The Addition of an Employee
The addition of an extra employee will cost the store manager $150 per week. With the help of the national office's marketing research group, the manager has determined that for each minute that customer waiting time is reduced, the store avoids a loss in sales of $75 per week. (That is, the store loses money when customers leave prior to shopping because of the long line, or when customers do not return.)

Increasing the service rate

If a new employee is hired, customers can be served in less time. In other words, the service rate, which is the number of customers served per time period, will *increase*. The previous service rate was

$\mu = 30$ customers served per hour

The addition of a new employee will increase the service rate to

$\mu = 40$ customers served per hour

It will be assumed that the arrival rate will remain the same ($\lambda = 24$ per hour), since the increased service rate will not increase arrivals but instead will minimize the loss of customers. (However, it is not illogical to assume that an increase in service might increase arrivals.)

Given the new λ and μ values, the operating characteristics can be recomputed as follows.

$$P_0 = \left(1 - \frac{\lambda}{\mu}\right)$$

$$= \left(1 - \frac{24}{40}\right)$$

$= .40$ probability of no customers in the system

$$L = \frac{\lambda}{\mu - \lambda}$$

$$= \frac{24}{40 - 24}$$

$= 1.5$ customers on the average in the queuing system

$$L_q = \frac{\lambda^2}{\mu(\mu - \lambda)}$$

$$= \frac{(24)^2}{40(16)}$$

$= .90$ customer on the average in the waiting line

$$W = \frac{1}{\mu - \lambda}$$

$$= \frac{1}{40 - 24}$$

$= .063$ hour (3.75 minutes) average time in the system per customer

$$W_q = \frac{\lambda}{\mu(\mu - \lambda)}$$

$$= \frac{24}{40(16)}$$

$= .038$ hour (2.25 minutes) average time in the waiting line per customer

$$U = \frac{\lambda}{\mu} = \frac{24}{40}$$

$= .60$ probability that the customer must wait

$$I = 1 - U$$

$= 1 - .60 = .40$ probability that the server will be idle and a customer can be served

Remember that these operating characteristics are *averages* that result over a period of time; they are not absolutes. In other words, customers who arrive at the Fast Shop Market checkout counter will not find .90 customer in line. There could be no customers, or 1, 2, or 3 customers, for example. The value .90 is simply an average that occurs over time, as do the other operating characteristics.

The average waiting time per customer has been reduced from 8 minutes to 2.25 minutes, a significant amount. The savings (that is, the decrease in lost sales) is computed as follows.

$$8.00 \text{ minutes} - 2.25 \text{ minutes} = 5.75 \text{ minutes}$$
$$5.75 \text{ minutes} \times \$75/\text{minute} = \$431.25$$

Since the extra employee costs management \$150 per week, the total savings will be

$$\$431.25 - \$150 = \$281.25 \text{ per week}$$

The store manager would probably welcome this savings and consider the above operating statistics preferable to the previous ones for the condition where the store had only one employee.

Alternative II: The Addition of a New Checkout Counter
Next we will consider the manager's alternative of constructing a new checkout counter. The total cost of this project would be \$6,000, plus an extra \$200 per week for an additional cashier.

The new checkout counter would be opposite the present counter (so that the servers would have their backs to each other in an enclosed counter area). There would be several display cases and racks between the two lines so that customers waiting in line would not move back and forth between the lines. (Such movement, called *jockeying*, would invalidate the queuing formulas we already developed.) We will assume that the customers would divide themselves equally between both lines, so the arrival rate for each line would be half of the prior arrival rate for a single checkout counter. Thus, the new arrival rate for each checkout counter is

$$\lambda = 12 \text{ customers per hour}$$

and the service rate remains the same for each of the counters,

$$\mu = 30 \text{ customers served per hour}$$

Substituting this new arrival rate and the service rate into our queuing formulas results in the following operating characteristics.

$P_0 = .60$ probability of no customers in the system
$L = .67$ customer in the queuing system
$L_q = .27$ customer in the waiting line
$W = .055$ hour (3.33 minutes) per customer in the system
$W_q = .022$ hour (1.33 minutes) per customer in the waiting line
$U = .40$ probability that a customer must wait
$I = .60$ probability that a server will be idle and a customer can be served

Deriving the savings
resulting from the
decreased arrival
rate

Using the same sales savings of \$75 per week for each minute's reduction in waiting time, we find that the store would save

$$8.00 \text{ minutes} - 1.33 \text{ minutes} = 6.67 \text{ minutes}$$
$$6.67 \text{ minutes} \times \$75/\text{minute} = \$500.00 \text{ per week}$$

Next we subtract the $200 per week cost for the new cashier from this amount saved.

$$\$500 - 200 = \$300$$

Since the capital outlay of this project is $6,000, it would take 20 weeks ($6,000/$300 = 20 weeks) to recoup the initial cost (ignoring the possibility of interest on the $6,000). Once the cost has been recovered, the store would save $18.75 ($300.00 − 281.25) more per week by adding a new checkout counter rather than simply hiring an extra employee. However, we must not disregard the fact that during the 20-week cost recovery period, the $281.25 savings incurred by simply hiring a new employee would be lost.

Table 14.1 presents a summary of the operating characteristics for each alternative.

Summary of the operating characteristics for each alternative

TABLE 14.1

Operating Characteristics for Each Alternative System

Operating Characteristics	Present System	Alternative I	Alternative II
L	4.00 customers	1.50 customers	.67 customer
L_q	3.20 customers	.90 customer	.27 customer
W	10.00 minutes	3.75 minutes	3.33 minutes
W_q	8.00 minutes	2.25 minutes	1.33 minutes
U	.80	.60	.40

For the store manager both of these alternatives seem preferable to the original conditions, which resulted in a lengthy waiting time of 8 minutes per customer. However, the manager might have a difficult time selecting between the two alternatives. It might be appropriate to consider other factors besides waiting time. For example, employee idle time is .40 with the first alternative and .60 with the second, which seems to be a significant difference. An additional factor is the loss of space resulting from a new checkout counter.

Decision making using the operating statistics

However, the final decision must be based on the manager's own experience and perceived needs. As we have noted previously, the results of queuing analysis provide information for decision making, but do not result in an actual recommended decision as an optimization model would.

Our two example alternatives illustrate the cost trade-offs associated with improved service. As the level of service increases, the corresponding cost of this service also increases. For example, when we added an extra employee in alternative I, the service was improved but the cost of providing service also increased. But when the level

The cost trade-offs related to improved service

of service was increased, the costs associated with customer waiting decreased. Maintaining an appropriate level of service should minimize the sum of these two costs as much as possible. This cost trade-off relationship is summarized in Figure 14.2. As the level of service increases, the cost of service goes up and the waiting cost goes down. The sum of these costs results in a total cost curve, and the level of service that should be maintained is where this total cost curve is at a minimum. (However, this does not mean we can determine an exact optimal minimum cost solution, since the service and waiting characteristics we can determine are averages, and thus uncertain.)

FIGURE 14.2

Cost Trade-offs for
Service Levels

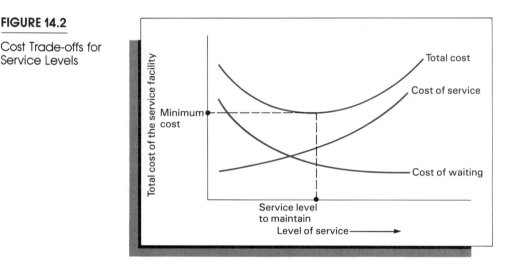

Computerized Analysis of the Single-Server System

A standard feature of most management science personal computer software packages is the capability to perform queuing analysis. The Micro Manager, Microcomputer Software for Quantitative Analysis for Management, and QSB+ packages, which have been used in different chapters in this text, all have queuing analysis capabilities. As an illustration of the computerized analysis of the single-server queuing system, we will use the Microcomputer Software package by Render and Stair to analyze the Fast Shop Market example. The model input and solution output are shown on page 499.

```
                    *** BASIC SINGLE SERVER MODEL ***

               **INPUT DATA ENTERED**

               PROBLEM TITLE: Fast Shop Market
               THE NUMBER OF CHANNELS = 1
               THE MEAN # OF ARRIVALS PER HR. = 24
               THE MEAN # OF PEOPLE OR ITEMS SERVED PER HR. = 30



          *** RESULTS *** BASIC SINGLE SERVER MODEL ***

     ------------------------------------------------------------------
     AVERAGE # OF UNITS IN THE SYSTEM =  4

     AVERAGE TIME PER UNIT SPENT IN THE SYSTEM IN HR.S
     (WAITING + SERVICE)= .1666

     AVERAGE # OF UNITS IN THE QUEUE =  3.2

     AVERAGE TIME PER UNIT SPENT WAITING IN THE QUEUE IN HR.S= .1333

     UTILIZATION RATE =  .8

     PROBABILITY THAT THE SYSTEM IS IDLE =  .1999
     ------------------------------------------------------------------

        ***END OF QUEUING ANALYSIS***
```

THE MULTIPLE-SERVER WAITING LINE

Slightly more complex than the single-server queuing system is the single waiting line being serviced by more than one server (i.e., multiple servers). As an example of this type of system, consider the customer service department of the Biggs Department Store.

The customer service department of the store has a waiting room in which chairs are placed along the wall, in effect forming a single waiting line. Customers come to this area with questions or complaints or to clarify matters regarding credit card bills. The customers are served by three store representatives, each located in a partitioned stall. Customers are treated on a first come, first served basis. Figure 14.3 presents a schematic of this queuing system.

A multiple-server system example

The store management wants to analyze this queuing system, because excessive waiting times can make customers angry enough to shop at other stores. Typically, customers who come to this area have some problem and thus are impatient anyway. Waiting a long time only serves to increase their impatience.

First the queuing formulas for a multiple-server queuing system will be presented. These formulas, like single-server model formulas, have been developed on the assumption of a *first-come, first-served queue discipline, Poisson arrivals, exponential service times,* and *an*

The characteristics of the multiple-server system

FIGURE 14.3

Customer Service
Queuing System

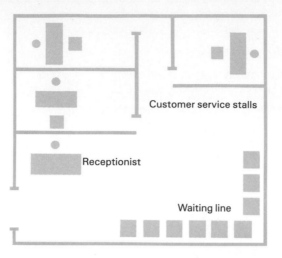

infinite calling population. The parameters of the multiple-server model are as follows.

λ = the arrival rate (average number of arrivals per time period)

μ = the service rate (average number served per time period) *per server* (channel)

c = the number of servers

$c\mu$ = the mean effective service rate for the system, which must exceed the arrival rate

The formulas for the operating characteristics of the multiple-server model are as follows.

The probability that there are no customers in the system (all servers are idle) is

Queuing formulas
for the
multiple-server
model

$$P_0 = \frac{1}{\left[\displaystyle\sum_{n=0}^{n=c-1} \frac{1}{n!}\left(\frac{\lambda}{\mu}\right)^n\right] + \frac{1}{c!}\left(\frac{\lambda}{\mu}\right)^c\left(\frac{c\mu}{c\mu - \lambda}\right)}$$

The probability of n customers in the queuing system is

$$P_n = \frac{1}{c!\,c^{n-c}}\left(\frac{\lambda}{\mu}\right)^n P_0, \quad \text{for } n > c \qquad P_n = \frac{1}{n!}\left(\frac{\lambda}{\mu}\right)^n P_0, \quad \text{for } n \le c$$

The average number of customers in the queuing system is

$$L = \frac{\lambda\mu(\lambda/\mu)^c}{(c-1)!\,(c\mu - \lambda)^2}P_0 + \frac{\lambda}{\mu}$$

The average time a customer spends in the queuing system (waiting and being served) is

$$W = \frac{L}{\lambda}$$

The average number of customers in the queue is

$$L_q = L - \frac{\lambda}{\mu}$$

The average time a customer spends in the queue waiting to be served is

$$W_q = W - \frac{1}{\mu}$$

$$= \frac{L_q}{\lambda}$$

The probability that a customer arriving in the system must wait for service (i.e., the probability that all the servers are busy) is

$$P_w = \frac{1}{c!} \left(\frac{\lambda}{\mu}\right)^c \frac{c\mu}{c\mu - \lambda} P_0$$

Notice in the formulas above that if $c = 1$ (i.e., if there is one server), then the formulas become the single-server formulas presented in the previous section.

Returning to our example, let us assume that a survey of the customer service department for a twelve-month period shows that the arrival rate and service rate are as follows:

   $\lambda = 10$ customers per hour arrive at the service department

   $\mu = 4$ customers per hour can be served by each store representative

In addition, recall that this is a three-server queuing system; therefore,

   $c = 3$ store representatives

Using the multiple-server model formulas, we can compute the following operating characteristics for the service department.

Computing the operating statistics for the multiple-server example

$$P_0 = \cfrac{1}{\left[\displaystyle\sum_{n=0}^{n=c-1} \frac{1}{n!}\left(\frac{\lambda}{\mu}\right)^n\right] + \frac{1}{c!}\left(\frac{\lambda}{\mu}\right)^c\left(\frac{c\mu}{c\mu - \lambda}\right)}$$

$$= \cfrac{1}{\left[\frac{1}{0!}\left(\frac{10}{4}\right)^0 + \frac{1}{1!}\left(\frac{10}{4}\right)^1 + \frac{1}{2!}\left(\frac{10}{4}\right)^2\right] + \frac{1}{3!}\left(\frac{10}{4}\right)^3 \frac{3(4)}{3(4) - 10}}$$

   $= .045$ probability that no customers are in the service department

$$L = \frac{\lambda\mu(\lambda/\mu)^c}{(c - 1)!\,(c\mu - \lambda)^2} P_0 + \frac{\lambda}{\mu}$$

$$= \frac{(10)(4)(10/4)^3}{(3 - 1)![3(4) - 10]^2}(.045) + \frac{10}{4}$$

   $= 6$ customers on the average in the service department

$$W = \frac{L}{\lambda}$$

$$= \frac{6}{10}$$

= .60 hour (36 minutes) average time in the service department per customer

$$L_q = L - \frac{\lambda}{\mu}$$

$$= 6 - \frac{10}{4}$$

= 3.5 customers on the average waiting to be served

$$W_q = \frac{L_q}{\lambda}$$

$$= \frac{3.5}{10}$$

= .35 hour (21 minutes) average time waiting in line per customer

$$P_w = \frac{1}{c!}\left(\frac{\lambda}{\mu}\right)^c \frac{c\mu}{c\mu - \lambda} P_0$$

$$= \frac{1}{3!}\left(\frac{10}{4}\right)^3 \frac{3(4)}{3(4) - 10}(.045)$$

= .703 probability that a customer must wait for service (i.e., that there are three or more customers in the system)

The department store's management has observed that customers are frustrated by the relatively long waiting time of 21 minutes and the .703 probability of waiting. To try to improve matters, management has decided to consider the addition of an extra service representative. The operating characteristics for this system must be recomputed with c = 4 service representatives.

Substituting this value along with λ and μ into our queuing formulas results in the following operating characteristics:

Recomputed operating statistics with an additional server

P_0 = .073 probability that no customers are in the service department

L = 3.0 customers on the average in the service department

W = .30 hour (18 minutes) average time in the service department per customer

L_q = .5 customer on the average waiting to be served

W_q = .05 hour (3 minutes) average time waiting in line per customer

P_w = .31 probability that a customer must wait for service

As in our previous example of the single-server system, the queuing operating characteristics provide input into the decision-making process, and the decision criteria are the waiting costs and service costs. The department store management would have to consider the cost of the extra service representative, as compared to the dramatic decrease in customer waiting time from 21 minutes to 3 minutes, in making a decision.

Computerized Analysis of the Multiple-Server System

The Microcomputer Software for Quantitative Analysis for Management package for the personal computer, used to analyze the single-server queuing system, can also be used to analyze the multiple-server system. The solution output for the Biggs Department Store example is as follows.

```
              *** MULTIPLE CHANNEL MODEL ***


           **INPUT DATA ENTERED**


           PROBLEM TITLE: Biggs Department Store
           THE NUMBER OF CHANNELS = 3
           THE MEAN # OF ARRIVALS PER HR. = 10
           THE MEAN # OF PEOPLE OR ITEMS SERVED PER HR. = 4




       *** RESULTS *** MULTIPLE CHANNEL MODEL ***


----------------------------------------------------------------
AVERAGE # OF UNITS IN THE SYSTEM = 6.011

AVERAGE TIME PER UNIT SPENT IN THE SYSTEM IN HR.S
(WAITING + SERVICE)= .6011

AVERAGE # OF UNITS IN THE QUEUE =  3.5112

AVERAGE TIME PER UNIT SPENT WAITING IN THE QUEUE IN HR.S= .3511

PROBABILITY THAT THE SYSTEM IS IDLE =  .0449
----------------------------------------------------------------

   ***END OF QUEUING ANALYSIS***
```

ADDITIONAL TYPES OF QUEUING SYSTEMS

The *single queue with a single server* and the *single queue with multiple servers* are two of the most common types of queuing systems. However, there are also two other general categories of queuing systems: *the single queue with single servers in sequence* and the *single queue with multiple servers in sequence.* Figure 14.4 presents a schematic of each of these two systems.

Single and multiple servers in sequence

FIGURE 14.4

Single Queues with Single and Multiple Servers in Sequence

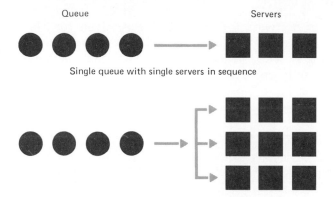

Queue   Servers

Single queue with single servers in sequence

Single queue with multiple servers in sequence

Examples of single servers in sequence

    An example of a queuing system that has a single queue leading into a sequence of single servers is the personnel office of a company where job applicants line up to apply for a specific job. All the applicants wait in one area and are called alphabetically. The application process consists of moving from one interview to the next in a single sequence to take tests, answer questions, fill out forms, and so on. Another example of this type of system is an assembly line, where products are queued up prior to being worked on by a sequenced line of machines.

Examples of multiple servers in sequence

    If, in the personnel office example above, an extra sequence of interviews were added, the result would be a queuing system with a single queue and multiple servers in sequence. Likewise, if products were lined up in a single queue prior to being worked on by machines in any one of three assembly lines, the result would be a sequence of multiple servers.

Other items that contribute to alternative queuing system forms

    These are four general categories of queuing systems. Other items that can contribute to the variety of possible queuing systems include:

Balking
Reneging

Finite calling populations

Queue systems in which customers *balk* from entering the system or leave the line if it is too long (i.e., *renege*)

Queues of limited capacity (such as a railhead with enough track for only five railroad cars or a bank teller drive-in window driveway that can accommodate only a few cars)

Servers who provide service on some basis other than first come, first served (such as alphabetical order or appointment, as in a doctor's office)

Service times that are not exponentially distributed

Arrival rates that are not Poisson distributed

Jockeying (i.e., movement between queues), which can often occur when there are multiple servers, each preceded by a separate queue (such as in a bank with several tellers, or a grocery store with several cash registers)

Jockeying

APPLICATIONS OF QUEUING ANALYSIS

Election Voting

The length of time a voter must wait in line prior to voting in an election is frequently a deterrent to voter turnout. The nationally recognized consulting firm of Pritsker and Associates was hired in 1976 by the Clearinghouse on Election Administration of the Federal Election Commission to develop a procedure for reducing the waiting time voters experienced at the polls. The firm could approach the problem in two ways. Service times could be decreased by educating the voter more thoroughly on machine use and on the candidates, or machine (server) utilization could be increased by a more effective allocation of available machines to polling stations based on expected voter turnout. The latter approach was selected, since it was more directly under the control of election officials than was the first alternative.

More effective allocation of voting machines

The firm employed queuing analysis in developing a manual that local election officials could use to allocate voting machines more effectively. The voting system was represented by a single queue, multiple-server queuing model. A study revealed that mean arrival rates varied according to the time of day; therefore, the day was segmented and a different mean arrival rate was defined for each segment. Four mean voting (service) times were identified for the election official to select from. A user-friendly manual was developed that enabled the election official to compute the number of machines to allocate given various voting time performance criteria. (For example, if election officials wanted to ensure that 90% of all voters in a specific precinct waited no more than three minutes to vote, the manual might indicate that two voting machines should be allocated.) The manual was distributed by the Clearinghouse on Election Administration.[1]

[1]F. Grant, "Reducing Voter Waiting Time," *Interfaces* 10, no. 5 (October 1980): 19–25.

Bank Teller Staffing

Reducing bank
labor costs

In 1976 the management of the Bankers Trust Company of New York became concerned about rising labor costs. The bank wanted to reduce labor costs but not at the expense of bank service. The bank's objective was to provide consistently good service to customers by matching the staff levels and work schedules at its branches to variable customer service demands. Using queuing analysis, the bank developed a teller staffing system to achieve this objective.

The teller staffing system encompassed three components: (1) a staff planning system that collected and analyzed data and determined staff requirements; (2) an administrative system that administered part-time staff, back-up personnel, and a management reporting system; and (3) an implementation plan that established service levels, line-staff interaction, control-performance evaluation, and follow-up action. The staff planning system indicated that arrival rates and service times conformed to standard queuing assumptions, although they varied from branch to branch. Once customer arrival rates and average service times had been estimated and the desired service level determined, the teller staffing model indicated the required number of open teller locations per hour for each hour of each day of the week. (Predetermined teller staffing tables used by the banking industry are available for this purpose.) Once these requirements had been determined, the bank arrived at a branch staffing plan that reflected the number of full- and part-time tellers required. The administrative system and implementation plan were employed to implement the staffing plan and manage it over time. The system was implemented in 1976 at 104 branches. As a result labor costs were reduced by approximately $1 million and service was improved. The total cost of the study and implementation was $110,000.[2]

Machine Operator Assignment

Increasing
production
capacity

The Becton Dickinson Division of the Becton Dickinson Company is a supplier of hypodermic needles and syringes for health care. The company's plant is located in a rural area, which means that the labor pool is small. This factor, combined with escalating costs, inhibited the company's ability to increase production capacity, maintain quality levels, and keep costs constant. It was determined that labor had a major impact on costs and that machine attendants comprised over 50% of the labor force. Further, it was discovered that although machine operators were responsible for five tasks, they spent most of their time clearing jams created by improper product

---

[2]H. Deutsch and V. Mabert, "Queueing Theory and Teller Staffing: A Successful Application," *Interfaces* 10, no. 5 (October 1980): 63–67.

flow, varying machine speeds, and production that was out of specification. The company viewed the problem as one of improving the way operators were assigned to machines.

A solution to this problem was developed using a single-server queuing model in which the jams were the arrivals (i.e., customers) and the operator was the server. Analysis of the system indicated that arrival rates (i.e., machine jam-ups) conformed to a Poisson distribution. The results of the queuing analysis indicated that operators should concentrate exclusively on maintaining product flow by clearing jams, and that all other tasks should be handled by indirect labor personnel. Further, the model was used to determine how many machines should be assigned to each attendant to minimize the total expected cost of operation. The queuing analysis enabled the company to reduce the machine operator work force by 115, which resulted in a $575,000 savings the first year. In addition, the plant was able to increase production levels by 80% to cope with an increased demand for syringes.[3]

A Telephone "Hotline" System

The New York State Child Abuse and Maltreatment Register Telephone Reporting System was designed to accept reports or inquiries about child abuse via a toll-free telephone system that operated twenty-four hours a day, seven days a week. For the system to be successful, the persons using the system for reporting or querying had to receive adequate service without lengthy delays. This required adequate equipment and staff. As a precaution against the system's becoming inadequate, a team of faculty and students from the State University of New York at Albany was asked to determine the necessary staff and equipment for the telephone system.

Providing telephone hotline service

The telephone system was identified as a queuing model, and queuing analysis was used to determine staff and equipment requirements. The analysis indicated the number of telephone lines and staff operators necessary to achieve a level of service (i.e., caller waiting time) specified by the New York State Department of Social Services. Although the existing telephone system had sufficient lines and operators at the time of analysis, sensitivity analysis indicated that population growth would soon require additional lines and staff to maintain an adequate system. Based on this study, in 1978 the director of the New York State Child Protective Services moved to increase the numbers of both lines and operators for the system. From 1974 to 1977, the number of calls increased from 29,000 per year to

[3]M. Vogel, "Queueing Theory Applied to Machine Manning," *Interfaces* 9, no. 4 (August 1979): 1–7.

40,000 per year and the number of telephone lines were increased from four to eleven.[4]

Summary

The various forms of queuing systems can make queuing a potentially complex field of analysis. However, because queues are encountered often in our everyday life, the analysis of queues is an important and widely explored area of management science. We have considered only the fundamentals of two basic types of queuing systems; a number of other analytical models have been developed to analyze the more complex queuing systems.

Some queuing situations, however, are so complex that it is impossible to develop an analytical model. When these situations occur, an alternative form of analysis is *simulation*, in which the real-life queuing system is simulated via a computerized mathematical model. The operating characteristics are determined by observing the simulated queuing system. This alternative technique, simulation, is the subject of the next chapter.

References

Buffa, E. S. *Operations Management: Problems and Models.* 3d ed. New York: John Wiley and Sons, 1972.

Deutsch, H., and Mabert, V. "Queueing Theory and Teller Staffing: A Successful Application." *Interfaces* 10, no. 5 (October 1980): 63–67.

Feller, W. *An Introduction to Probability Theory and Its Applications.* Vol. I. 3d ed. New York: John Wiley and Sons, 1968.

Grant, F. "Reducing Voter Waiting Time." *Interfaces* 10, no. 5 (October 1980): 19–25.

Hillier, F., and Lieberman, G. J. *Introduction to Operations Research.* 4th ed. San Francisco: Holden-Day, 1986.

Lee, Sang M.; Moore, Laurence J.; and Taylor, Bernard W. *Management Science.* 3d ed. Boston: Allyn and Bacon, 1990.

McKeown, P. "An Application of Queueing Analysis to the New York State Child Abuse and Maltreatment Register Telephone Reporting System." *Interfaces* 9, no. 3 (May 1979): 20–25.

Morse, P. M. *Queues, Inventories, and Maintenance.* New York: John Wiley and Sons, 1958.

Saaty, T. L. *Elements of Queueing Theory.* New York: McGraw-Hill, 1961.

Shamblin, J. E., and Stevens, G. T., Jr. *Operations Research: A Fundamental Approach.* New York: McGraw-Hill, 1974.

[4]P. McKeown, "An Application of Queueing Analysis to the New York State Child Abuse and Maltreatment Register Telephone Reporting System," *Interfaces* 9, no. 3 (May 1979): 20–25.

Taha, H. A. *Operations Research: An Introduction.* 4th ed. New York: Macmillan Co., 1987.

Vogel, M. "Queueing Theory Applied to Machine Manning." *Interfaces* 9, no. 4 (August 1979): 1–7.

EXAMPLE PROBLEM SOLUTION

The following example illustrates the analysis of both a single-server and a multiple-server queuing system, including the determination of the operating characteristics for each system.

Problem Statement

The new accounts loan officer of the Citizens Northern Savings Bank interviews all customers for new accounts. The customers desiring to open new accounts arrive at the rate of 4 per hour according to a Poisson distribution, and the accounts officer spends an average of 12 minutes with each customer setting up a new account.

a. Determine the operating characteristics (P_0, L, L_q, W, W_q, and P_w) for this system.

b. Add an additional accounts officer to the system described in this problem so that it is now a multiple-server queuing system with two channels, and determine the operating characteristics required in part a.

Step 1: Determine Operating Characteristics for the Single-Server System

$\lambda = 4$ customers per hour arrive

$\mu = 5$ customers per hour are served

$$P_0 = \left(1 - \frac{\lambda}{\mu}\right) = \left(1 - \frac{4}{5}\right)$$

$\quad = .20$ probability of no customers in the system

$$L = \frac{\lambda}{\mu - \lambda} = \frac{4}{5 - 4}$$

$\quad = 4$ customers on average in the queuing system

$$L_q = \frac{\lambda^2}{\mu(\mu - \lambda)} = \frac{(4)^2}{5(5 - 4)}$$

$\quad = 3.2$ customers on average in the waiting line

$$W = \frac{1}{\mu - \lambda} = \frac{1}{5 - 4}$$

$\quad = 1$ hour on average in the system

$$W_q = \frac{\lambda}{\mu(\mu - \lambda)} = \frac{4}{5(5 - 4)}$$

= .80 hour (48 minutes) average time in the waiting line

$$P_w = \frac{\lambda}{\mu} = \frac{4}{5}$$

= .80 probability that the new accounts officer will be busy and that a customer must wait

Step 2: Determine the Operating Characteristics for the Multiple-Server System

$\lambda = 4$ customers per hour arrive

$\mu = 5$ customers per hour are served

$c = 2$ servers

$$P_0 = \frac{1}{\left[\sum_{n=0}^{n=c-1} \frac{1}{n!}\left(\frac{\lambda}{\mu}\right)^n\right] + \frac{1}{c!}\left(\frac{\lambda}{\mu}\right)^c\left(\frac{c\mu}{c\mu - \lambda}\right)}$$

$$= \frac{1}{\left[\frac{1}{0!}\left(\frac{4}{5}\right)^0 + \frac{1}{1!}\left(\frac{4}{5}\right)^1\right] + \frac{1}{2!}\left(\frac{4}{5}\right)^2 \frac{(2)(5)}{(2)(5) - 4}}$$

= .429 probability that no customers are in the system

$$L = \frac{\lambda\mu\left(\frac{\lambda}{\mu}\right)^c}{(c - 1)!(c\mu - \lambda)^2}P_0 + \frac{\lambda}{\mu}$$

$$= \frac{(4)(5)\left(\frac{4}{5}\right)^2}{1![(2)(5) - 4]^2}(.429) + \frac{4}{5}$$

= .952 customer on average in the system

$$L_q = L - \frac{\lambda}{\mu} = .952 - \frac{4}{5}$$

= .152 customer on average waiting to be served

$$W = \frac{L}{\lambda} = \frac{.952}{4}$$

= .238 hour (14.3 minutes) average time in the system

$$W_q = \frac{L_q}{\lambda} = \frac{.152}{4}$$

= .038 hour (2.3 minutes) average time spent waiting in line

$$P_w = \frac{1}{c!}\left(\frac{\lambda}{\mu}\right)^c \frac{c\mu}{c\mu - \lambda}P_0 = \frac{1}{2!}\left(\frac{4}{5}\right)^2 \frac{(2)(5)}{(2)(5) - 4}(.429)$$

= .229 probability that a customer must wait for service

Problems

1. Identify ten real-life examples of queuing systems that you are familiar with.

2. Define the following components of a queuing system:
   a. Queue discipline
   b. Calling population
   c. Arrival rate
   d. Service rate

3. A single-server queuing system with an infinite calling population and a first-come, first-served queue discipline has an arrival rate of 50 customers per hour and a service rate of 70 customers per hour. Determine the following.
   a. The probability of no customers in the queuing system
   b. The average number of customers in the queuing system
   c. The average number of customers in the waiting line
   d. The average time a customer is in the queuing system
   e. The probability that the server is busy

4. A single-server queuing system with an infinite calling population and a first-come, first-served queue discipline has the following arrival and service rates:

   $\lambda = 16$ customers per hour
   $\mu = 24$ customers per hour

   Determine P_0, P_3, L, L_q, W, W_q, and P_w.

5. The ticket booth on the Tech campus is operated by one person, who is selling tickets for the annual Tech vs. State football game on Saturday. The ticket seller can serve an average of 12 customers per hour; on average, 10 customers arrive to purchase tickets each hour. Determine the average time a ticket buyer must wait and the portion of time the ticket seller is busy.

6. The Petroco Service Station has one pump for unleaded gas, which (with an attendant) can service 10 customers per hour. Cars arrive at the unleaded pump at a rate of 6 per hour. Determine the average queue length, the average time a car is in the system, and the average time a car must wait. If during a gasoline shortage the arrival rate increases to 12 cars per hour, what will be the effect on the average queue length?

7. The Dynaco Manufacturing Company produces a particular product in an assembly line operation. One of the machines on the line is a drill press that has a single assembly line feeding into it. A partially completed unit arrives at the press to be worked on every 7.5 minutes, on

the average. The machine operator can process an average of 10 parts per hour. Determine the average number of parts waiting to be worked on, the percentage of time the operator is working, and the percentage of time the machine is idle.

8. The management of Dynaco Manufacturing Company (problem 7) likes to have its operators working 90% of the time. What must the assembly line arrival rate be in order for the operators to be as busy as management would like?

9. The port of Hampton Roads has a facility where coal is loaded into ships. Railroad cars filled with coal presently arrive at the port facility at the rate of 120 per day. The facility operates 24 hours a day. A railroad car is emptied by automated equipment in an average of 8 minutes. The port authority is negotiating with a coal company for an additional 30 railroad cars per day. However, the coal company will not use this port unless the port authority can assure it that its cars will not have to wait at the unloading facility for more than 6 hours per car (on the average). Can the port authority provide this assurance?

10. The Peachtree Airport in Atlanta serves light aircraft. It has a single runway and one air traffic controller to land planes. It takes an airplane 12 minutes to land and clear the runway. Planes arrive at the airport at the rate of 4 per hour.

   a. Determine the average number of planes that will stack up waiting to land.

   b. Find the average time a plane must wait in line before it can land.

   c. Calculate the average time it takes a plane to clear the runway once it has notified the airport that it is in the vicinity and wants to land.

   d. The FAA has a rule that an air traffic controller can on the average land planes a maximum of 45 minutes out of every hour. There must be 15 minutes of idle time available to relieve the tension. Will this airport have to hire an extra air traffic controller?

11. The First American Bank of Rapid City presently has one outside drive-up teller. It takes the teller an average of 4 minutes to serve a bank customer. Customers arrive at the drive-up window at the rate of 12 per hour. The bank operations officer is currently analyzing the possibility of adding a second drive-up window at an annual cost of $20,000. It is assumed that arriving cars would be equally divided between both windows. The operations officer estimates that each minute's reduction in customer waiting time would increase the bank's revenue by $2,000 annually. Should the second drive-up window be installed?

12. During registration at State University every quarter, students in the College of Business must have their courses approved by the college advisor. It takes the advisor an average of 2 minutes to approve each schedule, and students arrive at the advisor's office at the rate of 28 per hour.

a. Compute L, L_q, W, W_q, and U.

b. The dean of the college has received a number of complaints from students about the length of time they must wait to have their schedules approved. The dean feels that waiting 10 minutes to get a schedule approved is not unreasonable. Each assistant the dean assigns to the advisor's office will reduce the average time required to approve a schedule by 0.25 minute, down to a minimum time of 1.0 minute to approve a schedule. How many assistants should the dean assign to the advisor?

13. All trucks traveling on Interstate 40 between Albuquerque and Amarillo are required to stop at a weigh station. Trucks arrive at the weigh station at a rate of 200 per 8-hour day, and the station can weigh, on the average, 220 trucks per day.

a. Determine the average number of trucks waiting, the average time spent at the weigh station by each truck, and the average waiting time before being weighed for each truck.

b. If the truck drivers find out they must remain at the weigh station longer than 15 minutes on the average, they will start taking a different route or traveling at night, thus depriving the state of taxes. The state of New Mexico estimates it loses $10,000 in taxes per year for each extra minute that trucks must remain at the weigh station. A new set of scales would have the same service capacity as the present set of scales, and it is assumed that arriving trucks would line up equally behind the 2 sets of scales. It would cost $50,000 per year to operate the new scales. Should the state install the new set of scales?

14. In problem 13, suppose passing truck drivers look to see how many trucks are waiting to be weighed at the weigh station. If they see 4 or more trucks in line, they will pass by the station and risk being caught and ticketed. What is the probability that a truck will pass by the station?

15. In the Fast Shop Market example in this chapter, alternative II was to add a new checkout counter at the market. This alternative was analyzed using the single-server model. Why was the multiple-server model not used?

16. A queuing system has a single queue, an arrival rate of 40 customers per hour, 3 servers, and a service rate of 20 customers per server per hour. Determine L, W, L_q, and P_w.

17. In problem 12, the dean of the College of Business at State University is considering the addition of a second advisor in the college advising office to serve students waiting to have their schedules approved. This new advisor could serve the same number of students per hour as the present advisor. Determine L, L_q, W, and W_q for this altered advising system. As a student, would you recommend adding the advisor?

18. The Cumberland River Carpet Mill has a warehouse with 2 loading docks, at which empty trucks are loaded with carpet to be shipped

around the country. It takes the loaders at a dock an hour to load a truck. The empty trucks arrive every 45 minutes at a parking lot adjacent to the warehouse to wait until a dock is vacated. The warehouse is open 12 hours per day. Determine the following:

a. The average number of trucks waiting to be loaded

b. The average number of trucks at the mill (both those waiting and those being loaded)

c. The average time a truck must wait in the parking lot

d. The average time a truck is at the mill

19. The Dynaco Manufacturing Company has an assembly line that feeds two drill presses. As partially completed products come off the line, they are lined up to be worked on as drill presses become available. The units arrive at the work station (containing both presses) at the rate of 100 per hour. Each press operator can process an average of 60 units per hour. Compute L, L_q, W, and W_q.

20. In problem 19, the Dynaco Company has found that if more than 3 units (average) are waiting to be processed at any one work station, then too much money is being tied up in in-process inventory (i.e., units waiting to be processed). The company estimates that (on the average) each unit waiting to be processed costs $50 per day. Alternatively, operating a third press would cost $150 per day. Should the company operate a third press at this work station?

21. Cakes baked by the Freshfood Bakery are transported from the ovens to be packaged by one of three wrappers. Each wrapper can wrap an average of 200 cakes per hour. The cakes are brought to the wrappers at the rate of 500 per hour. If a cake sits longer than 5 minutes before being wrapped, it will not be fresh enough to meet the bakery's quality control standards. Does the bakery need to hire another wrapper?

22. The Riverview Clinic has 2 general practitioners who see patients daily. An average of 6 patients arrive at the clinic per hour. Each doctor spends an average of 15 minutes with a patient. The patients wait in a waiting area until one of the 2 doctors is able to see them. However, since patients typically do not feel well when they come to the clinic, the doctors do not believe it is good practice to have a patient wait longer than an average of 15 minutes. Should this clinic add a third doctor, and if so, will this alleviate the waiting problem?

23. The Footrite Shoe Company is going to open a new branch at a mall, and company managers are attempting to determine how many salespeople to hire. Based on an analysis of mall traffic, the company estimates that customers will arrive at the store at the rate of 10 per hour, and from past experience at its other branches, the company knows that salespeople can serve an average of 6 customers per hour. How many

salespeople should the company hire in order to uphold a company policy that on average a customer should have to wait for service no more than 30% of the time?

24. When customers arrive at Gilley's Ice Cream Shop, they take a number and wait to be called to purchase ice cream from one of the counter servers. From experience in past summers, the store's staff knows that customers arrive at the rate of 40 per hour on summer days between 3:00 P.M. and 10:00 P.M. and a server can serve 15 customers per hour on average. Gilley's wants to make sure that customers wait no longer than 10 minutes for service. Gilley's is contemplating keeping 3 servers behind the ice cream counter during the peak summer hours. Will this number be adequate to meet the waiting time policy?

25. Moore's television repair service receives an average of 6 TV sets per 8-hour day to be repaired. The service manager would like to be able to tell customers that they can expect one-day service. What average repair time per set will the repair shop have to achieve to provide one-day service on the average? (Assume that the arrival rate is Poisson distributed and repair times are exponentially distributed.)

26. Partially completed products arrive at a work station in a manufacturing operation at a mean rate of 40 per hour (Poisson distributed). The processing time at the work station averages 1.2 minutes per unit (exponentially distributed). The manufacturing company estimates that each unit of in-process inventory at the work station costs $31 per day (on the average). However, the company can add extra employees and reduce the processing time to .90 minute per unit at a cost of $52 per day. Determine whether the company should continue the present operation or add extra employees.

27. The Atlantic Coast Shipping Company has a warehouse terminal in Spartanburg, South Carolina. The capacity of each terminal dock is 3 trucks. As trucks enter the terminal, the drivers receive numbers, and when one of the three dock spaces becomes available, the truck with the lowest number enters the vacant dock. Truck arrivals are Poisson distributed, and the unloading and loading times (service times) are exponentially distributed. The average arrival rate at the terminal is 5 trucks per hour, and the average service rate per dock is 2 trucks per hour (30 minutes per truck).

a. Compute L, L_q, W, and W_q.

b. The management of the shipping company is considering adding extra employees and equipment to improve the average service time per terminal dock to 25 minutes per truck. It would cost the company $18,000 per year to achieve this improved service. Management estimates that it will increase its profit by $750 per year for each minute it is able to reduce a truck's waiting time. Determine whether management should make the investment.

c. Now suppose that the managers of the shipping company have decided that truck waiting time is excessive and they want to reduce the waiting time. They have determined that there are two alternatives available for reducing the waiting time. They can add a fourth dock, or they can add extra employees and equipment at the existing docks, which will reduce the average service time per location from the original 30 minutes per truck to 23 minutes per truck. The costs of these alternatives are approximately equal. Management desires to implement the alternative that reduces waiting time by the greatest amount. Which alternative should be selected?

15

Simulation

Simulation represents a major divergence from the topics presented in the previous chapters of this text. Previous topics usually dealt with mathematical models and formulas that could be applied to certain types of problems. The solution approaches to these problems were, for the most part, analytical. However, not all real-world problems can be solved by applying a specific type of technique and then performing the calculations. Some problem situations are too complex to be represented by the concise techniques presented so far in this text. In such cases, *simulation* is an alternative form of analysis.

Analogue simulation is a form of simulation familiar to most people. In analogue simulation, an original physical system is replaced by an analogous physical system that is easier to manipulate. Much of the experimentation in manned space flight was conducted using physical simulation that re-created the conditions of space. For example, conditions of weightlessness were simulated using rooms filled with water. Other examples include wind tunnels that simulate the conditions of flight and treadmills that simulate automobile tire wear in a laboratory instead of on the road.

This chapter is concerned with an alternative type of simulation, *computerized mathematical simulation*. In this form of simulation, systems are replicated with mathematical models, which are analyzed with a computer. This form of simulation has become a very popular technique that has been applied to a wide variety of business problems.

An alternative form
of analysis for
complex systems

One reason for its popularity is because it offers a means of analyzing very complex systems that cannot be analyzed using the other management science techniques in this text. However, because such complex systems are beyond the scope of this text, we will not present actual simulation models; instead, we will present simplified simulation models of systems that can also be analyzed analytically. We will begin with one of the simplest forms of simulation models, which encompasses the "Monte Carlo" process for simulating random variables.

THE MONTE CARLO PROCESS

One characteristic of some systems that makes them difficult to solve analytically is that they consist of random variables represented by probability distributions. Thus, a large proportion of the applications of simulations are for probabilistic models.

A technique for
selecting numbers
randomly from a
probability
distribution

The term *Monte Carlo* has become synonymous with probabilistic simulation in recent years. However, the Monte Carlo technique can be more narrowly defined as a technique for selecting numbers *randomly* from a probability distribution (i.e., "sampling") for use in a *trial* (computer) run of a simulation. As such, the Monte Carlo technique is not a type of simulation model but rather a mathematical process used within a simulation.

A process
analogous to those
used in gambling
devices

The name Monte Carlo is appropriate, since the basic principle behind the process is the same as in the operation of a gambling casino in Monaco. In Monaco such devices as roulette wheels, dice, and playing cards are used. These devices produce numbered results at random from well-defined populations. For example, a 7 resulting from thrown dice is a random value from a population of 11 possible numbers (i.e., 2 through 12). This same process is employed, in principle, in the Monte Carlo process used in simulation models.

The Use of Random Numbers

The Monte Carlo process of selecting random numbers according to a probability distribution will be demonstrated using the following example. The manager of the Big T Supermarket must decide how many cases of milk to order each week. One of the primary considerations in the manager's decision is the amount of milk demanded each week. The number of cases of milk demanded is a random variable (which we will define as x) that ranges from 14 to 18 every week. From past records, the manager has determined the frequency of demand for cases of milk for the past 100 weeks. From this frequency distribution, a probability distribution of demand can be developed, as shown in Table 15.1.

A Monte Carlo example

TABLE 15.1
Probability Distribution of Demand for Milk

Cases Demanded per Week	Frequency of Demand	Probability of Demand $P(x)$
14	20	.20
15	40	.40
16	20	.20
17	10	.10
18	10	.10
	100	1.00

The purpose of the Monte Carlo process is to generate the random variable, demand, by "sampling" from the probability distribution, $P(x)$. The demand per week can be randomly generated according to the probability distribution by spinning a wheel that is partitioned into segments corresponding to the probabilities, as shown in Figure 15.1.

Since the surface area on the roulette wheel is partitioned according to the probability of each weekly demand value, the wheel replicates the probability distribution for demand if the values of de-

Generating values by spinning a roulette wheel

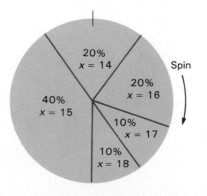

FIGURE 15.1

A Roulette Wheel for Demand

mand occur in a random manner. In order to simulate demand for one week, the manager spins the wheel; the segment at which the wheel stops indicates demand for one week. Over a period of weeks (i.e., many spins of the wheel), the frequency with which demand values occur will approximate the probability distribution, $P(x)$. This method of generating values of a variable, x, by randomly selecting from the probability distribution—the wheel—is the Monte Carlo process.

By spinning the wheel, the manager artificially reconstructs the purchase of milk during a week. In this reconstruction, a long period of *real time* (i.e., a number of weeks) is represented by a short period of *simulated time* (i.e., several spins of the wheel).

Now let us slightly reconstruct the roulette wheel. In addition to partitioning the wheel into segments corresponding to the probability of demand, we will put numbers along the outer rim as on a real roulette wheel. This reconstructed roulette wheel is shown in Figure 15.2.

Real time
Simulated time

FIGURE 15.2

Numbered Roulette Wheel

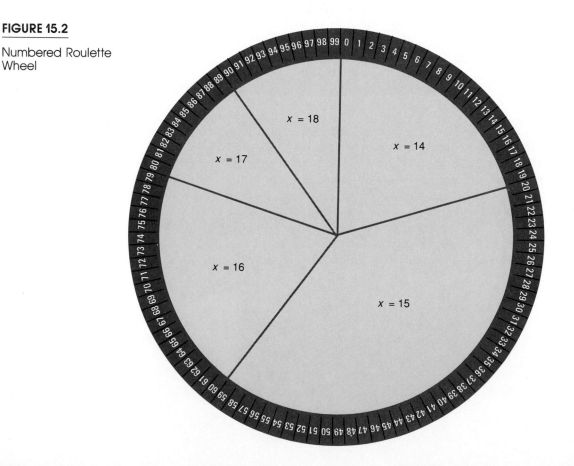

There are a total of 100 numbers from 0 to 99 on the outer rim of the wheel, and they have been partitioned according to the probability of each demand value. For example, 20 numbers from 0 to 19 (i.e., 20% of the total 100 numbers) correspond to a demand of 14 cases of milk. Now we can determine the value of demand by seeing which number the wheel stops at as well as by looking at the segment of the wheel.

When the manager spins this new wheel, the actual demand for cases of milk will be determined by a number. For example, if the number 71 comes up on a spin, the demand is 16 cases per week; the number 30 indicates a demand of 15. Since the manager does not know which number will come up prior to the spin and there is an equal chance of any of the 100 numbers' occurring, the numbers occur at random; that is, they are *random numbers.*

Obviously, it is not generally practical to generate weekly demand for milk by spinning a wheel. Alternatively, the process of spinning a wheel can be replicated using random numbers alone.

First, we will transfer the ranges of random numbers for each demand value from the roulette wheel to a table, as in Table 15.2. Next, instead of spinning the wheel to get a random number, we will select a random number from Table 15.3, which is referred to as a *random number table.* (These random numbers have been generated by computer so that they are all *equally likely to occur,* just as if we had spun a wheel. The development of random number tables will be discussed in more detail later in this chapter.) As an example, let us select the number 39 in Table 15.3. Looking again at Table 15.2, we can see that the random number 39 falls in the range 20–59, which corresponds to a weekly demand of 15 cases of milk.

Using a random number table

TABLE 15.2
Generating Demand from
Random Numbers

Demand x	Ranges of Random Numbers r	
14	0–19	
15 ‹	20–59 ←	*r* = 39
16	60–79	
17	80–89	
18	90–99	

By repeating this process of selecting random numbers from Table 15.3 (starting anywhere in the table and moving in any direction but not repeating the same sequence) and then determining weekly demand from the random number, we can simulate demand for a period of time. For example, Table 15.4 on page 523 shows demand for a period of 15 consecutive weeks.

TABLE 15.3

Random Number Table

39 65 76 45 45	19 90 69 64 61	20 26 36 31 62	58 24 97 14 97	95 06 70 99 00
73 71 23 70 90	65 97 60 12 11	31 56 34 19 19	47 83 75 51 33	30 62 38 20 46
72 18 47 33 84	51 67 47 97 19	98 40 07 17 66	23 05 09 51 80	59 78 11 52 49
75 12 25 69 17	17 95 21 78 58	24 33 45 77 48	69 81 84 09 29	93 22 70 45 80
37 17 79 88 74	63 52 06 34 30	01 31 60 10 27	35 07 79 71 53	28 99 52 01 41
02 48 08 16 94	85 53 83 29 95	56 27 09 24 43	21 78 55 09 82	72 61 88 73 61
87 89 15 70 07	37 79 49 12 38	48 13 93 55 96	41 92 45 71 51	09 18 25 58 94
98 18 71 70 15	89 09 39 59 24	00 06 41 41 20	14 36 59 25 47	54 45 17 24 89
10 83 58 07 04	76 62 16 48 68	58 76 17 14 86	59 53 11 52 21	66 04 18 72 87
47 08 56 37 31	71 82 13 50 41	27 55 10 24 92	28 04 67 53 44	95 23 00 84 47
93 90 31 03 07	34 18 04 52 35	74 13 39 35 22	68 95 23 92 35	36 63 70 35 33
21 05 11 47 99	11 20 99 45 18	76 51 94 84 86	13 79 93 37 55	98 16 04 41 67
95 89 94 06 97	27 37 83 28 71	79 57 95 13 91	09 61 87 25 21	56 20 11 32 44
97 18 31 55 73	10 65 81 92 59	77 31 61 95 46	20 44 90 32 64	26 99 76 75 63
69 08 88 86 13	59 71 74 17 32	48 38 75 93 29	73 37 32 04 05	60 82 29 20 25
41 26 10 25 03	87 63 93 95 17	81 83 83 04 49	77 45 85 50 51	79 88 01 97 30
91 47 14 63 62	08 61 74 51 69	92 79 43 89 79	29 18 94 51 23	14 85 11 47 23
80 94 54 18 47	08 52 85 08 40	48 40 35 94 22	72 65 71 08 86	50 03 42 99 36
67 06 77 63 99	89 85 84 46 06	64 71 06 21 66	89 37 20 70 01	61 65 70 22 12
59 72 24 13 75	42 29 72 23 19	06 94 76 10 08	81 30 15 39 14	81 33 17 16 33
63 62 06 34 41	79 53 36 02 95	94 61 09 43 62	20 21 14 68 86	84 95 48 46 45
78 47 23 53 90	79 93 96 38 63	34 85 52 05 09	85 43 01 72 73	14 93 87 81 40
87 68 62 15 43	97 48 72 66 48	53 16 71 13 81	59 97 50 99 52	24 62 20 42 31
47 60 92 10 77	26 97 05 73 51	88 46 38 03 58	72 68 49 29 31	75 70 16 08 24
56 88 87 59 41	06 87 37 78 48	65 88 69 58 39	88 02 84 27 83	85 81 56 39 38
22 17 68 65 84	87 02 22 57 51	68 69 80 95 44	11 29 01 95 80	49 34 35 36 47
19 36 27 59 46	39 77 32 77 09	79 57 92 36 59	89 74 39 82 15	08 58 94 34 74
16 77 23 02 77	28 06 24 25 93	22 45 44 84 11	87 80 61 65 31	09 71 91 74 25
78 43 76 71 61	97 67 63 99 61	30 45 67 93 82	59 73 19 85 23	53 33 65 97 21
03 28 28 26 08	69 30 16 09 05	53 58 47 70 93	66 56 45 65 79	45 56 20 19 47
04 31 17 21 56	33 73 99 19 87	26 72 39 27 67	53 77 57 68 93	60 61 97 22 61
61 06 98 03 91	87 14 77 43 96	43 00 65 98 50	45 60 33 01 07	98 99 46 50 47
23 68 35 26 00	99 53 93 61 28	52 70 05 48 34	56 65 05 61 86	90 92 10 70 80
15 39 25 70 99	93 86 52 77 65	15 33 59 05 28	22 87 26 07 47	86 96 98 29 06
58 71 96 30 24	18 46 23 34 27	85 13 99 24 44	49 18 09 79 49	74 16 32 23 02
93 22 53 64 39	07 10 63 76 35	87 03 04 79 88	08 13 13 85 51	55 34 57 72 69
78 76 58 54 74	92 38 70 96 92	52 06 79 79 45	82 63 18 27 44	69 66 92 19 09
61 81 31 96 82	00 57 25 60 59	46 72 60 18 77	55 66 12 62 11	08 99 55 64 57
42 88 07 10 05	24 98 65 63 21	47 21 61 88 32	27 80 30 21 60	10 92 35 36 12
77 94 30 05 39	28 10 99 00 27	12 73 73 99 12	49 99 57 94 82	96 88 57 17 91

From Table 15.4 the manager can compute the estimated average weekly demand.

$$\text{Estimated average demand} = \frac{241}{15}$$

$$= 16.1 \text{ cases per week}$$

Comparing the simulation result with the analytical result

The manager can then use this information to determine the number of cases of milk to order each week.

Although this example is convenient for illustrating how simulation works, the average demand could have more appropriately

TABLE 15.4
Randomly
Generated
Demand for
Fifteen Weeks

Week	r	Demand (x)
1	39	15
2	73	16
3	72	16
4	75	16
5	37	15
6	02	14
7	87	17
8	98	18
9	10	14
10	47	15
11	93	18
12	21	15
13	95	18
14	97	18
15	69	16
		$\Sigma = 241$

been calculated *analytically* using the formula for expected value. The *expected value* or average for weekly demand can be computed analytically from the probability distribution, $P(x)$.

$$E(x) = \sum_{i=1}^{n} P(x_i)x_i$$

where

x_i = demand value i

$P(x_i)$ = probability of demand

n = the number of different demand values

Therefore,

$$E(x) = (.20)(14) + (.40)(15) + (.20)(16) + (.10)(17) + (.10)(18)$$
$$= 15.5 \text{ cases per week}$$

The analytical result of 15.5 cases is close to the simulated result of 16.1 cases, but clearly there is some difference. The margin of difference (.6 case) between the simulated value and the analytical value is a result of the number of periods over which the simulation was conducted. The results of any simulation study are subject to the number of times the simulation occurred (i.e., the number of *trials*). Thus, the more periods for which the simulation is conducted, the more accurate the result. For example, if demand were simulated for 1,000 weeks, in all likelihood an average value exactly equal to the analytical value (15.5 cases of milk per week) would result.

The number of trials in a simulation

Once a simulation has been repeated enough times that it reaches an average result that remains constant, this result is analogous to the *steady-state* result, a concept we discussed previously in our discussion of Markov analysis and queuing. For this example, 15.5 cases is the long-run average or steady-state result, but we have seen that the simulation would have to be repeated more than 15 times (i.e., weeks) before this result was reached.

Validating the
simulation results

Comparing our simulated result with the analytical (expected value) result for this example points out one of the problems that can occur with simulation. It is often difficult to *validate* the results of a simulation model—i.e., to make sure the true steady-state average result has been reached. In this case we were able to compare the simulated result with the expected value (which is the true steady-state result), and we found there was a slight difference. We logically deduced that 15 trials of the simulation were not sufficient to determine the steady-state average. However, simulation most often is employed when analytical analysis is not possible (this is one of the reasons simulation is generally useful). In these cases, there is no analytical standard of comparison, and validation of results becomes more difficult. We will discuss this problem of validation in more detail later in the chapter.

COMPUTER SIMULATION

Computer vs.
manual simulation

The simulation we performed manually for our milk demand example was not too difficult. However, if we had performed the simulation for 1,000 weeks, it would have taken several hours. On the other hand, this simulation could be done on the computer in several seconds. Also, our simulation example was not very complex. As simulation models get progressively more complex, it becomes virtually impossible to perform them manually, thus making the computer a necessity.

Although we will not develop an actual computer model in a computer language for this example, we will demonstrate how a computerized simulation model is developed. (We will present a computer simulation model for the machine breakdown and maintenance example later in this chapter, however.) Figure 15.3 is a diagram of the structure of a computerized simulation model for the supermarket example.

The first step in developing a computer model is to generate a random number, r. There are numerous subroutines available on practically every computer system that generate random numbers. Most are quite easy to use and require the insertion of only a few statements in a program. These random numbers are generated by

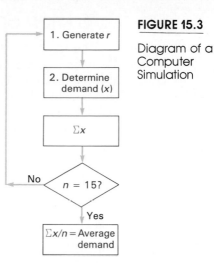

FIGURE 15.3

Diagram of a
Computer
Simulation

mathematical processes (which we will discuss later in the chapter) as opposed to a physical process, such as spinning a roulette wheel. For this reason, they are referred to as *pseudorandom numbers*.

Pseudorandom
numbers

Once a random number has been generated, a value for x, demand, is determined. This requires that computer statements be developed that will replicate the ranges of random numbers in Table 15.2. Such statements typically take the form of "If r is between 0 and 19, then x equals 14; otherwise go to the next statement, which specifies a range between 20 and 59," etc.

After each value for demand is determined, it is added to all previous values so that when the program is completed, the total sum of demand will exist.

At this point, demand has actually been simulated for one week. The program is constructed so that the number of weeks, n, is summed after each week is simulated. For our example, n equals 15 weeks. On each simulation the computer checks to see if n has reached 15. If it has not, the program is sent back to the beginning, another random number is generated, and a value for demand is determined. However, if n does equal 15, the program passes on to the next stage. At the final stage of the program, the average weekly demand is computed by dividing the sum for demand by n.

This example simulation model is relatively simple. The computer program for this simulation requires only a few statements and only a few seconds to run. One reason for its simplicity is that it contains only one random variable, x. As the number of random variables and the number of items being computed increase, so does the complexity of the simulation model. In the following example we will discuss a slightly more complex simulation model with two random variables.

SIMULATION OF A QUEUING SYSTEM

A simulation example with two random variables

In order to demonstrate the simulation of a queuing system, we will use a system similar to the Fast Shop Market example first introduced in Chapter 14. In this system a drive-in market consists of one cash register (the service facility) and a single queue of customers. In this example we will assume that the time intervals between customer arrivals and service times are *discrete* random variables defined by the probability distributions in Tables 15.5 and 15.6 (an assumption that will prohibit the use of the single-server queuing formulas developed in Chapter 14).

TABLE 15.5
Distribution of Arrival Intervals

Arrival Interval (minutes) x	Probability $P(x)$	Cumulative Probability	Random Number Range r_1
1.0	.20	.20	1–20
2.0	.40	.60	21–60
3.0	.30	.90	61–90
4.0	.10	1.00	91–99, 00

TABLE 15.6
Distribution of Service Times

Service Time (minutes) y	Probability $P(y)$	Cumulative Probability	Random Number Range r_2
0.5	.20	.20	1–20
1.0	.50	.70	21–70
2.0	.30	1.00	71–99, 00

Constructing the random number ranges using cumulative probabilities

Table 15.5 defines the interarrival time, or how often customers arrive at the cash register. For example, there is a .20 probability of a customer's arriving *one minute* after the previous customer. Table 15.6 defines the service time for a customer. Notice that cumulative probabilities have been included in Tables 15.5 and 15.6. The cumulative probability provides a convenient (visual) means for determining the ranges of random numbers associated with each probability. For example, in Table 15.5 the first random number range for r_1 is from 1 to 20, which corresponds to the cumulative probability of .20. The second range of random numbers is from 21 to 60, which corresponds to a cumulative probability of .60. Although the cumulative probability goes up to 1.00, Table 15.3 contains only random number values from 0 to 99. Thus, the number 0 is used in place of 100 in the last random number range of each table.

Table 15.7 illustrates the simulation of 10 customer arrivals to the cash register.

TABLE 15.7
Simulation of the Fast Shop Market Queuing System

Customer	r_1	Arrival Interval x	Arrival Clock	Enter Facility Clock	Waiting Time	Length of Queue After Entry	r_2	Service Time y	Depar- ture Clock	Time in System
1	—	—	0.0	0.0	0.0	0	65	1.0	1.0	1.0
2	71	3.0	3.0	3.0	0.0	0	18	.5	3.5	.5
3	12	1.0	4.0	4.0	0.0	0	17	.5	4.5	.5
4	48	2.0	6.0	6.0	0.0	0	89	2.0	8.0	2.0
5	18	1.0	7.0	8.0	1.0	1	83	2.0	10.0	3.0
6	08	1.0	8.0	10.0	2.0	1	90	2.0	12.0	4.0
7	05	1.0	9.0	12.0	3.0	2	89	2.0	14.0	5.0
8	18	1.0	10.0	14.0	4.0	2	08	.5	14.5	4.5
9	26	2.0	12.0	14.5	2.5	2	47	1.0	15.5	3.5
10	94	4.0	16.0	16.0	0.0	0	06	.5	16.5	.5
					12.5	8				24.5

The manual simulation process illustrated in Table 15.7 can be interpreted as follows.

Steps of the manual simulation process

1. Customer 1 arrives at time 0, which is recorded on an *arrival clock*. Since there are no customers in the system, customer 1 approaches the service facility (i.e., the cash register) immediately, also at time 0. The waiting time and queue length are 0.
2. Next, a random number, $r_2 = 65$, is selected from the second column in Table 15.3. Observing Table 15.6, we see that a random number of 65 results in a service time, y, of 1.0 minute. After checking out at the cash register, the customer departs at time 1.0 minute, having been in the queuing system a total of 1.0 minute.
3. A new random number, $r_1 = 71$, is selected from Table 15.3, which specifies that customer 2 arrives 3.0 minutes after customer 1, or at time 3.0 as shown on the arrival clock. Since customer 1 departed the service facility at time 1.0, customer 2 can be served immediately and thus incurs no waiting time.
4. Next a random number, $r_2 = 18$, is selected from Table 15.3, which indicates that customer 2 will spend .5 minute being served and will depart at time 3.5.

This process of selecting random numbers and generating arrival intervals and service times continues until ten customer arrivals have been simulated, as shown in Table 15.7.

Once the simulation is complete, we can compute operating characteristics from the simulation results as follows.

$$\text{Average waiting time} = \frac{12.5 \text{ minutes}}{10 \text{ customers}}$$

$$= 1.25 \text{ minutes per customer}$$

$$\text{Average queue length} = \frac{8 \text{ customers}}{10 \text{ customers}}$$

$$= .80 \text{ customer}$$

$$\text{Average time in the system} = \frac{24.5 \text{ minutes}}{10 \text{ customers}}$$

$$= 2.45 \text{ minutes per customer}$$

However, as in our previous example, these results must be viewed with skepticism. Ten trials of the system do not ensure steady-state results. In general, we can expect a considerable difference between the true average values and the values estimated from only ten random draws. One reason is that we cannot be sure that the random numbers we selected in this example replicated the actual probability distributions because we used so few random numbers. The stream of random numbers that was used might have had a preponderance of high or low values, thus biasing the final model results. For example, of nine arrivals, five had interarrival times of 1.0 minute. This corresponds to a probability of .55 (i.e., 5/9); however, the actual probability of an arrival interval of 1.0 minute is .20 (from Table 15.5). This excessive number of short interarrival times (caused by the sequence of random numbers) has probably artificially inflated the operating statistics of the system.

As the number of random trials is increased, the probabilities in the simulation will more closely conform to the actual probability distributions. That is, if we simulated the queuing system for 1,000 arrivals, we could more reasonably expect that 20% of the arrivals would have an interarrival time of 1.0 minute.

An additional factor that can affect simulation results is the starting conditions. If we start our queuing system with no customers in the system, we must simulate a length of time before the system replicates normal operating conditions. In this example, it is logical to start simulating at the time the market opens in the morning, especially if we simulate an entire working day. Some queuing systems, however, start with items already in the system. For example, a production plant typically starts each day with partially completed products from the previous day waiting at each machine. In this case, it is necessary to begin the simulation with items already in the system.

By adding a second random variable to a simulation model, such as the one just shown, we have substantially increased the complexity and therefore the manual operations. To simulate the example in Table 15.7 manually for 1,000 trials would require several hours. It would be far preferable to perform this type of simulation on the computer. A number of mathematical computations would be required to determine the various column values of Table 15.7. This would result in a computer model larger than the one diagrammed in Figure 15.3, since the number of statements in computer language would increase substantially. However, in the realm of computer models this would still be considered a relatively simple and easy model.

Computer Simulation of the Queuing Example

Some management science software packages for the personal computer include the capability to simulate specific systems. Micro Manager by Lee and Shim has the capability to simulate queuing systems with discrete probability distribution of arrivals and service times.

Following is a simulation, using Micro Manager, of the queuing example of the Fast Shop Market, which was simulated manually in Table 15.7. The following model input includes the discrete probability distributions for arrival intervals and service times shown in Tables 15.5 and 15.6.

```
PROGRAM: Simulation

***** INPUT DATA ENTERED *****

Queuing simulation

        Arrival Distribution
-----------------------------------------
  Arrival Interval    Probability
-----------------------------------------
      1.00               0.20
      2.00               0.40
      3.00               0.30
      4.00               0.10
-----------------------------------------


      Service Time Distribution

-----------------------------------------
      Service Time     Probability
-----------------------------------------
PROGRAM: Simulation
        0.50               0.20
        1.00               0.50
        2.00               0.30
-----------------------------------------
Number of simulation runs :    10
```

The initial simulation is for 10 arrivals. The tabular form in which the simulation results are displayed is identical to that of the manual results in Table 15.7, and the operating statistics that are computed are the same as those we calculated for our manual example (i.e., average waiting time, average queue length, and average time in the system).

```
*****   PROGRAM OUTPUT   *****


*** Simulation Results for  10 Arrivals ***
-----------------------------------------------------------------------
                      Enter          Length of
             Arvl Arvl Facil'y Wait'g Queue at        Service Dpture Time in
Arvls  r1   Intvl Time Time    Time   Entry    r2     Time    Time   System
-----------------------------------------------------------------------
    1  0.00  0.0  0.0   0.0    0.0      0     0.01    0.5     0.5    0.5
    2  0.75  3.0  3.0   3.0    0.0      0     0.66    1.0     4.0    1.0
    3  0.22  2.0  5.0   5.0    0.0      0     0.61    1.0     6.0    1.0
    4  0.47  2.0  7.0   7.0    0.0      0     0.20    0.5     7.5    0.5
    5  0.74  3.0  10.0  10.0   0.0      0     0.91    2.0    12.0    2.0

    6  0.19  1.0  11.0  12.0   1.0      0     0.41    1.0    13.0    2.0
    7  0.24  2.0  13.0  13.0   0.0      0     0.21    1.0    14.0    1.0
    8  0.09  1.0  14.0  14.0   0.0      0     0.57    1.0    15.0    1.0
    9  0.51  2.0  16.0  16.0   0.0      0     0.50    1.0    17.0    1.0
   10  0.27  2.0  18.0  18.0   0.0      0     0.16    0.5    18.5    0.5
                                ------   ----                       ------
                                 1.0      0                          10.5
-----------------------------------------------------------------------

Average waiting time              :     0.1
Average length of the queue at entry:   0.0
Average total time in the system  :     1.0
```

Notice that the results of this simulation are significantly different from the manual simulation results derived from Table 15.7. Recall that we speculated earlier, following the manual simulation, that they might be. From Table 15.7 the average waiting time was computed to be 1.25 minutes, whereas in this simulation the average waiting time is only .1 minute; likewise in the manual simulation the average queue length was .80 customer and in this simulation the average queue length is 0. These differences are primarily due to different random number streams. Over the span of a short simulation, such as in Table 15.7, the random numbers can be predominantly high or low. True randomness (i.e., a situation in which the probability of selecting each random number between 1 and 100 is the same) will occur only after a long run. Thus the 10-arrival simulation shown here is too short to ensure steady-state results. Close inspection of Table 15.7 and the simulation results shows that it is differences in the number streams that have caused the discrepancy in the results. Note that in Table 15.7 the average arrival interval (x) is 1.77 minutes and the average service time (y) is 1.2 minutes, whereas in the computer simulation the average arrival interval (x) is 2 minutes and the average service time (y) is .95 minute. In other words, the manual simulation (Table 15.7) has lower arrival intervals and higher service times than the computer simulation; the differences create the lower average waiting time and queue lengths in the computer simulation.

Running the Micro Manager simulation again for 100 arrivals results in the following output statistics.

```
*****   PROGRAM OUTPUT   *****

Average waiting time               :        0.0
Average length of the queue at entry:        0.0
Average total time in the system   :        1.2
```

Running the simulation again for 1,000 arrivals produces the following statistics, which we can be relatively confident are steady-state results (since they are close to the results obtained for the 100-arrival simulation).

```
*****   PROGRAM OUTPUT   *****

Average waiting time               :        0.1
Average length of the queue at entry:        0.0
Average total time in the system   :        1.3
```

Some personal computer software packages have the capability to analyze queuing systems that encompass continuous probability distributions, such as those presented in Chapter 14, with Poisson arrival rates and exponential service times. The QSB+ software package demonstrated in Chapter 3 has this capability.

CONTINUOUS PROBABILITY DISTRIBUTIONS

In the first example in this chapter, the supermarket manager considered a probability distribution of discrete demand values. In the first queuing example, the probability distributions were for discrete interarrival times and service times. However, applications of simulation models reflecting continuous distributions are more common than those of models employing discrete distributions.

The reason we have concentrated on examples with discrete distributions is that with a discrete distribution the ranges of random numbers can be explicitly determined and are thus easier to illustrate. When random numbers are being selected according to a continuous probability distribution, a continuous function must be used. For example, consider the following continuous probability function, $f(x)$, for time (minutes), x.

$$f(x) = \frac{x}{8}, \ 0 \leq x \leq 4$$

Integrating the continuous function

In order to determine the value of time, x, for a random number, r, this continuous function must be *integrated* over the range 0 to 4. This results in the following cumulative probability function.

$$F(x) = \frac{x^2}{16}$$

Cumulative probabilities are analogous to the discrete ranges of random numbers we used in previous examples. Thus, we let this function, $F(x)$, equal the random number, r,

$$r = \frac{x^2}{16}$$

and solve for x,

$$x = 4\sqrt{r}$$

By generating a random number, r, and substituting it into this function, we determine a value for x, "time." (However, for a continuous function, the range of random numbers must be between

0.0 and 1.00 to correspond to probabilities between 0.0 and 1.00.) For example, if $r = .25$, then

$x = 4\sqrt{.25}$
  $= 2$ minutes

The purpose of briefly presenting this example is to demonstrate the difference between discrete and continuous functions. This continuous function is relatively simple, but as functions become more complex, it becomes more difficult to develop the equation for determining the random variable, x, from r. Even this simple example required some calculus, and developing more complex models would require a higher level of mathematics.

Simulation of a Machine Breakdown and Maintenance System

In this example we will demonstrate the use of a continuous probability distribution. The Bigelow Manufacturing Company produces a product on a number of machines. The elapsed time between the breakdown of the machines is defined by the following continuous probability distribution.

$$f(x) = \frac{x}{8}, \ 0 \le x \le 4 \text{ weeks}$$

where

  x = weeks between machine breakdowns

As indicated in the previous section on continuous probability distributions, the equation for generating x given the random number, r_1, is

$x = 4\sqrt{r_1}$

When a machine breaks down it must be repaired, and it takes either 1, 2, or 3 days for the repair to be completed, according to the discrete probability distribution shown in Table 15.8.

Computer simulation

A continuous probability distribution of the time between breakdowns

Machine repair times

TABLE 15.8
Probability Distribution of Machine Repair Time

Machine Repair Time, *y* days	Probability of Repair Time, *P(x)*	Cumulative Probability	Random Number Range, r_2
1	.15	.15	1–15
2	.55	.70	16–70
3	.30	1.00	71–99, 00

Breakdown repair costs

Every time a machine breaks down, the cost to the company is an estimated $2,000 per day in lost production until the machine is repaired.

The company would like to know if it should implement a machine maintenance program at a cost of $20,000 per year that would reduce the frequency of breakdowns and thus the time for repair. The maintenance program would result in the following continuous probability function for time between breakdowns.

A machine maintenance program

A reduced time between breakdowns

$$f(x) = \frac{x}{18}, \quad 0 \le x \le 6 \text{ weeks}$$

where

x = weeks between machine breakdowns

The equation for generating x given the random number, r_1, for this probability distribution is

$$x = 6\sqrt{r_1}$$

Reduced repair time

The reduced repair time resulting from the maintenance program is defined by the discrete probability distribution shown in Table 15.9.

TABLE 15.9
Revised Probability Distribution of Machine
Repair Time with the Maintenance Program

Machine Repair Time, y days	Probability of Repair Time, $P(y)$	Cumulative Probability	Random Number Range, r_2
1	.40	.40	1–40
2	.50	.90	41–90
3	.10	1.00	91–99, 00

The modeling approach

In order to solve this problem, we must first simulate the existing system to determine an estimate of the average annual repair costs. Then, we must simulate the system with the maintenance program installed to see what the average annual repair costs will be with the maintenance program. We will then compare the average annual repair cost with and without the maintenance program and compute the difference, which will be the average annual savings in repair costs with the maintenance program. If this savings is more than the annual cost of the maintenance program ($20,000), we will recommend that it be implemented; if it is less, we will recommend that it not be implemented.

Manual simulation of machine breakdowns without the maintenance program

First, we will manually simulate the existing breakdown and repair system without the maintenance program, to see how the simulation model is developed. Table 15.10 illustrates the simulation of machine breakdowns and repair for one year (i.e., 52 weeks). Notice that the simulation in Table 15.10 ends once the cumulative time reaches 52 weeks, as shown in the last column in the table.

TABLE 15.10
Simulation of Machine Breakdowns and Repair

r_1	Time Between Breakdowns, x weeks	r_2	Repair Time, y days	Cost: $2,000y$	Cumulative Time, Σx weeks
.45	2.68	.19	2	4,000	2.68
.90	3.80	.65	2	4,000	6.48
.84	3.67	.51	2	4,000	10.15
.17	1.65	.17	2	4,000	11.80
.74	3.44	.63	2	4,000	15.24
.94	3.88	.85	3	6,000	19.12
.07	1.06	.37	2	4,000	20.18
.15	1.55	.89	3	6,000	21.73
.04	0.80	.76	3	6,000	22.53
.31	2.23	.71	3	6,000	24.76
.07	1.06	.34	2	4,000	25.82
.99	3.98	.11	1	2,000	29.80
.97	3.94	.27	2	4,000	33.74
.73	3.42	.10	1	2,000	37.16
.13	1.44	.59	2	4,000	38.60
.03	0.70	.87	3	6,000	39.30
.62	3.15	.08	1	2,000	42.45
.47	2.74	.08	1	2,000	45.19
.99	3.98	.89	3	6,000	49.17
.75	3.46	.42	2	4,000	52.63
				$84,000	

The simulation in Table 15.10 results in a total annual repair cost of $84,000. However, this is for only one year, and thus it is probably not very accurate (a matter we will deal with later).

Total annual repair cost

The next step in our simulation analysis is to simulate the machine breakdown and repair system with the maintenance program installed. We will use the revised continuous probability distribution for time between breakdowns and the revised discrete probability distribution for repair time shown in Table 15.9. Table 15.11 illustrates the manual simulation of machine breakdowns and repair for one year.

Manual simulation of machine breakdowns with the maintenance program

Table 15.11 shows that the annual repair cost with the maintenance program is $42,000. Recall that in the previous manual simulation in Table 15.10, the annual repair cost was $84,000 for the system without the maintenance program. The difference between the two annual repair costs is $84,000 − 42,000 = $42,000, which represents the savings in average annual repair cost with the maintenance program. Since the maintenance program will cost $20,000 per year, it would seem that the recommended decision would be to implement the maintenance program and generate an expected annual savings of $22,000 per year (i.e., $42,000 − 20,000 = $22,000).

Annual repair cost

A recommended decision

TABLE 15.11

Simulation of Machine Breakdowns and Repair with the Maintenance Program

r_1	Time Between Breakdowns, x weeks	r_2	Repair Time, y days	Cost: $2,000y	Cumulative Time, Σx weeks
.45	4.03	.19	1	2,000	4.03
.90	5.69	.65	2	4,000	9.72
.84	5.50	.51	2	4,000	15.22
.17	2.47	.17	1	2,000	17.69
.74	5.16	.63	2	4,000	22.85
.94	5.82	.85	2	4,000	28.67
.07	1.59	.37	1	2,000	30.29
.15	2.32	.89	2	4,000	32.58
.04	1.20	.76	2	4,000	33.78
.31	3.34	.71	2	4,000	37.12
.07	1.59	.34	1	2,000	38.71
.99	5.97	.11	1	2,000	44.68
.97	5.91	.27	1	2,000	50.59
.73	5.12	.10	1	2,000	55.71
				$42,000	

The limitations of manual simulation

However, let us now concern ourselves with the potential difficulties caused by the fact that we simulated each system (the existing one and the system with the maintenance program) only *once*. Since the time between breakdowns and the repair times are probabilistic, the simulation results could exhibit significant variation. The only way to be sure of the accuracy of our results is to simulate each system many times and compute an average result. Performing these many simulations manually would obviously require a great deal of time and effort. However, computer simulation can be used to accomplish the required simulation analysis.

Computer Simulation of the Machine Breakdown Example

BASIC programming language

IBM personal computer

In order to demonstrate the computer simulation of the machine breakdown example, we will first present the computer program for the simulation of the existing system. The program shown on page 538 was written in the IBM version of the BASIC computer language (referred to as BASICA) and solved on an IBM personal computer. The flowchart in Figure 15.4 illustrates the structure of the computer program and how it works.

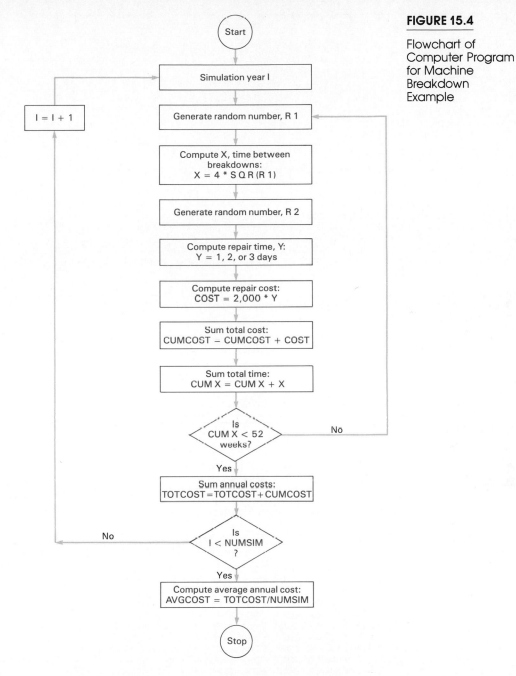

FIGURE 15.4

Flowchart of
Computer Program
for Machine
Breakdown
Example

```
LIST
10 REM BASIC PROGRAM TO SIMULATE MACHINE BREAKDOWN EXAMPLE
20 RANDOMIZE (9)
30 TOTCOST = 0
40 NUMSIM = 10
50 I = 0
60 I = I + 1
70 CUMX = 0
80 CUMCOST = 0
90 R1 = RND
100 X = 4*SQR(R1)
110 R2 = RND
120 IF R2 > 0 AND R2 <= .15 THEN Y = 1 ELSE 130
130 IF R2 > .15 AND R2 <= .7 THEN Y = 2 ELSE 140
140 IF R2 > .7 AND R2 <= 1 THEN Y = 3 ELSE 150
150 COST = 2000*Y
160 CUMCOST = CUMCOST + COST
170 CUMX = CUMX + X
180 IF CUMX < 52 THEN 90
190 TOTCOST = TOTCOST + CUMCOST
200 PRINT "MAINTENANCE COST FOR YEAR " I " IS " CUMCOST
210 IF I < NUMSIM THEN 60
220 AVGCOST = TOTCOST/NUMSIM
230 PRINT
240 PRINT " AVERAGE ANNUAL MAINTENANCE COST IS " AVGCOST
Ok
```

Simulating the breakdown system for ten years

We used the computer program to simulate the system for 10 years (as compared to one year in Table 15.10), in order to demonstrate the program output. The output of the program yields the maintenance cost for each of the 10 years (i.e., simulation runs) and the average annual maintenance cost for the 10-year period. This output is shown below.

Simulation output

```
RUN
MAINTENANCE COST FOR YEAR    1   IS   82000
MAINTENANCE COST FOR YEAR    2   IS   78000
MAINTENANCE COST FOR YEAR    3   IS   80000
MAINTENANCE COST FOR YEAR    4   IS   92000
MAINTENANCE COST FOR YEAR    5   IS   94000
MAINTENANCE COST FOR YEAR    6   IS   96000
MAINTENANCE COST FOR YEAR    7   IS   80000
MAINTENANCE COST FOR YEAR    8   IS   82000
MAINTENANCE COST FOR YEAR    9   IS   90000
MAINTENANCE COST FOR YEAR   10   IS   76000

  AVERAGE ANNUAL MAINTENANCE COST IS   85000
Ok
```

The average annual maintenance cost from this program is $85,000. This represents a difference of approximately 1% from the results of the manual simulation obtained in Table 15.10. To obtain more accurate results, the program can be run for more than 10 simulations. For example, running the program for 200 years (by changing line 40 to NUMSIM = 200) yields an average annual maintenance cost of $85,330, which is only slightly different from the results we obtained using 10 years. Running the program for even a greater number of years yields only a slight difference in the mean value. Thus, we can feel relatively confident that the average annual maintenance cost of $85,330 is close to the steady-state mean.

Average maintenance cost

Comparing the simulated results with the manual results

The next step in our simulation analysis is to alter the computer program to reflect the reduced time between machine breakdowns and the reduced repair time resulting from the proposed maintenance program. This requires that line 100 in the program be changed to reflect the new time between breakdowns function:

Simulating the breakdown system with the maintenance program

```
100 X = 6*SQR(R1)
```

Program changes

Also, lines 120, 130, and 140 must be changed for the revised probability distribution of repair times:

```
120 IF R2 > 0 AND R2 <= .4 THEN Y = 1 ELSE 130
130 IF R2 > .4 AND R2 <= .9 THEN Y = 2 ELSE 140
140 IF R2 > .9 AND R2 <= 1 THEN Y = 3 ELSE 150
```

These are the only changes in the program necessary to simulate the machine breakdown and repair times with the maintenance program. Running this revised program for 200 simulations results in an average annual maintenance cost of $46,160. Again, note that this is not significantly different from the annual cost we determined by manual simulation in Table 15.11.

Simulation results for the breakdown system with the maintenance program

This computer simulation now enables us to recommend a decision regarding the maintenance program that is based on more accurate results. The computer simulation indicated an average annual repair cost of $85,330 without the maintenance program, and an average annual repair cost of $46,160 with the maintenance program. Given these cost figures, the average annual repair cost savings are $39,170. Since the annual cost of the maintenance program is $20,000, it is clear that the company should implement the maintenance program.

Recommended decision based on computer simulation results

AN INVENTORY SIMULATION EXAMPLE

As noted in the discussion of the simulation of queuing systems, some management science software packages, such as QSB+, have the capability to simulate specific systems. A software package for personal computers that we have referred to previously in this text, Microcomputer Software for Quantitative Analysis for Management, has the capability to perform an inventory simulation with two random variables representing demand and lead time. This program simulates sales, demand, inventory levels, ordering, and lead time for a maximum of 100 time periods. The following example will illustrate the simulation capability of this package for inventory systems. (For additional insight into this type of problem, see Chapter 18, Inventory Analysis with Uncertain Demand.)

Simulation of an Inventory System with Uncertain Demand and Lead Time

The Videotech Store has the following probability distribution of weekly demand for VCRs.

Demand for VCRs	Probability
0	.10
1	.15
2	.30
3	.25
4	.20
	1.00

The time it takes for the store to receive an order of VCRs from its distributor (i.e., the lead time) is defined by the following distribution.

Lead Time (weeks)	Probability
1	.35
2	.45
3	.20
	1.00

The store must order 5 VCRs at a time, and the inventory level at which the store makes an order (i.e., the reorder point) is 3 VCRs.

The Microcomputer Software package can simulate this type of inventory system per time period (which in this example is one week) for up to 100 time periods. The simulation (1) generates weekly demand and attempts to fulfill that demand with items already in stock; (2) records the number of units left in inventory and any sales lost because there were not enough units (i.e., stockouts); (3) determines whether an order should be made (by comparing the reorder point to the inventory level); and, if an order is required, (4) generates a lead time (according to the probability distribution for lead time) and orders 5 VCRs.

The simulation requires as input the distribution of demand and lead time values and their corresponding random number ranges, as well as the order quantity and reorder point. The simulation output is provided in tabular form (as if it were done manually) and includes summary statistics. A summary of the input data and the solution output for a simulation of 10 weeks is shown below.

```
DEMAND PROBABILITY INTERVALS
-------------------------------
    VALUE      PROBABILITY
      0           0.10
      1           0.15
      2           0.30
      3           0.25
      4           0.20
-------------------------------


LEAD TIME PROBABILITY INTERVALS
-------------------------------
    VALUE      PROBABILITY
      1           0.35
      2           0.45
      3           0.20
-------------------------------
```

TIME PERIOD	BEG INVEN	RAND #	DEMAND #	SOLD #	ENDING INVEN	LOST SALE	PLACE ORDER	RAND #	LEAD TIME
1	5	44	2	2	3	0	YES	17	1
2	3	92	4	3	0	1	NO	0	0
3	5	2	0	0	5	0	NO	0	0
4	5	12	1	1	4	0	NO	0	0
5	4	25	1	1	3	0	YES	53	2
6	3	93	4	3	0	1	NO	0	0
7	0	46	2	0	0	2	NO	0	0
8	5	34	2	2	3	0	YES	21	1
9	3	22	1	1	2	0	NO	0	0
10	7	79	3	3	4	0	NO	0	0

```
------------------------------------------------------------
          AVG.# OF ORDERS PER PERIOD =  .3
          AVG.# OF UNITS SOLD PER PERIOD = 1.6
          AVG.# OF UNITS LOST SALE =  .4
          AVG.PER PERIOD INVENTORY =  2.4
------------------------------------------------------------

          ***** END OF SIMULATION ANALYSIS *****
```

RANDOM NUMBER GENERATORS

It should be apparent from the previous discussion that random numbers play a very important part in a probabilistic simulation. All the examples that were presented required random numbers. Some of the random numbers we used came from Table 15.3, a table of random numbers. However, random numbers do not come just from tables, and their generation is not as simple as one might initially think. If random numbers are not truly random, the validity of simulation results can be significantly affected.

The random numbers in Table 15.3 were generated using a *numerical technique.* Thus, they are not true random numbers, but *pseudorandom numbers.* True random numbers can be produced only by a physical process, such as spinning a roulette wheel over and over. However, a physical process, such as spinning a roulette wheel, cannot be conveniently employed in a computerized simulation model. Thus, there is a need for a numerical method that artificially creates random numbers.

In order to truly reflect the system being simulated, the artificially created random numbers must have the following characteristics.

1. The random numbers must be uniformly distributed. This means that each random number in the interval of random numbers (i.e., 0 to 1 or 0 to 100) has an equal chance of being selected. If this condition is not met, then the simulation results will be biased by the random numbers that have a *more likely* chance of being selected.

2. The numerical technique for generating random numbers should be efficient. This means that the random numbers should not degenerate into constant values or recycle too frequently. In addition, they should not require too much (computer) time and cost to generate.

3. The sequence of random numbers should not reflect any pattern. For example, the sequence of numbers 0, 1, 2, 3, 4, 5, 6, 7, 8, 9, 0, 1, 2, 3, 4, 5, 6, 7, 8, 9, 0, 1, 2, 3, 4, 5, 6, 7, 8, 9, 0, etc., although uniform, is not random.

You can determine whether the random numbers that are to be used in a simulation contain these characteristics by using any one of several statistical tests.

A number of efficient computer packages that easily generate random numbers with the above characteristics are now available for use on almost any computer system. One example is the random number generator contained in the computer program used to solve the machine breakdown example in the previous section. This random number generator, referred to as RND, is part of the BASICA programming language available on the IBM personal computer.

The BASICA command RND, shown in the program, yields a random number that is subsequently named R1 or R2 for descriptive purposes.

Notice that in the computer output for the machine breakdown example (shown on page 538), the number 9 in parentheses follows the "RANDOMIZE" command. This is the random number *seed value,* and it was selected arbitrarily from a range of thousands of possible seed values. The seed value starts a specific stream of random numbers. If the seed value of 9 is used each time the program is run, the same stream of random numbers will be employed by the program. This is very useful in that it enables us to compare the results from several different simulation experiments without having to worry about any variability created by different random numbers. (For the machine breakdown example, each of the simulation runs representing one year had a *different* stream of random numbers. In contrast, the two simulation experiments we conducted, with the maintenance program and without it, used the same random number stream created by the seed value 9.)

Seed value to generate a stream of random numbers

MODEL EXPERIMENTATION

A primary benefit of simulation analysis is that it enables us to experiment with the model. For example, in our queuing example we could expand the model to represent more service facilities, more queues, and different arrival and service times, and we could observe their effect on the results. In many analytical cases, such experimentation is limited by the availability of an applicable formula. That is, by changing various parts of the problem, we may create a problem for which we have no specific analytical formula. Simulation, however, is not subject to such limitations. Simulation is limited only by one's ability to develop a computer program.

Using the simulation model to test alterations in the system

OPTIMIZATION USING SIMULATION

Simulation is a management science technique that does not generally result in an optimal solution. Generally, a simulation model reflects the *operation of a system,* and the results of the model are in the form of operating statistics, such as averages. However, optimal solutions can sometimes be obtained for simulation models by employing *search techniques.*

A search technique is a method for searching sets of operating characteristics to a simulation model until the best set is found. Optimizing in this manner requires a series of computer simulation

Search techniques

runs, with predetermined changes in the decision variables from run to run.

The model presented earlier in this chapter for determining demand for milk at the Big T supermarket could be changed into an optimization model as follows. First, we would develop a cost function based on the profit from each case of milk sold and the loss from spoilage of unsold cases of milk. Given the fact that demand varies, we would simulate the system for various amounts of milk *ordered*. We would then determine the amount to order from the order quantity that resulted in the highest profit. In other words, the simulation would *search* through a sequence of order quantities and select the one that generated the greatest profit.

An example of searching for the best solution

VALIDATION OF SIMULATION RESULTS

Testing simulation results to make sure they are correct

A major problem of simulation is the difficulty of making sure the results of a simulation analysis are valid. In other words, does the model actually replicate what is going on in the real world? The user of simulation generally wants to be certain that the model is internally correct and that all the operations performed in the simulation are logical and mathematically correct. An old adage often associated with computer simulation is "garbage in, garbage out." In order to gain some assurances about the validity of simulation results, there are several testing procedures that the user of a simulation model can apply.

Checking the simulation model manually

First, the simulation model can be run for short periods of time or for only a few simulation trials. This allows the user to compare the results with manually derived solutions (as we did in the examples in this chapter) in order to check for discrepancies. Another means of testing is to divide the model into parts and simulate each part separately. This reduces the complexity of seeking out errors in the model. Similarly, the mathematical relationships in the simulation model can be simplified so that they can more easily be tested to see if the model is operating correctly.

Comparing the simulation results with real-world data

In order to determine if the model reliably represents the system being simulated, the simulation results can sometimes be compared with actual real-world data. Several statistical tests are available for performing this type of analysis. However, when a model is developed to simulate a *new* or *unique* system, there is no realistic way to ensure that the results are valid.

Starting conditions

An additional problem in determining if a simulation model is a valid representation of the system under analysis relates to starting conditions. Should the simulation be started with the system empty (e.g., should we start by simulating a queuing system with no customers in line), or should the simulation be started as close as possible to normal operating conditions? Another problem, as we have already seen, is the determination of how long the simulation should be run in order to reach true steady-state conditions, if indeed a steady state exists.

In general, a standard, foolproof procedure for validation is simply not possible. In many cases, the user of a simulation model must rely on the expertise and experience of whoever develops the model.

AREAS OF SIMULATION APPLICATION

Chapter 1 presented the results of two surveys that indicated the frequency of application of various management science techniques (see Tables 1.1 and 1.2). In both surveys, simulation ranked as the second most widely applied technique, and one of the surveys (Table 1.1) indicated that simulation was perceived as the most useful of all management science techniques. The reason for this popularity is that simulation can be applied to a number of problems that are too difficult to model and solve analytically. Some analysts feel that complex systems should be studied via simulation whether or not they can be analyzed analytically, because it provides such an easy vehicle for experimenting on the system. As a result, simulation has been applied to a wide range of problems.

Chapter 1 survey results related to simulation

Table 15.12 presents the results of a survey conducted by Christy and Watson and reported in a 1983 issue of *Interfaces*, which indicate the frequency of application of simulation in different functional areas within corporations. The survey was based on responses from nonacademic members of The Institute of Management Sciences and the Operations Research Society of America. Eighty-nine percent of the responding firms indicated they currently used simulation.

Percentage of companies using simulation

TABLE 15.12
Frequency of Simulation Application in
Functional Areas

Functional Area	Percentage of Respondents Indicating Simulation Application
Production	59%
Corporate Planning	53
Engineering	46
Finance	41
Research and Development	37
Marketing	24
Data Processing	16
Personnel	10

Reprinted by permission of D. Christy and H. Watson, "The Application of Simulation: A Survey of Industry Practice," in *Interfaces, 13*, 5, October 1983. Copyright 1983 The Institute of Management Sciences.

Following are descriptions of some of the more common applications of simulation.

Queuing

A major application of simulation has been in the analysis of queuing systems. As indicated in Chapter 14, the assumptions required to solve the operating characteristic formulas are relatively restrictive. For the more complex queuing systems (which result from a relaxation of these assumptions), it is not possible to develop analytical formulas, and simulation is often the only available means of analysis.

Inventory Control

Most people are aware that product demand is an essential component in determining the amount of inventory a commercial enterprise should keep. Most of the mathematical formulas used to analyze inventory systems make the assumption that this demand is certain (i.e., not a random variable). In practice, however, demand is rarely known with certainty. Simulation is one of the few means for analyzing inventory systems in which demand is a random variable, reflecting demand uncertainty. Inventory control will be discussed in Chapters 17 and 18.

Production and Manufacturing

Simulation is often applied to production problems, such as production scheduling, production sequencing, assembly line balancing (of in-process inventory), plant layout, and plant location analysis. It is surprising how often various production processes can be viewed as queuing systems that can only be analyzed using simulation. Since machine breakdowns typically occur according to some probability distributions, maintenance problems are also frequently analyzed using simulation.

In the last few years, several software packages for the personal computer have been developed to simulate all aspects of manufacturing operations. Two examples are SIMFACTORY and XCELL. SIMFACTORY is written in the SIMSCRIPT 11.5 simulation language, a highly acclaimed and powerful language. This package is very user friendly and requires no programming by the user; it has exceptional modeling and graphics capabilities. Applications of SIMFACTORY can be classified into two categories: evaluation of proposed systems (such as when an expansion of operations or a new manufacturing facility is contemplated) and evaluation of changes in existing operating policies, product mixes, scheduling strategies, and capacity. XCELL, although not as powerful as SIMFACTORY, is nevertheless an excellent package that enables the user to design a model of a factory, which can then be evaluated. While the model is being run, the "factory" can be changed to simulate different scenarios.

Finance

Capital budgeting problems require estimates of cash flows, which are often a result of many random variables. Simulation has been used to generate values of the various contributing factors to derive estimates of cash flows. Simulation has also been used to determine the inputs into rate of return calculations where the inputs are random variables, such as market size, selling price, growth rate, and market share.

Marketing

Marketing problems typically include numerous random variables, such as market size and type and consumer preferences. Simulation can be used to ascertain how a particular market might react to the introduction of a product or to an advertising campaign for an existing product. Another area in marketing where simulation is applied is the analysis of distribution channels to determine the most efficient distribution system.

Public Service Operations

Recently the operations of police departments, fire departments, post offices, hospitals, court systems, airports, and other public systems have been analyzed using simulation. Typically such operations are so complex and contain so many random variables that no technique except simulation can be employed for analysis.

Environmental and Resource Analysis

Some of the more recent innovative applications of simulation have been directed at problems in the environment. Simulation models have been developed to ascertain the impact of projects such as nuclear power plants, reservoirs, highways, and dams on the environment. In many cases, these models include measures to analyze the financial feasibility of such projects. Other models have been developed to simulate pollution conditions. In the area of resource analysis, numerous models have been developed in recent years to simulate energy systems and the feasibility of alternative energy sources.

SIMULATION LANGUAGES

Computer languages developed specifically to perform simulation operations

The computer programming aspects of simulation can be quite diffi-cult. Fortunately, generalized simulation languages have been devel-oped to perform many of the functions of a simulation study. Each of these languages requires at least some knowledge of a scientific or business-oriented programming language. Some of these simulation languages are GPSS, GASP, DYNAMO, SIMSCRIPT, SIMULA, GERT, Q-GERT, and SLAM. Each of these languages is more appli-cable to certain problems than others. For example, DYNAMO is useful when the random variables change over time (i.e., when they are dynamic); GPSS and GASP are useful languages for queuing problems; GERT, Q-GERT, and SLAM are "network" simulation packages applicable to systems that can be represented as networks.

Programming languages used most frequently for simulation

The survey on simulation applications conducted by Christy and Watson (mentioned in the previous section) also indicated the popu-larity of the various programming languages used for simulation modeling. Table 15.13 presents the results of this portion of the survey.

TABLE 15.13
Programming Languages Used for
Simulation Applications

Programming Language	Percent Using for Simulation Applications
FORTRAN	81%
GPSS	40
Special purpose financial planning (IFPS, SIMPLAN, EXPRESS, etc.)	35
BASIC	31
PL/I	25
SIMSCRIPT	19
APL	18
COBOL	16
SLAM	6
Q-GERT	5
Other	17

Reprinted by permission of D. Christy and H. Watson, "The Application of Simulation: A Survey of Industry Practice," in *Interfaces, 13,* 5, October 1983. Copyright 1983 The Insti-tute of Management Sciences.

APPLICATIONS OF SIMULATION

Wilderness Recreational Travel

Growth in the use of wilderness recreational areas has been very rapid, and the resulting congestion and damage to resources have created difficult problems for the managers of these areas. The problem is exacerbated by the uneven use of wilderness areas, with some areas experiencing heavy use and others experiencing little use. In addition, use increases or decreases according to the time of the year and day of the week, with summer weekends being the time of peak use. To solve these problems, managers have attempted to redistribute visitors away from heavily used areas to areas with little use, without reducing total use. However, because of the complexity of travel routes within wilderness areas, which overlap and intertwine, and the great variability in travel decisions, redistribution is difficult.

A simulation model was developed to provide a better way of formulating and evaluating policies for the management of wilderness area use. The model, written in the GPSS language, generates visitors of varying types and groups who arrive at various simulated times at different entrance points and move along selected routes of travel. The model provides information for simulations of particular use scenarios. The model has been applied in several wilderness areas. The Desolation Wilderness in California, encompassing over 64,000 acres, is one such area for which a use rationing plan was developed with the simulation model. Daily entrance quotas for each of sixteen entry points were determined that reduced visitor encounters with other groups.[1]

Evaluating policies for wilderness area use

Corporate Planning

Canterbury Timber Products Ltd. of New Zealand produces a medium-density fiberboard as its principal product at a plant that was completed in 1976. The company, faced with market and financial uncertainties in a technologically advanced, capital-intensive production environment, determined the need for more extensive planning. A simulation model was developed for this purpose. The simulation planning model was designed to assist management in developing medium-term (two to three years) corporate plans that encompassed all aspects of the company's operation from sales forecasting to cash flow analysis. The simulation model consisted of four submodels referred to as sales, production, cash flow, and print.

The sales submodel uses sales and price forecasts to develop input data for the other submodels. The production submodel uses the sales projections to generate a production schedule in addition to providing estimates of raw materials, inventory requirements, labor force, and so forth. The cash flow submodel is the main component of the planning model. Sales and production information is analyzed in this submodel, which enables analysis for marginal pricing and new market penetration. The print submodel generates relevant reports for sales, production, etc. The model increased profitability

[1]M. Schecter and R. Lucas, "Validating a Large Scale Simulation Model of Wilderness Recreational Travel," *Interfaces* 10, no. 5 (October 1980): 11–18.

by (1) enabling the company to explore more technological, production, and marketing alternatives; (2) improving the quality of decision making; (3) providing greater confidence in decisions; (4) enabling more effective planning; (5) providing more timely information; and (6) promoting a better understanding of the business.[2]

Restaurant Operations and Planning

In 1980 Burger King (a division of The Pillsbury Company) operated 3,000 fast-food restaurants in the United States and in other nations and was opening new restaurants at the rate of 300 per year. Eighty percent of the restaurants were owned independently. Although the corporation had to adhere to strict company policies, franchise owners had to be persuaded to adopt new products, systems, and procedures on a cost-benefit basis. Franchisers had to be shown that changes would increase sales and profits and thus provide an adequate return on their investment.

Since its inception in 1954, Burger King has exhibited innovative operational and marketing strategies that have led to growth and profitability. (For example, Burger King was the first fast-food hamburger system to introduce drive-thru service, which improved sales dramatically.) In 1978 Burger King decided to introduce specialty sandwiches, which by 1980 accounted for 20% of sales. However, the production of these sandwiches created operational problems, threatened service times, and rendered kitchen designs inadequate. This problem—together with a generally changing fast-food business, increasingly complex production systems, and changing customers—indicated the need for measures that would enhance efficiency and productivity. An operations research group was formed to develop a simulation model to assist in achieving this objective.

A general-purpose restaurant simulation model was developed that encompassed three subsystems: (1) the customer system, (2) the production system, and (3) the delivery system. The model was used to test new product service concepts and new restaurant configurations, to analyze labor and staffing needs, to solve operational problems, to analyze individual restaurant profitability and productivity, and to deal with a variety of other corporate activities. The model was implemented in 1980, and virtually no operational decision was made without the benefit of simulation model analysis. As an example of its success, the application of the simulation model to analyze the drive-thru system resulted in reduced customer waiting

[2]C. Kluyver and G. McNally, "Corporate Planning Using Simulation," *Interfaces* 10, no. 3 (June 1980): 1–7.

times, which generated an additional $15 million in annual sales capacity.[3]

Timber Processing

At Weyerhaeuser Company, processing timber requires decisions on cutting trees into logs and allocating these logs (called stems) to different mills to be manufactured into different end products such as paper or lumber. There may be hundreds of combinations of different log lengths and different allocations that can be made, and each combination can result in different revenues based on the resulting end product. Such decisions are made hundreds of times each day by operators in the field, who must consider the physical characteristics of the stems as well as varying economic factors in their decision making. Weyerhaeuser developed a "decision simulator," an interactive visual (rather than numeric) simulation of the decision-making scenario (somewhat similar to a videogame) to deal with this problem. The operator is provided a realistic visual display of each stem; the operator can then simulate cutting the stem and allocating it in various ways. The logs and profit contributions from these decisions are provided, as well as the stem cut and allocation generated from a dynamic programming algorithm constructed to maximize profit. This process can be repeated to explore alternative decisions. The system contributes several million dollars annually to company profits.[4]

CD Portfolio Management in a Bank

The First National Bank and Trust Company of Tulsa, Oklahoma developed a simulation model to assess the impact of different interest-rate conditions on its certificate of deposit (CD) portfolio for planning purposes. The simulation model computes the mean dollar weighted yield of the CD portfolio, which reflects the bank's cost of offering the CDs. In this statistic the interest rates of larger CDs are weighted more heavily than those of smaller CDs. The model results are in the form of alternative portfolio yields computed for different interest rates and different times to maturity, representing the manager's "what-if" analyses of future conditions. The model was developed using the SLAM simulation language. The authors of the article describing this model note that simulation appears to be the most

---

[3]W. Swart and L. Donno, "Simulation Modeling Improves Operations, Planning, and Productivity of Fast Food Restaurants," *Interfaces* 11, no. 6 (December 1981): 35–44.

[4]M. Lenbersky and U. Chi, "'Decision Simulators' Speed Implementation and Improve Operations," *Interfaces* 14, no. 4 (July–August 1984): 1–15.

widely used of all management science techniques in the banking industry.[5]

Summary

An important and widely used management science technique

Simulation has become an increasingly important management science technique in recent years. Various surveys have shown simulation to be one of the techniques most widely applied to real-world problems. Evidence of this popularity is the number of specialized simulation languages that have been developed by the computer industry and academia to deal with complex problem areas.

The popularity of simulation

The popularity of simulation is due in large part to the flexibility it allows in analyzing systems, compared to more confining analytical techniques. In other words, the problem does not have to fit the model (or technique)—the simulation model can be constructed to fit the problem. Simulation is popular also because it is an excellent experimental technique enabling systems and problems to be tested within a laboratory setting.

Limitations of simulation

However, in spite of its versatility, simulation has limitations and must be used with caution. One limitation is that simulation models are typically unstructured and must be developed for a system or problem that is also unstructured. Unlike some of the structured techniques presented in this text, they cannot simply be applied to a specific type of problem. As a result, developing simulation models often requires a certain amount of imagination and intuitiveness that is not required by some of the more straightforward solution techniques we have presented. In addition, the validation of simulation models is an area of serious concern. It is often impossible to realistically validate simulation results, to know if they accurately reflect the system under analysis. This problem has become an area of such concern that "output analysis" of simulation results is developing into a new field of study. Another limiting factor in simulation is the cost in money and time of model building. Because simulation models are developed for unstructured systems, they often take large amounts of staff, computer time, and money to develop and run. For many business companies, these costs can be prohibitive.

[5]R. Russell and R. Hickle, "Simulation of a CD Portfolio," *Interfaces* 16, no. 3 (May–June 1986): 49–54.

References

Christy, D., and Watson, H. "The Applications of Simulation: A Survey of Industry Practice." *Interfaces* 13, no. 5 (October 1983): 47–52.

Greenberg, S. *GPSS Primer.* New York: Wiley-Interscience, 1972.

Hammersly, J. M., and Handscomb, D. C. *Monte Carlo Methods.* New York: John Wiley and Sons, 1964.

Kluyver, C., and McNally, G. "Corporate Planning Using Simulation." *Interfaces* 10, no. 3 (June 1980): 1–7.

Markowitz, H. M.; Karr, H. W.; and Hausner, B. *SIMSCRIPT: A Simulation Programming Language.* Englewood Cliffs, N.J.: Prentice-Hall, 1963.

Meier, R. C.; Newell, W. T.; and Pazer, H. L. *Simulation in Business and Economics.* Englewood Cliffs, N.J.: Prentice-Hall, 1969.

Mize, J. and Cox, G. *Essentials of Simulation.* Englewood Cliffs, N.J.: Prentice-Hall, 1968.

Naylor, T. H.; Balintfy, J. L.; Burdinck, D. S.; and Chu, K. *Computer Simulation Techniques.* New York: John Wiley and Sons, 1966.

Pritsker, A. A. B. *Modeling and Analysis Using Q-GERT Networks.* 2d ed. New York: John Wiley and Sons, 1977.

———. *The GASP IV Simulation Language.* New York: John Wiley and Sons, 1974.

Schriber, T. J. *Simulation Using GPSS.* New York: John Wiley and Sons, 1974.

Shecter, M., and Lucas, R. "Validating a Large Scale Simulation Model of Wilderness Recreational Travel." *Interfaces* 10, no. 5 (October 1980): 11–18.

Swart, W., and Donno, L. "Simulation Modeling Improves Operations, Planning, and Productivity of Fast Food Restaurants." *Interfaces* 11, no. 6 (December 1981): 35–44.

Tocher, K. D. "Review of Computer Simulation." *Operational Research Quarterly* 16 (June 1965): 189–217.

Van Horne, R. L. "Validation of Simulation Results." *Management Science* 17 (January 1971): 247–257.

Wyman, F. P. *Simulation Modeling: A Guide to Using SIMSCRIPT.* New York: John Wiley and Sons, 1970.

EXAMPLE PROBLEM SOLUTION

The following example problem demonstrates a manual simulation using discrete probability distributions.

Problem Statement

Members of the Willow Creek Emergency Rescue Squad know from past experience that they will receive between 0 and 6 emergency calls each night, according to the following discrete probability distribution.

Calls	Probability
0	.05
1	.12
2	.15
3	.25
4	.22
5	.15
6	.06
	1.00

The rescue squad classifies each emergency call into one of three categories: minor, regular, or major emergency. The probability that a particular call will be each type of emergency is as follows.

Emergency Type	Probability
Minor	.30
Regular	.56
Major	.14
	1.00

The type of emergency call determines the size of the crew sent in response. A minor emergency requires a two-person crew, a regular call requires a three-person crew, and a major emergency requires a five-person crew.

Simulate the emergency calls received by the rescue squad for 10 nights, compute the average number of each type of emergency call each night, and determine the maximum number of crew members that might be needed on any given night.

Step 1: Develop Random Number Ranges for the Probability Distributions

Calls	Probability	Cumulative Probability	Random Number Range, r_1
0	.05	.05	1–5
1	.12	.17	6–17
2	.15	.32	18–32
3	.25	.57	33–57
4	.22	.79	58–79
5	.15	.94	80–94
6	.06	1.00	95–99, 00
	1.00		

Emergency Type	Probability	Cumulative Probability	Random Number Ranges, r_2
Minor	.30	.30	1–30
Regular	.56	.86	31–86
Major	.14	1.00	87–99, 00
	1.00		

Step 2: Set Up a Tabular Simulation

Use the second column of random numbers in Table 15.3.

Night	r_1	Number of Calls	r_2	Emergency Type	Crew Size	Total per Night
1	65	4	71	Regular	3	
			18	Minor	2	
			12	Minor	2	
			17	Minor	2	9
2	48	3	89	Major	5	
			18	Minor	2	
			83	Regular	3	10
3	08	1	90	Regular	3	3
4	05	0	—			
5	89	5	18	Minor	2	
			08	Minor	2	
			26	Minor	2	
			47	Regular	3	
			94	Major	5	14
6	06	1	72	Regular	3	3
7	62	4	47	Regular	3	
			68	Regular	3	
			60	Regular	3	
			88	Major	5	14
8	17	1	36	Regular	3	3
9	77	4	43	Regular	3	
			28	Minor	2	
			31	Regular	3	
			06	Minor	2	10
10	68	4	39	Regular	3	
			71	Regular	3	
			22	Minor	2	
			76	Regular	3	11

Step 3: Compute Results

$$\text{Average number of minor emergency calls per night} = \frac{10}{10} = 1.0$$

$$\text{Average number of regular emergency calls per night} = \frac{14}{10} = 1.4$$

$$\text{Average number of major emergency calls per night} = \frac{3}{10} = .30$$

If all the calls came in at the same time, the maximum number of squad members required during any one night would be 14.

Problems

1. Either 1, 2, 3, 4, or 5 customers come into the Fast Shop Market every hour, according to the following probability distribution.

Customers/Hour	Frequency of Occurrence	Probability
1	10	.10
2	40	.40
3	30	.30
4	15	.15
5	5	.05
	100	1.00

   a. Generate the number of customers per hour who arrive at the market for 20 hours, using the random number table in Table 15.3 (start with the fifth column from the left).
   b. Compute the average number of customers who arrive per hour, and compare this value with the expected value of the number of customers per hour computed from the probability distribution.

2. Cityside Realty gets either 2, 3, or 4 new listings for houses to sell every week, according to the following probability distribution.

Listings/Week	Probability
2	.30
3	.05
4	.20
	1.00

   Simulate the listings per week for 6 months, using the random numbers in Table 15.3, and compute the average listings per week.

3. The Hoylake Rescue Squad receives an emergency call every 1, 2, 3, 4, 5, or 6 hours, according to the following probability distribution.

Time Between Emergency Calls (hours)	Probability
1	.05
2	.10
3	.30
4	.30
5	.20
6	.05
	1.00

   The squad is on duty 24 hours per day, 7 days per week.

a. Simulate the emergency calls for 3 days (note that this will require a "running" or cumulative hourly clock), using the random number table.
b. Compute the average time between calls and compare this value with the expected value of the time between calls from the probability distribution. Why are the results different?
c. How many calls were made during the 3-day period? Can you logically assume that this is an average number of calls per 3-day period? If not, how could you simulate to determine such an average?

4. The time between arrivals of cars at the Petroco Service Station is defined by the following probability distribution.

Time Between Arrivals (minutes)	Probability
1	.15
2	.30
3	.40
4	.15
	1.00

a. Simulate the arrival of cars at the service station for 20 arrivals, and compute the average time between arrivals.
b. Simulate the arrival of cars at the service station for 1 hour using a different stream of random numbers from those used in part a, and compute the average time between arrivals.
c. Compare the results obtained in parts a and b.

5. The Dynaco Manufacturing Company produces a product in a process consisting of operations of 5 machines. The probability distribution of the number of machines that will break down in a week is as follows.

Machine Breakdowns per Week	Probability
0	.10
1	.10
2	.20
3	.25
4	.30
5	.05
	1.00

a. Simulate the machine breakdowns per week for 20 weeks.
b. Compute the average number of machines that will break down per week.

6. Every time a machine breaks down at the Dynaco Manufacturing Company (problem 5), either 1, 2, or 3 hours are required to fix it, according to the following probability distribution.

Repair Time (hours)	Probability
1	.30
2	.50
3	.20
	1.00

a. Simulate the repair time for 20 weeks and compute the average weekly repair time.
b. If the random numbers that are used to simulate breakdowns per week are also used to simulate repair time per breakdown, will the results be affected in any way? Explain.
c. If it costs $50 per hour to repair a machine when it breaks down (including lost productivity), determine the average weekly breakdown cost.
d. The Dynaco Company is considering a preventive maintenance program that would alter the probabilities of machine breakdowns per week as follows.

Machine Breakdowns per Week	Probability
0	.20
1	.30
2	.20
3	.15
4	.10
5	.05
	1.00

The weekly cost of the preventive maintenance program is $150. Using simulation, determine whether the company should institute the preventive maintenance program.

7. The Stereo Warehouse in Georgetown sells stereo sets, which it orders from Fuji Electronics in Japan. Because of shipping and handling costs, each order must be for 5 stereos. Because of the time it takes to receive an order, the warehouse outlet places an order every time the present stock drops to 5 stereos. It costs $100 to place an order. It costs the warehouse $400 in lost sales when a customer asks for a stereo and the warehouse is out of stock. It costs $40 to keep each stereo stored in the warehouse. If a customer cannot purchase a stereo when it is requested, the customer will not wait until one comes in but will go to a competitor. The following probability distribution for demand for stereos has been determined.

Demand per Month	Probability
0	.04
1	.08
2	.28
3	.40
4	.16
5	.02
6	.02
	1.00

The time required to receive an order once it is placed has the following probability distribution.

Time to Receive an Order (months)	Probability
1	.60
2	.30
3	.10
	1.00

The warehouse presently has 5 stereos in stock. Orders are always received at the beginning of the week. Simulate the Stereo Warehouse's ordering and sales policy for 20 months, using the first column of random numbers in Table 15.3. Compute the average monthly cost.

8. The First American Bank is trying to determine whether it should install one or two drive-in teller windows. The following probability distributions for arrival intervals and service times have been developed from historical data.

Time Between Automobile Arrivals (minutes)	Probability
1	.20
2	.60
3	.10
4	.10
	1.00

Service Time (minutes)	Probability
2	.10
3	.40
4	.20
5	.20
6	.10
	1.00

Assume that in the two-server system an arriving car will join the shorter queue. When the queues are of equal length, there is a 50–50 chance the driver will enter the queue for either window.

a. Simulate both the one- and the two-teller system. Compute the average queue length, waiting time, and percentage utilization for each system.
b. Discuss your results in part a and suggest the degree to which they could be used to make a decision about which system to employ.

9. The time between arrivals of oil tankers at a loading dock at Prudhoe Bay is given by the following probability distribution.

Time Between Ship Arrivals (days)	Probability
1	.05
2	.10
3	.20
4	.30
5	.20
6	.10
7	.05
	1.00

The time required to fill a tanker with oil and prepare it for sea is given by the following probability distribution.

Time to Fill and Prepare (days)	Probability
3	.10
4	.20
5	.40
6	.30
	1.00

a. Simulate the movement of tankers to and from the single loading dock for the first 20 arrivals. Compute the average time between arrivals, average waiting time to load, and the average number of tankers waiting to be loaded.
b. Discuss any hesitation you might have about using your results for decision making.

10. Differentiate between true random numbers and pseudorandom numbers.

11. Discuss the properties pseudorandom numbers must exhibit in order to be truly random.

12. The Saki automobile dealer in the Minneapolis–St. Paul area orders the Saki sport compact, which gets 50 miles per gallon of gasoline, from the manufacturer in Japan. However, the dealer never knows for sure how

many months it will take to receive an order once it is placed. It can take 1, 2, or 3 months with the following probabilities.

Months to Receive an Order	Probability
1	.50
2	.30
3	.20
	1.00

The demand per month is given by the following distribution.

Demand per Month (cars)	Probability
1	.10
2	.30
3	.40
4	.20
	1.00

The dealer orders when the number of cars on the lot gets down to a certain level. In order to determine the appropriate level of cars to use as an indicator of when to order, the dealer needs to know how many cars will be demanded during the time required to receive an order.

Simulate the demand for 30 orders and compute the average number of cars demanded during the time required to receive an order. At what level of cars in stock should the dealer place an order?

13. State University is playing Tech in their annual football game on Saturday. A sportswriter has scouted each team all season and accumulated the following data. State runs 4 basic plays—a sweep, a pass, a draw, and an off tackle; Tech uses 3 basic defenses—a wide tackle, an Oklahoma, and a blitz. The number of yards State will gain for each play against each defense is shown in the following table.

State Play	Wide Tackle	Tech Defense Oklahoma	Blitz
Sweep	−3	5	12
Pass	12	4	−10
Draw	2	1	20
Off tackle	7	3	−3

The probability that State will run each of its 4 plays is as follows.

Play	Probability
Sweep	.10
Pass	.20
Draw	.20
Off tackle	.50

The probability that Tech will use each of its defenses is as follows.

Defense	Probability
Wide tackle	.30
Oklahoma	.50
Blitz	.20

The sportswriter estimates that State will run 40 plays during the game. The sportswriter believes that if State gains 300 or more yards it will win; however, if Tech holds State to fewer than 300 yards it will win. Use simulation to determine which team the sportswriter will predict to win the game.

14. Each quarter, the students in the College of Business at State University must have their course schedules approved by the college advisor. The students line up in the hallway outside the advisor's office. The students arrive at the office according to the following probability distribution.

Time Between Arrivals (minutes)	Probability
4	.20
5	.30
6	.40
7	.10
	1.00

The time required by the advisor to examine and approve a schedule corresponds to the following probability distribution.

Schedule Approval (minutes)	Probability
3	.30
4	.50
5	.20
	1.00

Simulate this course approval system for 90 minutes. Compute the average queue length and the average time a student must wait, and discuss these results.

15. A new airport is being planned for a large urban area. The FAA has estimated the air traffic that will flow through the airport. You have been hired as a management scientist to develop a computerized simulation model that will provide information for the actual physical design of the airport. Identify the items you believe should be incorporated into the

simulation model, and discuss in general terms how you would design the simulation model.

16. A baseball game consists of plays that can be described as follows.

Play	Description
No advance	An out where no runners can advance. This includes strikeouts, popups, short flies, and the like.
Ground out	All runners can advance one base.
Possible double play	Double play if there is a runner on first base and fewer than two outs. The lead runner who can be forced is out; runners not out advance one base. If there is no runner on first or there are two outs, this play is treated as a "no advance."
Long fly	A runner on third base can score.
Very long fly	Runners on second and third base advance one base.
Walk	Includes a hit batter.
Infield single	All runners advance one base.
Outfield single	A runner on first base advances one base, but a runner on second or third base scores.
Long single	All runners can advance a maximum of two bases.
Double	Runners can advance a maximum of two bases.
Long double	All runners score.
Triple	
Home run	

Note: Singles also include a factor for errors allowing the batter to reach first base.

Distributions for these plays for two teams, the White Sox (visitors) and the Yankees (home), are as follows.

Team: White Sox

Play	Probability
No advance	.03
Groundout	.39
Possible double play	.06
Long fly	.09
Very long fly	.08
Walk	.06
Infield single	.02
Outfield single	.10
Long single	.03
Double	.04
Long double	.05
Triple	.02
Home run	.03
	1.00

Team: Yankees

Play	Probability
No advance	.04
Groundout	.38
Possible double play	.04
Long fly	.10
Very long fly	.06
Walk	.07
Infield single	.04
Outfield single	.10
Long single	.04
Double	.05
Long double	.03
Triple	.01
Home run	.04
	1.00

Simulate a nine-inning baseball game using the above information.[6]

---

[6]This problem was adapted from R. E. Trueman, "A Computer Simulation Model of Baseball: With Particular Application to Strategy Analysis," in R. E. Machol, S. P. Ladany, and D. G. Morrison, eds., *Management Science in Sports* (New York: North Holland Publishing Co., 1976), 1–14.

16

Forecasting

A forecast is a prediction of what will occur in the future. Meteorologists forecast the weather, sportscasters predict the winners of football games, and managers of business firms attempt to predict how much of their product will be demanded in the future. In fact, managers are constantly trying to predict the future regarding a number of factors, in order to make decisions in the present that will ensure the continued success of their firms. Often a manager will use judgment, opinion, or past experiences to forecast what will occur in the future. However, a number of mathematical methods are also available to aid the manager in making decisions. In this chapter, we will discuss two of the more traditional forecasting methods: time series analysis and regression. Although no technique will result in a totally accurate forecast (i.e., it is impossible to predict the future exactly), these forecasting methods can provide reliable guidelines for decision making.

Predicting what will
occur in the future

565

FORECASTING METHODS

There are a variety of forecasting methods, the applicability of which is dependent on the *time frame* of the forecast (i.e., how far in the future we are forecasting), the *existence of patterns* in the forecast (i.e., seasonal trends, peak periods, etc.), and the *number of variables* the forecast is related to. We will discuss each of these factors separately.

In general, forecasts can be classified according to three time frames: short-range, medium-range, and long-range. *Short-range* forecasts typically encompass the immediate future and are concerned with the daily operations of a business firm, such as daily demand or resource requirements. A short-range forecast rarely goes beyond a couple of months into the future. A *medium-range* forecast typically encompasses anywhere from one or two months to a year. A forecast of this length is generally more closely related to a yearly production plan and will reflect such items as peaks and valleys in demand and the necessity to secure additional resources for the upcoming year. A *long-range* forecast typically encompasses a period longer than one or two years. Long-range forecasts are related to management's attempt to plan new products for changing markets, build new facilities, or secure long-term financing. In general, the further into the future one seeks to predict, the more difficult forecasting is.

These classifications should be viewed as generalizations. The line of demarcation between medium- and long-range forecasts is often quite arbitrary and not always distinct. For some firms a medium-range forecast could be several years, and for other firms a long-range forecast could be in terms of months.

Forecasts often exhibit patterns or trends. A *trend* is a long-term movement of the item being forecast. For example, the demand for personal computers has shown an upward trend during the last several years without any long downward movement in the market. A *cycle* represents movement up or down during a trend. For example, new housing projects have shown a long, generally upward trend, but with cycles of up and down periods corresponding to economic conditions (high inflation, interest rates, etc.). A *seasonal pattern* is a movement that occurs periodically and is repetitive. For example, every winter the demand for sleds increases dramatically. Complicating the forecasting process is the fact that an item may exhibit *random movements*, which are not predictable and follow no pattern.

Some forecasts are related solely to time, whereas others are *dependent* on several variables. For example, the demand for gasoline is a function of the number of automobiles, the price and availability of gasoline, and the availability of alternative sources of transportation. An accurate forecast of the demand for gasoline would have to take these variables into consideration.

The factors discussed above determine the type of forecasting method that can or should be employed. In this chapter we are going to discuss two general types of forecasting methods that reflect these factors: *time series analysis* and *regression*.

TIME SERIES METHODS

Time series methods are statistical techniques that make use of historical data accumulated over a period of time. Time series methods assume that what has occurred in the past will continue to occur in the future. As the name *time series* suggests, these methods relate the forecast to only one factor—*time*. Time series methods tend to be most useful for short-range forecasting, although they can be used for longer range forecasting. We will discuss two types of time series methods: the *moving average* and *exponential smoothing*.

Forecasts related to time only

The Moving Average

To demonstrate the *moving average* forecasting method, we will use the following example. The Instant Paper Clip Office Supply Company sells and delivers office supplies to various companies, schools, and agencies within a 30-mile radius of its warehouse. The office supply business is extremely competitive, and the ability to deliver orders promptly is an important factor in getting new customers and keeping old ones. (Offices typically order not when their inventory of supplies is getting low, but when they completely run out. As a result, they need their orders immediately.) The manager of the company wants to be certain that enough drivers and delivery vehicles are available so that orders can be delivered promptly. Therefore, the manager wants to be able to forecast the number of orders that will occur during the next month (i.e., to forecast the demand for deliveries).

A moving average example

From records of delivery orders the manager has accumulated data for the past ten months. These data are shown in Table 16.1 and plotted in the graph in Figure 16.1.

TABLE 16.1

Orders for Ten-Month Period

Month	Orders Delivered per Month
January	120
February	90
March	100
April	75
May	110
June	50
July	75
August	130
September	110
October	90

FIGURE 16.1

Graph of Orders
per Month for the
Instant Paper Clip
Office Supply
Company

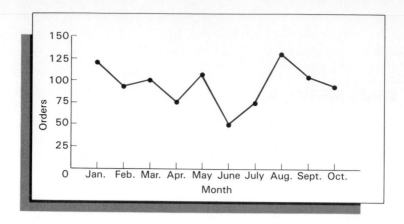

Computing the
moving average

The moving average forecast is computed by dividing the sum of the values of the forecast variable, orders per month for a sequence of months, by the number of months in the sequence. Frequently a moving average is calculated for three time periods. In our example a three-month moving average for February is computed by summing the number of orders for the three-month sequence of January, February, and March, of which February is the middle month.

A three-month
moving average

$$\text{February moving average} = \frac{120 + 90 + 100}{3}$$

$$= 103.3 \text{ orders per month}$$

The March moving average is computed as

$$\text{March moving average} = \frac{90 + 100 + 75}{3}$$

$$= 88.3 \text{ orders per month}$$

Notice that this approach results in no moving average for either January, the first month, or October, the last month. Only months that are in the middle of a sequence have moving averages.

The moving averages for the remaining months are shown in Table 16.2. In addition, this table includes the five-month moving average forecast in which a sequence of five months is employed.

The next period
forecast

For this example we are assuming that it is presently the end of October. The forecast resulting from either the three- or the five-month moving average is typically for the next month in the sequence, which in this case is November. The forecast for November is 110 orders using the three-month moving average, and 91 orders using the five-month moving average. Thus, the moving average method as used in this example generates a forecast for only the next immediate time period. (The actual forecast value is simply the last moving average computed in the sequence.)

TABLE 16.2

Three- and Five-Month Moving Averages

Month	Delivered Orders per Month	Three-Month Moving Average	Five-Month Moving Average
January	120	—	—
February	90	103.3	—
March	100	88.3	99.0
April	75	95.0	85.0
May	110	78.3	82.0
June	50	78.3	88.0
July	75	85.0	95.0
August	130	105.0	91.0
September	110	110.0	—
October	90	—	—

November forecasts

We can use the moving average to forecast further into the future than one period by determining if there is a pattern in the historical data. If a visible pattern appears (which would be most readily observed from a graph of the moving averages), then the last moving average value can be modified to reflect a more realistic forecast, rather than simply projected as the next period forecast. In addition, evidence of a moving average pattern can enable the forecaster to project the pattern several periods into the future rather than just the next period.

Forecasting into the future

Both moving average forecasts in Table 16.2 tend to *smooth* out the variability occurring in the actual data. This smoothing effect can be observed in Figure 16.2, in which the three-month and five-month averages have been superimposed on our graph of the original data (Fig. 16.1). The extremes in the actual orders per month have been reduced. This is beneficial if these extremes simply reflect

Smoothing the variability in the data

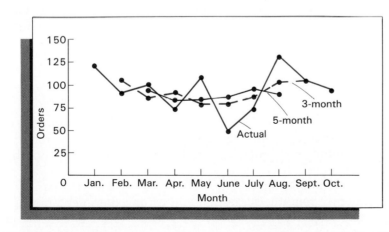

FIGURE 16.2

Three- and Five-Month Moving Averages

random fluctuations in orders per month, since our moving average forecast will not be strongly influenced by them.

Notice that the five-month moving average in Figure 16.2 smooths out fluctuations to a greater extent than the three-month moving average. However, the three-month average more closely reflects the most recent data available to the office supply manager. (The five-month average forecast considers data all the way back to June; the three-month average goes back only to August.) Therefore, forecasts made using the five-month moving average would be slower to react to a change in orders than would those made using the three-month moving average. The extra two months of data dampen the speed with which the forecast responds. Establishing the appropriate number of periods to use in a moving average forecast often requires an extensive amount of trial-and-error experimentation.

Disadvantage of the moving average

The major disadvantage of the moving average method is that it does not react well to variations that occur *for a reason,* such as cycles and seasonal effects (although this method does reflect long-term trends). Those factors that cause changes are generally ignored. It is basically a "mechanical" method, which reflects historical data in a consistent fashion. However, the moving average method does have the advantage of being easy to use, quick, and inexpensive. In general, this method can provide a relatively good forecast for the *immediate future*, but an attempt should not be made to push the forecast too far into the distant future.

The moving average method can be adjusted to more closely reflect more recent fluctuations in the data and seasonal effects. This adjusted method is referred to as a *weighted moving average* method. In this method, weights are assigned to the most recent data. For example, we will assign a weight of 3 to the October data, and weights of 2 and 1 to the September and August data. Next, the sum of the data values multiplied by the weights is divided by the sum of the weights to yield the forecast for November.

$$\text{Weighted three-month average} = \frac{3(90) + 2(110) + 1(130)}{6}$$

$$= 103.3 \text{ orders per month}$$

Notice that this forecast is slightly lower than our previously computed three-month average forecast of 110 orders, reflecting the lower number of orders in October (the most recent month in the sequence).

Determining the precise weights to use for each period of data frequently requires some trial-and-error experimentation, as does determining the exact number of periods to include in the moving average. If the most recent months are weighted too heavily, the forecast might overreact to a random fluctuation in orders; if they are weighted too lightly, the forecast might underreact to an actual change in the pattern of orders.

Exponential Smoothing

The *exponential smoothing* forecast method is actually a moving average method that weights the most recent past data more strongly than more distant past data. As such, the forecast will react more strongly to immediate changes in the data. This is very useful *if* the recent changes in the data are the results of an *actual* change (e.g., a seasonal pattern) instead of just random fluctuations (for which a simple moving average forecast would suffice).

We will consider two forms of exponential smoothing: *simple exponential smoothing* and *adjusted exponential smoothing* (i.e., adjusted for trends, seasonal patterns, etc.). We will discuss the simple exponential smoothing case first, followed by the adjusted form.

To demonstrate simple exponential smoothing, we will return to the Instant Paper Clip Office Supply Company example.

Simple exponential smoothing

The simple exponential smoothing forecast is computed using the formula

$$F_{t+1} = \alpha D_t + (1 - \alpha)F_t$$

where

F_{t+1} = the forecast for the next period

D_t = actual demand in the present period

F_t = the previously determined forecast for the present period

α = a weighting factor referred to as the *smoothing constant*

The smoothing constant, α, is between 0.0 and 1.0. It reflects the weight given to the most recent demand data. For example, if $\alpha = .20$,

The smoothing constant, α

$$F_{t+1} = .20D_t + .80F_t$$

which means that our forecast for the next period is based on 20% of recent demand (D_t) and 80% of past demand (in the form of the forecast F_t, since F_t is derived from previous demands and forecasts). If we go to one extreme and let $\alpha = 0.0$, then

$\alpha = 0.0$

$$F_{t+1} = 0D_t + 1F_t$$
$$= F_t$$

and the forecast for the next period is the same as for this period. In other words, *the forecast does not reflect the most recent demand at all.*

On the other hand, if $\alpha = 1.0$, then

$\alpha = 1.0$

$$F_{t+1} = 1D_t + 0F_t$$
$$= 1D_t$$

and we have considered only the most recent occurrence in our data (demand in the present period) and nothing else. Thus, we can conclude that the higher α is, the more sensitive the forecast will be to changes in recent demand. The most commonly used values of α are in the range from .01 to .30. However, the determination of α is usually judgmental and subjective and will often be based on extensive trial-and-error experimentation. An inaccurate estimate can limit the usefulness of this forecasting technique.

An exponential smoothing example

Using $\alpha = .10$, we will compute the March (i.e., period three) forecast for our example. From Table 16.3 we can see that

Demand in February, $D_2 = 90$ orders

Forecast for February, $F_2 = 120$ orders

TABLE 16.3
Exponential Smoothing Forecast

Period	Month	Delivered Orders per Month, D_t	Forecast, F_{t+1}	
			$\alpha = .10$	$\alpha = .30$
1	January	120	—	—
2	February	90	120.0	120.0
3	March	100	117.0	111.0
4	April	75	115.3	107.7
5	May	110	111.3	97.9
6	June	50	111.2	101.5
7	July	75	105.1	86.1
8	August	130	102.1	82.8
9	September	110	104.9	97.0
10	October	90	105.4	100.9
11	November	—	103.9 ←	97.6 ←

November forecasts

The March forecast

Notice that to begin the forecast we are using the actual January demand as the forecast for February (as a starting point). Alternatively, a subjective estimate could have been used. Thus, the forecast for March, F_3, is

$$F_3 = \alpha D_2 + (1 - \alpha)F_2$$
$$= (.10)(90) + (.90)(120)$$
$$= 117 \text{ orders}$$

The April forecast

The forecast for March ($F_3 = 117$) is subsequently used in the computation of the April forecast.

$$F_4 = \alpha D_3 + (1 - \alpha)F_3$$
$$= (.10)(100) + (.90)(117)$$
$$= 115.3 \text{ orders}$$

The remainder of the monthly forecasts are shown in Table 16.3. The final forecast is for November and is the forecast of interest to the manager, assuming that it is presently the end of October.

$F_{11} = .10(90) + .90(105.3)$

  = 103.9 orders for November

Summary of
monthly forecasts

Thus, the manager of the office supply company can estimate that there will be 103.9 delivery orders in November and make a decision regarding drivers and trucks accordingly.

Notice in Table 16.3 that a forecast for $\alpha = .30$ was also computed. The November forecast using this smoothing constant is 97.6 orders.

$F_{11} = .30(90) + .70(100.9)$

  = 97.6 orders for November

The purpose of computing this alternative forecast is to demonstrate the ability of the forecast to react to demand changes. This can be observed in Figure 16.3, which shows the two exponential smoothing forecasts for $\alpha = .10$ and .30 superimposed on the actual demand curve.

In Figure 16.3, the forecast using the higher smoothing constant, $\alpha = .30$, reacts more strongly to changes in demand than does the forecast with $\alpha = .10$. However, both tend to smooth out the random fluctuations in the forecast. Notice that both forecasts lag behind the actual demand. For example, a pronounced upward change in demand in July is not really reflected in the forecast until September. If these changes mark a change in trend (i.e., a long-term upward or downward movement) rather than just a random fluctuation, then the forecast will always lag behind this trend. Observing Figure 16.3, we can see a general downward trend in delivered orders from January through June. Notice that both forecasts tend to be consistently higher than the actual demand; that is, the forecasts lag the trend. Simple exponential smoothing forecasts, however, can be adjusted for the effects of a trend.

The effect of a
higher smoothing
constant

Forecast lag

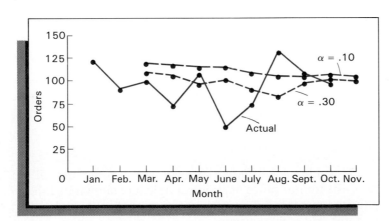

FIGURE 16.3

Exponential
Smoothing
Forecasts with
$\alpha = .10$ and $\alpha = .30$

Adjusted Exponential Smoothing

The adjusted exponential smoothing forecast consists of the simple exponential smoothing forecast with a *trend adjustment* factor added to it. The formula for the adjusted forecast is

$$\text{Adjusted } F_{t+1} = F_{t+1} + \left(\frac{1 - \beta}{\beta}\right)T_{t+1}$$

where

β = a smoothing constant for trend

T = an exponentially smoothed trend factor

Like α, β is a value between 0.0 and 1.0. It reflects the weight given to the most recent trend data. Also like α, β is often determined subjectively based on the judgment of the forecaster. A low β reflects trend changes more than a high β. It is not uncommon for β to equal α in this method.

The exponentially smoothed trend factor is computed much as the simple exponentially smoothed forecast is computed. It is, in fact, a forecast model for trend.

$$T_{t+1} = \beta(F_{t+1} - F_t) + (1 - \beta)T_t$$

where

T_t = the last period trend factor

As an example, we will compute the adjusted forecast for March using the simple exponentially smoothed forecast for $\alpha = .10$, shown in Table 16.3. The February trend, T_2, is assumed to equal zero, since we have no trend data for this month, and β is given a value of .10. Thus, the trend factor is computed as

$$
\begin{aligned}
T_3 &= \beta(F_3 - F_2) + (1 - \beta)T_2 \\
&= .10(117 - 120) + (.90)(0) \\
&= .10(-3) \\
&= -.30
\end{aligned}
$$

Using this trend factor, we next adjust our simple exponentially smoothed forecast for March.

$$
\begin{aligned}
\text{Adjusted } F_3 &= F_3 + \left(\frac{1 - 0.1}{0.1}\right)T_3 \\
&= 117 + (9)(-.30) \\
&= 114.3
\end{aligned}
$$

This adjusted forecast, as well as the other monthly adjusted forecasts for our office supply example, are shown in Table 16.4. The adjusted exponential smoothing forecast for November (F_{11}) shown in Table 16.4 is 95.6 orders.

TABLE 16.4

Adjusted Exponential Smoothing Forecast

Period t	Month	Delivered Orders for Month, D_t	Forecast, F_{t+1} $\alpha = .10$	Adjusted Forecast $\alpha = .10$	
1	January	120	—	—	
2	February	90	120.0	120.0	
3	March	100	117.0	114.3	
4	April	75	115.3	111.3	
5	May	110	111.3	104.1	
6	June	50	111.2	104.7	
7	July	75	105.1	93.7	
8	August	130	102.1	89.2	
9	September	110	104.9	95.8	
10	October	90	105.4	97.7	November
11	November	—	103.9 ⟵	95.6 ⟵	forecasts

Notice that the adjusted forecasts are consistently lower than the simple exponential smoothing forecasts. That is, the adjusted forecasts do not "lag" the actual demand as much as the simple exponential smoothing forecasts. This can also be observed in Figure 16.4.

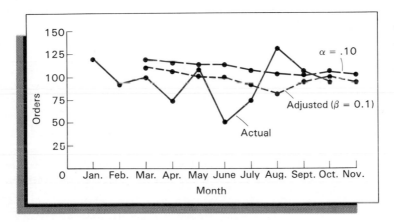

FIGURE 16.4

Adjusted Exponentially Smoothed Forecast

However, notice that although the adjusted forecast reacted bet- Reaction to trends
ter to the *downward trend* in the actual demand for delivered orders,
it did not react as well to the sudden upward turn at the end of
June. This demonstrates that the adjusted forecast is useful for *long-term trends* in the data, but not for sudden and short movements up
and down.

Since trends and seasonal patterns often tend to occur over a
relatively long period of time, the adjusted exponential smoothing
technique is sometimes used for medium-range forecasts. However,
in general, time series methods are used primarily for short-range
forecasts.

Forecast Reliability

As indicated in the introduction to this chapter, no forecast measure will result in a consistently perfect forecast. However, the person performing the forecast does hope it will be generally *reliable*. In order to test the forecast to see if it is accurately portraying what actually occurs, the forecaster can make use of several reliability measures. We will discuss the mean absolute deviation as an example of the reliability test.

Testing the forecast to see if it is accurate

The *mean absolute deviation* (referred to as *MAD*) is a measure of the difference between the forecast and what actually occurred. It is computed as follows.

The mean absolute deviation

$$\text{MAD} = \frac{\sum |\text{actual} - \text{forecast}|}{\text{number of periods}}$$

For our office supply example, the deviations between actual and forecast demand using the simple exponential smoothing forecast ($\alpha = .10$) in Table 16.3 are

$$\text{MAD} = \frac{17 + 40.3 + 1.3 + 61.2 + 30.1 + 27.9 + 5.2 + 15.3}{8}$$

$$= 24.8$$

Interpreting the MAD value

Interpreting the significance of the MAD value is somewhat judgmental. In general, however, the lower the MAD value, the better (i.e., a MAD value of zero means there is no forecast error). The MAD value for the adjusted forecast is 24.1. Although this is a slightly lower value than that obtained for the simple exponential smoothing forecast, the difference is not significant (it is due to the fact that the adjusted forecast did not react well to the sudden rise in the data in June).

Time Series Forecasting Using the Computer

The personal computer software packages we have demonstrated previously in this text all have the capability to perform time series forecasting.

We will demonstrate the use of Render and Stair's Microcomputer Software to perform exponential smoothing, using our example of the Instant Paper Clip Office Supply Company with $\alpha = .10$. The solution output, shown below, replicates the forecast obtained manually in Table 16.3. (However, note the slight numerical differences, which are the result of rounding in the manual process.)

```
ENTER THE PROBLEM TITLE? Instant Paper Clip

ENTER THE # OF PERIODS OF HISTORICAL DATA? 10

ENTER THE VALUE FOR PERIOD # 1 ? 120
ENTER THE VALUE FOR PERIOD # 2 ? 90
ENTER THE VALUE FOR PERIOD # 3 ? 100
ENTER THE VALUE FOR PERIOD # 4 ? 75
ENTER THE VALUE FOR PERIOD # 5 ? 110
ENTER THE VALUE FOR PERIOD # 6 ? 50
ENTER THE VALUE FOR PERIOD # 7 ? 75
ENTER THE VALUE FOR PERIOD # 8 ? 130
ENTER THE VALUE FOR PERIOD # 9 ? 110
ENTER THE VALUE FOR PERIOD # 10 ? 90

ENTER THE SMOOTHING CONSTANT ALPHA (O=<ALPHA<=1)? 0.1

ENTER THE ESTIMATE FOR PERIOD #1? 120

                        -- PROGRAM OUTPUT --


PROBLEM TITLE = Instant Paper Clip
NUMBER OF PERIODS - 10
SMOOTHING CONSTANT ALPHA = .1
ESTIMATE FOR PERIOD #1 = 120

              VALUE
              ----------
( 1 )          120
( 2 )           90
( 3 )          100
( 4 )           75
( 5 )          110
( 6 )           50
( 7 )           75
( 8 )          130
( 9 )          110
( 10 )          90

         *** RESULTS: EXPONENTIAL SMOOTHING ***
                   ALPHA = .1
         ---------------------------------------------
         PERIOD  ACTUAL     SMOOTHED FORECAST    ERROR
           1      120           120                0
           2       90           120               30
           3      100           117               17
           4       75           115.3             40.29
           5      110           111.26             1.26
           6       50           111.14            61.14
           7       75           105.02            30.02
           8      130           102.02           -27.98
           9      110           104.82            -5.18
          10       90           105.34            15.34

   MEAN ABSOLUTE DEVIATION (MAD) IS = 22.82
   MEAN SQUARED ERROR (MSE) = 849.95

THE EXPONENTIALLY SMOOTHED FORECAST FOR PERIOD # 11  IS = 103.8
         ---------------------------------------------
              *** END OF EXPONENTIAL SMOOTHING ***
```

Note that the solution output provides an exponentially smoothed forecast for period 11 (November) of 103.8. Also, the mean absolute deviation (MAD) measure of reliability is computed as 22.82.

REGRESSION FORECASTING METHODS

A forecasting technique that measures the relationship of one variable to one or more other variables

The time series techniques of exponential smoothing and moving average related a single variable being forecast (such as demand) to *time*. In contrast, *regression* is a forecasting technique that measures the relationship of one variable to one or more other variables. In effect, regression attempts to relate forecasts to the factors that *cause* trends, cycles, and seasonal patterns. (Regression is sometimes referred to as a *causal* technique.) If it is possible to identify the factors that cause trends and to develop a mathematical relationship that reflects these causes, often a very accurate forecast can be determined. Because regression can often be used to accurately forecast variables that reflect trends, it is frequently used as a medium-range forecasting technique. We will consider regression within the context of the following example.

A regression example

The vice-president for operations of the Blue Sox Professional Baseball Team of the National League believes that attendance at the team's home games is related to the amount spent on promotion by the team. Given that such a relationship exists, the vice-president would like to be able to use it to forecast attendance for various levels of promotional expenditures. In this example, the forecast for attendance will be based not solely on the pattern of the data over time, but on another variable, promotional expenditure.

Regression is a means of measuring the *relationship* of one variable, such as team attendance, to one or more other variables, such as promotional expenditures, won-lost record, or the fans' disposable income. The measure of this relationship is in the form of an equation, referred to as a *regression equation*. This regression equation can also be used to forecast the effect of one variable on another variable (e.g., the effect of promotional expenditure on attendance). Regression can be categorized as simple or multiple: *simple linear regression* reflects the relationship of *two* variables, and *multiple regression* encompasses *more than two* variables.

Simple Linear Regression

Components of the regression equation

Simple linear regression relates one dependent variable to one independent variable in the form of a linear equation.

$$y = a + bx$$

dependent variable

intercept

slope

independent variable

Now let us return to our example of the Blue Sox baseball team operation. The vice-president for operations has accumulated data (shown in Table 16.5) on promotional expenditures (in constant, noninflated dollars) and home attendance for the past ten years.

TABLE 16.5
Attendance and Promotional Expenditure Data

Year	Promotional Expenditures ($10,000s)	Home Attendance (100,000s)
1975	5.7	7
1976	5.5	10
1977	6.5	9
1978	9.0	12
1979	6.9	8
1980	8.1	14
1981	9.5	15
1982	10.2	17
1983	8.2	16
1984	10.6	18

The data on promotional expenditures and team attendance are diagramed in Figure 16.5.

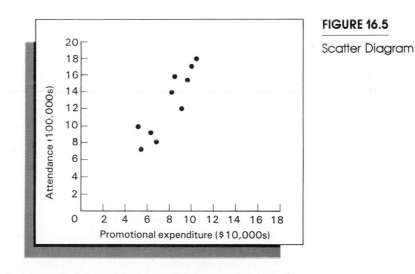

FIGURE 16.5

Scatter Diagram

The graph in Figure 16.5 is referred to as a *scatter diagram*. The points on the scatter diagram do not form an exact straight line, but they show a definite positive trend and seem to be linear in nature. We will develop the regression equation from these data. The two components in the regression equation that must be computed are *a*,

A scatter diagram

The slope and intercept of the regression equation

The slope of the linear equation

the intercept, and b, the slope. The slope represents the change in y per unit change in x (i.e., the amount that y changes—either positively or negatively—for a particular unit change in x). In other words, each increase in promotional expenditure results in a corresponding change in attendance, the magnitude of which is determined by the slope. The intercept is a constant value that represents the value of y when x is zero. As such, the intercept indicates the point at which the linear equation will intercept (i.e., intersect with) the y axis. These two components are computed using the following formulas:

$$a = \bar{y} - b\bar{x}$$

$$b = \frac{\Sigma xy - n\overline{xy}}{\Sigma x^2 - n\bar{x}^2}$$

where

n = the number of pieces of data

$\bar{x} = \dfrac{\Sigma x}{n}$ = the mean of the x data

$\bar{y} = \dfrac{\Sigma x}{n}$ = the mean of the y data

Table 16.6 gives the values that are used to compute a and b.

TABLE 16.6
Computations for Linear Regression Equation

x (expenditures)	y (attendance)	xy	x²
5.7	7	39.9	32.5
5.5	10	55.0	30.3
6.5	9	58.5	42.3
9.0	12	108.0	81.0
6.9	8	55.2	47.6
8.1	14	113.4	65.6
9.5	15	142.5	90.3
10.2	17	173.4	104.0
8.2	16	131.2	67.2
10.6	18	190.8	112.4
80.2	126	1,067.9	673.2

Recall that the linear regression equation is in the form

$$y = a + bx$$

Computing the slope, b

First we will compute the slope of this equation, b.

$$b = \frac{\Sigma xy - n\overline{xy}}{\Sigma x^2 - n\bar{x}^2}$$

From the values in Table 16.6 we determine that

$$\bar{x} = \frac{80.2}{10} = 8.02$$

$$\bar{y} = \frac{126}{10} = 12.6$$

Therefore,

$$b = \frac{1,067.9 - (10)(8.02)(12.6)}{673.2 - (10)(8.02)^2}$$

$$= \frac{57.4}{30.0}$$

$$= 1.91$$

Now that we know b, we can compute the intercept of our regression equation, a.

Computing the intercept, a

$$a = \bar{y} - b\bar{x}$$

$$= 12.6 - (1.91)(8.02)$$

$$= -2.72$$

Thus, our simple regression equation is

The regression equation

$$y = -2.72 + 1.91x$$

In Figure 16.6 the line defined by this equation is superimposed on the scatter diagram of the data.

The calculated linear regression line appears to fit the data in our example well, indicating that attendance, y, is linearly related to promotional expenditure, x. Now the vice-president for operations can

FIGURE 16.6

Regression Line

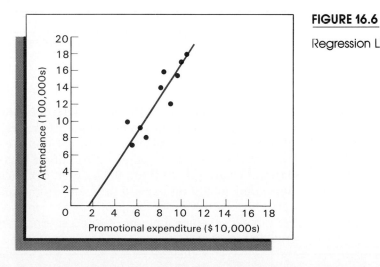

Attendance (100,000s) vs. Promotional expenditure ($10,000s)

Forecasting with the regression equation

use the regression equation to forecast attendance for a specific expenditure on promotion. For example, if the baseball team spends $100,000 ($x = 10$) on promotion, the forecasted attendance is computed as

$$y = -2.72 + 1.91(10)$$
$$= 16.4$$

which is interpreted as 1,640,000 in attendance at the home games.

From Figure 16.6 we can see that the regression line (and equation) is best suited for forecasting longer term trends. Because the regression equation is linear, it does not react to positive or negative trend changes in the data (i.e., it does not bend or change direction). It may flatten out or become steeper, but the line will not change direction if the data should change direction.

Limitation of regression

Coefficient of Determination

Testing the strength of the variable relationships

In order for the regression equation to be a reliable forecast method, there must be a relatively strong relationship between the two variables in the equation, and any other factors affecting the forecast must remain constant (or nearly so). An indicator of the strength of the relationship of the variables in the regression equation, and thus the reliability of the forecast, is the *coefficient of determination*. The formula for the coefficient of determination is

$$r^2 = \left[\frac{n\Sigma xy - \Sigma x \Sigma y}{\sqrt{[n\Sigma x^2 - (\Sigma x)^2][n\Sigma y^2 - (\Sigma y)^2]}} \right]^2$$

Computing the coefficient of determination

Although this equation looks formidable, for our example all of the components except Σy^2 have already been determined in Table 16.6. The value for Σy^2 is 1,728. Thus, the coefficient of determination for our example is

$$r^2 = \left[\frac{(10)(1,067.9) - (80.2)(126)}{\sqrt{[(10)(673.2) - (80.2)^2][(10)(1,728) - (126)^2]}} \right]^2$$
$$= (.89)^2$$
$$= .79$$

Interpreting the coefficient of determination

This value for the coefficient of determination means that 79% of the amount of variation in the attendance during the ten-year period of analysis can be explained by promotional expenditure. The remaining 21% is due to other unexplained factors related to attendance. A value of 1.00 (or 100%) would indicate that attendance depended totally on expenditures on promotion. Since 21% of the variation is a result of factors other than promotional expenditures, we can expect some amount of forecast error if the linear regression equation is used.

Multiple Regression

The fact that the coefficient of determination shows that 79% of the variation in attendance is related to promotional expenditures indicates that the remaining 21% is a result of other variables. These other variables could be the team's won-lost record, the fans' disposable income, or the population growth of the city where the team is located. *Multiple regression* is a method that reflects the relationships among a number of variables. However, computation of the multiple regression equation is quite a bit more complex than that of the simple linear regression equation. As a result, the only viable means of performing multiple regression analysis is by computer. The techniques are beyond the scope of this text; therefore, we will not pursue the topic of multiple regression.

Regression Analysis with the Computer

The development of the simple linear regression equation and the coefficient of determination for our baseball promotion example was not too difficult because the amount of data was relatively small. However, manual computation of the components of simple linear regression equations can become very time consuming and cumbersome as the amount of data increases. We have already indicated that the computation of the multiple regression equation is very complex, regardless of the amount of data.

The Microcomputer Software package that we used previously in this chapter to develop an exponentially smoothed forecast also has the capability to perform linear regression. To demonstrate this program we will use our example of the Blue Sox baseball team promotional expenditures. The program input data, which replicate the data shown in Table 16.6, and the resulting linear equation are shown below. (The slight differences between the manual result and this result are due to rounding in the manual process.) Notice that this output also displays the coefficient of determination.

```
                    *** LINEAR REGRESSION ***

    PROBLEM TITLE =Blue Sox Promotional Expenditures
    NUMBER OF OBSERVATIONS = 10

                  DEPENDENT      INDEPENDENT
                  VARIABLE        VARIABLE
                    (Y)             (X)
                -------------   -------------
    ( 1 )           7              5.7
    ( 2 )          10              5.5
    ( 3 )           9              6.5
    ( 4 )          12              9
    ( 5 )           8              6.9
```

```
( 6 )            14               8.100001
( 7 )            15               9.5
( 8 )            17               10.2
( 9 )            16               8.2
( 10 )           18               10.6


THE REGRESSION EQUATION IS :

Y = -2.793 + 1.9193 X

-------------------------------------------------
CORRELATION COEFFICIENT    (R)    =  .88
COEF. OF DETERMINATION     (R^2) =  .78
STANDARD ERROR OF ESTIM. (SEE) =  1.94
COMPUTED T-VALUE FOR THE SLOPE =  5.39
-------------------------------------------------
```

The program also has the capability to use the linear regression equation for forecasting, as we did in our earlier example. Recall that we determined the forecasted attendance for a promotional expenditure of $100,000 ($x = 10$) to be 1,640,000 ($y = 16.4$). This same computation can be done using this program as follows.

```
TO FORECAST, ENTER A VALUE OF X (O=STOP)? 10
THE PREDICTED VALUE OF Y FOR X= 10 IS  16.40026
```

There are also a number of powerful mainframe and personal computer statistical software packages that can perform not only simple regression but also multiple regression. Four of the most widely available such packages are BMD (Biomedical Computer Programs), SPSS (Statistical Package for the Social Sciences), SAS (Statistical Analysis System, and Minitab. At least one of these packages is typically available at most computer facilities. All four can be used for both simple and multiple regression.

Computer packages available for regression analysis

To demonstrate the capabilities of these statistical packages, we will use Minitab to solve our simple regression example for the Blue Sox Professional Baseball Team.[1] The first printout on page 585 shows the data input as it would appear on a computer display terminal. The data are the same as those in Table 16.5.

Minitab computer package

The Minitab program output in the second printout provides quite a bit more statistical information than was described in our presentation of simple linear regression. Only that portion of the output that was introduced in our discussion of regression is displayed.

[1]All Minitab printouts are reprinted with permission from Minitab, Inc., 3081 Enterprise Drive, State College, PA, 16801, (814) 238-3280, Telex 881612. Minitab is a registered trademark.

Input to the Minitab program

```
MTB > NOTE READ REGRESSION DATA
MTB > READ C1 C2
     10 ROWS READ
MTB > END
MTB > NAME C1 'X' C2 'Y'
MTB > PRINT 'X' 'Y'

 ROW      X      Y

   1     5.7      7
   2     5.5     10
   3     6.5      9
   4     9.0     12
   5     6.9      8
   6     8.1     14
   7     9.5     15
   8    10.2     17
   9     8.2     16
  10    10.6     18
```

```
MTB > DESCRIBE 'X' 'Y'

               N      MEAN    MEDIAN    TRMEAN     STDEV    SEMEAN
X             10     8.020     8.150     8.013     1.823     0.576
Y             10     12.60     13.00     12.62      3.95      1.25




  The regression equation is
  Y = - 2.79 + 1.92 X

  Predictor       Coef       Stdev
  Constant      -2.793       2.919
  X             1.9193      0.3558

  s = 1.945       R-sq = 78.4%
```

The first pieces of information provided are the means of the variables, x and y. Next, the y-intercept and the slope of the regression equation are presented. Recall that in our example the intercept was computed as -2.72; however, Minitab computes the intercept of the regression equation as -2.79294889. The discrepancy is again due to the fact that in the manual solution the values resulting from the various computations were consistently rounded to one decimal

Slope and
y-intercept

The coefficient of
determination

place, which created a rounding error. The final piece of information shown in the Minitab output is the coefficient of determination, defined as "R-sq." Again, the slight discrepancy between the manual value ($r^2 = .79$) and the Minitab result (R-sq = 0.784) is due to a rounding error.

As indicated above, the Minitab program provides much more statistical information than has been shown here. Only selected pieces of statistical information from the output have been presented. The Minitab package also has the capability to provide a graphical plot of the data and the regression line identical to the graph shown in Figure 16.6.

LONG-RANGE FORECAST METHODS

Time series analysis is most useful (and reliable) for short-range forecasting; regression analysis can be used for both short- and medium-range forecasting. However, neither method is generally appropriate for long-range forecasting.

An organization's long-range plans represent some of its most important decisions. The growth of the organization, the introduction of new products, and the construction of new facilities are just a few of the items typically considered in long-range planning that affect the continued life of the firm. However, analytical techniques (such as time series and regression) are, in general, not available for long-range forecasting. One reason is the lack of historical data that could be used in such models. The factors affecting the future are so diverse and complex that historical data are of little value for predictive purposes. These factors include technology, economic conditions, and political/social conditions, all three of which are the subject of intense forecasting by many business firms.

Technological
forecasting

Technological forecasting reflects an attempt to predict what types of technology will be available in the future. For example, several large electronics firms were able to successfully predict the development of microelectronics used in electronic products, such as calculators and computers, more than a decade before such products were introduced on the market. As a result, when the products were marketed, these electronics firms had the productive capabilities to enter the market themselves. At present, many firms are attempting to forecast the type of energy sources that will be available in the future and their effects on business.

Economic
forecasting

Economic forecasting is concerned with predicting the state of the economy in the future. The possibility of recessions, economic growth, high and low interest rates, and periods of unemployment is of vital importance to businesses. Although economic predictive models abound, their reliability is often suspect. One reason is that

future economic conditions are so closely related to political and
social factors.

Political/social forecasting is a relatively new and abstract form of
forecasting. World politics have become so volatile that their effect
on business firms has become immense. World trade is no longer
subject only to economic conditions but to political considerations as
well. In addition, social conditions now change rapidly and the
changes can have dramatic effects on businesses. Such develop-
ments as consumer protection and equal opportunity laws have had
a significant impact on the economy in general. As a result, more
and more firms are attempting to develop ways to predict such
changes in order to lessen their effects.

Political/social
forecasting

The forecasting models that have been developed to reflect these
long-range factors are qualitative in nature. They are typically based
on expert opinion, judgment, surveys of all types, and research results. However, since long-range forecasting is often an attempt to
predict future *events*, the reliability of such methods is limited.

APPLICATIONS OF FORECASTING

Work Force Forecasting

New York City's Department of Sanitation has an operating budget
of over $400 million and employs approximately 6,800 sanitation
workers. The Sanitation Department is responsible for collecting
household refuse, disposing of all refuse, cleaning streets, removing
snow, and enforcing the sanitary code. Measures of its performance
include a productivity index based on tons of garbage collected per
worker-hour, the number of loads not collected, the percentage of
night trucks needed, and a block cleanliness report. In 1978 all of
these performance measures were down, and the sanitation department was gaining undesirable media attention. Within a three-year
period, the new department commissioner was able to reverse this
performance trend and obtain substantial productivity improvement
with the assistance of a number of management science techniques
and models. A work force forecasting model was one of the models
employed to assist in planning.

The departmental workload was seasonal, and workload and
worker availability varied from month to month. As a result of good
data records, the department was able to compile all the factors
related to its work force requirements and worker availability. Historical data also enabled the department to determine seasonal fluctuations related to each of these factors. A forecasting model that
interrelated all of these factors was developed and used to predict

shortages and surpluses in the work force. The forecasting model was computerized and used in conjunction with an optimization model to yield an optimal hiring strategy that minimized total salary and overtime costs.[2]

Financial Forecasting

In 1978, the Texas Comptroller of Public Accounts was interested in forecasting quarterly tax revenues in order to optimize the state's tax flow management procedures. In addition, the Comptroller desired to obtain forecasts of electricity sales and nonagricultural employment that might prove useful in predicting certain components of total tax revenue. The Bureau of Business Research of the University of Texas was asked to prepare a pilot study applying time series analysis to forecast tax revenues, electricity sales, and nonagricultural employment. The time series models performed very well in forecasting growth in these variables.

Subsequently, the Texas Legislative Board read this study as a possible solution to a different problem. An amendment to the Texas constitution required that the Board establish a forecast of the growth rate of state personal income over each biennium, which would then become a constitutional limit on the growth rate of appropriations. Thus, another study was performed to evaluate the use of time series analysis to forecast the growth rate of personal income. The resulting forecast model was used to set the constitutionally mandated legislative spending limit for the 1982–1983 biennium.[3]

Forecasting Nursing Staff Requirements

Nursing salary costs typically represent at least 50% of the operating costs of a short-term acute-care hospital; thus, it is important that hospital administration manage and control these costs to the greatest extent possible. An important factor in managing these costs is estimating the nursing staff required to meet patient needs, the further in advance the better. A series of regression forecasting models was developed to assist hospital administrators at one 220-bed, nonprofit community hospital in an urban area. The modeling objective was to enable hospital management to predict nursing staff requirements for each ward per shift, each day of the week, each month. Since staff levels are a function of the number of patients re-

[2]L. Riccio, "Management Science in New York's Department of Sanitation," *Interfaces* 14, no. 2 (March–April 1984): 1–13.

[3]R. Ashley and J. Guerard, "Applications of Time Series Analysis to Texas Financial Forecasting," *Interfaces* 13, no. 4 (August 1983): 46–55.

quiring different levels of care and the standard hours required for those levels of care, the modeling effort focused on developing a patient forecast (i.e., a forecast of demand for the hospital's services).

Data on different levels of care were gathered from the hospital administration and used as input to the Statistical Package for the Social Sciences (SPSS) multiple regression computer program. A model was formulated to predict the number of patients by six intensity-of-care levels for each hospital ward by month, day, and shift. The model proved to be very useful in the distribution of nursing skills by ward and in planning nursing workloads.[4]

Sales Forecasting

The Packaging Division of the American Can Company is the company's major operating division, accounting for approximately 60% of company sales. The division consists of four marketing departments for food, beverages, meat and special products, and general packaging, each of which is a profit center with a general manager responsible for sales and profits. In 1974, none of the four profit centers was using computer-based forecasting models to develop monthly sales forecasts. Forecasts were prepared manually using judgmental factors and extrapolations from historical data. A senior manager determined the need for monthly forecasts for a small number of products in order to provide a benchmark against which to compare the frequently overoptimistic sales estimates from the field.

The management science group assigned this task faced several obstacles. First, a forecasting model developed in 1970 had performed poorly and thus had eroded management's confidence in such models. Second, this previous model was so technical that it was unintelligible to management and was therefore not trusted. As a result, the management science group believed the forecasting model to be developed had to be both accurate and simple to interpret. Such a forecasting model was developed.

The packaging forecast model consisted of elements of time series analysis (with trend and seasonal adjustments) and a moving average. The model was used to generate one-month and two-month forecasts which proved to be at least as good as the judgmental forecasts used previously. The simplicity of the forecasting model and its relative accuracy contributed to its successful implementation.[5]

[4]F. Helmer et al., "Forecasting Nursing Staffing Requirements by Intensity-of-Care Level," *Interfaces* 10, no. 3 (June 1980), 50–55.
[5]C. Kallina, "Development and Implementation of a Simple Short-Range Forecasting Model—Case Study," *Interfaces* 8, no. 3 (May 1978): 32–39.

Summary

This chapter presented several of the methods available for forecasting the short-, medium-, and long-term future. Two of the most popular and traditionally applied forecasting techniques, time series and regression, were discussed in detail. However, these methods are only two of the numerous forecasting methods available for each type of forecasting.

In general, the forecasts obtained from such methods are used as inputs to other decision models. For example, the probabilities of future states in a Markov model are forecasts. Another example of the use of forecasting results is in inventory models, the subject of the next two chapters. The primary factor in determining the amount of inventory a firm should order (i.e., prepare to have on hand) is the demand that will occur in the future—forecasted demand.

References

Ashley, R., and Guerard, J. "Applications of Time Series Analysis to Texas Financial Forecasting." *Interfaces* 13, no. 4 (August 1983): 46–55.

Benton, W. K. *Forecasting for Management.* Reading, Mass.: Addison-Wesley, 1972.

Box, G. E. P., and Jenkins, G. M. *Time Series Analysis, Forecasting and Control.* Rev. ed. San Francisco: Holden-Day, 1976.

Buffa, E. S., and Dyer, J. S. *Essentials of Management Science/Operations Research.* New York: John Wiley and Sons, 1978.

Helmer, F.; Oppermann, E.; and Suver, J. "Forecasting Nursing Staffing Requirements by Intensity-of-Care Level." *Interfaces* 10, no. 3 (June 1980): 50–55.

Huang, D. S. *Regression and Econometric Methods.* New York: John Wiley and Sons, 1970.

Kallina, C. "Development and Implementation of a Simple Short-Range Forecasting Model—Case Study." *Interfaces* 8, no. 3 (May 1978): 32–39.

Makridakis, S., and Wheelwright, S. C. *Forecasting, Methods and Applications.* New York: John Wiley and Sons, 1978.

Monks, J. G. *Operations Management: Theory and Problems.* 2d ed. New York: McGraw-Hill, 1982.

Nelson, C. R. *Applied Time Series Analysis for Managerial Forecasting.* San Francisco: Holden-Day, 1973.

Riccio, L. "Management Science in New York's Department of Sanitation." *Interfaces* 14, no. 2 (March–April 1984): 1–13.

Tersine, R. J. *Production/Operations Management.* 2d ed. New York: Elsevier North Holland, 1984.

Younger, M. S. *A Handbook for Linear Regression.* North Scituate, Mass.: Duxbury Press, 1979.

EXAMPLE PROBLEM SOLUTION

The following problem provides an example of the computation of exponentially smoothed and adjusted exponentially smoothed forecasts and linear regression.

Problem Statement

The Ramona Inn Hotel adjacent to the Atlanta–Fulton County Stadium has its highest occupancy rate during the summer months when school is out and the Atlanta Braves are playing. For the years 1982–1989, the occupancy rates for the summer months were as follows:

Year	Occupancy Rate
1982	83%
1983	78
1984	86
1985	85
1986	89
1987	93
1988	92
1989	91

a. Compute the exponentially smoothed forecast ($\alpha - .20$) and the adjusted exponentially smoothed forecast ($\beta - .10$) for 1990.
b. The hotel management believes that how well the Braves are playing has an impact on the occupancy rate at the hotel. Following are the numbers of victories for the Braves (in a 162-game schedule) during the years 1982–1989. Develop the simple linear regression equation for these data.

Year	Braves' Victories
1982	75
1983	70
1984	85
1985	91
1986	87
1987	90
1988	87
1989	67

Step 1: Exponentially Smoothed ($\alpha = .20$) and Adjusted ($\beta = .10$) Forecasts

1984 Forecast:

$$F_3 = \alpha D_2 + (1 - \alpha)F_2$$
$$= (.20)(78) + (.80)(83)$$
$$= 82$$

$$\text{Adjusted } F_3 = F_3 + \left(\frac{1 - \beta}{\beta}\right)T_3$$

where

$$T_3 = \beta(F_3 - F_2) + (1 - \beta)T_2$$
$$= .10(82 - 83) + (.90)(0)$$
$$= -.01$$

Thus,

$$\text{Adjusted } F_3 = 82 + \left(\frac{1 - .10}{.10}\right)(-.01)$$
$$= 82 - .09$$
$$= 81.91$$

The remaining forecast values are computed similarly and are summarized as follows:

t	Year	Occupancy Rate, P_t	Forecast $\alpha = .20$	Adjusted Forecast $\beta = .10$
1	1982	83%	—	—
2	1983	78	83.00	83.00
3	1984	86	82.00	81.50
4	1985	85	82.80	82.75
5	1986	89	83.24	83.42
6	1987	93	84.39	85.13
7	1988	92	86.11	87.64
8	1989	91	87.29	89.24
9	1990	—	88.03	90.16

Following is the exponentially smoothed forecast generated using Microcomputer Software.

```
                *** RESULTS: EXPONENTIAL SMOOTHING ***
                            ALPHA = .2
        --------------------------------------------------------
        PERIOD   ACTUAL     SMOOTHED FORECAST      ERROR
           1       83             83                0
           2       78             83                5
           3       86             82               -4
           4       85             82.8             -2.2
           5       89             83.24            -5.76
           6       93             84.39            -8.609999
           7       92             86.11            -5.89
           8       91             87.29            -3.71

     MEAN ABSOLUTE DEVIATION (MAD) IS = 4.39
     MEAN SQUARED ERROR (MSE) = 25.19

 THE EXPONENTIALLY SMOOTHED FORECAST FOR PERIOD # 9  IS = 88.03
 --------------------------------------------------------------
            *** END OF EXPONENTIAL SMOOTHING ***
```

Step 2: Compute the Linear Regression Model

The regression equation is computed as follows.

First compute $\bar{x}$ and $\bar{y}$.

$$\bar{x} = \frac{652}{8} = 81.50$$

$$\bar{y} = \frac{697}{8} = 87.125$$

Next compute the slope, b.

$$b = \frac{\Sigma xy - n\bar{x}\bar{y}}{\Sigma x^2 - n\bar{x}^2}$$

$$= \frac{56,944 - (8)(81.50)(87.125)}{53,758 - (8)(6,642.25)} = \frac{138.5}{620}$$

$$= .2233$$

$$a = \bar{y} - b\bar{x}$$

$$= 87.125 - (.2233)(81.50)$$

$$= 68.92$$

Thus, the simple regression equation is

$$y = 68.92 + .2233x$$

The computer solution for this example generated using Microcomputer Software is as follows.

```
                           *** LINEAR REGRESSION ***

   PROBLEM TITLE =Example Problem Solution
   NUMBER OF OBSERVATIONS = 8

                    DEPENDENT      INDEPENDENT
                    VARIABLE        VARIABLE
                      (Y)             (X)
                   -----------     -----------
   ( 1 )              83              75
   ( 2 )              78              70
   ( 3 )              86              85
   ( 4 )              85              91
   ( 5 )              89              87
   ( 6 )              93              90
   ( 7 )              92              87
   ( 8 )              91              67


   THE REGRESSION EQUATION IS :

   Y =  68.9189 + .2233 X


   ------------------------------------------------
   CORRELATION COEFFICIENT   (R)   =   .41
   COEF. OF DETERMINATION    (R^2) =   .16
   STANDARD ERROR OF ESTIM.  (SEE) =  5.03
   COMPUTED T-VALUE FOR THE SLOPE =  1.1
   ------------------------------------------------
```

Notice that the coefficient of determination is relatively small, implying that the linear regression equation is probably not a very good predictive model.

Problems

1. Distinguish among short-, medium-, and long-range forecasts.

2. Given the following demand for a six-period time frame,

Period	Units Demanded per Period
1	50
2	60
3	70
4	50
5	80
6	110

a. Compute a three-period moving average forecast for periods 4 through 7.

b. Plot the actual demand and the period forecasts graphically and compare the two.

3. Given the following demand data for a ten-period time frame,

Period	Units Demanded per Period
1	25
2	18
3	17
4	40
5	34
6	32
7	41
8	50
9	53
10	26

   a. Compute a three-period moving average forecast for periods 4 through 11.

   b. Compute a five-period moving average forecast for periods 6 through 11.

   c. Plot the actual demand and the forecasts determined in parts a and b on the same graph and compare them.

4. For the data in problem 3, compute a weighted three-period moving average for periods 4 through 11. Assign a weight of 3 to the most recent period, a weight of 2 to the next most recent period, and a weight of 1 to the most distant period in the moving average. Compare this forecast with the two obtained in parts a and b of problem 3. Which forecast appears to be the most accurate?

5. The Saki automobile dealer in the Minneapolis–St. Paul area wants to be able to accurately forecast demand for the Saki special compact car during the next month. Because the distributor is in Japan, it is difficult to send cars back or reorder if the proper number of cars is not ordered a month ahead. From sales records, the dealer has accumulated the following data for the past year.

Month	Cars Demanded per Month
January	6
February	7
March	5
April	4
May	8
June	10
July	12
August	16
September	14
October	10
November	16
December	18

a. Compute a three-month moving average forecast of demand for April through January (of the next year) and compare the forecast with the actual demand for each month.

b. Compute a five-month moving average forecast for April through January and compare the forecast with the actual demand for each month.

c. Compare the two forecasts computed in parts a and b. Which one should the dealer use for January of the next year?

6. Carpet City is a carpet outlet in Fresno. The manager of the outlet needs to be able to accurately forecast the demand for Soft Shag carpet (the dealer's biggest seller). If the dealer does not order enough carpet from the carpet mill, customers will buy their carpet from one of the dealer's many competitors. The dealer has collected the following demand data for the past eight months.

Month	Demand for Soft Shag Carpet (1,000 yards)
1	8
2	12
3	7
4	9
5	15
6	11
7	10
8	12

a. Compute a three-month moving average forecast for months 4 through 9.

b. Compute a weighted three-month moving average forecast for months 4 through 9. Assign weights of 5, 3, and 1 to the months in sequence, starting with the most recent month.

c. Compare the two forecasts graphically. Which forecast appears to be more accurate?

7. The Fastgro Fertilizer Company distributes fertilizer to various lawn and garden shops. The company must base its quarterly production schedule on a forecast of how many tons of fertilizer will be demanded from it. The company has gathered the following data for the past three years from its sales records.

Year	Quarter	Demand for Fertilizer (tons)
1	1	105
	2	150
	3	93
	4	121
2	5	140
	6	170
	7	105
	8	150
3	9	150
	10	170
	11	110
	12	130

a. Compute a three-quarter moving average forecast for quarters 4 through 13 and compare the forecast graphically with the actual demand.

b. Compute a five-quarter moving average forecast for quarters 6 through 13 and compare the forecast graphically with the actual demand.

c. Compute a weighted three-quarter moving average forecast using weights of 3, 2, and 1 for the most recent, next recent, and most distant data, respectively.

8. In problem 7 can you identify any trends, cycles, and/or seasonal patterns in the actual quarterly demand data?

9. Given the following demand data for a five-month time frame,

Period	Units Demanded per Period
1	40
2	30
3	45
4	60
5	55

compute exponentially smoothed forecasts for periods 2 through 6 using α values of .10 and .30.

10. The dean of the College of Business at State University wants to forecast the number of students who will enroll in Management Science 1 next quarter in order to determine how many sections to schedule. The dean has accumulated the following enrollment data for the past eight quarters.

Quarter	Students Enrolled in Management Science
1	400
2	450
3	350
4	420
5	500
6	575
7	490
8	650

Compute the exponentially smoothed forecast ($\alpha = .20$) for the enrollment in Management Science next quarter.

11. The manager of the Petroco service station wants to forecast the demand for unleaded gasoline next month so that the proper number of gallons can be ordered from the distributor. The owner has accumulated the following data on demand for unleaded gasoline from sales during the past ten months.

Month	Gasoline Demanded (gallons)
October	800
November	725
December	630
January	500
February	645
March	690
April	730
May	810
June	1,200
July	980

a. Compute an exponentially smoothed forecast using an α value of .10.
b. Compute an adjusted exponentially smoothed forecast (α = .10, β = .10).
c. Graphically plot the actual data and the forecasts obtained in parts a and b.

12. Compute an exponentially smoothed forecast (α = .20) for the monthly automobile demand data in problem 5. Graphically compare the exponentially smoothed forecast and the three-month moving average forecast obtained in problem 5 with the actual data. Does there appear to be a trend in the actual data? If so, which forecast seems to forecast the trend better?

13. Compute an exponentially smoothed forecast (α = .10) for the monthly carpet demand in problem 6.

14. Compute an exponentially smoothed forecast (α = .30) for the quarterly fertilizer demand in problem 7.

15. Compute an adjusted exponentially smoothed forecast (α = .30, β = .10) for the quarterly demand data for carpet in problem 7.

16. Compute an adjusted exponentially smoothed forecast (α = .20, β = .10) for the monthly automobile demand data in problem 5. Graphically plot the adjusted exponentially smoothed forecast together with the simple exponentially smoothed forecast obtained in problem 12 and the actual data. Which forecast do you believe would be more reliable?

17. Test the reliability of the three-month moving average forecast of automobile demand in problem 5, using the mean absolute deviation. Next, test the reliability of the simple exponentially smoothed forecast (problem 12) and the adjusted exponentially smoothed forecast (problem 16), using the mean absolute deviation. Which forecast appears to be the most reliable?

18. Test the reliability of the exponentially smoothed forecast of students enrolled in Management Science per quarter, obtained in problem 10, using the mean absolute deviation.

19. Test the reliability of the two forecasts of gasoline demand in problem 11, using the mean absolute deviation, and indicate the more reliable forecast.

20. Given the following data for a dependent variable, y, and an independent variable, x, develop the simple regression equation and superimpose the regression line on a scatter diagram of the data.

x	y
10	25
12	40
14	38
18	45
20	46
25	50
28	48
35	56
40	60
42	58

21. The job placement director at Tech believes that the salary offers for business administration graduates may be related to grade point averages. During the past two years the placement director has collected average salary and average grade point data as follows.

Grade Point Average	Average Annual Salary Offers
2.1	$13,500
2.4	14,100
2.7	15,000
2.9	15,200
3.2	16,000
3.5	16,300

Determine the regression equation for these data and superimpose the regression line on a scatter diagram of the actual data.

22. The Williamsburg Tourism Association is continually attempting to forecast the number of tourists who will visit the city. The association believes that the number of tourists is related to gasoline prices. The association has accumulated the following data on average monthly gasoline prices and the number of tourists visiting the city.

Monthly Gasoline Prices (per gallon)	Tourists/Month (1,000s)
$1.05	10.0
.90	17.0
1.17	9.0
1.21	8.0
.95	14.0
1.30	12.0
1.08	11.0
1.40	7.5
1.10	12.0
1.06	13.0

a. Develop the simple regression equation for these data.

b. Compute the coefficient of determination for the regression equation.

c. The tourist association estimates that the price of gasoline will be $1.25 next month. What will the expected number of tourists be next month?

23. The Fairface Cosmetics Firm believes its sales are directly related to the amount of money it spends on promotion. The firm has accumulated the following data on promotional expenditures and sales for the past ten years.

Annual Sales ($1,000s)	Annual Promotional Expenditures ($1,000s)
95	12
106	15
84	10
65	8
110	20
105	21
120	25
90	14
96	15
115	18

a. Develop a simple regression equation for these data.

b. Plot the actual data on a scatter diagram and superimpose the regression line on it.

c. For a promotional expenditure of $13,000, what level of sales would the firm expect?

d. What limiting factors do you feel are associated with this forecast equation?

24. The Ali Baba Carpet Store wants to develop a means to forecast its carpet sales. The store owner believes that the store's sales are directly related to the number of new housing starts in town. The store owner has

gathered data from city hall on monthly house construction permits and
from store records on monthly sales. These data are shown in the following table.

Monthly Sales (1,000 yards)	Monthly Construction Permits
5	21
10	35
4	10
3	12
8	16
2	9
12	41
11	15
9	18
14	26

a. Develop a simple regression equation for these data.

b. Compute the coefficient of determination. Does there appear to be a
   relationship between the number of construction permits and carpet sales?

c. What level of carpet sales can be expected next month if 30 housing
   construction permits are issued?

25. Compute the coefficient of determination for problem 23. Does there appear to be a relationship between money spent on promotion and sales?

17

Inventory Analysis with Certain Demand

All of the previous chapters have presented management science techniques that are applicable to decision-making problems in general. This chapter is slightly different in that a mathematical technique is developed that is applicable to a specific business function, inventory planning and control. However, to include the topic of inventory analysis is not inappropriate at all.

Inventory analysis is one of the most popular topics in management science. One reason is that almost all types of business organizations have inventory. Although we tend to think of inventory only in terms of stock on a store shelf, it can take on a variety of forms, such as partially finished products at different stages of a manufacturing process, raw materials, resources, labor, or cash. In addition, the purpose of inventory is not always simply to meet customer demand. For example, companies frequently stock large inventories of raw materials as a hedge against strikes. Whatever form inventory

All types of
organizations have
inventory

603

takes or whatever its purpose, it often represents a significant cost to a business firm. As such, it represents an important subject for the application of management science.

This chapter will present the classic economic order quantity models, which represent the most basic and fundamental form of inventory analysis. These models provide a means for determining how much to order (the order quantity) and when to place an order so that inventory-related costs are minimized. The underlying assumption of these models is that demand is known with certainty and is constant. Chapter 18 will present inventory models that do not include this assumption.

ECONOMIC ORDER QUANTITY

An inventory
example

The Armor Carpet Store stocks carpet in its warehouse and sells it through an adjoining showroom. The store keeps inventories of several brands of carpet; however, its biggest seller is Super Shag carpet. Since Super Shag is such an important product, the store does not allow the inventory of the carpet to run out; that is, the store always has Super Shag in stock.

Carrying and
ordering costs

The store incurs two costs associated with keeping this brand of carpet in inventory: the cost of holding the carpet in inventory and the cost of ordering the carpet from the carpet manufacturer. The manager of the store wants to know how much Super Shag should be ordered each time an order is placed in order to minimize the total sum of these costs. Our purpose will be to develop a model that helps the manager make this decision. This model is known as the *classical EOQ (economic order quantity) model.* It will be developed with the assumptions that demand is known with certainty, that demand is constant over time, and that orders are made and received instantaneously so that no shortages develop. (These assumptions will become more understandable as the model is developed.) In order to accomplish this, we will first analyze the two separate costs associated with inventory mentioned above.

The classical EOQ
model

The EOQ
assumptions

Carrying Cost

Items contributing
to carrying cost

The *carrying cost* (also known as holding cost) is the cost incurred by the store for carrying the carpet in inventory. The total carrying cost generally includes some or all of the following items:

Direct storage costs (rent, heat, lights, maintenance, security, handling, recordkeeping, labor, etc., in the warehouse)
Deferred profit on investment (i.e., carpet in inventory does not produce a profit)

Interest on the investment in inventory
Product obsolescence
Depreciation, taxes, insurance

Carrying cost is usually expressed on a per-unit basis for some period of time (although it is sometimes given as a percentage of average inventory). Traditionally, the carrying cost is referred to on an annual basis (i.e., per year).

The manager of the Armor Carpet Store has determined that the carrying cost, which we will represent symbolically as C_c, is

$C_c = \$ .75$ per yard of carpet per year

However, this value represents only the cost/unit and not the *total annual carrying cost*. The total carrying cost is determined by the amount of inventory on hand during the year. The amount of inventory available to the store during the year is illustrated in Figure 17.1.

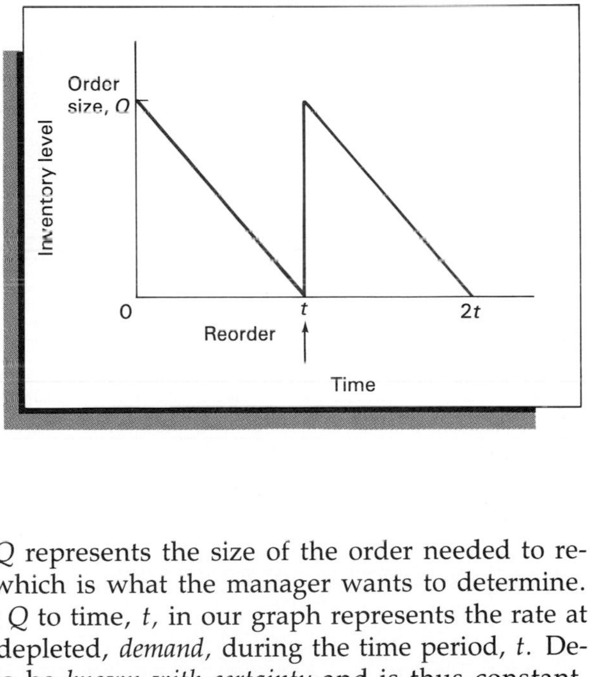

Carrying cost per unit

FIGURE 17.1

Inventory Usage

In Figure 17.1, Q represents the size of the order needed to replenish inventory, which is what the manager wants to determine. The line connecting Q to time, t, in our graph represents the rate at which inventory is depleted, *demand*, during the time period, t. Demand is assumed to be *known with certainty* and is thus constant, which explains why the line representing demand is straight. Also, notice that inventory never goes below zero—a condition the carpet store originally specified. In addition, when the inventory level does reach zero, it is assumed that an order arrives immediately after an infinitely small passage of time, a condition referred to as *instanta-*

The order size

neous receipt. This is a simplifying assumption that we will maintain for the moment.

Determining the average inventory level

Referring to Figure 17.1, we can see that the amount of inventory is Q, the size of the order, for an infinitely small period of time, since Q is always being depleted by demand. Similarly, the amount of inventory is zero for an infinitely small period of time, since the only time there is no inventory is at the specific time t. Thus the amount of inventory available is somewhere between these two extremes. A logical deduction is that the amount of inventory available is the *average inventory* level, defined as

$$\text{Average inventory} = \frac{Q}{2}$$

In order to verify this relationship, specify any number of points — values of Q — over the entire time period, t, and divide by the number of points. For example, if $Q = 5,000$, the six points designated from 5,000 to 0 yards, as shown in Figure 17.2, are summed and divided by 6.

$$\text{Average inventory} = \frac{5,000 + 4,000 + 3,000 + 3,000 + 2,000 + 1,000 + 0}{6}$$

$$= 2,500 \text{ yards}$$

FIGURE 17.2

Levels of Q

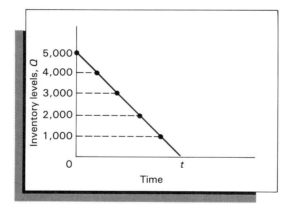

Alternatively, sum just the two extreme points (which also encompass the range of time, t) and divide by 2. This also equals 2,500 yards. This computation is the same, in principle, as adding Q and 0 and dividing by 2, which equals $Q/2$. This relationship for average inventory is maintained regardless of the size of the order, Q, or the frequency of orders (i.e., the time period, t). Thus, the average inventory on an *annual basis* is also $Q/2$, as shown in Figure 17.3.

Average annual inventory

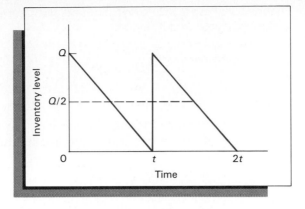

FIGURE 17.3

Average Inventory

Now that we know that the amount of inventory available *on an annual basis* is the average inventory, $Q/2$, we can determine the total annual carrying cost by multiplying the average number of yards in inventory by the carrying cost per yard per year, C_c:

Total annual carrying cost

$$\text{Total annual carrying cost} = C_c \frac{Q}{2}$$

Ordering Cost

The second inventory cost the carpet store incurs is the *cost of placing an order*. The total ordering cost generally includes some or all of the following items:

Items contributing to ordering cost

The cost of processing an order, including all recordkeeping
Transportation costs to get the order from the supplier
The cost of unloading the order and placing it in inventory
Salaries of employees involved in the ordering process
All supplies used in ordering, including forms, postage, telephone, and computer time

Ordering cost is expressed on a per-order basis. The manager of the Armor Carpet Store has determined that the cost of an order of Super Shag carpet, which we will represent symbolically as C_o, is

Cost per order

$$C_o = \$150 \text{ per order}$$

However, this value represents only the cost per order and not the *total ordering cost*. Just as we previously developed a formula for finding the total carrying cost on an annual basis, we will also determine the total ordering cost per year. The total ordering cost is derived from the *number of orders* that will be made during the year. Since the manager will not order more carpet than the amount de-

Determining the orders per year

manded *and* since we know demand with certainty, the number of orders per year is defined as

$$\text{Orders per year} = \frac{D}{Q}$$

where

$$D = \text{demand per year}$$

Total annual ordering cost

The total annual ordering cost per year can now be computed as the number of orders per year multiplied by the cost per order.

$$\text{Total annual ordering cost} = C_o \frac{D}{Q}$$

Total Inventory Cost

Summing the total annual carrying and ordering costs

The *total annual inventory cost* is computed by summing total annual carrying cost and total annual ordering cost.

$$\text{Total annual inventory cost} = C_c \frac{Q}{2} + C_o \frac{D}{Q}$$

Graphically illustrating inventory costs

Total inventory cost, ordering cost, and carrying cost are shown graphically in Figure 17.4. We will analyze each one of the three cost curves shown in Figure 17.4 separately.

FIGURE 17.4

Inventory Cost Model

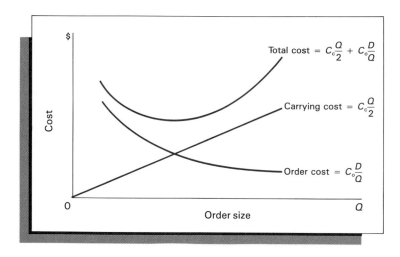

As Q increases, carrying cost increases

First observe the general upward trend of the total carrying cost curve. As the order size, Q (shown on the horizontal axis), increases, the total carrying cost (shown on the vertical axis) increases. This is logical, since larger orders will result in more units carried in inventory. For our carpet store example, recall that the carrying cost per yard, C_c, is $.75. Table 17.1 shows the total carrying cost computed for various (arbitrarily selected) increasing values of Q.

TABLE 17.1
Total Annual
Carrying Costs
for Selected
Order Sizes

Q	Total Annual Carrying Cost $C_c \dfrac{Q}{2}$
1,000	$ 375
2,000	750
3,000	1,125
4,000	1,500
5,000	1,875

Notice in Table 17.1 that as Q increases, so does total carrying cost, which is the trend shown by the carrying cost curve in Figure 17.4.

Next, observe the ordering cost curve in Figure 17.4. As the order size, Q, increases, the ordering cost *decreases* (just the opposite of what occurred with the carrying cost). This is logical, since an increase in the size of the orders will result in fewer orders' being placed each year. For our carpet store example, recall that the cost per order, C_o, is $150. We will assume that annual demand is for 10,000 yards of carpet. Table 17.2 shows the total ordering cost for the same example values of Q used in Table 17.1. Notice in Table 17.2 that as Q increases, the total ordering cost declines, a relationship reflected in the ordering cost curve in Figure 17.4.

As Q increases, ordering cost decreases

TABLE 17.2
Total Annual
Ordering Cost
for Selected
Order Sizes

Q	Total Annual Carrying Cost $C_o \dfrac{D}{Q}$
1,000	$1,500
2,000	750
3,000	500
4,000	375
5,000	300

Now we will combine the two costs for the selected values of Q to get the total annual inventory costs as shown in Table 17.3.

TABLE 17.3

Total Annual Inventory Cost for Selected Order Sizes

Q	Total Annual + Ordering Cost $C_o \dfrac{D}{Q}$	Total Annual = Carrying Cost $C_c \dfrac{Q}{2}$	Total Annual Inventory Cost	
1,000	$1,500	$ 375	$1,875	
2,000	750	750	1,500←	—— Minimum total
3,000	500	1,125	1,625	cost
4,000	375	1,500	1,875	
5,000	300	1,875	2,175	

Determining optimal Q graphically

In Table 17.3, the values in the total cost column represent points on the total cost curve in Figure 17.4. The total cost curve first declines as Q increases and then begins to increase after a point, as do the values in Table 17.3. The best, or *optimal*, value of Q is the one that results in the minimum total annual inventory cost. In Table 17.3, the optimal value of Q is 2,000, since $1,500 is the minimum total cost. This value of Q, which results in the total minimum inventory cost of $1,500, occurs at the point on the graph where the total cost curve is at its lowest, as shown in Figure 17.5.

FIGURE 17.5

Optimal Order Size, Q

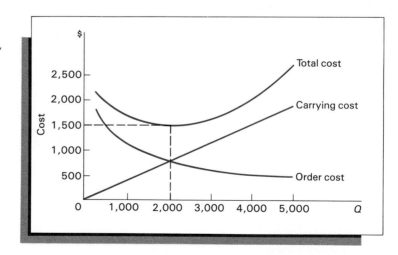

In this example, encompassing Tables 17.1, 17.2, and 17.3, we considered only increments of 1,000 yards of carpet as possible values of Q. Thus, it was a *coincidence* that we happened to test a value for Q (i.e., 2,000 yards) that turned out to correspond to the lowest point on the total cost curve. Some other value of Q could just as easily have been optimal. Of course, we could simply read the value of Q directly off the inventory graph in Figure 17.5 by locating the lowest point on the total cost curve. However, this is a rather time-consuming and cumbersome method and depends on a completely accurate graph. For these reasons we need some alternative mathematical method of determing total inventory cost that includes all possible values of Q (instead of the trial-and-error approach we used in our example) and does not require graphical analysis.

Computing Optimal Q

Observing Figure 17.5, we can see that the optimal value of Q corresponding to the minimum total inventory cost occurs not only where the total cost curve is lowest, but also where *total ordering cost equals total carrying cost* (where the two cost curves intersect). This relationship is expressed mathematically as

Equating ordering cost and carrying cost

$$C_c \frac{Q}{2} = C_o \frac{D}{Q}$$

Since the manager wants to know the value of Q, it is the decision variable we will solve for. First, we multiply both sides of this equation by Q, which yields

Solving for Q

$$C_c \frac{Q^2}{2} = C_o D$$

Next, we multiply both sides by 2 and divide both sides by C_c, which results in

$$Q^2 = \frac{2C_o D}{C_c}$$

Taking the square root of both sides gives

$$Q^* = \sqrt{\frac{2C_o D}{C_c}}$$

Q^* signifies that this value of Q, referred to as the *economic order quantity* (EOQ), is optimal.

Optimal Q*, the economic order quantity

The formula for the optimal value of Q can also be derived using calculus. Notice that Q^* corresponds to the minimum point on the total cost curve in Figure 17.5. At this point the slope of the total cost curve equals zero. Since the derivative of a curve (nonlinear function) equals the slope of the curve at any point, we can let the derivative of the total cost equation equal zero and solve for Q. This value of Q corresponds to the minimum point on the total cost curve; thus it is optimal.

Deriving Q* using calculus

For our carpet shop example, we will continue to assume that demand for Super Shag is 10,000 yards per year. Also, recall that car-

Computing Q*

rying cost per yard, C_c equals $.75 and ordering cost, C_o, equals $150 per order. Substituting these values into our economic order quantity formula, we get

$$Q^* = \sqrt{\frac{2(\$150)(10,000)}{(\$.75)}}$$

$$= 2,000 \text{ yards}$$

Computing the total minimum inventory cost

The total annual inventory cost is computed by using the value computed for the economic order quantity, Q^*, in our total cost formula.

$$\text{Total annual inventory cost} = C_c\frac{Q^*}{2} + C_o\frac{D}{Q^*}$$

$$= (\$.75)\frac{(2,000)}{2} + (\$150)\frac{(10,000)}{2,000}$$

$$= \$750 + 750$$

$$= \$1,500 \text{ per year}$$

Computing the orders per year

The number of orders that will be made annually can be computed as follows.

$$\text{Number of orders per year} = \frac{D}{Q^*}$$

$$= \frac{10,000 \text{ yards}}{2,000 \text{ yards}}$$

$$= 5 \text{ orders per year}$$

Computing the time between orders

Also, we can determine the time between orders as follows, assuming a year equals 365 days.

$$\text{Time between orders} = \frac{365 \text{ days}}{\text{Number of orders per year}}$$

$$= \frac{365 \text{ days}}{5 \text{ orders}}$$

$$= 73 \text{ days between orders}$$

EOQ Analysis over Time

One aspect of inventory analysis that can be confusing is the time frame encompassed by the analysis. Therefore, we will digress for just a moment to discuss this aspect of EOQ analysis.

Developing the EOQ model on a monthly basis

Recall that previously we developed the EOQ model "regardless of order size, Q, and time, t." Now we will verify this condition. We will do so by developing our EOQ model on a *monthly basis*. First, demand is equal to 833.3 yards per month (which we determined by dividing the annual demand of 10,000 yards by 12 months). Next, by dividing the annual carrying cost, C_c, of $.75 by 12, we get the monthly (per unit) carrying cost. $C_c - \$.0625$. (The ordering cost of $150 is not related to time.) We thus have the values

D = 833.3 yards per month
C_c = $.0625 per yard per month
C_o = $150 per order

which we can substitute into our EOQ formula:

Computing Q^*

$$Q^* = \sqrt{\frac{2C_o D}{C_c}}$$
$$= \sqrt{\frac{2(150)(833.3)}{(.0625)}}$$
$$= 2{,}000 \text{ yards}$$

This is the same optimal order size that we determined on an annual basis. Now we will compute total monthly inventory cost.

Q^* is the same regardless of the time frame

$$\text{Total monthly inventory cost} = C_c \frac{Q^*}{2} + C_o \frac{D}{Q^*}$$
$$= (\$.0625)\frac{(2{,}000)}{2} + (\$150)\frac{(833.3)}{(2{,}000)}$$
$$= \$125 \text{ per month}$$

In order to convert this monthly total cost to an annual cost, we multiply it by 12 (months).

$$\text{Total annual inventory cost} = (\$125)(12)$$
$$= \$1{,}500$$

This brief example demonstrates that regardless of the time period encompassed by EOQ analysis, the economic order quantity (Q^*) is the same.

Assumptions of the EOQ Model

In the development of the EOQ model we made several assumptions that tended to simplify the model. These assumptions were as follows:

Simplifying assumptions

1. Demand for inventory was known with certainty and was constant over time
2. When the inventory level reached zero, a new order was instantaneously placed and received (i.e., no shortages were allowed).

We will maintain the first assumption throughout the remainder of this chapter. However, by relaxing the second assumption we can develop variations of the EOQ model, which can be applied to more realistic inventory situations.

Relaxing the second assumption

THE EOQ MODEL WITH A REORDER POINT

Reorder lead time

One of the assumptions of our present EOQ model is that an order is received an infinitely short time after it is placed. However, a more realistic situation is that the store receives an order a certain amount of time after it is placed. The time between the placement of an order and its receipt is referred to as the *reorder lead time*. For our carpet store example, once the manager places an order with the manufacturer for Super Shag carpet, it takes 10 days to receive the order. This lead time of 10 days is assumed to be constant.

Ordering with inventory in stock to meet lead-time demand

The concept of lead time is illustrated graphically in Figure 17.6. Notice that the order must now be made prior to the time when the level of inventory falls to zero. Since the demand for the carpet is consuming the inventory while the order is being shipped, the order must be made while there is enough *inventory in stock* to meet demand during the lead-time period. This level of inventory is referred to as the *reorder point* and is so designated in Figure 17.6.

FIGURE 17.6

Reorder Point and Lead Time

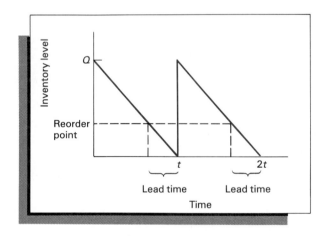

Computing the reorder point

The reorder point is computed by multiplying the lead time, L, by the demand per day. If we assume that a year consists of 365 days, then the demand per day is $D/365$. Thus, the formula for the reorder point, R, is

$$R = L\frac{D}{365}$$

Recall that for our example, L equals 10 days and demand is 10,000 yards of carpet per year. These values will yield the following reorder point.

$$R - L\frac{D}{365}$$

$$= (10)\frac{(10,000)}{365}$$

$$= 274 \text{ yards}$$

A reorder point of 274 yards means that an order should be placed whenever inventory falls to 274 yards. During the 10-day period while the order is being shipped, the 274 yards will be completely depleted, so at exactly the same time as the new order arrives the inventory level will reach zero. Notice, however, that the existence of a lead time does not affect the optimal order quantity at all. Thus, 2,000 units are still ordered regardless of the lead time and reorder point.

Q is independent of lead time

NONINSTANTANEOUS RECEIPT MODEL

The next assumption we will relax is that an order is received all at once. In many cases an order is received gradually over a period of time. This is what would occur if the carpet store were able to produce carpet as well as sell it. The carpet would go into inventory as it was produced. In fact, this form of inventory analysis is often referred to as the *production lot size model* because inventory is replenished directly from production. However, this model is applicable not only to a production situation, but to any situation where orders are not delivered all at once.

Gradual receipt of an order

Production lot size model

This type of model is graphically illustrated in Figure 17.7. Notice that inventory is not replenished instantaneously, but instead rises gradually to a point where the entire order, Q, has been re-

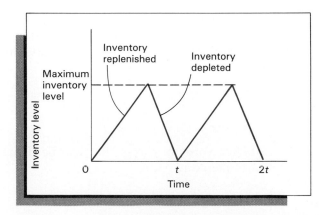

FIGURE 17.7

Noninstantaneous Receipt Model

Production rate
exceeds demand

Ordering cost is
unaffected

Determining
average inventory

The number of days
required to receive
an order

Daily demand rate

Demand during the
order receipt
period

ceived. As inventory is being replenished from production, the demand for the product is depleting the inventory stock at the same time. That is why the replenishment is gradual. However, replenishment could not occur at all if items were going out at a faster rate than they were coming in (i.e., if demand exceeded production). Thus, it must be assumed that *production exceeds demand* in this type of model.

Now we will develop an altered form of our EOQ model to compensate for the gradual replenishment of inventory by production. Our new model will consist of carrying cost and ordering cost, just as in our previous EOQ model. The ordering cost will not be affected by the gradual replenishment of inventory, since it is dependent only on the number of orders per year. However, carrying cost will be different, since it is dependent on *average inventory*, which is different for this model.

For this form of inventory analysis, it is necessary to reflect the rate of replenishment in the model. To do so, we will define the following variable:

r = daily rate of replenishment of inventory (also known as the
production rate)

Next, we must determine the maximum inventory level (as shown in Fig. 17.7) in order to compute average inventory. First, we will compute the number of days required to receive the order (which is also the length of time of a production run) as follows.

$$\text{Number of days to receive an order} = \frac{Q}{r}$$

For example, if Q equals 1,000 yards of carpet and 150 yards of carpet are produced per day, it will take

$$\frac{1,000}{150} = 6.7 \text{ days to receive an order}$$

Next we need to know how many yards of carpet will be demanded during this period. To determine this, we must use the daily rate of demand, d, which is found by dividing annual demand by 365 days.

$$d = \frac{10,000}{365 \text{ days}}$$
$$= 27.4 \text{ yards demanded per day}$$

The number of yards of carpet that will be demanded during the order receipt period is

$$\text{Demand during order receipt} = \frac{Q}{r} \cdot d$$

For our example, this amount is

6.7(27.4) = 183.6 yards demanded

The maximum amount of inventory that could be on hand if nothing were demanded during the order receipt period is Q (i.e., the total order). However, Q is depleted by the amount demanded. Thus, the maximum inventory level is

The maximum inventory level

$$Q - \frac{Q}{r} \cdot d$$

The average inventory level is one-half of this maximum inventory level (just as it was for our previous EOQ model).

The average inventory level

$$\text{Average inventory level} = \frac{1}{2}\left(Q - \frac{Q}{r}d\right)$$
$$= \frac{Q}{2}\left(1 - \frac{d}{r}\right)$$

Total carrying cost is computed by multiplying the per-unit carrying cost, C_c, by average inventory.

Total annual carrying cost

$$\text{Total carrying cost} = C_c\frac{Q}{2}\left(1 - \frac{d}{r}\right)$$

Notice that we can use annual carrying cost even though our equation uses daily demand and daily replenishment, because the latter two form a ratio that is independent of time.

Calculating the total inventory cost for this model requires the addition of total carrying cost and total ordering cost, as in our previous EOQ model.

Total annual inventory cost

$$\text{Total annual inventory cost} = C_o\frac{D}{Q} + C_c\frac{Q}{2}\left(1 - \frac{d}{r}\right)$$

The total inventory cost is a function of two other costs, just as in our previous EOQ model. Thus, the minimum inventory cost occurs when the total cost curve is lowest and where the carrying cost curve and ordering cost curve intersect (see Fig. 17.4). Therefore, to find optimal Q^*, we equate total carrying cost with total ordering cost.

Equating total ordering cost and total carrying cost

$$C_c\frac{Q}{2}\left(1 - \frac{d}{r}\right) = C_o\frac{D}{Q}$$
$$C_c\frac{Q^2}{2}\left(1 - \frac{d}{r}\right) = C_oD$$
$$Q^* = \sqrt{\frac{2C_oD}{C_c(1 - d/r)}}$$

Optimal Q^*

Computing Q^*

For our example, daily demand, d, is 27.4 yards; the daily production rate, r, is 150 yards; ordering cost, C_o, equals \$150; annual demand, D, is 10,000 yards (27.4 × 365 days); and carrying cost, C_c, is \$.75. Therefore, the economic order quantity is computed as follows.

$$Q^* = \sqrt{\frac{2(150)(10,000)}{(.75)(1 - 27.4/150)}}$$

$$= 2,212.2 \text{ yards per order}$$

Computing total minimum inventory cost

The total annual inventory cost is computed using the optimal order size, as follows.

$$\text{Total annual inventory cost} = C_o \frac{D}{Q} + C_c \frac{Q}{2}\left(1 - \frac{d}{r}\right)$$

$$= 150 \frac{(10,000)}{2,212.2} + (.75)\frac{2,212.2}{2}\left(1 - \frac{27.4}{150}\right)$$

$$= \$1,356.06 \text{ per year}$$

Computing the number of orders per year

The number of orders per year (which corresponds to the number of annual production runs) is computed the same way as in our original model, by using the formula

$$\text{Number of orders per year} = \frac{D}{Q}$$

$$= \frac{10,000}{2,212.2}$$

$$= 4.52 \text{ orders (production runs)}$$

Computing the number of days to receive an order

The length of time required to receive an order (the length of a production run) is one of the items we determined when we derived the average inventory level for this production model.

$$\text{Number of days to receive an order} = \frac{Q}{r}$$

$$= \frac{2,212.2}{150}$$

$$= 14.75 \text{ days}$$

Computing the maximum inventory level

The maximum inventory level was also determined during our derivation of the average inventory level for this model:

$$\text{Maximum inventory level} = Q - \frac{Q}{r}d$$

$$= 2,212.2 - \frac{2,212.2}{150}(27.4)$$

$$= 1,808.2 \text{ yards}$$

In this example, inventory (carpet) that was subsequently replenished by production was sold. However, the noninstantaneous receipt model is also widely used when the inventory is not sold but used internally. For example, this model would be appropriate for a manufacturing company that produces a part or item that is then used internally in another production process to produce a completed product, such as a furniture company that owns a sawmill to produce its own lumber for the furniture it makes.

THE EOQ MODEL WITH SHORTAGES AND BACK ORDERING

Recall that the manager of the carpet store specified that an inventory of Super Shag had to be available at all times; shortages could not exist. However, it is often more economical to allow shortages and back order demand and incur the cost associated with not being able to meet demand than to keep an excessive amount of inventory on hand to avoid shortages.

It can be more economical to allow shortages

An inventory model with shortages is shown in Figure 17.8. Notice that the time between order receipts has been divided into two other times: the time during which inventory is available, t_1, and the time during which there is a shortage, t_2, both *during one order cycle*. During the shortages, the carpet store will be unable to meet demand and will *back order* carpet. Typically, a cost is assigned to shortages. Shortage costs, which are primarily related to present and future sales lost because of customer dissatisfaction, are often referred to as *customer goodwill* costs. The longer a customer must wait, the more goodwill that is lost. In addition, shortage costs can include late delivery costs for back orders and special labor costs for handling back orders.

Dividing the order receipt period

Customer goodwill

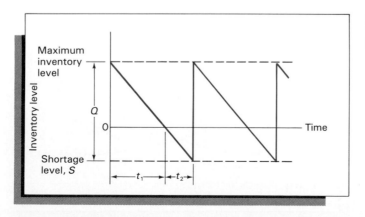

FIGURE 17.8

Shortage Model

Adding shortage
cost to the EOQ
model

In order to develop an EOQ model that includes shortages, a shortage cost must be added to our total cost equation. The development of both carrying cost and shortage cost for this model requires plane geometry, making this type of model more complex than our previous EOQ model. Therefore, we will bypass the lengthy derivation of these cost equations and present them only in their final form.

Defining the shortage cost per unit as C_s and the maximum shortage level as S (as shown in Fig. 17.8), we compute the total shortage cost as follows.

$$\text{Total shortage cost} = C_s\frac{S^2}{2Q}$$

The total carrying cost is defined as follows.

$$\text{Total carrying cost} = C_c\frac{(Q - S)^2}{2Q}$$

The total ordering cost is the same as in our previous EOQ model.

$$\text{Total ordering cost} = C_o\frac{D}{Q}$$

The total annual inventory cost is computed by summing all three of these costs.

$$\text{Total annual inventory cost} = C_s\frac{S^2}{2Q} + C_c\frac{(Q - S)^2}{2Q} + C_o\frac{D}{Q}$$

The total annual cost equation and all three of its component costs are illustrated graphically in Figure 17.9.

FIGURE 17.9

Cost Model with
Shortages

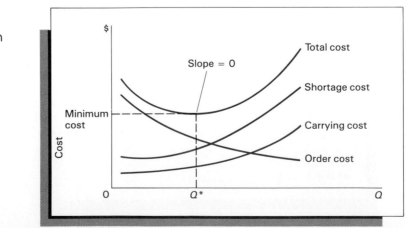

Notice in Figure 17.9 that the lowest point on the total cost curve no longer occurs where all the component cost curves intersect. This means that we cannot simply equate all the individual cost equations in order to determine the economic order quantity, Q^*. The only alternative method is to use calculus, as we did with the basic EOQ model.

The slope at any point on a curve can be found by taking the derivative of the equation of the curve at that point. At the lowest point of the total cost curve in Figure 17.9, the slope equals zero. Therefore, if we take the derivative of our total cost equation and set it equal to the slope, zero, we can solve for Q^*. Doing so results in the following EOQ formula.

$$Q^* = \sqrt{\frac{2C_oD}{C_c}\left(\frac{C_s + C_c}{C_s}\right)}$$

The maximum shortage level can also be computed as

$$S = Q^*\left(\frac{C_c}{C_c + C_s}\right)$$

For our carpet example, if we let C_s (the shortage cost per yard of carpet per year) equal \$2 and assume that all other costs and demand remain the same ($C_c = \$.75$, $C_o = \$150$, $D = 10,000$ yards), we can compute the economic order quantity as follows.

$$Q^* = \sqrt{\frac{2C_oD}{C_c}\left(\frac{C_s + C_c}{C_s}\right)}$$

$$= \sqrt{\frac{2(\$150)(10,000)}{(\$.75)}\left(\frac{\$2 + \$.75}{\$2}\right)}$$

$$= 2,345.2 \text{ yards per order}$$

The maximum shortage level is

$$S = Q^*\left(\frac{C_c}{C_c + C_s}\right)$$

$$= 2,345.2\left(\frac{\$.75}{\$2 + .75}\right)$$

$$= 639.6 \text{ yards per order}$$

The total annual cost is computed using both the optimal order quantity, Q^*, and the maximum shortage, S.

$$\text{Total annual inventory cost} = \frac{C_sS^2}{2Q} + C_c\frac{(Q - S)^2}{2Q} + C_o\frac{D}{Q}$$

$$= \frac{(\$2)(639.6)^2}{2(2,345.2)} + \frac{(\$.75)(1,705.6)^2}{2(2,345.2)}$$

$$+ \frac{150(10,000)}{2,345.2}$$

$$= \$174.44 + 465.16 + 639.60$$

$$= \$1,279.20$$

Optimal Q^* is no longer where all costs intersect

Using calculus to compute Q^*

Computing Q^*

Computing the shortage level

Computing total inventory cost

Computing the maximum inventory level

The maximum inventory level (shown in Fig. 17.8) can be determined as follows.

$$\text{Maximum inventory level} = Q - S$$
$$= 2,345.2 - 639.6$$
$$= 1,705.6 \text{ yards}$$

Computing the number of orders per year

The number of orders per year can be determined the same way as in our previous two models, by dividing total annual demand by the order quantity.

$$\text{Number of orders} = \frac{D}{Q}$$
$$= \frac{10,000}{2,345.2}$$
$$= 4.26 \text{ orders per year}$$

Computing the time between orders

Given the number of orders per year, we can also compute the time between orders, t, by dividing the number of days per year by the number of orders per year.

$$t = \frac{365}{4.26}$$
$$= 85.7 \text{ days between orders}$$

Computing the times during which inventory and shortages exist

The time during which there is inventory on hand (t_1 in Fig. 17.8) and the time during which there is a shortage (t_2 in Fig. 17.8) during each order cycle can be computed using the following formulas.

$$t_1 = \frac{Q - S}{D}$$
$$= \frac{2,345.2 - 639.6}{10,000}$$
$$= .171 \text{ year}$$
$$= 62.4 \text{ days}$$

and

$$t_2 = \frac{S}{D}$$
$$= \frac{639.6}{10,000}$$
$$= .064 \text{ year}$$
$$= 23.3 \text{ days}$$

To determine the total number of days each year during which inventory and shortages exist, multiply t_1 and t_2, respectively, by orders per year, D/Q.

Notice that by allowing shortages, the manager reduces total cost slightly from what it is when shortages are not allowed (i.e., $1,500). However, cases can occur where the difference in cost can be significant. Thus, the question of whether to allow shortages represents a major inventory decision.

Comparing the EOQ models with and without shortages

The Noninstantaneous Receipt Model with Shortages

The two previous models we developed were for the noninstantaneous receipt of an order and for allowed shortages. Both of these inventory characteristics can be combined in one model. Such a model represents the final and most complex form of the classical EOQ model. Since it is even more complex to develop than the model with shortages, we will not pursue it further in this text. However, this model is available in other, more advanced texts including those listed in the references at the end of this chapter. The interested reader can pursue this model using these references.

Combining the shortage and noninstantaneous receipt models

EOQ ANALYSIS WITH THE PERSONAL COMPUTER

Most management science software packages for the personal computer include the capability to perform EOQ analysis. As has been shown, EOQ analysis is based on a set of straightforward formulas, which makes programming relatively simple. We will use Microcomputer Software for Quantitative Analysis for Management to illustrate EOQ analysis using personal computer software.

Like other packages, this package can perform EOQ analysis for all the EOQ models presented in this chapter. However, for demonstration purposes we will apply it to our example of the EOQ model with shortages for Super Shag carpet.

Recall that the model parameters are as follows.

$$D = 10,000 \text{ yards}$$
$$C_o = \$150$$
$$C_s = \$2$$
$$C_c = \$.75$$

These values are input into the Microcomputer Software program in response to queries. The program output, which replicates the solution values we obtained using the formulas for the EOQ model with shortages, is presented in the following format.

```
          *** PLANNED SHORTAGE MODEL ***

               -- KEYBOARD INPUT --

ENTER THE PROBLEM TITLE? Super Shag carpet

ENTER THE ANNUAL DEMAND ? 10000

ENTER THE COST PER ORDER IN DOLLARS? 150

IS CARRYING COST EXPRESSED AS A % OF INVENTORY COST (Y/N) ? n
ENTER THE CARRYING COST IN DOLLARS ? 0.75

ENTER THE BACKORDER COST PER UNIT IN DOLLARS? 2

ENTER THE # OF WORKING DAYS IN THE INVENTORY YEAR (USE 365 IF NOT SURE) ? 365

          *** PLANNED SHORTAGE MODEL ***
**INPUT DATA ENTERED**


ANNUAL DEMAND =  10000
COST PER ORDER (IN $) =  150
CARRYING COST (IN $) =  .75
BACKORDER COST PER UNIT (IN $) =  2
NUMBER OF DAYS IN THE INVENTORY YEAR =  365


       ***** RESULTS : PLANNED SHORTAGE *****
------------------------------------------------------------
OPTIMUM ORDER QUANTITY =  2345.207
MAXIMUM INVENTORY =  1705.605

MAXIMUM QUANTITY BACKORDERED/CYCLE =  639.602

NUMBER OF ORDERS PER YEAR =  4.264
LENGTH OF INVENTORY CYCLE =  85.6  DAYS
TIME DURING WHICH UNITS ARE IN STOCK IN DAYS =  62.254

ANNUAL ORDERING COST = $ 639.602
ANNUAL CARRYING COST = $ 465.165
ANNUAL BACKORDER COST = $ 174.436

TOTAL ANNUAL INVENTORY COST
(EXCLUDING COST OF GOODS)=$ 1279.204
------------------------------------------------------------
      ***** END OF PLANNED SHORTAGE ANALYSIS *****
```

THE QUANTITY DISCOUNT MODEL

Receiving a
discount for making
a large order

Including item price
in the EOQ model

An additional variation of the classic EOQ model that does not include a relaxation of any of the original assumptions of the model is
the case where a store receives a discount from the supplier for placing a large order. Quantity discount analysis requires that the carrying cost be defined as a percentage of the price of the item paid to

the supplier. If we let price be represented symbolically as P, then our total annual inventory cost model becomes

$$\text{Total annual inventory cost} = C_o\frac{D}{Q} + C_cP\frac{Q}{2} + PD$$

The last term, PD (price multiplied by demand), represents the total annual amount paid to the supplier for all ordered units of the product.

Now we will consider two options open to the manager of the carpet store. We will assume that the carrying cost per unit, C_c, is 10% of the price of a yard of carpet, and that the price without discount is $3 per yard. The manager's first option is to purchase carpet from the supplier at the normal price. The second option is to purchase carpet at a price of $2 per yard (i.e., a $1 discount) by ordering a minimum of 4,000 yards.

Carrying cost as a percentage of price

In considering the first option, we compute the economic order quantity using a slightly altered version of our basic EOQ formula.

Optimal Q*

$$Q^* = \sqrt{\frac{2C_oD}{C_cP}}$$

For the first option, C_c = 10% of the price, P = $3, D = 10,000 yards, and C_o = $150.

Computing the discount options

$$Q^* = \sqrt{\frac{2(150)(10,000)}{(.10)(3)}}$$
$$= 3,162.3 \text{ yards}$$

The total annual inventory cost for this optimal value of Q^* is computed as follows.

$$\text{Total annual inventory cost} = C_o\frac{D}{Q} + C_cP\frac{Q}{2} + PD$$
$$= (150)\frac{10,000}{3,162.3} + (.10)(3)\frac{3,162.3}{2}$$
$$+ (3)(10,000)$$
$$= \$30,949 \text{ per year}$$

Next, we consider the second option. In order to receive the discount, the manager must order at least 4,000 yards. Thus, we will let Q = 4,000 yards and compute total cost with price equal to $2.00 per yard.

$$\text{Total annual inventory cost} = C_o\frac{D}{Q} + C_cP\frac{Q}{2} + PD$$
$$= (150)\frac{10,000}{4,000} + (.10)(2)\frac{4,000}{2}$$
$$+ (2)(10,000)$$
$$= \$20,775$$

Comparing the
discount options

The total costs of the two options are compared below.

	Option 1	*Option 2*
Q	3,162.3 yards	4,000 yards
P	$3.00	$2.00
Total annual cost	$30,949	$20,775

Although it appears that the selection of option 2 and the quantity discount is the best decision, we need to check one more condition to make sure there is not an even better decision. We must recompute Q^* with the new carrying cost to see if there is an order quantity *greater than* 4,000 yards that would result in an even lower cost. (In other words, 4,000 yards is just the minimum that must be ordered, and it is feasible that a larger order quantity could result in a lower cost.) The economic order quantity with the price discount is

$$Q^* = \sqrt{\frac{(2)(150)(10,000)}{(.10)(2)}}$$

$$= 3,873 \text{ yards}$$

Since this new order quantity is less than 4,000 yards, the option 2 decision is, in fact, the best one. Therefore, the manager would order 4,000 yards and receive the discount. Basically, this type of quantity discount analysis allows an assessment of the trade-off between the added carrying costs for holding the extra amount (necessary to get the discount) in inventory and the reduced price.

Quantity Discount Analysis with the Computer

The quantity discount analysis conducted in this section can also be performed using Microcomputer Software for Quantitative Analysis for Management, which was used earlier in this chapter for the analysis of the EOQ model with shortages. The EOQ parameters and the discount information are easily input, and the program output provided appears as follows.

```
ENTER THE ANNUAL DEMAND ? 10000

ENTER THE ORDERING COST PER UNIT (IN DOLLARS) ? 150

ENTER THE CARRYING COST AS % OF COST OF GOODS (ENTER AS A DECIMAL, E.G., ENTER
10% AS .10) ? .10

ENTER THE # OF PRICE DISCOUNTS ? 1

ENTER THE COST OF GOODS (PRICE WITH NO DISCOUNTS) ? 3

ENTER THE MAXIMUM ORDER (IN UNITS) BEFORE DISCOUNTS BEGIN ? 4000
----------------------------------------------------------------
```

```
THE OPTIMUM ORDER QUANTITY (UNADJUSTED) FOR THE BASIC PRICE =   3162.277

ADJUSTED OPTIMUM ORDER QUANTITY =  3162.277

TOTAL COST (NO DISCOUNT) =  30948.68
-------------------------------------------------------------


DISCOUNT #  1

ENTER THE DISCOUNTED PRICE ? 2

ENTER THE MINIMUM ORDER QUANTITY FOR THIS DISCOUNT ? 4000

THE OPTIMUM ORDER QUANTITY (UNADJUSTED) FOR THIS DISCOUNT =  3872.983

ADJUSTED OPTIMUM ORDER QUANTITY FOR THIS DISCOUNT =  4000

TOTAL COST FOR THIS DISCOUNT =  20775
-------------------------------------------------------------


OPTIMAL STRATEGY IS TO ORDER  4000
UNITS AT A TOTAL COST OF $  20775
-------------------------------------------------------------

********** END OF QUANTITY DISCOUNT ANALYSIS **********
```

MATERIAL REQUIREMENTS PLANNING

Material requirements planning (MRP) is a computer-based production and inventory planning and control system employed primarily for products in which the final product, or end item, is an assembly of component parts. The objectives of an MRP system are to ensure the availability of materials and components for assembly of the end item, to minimize the level of inventory, and to plan manufacturing activities, delivery schedules, and purchasing activities.

MRP

Objectives of an MRP system

The basic logic of an MRP system is to first analyze an end item (i.e., finished product) and break it down into its component parts, a procedure referred to as *exploding* the product. A schedule is then determined by employing the demand and lead time for a particular component to determine the demand and lead time for a subsequent component. In this manner, an MRP system determines *how much* of each component should be ordered and *when* the components should be ordered. The demand at each component level is dependent on the demand for the component at the next level of production.

Product explosion

The three major inputs to an MRP system are the *master production schedule*, the *product structure records*, and the *inventory status records*. The master production schedule outlines the production

Master production schedule

plans for all end items. The computerized MRP system then explodes this master schedule into individual time-phased component requirements. The product structure records (also called *bills of materials*) contain information on all raw materials, components, and subassemblies required for each end item. The bill of materials informs the MRP system about each item: its part number, its description, and the quantity demanded per end item. Finally, the inventory status records contain the on-hand and on-order status of all items in inventory plus information on lead times and order sizes for all components.

Bills of materials

Inventory status records

The MRP system determines a component's gross requirements by exploding the bill of materials according to the master production schedule. The exploding process is simply a multiplication of the number of end items by the quantity of each component necessary to produce an end item. The net requirements are determined by subtracting the available inventory (indicated by the inventory status reports) from the gross requirements. The timing of orders is then determined by offsetting the order receipts by their lead time. In this manner, an MRP system indicates what to order, how much to order, and when to order.

Gross requirements of a component part

The basic computer output of the MRP system is planned order releases that can be in the form of purchase orders to vendors or work orders to the internal production operations (or shops). These releases indicate the timing and quantity of the orders.

MRP computer output

Materials requirement planning has become a very popular and widely applied means of managing inventory. However, it does not necessarily supersede the EOQ models presented in this chapter. EOQ models are most applicable for single-product inventory control (not assembled end items) and for products with independent demand (not component-dependent demand). MRP systems tend to be alternatives to EOQ models for assembly-type manufacturing operations. In addition, MRP systems require order size determination, and EOQ models provide one of several alternatives for determining order sizes within the MRP framework.

EOQ models and MRP

Summary

In this chapter the classical economic order quantity model has been presented. The basic form of the EOQ model included simplifying assumptions regarding order receipt, no shortages, and constant demand known with certainty. By relaxing some of these assumptions, we were able to create increasingly complex but realistic models. These EOQ variations included the reorder point model, the noninstantaneous receipt model, and the model with shortages. However, all of these models maintained one assumption that was never relaxed—that demand was known with certainty and was constant. Although these EOQ models are quite useful in developing an inventory policy and are used extensively as approximations, they disregard the fact that demand is almost never known with certainty. Creating a truly realistic model involves dropping this last assumption. This is the topic of the next chapter—inventory analysis with uncertain demand.

Certain demand is always assumed in this chapter

References

Buchan, J., and Koenigsberg, E. *Scientific Inventory Management.* Englewood Cliffs, N.J.: Prentice-Hall, 1963.

Buffa, E. S., and Miller, Jeffrey G. *Production-Inventory Systems: Planning and Control.* 3d ed. Homewood, Ill.: Irwin, 1979.

Churchman, C. W.; Ackoff, R. L.; and Arnoff, E. L. *Introduction to Operations Research.* New York: John Wiley and Sons, 1957.

Hadley, G., and Whitin, T. M. *Analysis of Inventory Systems.* Englewood Cliffs, N.J.: Prentice-Hall, 1963.

Johnson, L. A., and Montgomery, D. C. *Operations Research in Production Planning, Scheduling, and Inventory Control.* New York: John Wiley and Sons, 1974.

Lee, Sang M.; Moore, Laurence J.; and Taylor, Bernard W. *Management Science.* 3d ed. Boston: Allyn and Bacon, 1990.

Magee, J. F., and Boodman, D. M. *Production Planning and Inventory Control.* 2d ed. New York: McGraw-Hill, 1967.

Shamblin, J. E., and Stevens, G. T., Jr. *Operations Research: A Fundamental Approach.* New York: McGraw-Hill, 1974.

Starr, M. K., and Miller, D. W. *Inventory Control: Theory and Practice.* Englewood Cliffs, N.J.: Prentice-Hall, 1962.

EXAMPLE PROBLEM SOLUTION

The following example will demonstrate EOQ analysis for the classical model and the model with shortages and back ordering.

Problem Statement

Electronic Village stocks and sells a particular brand of personal computer. It costs the store $450 each time it places an order with the manufacturer for the personal computers. The annual cost of carrying the PCs in inventory is $170. The store manager estimates that annual demand for the PCs will be 1,200 units.

a. Determine the optimal order quantity and the total minimum inventory cost.

b. Assume that shortages are allowed and the shortage cost is $600 per unit per year. Compute the optimal order quantity and the total minimum inventory cost.

Step 1 (part a): Determine the Optimal Order Quantity

$$D = 1{,}200 \text{ personal computers}$$
$$C_c = \$170$$
$$C_o = \$450$$

$$Q = \sqrt{\frac{2C_o D}{C_c}}$$

$$= \sqrt{\frac{2(450)(1{,}200)}{170}}$$

$$= 79.7 \text{ personal computers}$$

$$\text{Total cost} = C_2 \frac{Q}{2} + C_o \frac{D}{Q}$$

$$= 170\left(\frac{79.7}{2}\right) + 450\left(\frac{1{,}200}{79.7}\right)$$

$$= \$13{,}549.91$$

Step 2 (part b): Compute the EOQ with Shortages

$$C_s = \$600$$

$$Q = \sqrt{\frac{2C_o D}{C_c}\left(\frac{C_s + C_c}{C_s}\right)}$$

$$= \sqrt{\frac{2(150)(1{,}200)}{170}\left(\frac{600 + 170}{600}\right)}$$

$$= 90.3 \text{ personal computers}$$

$$S = Q\left(\frac{C_c}{C_c + C_s}\right)$$

$$= 90.3\left(\frac{170}{170 + 600}\right)$$

$$= 19.9 \text{ personal computers}$$

$$\text{Total cost} = \frac{C_s S^2}{2Q} + C_c \frac{(Q - S)^2}{2Q} + \frac{C_o D}{Q}$$

$$= \frac{(600)(19.9)^2}{2(90.3)} + 170\frac{(90.3 - 19.9)^2}{2(90.3)} + 450\left(\frac{1{,}200}{90.3}\right)$$

$$= \$1{,}315.65 + \$4{,}665.27 + 5{,}980.07$$

$$= \$11{,}960.98$$

Problems

1. Given the following annual demand, annual carrying cost, and cost per order, compute the economic order quantity and total minimum cost.

   D = 15,000 units per year
   C_o = $100 per order
   C_c = $.40 per unit per year

2. Given the following annual demand, annual carrying cost, and cost per order, compute the economic order quantity and total minimum cost.

   D = 750 units per year
   C_o = $50 per order
   C_c = $.15 per unit per year

3. An inventory system has an annual ordering cost of $200 per order, an annual per-unit carrying cost of $ .75, and an annual demand of 5,000 units (assuming a 365-day year). Compute the following:

   a. Economic order quantity
   b. Minimum total annual inventory cost
   c. Optimal number of orders per year
   d. Optimal time between orders

4. For the inventory system in problem 3, illustrate the optimal order size, average inventory, and time between orders in a graph relating inventory and time. Next, illustrate the economic order quantity in a graph relating inventory cost and order size.

5. The Western Jeans Company purchases denim from Cumberland Textile Mills. The Western Company uses 35,000 yards of denim per year (365 days) to make jeans. The cost of ordering denim from the textile company is $500 per order. It costs Western $.35 per yard annually to hold a yard of denim in inventory. Determine the optimal number of yards of denim the Western Company should order, the minimum total annual inventory cost, the optimal number of orders per year, and the optimal time between orders.

6. The Metropolitan Book Company purchases paper from the Atlantic Paper Company. Metropolitan produces magazines and paperbacks that require 215,000 yards of paper per year (365 days). The cost per order for the company is $1,200; the cost of holding one yard of paper in inventory is $.08 per year. Determine the following:

   a. Economic order quantity
   b. Minimum total annual cost
   c. Optimal number of orders per year
   d. Optimal time between orders

7. The Atlantic Paper Company produces paper from wood pulp, which it purchases from the Adirondack Lumber Products Company. Atlantic needs 450,000 pounds of wood pulp per year (365 days) to meet its customers' demand for paper. Each order of pulp costs Atlantic $700, and it costs $.30 per pound per year to carry a pound of pulp in inventory. It takes 8 days for Atlantic to receive an order from the Adirondack Company. Determine the following:

   a. Economic order quantity

   b. Minimum total annual inventory cost

   c. Reorder point

8. The Midtown Bookstore and Newsstand orders paperbacks from the Metropolitan Book Company. The demand at the Midtown store for paperbacks is 300 per month. The cost per order is $50; the cost per month of carrying a paperback on the shelf is $.02. Determine the optimal number of paperbacks to order per month, the total minimum monthly inventory cost, and the total minimum annual inventory cost.

9. The Big Buy Supermarket stocks Munchies Cereal. Demand for Munchies is 4,000 boxes per year (365 days). It costs the store $60 per order of Munchies, and it costs $.80 per box per year to keep the cereal in stock. Once an order for Munchies is placed, it takes 4 days to receive the order from a food distributor. Determine the following:

   a. Optimal order size

   b. Minimum total annual inventory cost

   c. Reorder point

10. Illustrate the optimal order size, time between orders, and reorder point for the inventory policy in problem 9 graphically.

11. In problem 5, if it takes the Western Jeans Company 6 days to receive an order of denim, at what level of inventory should the company reorder?

12. Given the following demand and replenishment rates per day, annual carrying cost per unit, and order cost, determine the economic order quantity and minimum total annual inventory cost for a noninstantaneous receipt model (one year equals 365 days).

   d = 200 units per day
   r = 500 units per day
   C_o = $300 per order
   C_c = $.80 per unit per year

13. Given an annual demand rate of 8,000 units and an annual replenishment rate of 12,000 units for a noninstantaneous receipt model, an annual carrying cost per unit of $1.15, and an order cost of $175 per order, determine the optimal order size and the minimum total annual inventory cost.

14. For the inventory system described in problem 13, graphically illustrate the optimal order size, the maximum inventory level, the time required to receive an order, and the time between orders.

15. The Adirondack Lumber Products Company produces wood pulp in its mill and then stores it in warehouses until it is shipped to customers. The company's customers demand 450,000 pounds of wood pulp per year. The company's mill is able to produce 600,000 pounds of wood pulp per year. Every time the mill starts a production run to produce wood pulp (i.e., an order), it costs $800. The annual carrying cost per pound is $.80. Determine the following:

   a. Optimal order size

   b. Minimum total annual inventory cost

   c. Maximum inventory level

16. The Petroco Oil Company refines oil into gasoline at its refinery in Corpus Christi and stores it in storage tanks until it is demanded by the company's distributors. The oil company refinery can produce 4,000 barrels of gasoline per day, and the demand for gasoline by the company's distributors is 3,500 barrels per day. The cost to make a production run is $2,000, and the annual carrying cost per barrel is $3. Determine the following:

   a. Economic order quantity

   b. Minimum total annual inventory cost

   c. Maximum inventory level

17. The Wood Valley Dairy makes cheese to supply to stores in its area. The dairy can make 250 pounds of cheese per day, and the demand at area stores is 180 pounds per day. Each time the dairy makes cheese, it costs $125 to set up the production process. The annual cost of carrying a pound of cheese in a refrigerated storage area is $12. Determine the optimal order size and the minimum total annual inventory cost.

18. The Rainwater Brewery produces Rainwater Light Beer, which it stores in barrels in its warehouse and supplies to its distributors on demand. The demand for Rainwater is 1,500 barrels of beer per day. The brewery can produce 2,000 barrels of Rainwater per day. It costs $6,500 to set up a production run for Rainwater. Once it is brewed, the beer is stored in a refrigerated warehouse at an annual cost of $50 per barrel. Determine the economic order quantity and the minimum total annual inventory cost.

19. The purchasing manager for the Atlantic Steel Company must determine a policy for ordering coal to operate 12 converters. Each converter requires exactly 5 tons of coal per day to operate, and the firm operates 360 days per year. The purchasing manager has determined that the ordering cost is $80 per order, and the cost of holding coal is 20% of the average dollar value of inventory held. The purchasing manager has negotiated a contract to obtain the coal for $12 per ton for the coming year.

a. Determine the optimal quantity of coal to receive in each order.

b. Determine the total inventory-related costs associated with the optimal ordering policy (do not include the cost of the coal).

c. If 5 days' lead time is required to receive an order of coal, how much coal should be on hand when an order is placed?

20. The Pacific Lumber Company and Mill processes 10,000 logs annually, operating 250 days per year. Immediately upon receiving an order, the logging company's supplier begins delivery to the lumber mill at the rate of 60 logs per day. The lumber mill has determined that the ordering cost per order is $62.50 and the cost of carrying logs in inventory before they are processed is $15 per log on an annual basis. Determine the following:

a. The optimal order size

b. The total inventory cost associated with the optimal order quantity

c. The number of operating days between orders

d. The number of operating days required to receive an order

21. The Northwoods Mail Order and General Retail Store in Vermont produces maple syrup to sell in its store on the premises and to ship. Setting up the syrup-making equipment to produce a batch of syrup costs $230. The annual cost of carrying a gallon of maple syrup in a temperature-controlled storeroom is $15 per gallon. Demand for maple syrup has been estimated at 7,500 gallons per year, and the store can produce 9,000 gallons per year. Shortages are not allowed.

a. Determine the optimal number of gallons to produce during each production run and the total minimum annual inventory cost for maple syrup.

b. Assume that the store reopens for the new year on January 2, and that the store and the maple syrup production facilities are open 365 days per year. The store begins the new year with no inventory and immediately begins a production run for maple syrup. Set up an approximate production schedule (rounding off fractional days to the nearest whole day) for the next six months based on the optimal production order size.

22. In the noninstantaneous receipt EOQ model, what would be the effect of the production rate's becoming increasingly large as the demand rate became increasingly small, until the ratio d/r was negligible?

23. Given the following information for an inventory system that allows shortages, compute the optimal order size and minimum total annual inventory cost.

$D = 25,000$ units per year

$C_o = \$300$ per order

$C_c = \$2$ per unit per year

$C_s = \$5$ per unit per year

24. Consider the inventory system of the Western Jeans Company described in problem 5. Assume that this company allows shortages and that the annual cost per unit of shortages is $2. Determine the optimal order size and minimum total annual inventory cost. Compare these results with those determined in problem 5, and indicate if shortages should be allowed.

25. Videoworld is a discount television store that sells color televisions. The annual demand for color television sets is 2,200. The cost per order from the manufacturer is $650. The carrying cost is $45 per set each year. The store has an inventory policy that allows shortages. The shortage cost per set is estimated at $60. Determine the following:

   a. Optimal order size

   b. Maximum shortage level

   c. Minimum total annual inventory cost

26. Graphically illustrate the optimal order size, maximum inventory level, and maximum shortage level for the inventory system described in problem 25.

27. Consider the inventory system of the Metropolitan Book Company described in problem 6. Assume that this company allows shortages and that the annual cost per shortage is $.12 per yard of paper. Determine the optimal order size and minimum total annual inventory cost, and compare these results with those determined in problem 6.

28. The Roadking Tire Store sells a brand of tire called the Roadrunner. The annual demand from the store's customers for Roadrunner tires is 3,700 per year. The cost to order tires from the tire manufacturer is $420 per order. The annual carrying cost is $1.75 per tire. The store allows shortages, and the annual shortage cost per tire is $4. Determine the following:

   a. Optimal order size

   b. Maximum shortage level

   c. Minimum total annual inventory cost

29. The Laurel Creek Lawn Shop sells Fastgro Fertilizer. The annual demand for the fertilizer is 270,000 pounds. The cost to order the fertilizer from the Fastgro company is $105 per order. The annual carrying cost is $.25 per pound. The store operates with shortages, and the annual shortage cost is $.70 per pound. Compute the optimal order size, minimum total annual inventory cost, and the maximum shortage level.

30. A car dealer who sells compact cars has an annual demand for 1,200 cars. It costs the dealer $1,800 per order to order cars from the manufacturer in Dearborn, and $700 per year to carry a car in inventory on the lot. The dealer is trying to decide whether to allow shortages. The dealer estimates that the cost of not having a car on the lot when a cus-

tomer wants to buy one is $1,200. Determine if the dealer should allow shortages and, if so, how much of a shortage.

31. The Texas Electronics Company manufactures personal computers in an assembly manufacturing process. At each work station electronic components are assembled for use in a PC. At one station, 7,200 units of a particular component are required monthly. The cost of ordering these components from the distributor is $1,600; the monthly cost of carrying the component in inventory in a climate-controlled warehouse is $12 per unit. If the company runs out of the component and the work station must be shut down, the entire manufacturing process is delayed. The cost of a shutdown is estimated to be $24 per unit per month. Determine the optimal order quantity and minimum total monthly and annual inventory costs.

32. At the Texas Electronics Company in problem 31, a work station produces several subassemblies that are used at subsequent stations in the manufacturing process. The monthly demand for one particular subassembly is 380 units. The monthly cost of holding the subassembly in inventory until it is used is $8. The cost of setting up the machinery at the work station to produce the subassembly is $700. If there are not enough units in inventory to meet demand at the subsequent work station, the monthly cost is $17 per unit. Determine the optimal number of subassemblies that should be produced at the work station per machine setup and the minimum total monthly and annual inventory costs.

33. Assume that in problem 5 the carrying cost per yard of denim is 29% of the price per yard and the price of denim from the Cumberland Mills is $1.20 per yard. Now suppose Western Company can get a discounted price of $1 per yard if it purchases 20,000 yards per order. Analyze both options and indicate what order policy the Western Jeans Company should follow.

34. Assume that in problem 7 the annual carrying cost per pound of wood pulp is 40% of the price per pound and the price per pound of wood pulp is $.75. Now suppose the Atlantic Paper Company can get a discounted price of $.60 per pound if it purchases a minimum of 60,000 pounds per order. Should Atlantic Paper Company purchase wood pulp at the normal price or at the discount?

35. Assume that in problem 9 the annual carrying cost is 80% of the price per box of Munchies and the price per box is $1. Now suppose the Big Buy Supermarket can get a discounted price of $.95 per box if it purchases 2,000 boxes per order. Should the market purchase at the normal price or at the discount?

36. The Uptown Bar and Grill buys Old World draft beer by the barrel from a local distributor. The grill has an annual demand for 900 barrels of beer, which it purchases from the distributor at a price of $205 per barrel. The annual carrying cost is 12% of the price, and the cost per order

is $160. The distributor has offered to give the grill a reduced price of $190 per barrel if it will order a minimum of 300 barrels. Should the grill maintain its normal ordering policy or take the discount?

37. Why does the general EOQ model not include the price of an item, and when does it become necessary to include the price in performing EOQ analysis?

38. By performing several mathematical manipulations, we can express the total cost equation for the general EOQ model as

Total annual inventory cost $= \sqrt{2C_o C_c D}$

Performing similar mathematical manipulations on the EOQ model with shortages and back ordering will result in the following total cost equation for that model:

Total annual inventory cost $= \sqrt{2C_o C_c D} \cdot \sqrt{\dfrac{C_s}{C_c + C_s}}$

Comparing these two total cost equations, what can you infer about the general relationship between the EOQ model with shortages and the model without shortages?

Inventory Analysis with Uncertain Demand

The EOQ Model with Safety Stocks
Determination of the Safety Stock
Determining Safety Stocks Using Service Levels

Determining the Order Quantity with Payoff Tables
Simulation of Inventory
Computer Simulation of the Flower Shop Example

Applications of Inventory Analysis

Parts and Raw Material Inventory in the Aircraft Industry
Raw Material Inventory Control in the Chemical Industry
Using a 95 Percent Service Rule for Inventory Control at a Phone Center
Payoff Tables for Inventory Control

Summary
References
Example Problem Solution
Problems

This chapter is a logical extension of the previous chapter on inventory analysis. In Chapter 17, several variations of a general technique (EOQ analysis) for inventory analysis were presented. These variations were created by selectively relaxing the general assumptions of the classical EOQ model. However, the assumption that demand was always constant and known with certainty was never dropped. Realistically, future demand can rarely be predicted with certainty. Thus, it will be beneficial for us to look at several ways to compensate for uncertain demand when determining the order quantity.

THE EOQ MODEL WITH SAFETY STOCKS

To begin our presentation of inventory analysis under conditions of uncertain demand, we will continue to work within the framework of the classic economic order quantity (EOQ) model developed in Chapter 17. One of the problems in performing EOQ analysis with

Determining a
reorder point given
uncertain demand

uncertain demand is that it is difficult to determine a *reorder point*. Recall that a reorder point is needed to prevent stockouts (i.e., shortages) during the time between the placement of an order and its receipt. The reorder point is a level of inventory remaining in stock that is equal to the demand during the time required to receive an order (i.e., *lead time*). When demand is certain, this inventory will be depleted at a known rate so the order will arrive at the same time that the inventory level reaches zero.

A reorder point
example

As an example, consider the Armor Carpet Store introduced in Chapter 17. Recall that the carpet store has a constant demand (D) of 10,000 yards of Super Shag carpet per year and a lead time (L) of 10 days. Thus, the reorder point, R, was computed as

$$R = L \frac{D}{365}$$
$$= \frac{(10)\,(10,000)}{365}$$
$$= 274 \text{ yards}$$

The manager of the carpet store places an order for the economic order quantity (Q^*) when the carpet in inventory reaches 274 yards, and this amount will be depleted by demand during the 10 days required to receive the order. However, although lead time may be constant, if demand is uncertain, then it is not possible to predict exactly the demand that will occur during these 10 days. Therefore, it is possible that even though we have a reorder point, shortages might occur anyway. As a hedge against stockouts when demand is uncertain, companies often use a buffer of extra inventory called a *safety stock*.

Safety stock

The occurrence of stockouts when demand is uncertain is illustrated graphically in Figure 18.1.

FIGURE 18.1

Inventory Model
with Uncertain
Demand

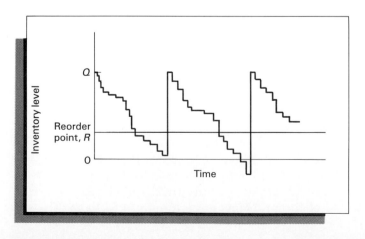

In the second order cycle, a stockout occurs because demand exceeds the *expected* reorder point during the lead time. Now let us add a safety stock to our graph, as shown in Figure 18.2. The reorder point is set so that the safety stock level is treated the same as the zero inventory level without a safety stock. In other words, we do not want inventory to go lower than the safety stock level. But when it does, as in the second order cycle, demand is still met.

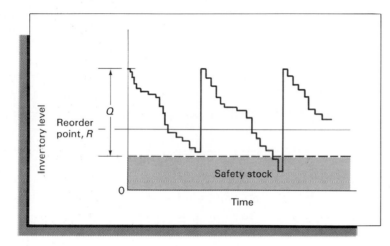

FIGURE 18.2

Inventory Model with Safety Stock

Maintaining a safety stock is not cost free, however. A carrying cost is charged on the safety stock as it is on regular inventory. It is generally assumed that the frequency and amount that actual demand is above the safety stock level equal the frequency and amount that it is below the safety stock level. Thus, the surpluses and deficits balance out over the year, so on the average the safety stock is unused. This means that to determine the annual cost of the safety stock, it is necessary only to multiply the annual carrying cost per unit by the safety stock level, S_s.

Total annual carrying cost of safety stock = $C_c S_s$

For our carpet store example, recall that C_c = \$.75 per yard. If we arbitrarily assume a safety stock of 300 yards, then the carrying cost is

$$\text{Total annual carrying cost of safety stock} = (\$.75)(300)$$
$$= \$225$$

However, this cost must be weighed against the cost of having a stockout. It is the objective of this form of inventory analysis to determine a safety stock level that minimizes the sum of the carrying cost and the stockout cost.

Determination of the Safety Stock

Probabilistic demand

Although demand is not known with certainty, we will assume that it can be described by a probability distribution. Based on the carpet store's records of demand, the manager has determined the following probability distribution for demand for carpet *during the lead-time period*.

Demand During Lead Time	Probability
500	.10
600	.20
700	.40
800	.20
900	.10
	1.00

Expected demand during lead time

Using this distribution, we will compute the *expected demand* during lead time, as follows.

$$E(\text{Demand}) = .10(500) + .20(600) + .40(700) + .20(800) + .10(900)$$
$$= 700 \text{ yards}$$

The initial reorder point

We will use this average value of 700 yards of carpet as the *initial* reorder point. The amount by which our finally determined reorder point exceeds 700 yards will be the safety stock.

With a reorder point of 700 yards and no safety stock, it is possible for the actual demand during lead time to exceed this amount by 100 yards (i.e., demand of 800 yards) 20% of the time and by 200 yards (i.e., demand of 900 yards) 10% of the time. On the other hand, if we established a reorder point of 800 yards including a safety stock of 100 yards, we could expect a stockout of 100 yards (i.e., demand of 900) only 10% of the time. If the reorder point were 900 yards including a safety stock of 200 yards, there would never be a stockout. The *expected shortages* for each of these possible reorder points with safety stock are computed in Table 18.1.

Computing expected shortages for each reorder point

TABLE 18.1

Computation of Expected Shortages per Reorder Point

Reorder Point	Safety Stock	Actual Demand During Lead Time	Resulting Shortage	Probability of Shortage	Expected Shortage	Total Expected Shortage per Reorder Point
700	0	700	0	.40	0	
		800	100	.20	20	40
		900	200	.10	20	
800	100	800	0	.20	0	
		900	100	.10	10	10
900	200	900	0	.10	0	0

From Table 18.1, we see that a reorder point of 700 yards and no safety stock will result in an expected shortage of 40 yards. A reorder point of 800 yards, which includes a safety stock of 100 yards, will result in an average shortage of 10 yards. A reorder point of 900 yards, which includes a safety stock of 200 yards, will result in no shortages.

In Table 18.1, the reorder points tested are for a single order, so the expected shortages are *per order*. From this information, we need to determine annual shortages. This is accomplished by multiplying the average shortages per order by the number of orders per year. Recall that the number of orders per year is computed as

Determining annual shortages

$$\text{Number of orders per year} = \frac{D}{Q}$$

Since demand is uncertain, we will use an *average demand* of 10,000 yards to compute both the order size, Q, and the number of orders per year. Recall that in Chapter 17 the carpet store manager had determined the following inventory costs for stocking Super Shag carpet.

Carrying cost, C_c = $.75 per yard per year
Ordering cost, C_o = $150 per order

Thus, the economic order quantity and number of orders per year are as follows:

$$Q^* = \sqrt{\frac{2C_o D}{C_c}}$$
$$= \sqrt{\frac{2(150)(10,000)}{0.75}}$$
$$= 2,000 \text{ yards per order}$$
$$\text{Number of orders per year} = \frac{10,000}{2,000}$$
$$= 5$$

Now we can compute the average annual shortages and the cost of these shortages for each of the reorder points. Assuming a shortage cost, C_s, of $2 per yard, the shortage costs per reorder point are as follows.

$$\begin{aligned}
\text{Total annual shortage cost} &= (\text{Shortage cost per yard}) \\
&\quad \times (\text{Number of orders}) \\
&\quad \times (\text{Average shortage per order}) \\
&= C_s \frac{D}{Q} (\text{Average shortage per order})
\end{aligned}$$

Total annual
shortage costs for
each safety stock

Using the average shortages for each reorder point shown in Table 18.1, we arrive at the total annual shortage costs:

Total annual shortage cost for safety stock of 0 yards = ($2) (5) (40)
= $400

Total annual shortage cost for safety stock of 100 yards = ($2) (5) (10)
= $100

Total annual shortage cost for safety stock of 200 yards = ($2) (5) (0)
= $0

Total annual
carrying costs for
each safety stock

Next, we must compare the cost of these shortages to the carrying cost for each level of safety stock, S_s.

Total annual carrying cost of safety stock = $C_c S_s$

Total annual carrying cost for safety stock of 0 yards = ($.75) (0)
= $0

Total annual carrying cost for safety stock of 100 yards = ($.75) (100)
= $75

Total annual carrying cost for safety stock of 200 yards = ($.75) (200)
= $150

Total annual safety
stock cost for each
safety stock

Now that we have determined *both costs* of having a safety stock for each safety stock level, we can compute the total safety stock cost by summing the two.

Total safety stock cost for safety stock of 0 yards = $400 + 0
= $400

Total safety stock cost for safety stock of 100 yards = $100 + 75
= $175

Total safety stock cost for safety stock of 200 yards = $0 + 150
= $150

Selecting the
minimum cost
safety stock and
reorder point

The minimum total safety stock cost is $150; thus the manager would maintain a safety stock of 200 yards, which requires a reorder point of 900 yards.

This example was relatively simple because we considered only six discrete values (between 500 and 900 yards) for demand during lead time. It would have been more realistic to include all possible demand values between 500 and 900 yards in our probability distribution, since yards are a continuous unit of measure. In other words, demand during lead time would have been more appropriately defined by a continuous probability distribution. However, this would have greatly complicated this example. By using discrete values for demand during lead time, we are, in effect, approximating actual occurrences.

Determining Safety Stocks Using Service Levels

An alternative way to determine a safety stock is to establish a safety stock level that will satisfy the demand of a specified percentage of total customers. This is an especially useful method for determining a safety stock when a shortage cost cannot be determined. For example, the manager of the carpet store might establish a reorder point of 1,000 yards of carpet, which would enable the store to meet the demand of 85% of the customers *during the lead time period*; 15% of the customers would not be able to buy the carpet because it would be out of stock. The percentage of customers the store is able to service during lead time (i.e., 85%) is referred to as the *service level*. By adding a safety stock to the reorder point, the store would be able to meet the demand of a larger percentage of the customers. In other words, the store is able to increase the service level by increasing the safety stock.

In order to develop a safety stock based on service level for our carpet store example, we will assume that demand is uncertain, but that it can be described by a *normal probability distribution*. Figure 18.3 is a graph of the normal distribution of carpet demand during lead time (assuming a lead time of 10 days). The mean of this distribution is 300 yards with a standard deviation of 50 yards. (See Chap. 10 for a discussion of the normal distribution.)

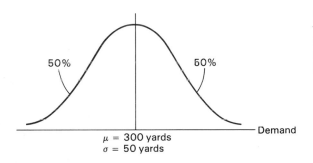

$\mu = 300$ yards
$\sigma = 50$ yards

Serving a specified percentage of customers during lead time

Normal probability distribution

FIGURE 18.3

Normal Distribution of Demand During Lead Time

Since the average demand during lead time is 300 yards, as shown in Figure 18.3, we will use this amount of inventory as the reorder point ($R = 300$ yards). However, this reorder point is simply an average; thus actual demand during the lead-time period will be more than 300 yards 50% of the time (i.e., 50% of the time customers will not be serviced) and less than 300 yards 50% of the time. Therefore, with a reorder point of 300 yards, the service level is 50% during the reorder lead time. To increase the service level, we must add a safety stock.

The average demand during lead time as the reorder point

A 50% service level

As an example, let us assume that the carpet store wants to establish a service level of 95%. This means that the reorder point must be set at the point labeled R in Figure 18.4. Notice that 5% of the probability distribution lies to the right of this point and 95% lies to the left of this point, indicating that demand will exceed the reorder point (on the average) 5% of the time. The safety stock is the amount between the mean of 300 yards and the reorder point, R.

The distance from the mean to the reorder point in Figure 18.4 is equal not only to the safety stock but also to the number of standard deviations corresponding to 45% of the normal curve between the mean and this point. Therefore, we can define the following relationship.

FIGURE 18.4

Normal Distribution of Demand During Lead Time with Safety Stock and Reorder Point

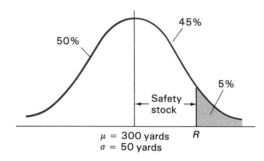

Safety stock = $Z\sigma$

where

Z = the number of standard deviations the reorder point is from the mean

σ = the standard deviation (50 yards)

Computing the safety stock

A probability of .4500 in Table A.1 of Appendix A corresponds to a Z value of 1.645. Thus, the safety stock is computed as

$$\text{Safety stock} = Z\sigma$$
$$= (1.645)(50)$$
$$= 82.25 \text{ yards}$$

The new reorder point with safety stock

The new reorder point is equal to the previously computed average demand during lead time plus the safety stock.

$$R = 300 + 82.25$$
$$= 382.25 \text{ yards}$$

For practical purposes we can round this value off to a reorder point of 382 yards. Therefore, every time the inventory level falls to 382 yards, a new order is made (regardless of what the economic order quantity actually is).

DETERMINING THE ORDER QUANTITY WITH PAYOFF TABLES

Chapter 11 on decision analysis presented the concept of a *payoff table*. A payoff table presents the various outcomes of a decision under alternative probabilistic conditions (states of nature). In this section we will use payoff tables (and thus decision analysis) in inventory analysis. In inventory analysis, the decisions are the possible order quantities, and the probabilistic states of nature are the possible levels of demand.

To demonstrate the application of decision analysis to inventory analysis, we will use the following example. The Petals and Plants Flower Shop orders carnations from a greenhouse on a weekly basis. (Since carnations are a perishable commodity, the order is placed at given intervals, typically corresponding to the life of the product, which in this case is one week. Hence, the decision as to when to place an order has already been determined.) The manager of the flower shop developed the following probability distribution for demand of carnations per week from past records.

Demand (dozens/week)	Probability
9	.15
10	.40
11	.25
12	.20
	1.00

The carnations cost the flower shop $1.50 per dozen and sell for $3.00 per dozen. The manager has determined that the carrying cost is $.50 per dozen per week and the shortage cost is $1.00 per dozen per week. The payoff table shown in Table 18.2 consists of four alternative decisions representing the four order sizes and four possible states of nature reflecting the four possible levels of demand for carnations.

TABLE 18.2
Payoff Table of Order Size

Decision (order size, Q)	States of Nature (demand, D)			
	9 .15	10 .40	11 .25	12 .20
9				
10				
11				
12				

Marginal notes: Decision analysis · Order quantities as decisions and demands as states of nature · A decision analysis example · Probability distribution of demand · Constructing the payoff table

Computing the payoff table values

Each payoff value in Table 18.2 equals the profit that will result from that specific order size and demand. For example, if the flower shop orders 9 dozen carnations and sells 9 dozen, then the profit is computed as follows.

$$\text{Profit} = (\text{Demand})(\text{Price}) - (\text{Order size})(\text{Cost})$$
$$- (\text{Average inventory})(\text{Carrying cost})$$
$$= (9)(\$3) - (9)(\$1.50) - (9/2)(\$.50)$$
$$= \$11.25$$

If we let D = demand, P = price per dozen, Q = order size, C = cost per dozen, $Q/2$ = average inventory, and C_c = carrying cost, then the above profit equation can be represented by the following formula.

$$\text{Profit} = DP - QC - \frac{Q}{2}C_c$$

A shortage cost

However, notice in this formula and in the above computation for profit that *shortage cost* was not included. Since demand equaled the order size, there was no shortage. Any time order size exceeds or equals demand, there is no shortage cost and the above formula for profit is applicable. If, on the other hand, *demand exceeds supply*, then the shortage cost must be included in the profit formula.

$$\text{Profit} = QP - QC - \frac{Q}{2}C_c - \boxed{C_s(D - Q)}$$
$$\nwarrow \text{shortage cost}$$

In this formula, shortage cost is computed by multiplying the amount by which demand exceeds the order size by the shortage cost. Also, notice that the first term in the profit equation has been changed from DP to QP, since all that can be sold is what is ordered. If the order size is 9 dozen carnations but demand is for 10 dozen, the profit is computed as follows (recall that C_s = \$1/dozen).

$$\text{Profit} = QP - QC - \frac{Q}{2}C_c - C_s(D - Q)$$

$$= (9)(\$3.00) - (9)(\$1.50) - \frac{9}{2}(\$.50) - (\$1.00)(10 - 9)$$

$$= \$10.25$$

Summary of profit formulas

The formulas for both conditions of order size and demand are summarized below.

Order Size ≥ Demand

$$\text{Profit} = DP - QC - \frac{Q}{2}C_c$$

Demand > Order Size

$$\text{Profit} = QP - QC - \frac{Q}{2}C_c - C_s(D - Q)$$

Using these formulas, we are able to compute profit for all the combinations of order quantity and profit shown in Table 18.2. These computed values are shown in Table 18.3.

The completed payoff table

TABLE 18.3

Payoff Table for Flower Shop Example

Decision (order size, Q)	Demand (D)			
	9 .15	10 .40	11 .25	12 .20
9	$11.25	$10.25	$ 9.25	$ 8.25
10	9.50	12.50	11.50	10.50
11	7.75	10.75	13.75	12.75
12	6.00	9.00	12.00	15.00

The values in Table 18.3 represent *certain profit* for each of the possible combinations of order size and demand. However, each demand has a probability of occurrence reflecting the uncertainty of demand. Therefore, instead of a certain profit for each order size, we will compute the *expected profit* based on the probability of each outcome (demand). The expected profit (EP) for each order size is computed by multiplying each profit for a specific order size by its corresponding probabilities and then summing these values.

Payoff table values represent certain profit

Computing the expected profit for each order size

$$EP(9) = \$(11.25)(.15) + (10.25)(.40) + (9.25)(.25) + (8.25)(.20)$$
$$= \$9.75$$
$$EP(10) = \$(9.50)(.15) + (12.50)(.40) + (11.50)(.25) + (10.50)(.20)$$
$$= \$11.40$$
$$EP(11) = \$(7.75)(.15) + (10.75)(.40) + (13.75)(.25) + (12.75)(.20)$$
$$= \$11.45$$
$$EP(12) = \$(6.00)(.15) + (9.00)(.40) + (12.00)(.25) + (15.00)(.20)$$
$$= \$10.50$$

The greatest expected profit ($11.45) results from an order size of 11 dozen carnations; thus, the optimal value of Q is 11. This means that if 11 dozen carnations are ordered every week for many weeks, the flower shop will make an average profit of $11.45 per week. The expected value does not mean that $11.45 will result every week. Since demand is uncertain, there will be shortages during some weeks and surpluses during others, as well as weeks when demand is exactly 11 dozen. However, notice that on the average shortages will occur only 20% of the time (since the only demand greater than 11 dozen is 12 dozen, which occurs 20% of the time).

Determining the optimal order size

Portion of time shortages occur

An additional item that could have been included in this payoff table example is a *salvage value* for items not sold. For example, if 11 dozen carnations are ordered but only 10 dozen are sold, then it is possible that the cost of the extra dozen not sold could be offset by

Including a salvage value

selling the carnations at a greatly reduced price at the end of the week to individual customers, hospitals, churches, or schools. This reduced price is the salvage value.

We also could have analyzed the effect of alternative selling prices on this model by developing additional payoff tables. For example, a selling price of $4 per dozen carnations could be considered in another payoff table, with the demand probabilities altered to reflect the effect of the new price on demand. The expected profit per week derived from a selling price of $4 could then be compared to the expected profit of $11.45 determined for the original price of $3, to see which price resulted in the greatest expected profit.

SIMULATION OF INVENTORY

We will now explore simulation as our final approach to inventory analysis under conditions of uncertain demand. Simulation was first presented in Chapter 15, where it was noted that simulation is a method of analysis often employed when uncertainty exists. In fact, the first simulation example in Chapter 15 was for the demand for milk at a grocery store, which was probabilistic.

To demonstrate how simulation is used for inventory analysis, we will use the Petals and Plants Flower Shop example from the previous section. The inventory cost, the selling price, and the cost of carnations remain the same. The probability distribution for demand is also the same, except now we will develop corresponding ranges for random numbers, as shown in Table 18.4.

TABLE 18.4

Random Number Ranges for Probability
Distribution of Demand

Demand (dozens/week)	Probability	Cumulative Probability	Random Numbers
9	.15	.15	1–15
10	.40	.55	16–55
11	.25	.80	56–80
12	.20	1.00	81–99, 00

Instead of testing all four order size values (9, 10, 11, and 12), we must select one of them and simulate demand based on that order size. As an example, we will simulate demand for an order size (Q) of 10, as shown in Table 18.5. The random numbers were selected from the first column of the random number table (Table 15.3) in Chapter 15.

TABLE 18.5

Simulation of Demand for $Q = 10$

Random Number	Demand	Sales DP or QP		Cost QC	Carrying Cost $(Q/2)C_c$	Shortage Cost $C_s(D - Q)$	Profit
39	10	$30		$15	$2.50	$0	$ 12.50
73	11		30	15	2.50	1	11.50
72	11		30	15	2.50	1	11.50
75	11		30	15	2.50	1	11.50
37	10	30		15	2.50	0	12.50
2	9	27		15	2.50	0	9.50
87	12		30	15	2.50	2	10.50
98	12		30	15	2.50	2	10.50
10	9	27		15	2.50	0	9.50
47	10	30		15	2.50	0	12.50
							$112.00

The profit for each demand value in Table 18.5 was computed using the same profit formulas developed in the previous section. For ten simulations, the total profit is $112; thus, the average profit is

Computing average profit for $Q = 10$

$$\text{Average profit} = \frac{\$112}{10}$$
$$= \$11.20$$

The expected profit computed from the payoff table in the previous section was $11.40, so our simulation result using only ten simulations is very close to the steady-state value average. If we increased the number of simulations, the simulation result should approach the expected (steady-state) value of $11.40.

In order to replicate the payoff table example, we would have to repeat the simulation for order sizes of 9, 11, and 12 dozen flowers. This would result in an average profit for each order size, with the optimal order size corresponding to the greatest average profit.

Replicating the payoff table example

This example is relatively simple and, as such, is probably more suited to analytical solution. However, notice that we considered only four demand values and four order sizes. If we had to consider perhaps 50 order sizes and 100 demands, then computerized simulation would be a more inviting alternative. Going a step further, if demand were defined by a continuous probability distribution (such as yards of carpet), then simulation would be especially appropriate.

Simulation is very useful as the problem increases in complexity

Computerized simulation becomes a necessity if more than one of the inventory model components is subject to uncertainty. For example, if *lead time* and *demand* are uncertain, then during each order cycle both order size and lead time vary. This is a situation very difficult to model and solve mathematically, especially if lead time and demand can equal a large range of values. In order to simulate this type of situation, one would typically simulate the inventory cost for a specific order size (as in Table 18.5), except that lead time as well as demand would vary.

Computer Simulation of the Flower Shop Example

To demonstrate the use of computer simulation, we will employ a slightly modified version of our Petals and Plants Flower Shop example. Instead of having the probability distribution for carnations encompass only four demand values (i.e., 9, 10, 11, or 12 dozen), we will employ a probability distribution that has twelve demand values, as shown in Table 18.6.

An expanded probability distribution of demand

TABLE 18.6
Probability Distribution of Demand fo Carnations

Demand (dozens/week)	Probability
1	.02
2	.02
3	.04
4	.10
5	.11
6	.14
7	.22
8	.18
9	.09
10	.05
11	.02
12	.01
	1.00

Considering a larger number of Q values

Since our example now encompasses a larger number of demand values, we must also evaluate a greater number of different order sizes, Q. The computer program that simulates the probability distribution of demand in Table 18.6 and evaluates Q values from 1 to 20 is shown on page 653. The program is written in the IBM version of the BASIC computer language and was run on the IBM personal computer. (See Chap. 15 for a more detailed explanation of computer simulation and simulation programs.)

The simulation program output indicates the average profit obtained for each of the 20 different values of Q.

Notice in this output that the highest profit, $5.06, is achieved with an order of 8 dozen carnations (i.e., Q = 8). (Do not be confused by the fact that the profit of $5.06 is significantly lower than the profit of $11.20 we derived from our manual simulation in the previous section. Recall that for this computerized simulation we

```
LIST
10 RANDOMIZE (15)
20 Q = 0
30 Q = Q + 1
40 SUMPROFIT = 0
50 SIMRUN = 0
60 SIMRUN = SIMRUN + 1
70 D = 0
80 PROFIT = 0
90 R = RND
100 IF R >= 0 AND R <= .02 THEN D = 1 ELSE 110
110 IF R > .02 AND R <= .04 THEN D = 2 ELSE 120
120 IF R > .04 AND R <= .08 THEN D = 3 ELSE 130
130 IF R > .08 AND R <= .18 THEN D = 4 ELSE 140
140 IF R > .18 AND R <= .29 THEN D = 5 ELSE 150
150 IF R > .29 AND R <= .43 THEN D = 6 ELSE 160
160 IF R > .43 AND R <= .65 THEN D = 7 ELSE 170
170 IF R > .65 AND R <= .83 THEN D = 8 ELSE 180
180 IF R > .83 AND R <= .92 THEN D = 9 ELSE 190
190 IF R > .92 AND R <= .97 THEN D = 10 ELSE 200
200 IF R > .97 AND R <= .99 THEN D = 11 ELSE 210
210 IF R > .99 AND R <= 1! THEN D = 12 ELSE 220
220 IF D <= Q THEN PROFIT = D*3 - Q*1.5 - (Q/2)*.5 ELSE PROFIT =
Q*3 - Q*1.5 - (Q/2)*.5 - 1*(D - Q)
230 SUMPROFIT = SUMPROFIT + PROFIT
240 IF SIMRUN < 100 THEN 60 ELSE 250
250 AVGPROFIT = SUMPROFIT/SIMRUN
260 PRINT " AVERAGE PROFIT FOR Q = " Q " IS $ " AVGPROFIT
270 IF Q < 20 THEN 30 ELSE 280
280 END
Ok

RUN
 AVERAGE PROFIT FOR Q =  1   IS $ -4.13
 AVERAGE PROFIT FOR Q =  2   IS $ -2.66
 AVERAGE PROFIT FOR Q =  3   IS $  .24
 AVERAGE PROFIT FOR Q =  4   IS $  1.83
 AVERAGE PROFIT FOR Q =  5   IS $  3.54
 AVERAGE PROFIT FOR Q =  6   IS $  4.66
 AVERAGE PROFIT FOR Q =  7   IS $  4.78
 AVERAGE PROFIT FOR Q =  8   IS $  5.06
 AVERAGE PROFIT FOR Q =  9   IS $  2.97
 AVERAGE PROFIT FOR Q = 10   IS $  1.72
 AVERAGE PROFIT FOR Q = 11   IS $  1.04
 AVERAGE PROFIT FOR Q = 12   IS $ -1.29
 AVERAGE PROFIT FOR Q = 13   IS $ -3.1
 AVERAGE PROFIT FOR Q = 14   IS $ -3.29
 AVERAGE PROFIT FOR Q = 15   IS $ -7.23
 AVERAGE PROFIT FOR Q = 16   IS $ -9.01
 AVERAGE PROFIT FOR Q = 17   IS $ -10.67
 AVERAGE PROFIT FOR Q = 18   IS $ -11.76
 AVERAGE PROFIT FOR Q = 19   IS $ -14.38
 AVERAGE PROFIT FOR Q = 20   IS $ -15.11
Ok
```

used a modified probability distribution that results in lower weekly demand, and thus lower sales, than in our manual simulation.) Based on this simulation, the recommended decision would be to order 8 dozen carnations per week.

Recommended decision

APPLICATIONS OF INVENTORY ANALYSIS

Parts and Raw Material Inventory in the Aircraft Industry

The Aircraft Division of Hindustan Aeronautics, Ltd., of India designs, develops, manufactures, and overhauls aircraft for the Indian Air Force. The company held high inventories as a result of poor planning, frequent design and production plan revisions, and acute shortages of raw materials, components, and spare parts, which are common in developing countries. Many items had to be imported from foreign vendors. Consequently, the proportion of capital tied up in inventory was very high (in 1975 the company's ending inventory was 162% of working capital excluding in-process inventories).

In order to control inventory, the company first developed an inventory classification scheme to ascertain the importance of different proprietary items, raw materials, and spare parts. This classification scheme was subsequently used to determine safety stocks (based on the importance of an inventory item) that achieved a specific service level. EOQ analysis was performed to determine order sizes. The inventory system was incorporated into a "materials information system" that provided accurate and timely inventory information. One year after implementation, inventory holdings had been reduced by 10%, resulting in an estimated annual savings of $400,000. In addition stockouts were reduced enough to increase the service level by 25%.[1]

Raw Material Inventory Control in the Chemical Industry

The Modesto plant of the FMC Corporation Industrial Chemical Group produces barium and strontium carbonate. Both products are produced on the same equipment; however, inventory control is difficult because of significant market fluctuations and the high costs of production changeover between products. An examination of raw materials indicated that three materials—coke, barite, and celestite—accounted for approximately 80% of the total dollar value of raw materials; hence, these three materials were the focus of inventory analysis. EOQ analysis with safety stocks was used to develop an inventory model for raw materials. The dollar value of celestite inventory was reduced by $36 million during 1977.[2]

[1]B. Lingaraj and R. Balasubramanian, "An Inventory Management and Materials Information System for Aircraft Production," *Interfaces* 13, no. 5 (October 1983): 65–70.

[2]M. Liberatore, "Using MRP and EOQ/Safety Stock for Raw Materials Inventory Control: Discussion and Case Study," *Interfaces* 9, no. 2, part 1 (February 1979): 1–7.

Using a 95% Service Rule for Inventory Control at a Phone Center

The Manitoba (Canada) Telephone System (MTS) operates phone centers that lease telephone equipment in large population centers. The product line includes 13 models of telephones in a variety of colors — a total of 62 different products. Each phone center is expected to meet at least 95% of customer demand. At the time of this study, the phone centers were carrying from 15 to 75 days of stock, which was thought to be excessive, given that stocks were replenished daily from the warehouse. Thus, MTS wanted to minimize inventory while maintaining the service level. MTS employed a simple approach that assumed no trends in demand (i.e., no forecast) and required each center to keep in stock 95% of the sets issued the previous year. A simple inventory rule that satisfied 95% of demand was established; i.e., the stock level for each phone set was set at the number corresponding to the 95 cumulative percentage point, based on the past year's data. In one year a single phone center recorded a 45% reduction in stock on hand with a capital investment savings of almost $5,000 and a reduction in holding costs of almost $1,000.[3]

Payoff Tables for Inventory Control

To deal with the problem of an increasing volume of discards (i.e., items remaining in inventory that would not be offered to dealers), Hallmark Cards Incorporated initiated a program that included the use of decision analysis and payoff matrices for inventory management. A case approach using a payoff matrix with revenues, demand, shortage costs, and salvage values was employed as part of an overall training program for inventory management. Managers trained using the payoff table approach subsequently applied both the concepts and direct knowledge to individual situations, with substantial savings and revenue generation. In one instance, a product manager made a last minute change in a production run for a promotional package (including napkins, puzzles, cards, and posters) based on a payoff table analysis; the change increased the gross margin by $200,000.[4]

[3]R. Cohen and F. Dunford, "Forecasting for Inventory Control: An Example of When 'Simple' Means 'Better'," *Interfaces* 16, no. 6 (November–December 1986): 95–99.

[4]F. Barron, "Payoff Matrices Pay Off at Hallmark," *Interfaces* 15, no. 4 (July–August 1985): 20–25.

Summary

This chapter presented four methods to compensate for conditions of uncertain demand in inventory analysis: safety stocks, safety stocks corresponding to service levels, payoff tables, and simulation. However, for very complex inventory models involving several components that are subject to uncertainty, computerized simulation becomes the only viable approach for analysis.

This concludes our two-chapter presentation of inventory analysis. The techniques for inventory analysis presented in these two chapters are not widely used to analyze other types of problems. Conversely, however, many of the techniques presented in this text are used for inventory analysis (in addition to the methods presented in these chapters). The wide use of management science techniques for inventory analysis attests to the importance of inventory to all types of organizations.

Conclusion of
presentation of
inventory analysis

References

Buchan, J., and Koenigsberg, E. *Scientific Inventory Management.* Englewood Cliffs, N.J.: Prentice-Hall, 1963.

Buffa, E. S., and Miller, Jeffrey G. *Production-Inventory Systems: Planning and Control.* 3d ed. Homewood, Ill.: Irwin, 1979.

Churchman, C. W.; Ackoff, R. L.; and Arnoff, E. L. *Introduction to Operations Research.* New York: John Wiley and Sons, 1957.

Hadley, G., and Whitin, T. M. *Analysis of Inventory Systems.* Englewood Cliffs, N.J.: Prentice-Hall, 1963.

Johnson, L. A., and Montgomery, D. C. *Operations Research in Production Planning, Scheduling, and Inventory Control.* New York: John Wiley and Sons, 1974.

Liberatore, M. "Using MRP and EOQ/Safety Stock for Raw Materials Inventory Control: Discussion and Case Study." *Interfaces* 9, no. 2. part 1 (February 1979): 1–7.

Lingaraj, B., and Balasubramanian, R. "An Inventory Management and Materials Information System for Aircraft Production." *Interfaces* 13, no. 5 (October 1983): 65–70.

Magee, J. F., and Boodman, D. M. *Production Planning and Inventory Control.* 2d ed. New York: McGraw-Hill, 1967.

Shamblin, J. E., and Stevens, G. T., Jr. *Operations Research: A Fundamental Approach.* New York: McGraw-Hill, 1974.

Starr, M. K., and Miller, D. W. *Inventory Control: Theory and Practice.* Englewood Cliffs, N.J.: Prentice-Hall, 1962.

EXAMPLE PROBLEM SOLUTION

The following example illustrates the solution procedure for determining the optimal order quantity with a payoff table.

Problem Statement

The Crumb and Custard Bakery bakes coconut cakes every morning. If the cakes are not sold during the day, they are discarded or given to employees. The bakery manager has developed the following probability distribution for daily demand for coconut cakes from past sales records.

Demand (cakes/day)	Probability
0	.07
1	.18
2	.35
3	.28
4	.12

Each coconut cake costs the bakery $2.25 to bake and sells for $7. The manager has estimated that although the cakes are kept for only one day, a carrying cost of $.75 per cake is incurred because of the special storage requirements for coconut. The manager has also determined that if a customer requests a coconut cake and none is available, the bakery incurs a shortage cost of $3.00 (in lost future sales). Determine the number of coconut cakes that should be baked each day using the payoff table approach.

Step 1: Develop the Payoff Value Formulas

Order Size $\geq$ Demand:

$$\text{Profit} = DP - QC - \frac{Q}{2}C_c$$

$$= 7D - 2.25Q - \frac{Q}{2}(.75)$$

Demand > Order Size:

$$\text{Profit} = QP - QC - \frac{Q}{2}C_c - C_s(D - Q)$$

$$= 7Q - 2.25Q - \frac{Q}{2}(.75) - 3(D - Q)$$

Step 2: Develop the Payoff Table

Decision (order size, Q)	Demand (D)				
	0 .07	1 .18	2 .35	3 .28	4 .12
0	$0.00	−$3.00	−$6.00	−$9.00	−$12.00
1	−2.63	4.37	1.37	−1.63	−4.63
2	−5.25	1.75	8.75	5.75	2.75
3	−7.88	−.88	6.12	13.12	10.12
4	−10.50	−3.50	4.50	11.50	18.50

Step 3: Compute the Expected Profit for Each Alternative

$EP(0) = -\$6.60$

$EP(1) = -\$.07$

$EP(2) = \$4.95$

$EP(3) = \$6.32$

$EP(4) = \$5.65$

The optimal decision is to bake three cakes per day.

Problems

1. An inventory system has an average yearly demand of 6,000 units and an ordering cost of $60 per order. The annual carrying cost is $2 per unit, and the shortage cost per unit is $1. The demand during lead time is defined by the following probability distribution.

Demand During Lead Time	Probability
100	.10
200	.20
300	.40
400	.20
500	.10
	1.00

Determine the safety stock, reorder point, and minimum total safety stock cost.

2. An inventory system has an average annual demand of 1,200 units and an ordering cost of $200 per order. The annual carrying cost is $5 per unit, and the shortage cost per unit is $10. The demand during lead time is defined by the following probability distribution.

Demand During Lead Time	Probability
50	.20
60	.30
70	.30
80	.10
90	.10
	1.00

Determine the safety stock, reorder point, and minimum total safety stock cost.

3. The Big Buy Supermarket stocks Munchies cereal. The average demand for Munchies is 4,000 boxes per year. It costs the store $90 per order of Munchies and $.30 per box per year to keep the cereal in inventory; the shortage cost is $1 per box. The demand during lead time for boxes of cereal is defined by the following probability distribution.

Demand During Lead Time	Probability
75	.05
100	.20
125	.40
150	.25
175	.10
	1.00

Determine the safety stock, reorder point, and minimum total safety stock cost.

4. The average annual demand for color television sets at Videoworld Discount Televisions is 2,200. The cost per order from the manufacturer is $650, the carrying cost is $45, and the shortage cost is $60 per set. The demand during lead time for television sets is defined by the following probability distribution.

Demand During Lead Time	Probability
20	.05
30	.10
40	.30
50	.40
60	.15
	1.00

Determine the safety stock, reorder point, and minimum total safety stock cost.

5. A car dealer who sells compact cars has an average annual demand for 1,200 cars. It costs the dealer $1,800 per order to order cars from the manufacturer in Dearborn and $700 per year to carry a car in inventory on the lot. The shortage cost is $1,200 per car. The demand during lead time for cars is defined by the following probability distribution.

Demand During Lead Time	Probability
10	.05
15	.15
20	.20
25	.30
30	.25
35	.05
	1.00

Determine the safety stock, reorder point, and minimum total safety stock cost.

6. A local distributor of Rainwater beer in Memphis has an average annual demand for 40,000 barrels of Rainwater. It costs the distributor $1,500 for an order of beer from the brewery. The annual cost of carrying a barrel of beer in inventory is $1.50. The shortage cost is $3 per barrel. The demand during lead time for barrels of beer is defined by the following distribution.

Demand During Lead Time	Probability
500	.05
600	.05
700	.10
800	.25
900	.30
1,000	.15
1,100	.10
	1.00

Determine the safety stock, reorder point, and minimum total safety stock cost.

7. Graphically illustrate the order size, safety stock, and reorder point for the inventory system in problem 1.

8. The demand during lead time for carpet at the Armor Carpet Store is normally distributed with a mean of 500 yards and a standard deviation of 80 yards. Determine a safety stock and a reorder point that will result in an average service level of 80% during lead time.

9. The production process of the Western Jeans Company uses an average of 3,000 yards of denim (with a standard deviation of 600 yards) to make

jeans during the time it takes to receive an order of denim from a textile mill. If the company wants to operate during 95% of the lead-time period, what safety stock and reorder point should it have?

10. Graphically illustrate the average demand during lead time, service level, safety stock, and reorder point for the inventory system in problem 8.

11. The Atlantic Paper Company produces paper from wood pulp ordered from a lumber products company. The paper company uses an average of 8,000 pounds of wood pulp (with a standard deviation of 1,500 pounds) during the time required to receive an order. What safety stock and reorder point should Atlantic Paper Company maintain so that the production process will be idle only 10% of the lead time?

12. The Uptown Bar and Grill serves Rainwater draft beer to its customers. The bar sells an average of 60 gallons of beer (with a standard deviation of 10 gallons) during the lead time required to receive an order of beer from the local distributor. If the bar runs out of beer, the customers are likely to stage a riot; therefore, the owner wants to maintain a 98% service level during lead time. What safety stock and reorder point should be used to meet this service level?

13. The Rainbow Paint Store in East Ridge sells an average of 110 gallons of paint (with a standard deviation of 35 gallons) during the lead time required to receive an order of paint from the manufacturer. However, since this is the only paint store in East Ridge, the owner is only interested in maintaining a 50% service level. What reorder point should be used to maintain this service level during lead time?

14. Suppose in problem 12 that the owner of the Uptown Bar and Grill has decided to use a reorder point of 75 gallons of beer. What level of service would this reorder point maintain?

15. The Uptown Bar and Grill orders either 5, 6, 7, or 8 barrels of beer each time it places an order with the distributor. Each barrel of beer costs $50 and sells for $100. The probability of demand for barrels of beer is shown below.

Demand	Probability
5	.10
6	.30
7	.40
8	.20
	1.00

Using the payoff table approach, determine the number of barrels of beer that should be ordered.

16. The Petals and Plants Flower Shop orders roses from a greenhouse on a weekly basis. The manager of the flower shop has developed the following probability distribution for demand for dozens of roses per week.

Demand (dozens/week)	Probability
6	.10
7	.20
8	.30
9	.30
10	.10
	1.00

The roses cost the flower shop $3 per dozen and sell for $5 per dozen. The carrying cost is $.60 per dozen per week, and the shortage cost is $2 per dozen per week. Determine the number of dozens of roses that should be stocked per week using the payoff table approach. Given this order size, how often will shortages occur?

17. The Loebuck Grocery orders milk from a dairy on a weekly basis. The manager of the store has developed the following probability distribution for demand per week (in cases).

Demand (cases)	Probability
15	.20
16	.25
17	.40
18	.15
	1.00

The milk costs the grocery $10 per case and sells for $16 per case. The carrying cost is $.50 per case per week, and the shortage cost is $1 per case per week. Determine the number of cases of milk that should be ordered from the dairy each week using the payoff table approach.

18. The Steak and Chop Butcher Shop orders steak from a local meat packing house. The meat is purchased on Monday at a price of $2 per pound, and it is sold for $3.50 per pound at the shop. The following probability distribution for the demand per week (in pounds) of steak has been developed.

Demand (lb)	Probability
20	.10
21	.20
22	.30
23	.30
24	.10
	1.00

The carrying cost is $.80 per pound per week, and the shortage cost is $1.25 per pound per week. Determine the number of pounds of steak that should be ordered each week using the payoff table approach.

19. The Roadway Paving Company purchases asphalt from Bay Petroleum Products Company in Mobile. The number of tons of asphalt used by Roadway to pave roads and driveways annually is given by the following probability distribution.

Demand (tons)	Probability
4	.20
5	.30
6	.40
7	.10
	1.00

Asphalt costs the paving company $9,500 per ton, and the company sells it for $15,000 per ton (the price is computed on the basis of yards of road laid). The annual carrying cost is $1,600 per ton, and the shortage cost is $4,000 per ton. Determine the number of tons that should be ordered each year using the payoff table approach.

20. The probability distribution of the cases of milk demanded each week at the Loebuck Grocery is as follows.

Demand Per Week (cases)	Probability
14	.20
15	.40
16	.20
17	.10
18	.10
	1.00

Using the random number table in Chapter 15 (Table 15.3), simulate demand for 15 weeks and compute the average demand.

21. Simulate the demand during lead time for the probability distribution in problem 4 for 20 reorder periods, and compute the average demand during lead time.

22. Simulate the shortages per reorder period that will occur in problem 3 using the reorder point computed in the problem. Simulate for 20 reorder periods and compute the probability that a shortage will occur. How does this result compare with the percentage of time a shortage would occur as determined in problem 3?

23. Using simulation, determine the average weekly profit from beer in problem 15 assuming an order size of 7 barrels of beer per week. Simu-

late for 20 weeks using the random number table in Chapter 15 (Table 15.3), and compute the average profit. How does this result compare with the results in problem 15?

24. Simulate the ordering system in problem 16 for 10 weeks using a weekly order size of 7 dozen roses, and compute the average weekly profit. (Use Table 15.3.) Compare the results with those determined in problem 16, and indicate how the optimal order size would be determined.

25. A store has the following probability distribution of demand per week.

Demand (units)	Probability
0	.10
1	.15
2	.30
3	.25
4	.20
	1.00

The lead time to receive an order (in weeks) is defined by the following distribution.

Lead Time (weeks)	Probability
1	.35
2	.45
3	.20
	1.00

Assume an initial starting inventory level of 4 units, and assume that units are not back ordered. The carrying cost is $2 per unit per week, the shortage cost is $10 per unit per week, and the cost per order is $20. Simulate the weekly inventory cost for 20 weeks using an order size of 5 units and a reorder point of 3 units. Compute the average weekly inventory cost. How would the optimal order size be determined using simulation?

Network Flow Models

A *network* is an arrangement of paths connected at various points, through which one or more items move from one point to another. Everyone is familiar with such networks as highway systems, telephone networks, railroad systems, and television networks. For example, a railroad network consists of a number of fixed rail routes (paths) connected by terminals at various junctions of the rail routes. In Chapter 7, the transportation problem illustrated in Figure 7.1 involves a network of transportation routes.

An arrangement of paths connected at various points

In recent years network models have become a very popular management science technique for analysis for a couple of very important reasons. First, a network is drawn as a diagram, which literally provides a *picture* of the system under analysis. This enables a manager to visually interpret the system and thus enhances the manager's understanding. Second, a large number of real-life systems can be modeled as networks, which are relatively easy to conceive and construct.

Reasons for the popularity of network models

In this and the next chapter we will look at several different types of network models. In this chapter we will present a class of network models directed at the *flow of items* through a system. As such, these models are referred to as *network flow models*. We will discuss the use of network flow models to analyze three types of problems: the shortest route problem, the minimal spanning tree problem, and the maximal flow problem. In Chapter 20 we will present the network techniques of PERT and CPM, which are used extensively for project analysis.

NETWORK COMPONENTS

Nodes
Branches

Networks are illustrated as diagrams consisting of two main components: nodes and branches. *Nodes* represent junction points—for example, an intersection of several streets. *Branches* connect the nodes and reflect the flow from one point in the network to another. Nodes are denoted in the network diagram by *circles*, and branches are represented by *lines* connecting the nodes. Nodes typically represent localities, such as cities, intersections, or air or railroad terminals; branches are the paths connecting the nodes, such as roads connecting cities and intersections, and railroad tracks or air routes connecting terminals. For example, the different railroad routes between Atlanta, Georgia, and St. Louis, Missouri, and the intermediate terminals are shown in Figure 19.1.

A network example

FIGURE 19.1

Network of
Railroad Routes

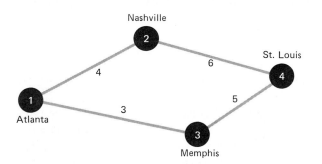

The network shown in Figure 19.1 has four nodes and four branches. The node representing Atlanta is referred to as the *origin*, and any of the three remaining nodes could be the *destination*, depending on what we are trying to determine from the network. Notice that a number has been assigned to each node. Numbers provide a more convenient means of identifying the nodes and branches than do names. For example, we can now refer to the origin (Atlanta) as node 1 and the branch from Atlanta to Nashville as branch 1–2.

Values assigned to
branches

Typically, a value that represents a distance, length of time, or cost is assigned to each branch. Thus, the purpose of the network is to determine the shortest distance, shortest length of time, or lowest cost between points in the network. In Figure 19.1, the values 4, 6, 3, and 5 corresponding to the four branches represent the lengths of time in hours between the attached nodes. Thus, a traveler can see that the route to St. Louis through Nashville requires 10 hours and the route to St. Louis through Memphis requires 8 hours.

THE SHORTEST ROUTE PROBLEM

The *shortest route problem* is to determine the shortest distance between an originating point and several destination points. For example, the Stagecoach Shipping Company transports oranges by six trucks from Los Angeles to six cities in the West and Midwest. The different routes between Los Angeles and the destination cities and the length of time in hours required by a truck to travel each route are shown in Figure 19.2.

The shortest distance between an originating point and several destination points

FIGURE 19.2

Shipping Routes from Los Angeles

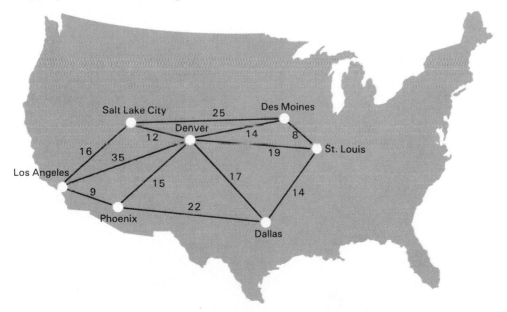

The shipping company manager wants to determine the best routes (in terms of the minimum travel time) for the trucks to take to reach their destinations. This problem can be solved using the shortest route solution technique. In applying this technique, it is conve-

Minimizing travel time

nient to represent the system of truck routes as a network, as shown in Figure 19.3.

FIGURE 19.3

Network of Shipping Routes

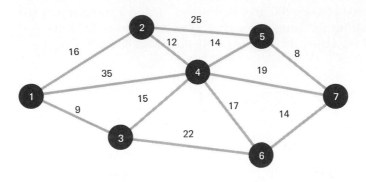

To repeat our objective as it relates to Figure 19.3, we want to determine the shortest routes from the origin (node 1) to the six destinations (nodes 2 through 7).

The Shortest Route Solution Approach

Determining the initial shortest route from node 1 to 3

We begin the shortest route solution technique by starting at node 1 (the origin) and determining the shortest time required to get to a directly connected (i.e., adjacent) node. The three nodes directly connected to node 1 are 2, 3, and 4, as shown in Figure 19.4. Of these three nodes, the shortest time is 9 hours to node 3. Thus, we have determined our first *shortest* route from node 1 to 3 (or from Los Angeles to Phoenix). We will now refer to nodes 1 and 3 as the *permanent set,* to indicate that we have found the shortest route to these nodes. (Since node 1 has no route to it, it is automatically in the permanent set.)

The permanent set nodes (1 and 3)

FIGURE 19.4

Network with Node 1 in the Permanent Set

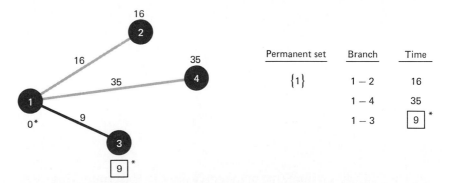

Permanent set	Branch	Time
{1}	1 − 2	16
	1 − 4	35
	1 − 3	9 *

Notice in Figure 19.4 that the shortest route to node 3 is drawn with a heavy line, and the shortest time to node 3 (9 hours) is enclosed by a box. The table accompanying Figure 19.4 describes the process of selecting the shortest route. The permanent set is shown to contain only node 1. The three branches from node 1 are 1–2, 1–4, and 1–3, and this last branch has the minimum time of 9 hours.

Next we will repeat the steps used to determine the shortest route to node 3 above. First, we must *determine all the nodes directly connected to the nodes in the permanent set* (nodes 1 and 3). Nodes 2, 4, and 6 are all directly connected to nodes 1 and 3, as shown in Figure 19.5.

Determine all nodes directly connected to the permanent set nodes

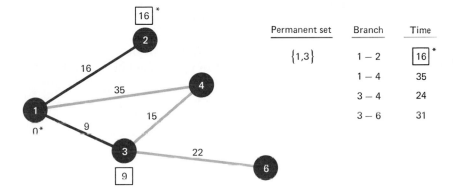

Permanent set	Branch	Time
$\{1,3\}$	1 – 2	16 *
	1 – 4	35
	3 – 4	24
	3 – 6	31

FIGURE 19.5

Network with Nodes 1 and 3 in the Permanent Set

The next step is to determine the shortest route to the three nodes (2, 4, and 6) directly connected to the permanent set nodes. There are two branches starting from node 1 (1–2 and 1–4) and two branches from node 3 (3–4 and 3–6). The branch with the shortest time is to node 2, with a time of 16 hours. Thus, node 2 becomes part of the permanent set. Notice in our computations accompanying Figure 19.5 that the time to node 6 (branch 3–6) is 31 hours, which was determined by adding the branch 3–6 time of 22 hours to the shortest route time of 9 hours at node 3.

Node 2 joins the permanent set

As we move to the next step, the permanent set consists of nodes 1, 2, and 3. This indicates that we have found the shortest route to nodes 1, 2, and 3. We must now determine which nodes are directly connected to the permanent set nodes. Node 5 is the only *adjacent* node not presently connected to the permanent set, so it is connected directly to node 2. In addition, node 4 is now connected directly to node 2 (since node 2 has joined the permanent set). These additions are shown in Figure 19.6.

The redefined permanent set

Five branches lead from the permanent set nodes (1, 2, and 3) to their directly connected nodes, as shown in the table accompanying Figure 19.6. The branch representing the route with the shortest time is 3–4, with a time of 24 hours. Thus, we have determined the shortest route to node 4, and it joins the permanent set. Notice that the shortest time to node 4 (24 hours) is the route from node 1

Node 4 joins the permanent set

FIGURE 19.6

Network with Nodes 1, 2, and 3 in the Permanent Set

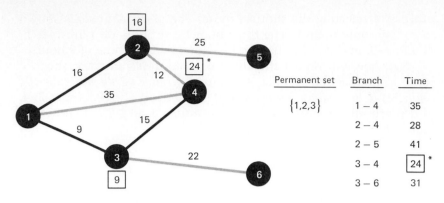

Permanent set	Branch	Time
$\{1,2,3\}$	1 – 4	35
	2 – 4	28
	2 – 5	41
	3 – 4	24 *
	3 – 6	31

through node 3. The other routes to node 4 from node 1 through node 2 are longer; therefore, we will not consider them any further as possible routes to node 4.

To summarize, the shortest routes to nodes 1, 2, 3, and 4 have all been determined, and these nodes now form the permanent set.

Next we repeat the process of determining the nodes directly connected to the permanent set nodes. These directly connected nodes are 5, 6, and 7, as shown in Figure 19.7. Notice in Figure 19.7 that we have eliminated the branches from nodes 1 and 2 to node 4, since we determined that the route with the shortest time to node 4 does not include these branches.

FIGURE 19.7

Network with Nodes 1, 2, 3, and 4 in the Permanent Set

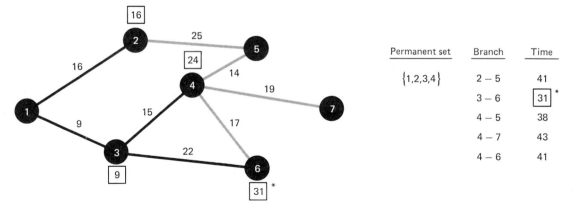

Permanent set	Branch	Time
$\{1,2,3,4\}$	2 – 5	41
	3 – 6	31 *
	4 – 5	38
	4 – 7	43
	4 – 6	41

Node 6 joins the permanent set

From the table accompanying Figure 19.7 we can see that of the branches leading to nodes 5, 6, and 7, branch 3–6 has the shortest *cumulative* time of 31 hours. Thus, node 6 is added to our permanent set. This means that we have now found the shortest routes to nodes 1, 2, 3, 4, and 6.

Repeating the process, we observe that the nodes directly connected (adjacent) to our permanent set are nodes 5 and 7, as shown

FIGURE 19.8

Network with Nodes 1, 2, 3, 4, and 6 in the Permanent Set

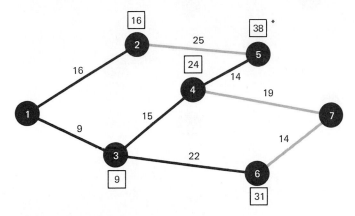

Permanent set	Branch	Time
{1,2,3,4,6}	2 – 5	41
	4 – 5	38 *
	4 – 7	43
	6 – 7	45

in Figure 19.8. (Notice that branch 4–6 has been eliminated, since the best route to node 6 goes through node 3 instead of node 4.)

Of the branches leading from the permanent set nodes to nodes 5 and 7, branch 4–5 has the shortest cumulative time of 38 hours. Thus, node 5 joins the permanent set. We have now determined the routes with shortest times to nodes 1, 2, 3, 4, 5, and 6 (as denoted by the heavy branches in Fig. 19.8).

Node 5 joins the permanent set

The only remaining node directly connected to the permanent set is node 7, as shown in Figure 19.9. Of the three branches connecting node 7 to the permanent set, branch 4–7 has the shortest time of 43 hours. Therefore, node 7 joins the permanent set.

Node 7 joins the permanent set

FIGURE 19.9

Network with Nodes 1, 2, 3, 4, 5, and 6 in the Permanent Set

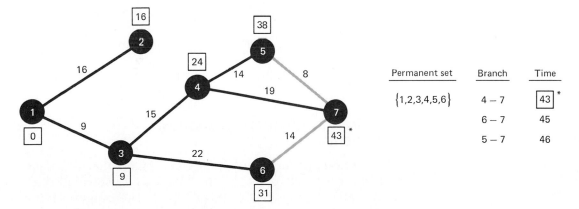

Permanent set	Branch	Time
{1,2,3,4,5,6}	4 – 7	43 *
	6 – 7	45
	5 – 7	46

The routes with the shortest times from the origin (node 1) to each of the other six nodes and their corresponding travel times are summarized in Figure 19.10 and Table 19.1.

Summary of the shortest routes

FIGURE 19.10

Network with Optimal Routes from Los Angeles to All Destinations

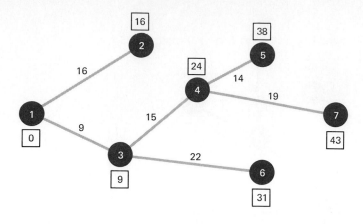

TABLE 19.1

Shortest Travel Time from Origin to Each Destination

From Los Angeles to:	Route	Total Hours
Salt Lake City (node 2)	1–2	16
Phoenix (node 3)	1–3	9
Denver (node 4)	1–3–4	24
Des Moines (node 5)	1–3–4–5	38
Dallas (node 6)	1–3–6	31
St. Louis (node 7)	1–3–4–7	43

Steps of the shortest route solution method

In summary, the steps of the shortest route solution method are as follows.

1. Select the node with the shortest direct route from the origin.
2. Establish a *permanent set* with the origin node and the node selected in step 1.
3. Determine all nodes directly connected to the permanent set nodes.
4. Select the node with the shortest route (branch) from the group of nodes directly connected to the permanent set nodes.
5. Repeat steps 3 and 4 until all nodes have joined the permanent set.

Computerized Solution of the Shortest Route Problem

The QSB+ software package for personal computers that was demonstrated in previous chapters has the capability to solve all three types of network flow models in this chapter. The program input and shortest route solution for the Stagecoach Shipping Company example used in this section are shown below. Notice that steps 1 through 7 in the QSB+ program output replicate the steps illustrated in Figures 19.4 through 19.10.

Branch Number	Branch Name	Start Node	End Node	Distance
1	< >	<1 >	<2 >	<16 >
2	< >	<1 >	<3 >	<9 >
3	< >	<1 >	<4 >	<35 >
4	< >	<2 >	<4 >	<12 >
5	< >	<2 >	<5 >	<25 >
6	< >	<3 >	<4 >	<15 >
7	< >	<3 >	<6 >	<22 >
8	< >	<4 >	<5 >	<14 >
9	< >	<4 >	<7 >	<19 >
10	< >	<4 >	<6 >	<17 >
11	< >	<5 >	<7 >	<8 >
12	< >	<6 >	<7 >	<14 >

Detailed Steps for the Shortest Route Algorithm:

Step 1 : Permanently label node 1
        Update the following nodes and labels (i.e., distance and from node):
            Node 2: (16; 1)
            Node 3: (9; 1)
            Node 4: (35; 1)

Step 2 : Permanently label node 3
        Update the following nodes and labels (i.e., distance and from node):
            Node 4: (24; 3)
            Node 6: (31; 3)

Step 3 : Permanently label node 2
        Update the following nodes and labels (i.e., distance and from node):
            Node 5: (41; 2)

Step 4 : Permanently label node 4
        Update the following nodes and labels (i.e., distance and from node):
            Node 5: (38; 4)
            Node 7: (43; 4)

Step 5 : Permanently label node 6
        Update the following nodes and labels (i.e., distance and from node):
            None

Step 6 : Permanently label node 5
        Update the following nodes and labels (i.e., distance and from node):
            None

Step 7 : Permanently label node 7
        Update the following nodes and labels (i.e., distance and from node):
            None

        The optimal solution has been found. Press any key to continue.

            The Final Shortest Routes for Stagecoach Shipping   Page: 1

Node	Distance	Shortest Route from Node 1
2	16	1- 2 (B1)
3	9	1- 3 (B2)
4	24	1- 3- 4 (B2-B6)
5	38	1- 3- 4- 5 (B2-B6-B8)
6	31	1- 3- 6 (B2-B7)
7	43	1- 3- 4- 7 (B2-B6-B9)

THE MINIMAL SPANNING TREE PROBLEM

Connecting all
nodes so that the
total branch
lengths are
minimized

In the shortest route problem presented in the previous section, the objective was to determine the shortest routes between the origin and the destination nodes in the network. In our example, we determined the best route from Los Angeles to each of the six destination cities. The *minimal spanning tree problem* is similar to the shortest route problem, except that the objective is to connect all the nodes in the network so that the total branch lengths are minimized. The resulting network *spans* (connects) all the points in the network at a minimum total distance (or length).

A minimal spanning
tree example

To demonstrate the minimal spanning tree problem, we will consider the following example. The Metro Cable Television Company is going to install a television cable system in a community consisting of seven suburbs. Each of the suburbs must be connected to the main cable system. The cable television company wants to lay out the main cable network in a way that will minimize the total length of cable that must be installed. The possible paths available to the cable television company (by consent of the town council) and the feet of cable (in thousands of feet) required for each path are shown in Figure 19.11.

FIGURE 19.11

Network of Possible
Cable TV Paths

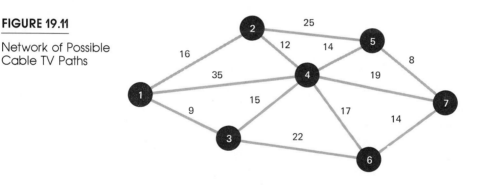

In Figure 19.11, the branch from node 1 to node 2 represents the available cable path between suburbs 1 and 2. The branch requires 16,000 feet of cable. Notice that the network shown in Figure 19.11 is identical to the network in Figure 19.2 that we used to demonstrate the shortest route problem. The networks were intentionally made identical in order to demonstrate the difference between the results of the two types of network models.

The Minimal Spanning Tree Solution Approach

The solution approach to the minimal spanning tree problem is actually easier than the shortest route solution method. In the minimal spanning tree solution approach, we can start at any node in the network. However, the conventional approach is to start with node 1. Beginning at node 1, we select the closest node (i.e., the shortest branch) to join our spanning tree. The shortest branch from node 1 is to node 3, with a length of 9 (thousand feet). This branch is indicated with a heavy line in Figure 19.12.

Start with any node in the network

Determining the initial spanning tree for nodes 1 and 3

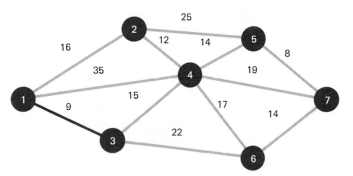

FIGURE 19.12

Spanning Tree with Nodes 1 and 3

Now we have a *spanning tree* consisting of two nodes: 1 and 3. The next step is to select the closest node not presently in the spanning tree. The node closest to either node 1 or node 3 (the nodes in our present spanning tree) is node 4, with a branch length of 15 thousand feet. The addition of node 4 to our spanning tree is shown in Figure 19.13.

Node 4 joins the spanning tree

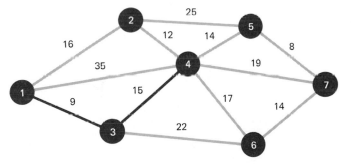

FIGURE 19.13

Spanning Tree with Nodes 1, 3, and 4

Next we repeat the process of selecting the closest node to our present spanning tree (nodes 1, 3, and 4). The closest node not presently connected to the nodes in our spanning tree is node 2. The length of the branch from node 4 to node 2 is 12 thousand feet. The addition of node 2 to the spanning tree is shown in Figure 19.14 on page 676.

Node 2 joins the spanning tree

Our spanning tree now consists of nodes 1, 2, 3, and 4. The node closest to this spanning tree is node 5, with a branch length of 14 thousand feet to node 4. Thus, node 5 joins our spanning tree, as shown in Figure 19.15, also on page 676.

Node 5 joins the spanning tree

FIGURE 19.14

Spanning Tree with Nodes 1, 2, 3, and 4

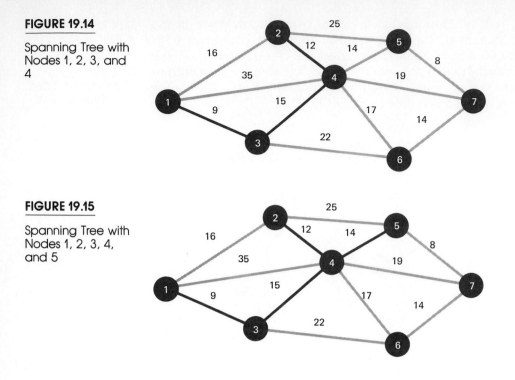

FIGURE 19.15

Spanning Tree with Nodes 1, 2, 3, 4, and 5

Node 7 joins the spanning tree

The spanning tree now contains nodes 1, 2, 3, 4, and 5. The closest node not currently connected to the spanning tree is node 7. The branch connecting node 7 to node 5 has a length of 8 thousand feet. Figure 19.16 shows the addition of node 7 to the spanning tree.

FIGURE 19.16

Spanning Tree with Nodes 1, 2, 3, 4, 5, and 7

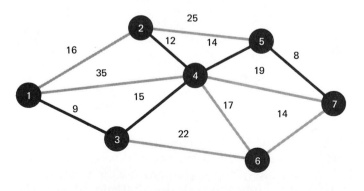

Node 6 joins the spanning tree

Now our spanning tree includes nodes 1, 2, 3, 4, 5, and 7. The only remaining node not connected to the spanning tree is node 6. The node in the spanning tree closest to node 6 is node 7, with a branch length of 14 thousand feet. The complete spanning tree, which now includes all seven nodes, is shown in Figure 19.17.

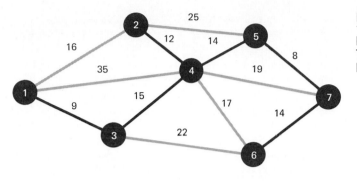

FIGURE 19.17

Minimal Spanning Tree for Cable TV Network

The spanning tree shown in Figure 19.17 requires the minimum amount of television cable to connect the seven suburbs—72,000 feet. This same minimal spanning tree could have been obtained by starting at any of the six nodes other than node 1.

Notice the difference between the minimal spanning tree network shown in Figure 19.17 and the shortest route network shown in Figure 19.10. The shortest route network represents the shortest paths between the origin and each of the destination nodes (i.e., six different routes). In contrast, the minimal spanning tree network shows how to connect all seven nodes so that the total distance (length) is minimized.

In summary, the steps of the minimal spanning tree solution method are as follows.

1. Select any starting node (conventionally node 1 is selected).
2. Select the node closest to the starting node to join the spanning tree.
3. Select the closest node not presently in the spanning tree.
4. Repeat step 3 until all nodes have joined the spanning tree.

The minimum total branch lengths

The difference between the minimal spanning tree network solution and shortest route network solution

Steps of the minimal spanning tree solution method

Computerized Solution of the Minimal Spanning Tree Problem

As noted earlier, the QSB+ software package has the capability to solve the minimal spanning tree problem. The minimal spanning tree solution steps and final solution for our Metro Cable Television Company example are shown on page 678. Notice that steps 1 through 7 in the solution output replicate the steps illustrated in Figures 19.12 through 19.17.

```
Detailed Steps for the Minimal Spanning Tree Algorithm:


Step 1 : Connect node  1
          The unconnected node closest to the connected nodes is: Node 3
          The shortest distance is from node 1 to node 3 with distance 9

Step 2 : Connect node  3
          The unconnected node closest to the connected nodes is: Node 4
          The shortest distance is from node 3 to node 4 with distance 15

Step 3 : Connect node  4
          The unconnected node closest to the connected nodes is: Node 2
          The shortest distance is from node 4 to node 2 with distance 12

Step 4 : Connect node  2
          The unconnected node closest to the connected nodes is: Node 5
          The shortest distance is from node 4 to node 5 with distance 14

Step 5 : Connect node  5
          The unconnected node closest to the connected nodes is: Node 7
          The shortest distance is from node 5 to node 7 with distance 8


Step 6 : Connect node  7
          The unconnected node closest to the connected nodes is: Node 6
          The shortest distance is from node 7 to node 6 with distance 14

Step 7 : Connect node  6
          The unconnected node closest to the connected nodes is: None

      The optimal solution has been found. Press any key to continue.

      The Final Minimal Spanning Tree for Metro Cable TV Co.   Page: 1

              Branch on the Tree              Distance

                    1 - 3 (B2)                    9
                    3 - 4 (B6)                   15
                    4 - 2 (B4)                   12
                    4 - 5 (B8)                   14
                    5 - 7 (B11)                   8
                    7 - 6 (B12)                  14

                    Total distance = 72
```

THE MAXIMAL FLOW PROBLEM

Maximizing the total flow from a source to a destination

In the shortest route problem, we determined the shortest truck route from the origin (Los Angeles) to six destinations. In the minimal spanning tree problem, we found the shortest connected network for television cable. In neither of these problems was the capacity of a branch limited to a specific number of items. However, there are network problems in which the branches of the network have limited flow capacities. The objective of these networks is to maximize the total amount of flow from an origin to a destination. These problems are referred to as *maximal flow problems.*

Maximal flow problems can involve the flow of water, gas, or oil through a network of pipelines; the flow of forms through a paper processing system (such as a government agency); the flow of traffic through a road network; or the flow of products through a production line system. In each of these examples, the branches of the network have limited and often different flow capacities. Given these conditions, the decision maker wants to determine the maximum flow that can be obtained through the system.

An example of a maximal flow problem is illustrated by the network of a railway system between Omaha and St. Louis shown in Figure 19.18. The Scott Tractor Company ships tractor parts from Omaha to St. Louis by railroad. However, a contract limits the number of railroad cars the company can secure on each branch during a week.

A maximal flow example

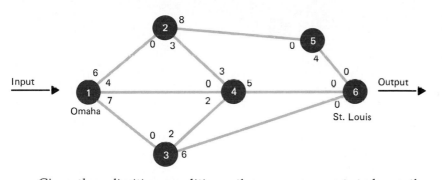

FIGURE 19.18

Network of Railway System

Given these limiting conditions, the company wants to know the maximum number of railroad cars containing tractor parts that can be shippped from Omaha to St. Louis during a week. The number of railroad cars available to the tractor company on each rail branch is indicated by the number on the branch to *the immediate right of each node* (which represents a rail junction). For example, 6 cars are available from node 1 (Omaha) to node 2, 8 cars are available from node 2 to node 5, 5 cars are available from node 4 to node 6 (St. Louis), etc. The number on each branch to the *immediate left* of each node is the number of cars available for shipping in the opposite direction. For example, no cars are available from node 2 to node 1. The branch from node 1 to node 2 is referred to as a *directed* branch, since flow is possible in only one direction (from node 1 to node 2, but not from 2 to 1). Notice that flow is possible in both directions on the branches between nodes 2 and 4 and nodes 3 and 4. These are referred to as *undirected branches.*

A directed branch

Undirected branches

The Maximal Flow Solution Approach

The first step in determining the maximum possible flow of railroad cars through the rail system is to *choose any path arbitrarily from origin to destination* and ship as much as possible on that path. In

Determine the maximum flow for any path through the system

Figure 19.19 we will arbitrarily select the path 1–2–5–6. The maximum number of railroad cars that can be sent through this route is 4. We are limited to 4 cars, since that is the maximum amount available on the branch between nodes 5 and 6. This path is shown in Figure 19.19.

The maximum flow for path 1–2–5–6

FIGURE 19.19

Maximal Flow for Path 1–2–5–6

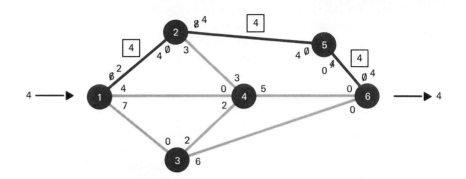

Recomputing branch capacities

Notice that the remaining capacities of the branches from node 1 to node 2 and from node 2 to node 5 are 2 and 4 cars, respectively, and that no cars are available from node 5 to node 6. These values were computed by subtracting the flow of 4 cars from the number available. The actual flow of 4 cars along each branch is shown enclosed in a box. Notice that the present input of 4 cars into node 1 and output of 4 cars from node 6 are also designated.

Determining branch flows in the opposite direction

The final adjustment on this path is to add the designated flow of 4 cars to the values at the immediate left of each node on our path, 1–2–5–6. These are the flows in the opposite direction. Thus, the value of 4 is added to the zeros at nodes 2, 5, and 6. It may seem incongruous to designate flow in a direction not possible; however, it is the means used in this solution approach to compute the *net flow* along a branch. (If, for example, a later iteration showed a flow of 1 car from node 5 to node 2, then the net flow in the correct direction would be computed by subtracting this flow of 1 in the wrong direction from the previous flow of 4 in the correct direction. The result would be a net flow of 3 in the correct direction.)

The maximum flow for path 1–4–6

We have now completed one iteration of the solution process and must repeat the steps above. Again, we arbitrarily select a path. This time we will select path 1–4–6, as shown in Figure 19.20. The maximum flow along this path is 4 cars, which is subtracted at each of the nodes. This increases the total flow through the network to 8 cars (because the flow of 4 along path 1–4–6 is added to the flow previously determined in Figure 19.19).

As a final step, the flow of 4 cars is added to the flow along the path in the opposite direction at nodes 4 and 6.

The maximum flow for path 1–3–6

Now we arbitrarily select another path. This time we will choose path 1–3–6, with a maximum possible flow of 6 cars. This flow of 6

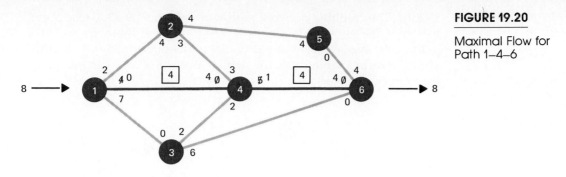

FIGURE 19.20

Maximal Flow for
Path 1–4–6

is subtracted from the branches along path 1–3–6 and added to the
branches in the opposite direction, as shown in Figure 19.21. The
flow of 6 for this path is added to the previous flow of 8, which results in a total flow of 14 railroad cars.

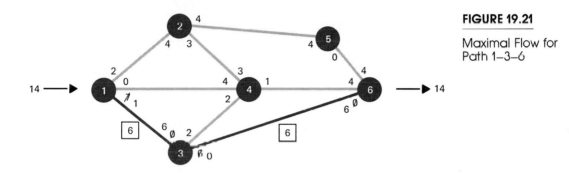

FIGURE 19.21

Maximal Flow for
Path 1–3–6

The next path we will select is 1–3–4–6. Notice that at this point
the number of paths we can take is restricted. For example, we cannot take the branch from node 3 to node 6, since zero flow capacity
is available. Likewise, no path — including the branch — from
node 1 to node 4 is possible.

The available flow capacity along the path 1–3–4–6 is 1 car, as
shown in Figure 19.22. This increases the total flow from 14 cars to

The maximum flow
for path 1–3–4–6

FIGURE 19.22

Maximal Flow for
Path 1–3–4–6

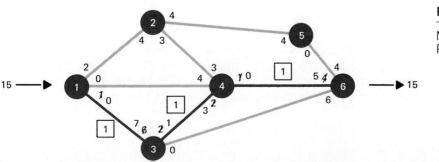
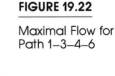

15 cars. The resulting network is shown in Figure 19.23. Close obser-vation of the network in Figure 19.23 shows that there are no more paths with available flow capacity. All paths out of nodes 3, 4, and 5 show zero available capacity, which prohibits any further paths through the network.

FIGURE 19.23

Maximal Flow for
Railway Network

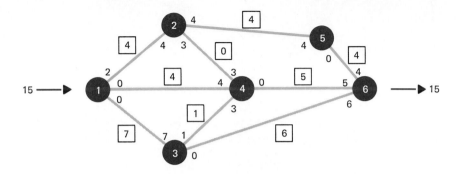

This completes the maximal flow solution for our example prob-lem. The maximum flow is 15 railroad cars. The flows that will occur along each branch appear in boxes in Figure 19.23.

In summary, the steps of the maximal flow solution method are as follows.

1. Arbitrarily select any path in the network from origin to destina-tion.
2. Adjust the capacities at each node by subtracting the maximal flow for the path selected in step 1.
3. Add the maximal flow along the path to the flow in the opposite direction at each node.
4. Repeat steps 1, 2, and 3 until there are no more paths with avail-able flow capacity.

Computerized Solution of the Maximal Flow Problem

As previously noted, the QSB+ software package has the capability to solve the maximal flow problem. The program input and maximal flow solution for the Scott Tractor Company example used in this section are shown below. Notice that the solution steps 1 through 6 in the QSB+ output differ from the steps shown in Figures 19.19 through 19.23, although the final solution is the same. This is be-cause the QSB+ program arbitrarily selected a different path to start with than we did in the manual solution in Figure 19.19.

NET Model Entry for Scott Tractor Co. Page 1

Branch Number	Branch Name	Start Node	End Node	Flow Capacity From Start Node	Flow Capacity From End Node
1	< >	<1 >	<2 >	<6 >	<0 >
2	< >	<1 >	<3 >	<7 >	<0 >
3	< >	<1 >	<4 >	<4 >	<0 >
4	< >	<2 >	<4 >	<3 >	<3 >
5	< >	<2 >	<5 >	<8 >	<0 >
6	< >	<3 >	<4 >	<2 >	<2 >
7	< >	<3 >	<6 >	<6 >	<0 >
8	< >	<4 >	<6 >	<5 >	<0 >
9	< >	<5 >	<6 >	<4 >	<0 >

Detailed Steps for the Maximal Flow Algorithm:

Step 1 : Flow = 3, determined by branch 2 - 4
         The path selected is: 1- 2- 4- 6

Step 2 : Flow = 3, determined by branch 1 - 2
         The path selected is: 1- 2- 5- 6

Step 3 : Flow = 2, determined by branch 3 - 4
         The path selected is: 1- 3- 4- 6

Step 4 : Flow = 5, determined by branch 1 - 3
         The path selected is: 1- 3- 6

Step 5 : Flow = 1, determined by branch 5 - 6
         The path selected is: 1- 4- 2- 5- 6

Step 6 : Flow = 1, determined by branch 3 - 6
         The path selected is: 1- 4- 3- 6

The Final Flow for Scott Tractor Co.   Page: 1

Branch	Net Flow
1 - 2 (B1)	6
1 - 3 (B2)	7
1 - 4 (B3)	2
2 - 4 (B4)	2
2 - 5 (B5)	4
3 - 4 (B6)	1
3 - 6 (B7)	6
4 - 6 (B8)	5
5 - 6 (B9)	4

    Maximal total flow = 15

Summary

In this chapter we examined the management science technique of network analysis. We concentrated specifically on a class of models referred to as network flow models. These included the shortest route network, the minimal spanning tree network, and the maximal flow network. These networks are all concerned with the flow of an item (or items) through an arrangement of paths (or routes).

Solution approaches were demonstrated for each of the three types of networks presented in this chapter. At times it may have seemed tiresome to go through the various steps of these solution methods when the solutions could have more easily been found by simply looking closely at the networks. However, as the sizes of networks increase, intuitive solution by observation becomes more difficult, thus creating the need for a solution procedure. Of course, as with the other techniques in this text, when a network gets extremely large and complex, computerized solution becomes the best approach.

In the next chapter we will continue our discussion of networks by presenting the network analysis techniques known as CPM and PERT. These network techniques are used primarily for project analysis and are not only the most popular types of network analysis, but also two of the most widely applied management science techniques.

References

Ford, L. R., Jr., and Fulkerson, D. R. *Flows in Networks*. Princeton, N.J.: Princeton University Press, 1962.

Hillier, F. S., and Lieberman, G. J. *Operations Research*. 4th ed. San Francisco: Holden-Day, 1986.

Hu, T. C. *Integer Programming and Network Flows*. Reading, Mass.: Addison-Wesley, 1969.

Lee, Sang M.; Moore, Laurence J.; and Taylor, Bernard W. *Management Science*. 3d ed. Boston: Allyn and Bacon, 1990.

Trueman, R. E. *Quantitative Methods for Decision Making in Business*. Hinsdale, Ill.: The Dryden Press, 1981.

EXAMPLE PROBLEM SOLUTION

The following example will illustrate the solution methods for the shortest route and minimal spanning tree network flow problems.

Problem Statement

A salesman for Healthproof Pharmaceutical Company travels each week from his office in Atlanta to one of five cities in the Southeast where he has clients. The travel time (in hours) between cities along interstate highways is shown along each branch in the following network.

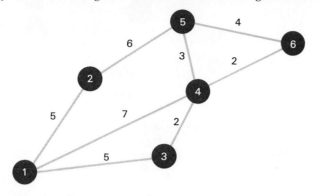

a. Determine the shortest route from Atlanta to each of the other five cities in the network.
b. Assume that the network now represents six different communities in a city, and that the local transportation authority wants to design a rail system that will connect all six communities with the minimum amount of track. The miles between each community are shown on each branch. Develop a minimal spanning tree for this problem.

Step 1 (part a): Determine the Shortest Route Solution

1. Permanent Set	Branch	Time
{1}	1–2	[5]
	1–3	5
	1–4	7

2. Permanent Set	Branch	Time
{1, 2}	1–3	[5]
	1–4	7
	2–5	11

3. Permanent Set	Branch	Time
{1, 2, 3}	1–4	[7]
	2–5	11
	3–4	7

4. Permanent Set	Branch	Time
{1, 2, 3, 4}	4–5	10
	4–6	[9]

5. Permanent Set	Branch	Time
{1, 2, 3, 4, 6}	4–5	[10]
	6–5	13

6. Permanent Set
{1, 2, 3, 4, 5, 6}

The shortest route network is shown below.

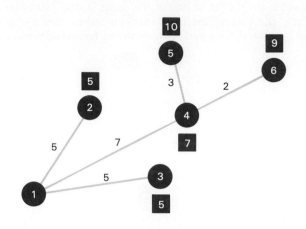

Step 2 (part b): Determine the Minimal Spanning Tree

1. The closest unconnected node to node 1 is 2.
2. The closest unconnected node to 1 and 2 is node 3.
3. The closest unconnected node to 1, 2, and 3 is node 4.
4. The closest unconnected node to 1, 2, 3, and 4 is node 6.
5. The closest unconnected node to 1, 2, 3, 4, and 6 is node 5.

The minimal spanning tree is shown below. The shortest total distance is 17 miles.

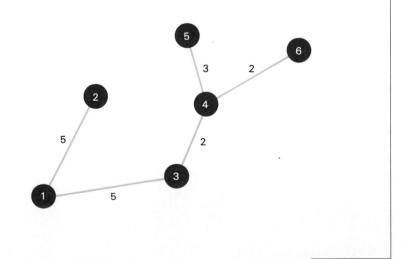

Problems

1. Given the following network with the indicated distances between nodes (in miles), determine the shortest route from node 1 to each of the other four nodes (2, 3, 4, and 5).

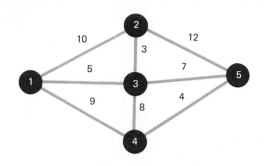

2. Given the following network with the indicated distances between nodes (in miles), determine the shortest route from node 1 to each of the other four nodes (2, 3, 4, and 5).

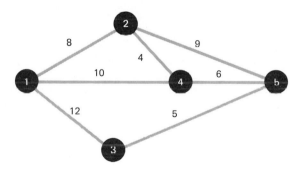

3. Given the following network with the indicated distances between nodes (in miles), determine the shortest route from node 1 to each of the other six nodes (2, 3, 4, 5, 6, and 7).

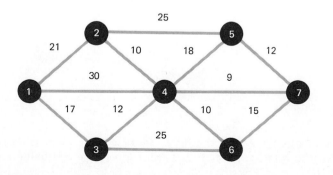

4. Frieda Millstone and her family live in Roanoke, Virginia, and they are planning an auto vacation across Virginia, their ultimate destination being Washington, D.C. The family has developed the following network of possible routes and cities they might like to visit on their trip. The time in hours between cities (which is affected by the type of road and the number of intermediate towns) is shown along each branch. Determine the shortest route the Millstone family can travel from Roanoke to Washington, D.C.

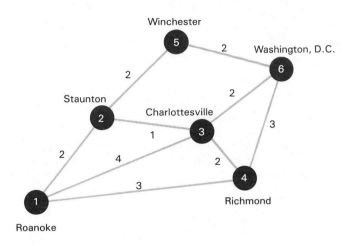

5. The Roanoke, Virginia, distributor of Rainwater Beer delivers beer by truck to stores in six other Virginia cities, as shown in the following network. The mileage between cities is shown along each branch. Determine the shortest truck route from Roanoke to each of the other six cities in the network.

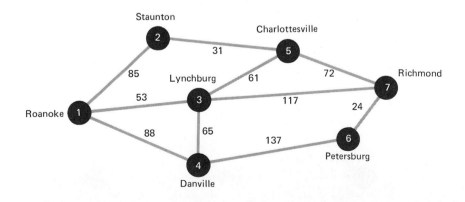

6. The plant engineer for the Bitco manufacturing plant is designing an overhead conveyor system that will connect the distribution/inventory

center to all areas of the plant. The network of possible conveyor routes through the plant, with the length (in feet) along each branch, is shown below. Determine the shortest conveyor route from the distribution/inventory center at node 1 to each of the other six areas of the plant.

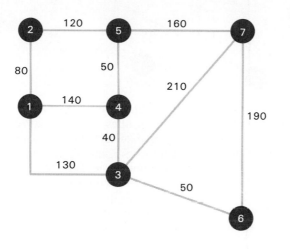

7. The Burger Doodle restaurant franchises in Los Angeles are supplied from a central warehouse in Inglewood. The location of the warehouse and its proximity in minutes of travel time to the franchise are shown in the following network. Trucks supply each franchise on a daily basis. Determine the shortest route from the warehouse at Inglewood to each of the seven franchises.

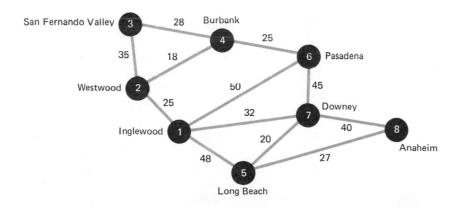

8. The Petroco gasoline distributor in Jackson, Mississippi, supplies service stations in six other southeastern cities, as shown in the following network. The distance in miles is shown on each branch. Determine the shortest route from Jackson to the six other cities in the network.

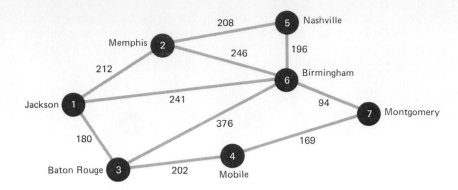

9. The administration at State University wants to connect eight campus buildings containing computer facilities to its central computer center via a coaxial cable system. A separate cable must be laid to each different building. The following network indicates the different paths the cable could follow from the computer center at node 1 to the eight buildings (nodes 2 through 9). The values accompanying each branch in the network are the distances in hundreds of feet between the various buildings. Determine the shortest cable path between the computer center and each of the eight buildings, and indicate the length of each of these paths.

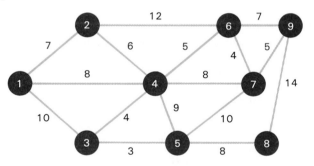

10. A steel mill in Gary supplies steel to manufacturers in seven other midwestern cities via truck as shown in the following network. The travel time between cities in hours is shown along each branch. Determine the shortest route from Gary to each of the other seven cities in the network.

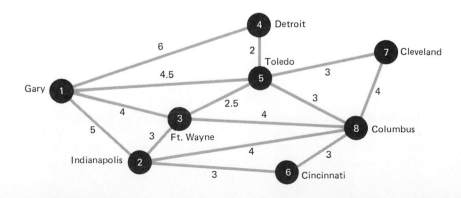

11. Determine the shortest route from node 1 (origin) to node 12 (destination) for the network given below. Distances are given along the network branches.

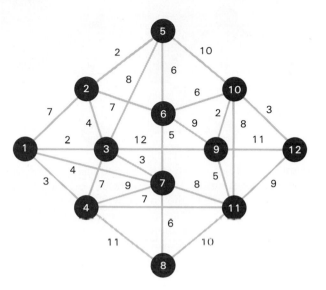

12. Given the following network with the indicated distances between nodes, develop a minimal spanning tree.

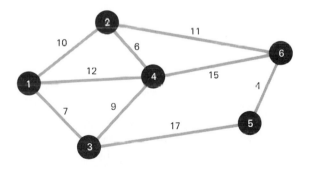

13. Given the following network with the indicated distances between nodes, develop a minimal spanning tree.

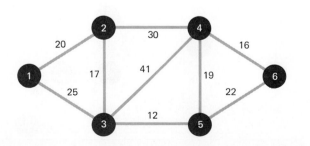

14. Given the following network with the indicated distances between nodes, develop a minimal spanning tree.

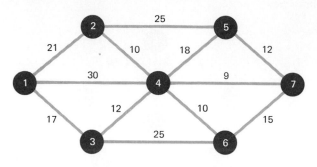

15. The community of Preston Forest is going to install a new sewer system to connect several suburbs. The network of possible sewage lines between the seven suburbs is shown below. The miles between suburbs are shown on each branch. Determine a sewer system that will connect all seven suburbs using the minimum number of miles of pipe, and indicate how many miles of pipe will be used.

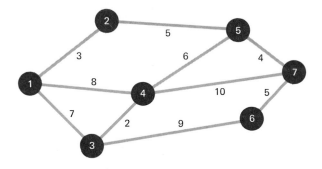

16. One of the opposing forces in a simulated army battle wishes to set up a communications system that will connect the eight camps in its command. The following network indicates the distances (in hundreds of yards) between the camps and the different paths over which a communications line can be constructed. Using the minimal spanning tree approach, determine the minimum-distance communication system that will connect all eight camps.

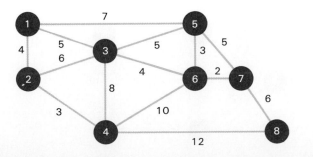

17. The management of the Dynaco manufacturing plant wants to connect the seven major manufacturing areas of its plant with a forklift route. Since the construction of such a route will take up a considerable amount of plant space and disrupt normal activities, management wants to minimize the total length of the route. The following network shows the distance in yards between the manufacturing areas (denoted by nodes 1 through 7). Determine the minimal spanning tree forklift route for the plant, and indicate the total yards the route will require.

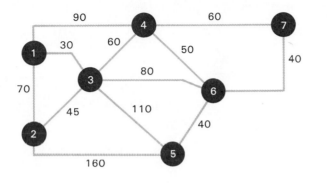

18. Several oil companies are jointly planning to build an oil pipeline to connect several southwestern and midwestern cities, as shown in the following network. The miles between cities are shown on each branch. Determine a pipeline system that will connect all eight cities using the minimum number of miles of pipe, and indicate how many miles of pipe will be used.

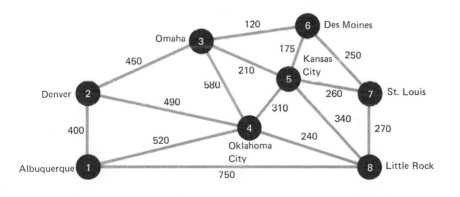

19. A major hotel chain is constructing a new resort hotel complex in Greenbranch Springs, West Virginia. The resort is in a heavily wooded area, and the developers want to preserve as much of the natural beauty as possible. To do so, the developers want to connect all the various facilities in the complex with a combination walking-riding path that will minimize the amount of pathway that will have to be cut through the woods. The following network shows possible connecting paths and corresponding distances (in yards) between the facilities. Determine the path that will connect all the facilities with the minimum amount of construction, and indicate the total length of the pathway.

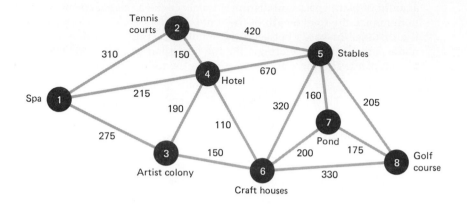

20. The Barrett Textile Mill is remodeling its plant and installing a new ventilation system. The possible ducts connecting the different rooms and buildings at the plant, with the length (feet) along each branch, are shown in the following network. Determine the ventilation system that will connect the various rooms and buildings of the plant using the minimum number of feet of ductwork, and indicate how many feet of ductwork will be used.

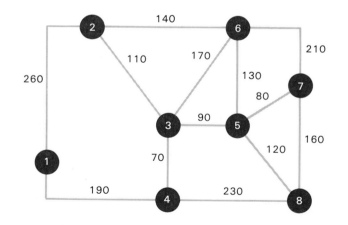

21. The town council of Whitesville has decided to construct a bicycle path that will connect the various suburbs of the town with the shopping center, the downtown area, and the local college. The council hopes the local citizenry will use the bike path, thus conserving energy and decreasing traffic congestion. The various paths that can be constructed and their lengths (in miles) are shown in the following network. Determine the bicycle pathway that will require the minimum amount of con-

struction to connect all the areas of the town. Indicate the total length of the path.

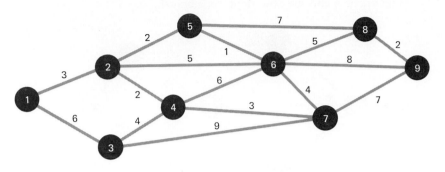

22. Determine the minimal spanning tree for the network in problem 11.

23. Given the following network with the indicated flow capacities of each branch, determine the maximum flow from source node 1 to destination node 6 and the flow along each branch.

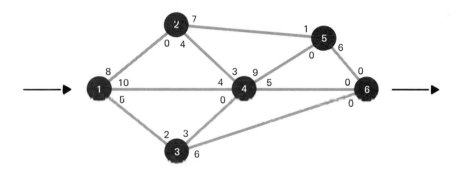

24. Given the following network with the indicated flow capacities along each branch, determine the maximum flow from source node 1 to destination node 7 and the flow along each branch.

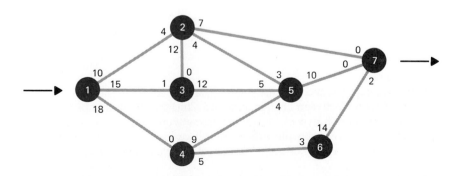

25. Given the following network with the indicated flow capacities along each branch, determine the maximum flow from source node 1 to destination node 6 and the flow along each branch.

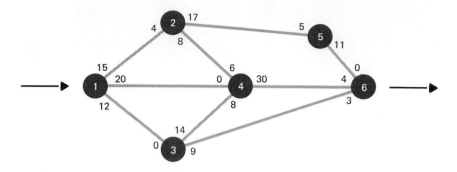

26. A new stadium complex is being planned for Denver, and the Denver traffic engineer is attempting to determine whether the city streets between the stadium complex and the interstate highway can accommodate the expected flow of 21,000 cars after each game. The various traffic arteries between the stadium (node 1) and the interstate (node 8) are shown in the following network. The flow capacities on each street are determined by the number of available lanes, the use of traffic police and lights, and whether any lanes can be opened or closed in either direction. The flow capacities are given in thousands of cars. Determine the maximum traffic flow the streets can accommodate and the amount of traffic along each street. Will the streets be able to handle the expected flow after a game?

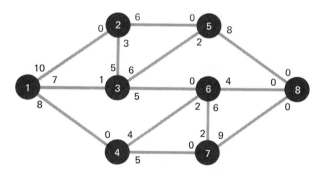

27. The FAA has granted a license to a new airline, Omniair, and awarded it several routes between Los Angeles and Chicago; the flights per day for each route are shown in the following network. Determine the maximum number of flights the airline can schedule per day from Chicago to Los Angeles, and indicate the number of flights along each route.

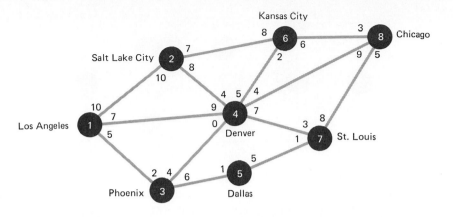

28. The National Express Parcel Service has established various truck and air routes around the country over which it ships parcels. The holiday season is approaching, which means a dramatic increase in the number of packages that will be sent. The service wants to know the maximum flow of packages it can accommodate (in tons) from station 1 to station 7. The network of routes and the flow capacities (in tons of packages per day) along each route are as follows. Determine the maximum tonnage of packages that can be transported per day from station 1 to station 7, and indicate the flow along each branch.

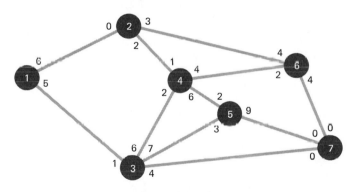

29. The traffic management office in Richmond is attempting to analyze the potential traffic flow from a new office complex under construction to an interstate highway interchange during the evening rush period. Cars leave the office complex via one of three exits, and then they travel through the city streets until they arrive at the interstate interchange. The following network shows the various street routes (branches) from the office complex (node 1) to the interstate interchange (node 9). All intermediate nodes represent street intersections, and the values accompanying the branches emanating from the nodes represent the traffic capacities of each street, expressed in thousands of cars per hour. Determine the maximum flow of cars that the street system can absorb during the evening rush hour.

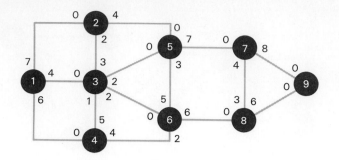

30. The Dynaco Company manufactures a product in five stages. Each stage of the manufacturing process is conducted at different plants. The following network shows the five different stages and the routes over which the partially completed products are shipped to the various plants at the different stages. Although each node represents a different plant, plants at the same stage perform the same operation. (For example, at stage 2 of the manufacturing process, plants 2, 3, and 4 all perform the same manufacturing operation.) The values accompanying the branches emanating from each node indicate the maximum number of units (in thousands) that a particular plant can produce and ship to another plant at the next stage. (For example, plant 3 has the capacity to process and ship 7,000 units of the product to plant 5.) Determine the maximum number of units that can be processed through the five-stage manufacturing process and the number of units processed at each plant.

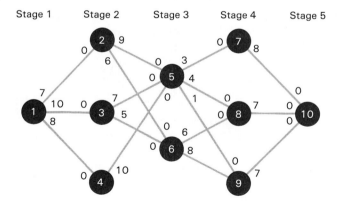

CPM and PERT Network Analysis

The CPM Network
Concurrent Activities
The Critical Path
Event Scheduling
Latest Event Times
Activity Slack

PERT Analysis
Probability Analysis of the PERT Network
Computerized PERT Analysis

Project Crashing and Time-Cost Trade-offs
Computerized Project Crashing

Formulating the CPM/PERT Network as a Linear Programming Model
Project Crashing with Linear Programming

Areas of Application of CPM/PERT Analysis
Project Management Software for the Personal Computer

Summary
References
Example Problem Solution
Problems

One of the most popular uses of networks is for project analysis. Such projects as the construction of a building, the development of a drug, or the installation of a computer system can be represented as networks. These networks illustrate the way in which the parts of the project are organized, and they can be used to determine the time duration of the projects. The network techniques that are used for project analysis are CPM and PERT. CPM stands for *Critical Path Method*, and PERT is an acronym for *Project Evaluation and Review Technique*. These two techniques are basically identical except that PERT is a probabilistic technique whereas CPM is a deterministic (i.e., nonprobabilistic) technique.

CPM and PERT were developed at approximately the same time (although independently) during the late 1950s. The fact that they have already been so frequently and widely applied attests to their value as management science techniques.

THE CPM NETWORK

Branches

Nodes
Activities and
events

A network example

The network flow models in the previous chapter consisted of nodes and branches. The *branches* represented routes (or paths) over which items flowed from one point in the network to other points, which were represented by *nodes*. A CPM network also consists of branches and nodes; however, the branches reflect *activities* of a project or operation, and the nodes represent the beginning and termination of activities, referred to as *events*.

As an example of a CPM network, we will consider the project of constructing a house. The network for building a house is shown in Figure 20.1.

FIGURE 20.1

Network for
Building a House

This network consists of three activities: designing the house, obtaining financing, and actually building the house. These activities are represented in the network by arrows (directed branches). The circles (nodes) in Figure 20.1 reflect events. For example, node 1 is the event of starting to design the house, and node 2 is an event representing the end of designing the house and the beginning of obtaining financing.

Precedence
relationships

The directed branches (arrows) in this network indicate *precedence relationships* among the three activities. In other words, the activity "design house" must precede the activity "obtain financing," which in turn precedes the activity "build house." These precedence relationships must be strictly followed. That is, an activity in this network cannot begin until the preceding activity has been totally completed. In network terminology, we say that when an activity is completed at a node, that node has been *realized*.

Realizing a node

Planning and
scheduling

The purpose of developing a network is to aid in *planning* and *scheduling* a project. The network for building a house in Figure 20.1 indicates to the home builder which activities are included in building a house and the order in which the activities must be undertaken. However, scheduling requires that times be associated with the activities. Therefore, we will designate estimated times for the duration of the activities in our home-building network, as shown in Figure 20.2.

In the network in Figure 20.2, the home builder has estimated that financing can be obtained after month 2, the house can be

FIGURE 20.2

Network for
Building a House
with Activity Times

started after month 3, and the entire project can be completed in 9 months. Based on this schedule, the home builder can plan when to vacate a present dwelling and move into the new house.

Concurrent Activities

Our home-building example has three activities occurring one after the other. However, a project often includes several activities that can occur at the same time (concurrently). To demonstrate concurrent activities, we will expand our home-building project network as shown in Figure 20.3.

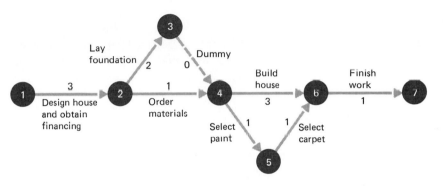

The expanded network in Figure 20.3 differs in several ways from the project network shown in Figure 20.1. First, the activities of designing the house and obtaining financing are now combined into activity 1 → 2 (where 1 and 2 are the nodes encompassing this activity). Next, the activity of ordering and receiving building materials follows the first activity. *In addition,* the activity of laying the foundation follows the first activity. In other words, the home builder can have the foundation laid *and* order the materials *concurrently.* Neither of these activities depends on the other; instead, both depend on the completion of the house design and financing.

When the activities of laying the foundation (2 → 3) and ordering materials (2 → 4) are completed, then activities 4 → 5 and 4 → 6 can begin simultaneously. However, before discussing these activities further, we will look more closely at activity 3 → 4, referred to in the network as a *dummy.*

A dummy activity is inserted into the network to show a precedence relationship, but it does not represent any actual passage of time. The activities could actually be represented in the network as shown in Figure 20.4 on page 702.

In a CPM network, however, two or more activities are not allowed to share the same starting and ending nodes. (The reason will become apparent later when we develop a schedule for the net-

FIGURE 20.4

Concurrent
Activities

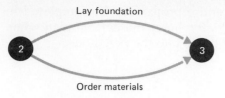

Lay foundation

Order materials

work.) Therefore, a *dummy* activity (3 → 4) is inserted to give two activities separate end nodes. Notice, though, that a time of zero months has been assigned to activity 3 → 4. Thus, the dummy activity, although it does not represent the passage of time, does show that activity 2 → 3 must be completed prior to any activities beginning at node 4.

Returning to the network (Fig. 20.3), we see that two activities start at node 4. Activity 4 → 6 is the actual building of the house, and activity 4 → 5 is the search for and selection of the paint for the exterior and interior of the house. Activity 4 → 6 and activity 4 → 5 can begin simultaneously and take place concurrently. Following the selection of the paint (activity 4 → 5) and the realization of node 5, the carpet can be selected (since the carpet color is dependent on the paint color). This activity can also occur concurrently with the building of the house (activity 4 → 6). When the building is completed and the paint and carpet are selected, the house can be finished (activity 6 → 7).

The Critical Path

Network paths

In our simpler network for building a house (before we expanded it), there was a single path with a duration of 9 months. However, the expanded network shown in Figure 20.3 has several paths. In fact, close observation of this network shows four paths, identified in Table 20.1 and Figure 20.5.

TABLE 20.1

Paths Through the
House-Building Network

Path	Events
A:	1 → 2 → 3 → 4 → 6 → 7
B:	1 → 2 → 3 → 4 → 5 → 6 → 7
C:	1 → 2 → 4 → 6 → 7
D:	1 → 2 → 4 → 5 → 6 → 7

The minimum time in which the project can be completed (i.e., the house can be built) is equal to the length of time required by the longest path in the network. The longest path is referred to as the

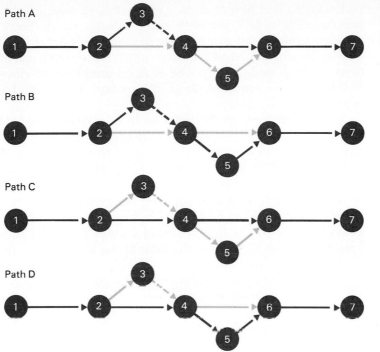

FIGURE 20.5

Alternative Paths in the Network

critical path. To better understand the relationship between the minimum project time and the longest network path, we will determine the length of each of the four paths shown in Figure 20.5.

By summing the activity times (shown in Fig. 20.3) along each of the four paths, we can compute the length of each path as follows.

Path A: $1 \rightarrow 2 \rightarrow 3 \rightarrow 4 \rightarrow 6 \rightarrow 7$
             $3 + 2 + 0 + 3 + 1 = 9$ months

Path B: $1 \rightarrow 2 \rightarrow 3 \rightarrow 4 \rightarrow 5 \rightarrow 6 \rightarrow 7$
             $3 + 2 + 0 + 1 + 1 + 1 = 8$ months

Path C: $1 \rightarrow 2 \rightarrow 4 \rightarrow 6 \rightarrow 7$
             $3 + 1 + 3 + 1 = 8$ months

Path D: $1 \rightarrow 2 \rightarrow 4 \rightarrow 5 \rightarrow 6 \rightarrow 7$
             $3 + 1 + 1 + 1 + 1 = 7$ months

Since path A is the longest path, it is also the critical path; thus the minimum completion time for the project is 9 months. Now let us analyze the critical path more closely. From Figure 20.3 we can see that event 2 will not occur until 3 months have passed. It is also relatively easy to see that event 3 will not occur until 5 months have passed. However, the realization of event 4 is dependent on two activities leading into node 4. Activity $3 \rightarrow 4$ is completed after 5 months (which we determine by adding the dummy activity time of zero to the time of 5 months until node 3 occurs), but activity $2 \rightarrow 4$ is com-

The longest path in the network

Determining the length of each path

Analyzing the critical path

pleted at the end of 4 months. Thus, we have two possible realization times for node 4: 5 months and 4 months. Recall, however, that a node represents the event of the next activity's occurring. Since no activity starting at node 4 can occur until *all* preceding activities have been finished, node 4 cannot be realized until *both* activities leading to it have been completed. Thus, the soonest node 4 can be realized is 5 months.

Now let us consider the activities leading from node 4. Using the same logic as above, we can see that node 6 will be realized either after 8 months (5 months at node 4 plus the 3 months required by activity 4 → 6) or after 7 months (5 months at node 4 plus the 2 months required by activities 4 → 5 and 5 → 6). Since all activities ending at node 6 must be completed before node 6 can be realized, the soonest node 6 can be realized is 8 months. Adding 1 month for activity 6 → 7 to the time at node 6 gives a project duration of 9 months. Recall that this is the time of the longest path in the network, or the critical path.

This brief analysis demonstrates the concept of a critical path and the determination of the minimum completion time of a project. Now we will look more closely at how each event in the network can be scheduled individually.

Event Scheduling

Earliest event time

In our analysis of the critical path in the previous section, we determined the soonest time that each event could be realized. For example, we found that the *earliest* time node 4 could be realized was 5 months. This time is referred to as the *earliest event time*, and it is expressed symbolically on the network as ET. The earliest times for all the events in our house-building network are shown in Figure 20.6.

FIGURE 20.6

Network with Earliest Event Times

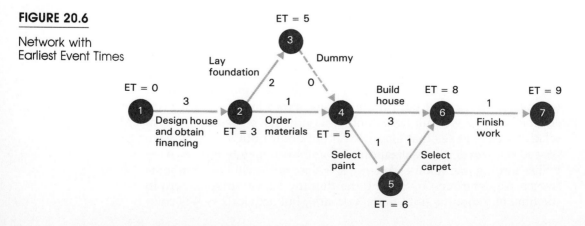

To determine the earliest time at every node, we make a *forward pass* through the network. That is, we start at the origin and move forward through the network. The earliest time at a node is the time when all activities ending at that node have been completed—the time when the node is realized. The earliest time at the final node in the network is always the project completion time, or the critical path time.

A forward pass

Observing node 2 in Figure 20.6, we can see that the earliest time of this event is 3 months. The only activity leading into node 2 has a duration of 3 months. Adding this amount to the earliest time of the immediately preceding node (zero at node 1) results in the earliest time of 3 months. At node 3, there is only one activity to be considered. Thus, the earliest time at node 3 is the activity time of 2 plus the earliest time of node 2, which equals 5 months.

At node 4, two activities terminate; thus, the earliest time is based on when *both* activities are completed. Activity $2 \rightarrow 4$ is completed at 4 months, but activity $3 \rightarrow 4$ is completed at 5 months. Therefore, 5 months is the earliest time event 4 can be realized. The remaining earliest event times are determined similarly.

In general, the earliest event time at a node, j, is computed as follows:

A formula for computing earliest event times

$$ET_j = \text{Maximum } (ET_i + t_{ij})$$

where i is the starting node number of all activities ending at node j and t_{ij} is the time for activity $i \rightarrow j$.

As an example, we will compute the earliest time at node 6 (i.e., $j = 6$).

$$
\begin{aligned}
ET_6 &= \text{Maximum } (ET_5 + t_{56}, ET_4 + t_{46}) \\
&= \text{Maximum } (6 + 1, 5 + 3) \\
&= \text{Maximum } (7, 8) \\
&= 8 \text{ months}
\end{aligned}
$$

which is the earliest time at node 6, as shown in Figure 20.6.

Latest Event Times

A companion to the earliest event time is the *latest event time*. The latest event time is the latest time an activity can start without delaying the completion of the project beyond the project critical path time. For our example, the project completion time (and earliest event time) at node 7 is 9 months. Thus, the objective of determining latest event times is to see how long each activity can be delayed without the project's exceeding 9 months.

Whereas a forward pass through the network is made to determine the earliest event times, the latest event times are computed

A backward pass

using a *backward pass*. We start at the end of the network at node 7 and work backward, computing the latest time at each event (node). Since we want to determine how long each activity in the network can be delayed *without extending the project time,* the latest time at node 7 cannot exceed the earliest time. Therefore, the latest time at node 7 (referred to as LT) is 9 months. This and all other latest event times are shown in Figure 20.7.

FIGURE 20.7

Network with Latest
Event Times

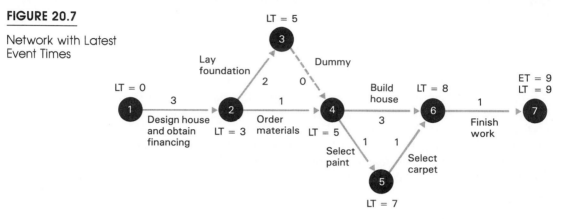

Moving backward through the network, we determine that the latest time at node 6 is 8 months, which is computed by subtracting the activity 6 → 7 time of 1 month from the latest time at node 7 (9 months). If event 6 is realized at any time later than 8 months, the overall project time will be increased beyond 9 months. For example, if node 6 is realized at month 9, then activity 6 → 7 will not be completed until *month 10.*

Next we compute the latest event time at node 5 the same way we did at node 6. Subtracting the activity 5 → 6 time of 1 month from the latest time at node 6 (8 months) results in a latest event time of 7 months at node 5.

At node 4 we have a choice as to the selection of the latest time. Either we can subtract the activity 4 → 6 time of 3 months from the latest time at node 6 (8 months), which results in a latest event time of 5 months, or we can subtract the activity 4 → 5 time of 1 month from the latest time at node 5, which results in a latest event time of 6 months. The latest time at node 4 can be either 5 months or 6 months. In such a case, we select the minimum latest event time, which is 5 months. The reason for this selection will become clear when we try using a latest time of 6 months at node 4.

If activity 4 → 6 starts at 6 months, then it will be completed after 9 months, which in turn will result in the project's being completed after 10 months. This is an obvious violation of our rule not to exceed the project (critical path) time. However, a latest event time of 5 months at node 4 will enable the project to be completed on time.

The remaining latest event times at nodes 3, 2, and 1 are determined similarly.

In general, the latest event time at node i is computed as follows:

$$LT_i = \text{Minimum } (LT_j - t_{ij})$$

A formula for computing the latest event times

where j is the ending node number of all activities starting at node i and t_{ij} is the time for activity $i \rightarrow j$.

As an example, we will compute the latest time at node 4 (i.e., $i = 4$).

$$LT_4 = \text{Minimum } (LT_6 - t_{46}, LT_5 - t_{45})$$
$$= \text{Minimum } (8 - 3, 7 - 1)$$
$$= \text{Minimum } (5, 6)$$
$$= 5 \text{ months}$$

which is the latest time at node 4, as shown in Figure 20.7.

Activity Slack

The network for building a house, with earliest and latest event times, is shown in Figure 20.8, which highlights the critical path $(1 \rightarrow 2 \rightarrow 3 \rightarrow 4 \rightarrow 6 \rightarrow 7)$ we determined earlier by inspection. Notice that for the events on the critical path, the earliest event times and latest event times are equal. This means that these events on the critical path must start exactly on time and cannot be delayed at all. If the start of any activity on the critical path is delayed, then the overall project time will be increased. As a result, we now have an alternative way to determine the critical path besides simply inspecting the network. The events on the critical path can be determined by seeing at which nodes the earliest event times equal the latest

Earliest and latest event times are equal on the critical path

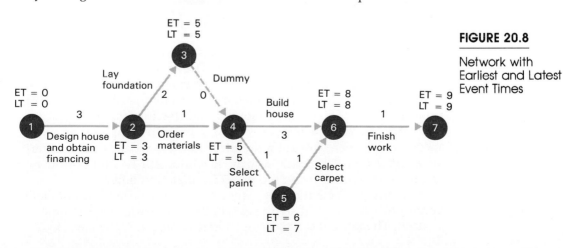

FIGURE 20.8

Network with Earliest and Latest Event Times

event times. In Figure 20.8, the nodes 1, 2, 3, 4, 6, and 7 all have earliest event times and latest event times that are equal; thus they are on the critical path.

A difficulty sometimes incurred in determining the critical path using solely the earliest and latest event times is that although the events on the critical path can be identified, it is possible to confuse the critical path activities with some activities not on the critical path. For example, nodes 2, 3, and 4 in Figure 20.8 all have equal earliest and latest event times. We might inadvertently designate the critical path as including activity $2 \rightarrow 4$ rather than activities $2 \rightarrow 3$ and $3 \rightarrow 4$, as the critical path actually does. Therefore, care must be taken in identifying the critical path.

There is, however, a way to tell exactly which activities are on the critical path. This alternative approach uses a concept known as *activity slack*. Slack is the amount of time an activity can be delayed without affecting the overall project duration. In effect, it is *extra time* available for completing an activity. The slack for each activity in our example network is shown in Figure 20.9.

Activity slack

Extra time available for completing an activity

FIGURE 20.9

Network with Slack

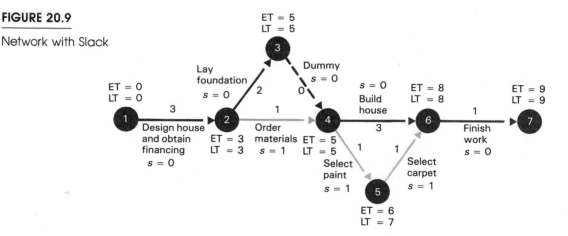

As an example of how slack is computed, we will look specifically at activity $2 \rightarrow 4$ in Figure 20.9. The earliest time this activity can start is at 3 months (i.e., the earliest event time at node 2). The latest this activity can be completed is at 5 months (the latest event time at node 4). This leaves 2 months available to complete the activity. Since the activity requires only 1 month to complete, an extra month is left over. This extra month is slack. If we delayed the start of activity $2 \rightarrow 4$ for one month, it could still be completed by month 5 without delaying the project completion time.

In contrast, activity $2 \rightarrow 3$ does not have any slack at all. The earliest this activity can start is at month 3 (the earliest event time at node 2). The latest it can be completed is at month 5 (the latest event time at node 3). Thus, 2 months are available for completion of this activity. Since activity $2 \rightarrow 3$ requires 2 months, no extra time is left over. Now recall that activity $2 \rightarrow 3$ is on the critical path. Careful inspection of Figure 20.9 shows that there is no slack for any of the activities on the critical path $(1 \rightarrow 2 \rightarrow 3 \rightarrow 4 \rightarrow 6 \rightarrow 7)$. All other activities not on the critical path do have slack. Therefore, as a general rule, the critical path encompasses those activities in the network that have no slack. In general, activity slack can be determined as follows.

Activities on the critical path have no slack

A formula for computing activity slack

Slack for activity $i \rightarrow j$ = Latest time (activity j)

$-$ earliest time (activity i)

$-$ activity time for activity $i \rightarrow j$

As an example, consider activity $5 \rightarrow 6$. The slack is computed as follows.

Slack for activity $5 \rightarrow 6 = LT_6 - ET_5 - t_{56}$

$- 8 - 6 - 1$

$= 1$ month

Before this discussion of slack is concluded, an additional aspect should be mentioned. Notice that activities $4 \rightarrow 5$ and $5 \rightarrow 6$ in Figure 20.9 both have slack time of 1 month. That means that either activity $4 \rightarrow 5$ *or* activity $5 \rightarrow 6$ can be delayed 1 month, but *both activities* cannot be delayed 1 month. If activity $4 \rightarrow 5$ starts at month 6 instead of month 5, then it will be completed at month 7, which will not allow the start of activity $5 \rightarrow 6$ to be delayed. The opposite is also true. If $4 \rightarrow 5$ starts at month 5, activity $5 \rightarrow 6$ can be delayed 1 month. The slack on these two activities is referred to as *shared slack*. This means that the *sequence of activities* $4 \rightarrow 5 \rightarrow 6$ can be delayed 1 month jointly without delaying the project.

Shared slack

PERT ANALYSIS

In the CPM network for building a house presented in the previous section, all of the activity time estimates were single values. By using only a single activity time estimate, we are, in effect, assuming that activity times are known with certainty (i.e., they are deterministic). For example, in Figure 20.9, the time estimate for activity $2 \rightarrow 3$ (laying the foundation) is shown to be 2 months. Since only this one value is given, we must assume that the activity time does not vary (or varies very little) from 2 months. In reality, however, it is rare that activity time estimates can be made with certainty. Projects that are networked are particularly likely to be unique, and thus there is little historical evidence that can be used as a basis to predict future occurrences. As an alternative to CPM, PERT (Project Evaluation and Review Technique) uses *probabilistic activity times*.

To demonstrate the PERT technique, we will employ a new example. (We could use the house-building network of the previous section; however, a network that is a little larger and more complex will provide more experience with different types of projects.) The Southern Textile Company has decided to install a new computerized order-processing system. In the past, orders for the cloth the company produces were processed manually, which contributed to delays in delivering orders and resulted in lost sales. The company wants to know how long it will take to install the new system.

The network for the installation of the new order-processing system is shown in Figure 20.10. We will briefly describe the activities.

FIGURE 20.10

Network for Installation of Order-Processing System

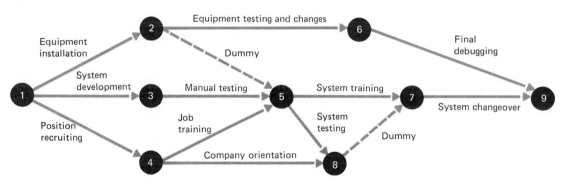

The network begins with three concurrent activities: the new computer equipment is installed (activity 1 → 2); the computerized order-processing system is developed (activity 1 → 3); and people are recruited to operate the system (activity 1 → 4). Once people are hired, they are trained for the job (activity 4 → 5), and other personnel in the company, such as marketing, accounting, and production personnel, are informed about the new system (activity 4 → 8). Once the system is developed (activity 1 → 3), it is tested manually to make sure that it is logical (activity 3 → 5). Following activity 1 → 2, the new equipment is tested and corrected (activity 2 → 6), and the newly trained personnel begin training on the computerized system (activity 5 → 7). Also, event 5 begins the testing of the system on the computer to check for errors (activity 5 → 8). The final activities include a trial run and changeover to the system (activity 7 → 9) and final debugging of the computer system (activity 6 → 9).

At this stage in a CPM network, we would assign a single-time estimate to each network activity. In a PERT network, however, we determine *three time estimates* for each activity, which will enable us to estimate the mean and variance for a *beta distribution* of the activity times. We are assuming that the activity times can be described by a beta distribution for several reasons. First, the beta distribution mean and variance can be approximated with three estimates. Second, the beta distribution is continuous, but it has no predetermined shape (such as the bell shape of the normal curve). It will take on the shape indicated—that is, be skewed—by the time estimates given. This is beneficial, since typically we have no prior knowledge of the shapes of the distributions of activity times in a unique project network. Third, although other types of distributions have been shown to be no more or less accurate than the beta, it has become traditional to use the beta distribution for PERT analysis.

Three time estimates for each activity

The beta distribution

The three time estimates for each activity are the most likely time, the optimistic time, and the pessimistic time. The *most likely time* is the time that would most frequently occur if the activity were repeated many times. The *optimistic time* is the shortest possible time within which the activity could be completed if everything went right. The *pessimistic time* is the longest possible time the activity would require to be completed assuming everything went wrong. In general, the person most familiar with an activity makes these estimates to the best of his or her knowledge and ability. (In other words, the estimate is subjective. See Chap. 10 on probability.)

The most likely time, the optimistic time, and the pessimistic time

These three time estimates can subsequently be used to estimate the mean and variance of a beta distribution. If we let

The mean and variance of a beta distribution

a = optimistic time estimate

m = most likely time estimate

b = pessimistic time estimate

then the mean and variance are computed as follows.

Mean (expected time): $t = \dfrac{a + 4m + b}{6}$

Variance: $v = \left(\dfrac{b - a}{6}\right)^2$

These formulas provide a reasonable estimate of the mean and variance of the beta distribution, a distribution that is continuous and can take on various shapes—i.e., exhibit skewness. (See Appendix D for a description of the beta distribution.)

The three time estimates, the mean, and the variance for all the activities in the network shown in Figure 20.10 are given in Table 20.2.

As an example of the computation of the individual activity mean times and variance, consider activity $1 \rightarrow 2$. The three time

Computing the activity mean and variance

TABLE 20.2
Activity Time Estimates for Figure 20.10

| Activity | Time Estimates (weeks) | | | Mean Time | Variance |
	a	m	b	t	v
$1 \rightarrow 2$	6	8	10	8	4/9
$1 \rightarrow 3$	3	6	9	6	1
$1 \rightarrow 4$	1	3	5	3	4/9
$2 \rightarrow 5$	0	0	0	0	0
$2 \rightarrow 6$	2	4	12	5	25/9
$3 \rightarrow 5$	2	3	4	3	1/9
$4 \rightarrow 5$	3	4	5	4	1/9
$4 \rightarrow 8$	2	2	2	2	0
$5 \rightarrow 7$	3	7	11	7	16/9
$5 \rightarrow 8$	2	4	6	4	4/9
$8 \rightarrow 7$	0	0	0	0	0
$6 \rightarrow 9$	1	4	7	4	1
$7 \rightarrow 9$	1	10	13	9	4

estimates ($a = 6$, $m = 8$, $b = 10$) are substituted in our formulas as follows.

$$t = \frac{a + 4m + b}{6}$$

$$= \frac{6 + 4(8) + 10}{6}$$

$$= 8 \text{ weeks}$$

$$v = \left(\frac{b - a}{6}\right)^2$$

$$= \left(\frac{10 - 6}{6}\right)^2$$

$$= 4/9 \text{ weeks}$$

The other values for the mean and variance in Table 20.2 are computed similarly. All of the means and variances for the activities in our example network are shown in Figure 20.11.

Once the expected activity times have been computed for each activity, we can determine the critical path the same way we did in the CPM network, except that we use the expected activity times, t. Recall that in the CPM network we identified the critical path as the one containing those activities with zero slack. This requires the determination of earliest and latest event times, as shown in Figure 20.12.

The critical path and expected project completion time

Observing Figure 20.12, we can see that the critical path encompasses activities $1 \rightarrow 3 \rightarrow 5 \rightarrow 7 \rightarrow 9$, since these activities have no available slack. We can also see that the *expected* project completion time (t_p) is 25 weeks. However, it is possible to compute the variance

FIGURE 20.11

Network with Mean Activity Times and Variances

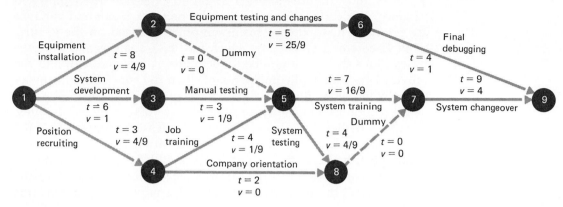

FIGURE 20.12

Network with Earliest and Latest Event Times and Slack

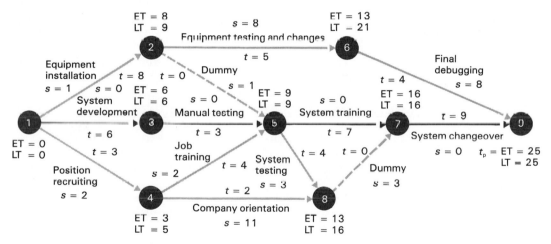

for project completion time. To determine the project variance, we *sum the variances for those activities on the critical path*. Using the variances computed in Table 20.2 and the critical path activities shown in Figure 20.12, we can compute the variance for project duration (v_p) as follows.

Project variance

Critical Path Activity	Variance
$1 \rightarrow 3$	1
$3 \rightarrow 5$	1/9
$5 \rightarrow 7$	16/9
$7 \rightarrow 9$	4
	62/9

$v_p = 62/9$

$\quad = 6.9$ weeks

The PERT method assumes that the activity times are statistically independent, which allows us to sum the individual expected activity times and variances in order to get an expected *project* time and variance. It is further assumed that the network mean and variance are normally distributed. This assumption is based on the Central Limit Theorem of probability, which for PERT analysis and our purposes states that if the number of activities is large enough and the activities are statistically independent, then the sum of the means of the activities along the critical path will approach the mean of a normal distribution. For the small examples in this chapter, it is questionable whether there are sufficient activities to guarantee that the mean project completion time and variance are normally distributed. Although it has become conventional in PERT analysis to employ probability analysis using the normal distribution regardless of the network size, the prudent user of PERT analysis should bear this limitation in mind.

Given these assumptions, we can interpret the expected project time (t_p) and variance (v_p) as the mean (μ) and variance (σ^2) of a normal distribution:

$\mu = 25$ weeks
$\sigma^2 = 6.9$ weeks

In turn, we can use these statistical parameters to make various probabilistic statements about the project.

Probability Analysis of the PERT Network

Recall from our discussion of the normal distribution in Chapter 10 that probabilities can be determined by computing the number of standard deviations (Z) a value is from the mean, as illustrated in Figure 20.13.

FIGURE 20.13

Normal Distribution of Network Duration

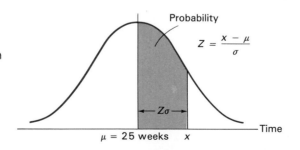

The value, Z, is computed using the following formula:

$$Z = \frac{x - \mu}{\sigma}$$

This value is then used to find the corresponding probability in Table A.1 of Appendix A.

For example, suppose the textile company manager told customers that the new order-processing system would be completely
installed in 30 weeks. What is the probability that it will, in fact, be
ready by that time? This probability is illustrated as the shaded area
in Figure 20.14.

Determining the
probability that the
project will be
completed within a
specific time

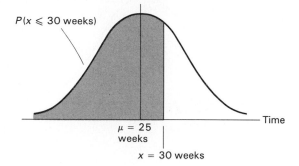

FIGURE 20.14

Probability the
Network Will Be
Completed in
30 Weeks or Less

To compute the Z value for a time of 30 weeks, we must first
compute the standard deviation (σ) from the variance (σ^2).

$$\sigma^2 = 6.9$$
$$\sigma = \sqrt{6.9}$$
$$\sigma = 2.63$$

Next we substitute this value for the standard deviation along
with the value for the mean and our proposed time project completion time (30 weeks), into the following formula.

$$Z = \frac{x - \mu}{\sigma}$$
$$= \frac{30 - 25}{2.63}$$
$$= 1.90$$

A Z value of 1.90 corresponds to a probability of .4713 in
Table A.1 in Appendix A. This means that there is a .9713 (.5000 +
.4713) probability of completing the project in 30 weeks or less.

Suppose one customer, frustrated with delayed orders, has told
the textile company that if the new ordering system is not working
within 22 weeks, she will trade elsewhere. The probability of the
project's being completed within 22 weeks is computed as follows.

$$Z = \frac{22 - 25}{2.63}$$
$$= \frac{-3}{2.63}$$
$$= -1.14$$

A Z value of 1.14 (the negative is ignored) corresponds to a probability of .3729 in Table A.1 of Appendix A. Thus, there is only a .1271 probability that the customer will be retained, as illustrated in Figure 20.15.

FIGURE 20.15

Probability the Network Will Be Completed in 22 Weeks or Less

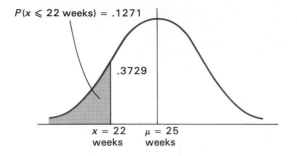

Computerized PERT Analysis

The capability to perform CPM/PERT network analysis is a standard feature of most management science software packages for the personal computer. To illustrate the application of such software to CPM/PERT analysis, we will employ the Microcomputer Software for Quantitative Analysis for Management package with our example of installing an order-processing system at the Southern Textile Company. The program input and network output are shown on page 717.

Notice that there is a distinct difference between this output and the manual results presented in conjunction with Figures 20.11 and 20.12, and this difference relates to network scheduling. There are two basic conventions for scheduling a network in which the activities are represented by branches (referred to as an "activity on arc" or AOA network, as opposed to an "activity on node" or AON network): event scheduling and activity scheduling. In this text we have used the event scheduling convention, whereas the Microcomputer Software package (as well as a number of other computer packages) uses activity scheduling. We employ the event scheduling method because it can be presented in a mathematically convenient manner.

Although the activity expected times and variances, activity slack, expected network completion time and variance, and critical path are all the same in the manual and the computer-generated solutions, the earliest and latest times are different. For example, note in Figure 20.12 that at node 1, ET = LT = 0. This means that the event represented by node 1 cannot occur earlier than time 0 or later than time 0 if the network is to be completed in 25 weeks. Next, observe that at node 4, ET = 3 and LT =5, indicating that this event

```
                       NETWORK ANALYSIS DATA:
        PROBLEM TITLE: Order Processing System
        ------------------------------------------------------------
                                          MOST
                            OPTIMISTIC PROBABLE PESSIMISTIC
           ACTIVITY      NODES        a         m          b
           --------      -----      ----------  --------  -----------
              1  |     1 -> 2        6.00      8.00      10.00
              2  |     1 -> 3        3.00      6.00       9.00
              3  |     1 -> 4        1.00      3.00       5.00
              4  |     2 -> 5        0.00      0.00       0.00
              5  |     2 -> 6        2.00      4.00      12.00
              6  |     3 -> 5        2.00      3.00       4.00
              7  |     4 -> 5        3.00      4.00       5.00
              8  |     4 -> 8        2.00      2.00       2.00
              9  |     5 -> 7        3.00      7.00      11.00
             10  |     5 -> 8        2.00      4.00       6.00
             11  |     8 -> 7        0.00      0.00       0.00
             12  |     6 -> 9        1.00      4.00       7.00
             13  |     7 -> 9        1.00     10.00      13.00
        ------------------------------------------------------------
                                     EXPECTED
           ACTIVITY     NODES         TIME      VAR.
        ------------------------------------------------------------
              1        1 -> 2        8.00      0.444
              2        1 -> 3        6.00      1.000
              3        1 -> 4        3.00      0.444
              4        2 -> 5        0.00      0.000
              5        2 -> 6        5.00      2.778
              6        3 -> 5        3.00      0.111
              7        4 -> 5        4.00      0.111
              8        4 -> 8        2.00      0.000
              9        5 -> 7        7.00      1.778
             10        5 -> 8        4.00      0.444
             11        8 -> 7        0.00      0.000
             12        6 -> 9        4.00      1.000
             13        7 -> 9        9.00      4.000
        ------------------------------------------------------------

                                  *** PERT ***
                                 PROGRAM OUTPUT
        ------------------------------------------------------------------
                                      ACTIVITY TIMES
           ACTIVITY     NODES       ES       EF       LS       LF      SLACK
        ------------------------------------------------------------------
              1        1 -> 2      0.00     8.00     1.00     9.00     1.00
              2        1 -> 3      0.00     6.00     0.00     6.00     0.00***
              3        1 -> 4      0.00     3.00     2.00     5.00     2.00
              4        2 -> 5      8.00     8.00     9.00     9.00     1.00
              5        2 -> 6      8.00    13.00    16.00    21.00     8.00
              6        3 -> 5      6.00     9.00     6.00     9.00     0.00***
              7        4 -> 5      3.00     7.00     5.00     9.00     2.00
              8        4 -> 8      3.00     5.00    14.00    16.00    11.00
              9        5 -> 7      9.00    16.00     9.00    16.00     0.00***
             10        5 -> 8      9.00    13.00    12.00    16.00     3.00
             11        8 -> 7     13.00    13.00    16.00    16.00     3.00
             12        6 -> 9     13.00    17.00    21.00    25.00     8.00
             13        7 -> 9     16.00    25.00    16.00    25.00     0.00***

                    (*** INDICATES CRITICAL PATH ACTIVITY)
        ------------------------------------------------------------------
                  EXPECTED PROJECT LENGTH = 25
                  VARIANCE OF THE CRITICAL PATH =  6.8888
                  STANDARD DEVIATION OF THE CRITICAL PATH =  2.6246

               ********** END OF NETWORK ANALYSIS **********
```

can occur no earlier than week 3 and no later than week 5. Now look at the computer output above and note the scheduled times for activity $1 \rightarrow 4$. For activity $1 \rightarrow 4$, the earliest start time is 0 and the latest start is week 2; the earliest finish is week 3 and the latest finish is week 5. In the computer output, the two weeks of slack associated with this activity are specifically reflected in the fact that this activity can have a "latest start" of week 2.

PROJECT CRASHING AND TIME-COST TRADE-OFF

To this point we have demonstrated the use of CPM and PERT network analysis for determining project time schedules. This in itself is valuable to the manager planning a project. However, in addition to scheduling projects, the project manager is frequently confronted with the problem of having to reduce the scheduled completion time of a project to meet a deadline. In other words, the manager must finish the project sooner than indicated by the CPM or PERT network analysis.

Project duration can be reduced by assigning more labor to project activities, often in the form of overtime, and by assigning more resources (i.e., material, equipment, etc.). However, additional labor and resources cost money and thus increase the overall project cost. Thus, the decision to reduce the project duration must be based on an analysis of the *trade-off* between time and cost.

Project crashing is a method for shortening the project duration by reducing the time of one or more of the critical project activities to a time that is less than the normal activity time. This reduction in the normal activity times is referred to as "crashing." Crashing is achieved by devoting more resources, measured in terms of dollars, to the activities to be crashed.

To demonstrate how project crashing works, we will employ the network for constructing a house first introduced in Figure 20.3. This network is repeated in Figure 20.16, except that the activity times previously shown as months have been converted to weeks. Although this example network encompasses only single activity time estimates, the project crashing procedure can be applied in the same manner to PERT networks with probabilistic activity time estimates.

In Figure 20.16, we will assume that the times (in weeks) shown on the network activities are the *normal activity times*. For example, normally, 12 weeks are required to complete activity $1 \rightarrow 2$. Further, we will assume that the cost required to complete this activity in the time indicated is $3,000. This cost is referred to as the *normal activity cost*. Next, we will assume that the building contractor has estimated

Reducing the project duration

A trade-off between time and cost

Project crashing

The house-building example

Normal activity times

Normal activity cost

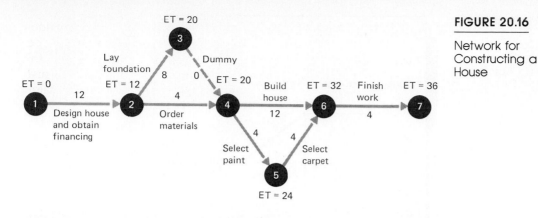

FIGURE 20.16

Network for
Constructing a
House

that activity $1 \rightarrow 2$ can be completed in 7 weeks but it will cost
$5,000 to complete the activity instead of $3,000. This new estimated
activity time is known as the *crash time,* and the revised cost is referred to as the *crash cost.*

Crash time
Crash cost

Activity $1 \rightarrow 2$ can be crashed a total of 5 weeks (normal time
crash time $= 12 - 7 = 5$ weeks) at a total crash cost of $2,000 (crash
cost $-$ normal cost $= \$5,000 - 3,000 = \$2,000$). Dividing the total
crash cost by the total allowable crash time yields the crash cost per
week:

Crash cost per unit
of time

$$\frac{\text{Total crash cost}}{\text{Total crash time}} = \frac{\$2,000}{5} = \$400 \text{ per week}$$

If we assume that the relationship between crash cost and crash
time is linear, then activity $1 \rightarrow 2$ can be crashed by any amount of
time (not exceeding the maximum allowable crash time) at a rate of
$400 per week. For example, if the contractor decided to crash ac-
tivity $1 \rightarrow 2$ by only 2 weeks (for an activity time of 10 weeks), the
crash cost would be $800 ($400 per week $\times$ 2 weeks). The linear relationships between crash cost and crash time and between normal
cost and normal time are illustrated in Figure 20.17 on page 720.

The linear
relationships
between crash cost
and time and
normal cost and
time

The normal times and costs, the crash times and costs, the total
allowable crash times, and the crash cost per week for each activity
in the network in Figure 20.16 are summarized in Table 20.3.

Recall that the critical path for the house-building network en-
compassed activities $1 \rightarrow 2 \rightarrow 3 \rightarrow 4 \rightarrow 6 \rightarrow 7$ and the project duration was 9 months, or 36 weeks. Suppose that the home builder
needed the house in 30 weeks and wanted to know how much extra
cost would be incurred to complete the house by this time. To analyze this situation, the contractor would crash the project network to
30 weeks using the information in Table 20.3.

Crashing the
network to
30 weeks

The objective of project crashing is to reduce the project duration while minimizing the cost of crashing. Since the project completion time can be shortened only by crashing activities on the critical

Objective of
project crashing

FIGURE 20.17

Time-Cost
Relationship for
Crashing Activity
$1 \rightarrow 2$

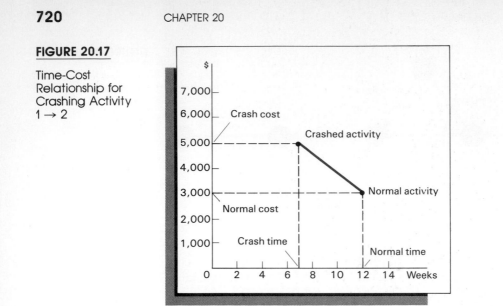

TABLE 20.3

Normal Activity and Crash Data for the Network in Figure 20.16

Activity	Normal Time (weeks)	Crash Time (weeks)	Normal Cost	Crash Cost	Total Allowable Crash Time (weeks)	Crash Cost per Week
$1 \rightarrow 2$	12	7	$ 3,000	$ 5,000	5	$ 400
$2 \rightarrow 3$	8	5	2,000	3,500	3	500
$2 \rightarrow 4$	4	3	4,000	7,000	1	3,000
$3 \rightarrow 4$	0	0	0	0	0	0
$4 \rightarrow 5$	4	1	500	1,100	3	200
$4 \rightarrow 6$	12	9	50,000	71,000	3	7,000
$5 \rightarrow 6$	4	1	500	1,100	3	200
$6 \rightarrow 7$	4	3	15,000	22,000	1	7,000
			$75,000	$110,700		

path, it may turn out that not all activities have to be crashed. However, as activities are crashed, the critical path may change, requiring crashing of previously noncritical activities to further reduce the project completion time.

Manually crashing the network

We start the crashing process by looking at the critical path and seeing which activity has the minimum crash cost per week. Observing Table 20.3 and Figure 20.18, we see that activity $1 \rightarrow 2$ has the minimum crash cost of $400 (excluding the dummy activity $3 \rightarrow 4$, which cannot be reduced). Thus, activity $1 \rightarrow 2$ will be reduced as much as possible. Table 20.3 shows that the maximum allowable reduction for activity $1 \rightarrow 2$ is 5 weeks, *but we can reduce activity $1 \rightarrow 2$*

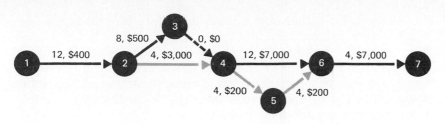

FIGURE 20.18

Network with Normal Activity Times and Weekly Activity Crashing Costs

only to the point where another path becomes critical. When two paths simultaneously become critical, activities on both must be reduced by the same amount. (If we reduce the activity time beyond the point where another path becomes critical, we may be incurring an unnecessary cost.) This last stipulation means that we must keep up with all of the network paths as we reduce individual activities, a condition that makes manual crashing very cumbersome. Later we will demonstrate an alternative method for project crashing using linear programming; however, for the moment we will pursue this example in order to demonstrate the logic of project crashing.

The difficulty of manual crashing

It turns out that activity $1 \rightarrow 2$ can be crashed by the total amount of 5 weeks without another path's becoming critical, since activity $1 \rightarrow 2$ is included in all four paths in the network. Crashing this activity results in a revised project duration of 31 weeks at a crashing cost of $2,000. The revised network is shown in Figure 20.19.

The network crashed to 31 weeks

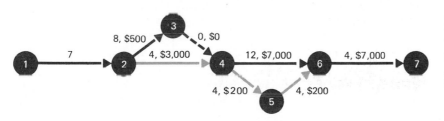

FIGURE 20.19

The Revised Network with Activity $1 \rightarrow 2$ Crashed

This process must now be repeated. The critical path in Figure 20.19 remains the same, and the minimum activity crash cost on the critical path is $500 for activity $2 \rightarrow 3$. Activity $2 \rightarrow 3$ can be crashed a total of 3 weeks, but since the contractor only desires to crash the network to 30 weeks, we only need to crash activity $2 \rightarrow 3$ by 1 week. Crashing activity $1 \rightarrow 2$ by 1 week does not result in any other path's becoming critical, so we can safely make this reduction. Crashing activity $2 \rightarrow 3$ to 7 weeks (i.e., a 1 week reduction) costs $500 and reduces the project duration to 30 weeks.

The network crashed to 30 weeks

The total cost of crashing the project to 30 weeks is $2,500. Thus, the contractor could inform the customer that an additional cost of only $2,500 would be incurred to finish the house in 30 weeks.

Cost of crashing

As indicated earlier, the manual procedure for crashing a network is very cumbersome and generally unacceptable for project crashing. It is basically a trial-and-error approach that is useful for demonstrating the logic of crashing; however, it quickly becomes unmanageable for larger networks. This approach would have become difficult if we had pursued even the house-building example to a crash time greater than 30 weeks.

Computerized Project Crashing

The QSB+ software package demonstrated previously in this text also has the capability to perform project crashing. Page 723 shows the crashing analysis for our house-building example encompassed by Table 20.3 and Figures 20.18 and 20.19.

Project crashing with linear programming An alternative procedure for project crashing is linear programming. Linear programming is a mathematical procedure that ensures an optimal crashing solution (i.e., a solution that minimizes the crashing cost). In this section we will show how a CPM/PERT network can be formulated as a linear programming model and how an expanded version of that model can be used for project crashing.

FORMULATING THE CPM/PERT NETWORK AS A LINEAR PROGRAMMING MODEL

Before we present the linear programming formulation of the project crashing network, it will be beneficial to look briefly at the formulation of the general CPM/PERT network model.

Formulating a linear programming model of a CPM/PERT network

As the first step in formulating the linear programming model, we will define the decision variables. In our general discussion of CPM/PERT networks, we designated an activity by its starting and ending node numbers. Thus, an activity starting at node 1 and ending at node 2 was referred to as activity $1 \rightarrow 2$. We will use a similar

Decision variables

designation to define the decision variables of our linear programming model. For an activity $i \rightarrow j$, the earliest event time of node i will be x_i, and the earliest event time of node j will be x_j.

The objective of the project network is to determine the earliest time the project can be completed (i.e., the critical path time). We have already determined from our discussion of CPM/PERT network analysis that the earliest event time of the last node in the network equals the critical path time. If we let x_m equal the earliest event time

Objective function

of the last node in the network, designated as node m, then the objective function can be expressed as

minimize $Z = x_m$

Next we must develop the model constraints. First we will define the time for activity $i \rightarrow j$ as t_{ij} (as we did earlier in this chapter).

```
                CPM Entry for Project Crash -- AOA Format     Page: 1

Activity  Activity  Start    End     Normal      Crash      Normal      Crash
 number     name    node    node    duration    duration     cost        cost
    1     <Design  > <1  > <2  > <12    > <7    > <3000   > <5000   >
    2     <Found   > <2  > <3  > <8     > <5    > <2000   > <3500   >
    3     <Order   > <2  > <4  > <4     > <3    > <4000   > <7000   >
    4     <Dummy   > <3  > <4  > <0     > <0    > <0      > <0      >
    5     <Paint   > <4  > <5  > <4     > <1    > <500    > <1100   >
    6     <Build   > <4  > <6  > <12    > <9    > <50000  > <71000  >
    7     <Carpet  > <5  > <6  > <4     > <1    > <500    > <1100   >
    8     <Finish  > <6  > <7  > <4     > <3    > <15000  > <22000  >
```

```
                CPM Analysis for Project Crash     Page  1
```

| Activity | | Activity | | Earliest | Latest | Earliest | Latest | Slack |
No.	Name	Exp.Time	Variance	Start	Start	Finish	Finish	LS-ES
1	Design	+12.0000	0	0	0	+12.0000	+12.0000	Critical
2	Found	+8.00000	0	+12.0000	+12.0000	+20.0000	+20.0000	Critical
3	Order	+4.00000	0	+12.0000	+16.0000	+16.0000	+20.0000	+4.00000
4	Dummy	0	0	+20.0000	+20.0000	+20.0000	+20.0000	Critical
5	Paint	+4.00000	0	+20.0000	+24.0000	+24.0000	+28.0000	+4.00000
6	Build	+12.0000	0	+20.0000	+20.0000	+32.0000	+32.0000	Critical
7	Carpet	+4.00000	0	+24.0000	+28.0000	+28.0000	+32.0000	+4.00000
8	Finish	+4.00000	0	+32.0000	+32.0000	+36.0000	+36.0000	Critical

```
        Expected completion time = 36    Total cost = 75000
```

```
                Crash Analysis for Project Crash
```

If you have not entered crash times and costs, please reply 'N' to the following question.

Have you entered crash times and crash costs (Y/N)? y

Completion time without crash for Project Crash is 36

By what time do you want to finish (0 to end) ? 30

Do you want to print the crash result (Y/N)? n

For this crash to reduce 6 time unit(s):

  Crash activity Design 5 time unit(s), New duration = 7 , Incremental cost =
2000

  Crash activity Found 1 time unit(s), New duration = 7 , Incremental cost =
500

Critical paths for Project Crash with completion time = 30   Total cost =
77500

CP # 1 : Design - Found - Dummy - Build - Finish

From our previous discussion of CPM/PERT network analysis, we know that the difference between the earliest event time at node j and the earliest event time at node i must be at least as great as the activity time t_{ij}. A set of constraints that expresses this condition is defined as

$$x_j - x_i \geq t_{ij}$$

The general linear programming model of formulation of a CPM/PERT network can be summarized as

minimize $Z = x_m$

subject to

$\quad x_j - x_i \geq t_{ij}, \quad$ for all activities $i \rightarrow j$

$\quad\quad x_i, x_j \geq 0$

where

$\quad x_i = $ earliest event time of node i

$\quad x_j = $ earliest event time of node j

$\quad t_{ij} = $ time of activity $i \rightarrow j$

$\quad m = $ number of the last node in the network

The solution of this linear programming model will indicate the earliest event time of each node in the network and the project duration.

As an example of the linear programming model formulation and solution of a project network, we will use our house-building network to demonstrate project crashing. This network, with activity times in weeks and earliest event times, is shown in Figure 20.20.

The linear programming model for the network in Figure 20.20 is

minimize $Z = x_7$

subject to

$\quad x_2 - x_1 \geq 12$

$\quad x_3 - x_2 \geq 8$

$\quad x_4 - x_2 \geq 4$

$\quad x_4 - x_3 \geq 0$

$\quad x_5 - x_4 \geq 4$

$\quad x_6 - x_4 \geq 12$

$\quad x_6 - x_5 \geq 4$

$\quad x_7 - x_6 \geq 4$

$\quad\quad x_i, x_j \geq 0$

Notice in this model that there is a constraint for every activity in the network.

This problem can be solved using the LINDO/PC computer package first introduced in Chapter 4. The computer output and solution for our example network are as follows.

```
: look all

MIN     X7
SUBJECT TO
        2)    X2 -  X1 >=    12
        3)  - X2 +  X3 >=     8
        4)  - X2 +  X4 >=     4
        5)  - X3 +  X4 >=     0
        6)  - X4 +  X5 >=     4
        7)  - X4 +  X6 >=    12
        8)  - X5 +  X6 >=     4
        9)    X7 -  X6 >=     4
END

: go

          OBJECTIVE FUNCTION VALUE

  1)        36.0000000

  VARIABLE          VALUE        REDUCED COST
        X7        36.000000          .000000
        X2        12.000000          .000000
        X1          .000000         1.000000
        X3        20.000000          .000000
        X4        20.000000          .000000
        X5        24.000000          .000000
        X6        32.000000          .000000

     ROW    SLACK OR SURPLUS       DUAL PRICES
      2)          .000000         -1.000000
      3)          .000000         -1.000000
      4)         4.000000           .000000
      5)          .000000         -1.000000
      6)          .000000           .000000
      7)          .000000         -1.000000
      8)         4.000000           .000000
      9)          .000000         -1.000000

  NO. ITERATIONS=         8
```

This computer output indicates that the earliest event time at node 7 is 36 weeks (i.e., $x_7 = 36$, the objective function value). The earliest event times indicated by the x_i variables are identical to the earliest event times we computed previously for this network, as shown in Figure 20.20.

Interpreting the computer solution

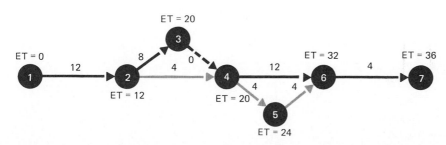

FIGURE 20.20

CPM/PERT Network for the House-Building Project with Earliest Event Times

This linear programming model for the general CPM/PERT network now provides us with a good foundation for developing a linear programming model for project crashing.

Project Crashing with Linear Programming

The linear programming model required to perform project crashing analysis differs from the linear programming model formulated for the general CPM/PERT network in the previous section. The linear programming model for project crashing is somewhat longer and more complex.

The objective for our general linear programming model was to minimize project duration; the objective of project crashing is to minimize the cost of crashing given the limits on how much individual activities can be crashed. As a result, the general linear programming model formulation must be expanded to include crash times and cost. We will continue to define the earliest event times for activity $i \rightarrow j$ as x_i and x_j. In addition, we will define the amount of

time each activity $i \rightarrow j$ is crashed as y_{ij}. Thus, the decision variables are defined as

x_i = earliest event time of node i

x_j = earliest event time of node j

y_{ij} = amount of time by which activity $i \rightarrow j$ is crashed (i.e., reduced)

The objective of project crashing is to reduce the project duration at the minimum possible crash cost. For our house-building net-

work, the objective function is written as

$$\text{minimize } Z = \$400y_{12} + 500y_{23} + 3{,}000y_{24} + 200y_{45} + 7{,}000y_{46} + 200y_{56}$$
$$+ 7{,}000y_{67}$$

The objective function coefficients are the activity crash costs per week from Table 20.3; the variables, y_{ij}, indicate the number of weeks each activity will be reduced. For example, if activity $1 \rightarrow 2$ is crashed by 2 weeks, then $y_{12} = 2$ and a cost of $800 is incurred.

The model constraints must specify the limits on the amount of time each activity can be crashed. Using the allowable crash times for each activity from Table 20.3 enables us to develop the following

set of constraints.

$y_{12} \leq 5$

$y_{23} \leq 3$

$y_{24} \leq 1$

$y_{34} \leq 0$

$y_{45} \leq 3$

$y_{46} \leq 3$

$y_{56} \leq 3$

$y_{67} \leq 1$

For example, the first constraint, $y_{12} \leq 5$, specifies that the amount of time that activity $1 \to 2$ is reduced cannot exceed 5 weeks.

The next group of constraints must mathematically represent the relationship between earliest event times for each activity in the network, as the constraint $x_j - x_i \geq t_{ij}$ did in our original linear programming model. However, we must now reflect the fact that activity times can be crashed by an amount y_{ij}. Recall the formulation of the activity $1 \to 2$ constraint for the general linear programming model formulation in the previous section:

Constraints for earliest event times

$$x_2 - x_1 \geq 12$$

This constraint can also be written

$$x_1 + 12 \leq x_2$$

This latter constraint indicates that the earliest event time at node 1 (x_1) plus the normal activity time (12 weeks) cannot exceed the earliest event time at node 2 (x_2). This is the same basic formulation of earliest event times as was presented at the start of this chapter: $ET_j = ET_i + t_{ij}$. To reflect the fact that this activity can be crashed, it is necessary only to subtract the amount by which it can be crashed from the left-hand side of the above constraint.

amount activity $1 \to 2$ can be crashed

$$x_1 + 12 - \boxed{y_{12}} \leq x_2$$

This revised constraint now indicates that the earliest event time at node 2 (x_2) is determined not only by the earliest event time at node 1 plus the activity time, but also by the amount the activity is crashed. Each activity in the network must have a similar constraint, as follows.

$$
\begin{aligned}
x_1 + 12 - y_{12} &\leq x_2 \\
x_2 + 8 - y_{23} &\leq x_3 \\
x_2 + 4 - y_{24} &\leq x_4 \\
x_3 + 0 - y_{34} &\leq x_4 \\
x_4 + 4 - y_{45} &\leq x_5 \\
x_4 + 12 - y_{46} &\leq x_6 \\
x_5 + 4 - y_{56} &\leq x_6 \\
x_6 + 4 - y_{67} &\leq x_7
\end{aligned}
$$

Finally, we must indicate the project duration we are seeking (i.e., the crashed project time). Because the housing contractor wants to crash the project from the 36-week normal critical path time to 30 weeks, our final model constraint specifies that the earliest event time at node 7 should not exceed 30 weeks:

Constraint for network crash time

$$x_7 \leq 30$$

A summary of this linear programming model for project crashing and the model solution are shown in the following LINDO/PC computer package output.

```
: look all

MIN      400 Y12 + 500 Y23 + 3000 Y24 + 200 Y45 + 7000 Y46 + 200 Y56
    + 7000 Y67
SUBJECT TO
        2)    Y12 <=     5
        3)    Y23 <=     3
        4)    Y24 <=     1
        5)    Y34 <=     0
        6)    Y45 <=     3
        7)    Y46 <=     3
        8)    Y56 <=     3
        9)    Y67 <=     1
       10)    Y12 + X2 - X1 >=     12
       11)    Y23 - X2 + X3 >=     8
       12)    Y24 - X2 + X4 >=     4
       13)    Y34 - X3 + X4 >=     0
       14)    Y45 - X4 + X5 >=     4
       15)    Y46 - X4 + X6 >=     12
       16)    Y56 - X5 + X6 >=     4
       17)    Y67 - X6 + X7 >=     4
       18)    X7 <=     30
END
:

            OBJECTIVE FUNCTION VALUE
    1)        2500.00000
    VARIABLE          VALUE             REDUCED COST
        Y12          5.000000              .000000
        Y23          1.000000              .000000
        Y24           .000000          3000.000000
        Y45           .000000           200.000000
        Y46           .000000          6500.000000
        Y56           .000000           200.000000
        Y67           .000000          6500.000000
        Y34           .000000              .000000
        X2           7.000000              .000000
        X1            .000000           500.000000
        X3          14.000000              .000000
        X4          14.000000              .000000
        X5          18.000000              .000000
        X6          26.000000              .000000
        X7          30.000000              .000000
```

This computer output indicates that $x_7 = 30$, which is the project duration crashed by the amount the contractor specified. Observing the solution values for the y_{ij} variables, we see that $y_{12} = 5$ and $y_{23} = 1$; the rest of the y_{ij} variables equal zero. This means that activity $1 \rightarrow 2$ has been crashed by 5 weeks and activity $2 \rightarrow 3$ has been crashed by 1 week, and none of the other activities have been crashed at all. The crash cost, referred to as the objective function value, is $2,500. The earliest event times for each activity for the crashed network are given by the x_i values. Notice that this is the same crashing solution we achieved earlier by the manual crashing procedure.

Another interesting application of linear programming is determining the cost of crashing the network by the maximum amount. The maximum amount a network can be crashed can be determined by assigning the maximum allowable crash time for each activity in the network and then computing the critical path time. For our example networks with total crash times for each activity, the critical path time is 24 weeks. In order to determine the cost of crashing the network to 24 weeks, only the final constraint in our model needs to be changed from $x_7 \leq 30$ to $x_7 \leq 24$. Solving this revised linear programming model using the LINDO/PC computer package results in the following computer output and solution.

Crashing the maximum amount

Alterations in the crashing model formulation

```
: look all

MIN      400 Y12 + 500 Y23 + 3000 Y24 + 200 Y45 + 7000 Y46 + 200 Y56
       + 7000 Y67
SUBJECT TO
        2)    Y12 <=    5
        3)    Y23 <=    3
        4)    Y24 <=    1
        5)    Y34 <=    0
        6)    Y45 <=    3
        7)    Y46 <=    3
        8)    Y56 <=    3
        9)    Y67 <=    1
       10)    Y12 + X2 - X1 >=    12
       11)    Y23 - X2 + X3 >=    8
       12)    Y24 - X2 + X4 >=    4
       13)    Y34 - X3 + X4 >=    0
       14)    Y45 - X4 + X5 >=    4
       15)    Y46 - X4 + X6 >=    12
       16)    Y56 - X5 + X6 >=    4
       17)    Y67 - X6 + X7 >=    4
       18)    X7 <=    24
END
:
          OBJECTIVE FUNCTION VALUE

     1)       31500.0000

     VARIABLE         VALUE          REDUCED COST
         Y12         5.000000            .000000
         Y23         3.000000            .000000
         Y24          .000000         3000.000000
         Y45          .000000          200.000000
         Y46         3.000000            .000000
         Y56          .000000          200.000000
         Y67         1.000000            .000000
         Y34          .000000            .000000
          X2         7.000000            .000000
          X1          .000000         7000.000000
          X3        12.000000            .000000
          X4        12.000000            .000000
          X5        16.000000            .000000
          X6        21.000000            .000000
          X7        24.000000            .000000
```

This computer output indicates that the cost of crashing the network to 24 weeks is $31,500. The total normal cost of constructing the house in 36 weeks is $75,000, so it would cost a total of $106,500 (i.e., $75,000 + 31,500) to complete the house in 24 weeks. The computer output shows that only activities $1 \rightarrow 2$, $2 \rightarrow 3$, $4 \rightarrow 6$, and $6 \rightarrow 7$ were crashed, since all other y_{ij} variables equal zero. This result illustrates that it is not necessary to incur the cost of crashing all activities in the network in order to crash the network the maximum amount possible.

AREAS OF APPLICATION OF CPM/PERT ANALYSIS

It was indicated at the beginning of this chapter that CPM/PERT network analysis is one of the most popular of all management science techniques. In the survey results on the usage and application of management science techniques, presented in Chapter 1, network analysis and CPM/PERT ranked behind only linear programming and simulation in frequency of use (see Tables 1.1 and 1.2).

The first formal documented application of PERT network analysis was in 1958, when PERT was applied as a management control procedure for the development of the Navy's Polaris missile system. (CPM was developed independently by another research group at approximately the same time.) Since that time CPM/PERT has been applied in a variety of government agencies concerned with project control, including various military agencies, NASA, the Federal Aviation Agency (FAA), and the General Services Administration (GSA). These agencies are frequently involved in large-scale projects involving millions of dollars and many subcontractors. Examples of such governmental projects include the development of weapons systems, aircraft, and such NASA space exploration projects as the Space Shuttle. It has become a common practice for these agencies to require subcontractors to develop and use a CPM/PERT analysis in order to maintain management control of the myriad of project components and subprojects.

CPM/PERT has also been widely applied in the private sector. Two of the major areas of application of CPM/PERT in the private sector have been research and development and construction. CPM/PERT has been applied to various R&D projects, such as developing new drugs, planning and introducing new products, and developing new and more powerful computer systems. CPM/PERT analysis has been particularly applicable to construction projects. Almost every type of construction project—from building a house to constructing a major sports stadium to building a ship to constructing the Alaska oil pipeline—has been the subject to network analysis.

Network analysis is also applicable to the planning and scheduling of major events, such as summit conferences, sports festivals, basketball tournaments, football bowl games, parades, political conventions, school registrations, or rock concerts.

Scheduling major events

This brief review of the various applications of CPM/PERT analysis indicates the broad popularity of this technique. One of the factors contributing to this popularity is that CPM/PERT can be easily understood by the layperson, primarily because the network provides a picture of what is occurring. Unlike some of the other management science techniques presented in this text, CPM/PERT networks are easily recognized and understood by most people. In addition, the benefits accruing from network analysis are readily apparent. CPM/PERT analysis provides a logical procedure for the often complex task of identifying and organizing the activities of a project.

Popularity of CPM and PERT

Project Management Software for the Personal Computer

A recent article by Wasil and Assad reported that during the period from 1985 to 1988, the number of commercially available project management software packages for personal computers increased from a few to over 100, and the cost of these packages ranged from several hundred to several thousand dollars. Total sales for these packages have been estimated at $51 million for 1987 alone. These figures indicate that project management has become probably the most visible and widely used management science technique. Some of the more popular packages include Harvard Total Project Manager, Microsoft Project, Super Project Plus, and Time Line (all of which are at the lower end of the cost scale), MacProject, Project Manager Workbench, Super Project Plus, OPEN PLAN, and PROMIS. The types of projects that such software packages have been applied to include the construction of a sawmill, installation of software systems at hospitals, departmental reorganizations, development of a communications satellite, military projects, facility and employee relocation, and highway construction. In addition, a number of applications have incorporated the use of project management within management information systems. The availability of powerful, user-friendly, project management software packages for the personal computer will only serve to increase the use of this technique.[1]

---

[1]E. Wasil and A. Assad, "Project Management on the PC: Software, Applications, and Trends," *Interfaces* 18, no. 2 (March–April 1988): 75–84.

Summary

In this chapter we discussed two of the most popular management science techniques—CPM and PERT networks. Their popularity is due primarily to the fact that a network forms a picture of the system under analysis that is easy for a manager to interpret. Sometimes it is difficult to explain a set of mathematical equations to a manager, but a network can often be easily explained.

CPM and PERT differ in how activity times are determined. In a CPM network, single (certain) activity times are used; in a PERT network, probabilistic activity times are used. At first glance, it is tempting to use only the PERT approach, as it seems more realistic to assume probabilistic activity times. However, PERT is subject to several limitations. First, it is often difficult to generate three accurate activity time estimates for the beta distribution. There is a strong tendency for the estimator to be conservative and to give a pessimistic time that is too high. Second, the PERT statistical results have been attacked as not always being theoretically correct. In general, such reservations have not diminished the popularity of PERT, as most people feel its usefulness far outweighs any theoretical drawbacks. (For a more thorough explanation of these theoretical difficulties, the reader should consult the references at the end of this chapter.)

Limitations of CPM and PERT

References

Lee, Sang M.; Moore, Laurence J.; and Taylor, Bernard W. *Management Science.* 3d ed. Boston: Allyn and Bacon, 1990.

Levy, F.; Thompson, G.; and Wiest, J. "The ABC's of the Critical Path Method." *Harvard Business Review* 41, no. 5 (October 1963).

Moder, J.; Phillips, C. R.; and Davis, E. W. *Project Management with CPM and PERT and Precedence Diagramming.* 3d ed. New York: Van Nostrand Reinhold, 1983.

O'Brian, J. *CPM in Construction Management.* New York: McGraw-Hill, 1965.

Wiest, J. D., and Levy, F. K. *A Management Guide to PERT/CPM.* 2d ed. Englewood Cliffs, N.J.: Prentice-Hall, 1977.

EXAMPLE PROBLEM SOLUTION

The following example will illustrate PERT network analysis and probability analysis.

Problem Statement

Given the following network and PERT activity time estimates, determine the expected project completion time and variance, and the probability that the project will be completed in 40 days or less.

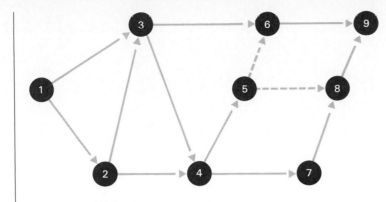

Activity	Time Estimates (days)		
	a	m	b
1 → 2	5	8	17
1 → 3	3	12	15
2 → 3	4	7	10
2 → 4	5	8	23
3 → 4	1	1	1
3 → 6	1	4	13
4 → 5	3	6	9
4 → 7	1	2.5	7
7 → 8	1	1	1
6 → 9	2	2	2
8 → 9	5	8	11

Step 1: Compute the Expected Activity Times and Variances

Using the following formulas, compute the expected time and variance for each activity.

$$t = \frac{a + 4m + b}{6}$$

$$v = \left(\frac{b - a}{6}\right)^2$$

For example, the expected time and variance for activity $1 \to 2$ are

$$t = \frac{5 + 4(8) + 17}{6} = 9$$

$$v = \left(\frac{17 - 5}{6}\right)^2 = 4$$

These values and the remaining expected times and variances for each activity are shown below.

Activity	t	v
1 → 2	9	4
1 → 3	11	4
2 → 3	7	1
2 → 4	10	9
3 → 4	1	0
3 → 6	5	4
4 → 5	6	1
4 → 7	3	1
7 → 8	1	0
6 → 9	2	0
8 → 9	8	1

Step 2: Determine the Earliest and Latest Time at Each Node

The earliest and latest time at each node and the activity slack are shown on the following network.

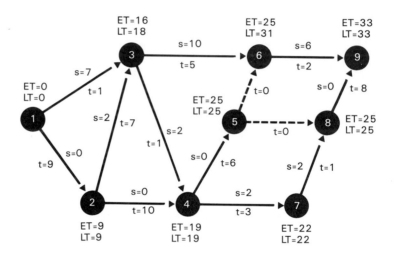

Step 3: Identify the Critical Path and Compute Expected Project Completion Time and Variance

Observing the network above and those activities with no slack (i.e., $s = 0$), we can identify the critical path as $1 \rightarrow 2 \rightarrow 4 \rightarrow 5 \rightarrow 8 \rightarrow 9$. The expected project completion time (t_p) is 33 days. The variance is computed by summing the variances for the activities in the critical path:

$$v_p = 4 + 9 + 1 + 1$$
$$= 15 \text{ days}$$

Step 4: Determine the Probability that the Project Will Be Completed in 40 Days or Less

The following normal probability distribution describes the probability analysis.

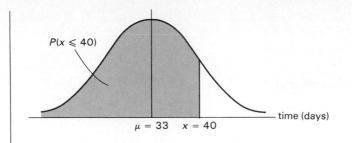

Compute Z using the following formula.

$$Z = \frac{x - \mu}{\sigma}$$

$$= \frac{40 - 33}{\sqrt{15}}$$

$$= 1.81$$

The corresponding probability from Table A.1 in Appendix A is .4649; thus,

$$P(x \leq 40) = .9649$$

Problems

1. Construct the CPM network described by the following set of activities, compute the length of each path in the network, and indicate the critical path.

Activity	Time (weeks)
1 → 2	5
1 → 3	4
2 → 4	3
3 → 4	6

2. Construct the CPM network described by the following set of activities, compute the length of each path in the network, and indicate the critical path.

Activity	Time (weeks)
1 → 2	3
1 → 3	7
2 → 4	2
3 → 4	5
3 → 5	6
4 → 6	1
5 → 6	4

3. Construct the CPM network described by the following set of activities, compute the length of each path in the network, and indicate the critical path.

Activity	Time (months)
1 → 2	4
1 → 3	7
2 → 4	8
2 → 5	3
3 → 5	9
4 → 5	5
4 → 6	2
5 → 6	6
3 → 6	5

4. Identify all of the paths in the following network, computer the length of each, and indicate the critical path. (Activity times are in weeks.)

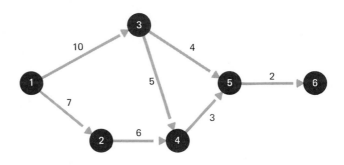

5. For the network in problem 4, determine the earliest event time, latest event time, and slack for each activity. Indicate how the critical path would be determined from this information.

6. Given the following network with activity times in months, determine the earliest event time, latest event time, and slack for each activity. Indicate the critical path and the project duration.

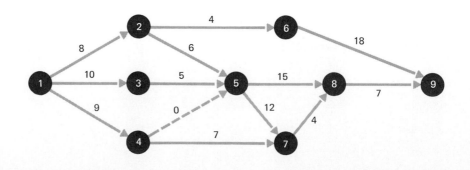

7. Given the following network with activity times in weeks, determine the earliest event time, latest event time, and slack for each activity. Indicate the critical path and the project duration.

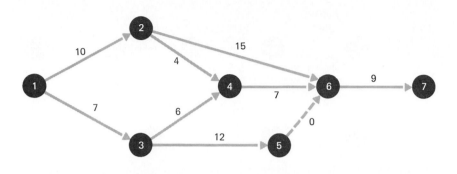

8. In one of the little known battles of the Civil War, General Tecumseh Beauregard lost the Third Battle of Bull Run because his preparations were not complete when the enemy attacked. If the critical path method had been available, the general could have planned better. Suppose that the following planning network with activity times in days had been available. Determine the earliest event times, latest event times, and activity slack for the network. Indicate the critical path and the time between the general's receipt of battle orders and the onset of battle.

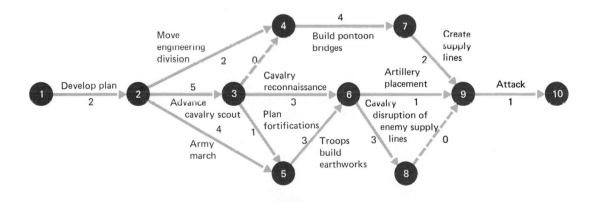

9. A group of developers is building a new shopping center. A consultant for the developers has constructed the CPM network shown on page 738 and assigned activity times in weeks. Determine the earliest event times, latest event times, activity slack, critical path, and duration for the project.

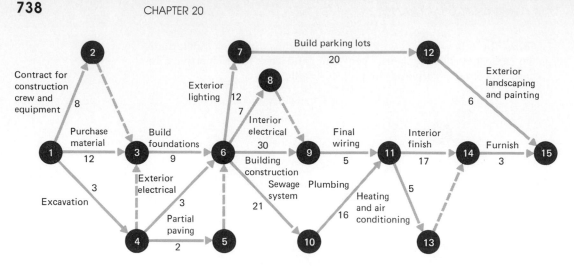

10. A farm owner is going to erect a maintenance building with a connecting electrical generator and water tank. The activities, activity descriptions, and estimated durations are given in the following table. (Notice that the activities are defined not by node numbers, but by activity descriptions. This alternative form of expressing activities and precedence relationships is often used in CPM.)

Activity	Activity Description	Activity Predecessor	Activity Duration (weeks)
a	Excavate	—	2
b	Erect building	a	6
c	Install generator	a	4
d	Install tank	a	2
e	Install maintenance equipment	b	4
f	Connect generator and tank to building	b, c, d	5
g	Paint on a finish	b	3
h	Check out facility	e, f	2

Construct the network for this project, identify the critical path, and determine the project duration time.

11. Given the following network and PERT activity time estimates, determine the expected time and variance for each activity and indicate the critical path.

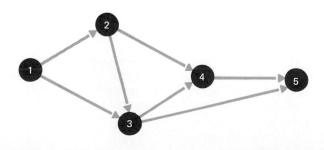

Activity	Time Estimates (weeks)		
	a	m	b
1 → 2	5	8	17
1 → 3	7	10	13
2 → 3	3	5	7
2 → 4	1	3	5
3 → 4	4	6	8
3 → 5	3	3	3
4 → 5	3	4	5

12. Given the following network and PERT activity time estimates, determine the expected time and variance for each activity and indicate the critical path.

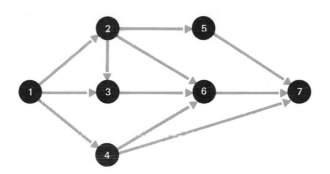

Activity	Time Estimates (weeks)		
	a	m	b
1 → 2	6	10	15
1 → 3	2	7	16
1 → 4	4	8	11
2 → 3	3	10	15
2 → 5	7	9	20
2 → 6	4	12	15
3 → 6	3	6	9
4 → 6	5	9	16
5 → 7	3	20	35
4 → 7	4	12	16
6 → 7	2	9	14

13. The following PERT activity time estimates are for the network in problem 6.

Activity	Time Estimates (months)		
	a	m	b
1 → 2	4	8	12
1 → 3	6	10	15
1 → 4	2	10	14
2 → 5	3	6	9
2 → 6	1	4	13
3 → 5	3	6	18
4 → 5	0	0	0
4 → 7	2	8	12
5 → 8	9	15	22
5 → 7	5	12	21
7 → 8	5	6	12
6 → 9	7	20	25
8 → 9	3	8	20

Determine the following:

a. Expected activity times

b. Earliest event times

c. Latest event times

d. Activity slack

e. Critical path

f. Expected project duration and variance

14. The following PERT activity time estimates are for the network in problem 8.

Activity	Time Estimates (days)		
	a	m	b
1 → 2	1	2	6
2 → 4	1	3	5
2 → 3	3	5	10
2 → 5	3	6	14
3 → 4	0	0	0
3 → 5	1	1.5	2
3 → 6	2	3	7
4 → 7	2	4	9
5 → 6	1	3	5
7 → 9	1	2	3
6 → 9	1	1	5
6 → 8	2	4	9
8 → 9	0	0	0
9 → 10	1	1	1

Determine the following:
a. Expected activity times
b. Earliest event times
c. Latest event times
d. Activity slack
e. Critical path
f. Expected project duration and variance

15. The Nevada Highway Department has developed the following PERT network and activity time estimates for a highway construction project.

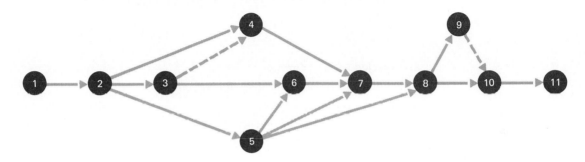

Activity	Time Estimates (months)		
	a	m	b
1 → 2	1	3	5
2 → 4	3	4	5
2 → 3	4	6	10
2 → 5	3	5	7
3 → 4	0	0	0
3 → 6	2	4	8
4 → 7	1	2	5
6 → 7	2	2	2
5 → 6	1	1	1
5 → 7	4	7	16
5 → 8	6	8	16
7 → 8	1	4	7
8 → 9	2	3	4
8 → 10	1	2	3
9 → 10	0	0	0
10 → 11	1	1	1

Determine the following:
a. Expected activity times
b. Earliest and latest event times
c. Activity slack
d. Critical path
e. Expected project duration and variance

16. The Stone River Textile Mill was inspected by OSHA and was found to be in violation of a number of safety regulations. The OSHA inspectors ordered the mill to alter some existing machinery to make it safer (i.e., add safety guards, etc.); purchase some new machinery to replace older, dangerous machinery; and relocate some machinery to make safer passages and unobstructed entrances and exits. OSHA gave the mill only 35 weeks to make the changes; if the changes were not made by then, the mill would be fined $300,000.

   The mill determined the activities in a PERT network that would have to be completed and then estimated the indicated activity times, as shown below.

   Construct the PERT network for this project and determine the following:

   a. Expected activity times

   b. Earliest and latest event times and activity slack

   c. Critical path

   d. Expected project duration and variance

   e. The probability that the mill will be fined $300,000

Activity	Description	Time Estimates (weeks)		
		a	m	b
1 → 2	Order new machinery	1	2	3
1 → 3	Plan new physical layout	2	5	8
1 → 4	Determine safety changes in existing machinery	1	3	5
2 → 6	Receive equipment	4	10	25
2 → 5	Hire new employees	3	7	12
3 → 7	Make plant alterations	10	15	25
4 → 8	Make changes in existing machinery	5	9	14
5 → 6	Dummy	0	0	0
6 → 7	Dummy	0	0	0
7 → 8	Dummy	0	0	0
6 → 9	Train new employees	2	3	7
7 → 9	Install new machinery	1	4	6
8 → 9	Relocate old machinery	2	5	10
9 → 10	Conduct employee safety orientation	2	2	2

17. The student center at State University has unexpectedly found out that the famous rock group Thunder and Lightning has had a cancellation and can appear at State. However, the concert will be scheduled for a date only 18 days in the future; therefore, the center must prepare quickly. The center has determined the following activities of a PERT network and estimated the activity times.

Activity	Description	Time Estimates (days)		
		a	m	b
1 → 2	Secure auditorium	2	4	7
1 → 3	Hire preliminary concert act	4	5	8
2 → 3	Print tickets	1	2	4
2 → 4	Make hotel and transportation arrangements	3	5	10
2 → 5	Complete employee union negotiations	1	3	8
5 → 6	Hire stagehands	2	4	7
5 → 7	Hire ushers	1	3	5
4 → 9	Arrange press conference	2	3	4
6 → 9	Set up stage	2	3	6
7 → 9	Assign ushers	1	2	3
3 → 9	Do advertising and promotion	2	6	12
3 → 8	Sell tickets	1	5	12
8 → 9	Dummy	0	0	0

Construct a PERT network and determine the following:

a. Expected activity times

b. Earliest and latest event times

c. Critical path

d. Expected project duration and variance

e. The probability that the concert preparations will be completed in time

18. On May 21, 1927, Charles Lindbergh landed at Le Bourget Field in Paris, completing his famous transatlantic solo flight. The preparation period prior to his flight was quite hectic and time was very critical, since several other famous pilots of the day were also planning transatlantic flights. Once Ryan Aircraft was contacted to build the *Spirit of St. Louis*, it took only a little over $2\frac{1}{2}$ months to construct the plane and fly it to New York for the takeoff. If CPM/PERT had been available to Charles Lindbergh, it no doubt would have been useful in helping him plan this project. Use your imagination and assume that a CPM/PERT network with the following estimated activity times was developed for the flight.

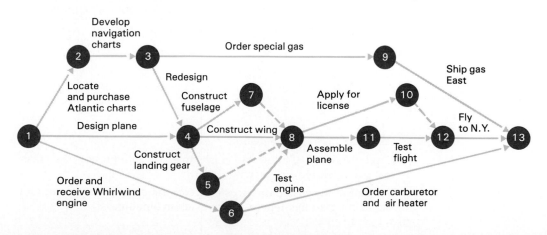

Activity	Time Estimates (days)		
	a	m	b
1 → 2	1	3	5
1 → 4	4	6	10
1 → 6	20	35	50
2 → 3	4	7	12
3 → 4	2	3	5
4 → 7	8	12	25
4 → 8	10	16	21
4 → 5	5	9	15
3 → 9	6	8	14
6 → 8	1	2	2
6 → 13	5	8	12
8 → 10	5	10	15
8 → 11	4	7	10
9 → 13	5	7	12
11 → 12	5	9	20
12 → 13	1	3	7

Determine the expected project duration and variance and the probability of completing the project in 67 days.

19. For the PERT network in problem 13, determine the probability that the network duration will exceed 50 months.

20. In the Third Battle of Bull Run, for which a PERT network was developed in problem 8, General Beauregard would have won if his preparations had been completed in 15 days. What would the probability of General Beauregard's winning the battle have been?

21. The following table provides the information necessary to construct a project network and project crash data.

Activity	(i, j)	Predecessor	Activity Time (weeks)		Activity Cost ($)	
			Normal	Crash	Normal	Crash
a	(1,2)	—	20	8	$1,000	$1,480
b	(1,4)	—	24	20	1,200	1,400
c	(1,3)	—	14	7	700	1,190
d	(2,4)	a	10	6	500	820
e	(3,4)	c	11	5	550	730

a. Construct the project network.

b. Compute the total allowable crash time per activity and the crash cost per week for each activity.

c. Determine the maximum possible crash time for the network and manually crash the network the maximum amount.

d. Compute the normal project cost and the cost of the crashed project.

e. Formulate the general linear programming model for this network.

f. Formulate the linear programming crashing model that would crash this network by the maximum amount.

22. The following table provides the information necessary to construct a project network and project crash data.

Activity	(i, j)	Predecessor	Activity Time (weeks)		Activity Cost ($)	
			Normal	Crash	Normal	Crash
a	(1,2)	—	16	8	$2,000	$4,400
b	(1,3)	—	14	9	1,000	1,800
c	(2,4)	a	8	6	500	700
d	(2,5)	a	5	4	600	1,300
e	(3,5)	b	4	2	1,500	3,000
f	(3,6)	b	6	4	800	1,600
g	(4,6)	c	10	7	3,000	4,500
h	(5,6)	d,e	15	10	5,000	8,000

a. Construct the project network.

b. Manually crash the network to 28 weeks.

c. Formulate the general linear programming model for this network.

d. Formulate the linear programming crashing model that would crash this model by the maximum amount.

23. Formulate the general linear programming model for problem 4.

24. Formulate the general linear programming model for the project network for installing an order processing system shown in Figure 20.12.

25. In problem 11, assume that the most likely times (m) are the normal activity times and the optimistic times (a) are the activity crash times. Further assume that the activities have the following normal and crash costs.

Activity	Costs (normal cost, crash cost)
$1 \rightarrow 2$	($100, 400)
$1 \rightarrow 3$	($250, 400)
$2 \rightarrow 3$	($400, 800)
$2 \rightarrow 4$	($200, 400)
$3 \rightarrow 4$	($150, 300)
$3 \rightarrow 5$	($100, 100)
$4 \rightarrow 5$	($300, 500)

a. Formulate the general linear programming model for this project network using expected activity times (t).

b. Formulate the linear programming crashing model that would crash this network by the maximum amount.

21

Dynamic Programming

In Chapter 19, Network Flow Models, we analyzed networks in *stages* to determine the shortest route through the network. That is, we determined the shortest of several routes to a particular node, then we determined the shortest route from this node to another node, and so on, until we reached the last node in the network. This process of analyzing a network in sequential stages instead of all at once is a potentially useful solution approach that can be applied to topics other than networks. Dynamic programming is a solution approach based on the principle of solving problems in *stages*.

Dynamic programming is a unique approach that you will find to be quite different from the other techniques presented in this text. One difference is that dynamic programming is a solution *approach* and not a technique (such as the simplex method in linear program-

A solution approach rather than a specific technique

747

ming). In fact, dynamic programming often uses other techniques within its overall solution approach. Because it is an approach and not a technique, it is not limited to certain classes of problems, as a technique often is. Thus, dynamic programming is applicable to a wide variety of problems. In this chapter we will present the basic fundamentals of the dynamic programming solution approach through several popular examples of dynamic programming.

THE DYNAMIC PROGRAMMING SOLUTION APPROACH

Breaking down a problem into stages

The solution approach encompassed by dynamic programming is to break down a problem into smaller subproblems called *stages* and then solve these stages sequentially. The outcome of a decision (i.e., the solution) at one stage will affect the decision made at the next stage in the sequence. This process is very difficult to visualize from a written description; therefore, we will demonstrate the dynamic programming solution approach within the context of an example problem.

A dynamic programming example

The Wood Valley Cosmetics Company has subdivided its sales area into 3 regions—north, east, and south. The company has 3 salespeople it wants to allocate to these 3 regions. The company wants to allocate these salespeople in a manner that will result in maximum dollar sales. To achieve this objective in the most efficient manner, the company will not restrict the number of salespeople that can be assigned to any one region. In the extreme case, all 3 salespeople could be assigned to one region.

The sales returns that will be generated in each region from each possible combination of salespeople are shown in Table 21.1.

TABLE 21.1

Sales Return for Combinations of Salespeople per Region

Decision Alternatives Salespeople/Territory	Return for Each Territory ($1,000s)		
	North	East	South
0	$ 0	$ 0	$ 2
1	7	9	6
2	12	15	10
3	20	18	16

Table 21.1 shows that no sales will be made in the north and east regions if no salespeople are assigned to these regions. However, in the southern region, $2,000 in sales will result from direct customer-

to-company orders even without any salespeople in the field. If all 3 salespeople are assigned to the eastern region, sales of $18,000 will occur; and if all 3 salespeople are allocated to the southern region, sales of $16,000 will result. An allocation of 2 salespeople to the northern region and 1 salesperson to the southern region will result in sales of $18,000.

The objective of this problem is to maximize total sales subject to the limited number of salespeople available to be allocated to the 3 regions. We can express this problem statement mathematically as

maximize $R_1 + R_2 + R_3$

subject to

$D_1 + D_2 + D_3 \leq 3$

where

$R_1, R_2,$ and $R_3 = returns$ (i.e., sales) from each of the 3 regions

$D_1, D_2,$ and $D_3 = decisions$ to assign a number of salespeople to each of the 3 regions

As noted at the beginning of this section, the dynamic programming solution approach is to subdivide a problem into smaller subproblems called *stages*. The stages of our example problem correspond to the 3 regions to which we can allocate salespeople. We will solve for the best solution at each stage (i.e., region), which will, in turn, be used as an input into the next stage of the problem.

Stage 1—Allocation to the Southern Region

We will *arbitrarily* select the southern region as the *first stage* of our problem. The decision at the first stage is how many salespeople to allocate to this region. In dynamic programming we assume that the stage 1 decision is the final decision of a sequence of decisions. Therefore, if we consider the other 2 regions as the second and third stages, then the decision at stage 1 is based on how many salespeople *might already have been allocated to the other 2 regions*. That is, either 0, 1, 2, or 3 salespeople can be allocated to the southern region, depending on how many might already have been allocated to the other 2 regions. The possible stage 1 allocations are shown in Table 21.2.

Observing Table 21.2, we see that if no (zero) salespeople are available (which means all 3 salespeople have been allocated to the other two regions), then the *decision* at stage 1 is to allocate zero salespeople to the southern region. This decision results in a return of $2,000. If 1 salesperson is available, then either 0 or 1 salesperson can be allocated, with a corresponding return of $2,000 or $6,000. If 2 salespeople are available, then 0, 1, or 2 salespeople can be allo-

TABLE 21.2

Stage 1 (Southern Region): Decision
Alternatives for Each State

State 1 (S_1): Salespeople Available	Decision 1 (D_1): Salespeople to Allocate	Return 1 (R_1): Amount of Sales
0	0	$ 2
1	0	2
	1	6
2	0	2
	1	6
	2	10
3	0	2
	1	6
	2	10
	3	16

System state at each stage

The best decision for each possible state

cated to the southern region, and if 3 salespeople are available, 0, 1, 2, or 3 salespeople can be allocated.

Notice in Table 21.2 the use of symbolic notation that is common to dynamic programming: S_1, D_1, and R_1. S_1 represents the *state of the system* at stage 1. The states of the system for this problem are the number of salespeople available to be allocated to each region. As can be seen from Table 21.2, a stage contains several possible state values. D_1 represents the decision at stage 1; R_1 is the return at stage 1 for each decision.

The next step in the dynamic programming solution approach is to determine the *best decision for each possible state*. The best decision at each state is the one that results in the *greatest return*. The best decisions for stage 1, in terms of the number of salespeople to allocate given each state (the salespeople available), are shown in Table 21.3.

TABLE 21.3

Stage 1: Optimal Decisions for Each State

State 1 (S_1): Salespeople Available	Decision 1 (D_1): Salespeople to Allocate	Return 1 (R_1): Amount of Sales
0	0	$ 2*
1	0	2
	1	6*
2	0	2
	1	6
	2	10*
3	0	2
	1	6
	2	10
	3	16*

In Table 21.3, the best decision for each state and the corresponding return are shaded and designated by asterisks (*). There is only one possible decision if no salespeople are available; therefore, it must be the best decision. If 1 salesperson is available, then the best decision is to allocate 1 salesperson to the southern region; if 2 or 3 salespeople are available, 2 or 3 should be allocated, respectively. *These decisions for the various states at stage 1 will subsequently be used as input for the set of decisions at stage 2.*

Stage 1 decisions will be used as inputs to determine stage 2 decisions

Stage 2—Allocation to the Eastern Region

Now that the best decisions for stage 1 have been determined, we move to stage 2 in the solution approach, which we will arbitrarily designate as the allocation of salespeople to the eastern region.

The stage 2 decision choices and states are basically the same as those for stage 1. However, the best decision for each state is not determined in the same way. The states and decisions for stage 2 are shown in Table 21.4.

TABLE 21.4

Stage 2 (Eastern Region): Decision Alternatives for Each State

State 2 (S_2): Salespeople Available	Decision 2 (D_2): Salespeople to Allocate	Return 2 (R_2): Amount of Sales	State 1 (S_1): Salespeople Available at Stage 1	Return (R_1) for Best State 1 Decision	Total Return: $R_1 + R_2$
0	0	$ 0	0	$ 2	$ 2
1	0	0	1	6	6
	1	9	0	2	11
2	0	0	2	10	10
	1	9	1	6	15
	2	15	0	2	17
3	0	0	3	16	16
	1	9	2	10	19
	2	15	1	6	21
	3	18	0	2	20

The states (S_2) for stage 2 are the same as those for stage 1. In other words, we will assume that *depending on what might have occurred at stage 3* (the northern region), either 0, 1, 2, or 3 salespeople can be allocated to the eastern region. The decision alternatives for each state are also the same as those for stage 1. For example, if 2 salespeople are available to be allocated in the eastern region (i.e., 2 are left over from previous allocations), then *either 0, 1, or 2 can be*

Interpreting the stage 2 states

allocated. The returns (labeled R_2) for each of these possible decisions are $0, $9,000, and $15,000 (from Table 21.1). This information is presented in the first three columns of Table 21.4.

The fourth column in Table 21.4 reflects the number of salespeople remaining to be allocated at stage 1 *given the allocation at stage 2*. For example, if 0 salespeople are available at stage 2, then 0 salespeople are available at stage 1 (as shown in column 4). If 1 salesperson is available at stage 2 and 0 salespeople are allocated at stage 2, then 1 salesperson is available at stage 1. Alternatively, if the 1 salesperson available at stage 2 is allocated at stage 2, this leaves 0 salespeople available at stage 1. Thus, we can see that the number of salespeople available at stage 1 is a function of *both the salespeople available at stage 2 and the decision at stage 2*.

A transition function

This relationship between the stages of a problem is referred to as a *transition function*. The transition function defines how the stages of a dynamic programming model are interrelated. Given a stage n, the functional relationship between the states in this stage and the previous stage states can be expressed mathematically as

$$S_{n-1} = S_n - D_n$$

where (you will recall) S_n and D_n are the state and the decision, respectively, at stage n.

For example, if the state at stage 2 (S_2) equals 3 available salespeople and the decision is to allocate 2 salespeople, then the remaining state at stage 1 is determined as follows:

$$S_{n-1} = S_n - D_n$$
$$S_1 = S_2 - D_2$$
$$S_1 = 3 - 2$$
$$S_1 = 1 \text{ salesperson}$$

This result can be seen in Table 21.4. If $S_2 = 3$ (the available salespeople) and 2 are allocated, then only 1 salesperson is available to be allocated at stage 1.

The fifth column in Table 21.4 shows the return for *the best decision* given a state at stage 1 (S_1). Calculating this return requires that we observe both stages simultaneously. For example, we saw above that if 3 salespeople are available at stage 2, a decision to allocate 2 salespeople will result in 1 salesperson's being available at stage 1. A look at Table 21.3 (stage 1) reveals that the best decision *given 1 salesperson* ($S_1 = 1$) is to allocate 1 salesperson, which results in a return of $6,000.

Now we must add this $6,000 to the return at stage 2 of $15,000, which will result in a total return of $21,000 for this combination of decisions — the allocation of 2 salespeople to the eastern region and 1 salesperson to the southern region. This value is shown in the last column of Table 21.4. This total accumulated return is referred to as the *recursive return*. The recursive return function is the return at stage n plus the sum of returns for previous decisions. Mathematically it is expressed as

The recursive return function

$$\text{Total recursive return} = R_n + R_{n-1} + R_{n-2} + \cdots + R_1$$

Next we select the decision that results in the *best total return* for each state at stage 2. These four best decisions are shaded and marked by asterisks in Table 21.5.

Selecting the best decision for each stage 2 state

TABLE 21.5
Stage 2: Optimal Decision for Each State

State 2 (S_2): Salespeople Available	Decision 2 (D_2): Salespeople to Allocate	Return 2 (R_2): Amount of Sales	State 1 (S_1): Salespeople Available at Stage 1	Return (R_1) for Best State 1 Decision	Total Return: $R_1 + R_2$
0	0	$ 0	0	$ 2	$ 2*
1	0	0	1	6	6
	1	9	0	2	11*
2	0	0	2	10	10
	1	9	1	6	15
	2	15	0	2	17*
3	0	0	3	16	16
	1	9	2	10	19
	2	15	1	6	21*
	3	18	0	2	20

The optimal decisions for each state at both stage 2 and stage 1 have now been determined. This process is referred to as *stage optimization*.

Stage optimization

Stage 3—Allocation to the Northern Region

We now have only stage 3 to consider—the allocation of salespeople to the northern region. Stage 3 actually reflects the first decision regarding the allocation of salespeople. In other words, at stage 3 we assume that all 3 salespeople are available to be allocated. This situation is shown in Table 21.6 on page 754.

The last stage reflects the first actual decision

Notice in Table 21.6 that we are assuming that all 3 salespeople are available for allocation. The decision is how many of these 3 salespeople to allocate to this region. The returns (R_3) for each of the possible decisions (D_3) are from Table 21.1. The states for stage 2 (S_2) are determined from the transition function between stages 2 and 3.

All resources are available at stage 3

$$S_2 = S_3 - D_3$$

TABLE 21.6

Stage 3 (Northern Region): Decision Alternatives for Each State

State 3 (S_3): Salespeople Available	Decision 3 (D_3): Salespeople to Allocate	Return 3 (R_3): Amount of Sales	State 2 (S_2): Salespeople Available at Stage 2	Return ($R_1 + R_2$) for Best State 2 Decision	Total Return: ($R_1 + R_2$) + R_3
3	0	$ 0	3	$21	$21
	1	7	2	17	24
	2	12	1	11	23
	3	20	0	2	22

For example, since $S_3 = 3$, if we allocate 1 salesperson ($D_3 = 1$), then S_2 equals 2 salespeople, as shown in the fourth column of Table 21.6. The optimal return for each of the S_2 states is selected from Table 21.5. If 2 salespeople are available at stage 2 (which means 1 salesperson is allocated at stage 3), the best decision is to allocate 2, with a return of $17,000. This amount, added to the stage 3 return of $7,000, results in a recursive return value of $24,000. All four decisions and their recursive returns are determined similarly at stage 3, as shown in Table 21.6.

The optimal stage 3 decision

The optimal decision at stage 3 is the one that results in the maximum total recursive return. Since the maximum total return is $24,000, the best decision is to allocate 1 salesperson to the northern region, as shown in Table 21.7.

TABLE 21.7

Stage 3: Optimal Decision for State 3

State 3 (S_3): Salespeople Available	Decision 3 (D_3): Salespeople to Allocate	Return 3 (R_3): Amount of Sales	State 2 (S_2): Salespeople Available at Stage 2	Return 2 ($R_1 + R_2$) for Best State 2 Decision	Total Return: ($R_1 + R_2$) + R_3
3	0	$ 0	3	$21	$21
	1	7	2	17	24*
	2	12	1	11	23
	3	20	0	2	22

The sequence of optimal decisions

The optimal decision to allocate 1 salesperson to the northern region (stage 3) corresponds to a stage 2 decision to allocate 2 salespeople to the eastern region. Now, returning to Table 21.5, we see that if 2 salespeople are available at stage 2 ($S_2 = 2$) and 2 salespeople are allocated (the optimal decision for this state), then 0 salespeople are allocated to the southern region. This decision sequence is summarized as follows.

Summarizing the decision sequence

Stage (region)	Allocation of Salespeople	Return (sales)
1. South	0	$ 2,000
2. East	2	15,000
3. North	1	7,000
Totals	3 Salespeople	$24,000 Sales

The steps of the sequential decision process for this dynamic programming problem are illustrated in Figure 21.1. The nodes at each stage in Figure 21.1 correspond to the possible decisions at each stage. Notice that at stage 1 in Figure 21.1 there are 10 nodes reflecting the 10 possible decisions shown in Table 21.2. Thus, it is beneficial to analyze Figure 21.1 in conjunction with the tables representing each of the three stages of our problem.

Illustrating the sequential decision process

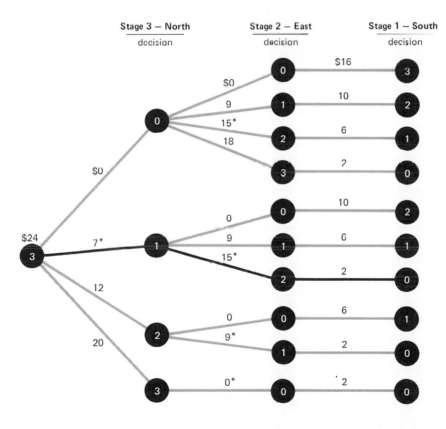

Stage 3 — North decision   Stage 2 — East decision   Stage 1 — South decision

FIGURE 21.1

Decision Network and Optimal Allocation for Salesperson Allocation Example

This completes our analysis of the use of the dynamic programming approach to solve our example problem of allocating salespeople to sales regions. The general solution steps, however, can be applied to all dynamic programming problems. Therefore, we will review the steps of the dynamic programming solution approach in general terms.

REVIEW OF THE SOLUTION STEPS FOR DYNAMIC PROGRAMMING

Stages transform a decision into a sequential process

The main principle encompassed by dynamic programming is the subdivision of a problem into smaller subproblems referred to as *stages*. In effect, the subdivision of a problem into stages transforms a decision into a sequential process. This concept is illustrated in Figure 21.2 for a three-stage problem (like our example).

FIGURE 21.2

Subdivision of a Problem into Sequential Stages

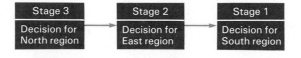

Information flows from left to right

The diagram in Figure 21.2 illustrates the interrelationships between stages, with arrows reflecting the flow of information from left to right, from one stage to the next. However, the stages are numbered in reverse, from right to left. The numbering reflects the solution sequence, in which stage 1 solutions are considered first, then stage 2 solutions, and so on. We consider stages in reverse order so as to be able to observe the *last decision* (i.e., stage 1) in terms of all possible outcomes.

States as resource levels

States are identified at each stage. Dynamic programming (like linear programming) is often concerned with the allocation of scarce resources. Thus, the states at a stage are often the different levels of resources available at that stage. For example, in our problem of allocating salespeople to regions, the states were the possible numbers of salespeople (i.e., the resource) available at each stage.

Decision returns

Given each state, a number of *decisions* are possible, each of which results in a *return*. The relationships among stages, decisions, and returns are illustrated in Figure 21.3.

FIGURE 21.3

The Stage Decision Process

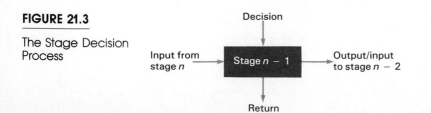

For each state, the best decision is the one that results in the greatest return. These states and decisions are then related to the next stage in the solution process through a *transition function.* Figure 21.4 illustrates how the transition function connects the three stages of our example problem.

Stages are related by the transition function

FIGURE 21.4

The Transitions Between Problem Stages

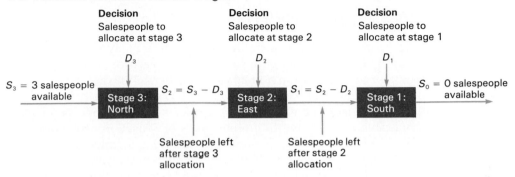

For example, if one of the states at stage 2 is the availability of 2 salespeople and we make a decision to allocate 1 salesperson at stage 2, then we can allocate either 0 or 1 salesperson at stage 1. The decision we make at stage 2 is based on the total return resulting from our decision at stage 2 and the best corresponding decision (either 0 or 1 salesperson) at stage 1. In other words, we make the *best combination* of decisions for the two stages. The total return is determined by using a *recursive return function* that computes the return from a *sequence of optimal decisions.*

The best combination of decisions is made for two stages

At the last stage of our problem, all resources are considered available. That is, theoretically we are on the threshold of making our sequence of decisions and all the resources are available to us. There is typically only one state at this final level of resources — the maximum level.

The last stage is the threshold of a sequence of decisions

Since we have already determined the returns that can be obtained for *all* combinations of decisions up to (but not including) the final stage, we can determine the return for a sequence of decisions given any decision at the final stage. This is accomplished by computing the recursive return from the decision at the final stage and the *previous best decisions* from the states that will result from this decision at the final stage.

In the example problem all 3 salespeople were available to be allocated at stage 3, the final stage. Any number of salespeople we decided to allocate at stage 3 would leave a number of salespeople available to be allocated in the other regions. If we allocated 2 salespeople at stage 3, we would have 1 salesperson left to allocate at the other two stages. The number of salespeople we actually allocated at stage 3 was determined by the returns. We selected the decision at stage 3 that triggered the sequence of best decisions with the highest return. Now that we have presented the dynamic programming solution approach within the context of an example problem and in general terms, we will apply dynamic programming to two traditional examples: the knapsack problem and the stagecoach problem.

THE KNAPSACK PROBLEM

An allocation problem

The *knapsack problem* is a traditional example of dynamic programming that is concerned with how many of each of several different kinds of items to put in a knapsack in order to maximize the return from the items. The knapsack typically has some capacity in terms of weight or size. The general framework of the knapsack problem is applicable to a variety of different types of allocation problems.

A knapsack example

To demonstrate the dynamic programming solution approach to the knapsack problem, we will use the following example. Travelers from the U.S.S.R. who visit the United States and Europe on a frequent basis (such as athletes, musicians, and dancers) are allowed to return with a limited number of consumer items not generally available in the U.S.S.R. The items, which are carried into the U.S.S.R. in a duffel bag, cannot exceed a weight of 5 pounds. Once the traveler is inside the country, the items are sold on the black market at a highly inflated price.

The three most popular items in the U.S.S.R. (that are not considered security risks by the police) are denim jeans, radio/tape cassette players, and tape cassettes of popular rock groups. The black market profit (in U.S. dollars) and weight for each of these items are shown in Table 21.8.

TABLE 21.8

Black Market Items

Item	Weight (lb)	Profit ($)
1. Denim jeans	2	$ 90
2. Radio/tape players	3	150
3. Tape cassettes	1	30

The objective of the traveler

A mathematical model of the problem

The objective of the traveler is to determine the combination of items to put in the duffel bag that will maximize the total return from the black market without exceeding the 5-pound limit. (Failure to adhere to the 5-pound limit will result in revocation of the travel permit.) We can express this problem statement mathematically as follows.

maximize $R_1 D_1 + R_2 D_2 + R_3 D_3$

subject to

$W_1 D_1 + W_2 D_2 + W_3 D_3 \leq 5$ pounds

where

R_1, R_2, and R_3 = *return* (profit) from each item

D_1, D_2, and D_3 = *decision* on the number of each item to include

W_1, W_2, and W_3 = *weight* of each item

The first step in the dynamic programming solution approach is to divide the problem into stages. This problem can be divided conveniently into three stages representing the three consumer items to be put into the duffel bag.

Stage 1—Denim Jeans

We will arbitrarily select the number of denim jeans to include in the duffel bag as stage 1. At stage 1 there are 5 states corresponding to the number of pounds that might be available at this stage. The states go from 0 to 5 pounds, as shown in Table 21.9. Notice that state 1 (S_1) consists only of integer weights (i.e., 0, 1, 2, 3, 4, and 5 pounds). Since the consumer items have only integer weights (i.e., 2, 3, and 1 pound), the remaining weight available at stage 1 must also be an integer, regardless of how many items are selected at stages 2 and 3.

States of the problem

TABLE 21.9

Stage 1 (Denim Jeans): Decision Alternatives

State 1 (S_1): Available Weight	Decision 1 (D_1): Number of Items	Weight (lb) of Items	Return (R_1)
5	2	4	$180
4	2	4	180
3	1	2	90
2	1	2	90
1	0	0	0
0	0	0	0

The first column in Table 21.9 represents the possible values that S_1 can assume. After making decisions regarding the number of the other types of items to pack, we will have either 0, 1, 2, 3, 4, or 5 pounds available for denim jeans. The actual decision (D_1) is constrained by the weight limitation.

For example, if $S_1 = 5$ pounds (i.e., 5 pounds are available), then we can pack 2 pairs of jeans, which would use a total of 4 pounds of the allowed weight. One more pair of jeans would bring the weight to 6 pounds, which would exceed the 5-pound limit. The weight cor-

Only optimal
decisions are
considered at
stage 1

responding to each decision in the second column is shown in the third column in Table 21.9. The return (R_1) for each decision (i.e., each quantity of jeans packed) is given in the last column. For example, 2 pairs of jeans will result in a profit of $180.

We have simplified our stage 1 decision model (Table 21.9) by excluding some of the possible decisions. Since we will eventually consider only the optimal decisions at stage 1, all other nonoptimal decisions have been deleted. For example, if $S_1 = 5$ pounds, then there would be 3 possible decisions; pack 0, 1, or 2 pairs of jeans. However, since we want to maximize the return, we would obviously pack the greatest number of items possible (2 pairs). In other words, the optimal decisions at this stage are all the maximum number of items possible. *Thus, only the optimal decision for each state 1 value is contained in Table 21.9.* (This could also have been done in the salesperson allocation problem; however, in that case we included more detail for explanatory purposes.)

Stage 2—Radio/Tape Cassette Players

The number of radio/tape players is arbitrarily selected as stage 2. The possible states, decisions, weights, and returns for this stage are contained in the first four columns of Table 21.10.

TABLE 21.10

Stage 2 (Radio/Tape Players): Decision Alternatives

State 2 (S_2): Available Weight	Decision 2 (D_2): Number of Items	Weight (lb) of Items	Return (R_2)	State 1 (S_1): Available Weight at Stage 1	Best State 1 Decision	Return (R_1) for Best State 1 Decision	Total Return: $R_1 + R_2$
5	1	3	$150	2	1	$ 90	$240*
	0	0	0	5	2	180	180
4	1	3	150	1	0	0	150
	0	0	0	4	2	180	180*
3	1	3	150	0	0	0	150*
	0	0	0	3	1	90	90
2	0	0	0	2	1	90	90*
1	0	0	0	1	0	0	0*
0	0	0	0	0	0	0	0*

Notice in Table 21.10 that we are considering all possible decisions for each state (as opposed to considering only the optimal decisions, as we did at stage 1). This is because the optimal decision for each state 2 value may not be the maximum number of items (i.e., radio/

tape players), since the best return will be a function of the decisions at this stage *and* at the previous stage (stage 1).

The weight available at stage 1 is determined by the transition function between stages 1 and 2.

The transition function

$$S_1 = S_2 - D_2 W_2$$

For example, if $S_2 = 4$ pounds and $D_2 = 1$ radio/tape player, then W_2 automatically equals 3 pounds and

$$S_1 = 4 - (1)(3)$$
$$= 1 \text{ pound}$$

which is the amount shown in the S_1 column for this decision in Table 21.10.

The best decision for each of the values in the S_1 column is determined from Table 21.9. For example, if $S_1 = 1$, then from Table 21.9 the best decision is $D_1 = 0$.

The recursive returns are computed by summing the returns from the combination of best decisions at stages 1 and 2. For example, if 5 pounds are available at stage 2 ($S_2 = 5$) and 1 radio/tape player is packed, the return is $150. Given the 2 pounds remaining at stage 1 ($S_1 = 2$), the best decision is to pack 1 pair of denim jeans, with a return of $90. The total recursive return is the sum of these two returns, $240.

The recursive returns at stage 2

The optimal decision for each state in Table 21.10 is shaded and marked by an asterisk.

Stage 3—Tape Cassettes

The number of tape cassettes is selected as stage 3. The states, decisions, and returns for this stage are shown in Table 21.11.

TABLE 21.11
Stage 3 (Tape Cassettes): Decision Alternatives

State 3 (S_3): Available Weight	Decision 3 (D_3): Number of Items	Weight (lb) of Items	Return (R_3)	State 2 (S_2): Available Weight at Stage 2	Best State 2 Decision	Return ($R_1 + R_2$) for Best State 2 Decision	Total Return: ($R_1 + R_2$) + R_3
5	5	5	$150	0	0	$ 0	$150
	4	4	120	1	0	0	120
	3	3	90	2	0	90	180
	2	2	60	3	1	150	210
	1	1	30	4	1	180	210
	0	0	0	5	1	240	240*

The optimal
decision at stage 3

Since stage 3 theoretically represents the first decision that will
be made by the traveler, the total weight of 5 pounds is available.
The values in Table 21.11 for stage 3 are determined in the same way
as our stage 2 values. The optimal decision is to pack 0 tape cassettes, which will result in all 5 pounds' being available at stage 2.
The best decision, given that $S_2 = 5$, is to pack 1 radio/tape player.
This leaves 2 pounds for stage 1 (i.e., $S_1 = 2$), and given this state
the best decision (from Table 21.9) is to pack 1 pair of denim jeans.

Summarizing the
optimal decision
sequence

The solution is summarized below.

Item	Decision	Weight	Return
Denim jeans	1	2 lb	$ 90
Radio/tape players	1	3 lb	150
Tape cassettes	0	0 lb	0
		5 lb	$240

THE STAGECOACH PROBLEM

A network routing
problem

The *stagecoach problem* is a network routing problem in which a stagecoach traveler in the nineteenth century wants to determine the
shortest route between two cities, given that several alternative routes
exist. For the stagecoach problem we will use an example similar to
the one introduced in Chapter 19, Network Flow Models, to demonstrate the *shortest route problem*.

A stagecoach
example

In this example, the Stagecoach Shipping Company transports
oranges by truck from Los Angeles to six other cities in the West and
Midwest. The routes and the travel time in hours for each branch
are shown in Figure 21.5. We will assume that the manager of the
company wants to determine the shortest route (in terms of travel
time) from Los Angeles to St. Louis (i.e., from node 1 to node 7).

FIGURE 21.5

Network of Travel
Routes

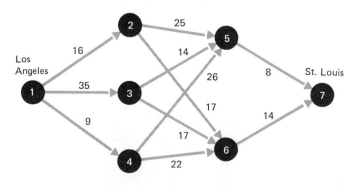

Careful observation of the network of routes in Figure 21.5
shows that there is a maximum of 3 legs for each possible journey
from node 1 to node 7. For example, a truck could go from node 1 to

2 to 5 to 7, which encompasses three *branches* in the network. We will decompose this problem into three dynamic programming stages representing the legs of the journey.

Stage 1—The Last Leg of the Journey

The last leg of the journey is selected as stage 1 in the stagecoach problem. Figure 21.5 shows that there are two possible branches the truck can take on the last leg. That is, two branches end at node 7. These two branches are $5 \rightarrow 7$ and $6 \rightarrow 7$. The *state* at stage 1 is the location of the truck as it is about to take the last leg of the journey. Thus, the two states are nodes 5 and 6, as shown in Table 21.12.

The branches that end at node 7

TABLE 21.12
Stage 1 (Last Leg): Decision Alternatives

State 1 (S_1): Location of Truck	Decision 1 (D_1): Route to Take	Return 1 (R_1): Time of Route
5	$5 \rightarrow 7$	8
6	$6 \rightarrow 7$	14

In Table 21.12, state 1 (S_1) represents the two locations the truck could be at as the end of the journey (node 7) approaches. Decision 1 (D_1) is the branch to take from the state 1 location to the ending node. There is only one decision from each state 1 node to node 7, because there is only one branch from each. Thus, each of the two decisions is optimal. The time for each in hours is the return shown in the last column of Table 21.12.

State 1

Stage 2—The Second Leg

The second leg of the journey is designated as stage 2. The state 2 nodes are the possible locations of the truck as it approaches our state 1 nodes. In Figure 21.5, nodes 2, 3, and 4 all connect directly to our state 1 nodes 5 and 6. Thus, nodes 2, 3, and 4 represent the state 2 locations of the truck, as shown in Table 21.13.

TABLE 21.13
Stage 2 (Second Leg): Decision Alternatives

State 2 (S_2): Location of Truck	Decision 2 (D_2): Route to Take	Return 2 (R_2): Time of Route	State 1 (S_1): Locations of Truck at Stage 1	Return 1 (R_1) from State 1 Route	Total Return: $R_1 + R_2$
2	$2 \rightarrow 5$	25	5	8	33
	$2 \rightarrow 6$	17	6	14	31*
3	$3 \rightarrow 5$	14	5	8	22*
	$3 \rightarrow 6$	17	6	14	31
4	$4 \rightarrow 5$	26	5	8	34*
	$4 \rightarrow 6$	22	6	14	36

If the truck is at node 2, it has two alternative branches it can take: $2 \rightarrow 5$ or $2 \rightarrow 6$. The returns of 25 and 17 hours, respectively, are shown in Table 21.13. Similarly, if the truck is at node 3 or 4, two possible branches extend from each of these nodes. If, for example, the truck takes branch $2 \rightarrow 6$, it must take $6 \rightarrow 7$ at stage 1. This combination of branches represents the transition function between stages 1 and 2. The recursive return is the sum of the times for these two branches: $17 + 14 = 31$ hours.

The recursive return at stage 2

The optimal decision (i.e., route) for each state 2 location is indicated by an asterisk and shaded.

Stage 3 — The First Leg

The first leg of the journey, designated as stage 3, is shown in Table 21.14. The location of the truck is at the start of the journey, which is represented by node 1. Node 1 connects directly (i.e., with one branch) with the three state 2 nodes at stage 2: nodes 2, 3, and 4.

TABLE 21.14

Stage 3 (First Leg): Decision Alternatives

State 3 (S_3): Location of Truck	Decision 3 (D_3): Route to Take	Return 3 (R_3): Time of Route	State 2 (S_2): Location of Truck at Stage 2	Return 2 $(R_1 + R_2)$ from State 2 Route	Total Return: $(R_1 + R_2) + R_3$
1	$1 \rightarrow 2$	16	2	31	47
	$1 \rightarrow 3$	35	3	22	57
	$1 \rightarrow 4$	9	4	34	43*

The optimal network route

The total recursive return shows that the minimum time of 43 hours is achieved by going from node 1 to node 4. Looking back to Table 21.13, we see that the optimal branch from node 4 is to node 5. Next, Table 21.12 shows that the optimal branch from node 5 is to node 7. Thus, the shortest route is $1 \rightarrow 4 \rightarrow 5 \rightarrow 7$, with a minimum time of 43 hours, as shown in Figure 21.6 on page 765. (Notice that the dynamic programming approach used in this example represents an alternative to the methods shown in Chap. 19 for solving the shortest route problem.)

Computerized Solution of Dynamic Programming Problems

Management science software packages for the personal computer do not always have the capability to solve dynamic programming

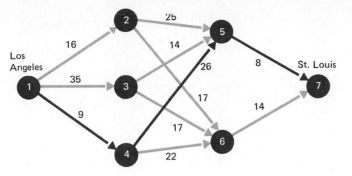

FIGURE 21.6

The Optimal
Shortest Route

problems. When such a solution capability is included, it is sometimes limited to specific types of problems such as the examples in
this chapter. For example, the QSB+ software package that we have
demonstrated in previous chapters has the capability to solve only
the knapsack and stagecoach problems and a production and inventory control problem. The Micro Manager software package, on the
other hand, has the capability to solve general dynamic programming problems. In this section we will employ Micro Manager to
solve the Wood Valley Cosmetics Company salesperson allocation
problem introduced at the beginning of this chapter. Notice that the
stage tables in the following computer output replicate Tables 21.2,
21.4, and 21.6 in this chapter.

```
PROGRAM: Dynamic Programming

Enter 1 for maximization or 2 for minimization: 1
Enter 1 for network or 2 for nonnetwork problem: 2
Enter number of stages: 3


    1.    S(n-1) = S(n) - D(n)
    2.    S(n-1) = S(n) + D(n)
    3.    S(n-1) = S(n) * D(n)
    4.    S(n-1) = D(n)
    5.    S(n-1) = a(n)*S(n) + b(n)*D(n) + c(n)


To define the transition function, enter a number: 1

Enter maximum value of decisions in integer: 3
Enter value of state in stage 3 in integer: 3


    1.    f(n) = R(n) + f(n-1)
    2.    f(n) = R(n) - f(n-1)
    3.    f(n) = R(n) * f(n-1)
    4.    f(n) = a(n)*R(n) + b(n)*f(n-1) + c(n)


To define the recursion function, enter a number: 1
```

```
        1.    R(n) = known value
        2.    R(n) = a(n)*S(n) + b(n)*D(n) + c(n) ; function value

To define the return function, enter a number: 1

Enter return value for decision 0 in stage 3 : 0
Enter return value for decision 1 in stage 3 : 7
Enter return value for decision 2 in stage 3 : 12
Enter return value for decision 3 in stage 3 : 20

Enter return value for decision 0 in stage 2 : 0
Enter return value for decision 1 in stage 2 : 9
Enter return value for decision 2 in stage 2 : 15
Enter return value for decision 3 in stage 2 : 18

Enter return value for decision 0 in stage 1 : 2
Enter return value for decision 1 in stage 1 : 6
Enter return value for decision 2 in stage 1 : 10
Enter return value for decision 3 in stage 1 : 16


PROGRAM: Dynamic Programming

***** INPUT DATA ENTERED *****

Nonnetwork/Maximization problem

Maximum value of decisions:  3
Value of state in stage 3 :  3

Transition function: S(n-1) = S(n) - D(n)

Recursion function:  f(n) = R(n) + f(n-1)

Return function
---------------------------------------------------
                              Stages
   Decisions        3            2            1
---------------------------------------------------
       0           0.00         0.00         2.00
       1           7.00         9.00         6.00
       2          12.00        15.00        10.00
       3          20.00        18.00        16.00


---------------------------------------------------

*****    PROGRAM OUTPUT    *****
                     Stage 1
-------------------------------------------------------------
   S(n)     D(n)        R(n)     S(n-1)   f(n-1)        f(n)
-------------------------------------------------------------
    0        0         2.000       0       0.000       2.000
-------------------------------------------------------------
    1        0         2.000       0       0.000       2.000
    1        1         6.000       0       0.000       6.000
-------------------------------------------------------------
    2        0         2.000       0       0.000       2.000
    2        1         6.000       0       0.000       6.000
    2        2        10.000       0       0.000      10.000
-------------------------------------------------------------
    3        0         2.000       0       0.000       2.000
    3        1         6.000       0       0.000       6.000
    3        2        10.000       0       0.000      10.000
    3        3        16.000       0       0.000      16.000
-------------------------------------------------------------
```

```
                          Stage 2
-----------------------------------------------------------------
   S(n)      D(n)         R(n)      S(n-1)    f(n-1)      f(n)
-----------------------------------------------------------------
    0         0          0.000        0       2.000      2.000
-----------------------------------------------------------------
    1         0          0.000        1       6.000      6.000
    1         1          9.000        0       2.000     11.000
-----------------------------------------------------------------
    2         0          0.000        2      10.000     10.000
    2         1          9.000        1       6.000     15.000
    2         2         15.000        0       2.000     17.000
-----------------------------------------------------------------
    3         0          0.000        3      16.000     16.000
    3         1          9.000        2      10.000     19.000
    3         2         15.000        1       6.000     21.000
    3         3         18.000        0       2.000     20.000
-----------------------------------------------------------------


PROGRAM: Dynamic Programming

                          Stage 3
-----------------------------------------------------------------
   S(n)      D(n)         R(n)      S(n-1)    f(n-1)      f(n)
-----------------------------------------------------------------
    3         0          0.000        3      21.000     21.000
    3         1          7.000        2      17.000     24.000
    3         2         12.000        1      11.000     23.000
    3         3         20.000        0       2.000     22.000
-----------------------------------------------------------------

             Final Solution
----------------------------------------------
 Stage    Optimal Dn    Optimal Rn
----------------------------------------------
   3        1.000        7.000
   2        2.000       15.000
   1        0.000        2.000
----------------------------------------------
 Total      3.000       24.000


** End of the analysis **
```

ADDITIONAL EXAMPLES OF DYNAMIC PROGRAMMING

The examples presented in this chapter to demonstrate the dynamic programming solution approach reflect popular applications of dynamic programming. For the most part, these examples were similar and not very complex. In fact, however, dynamic programming can be applied to a wide variety of complex problems. Dynamic programming has been applied to problems in capital investment analysis, inventory control, job-shop scheduling, plant maintenance, sales planning, energy development, and many other problem areas.

Dynamic programming has been applied to a wide variety of problems

Problems with more
than one state
variable

Probabilistic
dynamic
programming

Problems in which
time increments are
the stages

All three examples in this chapter contained only one state variable. That is, the states at each stage represented only one type of item, such as weight, available salespeople, or travel time. Dynamic programming can encompass problems with more than one state variable. For example, in our knapsack problem, the consumer items taken into the U.S.S.R. could have been subject to volume limitations as well as weight limitations.

Our examples can be referred to as *deterministic* dynamic programming problems. The possible outcomes at each stage were deterministic — that is, we could specifically determine the optimal decision for each state at a stage. In some dynamic programming problems, the decision made at stage n influences the probability distribution of states at stage $n - 1$.

One of the most popular applications of dynamic programming is to classes of problems in which time is one of the essential components. In such problems the time increments are the stages of the dynamic programming model. For example, consider a company that plans to invest in plant expansion over the next five years. During each year several projects compete for limited investment funds. For this problem the stages are the years, the states are the available funds, and the decisions are the projects to select.

APPLICATIONS OF DYNAMIC PROGRAMMING

Transportation Fleet Replacement Analysis

The transportation fleet of the Phillips Petroleum Company included approximately 1,500 passenger cars and 3,800 trucks. An important decision for company management was determining when various vehicles in its fleet should be replaced. For a number of years the company employed a replacement policy based on a model that assumed that vehicle operation costs were related solely to a vehicle's age. The model was used to develop a blanket replacement schedule that indicated vehicle replacement after a certain number of miles or months of operation, whichever came first.

Increasing operating costs of the transportation fleet incited management to begin examining the replacement policy. Management wanted to know whether vehicles should be replaced after the first of the year (since depreciation could thereby be realized more quickly than if replacement occurred before the first of the year), whether some vehicle replacements should be delayed to realize a more favorable tax depreciation schedule, and whether some vehicles should be replaced sooner to take advantage of better fuel efficiency on newer model vehicles. Management was also concerned about purchasing licenses for vehicles immediately before replacing them. An examination of these questions led to a new model for replacement analysis. This model resulted in more careful replacement decisions for individual vehicles than had the blanket replacement policy previously used. The main component of this new policy was a computer-based dynamic programming model.

The new replacement model determines if and when a particular vehicle should be replaced. The states of the dynamic programming model are vehicle ages, broken down into finite times. The fleet manager has fixed opportunities for replacement, and the interval from one replacement opportunity to the next defines the stages of the model. The model attempts to minimize the discounted outgoing cash flow (i.e., cost) associated with vehicle replacement. Components of the discounted outgoing cash flow include maintenance and operating costs (fuel, salaries, etc.), any leasing or purchase costs, license fees, and road use taxes, in addition to tax savings gained and lost, depreciation, and so forth.

The dynamic programming model was incorporated into a computer program designed to provide replacement opportunities at the end of each month. The program generates a decision network that indicates both replacement and retention paths for individual vehicles. This program was used for tractor replacement at Phillips Petroleum Company for six years and in 1983 was implemented for replacement analysis of all vehicles. Annual cost savings of $90,000 were expected.[1]

Pumping Policy at a Water Plant

The Lancaster, Ohio, water distribution system has two reservoirs that serve a population of 39,000. The system has one pumping station, with four pumps in parallel, that delivers treated water to a common main. Water is pumped from wells located near the plant and sent to the treatment plant. Over a long period of time, the water in these wells was depleted, and new wells were opened every two years. Water was supplied to the customer from these wells until demand peaked; then water was pulled from the two reservoirs. Thus, the main function of the reservoirs was to offset fluctuations in demand and to provide reserves in case of emergencies.

The objective of the city was to determine how best to divide the amount of water to be pumped among the four pumps in order to meet customer demand while minimizing pumping costs. Pumping costs result from the electricity used to operate the pumps and from fuel adjustment costs that are subject to change on a monthly basis.

[1]R. Waddell, "A Model for Equipment Replacement Decisions and Policies," *Interfaces* 13, no. 4 (August 1983): 1–7.

A dynamic programming model was developed to determine the optimal pump combination for a one-week planning horizon. A week was divided into 42 four-hour periods, and optimal decisions were determined from the model for each of these periods. Future water demand was determined using an exponential smoothing forecasting model (see Chap. 16). The model was tested using historical data from 1977 and 1979. The optimal pumping policy reduced costs by 7 to 20%.[2]

Summary

Dynamic programming is a very flexible solution technique that can be applied to a wide variety of problems. The example problems presented in this chapter represent only a small sample of the types of problems to which dynamic programming can be applied. The solution approach of decomposing problems into smaller subproblems called stages and solving these stages sequentially allows solution of complex problems that could not be easily solved otherwise. In fact, many of the more complex problems that are encountered in the topic areas covered by other chapters in this text can be solved with dynamic programming.

Limitations of dynamic programming

A limitation of dynamic programming is that it is an *approach*, and not a *technique* (such as linear programming). As a result, often a great deal of ingenuity, expertise, and insight are required to develop a dynamic programming model, including the stages, transition function, states, and recursive function. An additional limiting factor is the symbolic (mathematical) notation that often accompanies more complex dynamic programming models. A concerted effort was made to avoid a great deal of symbolic notation in this chapter so that the basic principles of the dynamic solution approach could be more easily understood. However, anyone seeking a more advanced presentation of dynamic programming will confront this often confusing notation. The nature of the notation has prevented dynamic programming from being applied in many cases where it would be very beneficial. Many potential users of dynamic programming are scared off by the impression of complexity that the extensive notation lends to dynamic programming.

[2]S. Sarin and W. El Benni, "Determination of Optimal Pumping Policy of a Municipal Water Plant," *Interfaces* 12, no. 2 (April 1982): 43–49.

References

Bellman, R. *Dynamic Programming*. Princeton, N.J.: Princeton University Press, 1957.

Bellman, R., and Dreyfus, S. E. *Applied Dynamic Programming*. Princeton, N.J.: Princeton University Press, 1962.

Dallenbach, H. G.; George, J. A.; and McNickle, Donald C. *Introduction to Operations Research Techniques*. 2d ed. Boston: Allyn and Bacon, 1983.

Howard, R. A. *Dynamic Programming and Markov Processes*. New York: John Wiley and Sons, 1960.

Lee, Sang M.; Moore, Laurence J.; and Taylor, Bernard W. *Management Science*. 3d ed. Boston: Allyn and Bacon, 1990.

Loomba, N. P., and Turban, E. *Applied Programming for Management*. New York: Holt, Rinehart and Winston, 1974.

Nemhauser, G. L. *Introduction to Dynamic Programming*. New York: John Wiley and Sons, 1966.

Sarin, S., and El Benni, W. "Determination of Optimal Pumping Policy of a Municipal Water Plant." *Interfaces* 12, no. 2 (April 1982): 43–49.

Waddell, R. "A Model for Equipment Replacement Decisions and Policies." *Interfaces* 13, no. 4 (August 1983): 1–7.

Wagner, H. M. *Principles of Operations Research*. 2d ed. Englewood Cliffs, N.J.: Prentice-Hall, 1975.

EXAMPLE PROBLEM SOLUTION

The following example of a resource allocation problem will demonstrate the solution procedure for a dynamic programming problem.

Problem Statement

The Dynaco manufacturing company has budgeted $4 million for capital improvements for next year, to be allocated (in $1 million blocks) among three plants in Atlanta, Birmingham, and Charlotte. Each plant needs at least $1 million to undertake a project; the company has limited investments to $3 million per plant. The expected return accruing from each investment is estimated as follows:

Allocation ($ millions)	Expected Return ($ millions)		
	Atlanta	Birmingham	Charlotte
1	$ 2	$ 4	$ 3
2	5	5	6
3	10	7	9

If the company decides not to invest in a plant, the return is zero. The company wants to invest the entire $4 million. Determine the investment decision at each plant using dynamic programming.

Step 1: Stage 1—Allocation to Charlotte Plant

S_1: Capital Available	D_1: Allocation	R_1: Return
$0	$0	$0
1	1	3
2	2	6
3	3	9
4	3	9

Step 2: Stage 2—Allocation to Birmingham Plant

S_2: Capital Available	D_2: Allocation	R_2: Return	Best S_1	R_1	$R_1 + R_2$
$0	$0	$0	$0	$0	$ 0
1	0	0	1	3	3
	1	4	0	4	4
2	0	0	2	6	6
	1	4	1	3	7
	2	5	0	0	5
3	0	0	3	9	9
	1	4	2	6	10
	2	5	1	3	8
	3	7	0	0	7
4	0	0	4	9	9
	1	4	3	9	13
	2	5	2	6	11
	3	7	1	3	10

Step 3: Stage 3—Allocation to Atlanta Plant

S_3: Capital Available	D_3	R_3	Best S_2	$R_1 + R_2$	$(R_1 + R_2) + R_3$
$4	$0	0	4	13	13
	1	2	3	10	12
	2	5	2	7	12
	3	10	1	4	14
	4	10	0	0	10

Step 4: Identify the Optimal Decision

Decision sequence:

Stage	Plant	Allocation	Return
3	Atlanta	$3	$10
2	Birmingham	1	4
1	Charlotte	0	0
		$4 million	$14 million

Problems

1. The Barnes and Ewing Pharmaceutical Firm has divided its sales area into 2 regions: East and West. The company has 3 salespeople it wants to allocate to these 2 regions so as to generate maximum dollar sales. The company will not restrict the number of salespeople that can be assigned to any one region. The sales returns that will be generated in each region from each possible combination of salespeople are shown in the following table.

Salespeople per Region	Return per Region ($1,000s)	
	East	West
0	$ 0	$ 1
1	8	6
2	20	23
3	31	36

   a. Express this problem as a mathematical model and explain how it would be solved using the dynamic programming approach.

   b. Determine the optimal number of salespeople to assign to each region using the dynamic programming approach.

2. The Universal Encyclopedia Company has divided its sales area into 3 regions: East, Midwest, and West. The company has 4 sales representatives who are to be assigned to these 3 regions in a manner that will result in maximum dollar sales. The company will not restrict the number of sales representatives that can be assigned to any one region. The sales returns that will be generated in each region from each possible combination of sales representatives are shown in the following table.

Sales Representatives per Region	Return per Region ($1,000s)		
	East	Midwest	West
0	$ 0	$ 0	$ 0
1	22	17	25
2	51	48	45
3	65	71	58
4	82	90	75

Determine the optimal number of sales representatives to assign to each region in order to maximize the total sales returns.

3. The captain of a whaling ship in the nineteenth century allowed each member of the crew to carry a bag full of items to trade with natives of the South Sea Islands; however, the bag of items could not exceed 5 pounds in weight. One crew member, Ishmael, decided to take mirrors and pocketknives to trade. The profit (in gold) and the weight for each trade item are shown in the following table.

Item	Weight (lb)	Profit ($)
1. Mirrors	1	$20
2. Knives	2	24

Using the dynamic programming solution approach, determine the optimal number of each item Ishmael should carry in his bag in order to maximize his total profit.

4. A member of the diplomatic staff for the East German Embassy in Washington, D.C., makes several trips per month to East Berlin to carry classified documents. On each trip the diplomat carries several black market items to sell for a high profit. To avoid suspicion, the diplomat limits the weight of the items to 7 pounds, so that they can be conveniently hidden in a briefcase. The items that the diplomat smuggles are denim jackets, perfume, and bourbon. The weight and profit for each item are shown in the following table.

Item	Weight (lb)	Profit ($)
1. Denim jackets	3	$120
2. Bourbon	2	90
3. Perfume	1	70

Determine the optimal number of each item the diplomat should smuggle in a briefcase in order to maximize profit.

5. A cargo plane is leaving Philadelphia for Spokane. The plane has a cargo capacity of 5 tons. A company wishes to transport several pieces of heavy machinery on the plane. The weights and values of the 3 types of machinery are as follows.

Item	Weight (tons)	Value ($1,000s)
A	2	$65
B	3	80
C	1	30

Determine how many of each piece of machinery to ship on the cargo plane in order to maximize the value of the shipment.

6. A company has budgeted $5 million for the coming fiscal year to be allocated among its plants in Akron, Baltimore, and Chicago. The $5 million is to be allocated in $1 million block amounts, with a maximum of $4 million going to any one plant. The expected annual return from each level of capital investment at each plant is as follows.

Capital Investment ($ millions)	Expected Annual Cash Return ($ millions)		
	Akron	Baltimore	Chicago
0	$0	$0	$0
1	2	3.5	4
2	6	5	7
3	8	7	10
4	9	9	11

Using dynamic programming, determine the optimal allocation of capital among the 3 plants.

7. In problem 6, determine the optimal allocation of capital among the 3 plants if only $4 million is available for investment.

8. Illustrate the optimal solution in problem 2 using a decision network, as shown in Figure 21.1.

9. The Rountown Bus Company has purchased 6 additional buses, which it plans to use on 3 routes. In order to decide how many of the new buses to assign to each of the 3 routes, the bus line has developed the following estimates of the additional profit per day that would be generated on the various routes.

Number of Buses Assigned	Profit per Week ($)		
	Route A	Route B	Route C
0	$ 0	$ 0	$ 0
1	350	100	225
2	450	250	300
3	500	450	475
4	525	650	600
5	450	700	650
6	400	750	650

Use dynamic programming to determine the optimal number of buses to assign to each route.

10. In problem 9, determine the optimal assignment of buses to routes if only 5 buses are available.

11. The police department of a city must determine the optimal allocation of 5 new officers to 4 precincts. The police department has developed estimates of the number of crimes per 8-hour period that can be expected to occur, given the various assignments of officers to precincts.

Number of Officers Allocated	Crimes per 8-hour Period			
	North Precinct	South Precinct	East Precinct	West Precinct
0	40	35	32	27
1	27	31	25	23
2	18	23	20	19
3	12	15	17	16
4	10	10	12	14
5	8	9	10	12

Use dynamic programming to determine the optimal allocation of officers to precincts that will minimize the total number of crimes per 8-hour period.

12. The Pyrotec Company has 4 machines on which it can produce 3 products (A, B, and C). All 4 machines can be set up to produce any of the 3 products. However, once a machine is set up to produce one of the 3 products, a production run of one week is always used. Each week the company must determine how many machines to schedule for each of the 3 products. The expected return from each product (based on a weekly demand forecast) is shown in the following table.

Machines Scheduled	Forecasted Profit ($)		
	Product A	Product B	Product C
0	$ 0	$ 0	$ 0
1	1,000	1,500	500
2	1,900	2,500	1,600
3	2,700	3,200	2,800
4	3,400	3,500	4,000

Use dynamic programming to determine the optimal number of machines to schedule for the production of each of the 3 products for the coming week.

13. The Reserve Milling Company, a large industrial firm, has plants in Lincoln, Dubuque, and Terre Haute. Recently a competing firm went bankrupt, and Reserve purchased 5 large machines at an auction of the

bankrupt company's equipment. The company wants to determine the optimal allocation of the new machines to its 3 plants. The expected profits the machines will earn at the plants are shown in the following table.

Machines Allocated	Profit per Plant ($1,000s)		
	Lincoln	Dubuque	Terre Haute
0	$ 0	$ 0	$ 0
1	40	35	50
2	65	52	60
3	72	66	70
4	80	92	80
5	105	115	90

Using dynamic programming, determine the optimal allocation of machines to plants so as to maximize profit.

14. The federal Department of Energy has 4 teams working on 4 energy research projects in a research program. The DOE is concerned with minimizing the probability of failure of the energy research program. The estimated probability of failure for each research team is as follows:

	Research Team		
1	2	3	4
.60	.80	.45	.75

Thus, the overall probability of total failure of the research program is the product of the individual failure probabilities of the projects, or .162.

The DOE has decided that this probability of research failure is too high and has allocated 3 more scientists to the research program. The estimated probabilities of failure for each research team given 0, 1, 2, and 3 additional scientists are as follows:

Number of Additional Scientists	Probability of Failure of Each Research Team			
	1	2	3	4
0	.60	.80	.45	.75
1	.40	.50	.20	.45
2	.20	.30	.15	.30
3	.10	.20	.10	.15

Using dynamic programming, determine how many scientists to allocate to which teams so as to minimize the overall probability of failure.

15. The Apco manufacturing firm produces small quantities of a specialized piece of equipment. The company currently has orders for 14 units of the equipment, with no expectation of receiving any further orders within the next several months. The firm's customers have requested delivery according to the following schedule:

Delivery Month	Number of Items
January	2
February	5
March	3
April	4

Apco can manufacture a maximum of 5 pieces of equipment per month at a cost of $50 for setup plus $20 per unit for production. It has storage capacity for a maximum of 4 pieces of equipment; carrying costs are estimated to be $4 per unit held from one month to the next.

The firm wishes to determine the optimal production and inventory holding schedule for the planning period of January through April. It currently has zero units in inventory, and it wants to have zero ending inventory in April. Use dynamic programming to solve this problem.

The problem can be solved by beginning with the last month, April, as stage 1 and working backward to the first month, January, as stage 4. Since the firm wishes to have zero ending inventory in April, the optimal stage 1 decision is to produce the quantity differential between beginning inventory (S_1) and the amount required to meet demand in that month (4 units).

16. The Rainwater Brewery ships beer by truck from Indianapolis to Columbus. The possible routes a truck can take and the mileage for each route are shown in the following network. Determine the shortest route from Indianapolis to Columbus using dynamic programming.

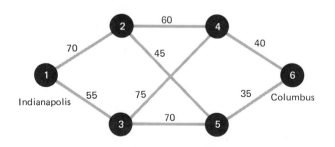

17. A traveler during the 1800s wishes to determine the shortest stagecoach route from San Francisco to New York. The traveler has to travel by 4 different stagecoaches to complete the journey. The different routes from San Francisco to New York and the times in hours are shown in the following network.

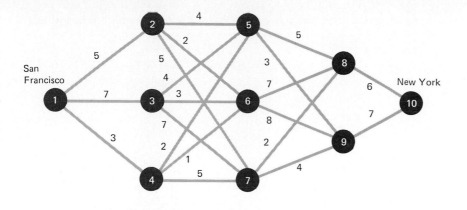

Using dynamic programming, determine the optimal route from San Francisco to New York.

18. The Black Diamond Coal Company transports coal from a railyard in Charleston, West Virginia, to the port of Norfolk, Virginia. The following network shows the various rail routes between these 2 cities and the times (in hours).

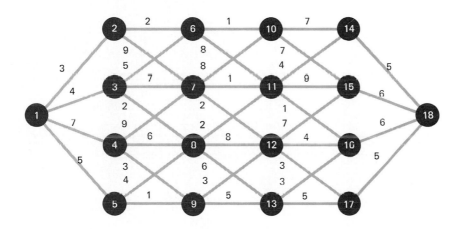

Using dynamic programming, determine the optimal (shortest) route from Charleston to Norfolk.

Break-Even Analysis

As has already been indicated in previous chapters, the objective of most business enterprises is to make as much profit as possible. The topic of this chapter, break-even analysis, is often referred to as *profit analysis*. The purpose of break-even analysis is to determine the number of units of a product (i.e., the volume) to produce that will equate total revenue with total cost. At this point, referred to as the break-even point, profit is zero. The break-even point gives the manager a point of reference in determining how many units will be needed to ensure a profit.

Because break-even analysis deals with a profit, a topic of direct concern to managers, and because it is a relatively easy form of analysis to learn (as will be seen in this chapter), it is a popular management science technique. An additional reason for studying this topic, especially at this point in the text, is that the more complex forms of break-even analysis require solutions using calculus techniques. Thus, the topic provides a useful introduction to the classical optimization techniques that will be considered in the next chapter.

Profit analysis

Determining the product volume that equates total revenue and total cost

COMPONENTS OF BREAK-EVEN ANALYSIS

The three components of break-even analysis are volume, cost, and profit. Because each of these three factors is a function of several other components, we will analyze each component of break-even analysis individually.

Volume

The level of production

Volume is the level of production by a company. Volume can be expressed as the *number of units* (i.e., quantity) produced and sold, as the *dollar volume* of sales, or as a *percentage* of total capacity available.

Costs

Fixed costs

Two types of costs are typically incurred in the production of a product: *fixed costs* and *variable costs*. Fixed costs are generally independent of the volume of units produced. That is, fixed costs remain constant regardless of how many units of product are produced within a given range. The costs of items such as the following, taken together, result in total fixed costs:

Rent on plant and equipment
Taxes
Insurance
Management and staff salaries
Advertising
Interest on investment
Depreciation on plant and equipment
Heat and light
Janitorial services

Variable costs per unit

Variable costs are determined on a per-unit basis. Thus, total variable costs depend on the number of units produced. The costs of the following items are variable costs:

Raw materials and resources
Direct labor
Packaging
Material and product handling
Maintenance
Freight

Total variable costs

Total variable costs are a function of the *volume* and the *variable cost per unit*. This relationship can be expressed mathematically as

Total variable cost = vc_v

where

c_v = variable cost per unit

v = volume (number of units)

The total cost of an operation is computed by summing total fixed cost and total variable cost, as follows:

Total cost = total fixed cost + total variable cost

Total cost

or

$$TC = c_f + vc_v$$
where
$$c_f = \text{fixed cost}$$

As an example, consider the Western Clothing Company, which produces denim jeans. The company incurs the following monthly costs to produce denim jeans.

Computing total cost

Fixed costs = c_f = $10,000
Variable cost = c_v = $8 per pair

If we arbitrarily let the volume, v, equal 400 pairs of denim jeans, the total cost is

$$TC = c_f + vc_v$$
$$= \$10,000 + (400)(8)$$
$$= \$13,200$$

Since the equations for total costs, fixed costs, and variable costs are all linear equations, we can illustrate these relationships graphically as shown in Figure 22.1.

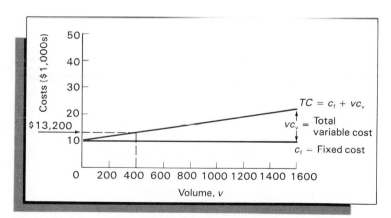

FIGURE 22.1

Cost Relationships for the Break-Even Model

In Figure 22.1, the fixed cost, c_f, has a constant value of $10,000, regardless of the volume. The total cost line, TC, represents the sum of variable cost and fixed cost. The total cost line increases because variable cost increases as the volume increases. Our example volume of 400 pairs of jeans, which results in $13,200 in total cost, is also illustrated in Figure 22.1.

Profit

Total revenue

The third component in our break-even model is *profit*. Profit is the difference between *total revenue* and total cost. Total revenue is the volume multiplied by the price per unit.

Total revenue = vp

where

p = price per unit

Computing total revenue

For our clothing company example, if denim jeans sell for $23 per pair and we sell 400 pairs per month, then the total monthly revenue is

$$\text{Total revenue} = vp$$
$$= (400)(23)$$
$$= \$9,200$$

The graph of total revenue for our example is shown in Figure 22.2.

FIGURE 22.2

Revenue
Relationship for the
Break-Even Model

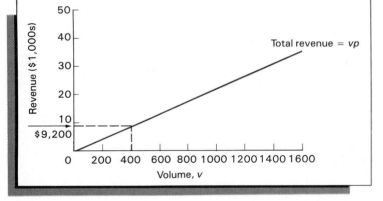

We have already determined total cost to be

Total cost = $c_f + c_v$

Now that we have developed relationships for total revenue and total cost, profit (Z) can be computed as follows.

Total profit equals revenue minus cost

$$\text{Total profit} = \text{total revenue} - \text{total cost}$$
$$Z = vp - [c_f + vc_v]$$
$$Z = vp - c_f - vc_v$$

The Break-Even Point

Computing total profit

For our clothing company example, we have determined total revenue and total cost to be $9,200 and $13,200, respectively. With these values, there is no profit, but instead a loss of $4,000.

Total profit = total revenue − total cost
$$= \$9,200 - 13,200$$
$$= -\$4,000$$

We can verify this result by using our total profit formula,

$$Z = vp - c_f - vc_v$$

and the values $v = 400$, $p = \$23$, $c_f = \$10,000$, and $c_v = \$8$.

$$Z = vp - c_f - vc_v$$
$$= \$(400)(23) - 10,000 - (400)(8)$$
$$= \$9,200 - 10,000 - 3,200$$
$$= -\$4,000$$

Obviously, the clothing company does not want to operate with a monthly loss of $4,000, since doing so might eventually result in bankruptcy. If we assume that price is static because of market conditions and that fixed costs and the variable cost per unit are not subject to change, then the only part of our model that can be varied is *volume*. Thus, in order to avoid a loss, *the company must produce more units*. This may not be immediately obvious, since costs as well as profit increase if more items are produced. However, Figure 22.3, which is actually a composite graph of Figures 22.1 and 22.2, illustrates that profit increases with an increase in volume.

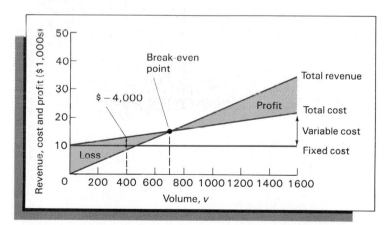

FIGURE 22.3

Break-Even Model

Notice in Figure 22.3 that a volume of 400 pairs of denim jeans results in a loss of $4,000. This loss occurs because the total cost line is above the total revenue line at the point representing 400 pairs of jeans. However, as volume increases, the loss area in Figure 22.3 decreases until a point is reached where the two lines intersect, which indicates that total revenue equals total cost. The volume, v, that corresponds to this point is the *break-even volume*. The break-even volume in Figure 22.3 is 666.7 pairs of denim jeans.

Computing
break-even volume

We can also determine the break-even volume mathematically (and more conveniently). At the break-even point where total revenue equals total cost, the profit, Z, equals zero. Thus, if we let profit, Z, equal zero in our total profit equation and solve for v, we can determine the break-even volume.

$$Z = vp - c_f - vc_v$$
$$0 = v(23) - 10,000 - v(8)$$
$$0 = 23v - 10,000 - 8v$$
$$15v = 10,000$$
$$v = 666.7 \text{ pairs of jeans}$$

In other words, if the company produces 666.7 pairs of jeans, the profit (and loss) will be zero and the company will *break even*. This gives the company a point of reference from which to determine how many pairs of jeans to produce in order to gain a profit (subject to any capacity limitations). For example, a volume of 800 pairs of denim jeans will result in the following monthly profit.

$$Z = vp - c_f - vc_v$$
$$= \$(800)(23) - 10,000 - (800)(8)$$
$$= \$2,000$$

A break-even
formula

In general, the break-even volume can be determined using the following formula.

$$Z = vp - c_f - vc_v$$
$$0 = v(p - c_v) - c_f$$
$$v(p - c_v) = c_f$$
$$v = \frac{c_f}{p - c_v}$$

For our example,

$$v = \frac{c_f}{p - c_v}$$
$$= \frac{10,000}{23 - 8}$$
$$= 666.7 \text{ pairs of jeans}$$

Variations in Volume

When we first introduced the break-even component volume, we mentioned that it could be expressed in three forms: quantity volume, dollar volume, and volume as a percentage of available capacity. The general break-even formula we developed was for *quantity volume*. Now we will alter the general break-even formula to reflect these other two ways of expressing volume.

First we will consider volume expressed in terms of dollar sales.

We calculate this value by multiplying the break-even quantity volume by the price, p.

Break-even sales volume $= pv$

Thus, for our example,

$$pv = \$(23)(666.7)$$
$$= \$15,334$$

Next we will consider volume expressed as a percentage of total capacity. This value is determined by dividing the break-even quantity volume by the maximum operating capacity, k.

Break-even volume as a percentage of capacity $= \dfrac{v}{k}$

If in our example the maximum capacity, k, equals 1,000 pairs of denim jeans, then the break-even volume as a percentage of total capacity is

$$\frac{v}{k} = \frac{666.7}{1,000}$$
$$= 66.7\%$$

Both of these variations of break-even volume are illustrated in Figure 22.4.

FIGURE 22.4

Break-Even Point Expressed in Terms of Sales Volume and Percentage of Capacity

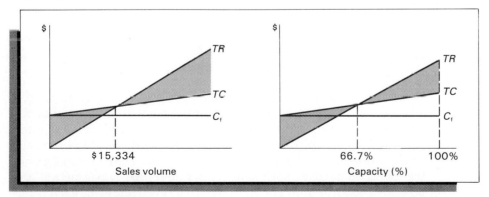

PROFIT ANALYSIS

We have now developed a general relationship for determining the break-even volume. This relationship has enabled us to see how the level of profit (and loss) is directly affected by changes in volume. When we developed this model, we assumed that both fixed and variable (per-unit) costs as well as selling price were constant. Any changes in these three items, though, can affect profit. Thus, we will now observe the effects of changes in these items on our general break-even relationship.

Price

The first item we will analyze is price. As an example, we will increase the price for denim jeans from $23 to $30. As expected, this increases the total revenue, and therefore reduces the break-even point from 666.7 pairs of jeans to 454.5 pairs of jeans.

$$v = \frac{c_f}{p - c_v}$$

$$= \frac{10,000}{30 - 8}$$

$$= 454.5 \text{ pairs of denim jeans}$$

The effect of the price change on break-even volume is illustrated in Figure 22.5.

FIGURE 22.5

Break-Even Model with a Change in Price

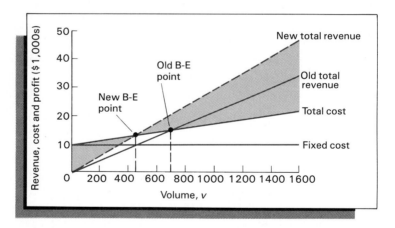

Although a decision to increase price looks inviting from a strictly analytical point of view, it must be remembered that the lower break-even volume and higher profit are *possible*, but not guaranteed. A higher price can make it more difficult to sell the product. Thus, a change in price often must be accompanied by corresponding increases in costs, such as those for advertising, packaging, and possibly production (to enhance quality). However, even such direct changes as these may have little effect on product demand, since price is often sensitive to numerous factors, such as the type of market, monopolistic elements, and product differentiation.

Variable Costs

The effect of an
increase in variable
costs

In our consideration of an increase in price, we mentioned the possibility of raising the quality of the product to offset a potential loss of sales due to the price increase. For example, suppose the stitching on the denim jeans is changed to make the jeans more attractive and stronger. This change results in an increase in variable costs of $4 per pair of jeans, thus raising the variable costs per unit, c_v, to $12 per pair. This change (in conjunction with our previous price change to $30) results in a new break-even volume.

$$v = \frac{c_f}{p - c_v}$$

$$= \frac{10,000}{30 - 12}$$

$$= 555.5 \text{ pairs of denim jeans}$$

This new break-even volume and the change in the total cost line that occurs as a result of the variable cost change are shown in Figure 22.6.

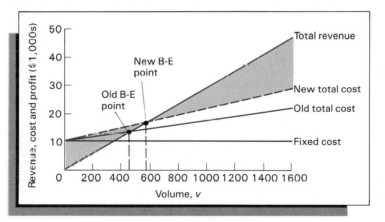

FIGURE 22.6

Break-Even Model with a Change in Variable Cost

Fixed Costs

Next we will consider an increase in advertising expenditures to off-set the potential loss in sales resulting from a price increase. An in-crease in advertising expenditures is an addition to fixed costs. For example, if the clothing company increases its monthly advertising budget by $3,000, then the total fixed cost, c_f, becomes $13,000. Us-ing this fixed cost, as well as the increased variable cost per unit of $12 and the increased price of $30, we compute the break-even vol-ume as follows.

The effect of an increase in fixed costs

$$v = \frac{c_f}{p - c_v}$$

$$= \frac{13,000}{30 - 12}$$

$$= 722.2 \text{ pairs of denim jeans}$$

This new break-even volume, representing changes in price, fixed costs, and variable costs, is illustrated in Figure 22.7. Notice that the

FIGURE 22.7

Break-Even Model
with a Change in
Fixed Cost

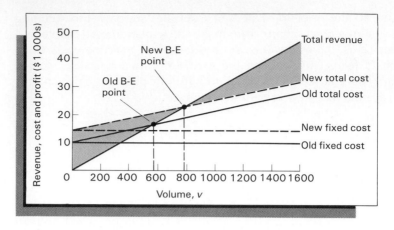

break-even volume is now higher than the original volume of 666.7 pairs of jeans, as a result of the increased costs necessary to offset the potential loss in sales. This indicates the necessity to analyze the effect of a change in one of the break-even components on the whole break-even model. In other words, generally it is not sufficient to consider a change in one model component without considering the overall effect.

PROBABILISTIC ANALYSIS OF THE BREAK-EVEN MODEL

Some of the
break-even model
components are
usually uncertain

Assuming volume is
uncertain

In the preceding discussion of break-even analysis, the assumption was made that the model components—costs, volume, and profit—were known with certainty (i.e., they were deterministic). However, it is more realistic to assume that some or all of these components are uncertain. Sales volume is typically the component most subject to uncertainty, because it is beyond the control of the company to a greater degree than costs. If we assume that volume is uncertain but that the probability distribution of volume is defined by a normal distribution, we can perform probabilistic analysis of the break-even model.

Recall our example of the Western Clothing Company, which produces denim jeans. The model components were defined as

$$c_f = \$10,000$$
$$c_v = \$8 \text{ per pair}$$
$$p = \$23 \text{ per pair}$$

Figure 22.8 illustrates the break-even model and designates the break-even point of (approximately) 667 pairs of denim jeans.

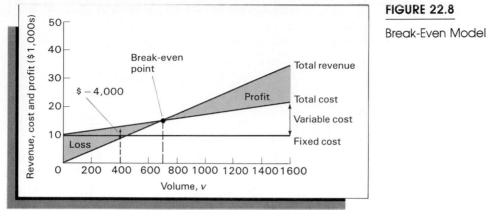

FIGURE 22.8

Break-Even Model

Now let us assume that volume is defined by the normal probability distribution shown in Figure 22.9, with a mean of 800 pairs of jeans and a standard deviation of 267 pairs of jeans.

Normal probability distribution of sales volume

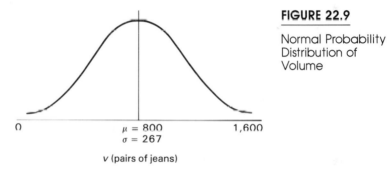

v (pairs of jeans)

FIGURE 22.9

Normal Probability Distribution of Volume

Suppose the manager of the clothing company wants to determine the probability that the break-even point of 667 pairs of jeans will be achieved and a profit will result. Figure 22.10 illustrates the area under the normal curve and hence the probability the manager wants to know.

The probability of breaking even

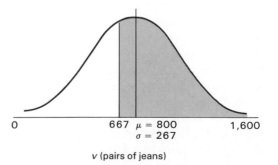

v (pairs of jeans)

FIGURE 22.10

Probability That the Volume Will Be Greater Than the Break-Even Point

The probability that the volume will be at least 667 pairs of jeans is determined by first computing Z, the number of standard deviations 667 is from the mean (see Chap. 10 on probability).

$$Z = \frac{x - \mu}{\sigma}$$
$$= \frac{667 - 800}{267}$$
$$= -.50$$

The Z value of .50 corresponds to a probability of .1915 in Table A.1 in Appendix A. This indicates that the probability that sales volume will be between 667 and 800 pairs of jeans is .1915. To find the desired probability, we add this probability to .5000,

$$P(x \geq 667) = .1915 + .5000$$
$$= .6915$$

Thus, there is a .6915 probability that the company will achieve the break-even point.

Next, let us suppose the manager wants to analyze the profit capabilities of the company subject to the probability distribution of volume shown in Figure 22.10. For example, let us assume the manager wants to know the probability that a profit of $5,000 per month can be achieved. In order to proceed with this analysis, the probability distribution of volume must be converted to a probability distribution of profit. This is accomplished by computing the mean profit and standard deviation, using the mean volume and standard deviation. The mean profit is computed as follows, by substituting the mean volume into the profit equation.

$$\mu = vp - c_f - vc_v$$
$$= \$(800)(23) - 10,000 - (800)(8)$$
$$= \$2,000$$

The standard deviation of profit is determined somewhat differently. First we must compute the upper and lower limits of the normal distribution corresponding to the upper and lower volume limits in Figure 22.10. Substituting 1,600 units into the profit equation gives an upper profit limit of $14,000, and substituting 0 units in the profit equation gives a lower limit of −$10,000. From our knowledge of the normal distribution, we know that the area under the curve between these limits is approximately 1.0, or 100%. We also know that the distance from the mean to either of the limits of the distribution is approximately 3 standard deviations. Since the distance between the mean and the upper limit is $12,000, the standard deviation is approximately one-third of this distance, or $4,000. The probability distribution for profit defined by this mean and standard deviation is shown in Figure 22.11.

FIGURE 22.11

Normal Probability
Distribution of Profit

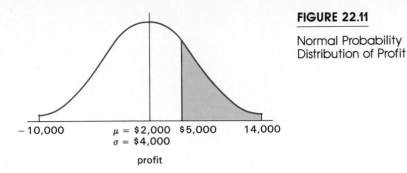

To determine the probability that a profit of $5,000 or more will be achieved, we must determine how many standard deviations this value is from the mean.

$$Z = \frac{x - \mu}{\sigma}$$
$$= \frac{5,000 - 2,000}{4,000}$$
$$= .75$$

The Z value of .75 corresponds to a probability of .2734 in Table A.1 in Appendix A. This indicates that the probability that profit will be between $2,000 and $5,000 is .2734. To find the desired probability, we subtract this probability from .5000.

$$P(x \geq \$5,000) = .5000 - .2734$$
$$= .2266$$

Thus, there is a .2266 probability that the company will realize a profit of $5,000 or more per month.

This same type of analysis of the probability distribution of profit can be used to evaluate potential losses. Such analyses are especially beneficial when a company is contemplating the introduction of a new product, such as a new line of denim jeans, and product demand and thus volume are subject to uncertainty. The break-even model can be employed on a monthly basis to forecast potential losses and profits in the short run.

Computerized Break-Even Analysis

Both the Micro Manager software package and Microcomputer Software for Quantitative Analysis for Management have the capability to perform break-even analysis. We will use the latter to perform break-even analysis for the Western Clothing Company example.

```
                              *** REGULAR BREAK-EVEN ANALYSIS ***

                                    -- PROGRAM OUTPUT --


        DATA ENTERED:

        PROBLEM TITLE          =  Western Clothing Company
        TOTAL FIXED COST       =  10000
        UNIT VARIABLE COST     =  8
        UNIT SELLING PRICE     =  23



                         ********* BREAK-EVEN RESULTS *********

                         THE BREAK-EVEN POINT (IN UNITS) =  666.667
                         THE BREAK-EVEN POINT (IN DOLLARS) =  15333.33



                         ***** END OF BREAK-EVEN ANALYSIS *****
```

This package also has the capability to perform limited probabilistic analysis. For example, the following computer analysis indicates the probability of making a profit (i.e., achieving the break-even point), given a mean volume of 800 pairs of jeans with a standard deviation of 267.

```
        UNIT VARIABLE COST     =  8
        UNIT SELLING PRICE     =  23
        MEAN OF DISTRIBUTION    =  800
        STANDARD DEVIATION     =  267

        ********* BREAK-EVEN RESULTS *********

        THE BREAK-EVEN POINT (IN UNITS) =  666.667

        THE EXPECTED PROFIT FOR THIS
        DEMAND DISTRIBUTION (IN$) IS =  2000


        **********************************************************
        THE # OF STANDARD DEVIATIONS (Z VALUE)= -.4994

        THE PROBABILITY OF NOT BREAKING EVEN IS = 0.3088

        THE PROBABILITY OF MAKING A PROFIT IS = 0.6912

        **********************************************************
```

Finally, we can determine the probability of realizing a profit of $5,000 or more.

```
ENTER THE PROFIT ($) TO ANALYZE (RETURN WHEN DONE)? 5000

THE DEMAND NEEDED FOR A PROFIT OF   5000   IS =   1000

**********************************************************
THE # OF STANDARD DEVIATIONS (Z VALUE)=   .749

THE PROBABILITY OF NOT BREAKING EVEN IS = 0.7731

THE PROBABILITY OF MAKING A PROFIT IS = 0.2269

**********************************************************
```

NONLINEAR PROFIT ANALYSIS

One important but somewhat unrealistic assumption of the break-even model as we have constructed it is that demand is independent of price (i.e., *volume remains constant* regardless of the price of the product). It would be more realistic for the volume to vary as price increased or decreased. For example, let us suppose that the dependency of volume on price is defined by the following linear function:

Volume as a function of price

$$v = 1,500 - 24.6p$$

This linear relationship is illustrated in Figure 22.12. The figure illustrates the fact that as price increases, volume decreases, up to a particular price level ($60.98) that will result in no sales volume.

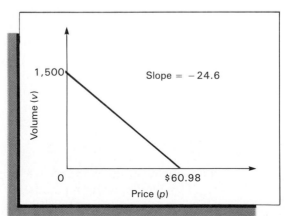

FIGURE 22.12

Linear Relationship of Volume to Price

Now we will insert our new relationship for volume (v) into our original profit equation.

$$Z = vp - c_f - vc_v$$
$$= (1,500 - 24.6p)p - c_f - (1,500 - 24.6p)c_v$$
$$= 1,500p - 24.6p^2 - c_f - 1,500c_v + 24.6pc_v$$

A nonlinear profit function

Substituting the values for fixed cost ($c_f = \$10,000$) and variable cost ($c_v = \$8$) into this new profit function results in the following equation.

$$Z = 1,500p - 24.6p^2 - 10,000 - 1,500(8) + 24.6p(8)$$
$$= 1,696.8p - 24.6p^2 - 22,000$$

This equation for profit is now a nonlinear function that relates profit to price, as shown in Figure 22.13.

FIGURE 22.13

The Nonlinear Profit Function

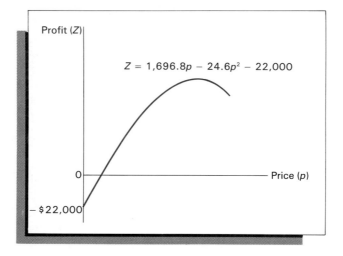

$Z = 1,696.8p - 24.6p^2 - 22,000$

In Figure 22.13, the greatest profit will occur at the point where the profit curve is at its highest. At this point the slope of the curve will equal zero, as shown in Figure 22.14.

Differentiating the profit function

Recall that the slope of a curve at any point is equal to the derivative of the mathematical function that defines the curve. The derivative of our profit function is determined as follows. (For a review of the rules of differentiation, see Appendix E.)

$$Z = 1,696.8p - 24.6p^2 - 22,000$$
$$\frac{\partial Z}{\partial p} = 1,696.8 - 49.2p$$

Setting the derivative equal to zero

Given this derivative, the slope of the profit curve at its highest point is defined by the following relationship.

$$0 = 1,696.8 - 49.2p$$

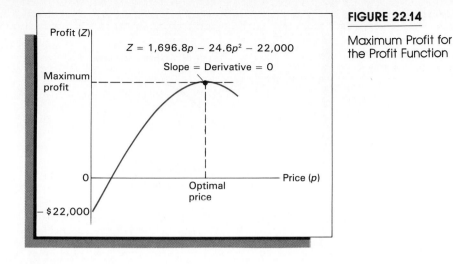

FIGURE 22.14

Maximum Profit for
the Profit Function

Now we can solve this relationship for the optimal price, p, which will maximize total profit.

Solving for the optimal price

$$0 = 1{,}696.8 - 49.2p$$
$$49.2p = 1{,}696.8$$
$$p = 1{,}696.8/49.2$$
$$= \$34.49$$

The optimal volume of denim jeans to produce is computed by substituting this price into our previously developed linear relationship for volume.

The optimal break-even volume

$$v = 1{,}500 - 24.6p$$
$$- 1{,}500 - 24.6(34.49)$$
$$= 651.6 \text{ pairs of denim jeans}$$

The maximum total profit is computed as follows.

Maximum profit

$$Z = \$1{,}696.8p - 24.6p^2 - 22{,}000$$
$$= \$1{,}696.8(34.49) - 24.6(34.49)^2 - 22{,}000$$
$$= \$7{,}259.45$$

The maximum profit, optimal price, and optimal volume are shown graphically in Figure 22.15 on page 798.

An important concept we have yet to mention is that by extending the break-even model this way, we have converted it into an *optimization* model. In other words, we are now able to maximize an objective function (profit) by determining the optimal value of a variable (price). This is exactly what we did in linear programming when we determined the values of decision variables that optimized an ob-

FIGURE 22.15

Maximum Profit, Optimal Price, and Optimal Volume

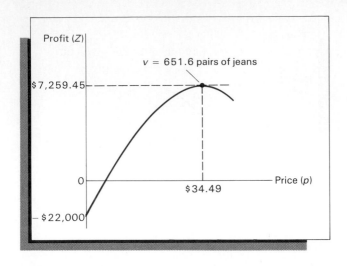

jective function. The use of calculus to find optimal values for variables is often referred to as *classical optimization;* the term *classical* is used because calculus is one of the oldest mathematical techniques.

Classical optimization

Summary

Break-even analysis can be very helpful to managers in making decisions in the short run. The fact that it is basically a simple type of analysis, using data that are generally available to the manager, enhances it usefulness. Break-even analysis can be used not only for determining the level of production, the application illustrated in this chapter, but also for product planning (i.e., determining whether to add a new product or discontinue an old product, determining the appropriate price for a product, and determining when to purchase new equipment and operating facilities, among other applications).

As indicated in the introduction, an additional reason for studying break-even analysis at this point in the text is that it provides an excellent vehicle for introducing calculus-based solution techniques, the topic of the next chapter. The break-even model in this chapter included only linear relationships. However, break-even analysis can be extended to include nonlinear profit and cost relationships, which require a calculus solution. We will use the extension of break-even analysis as the introductory material for the next chapter on nonlinear programming.

Break-even analysis is used to introduce calculus-based techniques

References

Childress, R. L. *Mathematics for Managerial Decisions.* Englewood Cliffs, N.J.:
    Prentice-Hall, 1974.
Lee, S. M., and Moore, L. J. *Introduction to Decision Science.* 2d ed. New York:
    Petrocelli/Charter, 1975.
Levin, R. I., and Kirkpatrick, C. A. *Quantitative Approaches to Management.*
    5th ed. New York: McGraw-Hill, 1982.
Loomba, N. P. *Management: A Quantitative Perspective.* New York: Macmillan,
    1978.
Loomba, N. P., and Turban, E. *Applied Programming for Management.* New
    York: Holt, Rinehart and Winston, 1974.
Monks, J. G. *Operations Management: Theory and Problems.* 2d ed. New York:
    McGraw-Hill, 1982.

EXAMPLE PROBLEM SOLUTION

The following example will demonstrate break-even analysis as a prelude
to the problems.

Problem Statement

The Texas Electronics Company produces calculators. The annual fixed
cost of producing calculators is $280,000. The variable cost of producing a
calculator is $8. The company sells the calculators for $26. Given an annual volume of 60,000 calculators, determine the total cost, total revenue,
profit, break-even volume, and break-even sales volume. If production
capacity is 80,000 calculators, determine the break-even volume as a percentage of capacity.

Step 1: Determine Total Cost

$$v = 60,000$$
$$c_f = \$280,000$$
$$c_v = \$8 \text{ per calculator}$$
$$p = \$26$$
$$\text{TC} = c_f + vc_v$$
$$= \$280,000 + (60,000)(8)$$
$$= \$760,000$$

Step 2: Determine Total Revenue

$$\text{TR} = vp$$
$$= (60,000)(26)$$
$$= \$1,560,000$$

Step 3: Determine Profit

$$Z = TR - TC$$
$$= \$1,560,000 - 760,000$$
$$= \$800,000$$

Step 4: Determine Break-Even Volume

$$v = \frac{c_f}{p - c_v}$$
$$= \frac{280,000}{26 - 8}$$
$$= 15,555.56 \text{ calculators}$$

Step 5: Determine Break-Even Sales Volume

$$\text{B-E sales volume} = pv$$
$$= (26)(15,555.56)$$
$$= \$404,470.56$$

Step 6: Determine Break-Even Volume as a Percentage of Capacity

$$\text{B-E volume as a \% of capacity} = \frac{v}{k}$$
$$= \frac{15,555.56}{80,000}$$
$$= .194$$
$$= 19.4\%$$

Problems

1. The Willow Furniture Company produces tables. The fixed monthly cost of production is $8,000, and the variable cost per table is $65. The tables sell for $180 apiece. For a monthly volume of 300 tables, determine the total cost, total revenue, and profit.

2. The Retread Tire Company recaps tires. The fixed annual cost of the recapping operation is $60,000. The variable cost of recapping a tire is $9. The company charges $25 to recap a tire. For an annual volume of 12,000 tires, determine the total cost, total revenue, and profit.

3. The Rolling Creek Textile Mill produces cotton denim. The fixed monthly cost is $21,000, and the variable cost per yard of denim is $.45. The mill sells a yard of denim for $1.30. For a monthly volume of 18,000 yards of denim, determine the total cost, total revenue, and profit.

4. Determine the monthly break-even volume for the Willow Furniture Company operation described in problem 1.

5. Determine the annual break-even volume for the Retread Tire Company operation described in problem 2.

6. Determine the monthly break-even volume for the Rolling Creek Textile Mill operations described in problem 3.

7. The Evergreen Fertilizer Company produces fertilizer. The fixed monthly cost is $25,000, and the variable cost per pound of fertilizer is $.15. The fertilizer sells for $.40 per pound. Determine the monthly break-even volume for the company.

8. Graphically illustrate the break-even volume for the Retread Tire Company determined in problem 5.

9. Graphically illustrate the break-even volume for the Evergreen Fertilizer Company determined in problem 7.

10. Determine the break-even sales volume for the Willow Furniture Company described in problem 1.

11. Determine the break-even sales volume for the Retread Tire Company described in problem 2.

12. Determine the break-even sales volume for the Evergreen Fertilizer Company described in problem 7.

13. If the maximum operating capacity of the Retread Tire Company described in problem 2 is 8,000 tires annually, determine the break-even volume as a percentage of capacity.

14. If the maximum operating capacity of the Rolling Creek Textile Mill described in problem 3 is 25,000 yards of denim per month, determine the break-even volume as a percentage of capacity.

15. If the maximum operating capacity of the Evergreen Fertilizer Company described in problem 7 is 120,000 pounds of fertilizer per month, determine the break-even volume as a percentage of capacity.

16. If the Retread Tire Company changes its price for recapping a tire from $25 to $31, what effect will the change have on the break-even volume determined in problem 5?

17. If the Evergreen Fertilizer Company changes the price of its fertilizer from $.40 per pound to $.60 per pound, what effect will the change have on the break-even volume determined in problem 7?

18. If Evergreen Fertilizer Company changes its production process to add a weed killer to the fertilizer in order to make it sell better, the variable cost per pound will increase from $.15 to $.22. What effect will this change have on the break-even volume computed in problem 17?

19. If the Evergreen Fertilizer Company increases its advertising expenditures by $14,000 per year, what effect will the increase have on the break-even volume computed in problem 18?

20. The Pastureland Dairy makes cheese, which it sells at local supermarkets. The fixed monthly cost of production is $4,000, and the variable cost per pound of cheese is $.21. The cheese sells for $.75 per pound; however, the dairy is considering raising the price to $.95 per pound. The dairy presently produces and sells 9,000 pounds of cheese per month, but if it raises its price per pound, sales will decrease to 5,700 pounds per month. Should the dairy raise the price?

21. The break-even volume of tables for the Willow Furniture Company (described in problem 1) was computed in problem 4. Now suppose the company has determined that volume is normally distributed with a mean of 90 tables per month and a standard deviation of 30 tables.

    a. Determine the probability that the company will break even.

    b. Determine the probability that the company will make a profit of $8,000 or more per month.

22. The break-even volume of fertilizer for the Evergreen Fertilizer Company was computed in problem 7. Now suppose the company has determined that volume is normally distributed with a mean of 120,000 pounds per month and a standard deviation of 40,000 pounds.

    a. Determine the probability that the company will break even.

    b. Determine the probability that the company will incur a loss of $3,000 or more per month.

23. The Evergreen Fertilizer Company (problem 22) is considering the introduction of a new product, a fertilizer with an additive that kills crabgrass. The fixed cost per month is estimated to be $14,000, the variable cost per pound of fertilizer is estimated to be $.17 per pound, and the fertilizer will sell for $.70 per pound. The company estimates that the volume of the new fertilizer will be normally distributed with a mean of 36,000 pounds per month and a standard deviation of 12,000 pounds.

    a. Should the company produce the new product? Explain your answer.

    b. If the company had a choice of producing either its original fertilizer or its new brand, which should it select? Explain your answer.

24. Recall that the Western Clothing Company described in this chapter manufactures denim jeans. For a variable cost per pair of jeans of $8, a fixed cost of $10,000, and a price per pair of jeans of $23, the break-even volume was computed to be approximately 667 pairs of jeans. Further

recall that in the probabilistic analysis of this example, product volume was assumed to be normally distributed with a mean of 800 pairs of jeans and a standard deviation of 267 pairs. The manager would like for the break-even probability to be .90. To achieve this probability, the manager would have to reduce the variable cost per unit. What variable cost would have to be achieved in order to attain a .90 probability of breaking even?

25. The manager of the Western Clothing Company (problem 24) has determined that it is not possible to reduce variable cost in order to achieve a .90 probability of breaking even. However, the manager believes it might be possible to raise the price of a pair of jeans somewhat without affecting sales adversely. What price per pair would the company have to charge in order to attain an .80 probability of breaking even?

26. The Hickory Cabinet and Furniture Company makes chairs. The fixed cost per month of making chairs is $7,500, and the variable cost per chair is $40. Price is related to volume according to the following linear equation:

$$v = 400 - 1.2p$$

Develop the nonlinear profit function for this company and determine the price that will maximize profit, the optimal volume, and the maximum profit per month.

27. Graphically illustrate the profit curve developed in problem 26. Indicate the optimal price and the maximum profit per month.

28. The Rainwater Brewery produces beer. The annual fixed cost is $150,000, and the variable cost per barrel is $16. Price is related to volume according to the following linear equation:

$$v = 75,000 - 1,153.8p$$

Develop the nonlinear profit function for the brewery and determine the price that will maximize profit, the optimal volume, and the maximum profit per year.

29. The Rolling Creek Textile Mill makes denim. The monthly fixed cost is $8,000, and the variable cost per yard of denim is $.35. Price is related to volume according to the following linear equation:

$$v = 17,000 - 5,666p$$

Develop the nonlinear profit function for the textile mill and determine the optimal price, the optimal volume, and the maximum profit per month.

30. The Grady Tire Company recaps tires. The weekly fixed cost is $2,500, and the variable cost per tire is $9. Price is related to volume according to the following linear equation:

$$v = 200 - 4.75p$$

Develop the nonlinear profit function for the tire company and determine the optimal price, the optimal volume, and the maximum profit per week.

31. Suppose Grady Tire Company (problem 30) has determined that its variable cost per tire decreases as volume increases (because the company receives discounts for ordering larger quantities of rubber). Variable cost is related to volume according to the following linear function:

$c_v = 6 + .03v$

Assume the company charges $25 to recap a tire. Develop the nonlinear profit function for the tire company and determine the optimal volume and maximum profit.

Nonlinear Programming

A substantial proportion of this text has been devoted to linear programming. Chapters 2 through 9 relate directly to linear programming techniques. This emphasis is due in large part to the popularity and applicability of linear programming in the real world, and in part to the very efficient methods of solution that have been developed for linear programming problems. However, not all problems that can be classified as *mathematical programming* problems consists solely of linear relationships. Some problems have the general form of a mathematical programming model with an objective function and constraints, but the relationships involved in the problems are not linear. Such problems are referred to as *nonlinear programming*, which is the topic of this chapter.

Mathematical programming models with nonlinear relationships

In the preceding chapter, the profit analysis model contained a nonlinear function. It was demonstrated that the solution of a problem with nonlinear relationships requires the application of calculus. As might be expected, the solution approaches for nonlinear programming problems are also based on calculus methods. The topic

805

of nonlinear programming represents a convergence of the topics of mathematical programming and calculus. Unlike those for linear programming, however, the solution methods for nonlinear programming are not very efficient and are very complex. As a result, the topic of nonlinear programming is too broad and advanced for more than a cursory introduction in this chapter. Therefore, we will simply introduce the basic principles underlying nonlinear programming and offer some insight into how the solution of such problems is approached.

CONSTRAINED OPTIMIZATION

The total profit equation

In the preceding chapter, the profit analysis model was developed as an extension of the break-even model. Recall that the total profit function was

$$Z = vp - c_f - vc_v$$
where
v = volume
p = price
c_f = fixed cost
c_v = variable cost

and the demand function (i.e., volume as a function of price) was

$$v = 1,500 - 24.6p$$

The nonlinear profit function

By substituting this demand function into our total profit equation, we developed a nonlinear function.

$$Z = 1,500p - 24.6p^2 - c_f - 1,500c_v + 24.6pc_v$$

Then, by substituting values for c_f ($10,000) and c_v ($8) into this function, we obtained

$$Z = 1,696.8p - 24.6p^2 - 22,000$$

You will recall that we then differentiated this function, set it equal to zero, and solved for the value of p ($34.49), which corresponded to the maximum point on the profit curve (where the slope equaled zero).

Unconstrained optimization

Constrained optimization

This type of model is referred to as an *unconstrained optimization problem.* It consists of a single nonlinear objective function and *no* constraints—hence the name "unconstrained." If we add one or more constraints to this model, it becomes a *constrained optimization model.* A constrained optimization model is more commonly referred to as a *nonlinear programming model.* The reason this type of model is designated as a form of mathematical programming is because all types of mathematical programming models are actually constrained optimization models. That is, they all have the general form of an objective function that is *subject to one or more constraints*. In linear programming there is an objective function and constraints that happen to be linear. A nonlinear programming model has the same general form as a linear programming model, except that the objective function *and/or* the constraint(s) are nonlinear.

Nonlinear programming differs from linear programming, however, in one other critical aspect: the solution of nonlinear programming problems is much more complex. In linear programming a particular procedure is guaranteed to lead to a solution if the problem has been correctly formulated, whereas in nonlinear programming no guaranteed procedure exists. The reason for this complexity can be illustrated by a graph of our profit analysis model. Figure 23.1 shows the nonlinear profit curve for the example model.

Solving nonlinear programming problems is very complex

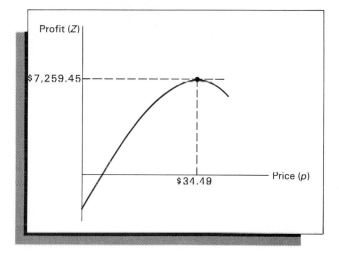

FIGURE 23.1

Nonlinear Profit Curve for the Profit Analysis Model

As stated previously, the solution is found by taking the derivative of the profit function, setting it equal to zero, and solving for p (price). This results in an optimal value for p, which corresponds to the maximum profit, as shown in Figure 23.1.

Now we will transform this unconstrained optimization model into a nonlinear programming model by adding the constraint

A nonlinear programming model

$$p \le \$20$$

In other words, because of market conditions, we are restricting the price to a maximum of $20. This constraint results in a feasible solution space, as shown in Figure 23.2.

As in a linear programming problem, the solution is on the boundary of the feasible solution space formed by the constraint. Thus, in Figure 23.2, point A is the optimal solution. It corresponds

FIGURE 23.2

A Constrained
Optimization Model

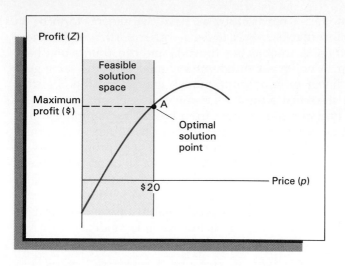

to the maximum value of the portion of the objective function that is still feasible. However, the difficulty with nonlinear programming is that the solution is not always on the boundary of the feasible solution space formed by the constraint. For example, consider the addition of the following constraint to our original nonlinear objective function:

$$p \leq \$40$$

This constraint also creates a feasible solution space, as shown in Figure 23.3.

FIGURE 23.3

Constrained
Optimization Model
with a Solution Point
Not on the
Constraint
Boundary

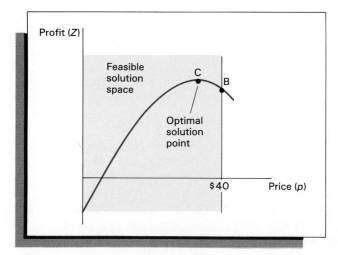

But notice in Figure 23.3 that the solution is no longer on the boundary of the feasible solution space, as it would be in linear programming. Point C represents a greater profit than point B, and it is also in the feasible solution space. This means that we cannot simply look at points on the solution space boundary to find the solution; instead, we must also consider other points on the surface of the objective function. This greatly complicates the process of finding a solution to a nonlinear programming problem, and this difficulty is aggravated by an increased number of variables and constraints and nonlinear functions of a higher order. You can imagine the difficulties of solution if you contemplate a model in space that is made up of intersecting cones, ellipses, and undulating surfaces, as well as planes, and a solution that is not even on the boundary of the solution space.

The difficulty of locating the solution point for a nonlinear programming problem

A number of different solution approaches to nonlinear programming problems are available. As we have already indicated, they typically represent a convergence of the principles of calculus and mathematical programming. However, as noted above, the solution techniques can be very complex. Thus, we will confine the following discussion of nonlinear programming solution methods to the simplest cases.

THE SUBSTITUTION METHOD

The least complex method for solving nonlinear programming problems is referred to as *substitution*. This method is restricted to models that contain only equality constraints, and typically only one of these. The method involves solving the constraint equation for one variable in terms of another. This new expression is then substituted into the objective function, effectively eliminating the constraint. In other words, a constrained optimization model is transformed into an unconstrained model.

Substituting the constraint equation into the objective function

For an example of the substitution method we will return to our profit analysis model. This model is actually a nonlinear programming model that we solved by the substitution method. The demand function is a constraint. Thus, the nonlinear programming model is formulated as

An example of the substitution method

maximize $Z = vp - c_f - vc_v$
subject to
$v = 1,500 - 24.6p$

The objective function in this model is nonlinear, since both v (volume) and p (price) are variables and multiplying them (i.e., vp) creates a curvilinear relationship.

The constraint has already been solved for one variable (v) in terms of another (p); thus, we can substitute this expression directly into the objective function. This results in the following uncon-strained function:

$$Z = 1{,}500p - 24.6p^2 - c_f - 1{,}500c_v + 24.6pc_v$$

By substituting the constant values for c_f ($10,000) and c_v ($8), we obtain

$$Z = 1{,}696.8p - 24.6p^2 - 22{,}000$$

Next, we solve this problem by differentiating the function, Z, and setting it equal to zero, as we did in Chapter 22.

$$\frac{\partial Z}{\partial p} = 1{,}696.8 - 49.2p$$
$$0 = 1{,}696.8 - 49.2p$$
$$49.2p = 1{,}696.8$$
$$p = \$34.49$$

Since you have become very familiar with this example, we will present another example as a further illustration of a nonlinear pro-gramming problem and the substitution method. This example is a modified version of the Colonial Pottery Company example first in-troduced in Chapter 2. Recall that the company produced bowls (x_1) and mugs (x_2), which generated unit profits of $4 and $5, respec-tively. The linear objective function was formulated as

$$\text{maximize } Z = \$4x_1 + 5x_2$$

However, now we will assume that the profit contribution for each product *declines* as the quantity of each item produced in-creases. Thus, for bowls the per-unit profit contribution is now ex-pressed according to the relationship

$$\$4 - .1x_1$$

For mugs, the profit contribution per unit is

$$\$5 - .2x_2$$

(These relationships express the fact that production costs for each product increase as the number of units sold increases.)

These profit relationships are on a per-unit basis. Thus, the total profit contribution from each product is determined by multiplying these relationships by the number of units produced. For bowls, the profit contribution is

$$(4 - .1x_1)x_1$$

or

$$4x_1 - .1x_1^2$$

For mugs, the profit contribution is

$$(5 - .2x_2)x_2$$

or

$$5x_2 - .2x_2^2$$

Total profit is the sum of these two terms.

A nonlinear objective function

$$Z = \$4x_1 - .1x_1^2 + 5x_2 - .2x_2^2$$

The original linear programming model had constraints for labor and pounds of clay. In this model, we will consider only the labor constraint, and we will treat it as an equality rather than an inequality.

Adding a labor constraint

$$x_1 + 2x_2 = 40 \text{ hr}$$

The complete nonlinear programming model is as follows.

maximize $Z = \$4x_1 - .1x_1^2 + 5x_2 - .2x_2^2$
subject to
$$x_1 + 2x_2 = 40$$

The first step in the substitution method is to solve the constraint equation for one variable in terms of another. We will arbitrarily decide to solve for x_1 as follows.

Substituting the constraint into the objective function

$$x_1 = 40 - 2x_2$$

Now wherever x_1 appears in the nonlinear objective function, we will substitute the expression $40 - 2x_2$.

$$
\begin{aligned}
Z &= 4(40 - 2x_2) - .1(40 - 2x_2)^2 + 5x_2 - .2x_2^2 \\
&= 160 - 8x_2 - .1(1{,}600 - 160x_2 + 4x_2^2) + 5x_2 - .2x_2^2 \\
&\quad\ 160 - 8x_2 - 160 + 16x_2 - .4x_2^2 + 5x_2 - .2x_2^2 \\
&= 13x_2 - .6x_2^2
\end{aligned}
$$

This is an unconstrained optimization function, and we can solve it by differentiating it and setting it equal to zero.

Differentiating the objective function

$$
\begin{aligned}
\frac{\partial Z}{\partial x_2} &= 13 - 1.2x_2 \\
0 &= 13 - 1.2x_2 \\
1.2x_2 &= 13 \\
x_2 &= 10.8 \text{ mugs}
\end{aligned}
$$

To determine x_1, we can substitute x_2 into the constraint equation.

$$
\begin{aligned}
x_1 + 2x_2 &= 40 \\
x_1 + 2(10.8) &= 40 \\
x_1 &= 18.4 \text{ bowls}
\end{aligned}
$$

Substituting the values of x_1 and x_2 into the original objective function gives the total profit, as follows.

$$
\begin{aligned}
Z &= \$4x_1 - .1x_1^2 + 5x_2 - .2x_2^2 \\
&= \$4(18.4) - .1(18.4)^2 + 5(10.8) - .2(10.8)^2 \\
&= \$70.40
\end{aligned}
$$

Both of the examples presented in this section for solving non-linear programming problems exhibit the limitations of this approach. The objective functions were not very complex (i.e., the highest order of a variable was a power of 2 in the second example), there were only two variables, and the single constraint in each example was an equation. This method becomes very difficult if the constraint becomes complex. An alternative solution approach that is not quite as restricted is the method of Lagrange multipliers.

THE METHOD OF LAGRANGE MULTIPLIERS

The method of Lagrange multipliers is a general mathematical technique that can be used for solving constrained optimization problems consisting of a nonlinear objective function and one or more linear or nonlinear constraint equations. In this method, the constraints as multiples of a Lagrange multiplier, λ, are subtracted from the objective function.

A Lagrange example

To demonstrate this method, we will use our modified pottery company example developed in the preceding section. This model was formulated as

maximize $Z = 4x_1 + .1x_1^2 + 5x_2 - .2x_2^2$
subject to
$$x_1 + 2x_2 = 40$$

The Lagrangian function

The first step is to transform the nonlinear objective function into a *Lagrangian function*. This is accomplished by first transforming the constraint equation as follows.

$$x_1 + 2x_2 - 40 = 0$$

The Lagrangian multiplier, λ

Next, this expression is multiplied by λ, the *Lagrangian multiplier*, and subtracted from the objective function to form the Lagrangian function.

$$L = 4x_1 - .1x_1^2 + 5x_2 - .2x_2^2 - \lambda(x_1 + 2x_2 - 40)$$

Since the constraint equation now equals zero, the subtraction of the constraint, multiplied by λ, from the objective function does not affect the value of the function. (We will explain the exact meaning of λ after a solution has been determined.)

Differentiation of the Lagrangian function

Now we must determine the partial derivatives of the Lagrangian function with respect to each of the three variables, x_1, x_2, and λ.

$$\frac{\partial L}{\partial x_1} = 4 - .2x_1 - \lambda$$

$$\frac{\partial L}{\partial x_2} = 5 - .4x_2 - 2\lambda$$

$$\frac{\partial L}{\partial \lambda} = -x_1 - 2x_2 + 40$$

These three equations are all set equal to zero and solved simultaneously to determine the values of x_1, x_2, and λ.

$$4 - .2x_1 - \lambda = 0$$
$$5 - .4x_2 - 2\lambda = 0$$
$$-x_1 - 2x_2 + 40 = 0$$

To solve these equations simultaneously, we multiply the first equation by -2 and add it to the second equation, which eliminates λ.

$$-8 + .4x_1 + 2\lambda = 0$$
$$\underline{5 - .4x_2 - 2\lambda = 0}$$
$$-3 + .4x_1 - .4x_2 = 0$$

This new equation and the original third equation above represent two equations with two unknowns (x_1 and x_2). We multiply the third equation above by .4 and add it to the new equation in order to eliminate x_1.

$$-.4x_1 - .8x_2 + 16 = 0$$
$$\underline{.4x_1 - .4x_2 - 3 = 0}$$
$$-1.2x_2 + 13 = 0$$

The resulting equation is solved for x_2 as follows.

$$-1.2x_2 + 13 = 0$$
$$-1.2x_2 = -13$$
$$x_2 = 10.8 \text{ mugs}$$

Substituting this value back into previous equations gives the values of x_1 and λ.

$$-x_1 - 2x_2 + 40 = 0$$
$$-x_1 - 2(10.8) = -40$$
$$x_1 = 18.4 \text{ bowls}$$
$$5 - .4x_2 - 2\lambda = 0$$
$$5 - .4(10.8) = 2\lambda$$
$$\lambda = .35$$

Substituting the values for x_1 and x_2 into the original objective function yields the total profit.

$$Z = \$4x_1 - .1x_1^2 + 5x_2 - .2x_2^2$$
$$= \$4(18.4) - .1(18.4)^2 + 5(10.8) - .2(10.8)^2$$
$$= \$70.40$$

This result can also be obtained by using the Lagrangian function, L, and multiplier, λ.

$$L = \$4x_1 - .1x_1^2 + 5x_2 - .2x_2^2 - \lambda(x_1 + 2x_2 - 40)$$
$$= \$4(18.4) - .1(18.4)^2 + 5(10.8) - .2(10.8)^2 - 0.35(0)$$
$$= \$70.40$$

To summarize, we have $x_1 = 18.4$ bowls, $x_2 = 10.8$ mugs, $Z = \$70.40$, and $\lambda = .35$. This is the same answer obtained previously using the substitution method. However, unlike the substitution method, the Lagrange multiplier approach can be used to solve nonlinear programming problems with more complex constraint equations and *inequality constraints*. In addition, it can encompass problems with more than two variables. We will not pursue any examples, though, that demonstrate the complexities involved. The Lagrange multiplier method must be altered to compensate for inequality constraints and additional variables, and the resulting mathematics are very difficult. Even though the Lagrange multiplier method is more flexible than the substitution method, it is practical for solving only small problems. As the size of the problem increases, the mathematics become overwhelmingly difficult. Several computerized approaches have been developed to deal with larger problems, and we will discuss these later in the chapter.

The Meaning of λ

The Lagrange multiplier, λ, in nonlinear programming problems is analogous to the dual variables in a linear programming problem. It reflects the approximate change in the objective function resulting from a unit change in the quantity (right-hand-side) value of the constraint equation. For our example, we will increase the quantity value in the constraint equation from 40 to 41 hours of labor. (You will recall from the preceding calculations that $\lambda = .35$.)

$$x_1 + 2x_2 = 41 \quad \text{or} \quad x_1 + 2x_2 - 41 = 0$$

This constraint equation will result in the following Lagrangian function.

$$L = 4x_1 - .1x_1^2 + 5x_2 - .2x_2^2 - \lambda(x_1 + 2x_2 - 41)$$

Solving this problem the same way we solved the original model gives the following solution.

$$x_1 = 18.68$$
$$x_2 = 11.16$$
$$\lambda = .27$$
$$Z = \$74.75$$

This value for Z is $\$.35$ greater than the previous Z value of $\$74.40$. Thus, a one-unit increase in the right-hand side of the constraint equation results in a λ increase in the objective function. More specifically, a unit increase in a resource (labor) results in a $\$.35$ increase in profit. Thus, we would be willing to pay $\$.35$ for one additional hour of labor. This is the same interpretation as that given for a dual variable in Chapter 6.

In general, if λ is positive, the optimal objective function value will increase if the quantity (absolute) value in the constraint equation is increased, and it will decrease if the quantity (absolute) value is decreased. On the other hand, if λ is negative, the optimal objective function value will increase if the quantity (absolute) value is decreased, and it will decrease if the quantity (absolute) value is increased.

NONCONVEX AND NONCONCAVE FUNCTIONS

In all of the examples in this and the preceding chapter, the nonlinear objective functions were either completely convex or completely concave. That is, the curves formed by the functions were in the shape of either upright or inverted "bowls," as shown in Figure 23.4. This means that there could be only one maximum or minimum point on the curve, and thus only one possible solution point. However, this is not always the case, because the objective function can define an undulating curve that contains both convex and concave portions. Such a curve is shown in Figure 23.5.

Nonlinear objective functions that are not totally convex or concave

FIGURE 23.4

Convex and Concave Functions

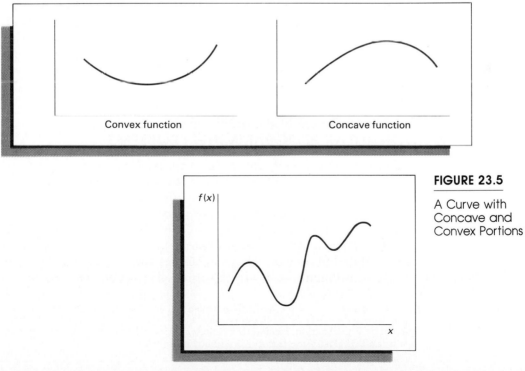

Convex function   Concave function

FIGURE 23.5

A Curve with Concave and Convex Portions

When this type of nonlinear function exists in a problem, simply taking the derivative of the function will not automatically identify the optimal solution, because there are several points on the curve where the slope equals zero. Several additional calculus steps must be performed to exactly determine the optimal solution. These steps require the use of higher-order derivatives. Since these steps are necessary only for more complex nonlinear functions than we have demonstrated in this chapter, we will not pursue this topic. However, Appendix F presents the basic principles for determining optimality for nonlinear functions.

ADVANCED SOLUTION METHODS FOR NONLINEAR PROGRAMMING

Gradient search methods

Most of the modern-day solution methods for nonlinear programming problems are iterative search procedures that have been developed rather recently. These procedures, referred to as *gradient search methods*, are conducted almost exclusively on the computer. The process used is analogous to locating the highest peak in a mountain range by successively searching from peak to peak. The search starts at point A and proceeds to point B, when B appears to be the highest point in the immediate vicinity of A. The search continues until the summit (optimal solution) is reached. At this point no additional improvement in the objective function can be made. A number of these search techniques have been documented and used. The interested reader is referred to the references at the end of this chapter (especially the text by Luenberger) for a more thorough presentation of these techniques.

COMPUTERIZED SOLUTION OF NONLINEAR PROGRAMMING PROBLEMS

Typically, management science software packages for the personal computer do not have the capability to solve nonlinear programming problems. Thus, the user is required to employ a computer package specifically designed to solve nonlinear programming problems. One such software package is GINO, by Lasdon, Waren, and LINDO Systems, Inc.[1] GINO is a relative of LINDO, which we have demonstrated in previous chapters, and as such is very similar in its input requirements and output format. However, because of the

---

[1]L. Lasdon, A. Waren, and LINDO Systems, Inc., GINO (General Interactive Optimizer) (Chicago: LINDO Systems, Inc., 1986). Also see the associated textbook manual by J. Liebman, L. Lasdon, L. Schrage, and A. Waren, *Modeling and Optimization with GINO* (Palo Alto, CA: The Scientific Press, 1986).

complexity of nonlinear programming problems, GINO may impose some hardware restrictions on the user, such as the necessity of a math coprocessor.

To demonstrate GINO we will first use the nonlinear profit analysis model we solved using the substitution method. You will recall that we simply solved a nonlinear objective function,

$$Z = 1,696.8p - 24.6p^2 - 22,000$$

The following GINO output shows the model input and solution format.

```
MODEL:
    1) MAX= 1696.8 * P - 24.6 * P ^ 2 - 22000 ;
END


SOLUTION STATUS:  OPTIMAL TO TOLERANCES.  DUAL CONDITIONS:  UNSATISFIED.

            OBJECTIVE FUNCTION VALUE

    1)       7259.454889

    VARIABLE         VALUE          REDUCED COST
        P         34.487805           .000841
```

You will notice that the input for GINO differs slightly from that for LINDO. We start by typing the term "Model." Next, note that an asterisk signifies the product of a variable and constant (i.e., of 1696.8 and p). Also, terms raised to a power, such as "p^2," are input using $\wedge$, as in $p \wedge 2$.

Next, we will use GINO to solve the Colonial Pottery Company example we solved using the method of Lagrange multipliers. The GINO input and solution output for this model are shown below.

```
:
:
: look all

    MODEL:
        1) MAX= 4 * X1 - .1 * X1 ^ 2 + 5 * X2 - .2 * X2 ^ 2 ;
        2) X1 + 2 * X2 = 40 ;
    END


: go
SOLUTION STATUS:  OPTIMAL TO TOLERANCES.  DUAL CONDITIONS:  SATISFIED.
```

```
            OBJECTIVE FUNCTION VALUE

        1)        70.416666

   VARIABLE         VALUE        REDUCED COST
       X1         18.333333          .000001
       X2         10.833333          .000000

      ROW      SLACK OR SURPLUS         PRICE
       2)          .000000            .333332
```

AN APPLICATION OF NONLINEAR PROGRAMMING

Gas Production Planning in Australia

SANTOS, Ltd., a publicly owned mineral exploration and production company in Australia, has developed a nonlinear mathematical programming model to determine how to manage its Cooper Basin oil and gas reservoirs in the eastern half of Australia. The basic questions the company needs to answer are

How many oil and gas wells should be drilled and when?
How much compressor capacity should be installed and when?
At what rate should each reservoir be produced in order to meet demand?

The nonlinear mathematical programming model determines the production schedule that meets physical and logistical constraints while maximizing net present value (subject to a requirement that the incremental present value ratio of each reservoir investment exceed a minimum value). It is estimated the model saves the company approximately $43.6 million per year.[2]

Summary

There is no efficient solution method for nonlinear programming problems

The purpose of this chapter has been to provide a general overview of and introduction to the topic of nonlinear programming. An in-depth discussion of the solution methods for nonlinear programming, however, has not been presented. At this time, there is really no single efficient generalized solution method

[2]E. Dougherty, D. Dare, P. Hutchison, and E. Lombardino, "Optimizing SANTOS's Gas Production and Processing Operations in Central Australia Using the Decomposition Method," *Interfaces* 17, no. 1 (January–February 1987): 65–93.

available for nonlinear programming problems. What is available (and what was introduced) are several analytical approaches that are applicable to problems of very small magnitude, as well as more advanced computerized search methods for more complex problems. Nonlinear programming is a technique in transition, and new approaches and techniques are continually being researched.

References

Gottfried, B. S., and Weisman, J. *Introduction to Optimization Theory.* Englewood Cliffs, N.J.: Prentice-Hall, 1973.

Hillier, F. S., and Lieberman, G. J. *Operations Research.* 4th ed. San Francisco: Holden-Day, 1986.

Kuhn, H. W., and Tucker, A. W. "Non-Linear Programming." In *Proceedings of the Second Berkeley Symposium on Mathematical Statistics and Probability,* edited by Jerzy Neyman, pp. 481–92. Berkeley: University of California Press, 1951.

Loomba, N. P., and Turban, E. *Applied Programming for Management.* New York: Holt, Rinehart & Winston, 1974.

Luenberger, David G. *Introduction to Linear and Non-Linear Programming.* Reading, Mass.: Addison-Wesley, 1973.

McMillan, Claude, Jr. *Mathematical Programming.* 2d ed. New York: John Wiley & Sons, 1975.

Taha, Hamdy A. *Operations Research.* 4th ed. New York: Macmillan, 1987.

EXAMPLE PROBLEM SOLUTION

The following example illustrates the use of the substitution method and the method of Lagrange multipliers for solving a nonlinear programming problem.

Problem Statement

The Hickory Cabinet and Furniture Company makes chairs and tables. The company has developed the following nonlinear programming model to determine the optimal number of chairs (x_1) and tables (x_2) to produce each day in order to maximize profit, given a constraint for available mahogany wood.

$$\text{maximize } Z = \$280x_1 - 6x_1^2 + 160x_2 - 3x_2^2$$
$$\text{subject to}$$
$$20x_1 + 10x_2 = 800 \text{ board ft}$$

Determine the optimal solution to this model using (a) the substitution method and (b) the method of Lagrange multipliers.

Step 1 (part a): Solve Using the Substitution Method

Solve the constraint for x_1,

$$x_1 = 40 - .5x_2$$

and substitute this term into the objective function.

$$
\begin{aligned}
Z &= 280(40 - .5x_2) - 6(40 - .5x_2)^2 + 160x_2 - 3x_2^2 \\
&= 11{,}200 - 140x_2 - 9{,}600 + 240x_2 - 1.5x_2^2 + 160x_2 - 3x_2^2 \\
&= 1{,}600 + 260x_2 - 4.5x_2^2
\end{aligned}
$$

Differentiate Z, set it equal to zero, and solve for x_2.

$$\frac{\partial Z}{\partial x_2} = 260 - 4.5x_2^2 = 0$$

$$x_2 = 28.88 \text{ chairs}$$

Substitute this value for x_2 into the original constraint.

$$
\begin{aligned}
x_1 &= 40 - .5x_2 \\
&= 40 - .5(28.88) \\
&= 25.56 \text{ tables}
\end{aligned}
$$

Then,

$$
\begin{aligned}
Z &= 280(25.56) - 6(25.56)^2 + 160(28.88) - 3(28.88)^2 \\
&= \$5{,}355.56
\end{aligned}
$$

Step 2 (part b): Solve Using the Method of Lagrange Multipliers

Develop the Lagrangian function:

$$L = 280x_1 - 6x_1^2 + 160x_2 - 3x_2^2 - \lambda(20x_1 + 10x_2 - 800)$$

Differentiate L with respect to x_1, x_2, and λ.

$$\frac{\partial L}{\partial x_1} = 280 - 12x_1 - 20\lambda$$

$$\frac{\partial L}{\partial x_2} = 160 - 6x_2 - 10\lambda$$

$$\frac{\partial L}{\partial \lambda} = -20x_1 - 10x_2 + 800$$

Solve simultaneously by setting all three equations equal to zero. Eliminate λ in the first two equations.

$$
\begin{aligned}
280 - 12x_1 - 20\lambda &= 0 \\
\underline{-320 + 12x_2 + 20\lambda} &= 0 \\
40 - 12x_1 + 12x_2 &= 0
\end{aligned}
$$

and

$$-12x_1 + 12x_2 - 40 = 0$$
$$\underline{-24x_1 - 12x_2 + 960 = 0}$$
$$-36x_1 - 920 = 0$$
$$x_1 = 25.56 \text{ tables}$$

Solve for x_2.

$$20x_1 + 10x_2 = 800$$
$$20(25.56) + 10x_2 = 800$$
$$x_2 = 28.88 \text{ chairs}$$

Then

$$Z = \$5,355.56$$

Problems

1. Explain why the addition of one or more constraints to a problem with a nonlinear objective function complicates the process of finding a solution to the problem.

2. Explain the substitution method for solving nonlinear programming problems and its limitations as a solution approach.

3. The Rainwater Brewery produces beer, which it sells to distributors in barrels. The brewery incurs a monthly fixed cost of \$12,000, and the variable cost per barrel is \$17. The brewery has developed the following profit function and demand constraint.

   maximize $Z = vp - \$12,000 - 17v$
   subject to
   $v = 800 - 15p$

   Solve this nonlinear programming model for the optimal price (p) using the substitution method.

4. The Colonial Pottery Company has developed the following nonlinear programming model to determine the optimal number of bowls (x_1) and mugs (x_2) to produce each day.

   maximize $Z = \$7x_1 - .3x_1^2 + 8x_2 - .4x_2^2$
   subject to
   $4x_1 + 5x_2 = 100 \text{ hr}$

   Determine the optimal solution to this model using the substitution method.

5. The Evergreen Fertilizer Company produces two types of fertilizers, Fastgro and Super Two. The company has developed the following non-linear programming model to determine the optimal number of bags of Fastgro (x_1) and Super Two (x_2) to produce each day in order to maximize profit, given a constraint for available potassium.

maximize $Z = \$30x_1 - 2x_1^2 + 25x_2 - .5x_2^2$

subject to

$\quad 3x_1 + 6x_2 = 300$ lb

Determine the optimal solution to this model using the substitution method.

6. The Rolling Creek Textile Mill produces denim and brushed cotton cloth. The company has developed the following nonlinear programming model to determine the optimal number of yards of denim (x_1) and brushed cotton (x_2) to produce each day in order to maximize profit, subject to a labor constraint.

maximize $Z = \$10x_1 - .02x_1^2 + 12x_2 - .03x_2^2$

subject to

$\quad .2x_1 + .1x_2 = 40$ hr

Determine the optimal solution to this model using the substitution method.

7. Solve problem 4 using the method of Lagrange multipliers.

8. Solve problem 5 using the method of Lagrange multipliers.

9. Solve problem 6 using the method of Lagrange multipliers.

10. The Riverwood Paneling Company makes two kinds of wood paneling, Colonial and Western. The company has developed the following non-linear programming model to determine the optimal number of sheets of Colonial paneling (x_1) and Western paneling (x_2) to produce in order to maximize profit, subject to a labor constraint.

maximize $Z = \$25x_1 - .8x_1^2 + 30x_2 - 1.2x_2^2$

subject to

$\quad x_1 + 2x_2 = 40$ hr

Determine the optimal solution to this model using the method of Lagrange multipliers.

11. Interpret the meaning of λ, the Lagrange multiplier, in problem 10.

12. Explain the difficulties in determining an optimal solution when the nonlinear objective function in a model is not completely convex or completely concave.

The Manager and Management Science

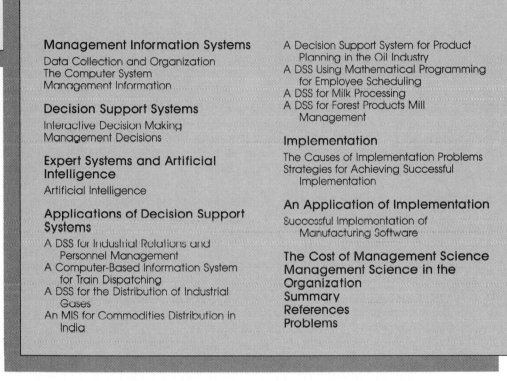

In all of the preceding chapters of this text we have presented management science *techniques*. These techniques do not actually make decisions, but they provide information that can aid the manager in making decisions. However, we have not discussed how this information generated from management science techniques is assimilated into the business organization. In other words, where in the organization is this information generated, how does it get to the manager,

Two types of
information systems

and how does the manager use it to make decisions? Many organizations employ some form of computer-based information system to accumulate, organize, and distribute information for decision-making purposes. In this chapter we will present and discuss two types of information systems, a *management information system* and a *decision support system*.

The fact that information is provided in most organizations through a computer-based information system does not ensure that this information will be used in an effective manner by the manager. The manager may simply ignore the information altogether. When the information generated from management science techniques is not used by the recipient to make decisions, we say the technique results are not *implemented*. Failure to implement model results can be a serious problem in organizations, and thus it will be the second topic we will discuss in this chapter.

MANAGEMENT INFORMATION SYSTEMS

A system designed
to channel
information through
an organization

A *management information system* (also known as an *MIS*) is a system specifically designed to channel large quantities and numerous types of information through an organization. In a management information system, data are collected, organized, processed, and made conveniently accessible to the manager so that the information will be of assistance to the manager in his or her daily operations. Much

Report generation

of this information is in the form of reports that are posted according to a predetermined schedule. Examples include payroll and sales reports generated on a weekly or monthly basis, or monthly inventory reports. Such reports enable the company to maintain control and also serve as a communication system, linking the various units (or departments) of an organization so that managerial actions are cooperative and made in concert.

The components of
an MIS

The essential components of a management information system are the data base, the computer system, and the form in which the data are distributed. In order to provide an idea of how a management information system is constructed and how it operates, we will discuss each component separately.

Data Collection and Organization

A data base

The first component in a management information system is the *data base*, which is an organized collection of numerical information. Prices, production output and rates, numbers of orders, available resources, capacities, and labor rates are examples of the pieces of information that form a data base.

For a management information system to be efficient and effective, the data base must contain the right amount and the right type of relevant, high-quality information. In addition, this information must be properly organized. Since most modern organizations have access to a large quantity and variety of information, maintaining an efficient and organized data base requires the use of a computer.

The Computer System

Modern management information systems generally are computerized. The vast amounts of data available to organizations make the computer an essential component of most management information systems (although manual systems do exist in smaller organizations).

MIS is generally computerized

Essentially a computer is an electrical machine that performs arithmetic operations very rapidly. The actual machine and the ancillary equipment, such as printers and display terminals, are referred to as *hardware*. The mathematical and written codes that instruct the computer how to perform operations are referred to as *software*. In order for the computer to perform a specific task, a *program* must be fed into the computer to tell it what to do.

Hardware
Software

A number of programs, also referred to as *software packages*, that organize and distribute information in report form are commercially available from computer software vendors. A large proportion of these software packages have been developed specifically for use on personal computers. Thus, it is no longer necessary for many companies to gain access to large *mainframe* computers and hire individuals specifically to write the programs that form an information system. Companies can purchase personal computers and compatible information system software packages at relatively moderate prices.

Software packages

Mainframe computers
Personal computers

Programs can also be developed internally by management scientists or by other individuals in the firm who are skilled in computer programming. Programs are written in computer languages such as FORTRAN, COBOL, or BASIC, among others. Frequently a company will develop a management information system from a combination of commercially available software packages and internally developed programs. These information systems are customized to fit the company's specific needs.

Programming languages

Management Information

The computer in a management information system processes data and generates information for use by the different units in the organization. The information flowing from the computer to the different departments can take several forms. It can be in the form of *reports* that summarize and organize the data, such as accounts receivable, order, work force, inventory level, resource level, market behav-

Information flows
Types of information flows

ior, or production output reports. These reports can provide recent information or historical information that might be relevant for present or future decisions. Reports typically do not reflect any form of management science analysis, but are simply collections of data organized so as to be useful and easily interpreted. They can be generated at the request of management or on a regular basis as a matter of policy. For example, the manager of the production area might request a report on the frequency of machine breakdowns during a particular month, whereas a report on monthly production output would be provided on a regular basis without request.

Management science model results

Information can also take the form of *management science model results or solutions*. Like reports, this information can be generated on a regular basis or by request. Most frequently, the information is compiled at the request of a manager who wants to solve a specific problem. However, it is important to point out that the management information system generally cannot formulate the management science model itself. This must be accomplished by the manager, a management scientist, or a management science staff skilled in management science techniques. (The development of these skills has been the purpose of this text.) The computer system can only provide the solution to the model that represents the problem.

DECISION SUPPORT SYSTEMS

A decision support system (DSS) is an information system with the capability of supporting the manager in the decision-making process. It differs from a management information system in that the manager typically acts as an *internal* component in a DSS, rather than an *external* component as in an MIS. In other words, the manager interacts with the computer-based information system so as to reach a decision through an iterative process.[1] Therefore, decision support systems are typically thought of as having interactive capabilities whereby the manager can establish a dialogue with the information system. In addition, a DSS frequently integrates management science models within its framework as the primary system components with which the decision maker interacts.

The manager is internal in a DSS, external in an MIS

Interactive capabilities

Turban has summarized the differences between MIS and DSS as follows.[2]

Management Information Systems

- The impact is on structured tasks, where standard operating procedures, decision rules, and information flows can be reliably predefined.

[1] D. Couger, "Question Yet Unresolved: What Is a Decision Support System?" *Computer Newsletter* 16, no. 2 (October 1982): 1.

[2] E. Turban, *Decision Support and Expert Systems* (New York: Macmillan, 1988), p. 18.

- The payoff is on improving efficiency by reducing costs, turnaround time, etc., and by replacing clerical personnel.
- The relevance for managers' decision making has been indirect—i.e., providing reports and access to data.

Decision Support Systems

- The impact is on decisions in which there is sufficient structure for computer and analytic aids to be of value but where managers' judgment is essential.
- The payoff is in extending the range and capability of computerized decision processes to help managers improve their effectiveness.
- The relevance for managers is the creation of a supportive tool, under their own control, that does not attempt to automate the decision process, predefine objectives, or impose solutions.

A general framework of a decision support system is illustrated in Figure 24.1. Notice that the blocks designated as *data, computer system–data processing*, and *information*, and the various information flows to management comprise the management information system. The added components that form a DSS are the decision-making capabilities, the management science techniques, and the interactive capabilities (i.e., what-if? analysis). To clarify the operation of a decision support system, we will explain the interactive capabilities of a DSS in greater detail.

General framework of a DSS

FIGURE 24.1

A Decision Support System

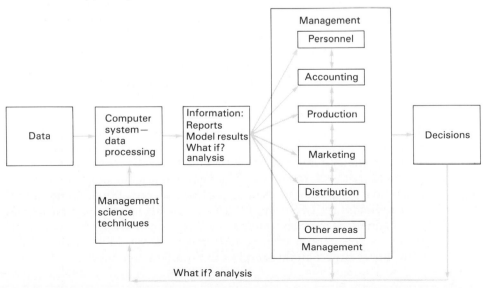

Interactive Decision Making

The information flows shown in Figure 24.1 reflect the interaction between the manager and the computer system, or what is more commonly referred to as *what-if? analysis*. That is, the computer system generates the results of a management science model and the manager asks the computer, What if something were changed in the model? For example, the computer system might generate an economic order quantity (Q) based on data provided in the EOQ model. The manager might then speculate that the order cost will change, and ask the computer for new results based on this change. Such experimentation with possible changes educates the manager regarding the possible courses of action that can be taken as a result of occurrences in the future. The manager can also test possible decisions to see their potential results before actually making them.

As shown in Figure 24.1, what-if? analysis takes the form of *interactive feedback* with the computer. In other words, such analysis occurs only at the request of management. Computer hardware and software packages are available that can perform this type of analysis very efficiently. With the use of *remote terminals* and *interactive computer programs*, managers can work directly with the computer, bypassing intermediate personnel or procedures. A remote terminal or CRT (cathode ray tube) display is a video screen that looks and acts like a television. The results of the DSS or MIS are displayed on this terminal either in color or in black and white, depending on the capabilities of the display terminal. The user types the request for information, or a command for the processing of information, via a keyboard similar to that of a typewriter. The request or command is passed to the computer, which performs the computational operations and returns the desired information to the user via the display terminal. The computer may be connected directly to the display terminal in the form of a personal computer, or it may be a larger unit housed in another location.

As in the case of management information systems, a number of interactive software packages are commercially available for use on mainframe or personal computers. Some of these packages serve only as decision support systems. In other cases, these packages can be integrated within a company's own customized DSS to perform specific operations. Examples of such commercially available decision support systems include IFPS and Lotus 1-2-3. Other software packages that perform specific management science operations in an interactive mode can be used as part of a larger DSS or stand alone as a rudimentary DSS. The LINDO and QSB+ computer packages for solving linear programming models, which we used in several previous chapters, are such software packages. Recall that they solve linear programming models in an interactive mode.

Margin notes:

What-if? analysis

Interactive feedback

Interactive computer programs

Video display monitor

Interactive software packages

These programs are designed to request the necessary input data from the manager by asking questions. The computer actually carries on a dialogue with the manager. For example, if the manager is performing inventory analysis, the computer might print the following question on the terminal screen:

WHAT IS THE ORDER COST PER UNIT, C_o?

The manager would then type in the order cost,

$C_o = 200$

and the computer would type out the optimal order quantity on the screen:

$Q = 500$

One additional aspect of a decision support system is the interaction between departments. Notice in Figure 24.1 that information flows between the departments. Decisions rarely affect only one unit in an organization. For example, inventory decisions affect not only the production operation but also the marketing department (which wants to be able to promise customers immediate delivery), the distribution department (because the availability of units of product affects shipping loads), and accounting (because the inventory on hand represents both an investment and a cost). The flow of information between areas must be coordinated in order to develop cooperative decisions, and this coordination is the function of top management that pervades all departments.

Departmental interaction

Management Decisions

The final stage in the decision support system shown in Figure 24.1 reflects the actual decisions made by management. Based on the information contained in reports, the solution results from management science models, and what-if? analysis, managers make decisions. However, these decisions are not an end in themselves; the decisions and their results in the form of *feedback* provide additional data for the data base. An ideal decision support system is an ongoing, dynamic system that continuously updates itself.

Although decision support systems can vary dramatically in sophistication, they are generally similar to the system shown in Figure 24.1. Regardless of the type of management information system or decision support system a business firm employs, however, *the generation of information does not ensure its use* for decision making. We will consider the problem of implementation later in this chapter.

Availability of information does not ensure its use

EXPERT SYSTEMS AND ARTIFICIAL INTELLIGENCE

A decision support system has already been defined as an interactive, computer-based information system that uses rules, models, and data to assist decision makers in making decisions. In comparison, Turban defines an expert system as a computer program that includes a *knowledge base* containing an expert's knowledge on a particular type of problem and a mechanism for reasoning that allows inferences to be made from the knowledge base.[3] In addition, he notes that an expert system provides the user with some detail about the reasoning process. Further, most expert systems are independent computer systems that advise users on specific problem areas. As such, they are often referred to as intelligent DSS. Table 24.1 shows the differences between decision support systems and expert systems as outlined by Turban.

TABLE 24.1

Difference Between Decision Support Systems and Expert Systems

Attributes	Decision Support System	Expert System
Objectives	Assist decision maker	Replicate an adviser
Who makes the decisions?	The decision maker and/or the system	The system
Major orientation	Decision making	Transfer of expertise and rendering of advice
Major query direction	Decision maker queries the machine	Machine queries the decision maker
Nature of support	Personal, groups, and institutional	Personal and groups
Data manipulation method	Numerical	Symbolic (mainly)
Characteristics of problem area	Complex, broad	Narrow
Type of problems treated	Ad hoc, unique	Repetitive
Content of data base	Factual knowledge	Procedural and factual knowledge
Reasoning capability	No	Yes, limited
Explanation capability	Limited	Yes

Because a knowledge base is central to the concept of an expert system, such a system is often called a *knowledge-based expert system*. The knowledge base is a large amount of knowledge about the problem that is stored in the system. Researchers have found that using masses of knowledge in an effective manner is more conducive to success than using a specific solution technique.[4] The term "expert"

---

[3]E. Turban, *Decision Support and Expert Systems*, p. 546.
[4]H. Ranch, "Probability Concepts for an Expert System Used for Data Fusion," *AI Magazine* 5, no. 3, 55–60.

is used because the system addresses problems typically thought to require an expert or specialist to solve.

Expert systems can be viewed as computerized "consultants" for decision making that have a collection of facts, knowledge, and *rules* used to make inferences about a problem area. The following brief example illustrates the use of a single rule (out of several) by an expert system to classify animals: If the variable EYES has the value *face forward*, the variable TEETH has the value *sharp*, the variable CLAWS has the value *has*, and the variable CLASS has the value *mammal*, then the variable CARNIVORE can be assigned the value *true*.[5] This rule has four input variables, EYES, TEETH, CLAWS, and CLASS, and one output variable, CARNIVORE. Each of the variables is assigned a *value* (e.g., for EYES a value "face forward" is assigned). If each input variable has the appropriate value specified in the rule, then the output variable, CARNIVORE, is assigned a value "true." In other words, knowledge is used in conjunction with a rule to make an inference regarding animal classification. This particular rule is only one of a number of rules that might be part of an expert system that would classify animals. Figure 24.2 illustrates the general structure of a rule-based expert system such as an animal classification system.

FIGURE 24.2

The General Structure of a Rule-Based Expert System for Classification

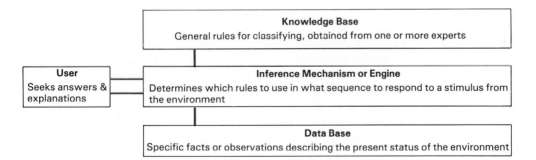

SOURCE: Adapted from K. Fordyce, P. Norden, G. Sullivan, "Review of Expert Systems for the Management Science Practitioner," *Interfaces* 17, no. 2 (March–April 1987): 64–77.

[5]P. Winston, *Artificial Intelligence* (Reading, Mass.: Addison Wesley, 1983), in K. Fordyce, P. Norden, and G. Sullivan, "Review of Expert Systems for the Management Science Practitioner," *Interfaces* 17, no. 2 (March–April 1987): 64–77.

The reader will notice in the discussion in this section and in Figure 24.2 the use of several terms whose meaning is not self-evident, such as "knowledge base," "inference engine," and "knowledge engineering." In recent years the field of expert systems has grown very rapidly, along a separate path that has not been incorporated within any other single discipline, such as management science. As a result, an entire nomenclature has been developed for expert systems and artificial intelligence that is peculiar to these areas and that may be intimidating to the casual but interested observer. Gaining real knowledge of and ability to use expert systems requires a commitment that will enable one to overcome the complex terminologies and philosophies that are part of expert systems and artificial intelligence.

Artificial Intelligence

Artificial intelligence is a concept that is difficult to define specifically, yet it appears to have certain characteristics. The objective of those interested in artificial intelligence is to study and understand human thought processes (i.e., intelligence) and to develop computational processes (using computers, robots, etc.) that will simulate those thought processes. Artificial intelligence allows machines to exhibit behavior, such as solving problems or carrying out tasks, similar to that of human beings. Such behavior would be viewed as intelligent if a human rather than a machine exhibited it. Some of the earliest (and still most popular) examples of artificial intelligence have been the use of computers to play games like chess and checkers. In general, expert systems are viewed as a subspecialty of artificial intelligence.

A central characteristic of artificial intelligence is that it represents knowledge gained by using *heuristics* (or rules of thumb) rather than *algorithms* to process information. An algorithm is a step-by-step solution approach that guarantees a solution, such as the simplex method to solve linear programming problems introduced in Chapter 4. In contrast, heuristic reasoning invokes intuition, plausible arguments, or rules of thumb to make decisions, and as such it reflects human reasoning more closely than do algorithms.

Another important characteristic of artificial intelligence is that it employs symbols as well as, and sometimes in place of, numbers. Computers were originally designed to process numbers; however, human reasoning appears to be based on the use and manipulation of symbols as much as numbers.

The use of artificial intelligence and its subset of expert systems merges with and affects management science in several ways. Expert systems with heuristic reasoning have found applications in such areas as developing, reviewing, and monitoring plans; production and manufacturing; and maintenance—areas where management science solutions based on algorithms were not possible. Expert systems provide a vehicle for using management science models in an effective way: the expert system can use the model results to establish guidelines or make recommendations. Expert systems can also select the appropriate management science model to use for a particular problem and assist the management scientist in interpreting the model results.[6]

APPLICATIONS OF DECISION SUPPORT SYSTEMS

A DSS for Industrial Relations and Personnel Management

In 1972 RCA decided to upgrade its employee benefits programs, and an evaluation of the retirement plan was initiated. In order to test the existing retirement plan, a mathematical model was constructed; however, problems were encountered in obtaining data support to use the model. The corporate industrial relations staff requested personnel information from RCA operating units, but the data received were often inaccurate, dated, incomplete, and unreliable. In 1974 the corporate operations research group was requested to develop a new information system that would provide a vehicle for interactive inquiry and analysis on the part of all levels of industrial relations management, and that would provide all regular clerical functions and procedures required by the industrial relations staff.

The new information system encompassed four major design components. (1) Data base management (DBM) technology was used to create and maintain a repository for employee information; (2) the user portion of the system (i.e., the "front end") was designed to be interactive and to provide procedures for receiving and manipulating data on-line; (3) a "back office" of the system was created to update and maintain the data base and provide all standard reports; and (4) the system was equipped to receive and process all personnel-related transactions.

A successful pilot system was created and demonstrated by mid-1974; five years were then required to install the system at the nineteen RCA operating units. By 1979 the entire company was using the system, referred to as IRIS (Industrial Relations Information Sys-

---

[6]K. Fordyce, P. Norden, and G. Sullivan, "Artificial Intelligence and the Management Science Practitioner: Links Between Operations Research and Expert Systems," *Interfaces* 17, no. 4 (July–August 1987): 34–40.

tem). During the implementation period, the company employed an intricate cost evaluation system to compare those units of the company not using the system with those using the system. At the end of 1978, the cost of personnel information per employee was $27 less for those units using IRIS than for those units not using it. This represented an annual "cost avoidance" rate of approximately $2.5 million. Beyond cost savings, the system had a significant impact on the effectiveness and managerial efficiency of the industrial relations function in the company.[7]

A Computer-Based Information System for Train Dispatching

The Alabama Division of Southern Railway, headquartered in Birmingham, Alabama, is a complex operating division encompassing 800 miles of mainline track and 80 to 90 trains in daily operation. The division headquarters is responsible for daily operations, including the safe and efficient dispatching of trains throughout the division. Trains generally operate on single tracks, and opposing trains "meet" at strategically placed sidings, which are arranged by division dispatchers with safety as the paramount consideration.

System simulation

In 1975 the operations research staff began the development of a computer-based information system to assist train dispatchers. The staff initially developed a minicomputer-based simulator that emulated a centralized traffic control office environment and allowed designers and dispatchers to re-create real-life scenarios. The simulator encompassed four CRT color monitors. Two of these CRTs displayed the movement of trains along track layouts based on route decisions made interactively by the train dispatcher. A third CRT monitor served as a worksheet for updating train-data files. The final color monitor was used to indicate how trains should be routed.

Branch-and-bound optimization

A "meet/pass" plan based on a branch-and-bound optimization algorithm was integrated into this simulator. This on-line interactive system considered all feasible future train meetings in the division territory and advised the dispatcher of the combination that would minimize total train delay. This plan reflected all realistic operating conditions, including travel times, speed limits and restrictions, schedules, and cargo handling. The meet/pass plan was designed to reevaluate the combination whenever conditions changed and to generate and display a new plan projecting up to eight hours in the future. The dispatcher could also override the plan to reflect dispatcher experience and judgment and to interact with the planning system to perform what-if? analysis.

[7]F. Edelman, "Managers, Computer Systems, and Productivity," *Interfaces* 12, no. 5 (October 1982): 35–46, reprinted from *MIS Quarterly* 5, no. 3 (September 1981).

The system was implemented in 1980 at the North Alabama district of the division. In the first two years of operation, use of the system resulted in a 15% reduction in train delays, reflecting a savings of $316,000 each year in the district. It was estimated that future savings for the entire Alabama district would be $675,000 per year.[8]

A DSS for the Distribution of Industrial Gases

Air Products and Chemicals, Inc., one of the world's largest suppliers of industrial gases, manufactures liquid oxygen and nitrogen at highly automated plants which also serve as supply depots where gases are stored. The gases are subsequently distributed by tankers to industrial users and hospitals equipped with storage tanks provided by the supplier, which monitors the inventory levels in the tanks and delivers gases as needed. Because of relatively uniform manufacturing costs among gas suppliers, industry competition is significantly affected by efficient distribution.

The scheduling and distribution of gases by Air Products was an extremely complex function complicated by several factors. It was necessary to integrate inventory management at customer locations with vehicle scheduling and dispatching. Customer demand was uncertain; therefore, safety stocks were required to ensure that no shortages developed, yet customers were not always open for deliveries. The complicated scheduling function was performed manually by staff members at the depots.

A new computerized vehicle scheduling system was implemented in 1981. This new system is accessed interactively by schedulers at the plants/depots using CRT monitors linked by dedicated telephone lines to the main computer. Detailed schedules for two- to five-day horizons are produced daily at each plant, and delivery data and customer requirements are updated interactively upon receipt.

The system encompasses six data files. A customer file containing relevant data about each customer interacts with a demand forecaster that uses a time series model to forecast customer demand. This forecast is then used by an inventory level calculator to project customer tank inventory at any point in time. A resource data file contains all relevant information about trucks in the fleet and information on the availability of gases for at least five days in the future, and a cost file contains all relevant distribution system costs. A mileage file contains a network representation of the road system of the United States, which is used with a shortest route algorithm to determine the distance, travel time, and toll costs between any two

Network analysis

[8]R. Sauder and W. Westerman, "Computer Aided Train Dispatching: Decision Support Through Optimization," *Interfaces* 13, no. 6 (December 1983): 24–37.

Mixed integer
programming

customers. This information is subsequently stored in a time and distance file. The data from these files are used by a scheduling module called ROVER (Realtime Optimizer for Vehicle Routing) to produce a schedule for distribution during a two- to five-day period. ROVER determines the schedule by solving an extremely large mixed integer programming model that can encompass up to 800,000 variables and 200,000 constraints. As indicated, the entire decision support system is user-friendly and interactive.

In 1983 the vehicle scheduling system was used by eleven depots. Average savings for a system of sixteen depots was estimated at between $1.54 million and $1.72 million annually. The savings in capital expenditures for new tankers was estimated at $3.1 million.[9]

An MIS for Commodities Distribution in India

In 1954, the government of India established a public distribution system (PDS) to provide essential commodities such as rice, wheat, and vegetable oil to the poor. By 1985 this system had grown to approximately 320,000 retail outlets and 6,000 warehouses, the management of which required several agencies. A management information system was designed to assist in production and procurement planning, agency coordination, and shipping to warehouses. The MIS is based on two reports, one from the stores and a monthly report from the warehouses. Both of these reports encompass data on system operations. Performance reports are subsequently generated based on the base reports. The MIS helps the state government of India to plan and monitor the distribution of commodities.[10]

A Decision Support System for Product Planning in the Oil Industry

Citgo Petroleum Corporation, a subsidiary of The Southland Corporation, is one of the nation's largest industrial companies. During the early 1980s, as the price of crude oil and interest rates increased, Citgo determined to develop a supply, distribution, and marketing (SDM) modeling system to integrate the company's key economic and physical characteristics on an 11-week planning horizon. The system is based on a network optimization methodology encompassing a maximum profit flow (transshipment) network model for the motor fuel and fuel oil products of the firm. (Transshipment

---

[9]W. Bell et al., "Improving the Distribution of Industrial Gases with an On-line Computerized Routing and Scheduling Optimizer," *Interfaces* 13, no. 6 (December 1983): 4–23.

[10]K. Ramani and S. Bhatnagar, "A Management Information System to Plan and Monitor the Distribution of Essential Commodities in India," *Interfaces* 18, no. 2 (March–April 1988): 56–63.

models are a special case of the transportation problem.) The mathematical model includes an objective function that maximizes profit, calculated as total revenue from sales less expenses, and constraints representing product flow balances for each distribution center. The final mathematical model includes approximately 3,000 equations and 15,000 variables. The model assists management in making weekly decisions regarding refinery run levels, establishing prices, determining where to buy and sell products, and setting inventory and shipment levels. It is also used by schedulers for operational decisions. The primary benefit of the system has been the reduction of product inventories by over $116 million, which is equivalent to an annual reduction of $14 million in interest expenses.[11]

A DSS Using Mathematical Programming for Employee Scheduling

United Airlines initiated its Station Manpower Planning Project in 1982 for work scheduling primarily among its reservations office personnel and airport groups working shift schedules. The project objectives were to determine the numbers of employees needed, to identify excess employees for reallocation, to reduce schedule preparation time, to render employee allocation more day and time sensitive, and to quantify scheduling costs. These objectives were essentially achieved by developing monthly employee shift schedules. The system consists of a mixed integer linear programming model used to determine the times of day that shifts should start; these times, in turn, are inputs to a continuous linear programming model that identifies monthly shift schedules that minimize labor cost while meeting employee and operating preferences. Also included are a heuristic rounding routine, which converts the fractional linear programming solution into a workable shift schedule; a report module, which produces monthly shift schedules and places them in an interactive data base where they can be accessed by schedulers; and various cost reports. Finally, a network assignment model is used in a day-off pairing module to combine monthly shift schedules into trimester work assignments based on transitions between types of shifts and assigned days off in two adjoining months. The system was implemented during 1983 and 1984. Used to schedule approximately 4,000 employees, the system has resulted in annual savings in direct salary and benefit costs of $6 million.[12]

[11]D. Klingman, N. Phillips, D. Steiger, R. Wirth, and W. Young, "The Challenges and Success Factors in Implementing an Integrated Products Planning System for Citgo," *Interfaces* 16, no. 3 (May–June 1986): 1–19.

[12]T. Holloran and J. Byrn, "United Airlines Station Manpower Planning System," *Interfaces* 16, no. 1 (January–February 1986): 39–50.

A DSS for Milk Processing

The Dairyman's Cooperative Creamery Association (DCCA) in Tulare, California, developed a decision support system that has as its primary component an interactive linear programming model. DCCA, the largest single milk processing plant in the United States, receives approximately 5 million pounds of raw milk per day, which is stored in silos and then transferred to different product stations for processing into approximately 50 products. Plant supervisors are responsible for allocating and estimating milk flow demand and supply; estimating total available storage and equipment capacities; anticipating personnel availability, maintenance requirements, and customer demand; and specifying quality standards—all of which vary daily and during the day. Previously supervisors were required to develop these relationships by hand. The decision support system consists of two components: a preprocessor, which elicits the production information and estimates and uses these data to develop linear flow and capacity constraints, and a linear programming module, which determines the daily production and inventory levels that will maximize plant throughput. The system enables supervisors to make daily production plans and adjust them rapidly. The system development cost was $15,000, and it is estimated that the system has increased daily plant throughput by 150,000 pounds per day, resulting in an estimated annual net increase in profits of $48,000. Including the savings in time to supervisors, which enables them to concentrate their efforts on related production problems, total savings are expected to be $100,000 annually.[13]

A DSS for Forest Products
Mill Management

At the Weyerhaeuser Company, logs (referred to as stems) are shipped randomly to the log mill from inventory at a machine center (referred to as a merchandiser), where they have been sawed and cut to various lengths. This process requires that operators decide where to cut the stem. This seemingly simple decision is actually quite crucial in terms of maximizing return. The company has developed a decision support system that includes a merchandiser decision system (MDS) and a concurrent simulation system (COMPASS). The MDS encompasses a data acquisition system, which acquires information about the physical characteristics of a stem; a processor, which determines an optimal decision (where to cut); and a control system, which interfaces the operator with the saws. COMPASS includes a

[13]R. Sullivan and S. Secrest, "A Simple Optimization DSS for Production Planning at Dairyman's Cooperative Creamery Association," *Interfaces* 15, no. 5 (September–October 1985): 46–53.

data base, simulation models, and interfaces that act concurrently with MDS to help managers determine the effects of the system's logic and explore alternative merchandising strategies. Among other things, the MDS predicts the amount of lumber that will be extracted from a log. The company estimated that the system's return on investment is over 40%.[14]

IMPLEMENTATION

A major consideration in designing a decision support system is ensuring that the manager will use the information provided as efficiently as possible to make decisions. If the information is not used or is ignored altogether, then it represents a total loss. In other words, there is only the cost of providing the information and not any benefit received from it.

Ensuring that the manager uses the information provided to make more efficient decisions

The application of information generated from management science models is referred to as *implementation*. The fact that implementation is not always achieved poses a potential problem for the top management of an organization. The problem of implementing management science results has received a great deal of attention in recent years. Management information systems have become more sophisticated, and the number and types of management science techniques have increased. However, evidence indicates that these advancements have not been accompanied by a corresponding increase in implementation. The results of management science techniques are not being used to the fullest extent possible, and thus their total potential is not being realized. We will explore some of the causes of the failure to implement management information and offer some possible remedies.

The Causes of Implementation Problems

When the problem of implementation first came to the attention of managers and management scientists, the causes identified were somewhat superficial. These causes included the following (among others).

The personalities and training of managers
Ill-defined problems and improper model formulation
Models that are too sophisticated (and complicated) for the problems to be solved

[14]M. Hehnen, S. Chou, H. Scheurman, G. Robinson, T. Luken, and D. W. Baker, "An Integrated Decision Support and Manufacturing Control System," *Interfaces* 14, no. 5 (September–October 1984): 44–52.

A lack of understanding of management and decision-making processes by the management scientist

A lack of understanding of management science techniques by managers

Too much time required to develop models for decisions that must be made immediately

Models that do not reflect the reality of the actual problem

The appropriate data are not always available in the management information system

An improperly designed management information system

Resistance on the part of the manager to using new tools of analysis (such as a management science technique)

These are typical of the explanations given for problems in implementing the results of management science models. Although these criticisms are often valid, as opinions based in many cases on practical experiences, they tend to be too general to be applied to the problem of implementation as a whole.

As is the case with many types of problem analysis, attempts to explain the problems of implementation eventually passed from generalization to directed research. Such research typically revealed that implementation problems are rooted in the relationship of the management science staff to the surrounding organization. Some of the more subtle factors relating to implementation problems are

Factors related to implementation problems

The level of support for management science in the organization

The success of prior uses of management science

The "political" opposition to or support for management science

The amount of power and influence the management science staff has in the organization

The size of the management science staff and the amount of resources it commands

The climate for innovation and change within the organization

The time frame for decision making

The location of the responsibility for implementation

Management's experience with management science techniques

These are only a few of the many factors that have been identified as being related to implementation. These lists of factors demonstrate that there is no one cause or set of causes for implementation failure. As a result, it is difficult to propose a specific strategy for ensuring successful implementation. An implementation strategy must be tailored to fit the particular organization.

Strategies for Successful Implementation

Numerous strategies have been proposed to ensure successful implementation, as might be expected given the many causes of the problem that have been identified. A common thread running through the various proposals for achieving success is that the implementation process must be viewed as a *continuous, ongoing process*. This means that implementation encompasses not only the final decision but also problem formulation, model development, and construction and model testing.

In this framework, the experiences gained from implementation provide feedback to different stages in the management science modeling process. Thus, the model evolves through the implementation process. The basic premise underlying this approach is that successful implementation is dependent on success at each stage of the modeling process. If the management problem is not formulated properly, if the model is constructed improperly, if the results are not realistic or applicable, then implementation will never occur.

Within this framework, management involvement in the management science process enhances the possibility of successful implementation. This means that the manager must be an active participant in the development and use of the management science model. If this interaction takes place, then there is a better chance that the model will be designed with the proposed use closely in mind and that the model will not be too sophisticated for the user.

Another strategy for achieving successful implementation is to create a situation in which the manager is receptive and conducive to change. Behavioral change on the part of the manager is a major factor in implementation. For the manager, a *lack of change* promotes stability and continuity, leading to feelings of comfort and safeness. Management and labor functions tend to become routinized and habitual in this environment. When change becomes imminent, it is resisted, since it is perceived as a threat to the normal safe routine. In this scenario the management science technique is a potential change, since it often represents a new and different way of doing things.

In order to overcome this resistance to change, an organized process must be established to introduce the management science model and to create a new feeling of routine that will reinforce the use of the model. There are several ways to achieve these goals, but basically they require a joint effort by both the manager and the management scientist. Regardless of the means used, the important point is that the information generated from management science models cannot simply be *dumped* on the manager without some prior preparation.

Margin notes:

Implementation as a continuous, ongoing process

Implementation experiences provide feedback to the modeling process

Management involvement in the management science process

Implementation creates changes for the manager

Overcoming the resistance to change

AN APPLICATION OF IMPLEMENTATION

Successful Implementation of Manufacturing Software

Geisler and Rubenstein conducted a study of eighteen manufacturing companies in order to determine factors that might contribute to the successful implementation of manufacturing-related software. The development of such software frequently requires a large capital investment; thus its successful implementation is of particular importance. The study revealed that successful implementation is dependent on the degree of interaction between the software developers and users, on the support from upper management, and on the quality of the planning and objectives related to implementation. Three implications were developed from the study for improving implementation. First, top management should encourage interaction between the software producers and users (production personnel). Second, management should support the implementation of the software and not be preoccupied exclusively with the productivity of the software. Clear and feasible goals and policies should be set for the software. Third, management should support the (production) user before, during, and after implementation with resources, training, support for risk-taking, and autonomy in making related decisions. In addition, management should encourage manufacturing and other company functions (such as MIS) to work together in the planning process and in the selection and evaluation of software.[15]

THE COST OF MANAGEMENT SCIENCE

The cost in time and resources of developing management science models

An often overlooked but important aspect of management science is the cost in time and resources of developing and using management science models. The costs of the staff skills and computer time required to develop and use management science can sometimes be high. Thus, any consideration of the use of management science techniques should also include an estimate of the benefits and costs involved.

The easiest costs to estimate are those for the staff necessary to develop a model; however, even these costs cannot be forecast with complete certainty. Such costs include the cost of the management science personnel and the cost of teaching management personnel

[15]E. Geisler and A. Rubenstein, "The Successful Implementation of Application Software in New Production Systems,"*Interfaces* 17, no. 3 (May–June 1987): 18–24.

the techniques. It is even more difficult to determine the costs resulting from the disruption of normal operating conditions, which can
temporarily cause decreased output and productivity, lost sales, and
disrupted schedules.

The benefits accruing from a management science model are
measured in terms of increased productivity, profits, or efficiency, or
reduced cost or time. Failure to implement the results of a management science model results in little or no benefit.

MANAGEMENT SCIENCE IN THE ORGANIZATION

The location of management science within the organization structure, the size of the management science staff (assuming there is
one), and the status of the management scientist are all factors affecting the degree of implementation of management science results.
Many large and medium-sized business firms have management science departments or staffs concerned exclusively with problem solving and model development. Although these staffs can be quite
large, containing as many as thirty members, their success is dependent primarily on the quality of their efforts.

The management science staff can exist at several locations
within the organization structure. It can be at the top management
level, the corporate level, or the operational level. Some firms have
management science groups at each level of the organization. The
officer to whom the management science staff reports is determined
basically by the location of the staff in the organization. There does
not appear to be a typical organizational location for a management
science staff.

This discussion of the management science staff should not leave
the impression that management science is not important in firms
where there is no management science staff or department. In many
instances, a member (or several members) of the management staff
who is well versed in management science will apply management
science techniques to the firm's problems. This will become more
common in the future as a result of the increased training in management science techniques being provided in college business programs. Undergraduate business majors will be better prepared in
the future to apply management science techniques to business
problems. Although the managers/management scientists of the future will be constrained by a lack of time and resources, they will
have the advantage of being directly involved in the problem situation, which can enhance implementation.

The location of the management science staff in the organization

Summary

In this concluding chapter we have explained how management science is made available to the manager through computer-based information systems and indicated some of the problems that can prevent the implementation of management science results that are obtained from such systems. Even though management science techniques have tremendous potential for solving business problems, their actual use is dependent on an efficient management information system and a concerted emphasis on implementation. Although there are many documented instances of the successful use of management science and more successes will be forthcoming in the future, information systems and implementation efforts must continue to be refined. It would be regretable if the full potential offered by management science techniques remained unrealized because obstacles to their assimilation into the organization by management could not be overcome. However, as this chapter has indicated, the problems have been recognized and solutions will continue to be sought in the future.

References

Bell, W.; Dalberto, L.; Fisher, M.; Greenfied, A.; Jaikumar, R.; Kedia, P.; Mack, R.; and Prutzman, P. "Improving the Distribution of Industrial Gases with an On-line Computerized Routing and Scheduling Optimizer." *Interfaces* 13, no. 6 (December 1983): 4–23.

Churchman, C., and Shainblatt, A. A. "The Researcher and the Manager: A Dialectic of Implementation." *Management Science* 11, no. 4 (February 1965): 869–87.

Couger, D. "Question Yet Unresolved: What Is a Decision Support System?" *Computing Newsletter* 16, no. 2 (October 1982): 1.

Davis, G. B. *Management Information Systems: Conceptual Foundations, Structure and Development.* New York: McGraw-Hill, 1974.

Davis, K. R., and Taylor, B. W. "Addressing the Implementation Problem: A Gaming Approach." *Decision Sciences* 7, no. 4 (October 1976): 677–87.

Edelman, F. "Managers, Computer Systems, and Productivity." *Interfaces* 12, no. 5 (October 1982): 35–46; reprinted from *MIS Quarterly* 5, no. 3 (September 1981).

Fordyce, K.; Norden, P.; and Sullivan, G. "Review of Expert Systems for the Management Science Practitioner." *Interfaces* 17, no. 2 (March–April 1987): 64–77.

Fordyce, K.; Norden, P.; and Sullivan, G. "Artificial Intelligence and the Management Science Practitioner: Links Between Operations Research and Expert Systems." *Interfaces* 17, no. 4 (July–August 1987): 34–40.

Gaither, N. "The Adoption of Operations Research Techniques by Manufacturing Organizations." *Decision Sciences* 6, no. 4 (October 1975): 797–813.

Grayson, C. J., Jr. "Management Science and Business Practice." *Harvard Business Review* 51, no. 4 (July–August 1973): 41–48.

Harvey, A. "Factors Making for Implementation Success and Failure." *Management Science* 16, no. 6 (February 1970): B312–21.

Keen, P., and Scott-Morton, M. *Decision Support Systems, An Organizational Perspective.* Reading, Mass.: Addison-Wesley, 1978.

Lee, Sang M.; Moore, Laurence J.; and Taylor, Bernard W. *Management Science.* 3d ed. Boston: Allyn and Bacon, 1990.

McLeod, R., Jr. *Management Information Systems.* 3d ed. Chicago: SRA, 1986.

Murdick, R. G., and Ross, J. E. *Introduction to Management Information Systems.* Englewood Cliffs, N.J.: Prentice-Hall, 1977.

Rubenstein, A. H.; Radnor, M.; Baker, N. R.; Heiman, D. K.; and McColly, J. B. "Some Organizational Factors Related to Effectiveness of Management Science Groups in Industry." *Management Science* 13, no. 8 (April 1967): B508–18.

Sauder, R., and Westerman, W. "Computer Aided Train Dispatching: Decision Support Through Optimization." *Interfaces* 13, no. 6 (December 1983): 24–37.

Schultz, R. L., and Slevin, D. P., eds. *Implementing Operations Research/Management Science.* New York: Elsevier, 1975.

Simon, H. "Two Heads Are Better Than One: The Collaboration Between AI and OR." *Interfaces* 17, no. 4 (July–August 1987): 8–15.

Sprague, R. H., and Watson, H. J. "MIS Concepts." *Journal of Systems Management* (January and February 1975).

Turban, E. *Decision Support and Expert Systems.* New York: Macmillan, 1988.

Problems

1. What is a management information system?

2. Explain the function of a data base in a management information system.

3. Why are management information systems typically computerized?

4. Define a decision support system and describe the difference between an MIS and a DSS.

5. Explain what the term "what-if? analysis" means.

6. Explain what an interactive computer program does.

7. What is the function of information feedback in a decision support system?

8. Using the general form of Figure 24.1, design a theoretical decision support system that encompasses one or more management science techniques and assists the manager in making a specific decision.

9. Define an expert system.

10. Discuss the differences between a decision support system and an expert system.

11. Explain the difference between a heuristic and an algorithm.

12. Define implementation.

13. List and discuss the three biggest causes of implementation problems, in your opinion.

14. Why must implementation be viewed as a continuous process?

15. What effect does change have on the implementation process?

16. Describe some of the costs associated with management science.

17. Discuss the relationship of management science to the organization as a whole and the effect of this relationship on implementation.

A

Tables

Table A.1 Normal Curve Areas

Z	.00	.01	.02	.03	.04	.05	.06	.07	.08	.09
0.0	.0000	.0040	.0080	.0120	.0160	.0199	.0239	.0279	.0319	.0359
0.1	.0398	.0438	.0478	.0517	.0557	.0596	.0636	.0675	.0714	.0753
0.2	.0793	.0832	.0871	.0910	.0948	.0987	.1026	.1064	.1103	.1141
0.3	.1179	.1217	.1255	.1293	.1331	.1368	.1406	.1443	.1480	.1517
0.4	.1554	.1591	.1628	.1664	.1700	.1736	.1772	.1808	.1844	.1879
0.5	.1915	.1950	.1985	.2019	.2054	.2088	.2123	.2157	.2190	.2224
0.6	.2257	.2291	.2324	.2357	.2389	.2422	.2454	.2486	.2517	.2549
0.7	.2580	.2611	.2642	.2673	.2704	.2734	.2764	.2794	.2823	.2852
0.8	.2881	.2910	.2939	.2967	.2995	.3023	.3051	.3078	.3106	.3133
0.9	.3159	.3186	.3212	.3238	.3264	.3289	.3315	.3340	.3365	.3389
1.0	.3413	.3438	.3461	.3485	.3508	.3531	.3554	.3577	.3599	.3621
1.1	.3643	.3665	.3686	.3708	.3729	.3749	.3770	.3790	.3810	.3830
1.2	.3849	.3869	.3888	.3907	.3925	.3944	.3962	.3980	.3997	.4015
1.3	.4032	.4049	.4066	.4082	.4099	.4115	.4131	.4147	.4162	.4177
1.4	.4192	.4207	.4222	.4236	.4251	.4265	.4279	.4292	.4306	.4319
1.5	.4332	.4345	.4357	.4370	.4382	.4394	.4406	.4418	.4429	.4441
1.6	.4452	.4463	.4474	.4484	.4495	.4505	.4515	.4525	.4535	.4545
1.7	.4554	.4564	.4573	.4582	.4591	.4599	.4608	.4616	.4625	.4633
1.8	.4641	.4649	.4656	.4664	.4671	.4678	.4686	.4693	.4699	.4706
1.9	.4713	.4719	.4726	.4732	.4738	.4744	.4750	.4756	.4761	.4767
2.0	.4772	.4778	.4783	.4788	.4793	.4798	.4803	.4808	.4812	.4817
2.1	.4821	.4826	.4830	.4834	.4838	.4842	.4846	.4850	.4854	.4857
2.2	.4861	.4864	.4868	.4871	.4875	.4878	.4881	.4884	.4887	.4890
2.3	.4893	.4896	.4898	.4901	.4904	.4906	.4909	.4911	.4913	.4916
2.4	.4918	.4920	.4922	.4925	.4927	.4929	.4931	.4932	.4934	.4936
2.5	.4938	.4940	.4941	.4943	.4945	.4946	.4948	.4949	.4951	.4952
2.6	.4953	.4955	.4956	.4957	.4959	.4960	.4961	.4962	.4963	.4964
2.7	.4965	.4966	.4967	.4968	.4969	.4970	.4971	.4972	.4973	.4974
2.8	.4974	.4975	.4976	.4977	.4977	.4978	.4979	.4979	.4980	.4981
2.9	.4981	.4982	.4982	.4983	.4984	.4984	.4985	.4985	.4986	.4986
3.0	.4987	.4987	.4987	.4988	.4988	.4989	.4989	.4989	.4990	.4990

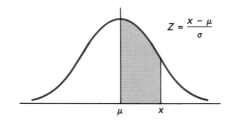

$$Z = \frac{x - \mu}{\sigma}$$

Table A.2 The Binomial Distribution for Selected Values of *n*

r	.01	.02	.03	.04	.05	.10	.15	.20	.30	.40	.50
						p					

n = 1

r	.01	.02	.03	.04	.05	.10	.15	.20	.30	.40	.50
0	.9900	.9800	.9700	.9600	.9500	.9000	.8500	.8000	.7000	.6000	.5000
1	.0100	.0200	.0300	.0400	.0500	.1000	.1500	.2000	.3000	.4000	.5000

n = 2

r	.01	.02	.03	.04	.05	.10	.15	.20	.30	.40	.50
0	.9801	.9604	.9409	.9216	.9025	.8100	.7225	.6400	.4900	.3600	.2500
1	.0198	.0392	.0582	.0768	.0950	.1800	.2550	.3200	.4200	.4800	.5000
2	.0001	.0004	.0009	.0016	.0025	.0100	.0225	.0400	.0900	.1600	.2500

n = 3

r	.01	.02	.03	.04	.05	.10	.15	.20	.30	.40	.50
0	.9704	.9412	.9127	.8847	.8574	.7290	.6141	.5120	.3430	.2160	.1250
1	.0294	.0576	.0847	.1106	.1354	.2430	.3251	.3840	.4410	.4320	.3750
2	.0003	.0012	.0026	.0046	.0071	.0270	.0574	.0960	.1890	.2880	.3750
3	.0000	.0000	.0000	.0001	.0001	.0010	.0034	.0080	.0270	.0640	.1250

n = 4

r	.01	.02	.03	.04	.05	.10	.15	.20	.30	.40	.50
0	.9606	.9224	.8853	.8493	.8145	.6561	.5220	.4096	.2401	.1296	.0625
1	.0388	.0753	.1095	.1416	.1715	.2916	.3685	.4096	.4116	.3456	.2500
2	.0006	.0023	.0051	.0088	.0135	.0486	.0975	.1536	.2646	.3456	.3750
3	.0000	.0000	.0001	.0002	.0005	.0036	.0115	.0256	.0756	.1536	.2500
4	.0000	.0000	.0000	.0000	.0000	.0001	.0005	.0016	.0081	.0256	.0625

n = 5

r	.01	.02	.03	.04	.05	.10	.15	.20	.30	.40	.50
0	.9510	.9039	.8587	.8154	.7738	.5905	.4437	.3277	.1681	.0778	.0312
1	.0480	.0922	.1328	.1699	.2036	.3280	.3915	.4096	.3602	.2592	.1562
2	.0010	.0038	.0082	.0142	.0214	.0729	.1382	.2048	.3087	.3456	.3125
3	.0000	.0001	.0003	.0006	.0011	.0081	.0244	.0512	.1323	.2304	.3125
4	.0000	.0000	.0000	.0000	.0000	.0004	.0022	.0064	.0284	.0768	.1562
5	.0000	.0000	.0000	.0000	.0000	.0000	.0001	.0003	.0024	.0102	.0312

n = 6

r	.01	.02	.03	.04	.05	.10	.15	.20	.30	.40	.50
0	.9415	.8858	.8330	.7828	.7351	.5314	.3771	.2621	.1176	.0467	.0156
1	.0571	.1085	.1546	.1957	.2321	.3543	.3993	.3932	.3025	.1866	.0938
2	.0014	.0055	.0120	.0204	.0305	.0984	.1762	.2458	.3241	.3110	.2344
3	.0000	.0002	.0005	.0011	.0021	.0146	.0415	.0819	.1852	.2765	.3125
4	.0000	.0000	.0000	.0000	.0001	.0012	.0055	.0154	.0595	.1382	.2344
5	.0000	.0000	.0000	.0000	.0000	.0001	.0004	.0015	.0102	.0369	.0938
6	.0000	.0000	.0000	.0000	.0000	.0000	.0000	.0001	.0007	.0041	.0156

n = 7

r	.01	.02	.03	.04	.05	.10	.15	.20	.30	.40	.50
0	.9321	.8681	.8080	.7514	.6983	.4783	.3206	.2097	.0824	.0280	.0078
1	.0659	.1240	.1749	.2192	.2573	.3720	.3960	.3670	.2471	.1306	.0547
2	.0020	.0076	.0162	.0274	.0406	.1240	.2097	.2753	.3177	.2613	.1641
3	.0000	.0003	.0008	.0019	.0036	.0230	.0617	.1147	.2269	.2903	.2734
4	.0000	.0000	.0000	.0001	.0002	.0026	.0109	.0287	.0972	.1935	.2734
5	.0000	.0000	.0000	.0000	.0009	.0002	.0012	.0043	.0250	.0774	.1641
6	.0000	.0000	.0000	.0000	.0000	.0000	.0001	.0004	.0036	.0172	.0547
7	.0000	.0000	.0000	.0000	.0000	.0000	.0000	.0000	.0002	.0016	.0078

Table A.2 *Continued*

						p					
r	.01	.02	.03	.04	.05	.10	.15	.20	.30	.40	.50
						n = 8					
0	.9227	.8508	.7837	.7214	.6634	.4305	.2725	.1678	.0576	.0168	.0039
1	.0746	.1389	.1939	.2405	.2793	.3826	.3847	.3355	.1977	.0896	.0312
2	.0026	.0099	.0210	.0351	.0515	.1488	.2376	.2936	.2965	.2090	.1094
3	.0001	.0004	.0013	.0029	.0054	.0331	.0839	.1468	.2541	.2787	.2188
4	.0000	.0000	.0001	.0002	.0004	.0046	.0185	.0459	.1361	.2322	.2734
5	.0000	.0000	.0000	.0000	.0000	.0004	.0026	.0092	.0467	.1239	.2188
6	.0000	.0000	.0000	.0000	.0000	.0000	.0002	.0011	.0100	.0413	.1094
7	.0000	.0000	.0000	.0000	.0000	.0000	.0000	.0001	.0012	.0079	.0312
8	.0000	.0000	.0000	.0000	.0000	.0000	.0000	.0000	.0001	.0007	.0039
						n = 9					
0	.9135	.8337	.7602	.6925	.6302	.3874	.2316	.1342	.0404	.0101	.0020
1	.0830	.1531	.2116	.2597	.2985	.3874	.3679	.3020	.1556	.0605	.0176
2	.0034	.0125	.0262	.0433	.0629	.1722	.2597	.3020	.2668	.1612	.0703
3	.0001	.0006	.0019	.0042	.0077	.0446	.1069	.1762	.2668	.2508	.1641
4	.0000	.0000	.0001	.0003	.0006	.0074	.0283	.0661	.1715	.2508	.2461
5	.0000	.0000	.0000	.0000	.0000	.0008	.0050	.0165	.0735	.1672	.2461
6	.0000	.0000	.0000	.0000	.0000	.0001	.0006	.0028	.0210	.0743	.1641
7	.0000	.0000	.0000	.0000	.0000	.0000	.0000	.0003	.0039	.0212	.0703
8	.0000	.0000	.0000	.0000	.0000	.0000	.0000	.0000	.0004	.0035	.0176
9	.0000	.0000	.0000	.0000	.0000	.0000	.0000	.0000	.0000	.0003	.0020
						n = 10					
0	.9044	.8171	.7374	.6648	.5987	.3487	.1969	.1074	.0282	.0060	.0010
1	.0914	.1667	.2281	.2770	.3151	.3874	.3474	.2684	.1211	.0403	.0098
2	.0042	.0153	.0317	.0519	.0746	.1937	.2759	.3020	.2335	.1209	.0439
3	.0001	.0008	.0026	.0058	.0105	.0574	.1298	.2013	.2668	.2150	.1172
4	.0000	.0000	.0001	.0004	.0010	.0112	.0401	.0881	.2001	.2508	.2051
5	.0000	.0000	.0000	.0000	.0001	.0015	.0085	.0264	.1029	.2007	.2461
6	.0000	.0000	.0000	.0000	.0000	.0001	.0012	.0055	.0368	.1115	.2051
7	.0000	.0000	.0000	.0000	.0000	.0000	.0001	.0008	.0090	.0425	.1172
8	.0000	.0000	.0000	.0000	.0000	.0000	.0000	.0001	.0014	.0106	.0439
9	.0000	.0000	.0000	.0000	.0000	.0000	.0000	.0000	.0001	.0016	.0098
10	.0000	.0000	.0000	.0000	.0000	.0000	.0000	.0000	.0000	.0001	.0010
						n = 15					
0	.8601	.7386	.6333	.5421	.4633	.2059	.0874	.0352	.0047	.0005	.0000
1	.1303	.2261	.2938	.3388	.3658	.3432	.2312	.1319	.0305	.0047	.0005
2	.0092	.0323	.0636	.0988	.1348	.2669	.2856	.2309	.0916	.0219	.0032
3	.0004	.0029	.0085	.0178	.0307	.1285	.2184	.2501	.1700	.0634	.0139
4	.0000	.0002	.0008	.0022	.0049	.0428	.1156	.1876	.2186	.1268	.0417
5	.0000	.0000	.0001	.0002	.0006	.0105	.0449	.1032	.2061	.1859	.0916
6	.0000	.0000	.0000	.0000	.0000	.0019	.0132	.0430	.1472	.2066	.1527
7	.0000	.0000	.0000	.0000	.0000	.0003	.0030	.0138	.0811	.1771	.1964
8	.0000	.0000	.0000	.0000	.0000	.0000	.0005	.0035	.0348	.1181	.1964
9	.0000	.0000	.0000	.0000	.0000	.0000	.0001	.0007	.0116	.0612	.1527
10	.0000	.0000	.0000	.0000	.0000	.0000	.0000	.0001	.0030	.0245	.0916
11	.0000	.0000	.0000	.0000	.0000	.0000	.0000	.0000	.0006	.0074	.0417
12	.0000	.0000	.0000	.0000	.0000	.0000	.0000	.0000	.0001	.0016	.0139
13	.0000	.0000	.0000	.0000	.0000	.0000	.0000	.0000	.0000	.0003	.0032
14	.0000	.0000	.0000	.0000	.0000	.0000	.0000	.0000	.0000	.0000	.0005

Table A.2 *Continued*

r	.01	.02	.03	.04	.05	.10	.15	.20	.30	.40	.50
								p			

n = 20

r	.01	.02	.03	.04	.05	.10	.15	.20	.30	.40	.50
0	.8179	.6676	.5438	.4420	.3585	.1216	.0388	.0115	.0008	.0000	.0000
1	.1652	.2725	.3364	.3683	.3774	.2702	.1368	.0576	.0068	.0005	.0000
2	.0159	.0528	.0988	.1458	.1887	.2852	.2293	.1369	.0278	.0031	.0002
3	.0010	.0065	.0183	.0364	.0596	.1901	.2428	.2054	.0716	.0123	.0011
4	.0000	.0006	.0024	.0065	.0133	.0898	.1821	.2182	.1304	.0350	.0046
5	.0000	.0000	.0002	.0009	.0022	.0319	.1028	.1746	.1789	.0746	.0148
6	.0000	.0000	.0000	.0001	.0003	.0089	.0454	.1091	.1916	.1244	.0370
7	.0000	.0000	.0000	.0000	.0000	.0020	.0160	.0545	.1643	.1659	.0739
8	.0000	.0000	.0000	.0000	.0000	.0004	.0046	.0222	.1144	.1797	.1201
9	.0000	.0000	.0000	.0000	.0000	.0001	.0011	.0074	.0654	.1597	.1602
10	.0000	.0000	.0000	.0000	.0000	.0000	.0002	.0020	.0308	.1171	.1762
11	.0000	.0000	.0000	.0000	.0000	.0000	.0000	.0005	.0120	.0710	.1602
12	.0000	.0000	.0000	.0000	.0000	.0000	.0000	.0001	.0039	.0355	.1201
13	.0000	.0000	.0000	.0000	.0000	.0000	.0000	.0000	.0010	.0146	.0739
14	.0000	.0000	.0000	.0000	.0000	.0000	.0000	.0000	.0002	.0049	.0370
15	.0000	.0000	.0000	.0000	.0000	.0000	.0000	.0000	.0000	.0013	.0148
16	.0000	.0000	.0000	.0000	.0000	.0000	.0000	.0000	.0000	.0003	.0046
17	.0000	.0000	.0000	.0000	.0000	.0000	.0000	.0000	.0000	.0000	.0011
18	.0000	.0000	.0000	.0000	.0000	.0000	.0000	.0000	.0000	.0000	.0002

n = 25

r	.01	.02	.03	.04	.05	.10	.15	.20	.30	.40	.50
0	.7778	.6035	.4670	.3604	.2774	.0718	.0172	.0038	.0001	.0000	.0000
1	.1964	.3079	.3611	.3754	.3650	.1994	.0759	.0236	.0014	.0000	.0000
2	.0238	.0754	.1340	.1877	.2305	.2659	.1607	.0708	.0074	.0000	.0000
3	.0018	.0118	.0318	.0600	.0930	.2265	.2174	.1358	.0243	.0019	.0001
4	.0001	.0013	.0054	.0137	.0269	.1384	.2110	.1867	.0572	.0071	.0004
5	.0000	.0001	.0007	.0024	.0060	.0646	.1564	.1960	.1030	.0199	.0016
6	.0000	.0000	.0001	.0003	.0010	.0239	.0920	.1633	.1472	.0442	.0053
7	.0000	.0000	.0000	.0000	.0001	.0072	.0441	.1108	.1712	.0800	.0143
8	.0000	.0000	.0000	.0000	.0000	.0018	.0175	.0623	.1651	.1200	.0322
9	.0000	.0000	.0000	.0000	.0000	.0004	.0058	.0294	.1336	.1511	.0609
10	.0000	.0000	.0000	.0000	.0000	.0001	.0016	.0118	.0916	.1612	.0974
11	.0000	.0000	.0000	.0000	.0000	.0000	.0004	.0040	.0536	.1465	.1328
12	.0000	.0000	.0000	.0000	.0000	.0000	.0001	.0012	.0268	.1140	.1550
13	.0000	.0000	.0000	.0000	.0000	.0000	.0000	.0003	.0115	.0760	.1550
14	.0000	.0000	.0000	.0000	.0000	.0000	.0000	.0001	.0042	.0434	.1328
15	.0000	.0000	.0000	.0000	.0000	.0000	.0000	.0000	.0013	.0212	.0974
16	.0000	.0000	.0000	.0000	.0000	.0000	.0000	.0000	.0004	.0088	.0609
17	.0000	.0000	.0000	.0000	.0000	.0000	.0000	.0000	.0001	.0031	.0322
18	.0000	.0000	.0000	.0000	.0000	.0000	.0000	.0000	.0000	.0009	.0143
19	.0000	.0000	.0000	.0000	.0000	.0000	.0000	.0000	.0000	.0002	.0053
20	.0000	.0000	.0000	.0000	.0000	.0000	.0000	.0000	.0000	.0000	.0016
21	.0000	.0000	.0000	.0000	.0000	.0000	.0000	.0000	.0000	.0000	.0004
22	.0000	.0000	.0000	.0000	.0000	.0000	.0000	.0000	.0000	.0000	.0001

Table A.2 *Continued*

r	.01	.02	.03	.04	.05	.10	.15	.20	.30	.40	.50
						$n = 30$					
0	.7397	.5455	.4010	.2939	.2146	.0424	.0076	.0012	.0000	.0000	.0000
1	.2242	.3340	.3721	.3673	.3389	.1413	.0404	.0093	.0003	.0000	.0000
2	.0328	.0988	.1669	.2219	.2586	.2277	.1034	.0337	.0018	.0000	.0000
3	.0031	.0188	.0482	.0863	.1270	.2361	.1703	.0785	.0072	.0003	.0000
4	.0002	.0026	.0101	.0243	.0451	.1771	.2028	.1325	.0208	.0012	.0000
5	.0000	.0003	.0016	.0053	.0124	.1023	.1861	.1723	.0464	.0041	.0001
6	.0000	.0000	.0002	.0009	.0027	.0474	.1368	.1795	.0829	.0115	.0006
7	.0000	.0000	.0000	.0001	.0005	.0180	.0828	.1538	.1219	.0263	.0019
8	.0000	.0000	.0000	.0000	.0001	.0058	.0420	.1106	.1501	.0505	.0055
9	.0000	.0000	.0000	.0000	.0000	.0016	.0181	.0676	.1573	.0823	.0133
10	.0000	.0000	.0000	.0000	.0000	.0004	.0067	.0355	.1416	.1152	.0280
11	.0000	.0000	.0000	.0000	.0000	.0001	.0022	.0161	.1103	.1396	.0509
12	.0000	.0000	.0000	.0000	.0000	.0000	.0006	.0064	.0749	.1474	.0806
13	.0000	.0000	.0000	.0000	.0000	.0000	.0001	.0022	.0444	.1360	.1115
14	.0000	.0000	.0000	.0000	.0000	.0000	.0000	.0007	.0231	.1101	.1354
15	.0000	.0000	.0000	.0000	.0000	.0000	.0000	.0002	.0106	.0783	.1445
16	.0000	.0000	.0000	.0000	.0000	.0000	.0000	.0000	.0042	.0489	.1354
17	.0000	.0000	.0000	.0000	.0000	.0000	.0000	.0000	.0015	.0269	.1115
18	.0000	.0000	.0000	.0000	.0000	.0000	.0000	.0000	.0005	.0129	.0806
19	.0000	.0000	.0000	.0000	.0000	.0000	.0000	.0000	.0001	.0054	.0509
20	.0000	.0000	.0000	.0000	.0000	.0000	.0000	.0000	.0000	.0020	.0280
21	.0000	.0000	.0000	.0000	.0000	.0000	.0000	.0000	.0000	.0006	.0133
22	.0000	.0000	.0000	.0000	.0000	.0000	.0000	.0000	.0000	.0002	.0055
23	.0000	.0000	.0000	.0000	.0000	.0000	.0000	.0000	.0000	.0000	.0019
24	.0000	.0000	.0000	.0000	.0000	.0000	.0000	.0000	.0000	.0000	.0006
25	.0000	.0000	.0000	.0000	.0000	.0000	.0000	.0000	.0000	.0000	.0001

Table A.3 Values of e^a and e^{-a}

a	e^a	e^{-a}	a	e^a	e^{-a}	a	e^a	e^{-a}
0.00	1.000	1.000	2.10	8.166	0.122	4.10	60.340	0.017
0.10	1.105	0.905	2.20	9.025	0.111	4.20	66.686	0.015
0.20	1.221	0.819	2.30	9.974	0.100	4.30	73.700	0.014
0.30	1.350	0.741	2.40	11.023	0.091	4.40	81.451	0.012
0.40	1.492	0.670	2.50	12.182	0.082	4.50	90.017	0.011
0.50	1.649	0.607	2.60	13.464	0.074	4.60	99.484	0.010
0.60	1.822	0.549	2.70	14.880	0.067	4.70	109.95	0.009
0.70	2.014	0.497	2.80	16.445	0.061	4.80	121.51	0.008
0.80	2.226	0.449	2.90	18.174	0.055	4.90	134.29	0.007
0.90	2.460	0.407	3.00	20.086	0.050	5.00	148.41	0.007
1.00	2.718	0.368	3.10	22.198	0.045	5.10	164.02	0.006
1.10	3.004	0.333	3.20	24.533	0.041	5.20	181.27	0.006
1.20	3.320	0.301	3.30	27.113	0.037	5.30	200.34	0.005
1.30	3.669	0.273	3.40	29.964	0.033	5.40	221.41	0.005
1.40	4.055	0.247	3.50	33.115	0.030	5.50	244.69	0.004
1.50	4.482	0.223	3.60	36.598	0.027	5.60	270.43	0.004
1.60	4.953	0.202	3.70	40.447	0.025	5.70	298.87	0.003
1.70	5.474	0.183	3.80	44.701	0.022	5.80	330.30	0.003
1.80	6.050	0.165	3.90	49.402	0.020	5.90	365.04	0.003
1.90	6.686	0.150	4.00	54.598	0.018	6.00	403.43	0.002
2.00	7.389	0.135						

B

Matrix Multiplication

The dimensions of a matrix relate to the number of rows and columns contained in the matrix. A matrix is typically referred to in terms of its dimensions expressed as m rows by n columns. For example, the following are examples of a 2×3, 3×2, and 1×2 matrix.

Dimensions of a matrix

2×3 matrix: $\begin{bmatrix} a_1 & a_2 & a_3 \\ b_1 & b_2 & b_3 \end{bmatrix}$

3×2 matrix: $\begin{bmatrix} a_1 & a_2 \\ b_1 & b_2 \\ c_1 & c_2 \end{bmatrix}$

1×2 matrix: $\begin{bmatrix} a_1 & a_2 \end{bmatrix}$

The symbols a, b, and c within each matrix above represent values, either integer or fractional (e.g., probabilities).

In order to multiply two matrices, the number of columns, n, in the first matrix must equal the number of rows, m, in the second

Multiplying two matrices

matrix. It is not possible to multiply two matrices of dimensions 1×2 and 3×3, for example. It is possible, however, to multiply a 2×3 matrix and a 3×2 matrix, since the number of columns in the first matrix, 3, equals the number of rows in the second, also 3.

$$\begin{bmatrix} a_1 & a_2 & a_3 \\ b_1 & b_2 & b_3 \end{bmatrix} \qquad \begin{bmatrix} c_1 & c_2 \\ d_1 & d_2 \\ e_1 & e_2 \end{bmatrix}$$

Two matrices of compatible dimensions are multiplied together by multiplying the values in the rows of the first matrix by the values in the columns of the second matrix and summing each of these sets of values. The resulting matrix will have the same number of rows as the first matrix and the same number of columns as the second matrix. As examples, we will use several matrices from the discussion of Markov analysis in Chapter 13.

First, consider the multiplication of a 2×2 matrix by a 1×2 matrix. This will result in a 1×2 matrix.

$$\begin{bmatrix} a_1 & a_2 \end{bmatrix} \begin{bmatrix} b_1 & b_2 \\ c_1 & c_2 \end{bmatrix} = [(a_1b_1 + a_2c_1) \quad (a_1b_2 + a_2c_2)]$$

Examples of matrix multiplication

The matrix for the gasoline service station example in Chapter 13 is computed as follows.

$$\begin{bmatrix} .60 & .40 \end{bmatrix} \begin{bmatrix} .60 & .40 \\ .20 & .80 \end{bmatrix}$$

$$= [(.60)(.60) + (.40)(.20) \quad (.60)(.40) + (.40)(.80)]$$
$$= [.44 \quad .56]$$

Next, consider the multiplication of two 2×2 matrices, which will result in another 2×2 matrix.

$$\begin{bmatrix} a_1 & a_2 \\ b_1 & b_2 \end{bmatrix} \begin{bmatrix} c_1 & c_2 \\ d_1 & d_2 \end{bmatrix} = \begin{bmatrix} (a_1c_1 + a_2d_1) & (a_1c_2 + a_2d_2) \\ (b_1c_1 + b_2d_1) & (b_1c_2 + b_2d_2) \end{bmatrix}$$

For the service station example from Chapter 13, the 2×2 matrix is computed as follows.

$$\begin{bmatrix} .44 & .56 \\ .28 & .72 \end{bmatrix} \begin{bmatrix} .60 & .40 \\ .20 & .80 \end{bmatrix}$$

$$= \begin{bmatrix} (.44)(.60) + (.56)(.20) & (.44)(.40) + (.56)(.80) \\ (.28)(.60) + (.72)(.20) & (.28)(.40) + (.72)(.80) \end{bmatrix}$$

$$= \begin{bmatrix} .38 & .62 \\ .31 & .69 \end{bmatrix}$$

Notice in the above case that the values in the first row are multiplied by the values in the first column and then summed. Next, the values in the first row are multiplied by the values in the second column and summed. This produces the first row of the new matrix. The process is then repeated using the second row of the first matrix.

Now consider the multiplication of two 3×3 matrices.

$$\begin{bmatrix} a_1 & a_2 & a_3 \\ b_1 & b_2 & b_3 \\ c_1 & c_2 & c_3 \end{bmatrix} \begin{bmatrix} d_1 & d_2 & d_3 \\ e_1 & e_2 & e_3 \\ f_1 & f_2 & f_3 \end{bmatrix}$$

$$= \begin{bmatrix} (a_1d_1 + a_2e_1 + a_3f_1) & (a_1d_2 + a_2e_2 + a_3f_2) & (a_1d_3 + a_2e_3 + a_3f_3) \\ (b_1d_1 + b_2e_1 + b_3f_1) & (b_1d_2 + b_2e_2 + b_3f_2) & (b_1d_3 + b_2e_3 + b_3f_3) \\ (c_1d_1 + c_2e_1 + c_3f_1) & (c_1d_2 + c_2e_2 + c_3f_2) & (c_1d_3 + c_2e_3 + c_3f_3) \end{bmatrix}$$

As an example, consider the squaring of the 3×3 matrix used in the truck rental example in Chapter 13.

$$\begin{bmatrix} .6 & .2 & .2 \\ .3 & .5 & .2 \\ .4 & .1 & .5 \end{bmatrix} \begin{bmatrix} .6 & .2 & .2 \\ .3 & .5 & .2 \\ .4 & .1 & .5 \end{bmatrix}$$

$$= \begin{bmatrix} (.6)(.6) + (.2)(.3) + (.2)(.4) & (.6)(.2) + (.2)(.5) + (.2)(.1) & (.6)(.2) + (.2)(.2) + (.2)(.5) \\ (.3)(.6) + (.5)(.3) + (.2)(.4) & (.3)(.2) + (.5)(.5) + (.2)(.1) & (.3)(.2) + (.5)(.2) + (.2)(.5) \\ (.4)(.6) + (.1)(.3) + (.5)(.4) & (.4)(.2) + (.1)(.5) + (.5)(.1) & (.4)(.2) + (.1)(.2) + (.5)(.5) \end{bmatrix}$$

$$= \begin{bmatrix} .50 & .24 & .26 \\ .41 & .33 & .26 \\ .47 & .18 & .35 \end{bmatrix}$$

THE INVERSE OF A MATRIX

The inverse of the 2×2 matrix

$$M = \begin{bmatrix} a_1 & a_2 \\ b_1 & b_2 \end{bmatrix}$$

is denoted as M^{-1} and is computed according to the following formulation.

$$M^{-1} = \begin{bmatrix} b_2/D & -a_2/D \\ -b_1/D & a_1/D \end{bmatrix}$$

D is the *determinant* of the matrix, M, and is computed as follows.

$$D = a_1b_2 - b_1a_2$$

In the debt example in Chapter 13, we computed the fundamental matrix by taking the inverse of the $(I - Q)$ matrix,

$$I - Q = \begin{bmatrix} 1 & -.30 \\ 0 & 1 \end{bmatrix}$$

The determinant of this matrix is

$$D = (1)(1) - (0)(-.30)$$
$$D = 1$$

Thus, according to our formula, the inverse is computed as follows.

$$(I - Q)^{-1} = \begin{bmatrix} 1/1 & -(-.30)/1 \\ -0/1 & 1/1 \end{bmatrix}$$
$$= \begin{bmatrix} 1 & .30 \\ 0 & 1 \end{bmatrix}$$

The Poisson and Exponential Distributions

THE POISSON DISTRIBUTION

The formula for a Poisson distribution is

The Poisson distribution formula

$$P(x) = \frac{a^x e^{-\lambda}}{x!}$$

where

λ = average arrival rate (i.e., arrivals during a specified period of time)

x = number of arrivals during the specified time period

e = 2.71828

$x!$ = the factorial of a value, x

[i.e., $x! = x(x - 1)(x - 2) \cdots (3)(2)(1)$]

As an example of this distribution, consider a service facility that has an average arrival rate of 5 customers per hour ($\lambda = 5$). The

An example of the Poisson distribution

probability that exactly 2 customers will arrive at the service facility is found by letting $x = 2$ in the above Poisson formula.

$$P(x = 2) = \frac{5^2 e^{-5}}{2!}$$

$$= \frac{25(.007)}{(2)(1)}$$

$$= .084$$

The value for e^{-5} was found by using Table A.3 in Appendix A, a table with selected $e^{-\lambda}$ values. The value .084 is the probability of exactly 2 customers' arriving at the service facility.

A distribution of customer arrivals

By substituting values of x into the Poisson formula, we can develop a distribution of customer arrivals during a 1-hour period, as shown in Figure C.1. However, remember that this distribution is for an arrival rate of 5 customers per hour. Other values of λ will result in distributions different from the one in Figure C.1.

FIGURE C.1

Poisson Distribution for $\lambda = 5$

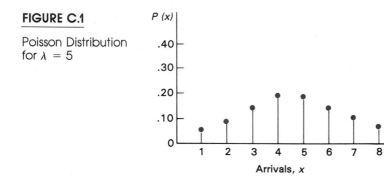

THE EXPONENTIAL DISTRIBUTION

The exponential distribution formula

The formula for the exponential distribution is

$$f(t) = \mu e^{-\mu t}, \qquad t \geq 0$$

where

μ = average number of customers served during a specified period of time

t = service time

e = 2.71828

The *probability* that a customer will be served within a specified time period can be determined by using the exponential distribution in the following form:

$$P(T \leq t) = 1 - e^{-\mu t}$$

If, for example, the service rate is 6 customers per hour, then the probability that a customer will be served within 10 minutes (0.17 hour) is computed as follows.

$$P(T \leq .17) = 1 - e^{-6(.17)}$$
$$= 1 - e^{-1.0}$$
$$= 1 - .368$$
$$= .632$$

Thus, the probability of a customer's being served within 10 minutes is .632. Figure C.2 is the exponential probability distribution for this service rate ($\mu = 6$).

FIGURE C.2

Exponential Distribution for $\mu = 6$

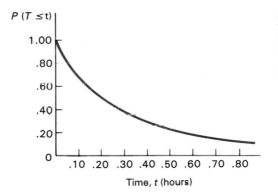

An exponential distribution example

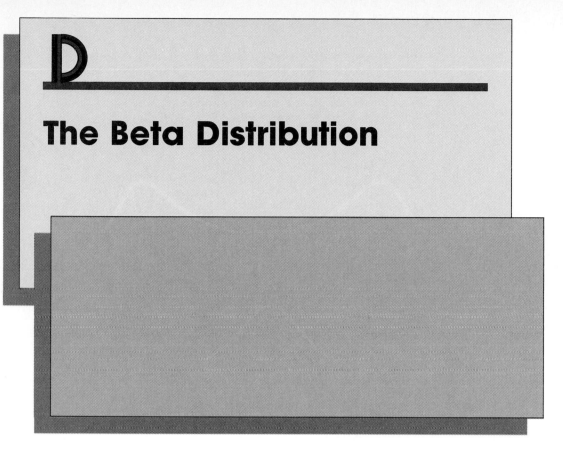

The Beta Distribution

In order to estimate the mean of the probability distribution of activity time, a functional form for the probability distribution must be assumed. A good candidate is the *beta distribution*. The beta distribution has the desirable properties that it can be contained entirely within a finite interval such as the one between a, the optimistic activity time, and b, the pessimistic activity time, and it can be symmetric or skewed in either direction depending on the location of m, the mode (most likely time), relative to a and b. Because there usually is no empirical data base for project activities that would enable the selection of a specific distribution, the beta distribution has been traditionally accepted as a distribution for activity times.

The mean and variance of the beta distribution are *estimated* using the following formulas.

$$t = \frac{a + 4m + b}{6}$$

$$v = \left(\frac{b - a}{6}\right)^2$$

Three examples of the beta distribution, showing the relative locations of *a*, *m*, *b*, and *t*, are illustrated in Figure D.1. Figure D.1 shows that the beta distribution is unimodal (i.e., has a single high point) and continuous and has finite lim ts. It also shows that the beta distribution can be symmetrical (as in part C) or skewed in either direction (as in parts A and B).

FIGURE D.1

Beta Distribution for Activity Times: (A) skewed to right, (B) skewed to left, and (C) symmetrical

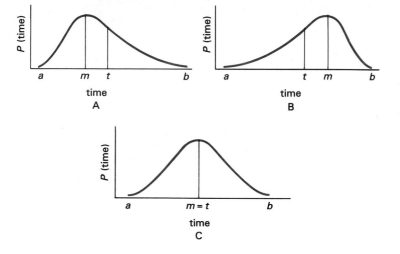

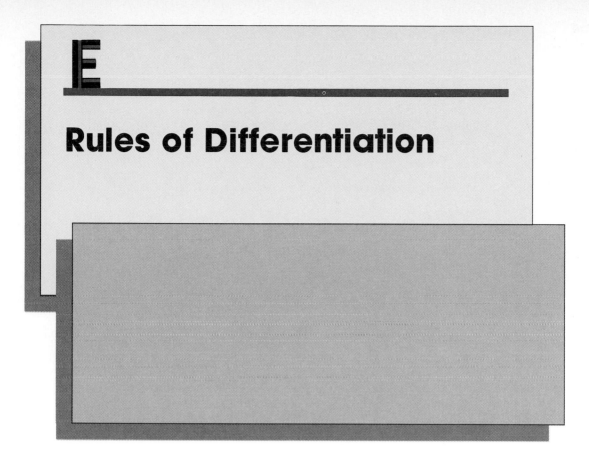

Rules of Differentiation

The derivative of a function

$$y = f(x)$$

is expressed as

$$\frac{\partial y}{\partial x} = f'(x)$$

Following is a set of rules for determining the derivatives of several different types of functions.

Rule 1: The derivative of a constant equals zero. In functional notation, if

$$y = k$$

where k is a constant, then the derivative is

$$\frac{\partial y}{\partial x} = 0$$

For example, if $y = 10$, then

$$\frac{\partial y}{\partial x} = 0$$

Rule 2:   The derivative of a variable equals one. In functional notation, if

$$y = x$$

then the derivative is

$$\frac{\partial y}{\partial x} = 1$$

Rule 3:   For a variable raised to a power n,

$$y = x^n$$

the derivative is

$$\frac{\partial y}{\partial x} = nx^{n-1}$$

For example, if $y = x^3$, the derivative is

$$\frac{\partial y}{\partial x} = 3x^2$$

We can verify Rule 2 using this formula. For a variable x, the power (n) is one.

$$y = x^1$$

The derivative of this function is

$$\frac{\partial y}{\partial x} = 1x^0$$
$$= 1$$

which is the result given in Rule 2.

Rule 4:   For a function multiplied by a constant, the derivative is

$$\frac{\partial y}{\partial x} = k \cdot f'(x)$$

For example, if $f(x) = x^4$ and $k = 10$ (i.e., $f(x) = 10x^4$), the derivative is

$$\frac{\partial y}{\partial x} = 10[4x^3]$$
$$= 40x^3$$

Rule 5:   For two functions that are added (or subtracted),

$$y = f(x) + g(x)$$

the derivative is the sum (or difference) of the derivatives of the two functions.

$$\frac{\partial y}{\partial x} = f'(x) + g'(x)$$

For example, if $y = x^3 + 3x^4$, the derivative is

$$\frac{\partial y}{\partial x} = 3x^2 + 12x^3$$

Rule 6:   For two functions that are multiplied,

$$y = f(x) \cdot g(x)$$

the derivative is the first function multiplied by the derivative of the second, plus the second function times the derivative of the first.

$$\frac{\partial y}{\partial x} = f(x)g'(x) + f'(x)g(x)$$

For example, if $f(x) = x^3$ and $g(x) = 4x^4$, the derivative is

$$\frac{\partial y}{\partial x} = (x^3)(16x^3) + (3x^2)(4x^4)$$

$$= 16x^6 + 12x^6$$

$$= 28x^6$$

Rule 7:   For two functions that are divided,

$$y = \frac{f(x)}{g(x)}$$

the derivative is determined by multiplying the denominator by the derivative of the numerator, subtracting from this product the numerator multiplied by the derivative of the denominator, and then dividing the result by the denominator squared.

$$\frac{\partial y}{\partial x} = \frac{g(x)f'(x) - g'(x)f(x)}{[g(x)]^2}$$

For example, if $f(x) = x^3$ and $g(x) = 5x^2$, the derivative is

$$\frac{\partial y}{\partial x} = \frac{(5x^2)(3x^2) - (x^3)(10x)}{[5x^2]^2}$$

$$= \frac{15x^4 - 10x^4}{25x^4}$$

$$= \frac{1}{5}$$

Global Maximums and Minimums

In Chapter 23, the nonlinear functions that were included in the examples of the break-even model and inventory models were either *concave* or *convex*. For a convex function, a straight line connecting any two points on the curve will be entirely *above* the curve. For a concave function, a straight line connecting any two points on the curve will be entirely *below* the curve. Examples of convex and concave functions are illustrated in Figure F.1.

Concave and convex functions

FIGURE F.1

Convex and Concave Functions

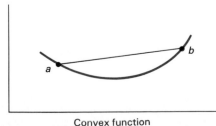

Convex function

Concave function

If a function is either convex or concave, there will be only one minimum or one maximum point on the curve. The values of the variables corresponding to these maximum and minimum points can be computed by determining the first derivative of the nonlinear function and setting it equal to zero (as demonstrated in Chaps. 23 and 24). This is a rather simple procedure when the nonlinear function is either convex or concave. However, it is possible for a nonlinear function to be neither totally convex nor totally concave, but instead a curve that contains several minimum and/or maximum points. Such a curve is shown in Figure F.2. When a problem involves this type of nonlinear function, we must go beyond the first derivative of the function and apply additional calculus steps.

FIGURE F.2

A Nonlinear Function with Several Maximum and Minimum Points

The nonlinear function in Figure F.2 contains two minimum points and two maximum points. These points are referred to as *extreme points*. Extreme points are further classified as *local* or *global* and *maximum* or *minimum*. The points a, b, c, and d in Figure F.3 are relative extreme points. Points a and c are relative maximums; points b and d are relative minimums. Since point c is the maximum of the two relative maximum points, it is known as the global (or absolute) maximum; point a is a local maximum. Similarly, since point b is the minimum of the two relative minimum points, it is known as the global (or absolute) minimum; point d is a local minimum. In nonlinear programming, we are most interested in the

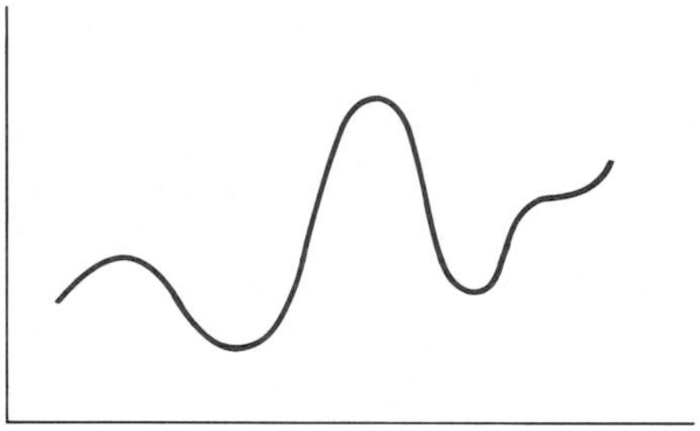

Extreme points

Relative maximums and minimums

Global maximums and minimums

FIGURE F.3

A Nonlinear Function with Global Maximum and Minimum Points

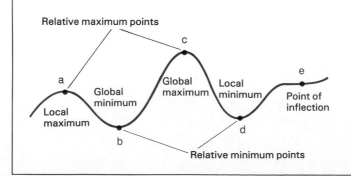

global maximum and minimum points, since they correspond to such items as maximum profit and minimum cost.

In the example problems in Chapter 23 it was unnecessary to worry about whether a maximum point on the curve was a global maximum (or whether a minimum point was a global minimum). Since the curves were either convex or concave, there was only one maximum or minimum point, so it had to be the global point. Thus, it was necessary only to compute the first derivative and solve for the values of the variables. However, for the function in Figure F.3, we do not actually determine the global points simply by determining the first derivative at points a, b, c, and d. To find the global maximum or minimum point, we must apply several additional calculus steps, which will be outlined in the following discussion.

First, we must determine the first derivative and set it equal to zero, as we have done in the past. This enables us to solve for the value of the variable corresponding to a relative extreme point. This step is referred to as a *necessary condition* for identifying relative extreme points. However, determining whether we have a relative maximum or minimum requires that we take the *second derivative* of the function.

A necessary condition

The second derivative

The second derivative of a nonlinear function is determined by applying the rules of differentiation to the first derivative. The symbolic notation for the second derivative of a function y with respect to a variable x is

$$\frac{\partial^2 y}{\partial x^2}$$

Once the second derivative has been determined, the value of the variable x determined from the first derivative is substituted into the second derivative function. If the resulting value of the second derivative is greater than zero, the point (defined by the variable values) is a relative minimum. If the value of the second derivative is less than zero, the point is a relative maximum. (If the second derivative value equals zero, the point is generally known as a *point of inflection*, which is a point on the curve where it flattens out, but is neither a maximum nor a minimum. Point e in Fig. F.3 is a point of inflection.) This step is referred to as a *sufficient condition*.

A point of inflection

A sufficient condition

In order to determine whether a relative maximum or minimum point is a global point, the value of the variable at this point must be substituted into the original function (y) and the function must be solved for y. All other relative points are treated similarly and then compared to determine which one is global. This comparison should also include the end points of the function.

These steps are summarized as follows.

Steps for determining maximum and minimum points

1. Determine the first derivative $\partial y / \partial x$ of a function y with respect to the variable x. Set it equal to zero, and solve for the value of the variable x. This step is called a *necessary condition*.

2. Determine the second derivative $\partial^2 y/\partial x^2$ of the function, and substitute the value of x determined in step 1 into this second derivative. If $\partial^2 y/\partial x^2 \geq 0$, the point is a relative minimum; if $\partial^2 y/\partial x^2 < 0$, the point is a relative maximum.
3. Substitute the variable values computed at all relative maximum (or minimum) points into the original function, and compare the results to all other relative points to see which is the global point (i.e., the maximum or minimum).

The profit model example

As an example, consider the profit analysis model in Chapter 23. We will go through the above steps for the function

$$Z = 1,696.8p - 24.6p^2 - 22,000$$

1. Determine the first derivative, set it equal to zero, and solve.

$$\frac{\partial z}{\partial p} = 1,696.8 - 49.2p$$

$$0 = 1,696.8 - 49.2p$$

$$p = \$34.49$$

2. Determine the second derivative.

$$\frac{\partial^2 Z}{\partial p^2} = -49.2$$

Since no values can be substituted into this relationship, we perform our test,

$$\frac{\partial^2 Z}{\partial p^2} = -49.2 < 0$$

which indicates that point p is a relative maximum.
3. Since this solution point, $p = \$34.49$, is the only solution available, it is the global maximum.

These basic principles of calculus are the foundation on which some of the more complex extensions of the Lagrangian solution method are based. However, the calculus steps presented in this appendix are for functions with a single variable. As more variables are introduced into nonlinear programming, these steps must be extended somewhat, although the basic approach remains the same.

Solutions to Odd-Numbered Problems

1

1. See p. 1.
3. See Fig. 1.1.
5. See p. 3, "Definition of the Problem."
7. See p. 4, "Model Construction."
9. See p. 4.
11. See pp. 5–7, "Model Solution."
13. See p. 7, "Management Science as an Ongoing Process."
15. See Fig. 1.2.

2

1. max. $Z = 12x_1 + 16x_2$; s.t. $3x_1 + 2x_2 \leq 500$, $4x_1 + 5x_2 \leq 800$, $x_1 \geq 0$, $x_2 \geq 0$
3. min. $Z = 4x_1 + 3x_2 + 2x_3$; s.t. $2x_1 + 4x_2 + x_3 \geq 16$, $3x_1 + 2x_2 + x_3 \geq 12$, $x_1 \geq 0$, $x_2 \geq 0$, $x_3 \geq 0$
5. max. $Z = 8x_1 + 10x_2 + 7x_3$; s.t. $7x_1 + 10x_2 + 5x_3 \leq 2,000$, $2x_1 + 3x_2 + 2x_3 \leq 660$, $x_1 \leq 200$, $x_2 \leq 300$, $x_3 \leq 150$, $x_1 \geq 0$, $x_2 \geq 0$, $x_3 \geq 0$
7. max. $Z = 7x_1 + 5x_2 + 5x_3 + 4x_4$; s.t. $2x_1 + 4x_2 + 2x_3 + 3x_4 \leq 45,000$, $x_1 + x_2 \leq 6,000$, $x_3 + x_4 \leq 7,000$, $x_1 + x_3 \leq 5,000$, $x_2 + x_4 \leq 6,000$, $x_1 \geq 0$, $x_2 \geq 0$, $x_3 \geq 0$, $x_4 \geq 0$
9. max. $Z = 3,000x_1 + 3,500x_2 + 2,500x_3$; s.t. $8,000x_1 + 5,000x_2 + 4,500x_3 \leq 210,000$, $50x_1 + 35x_2 + 25x_3 \leq 8,000$, $x_1 \leq 80$, $x_2 \leq 175$, $x_3 \leq 250$, $x_1 \geq 0$, $x_2 \geq 0$, $x_3 \geq 0$
11. max. $Z = 300x_1 + 520x_2$; s.t. $x_1 + x_2 \leq 410$, $105x_1 + 210x_2 \leq 52,500$, $x_2 \leq 100$, $x_1 \geq 0$, $x_2 \geq 0$
13. max. $Z = .02x_1 + .09x_2 + .06x_3 + .04x_4$; s.t. $x_1 + x_2 + x_3 + x_4 = 4,000,000$, $x_1 \leq 1,600,000$, $x_2 \leq 1,600,000$, $x_3 \leq 1,600,000$, $x_4 \leq 1,600,000$, $x_2 - x_3 - x_4 \leq 0$, $x_1 - x_3 \geq 0$, $x_1 \geq 0$, $x_2 \geq 0$, $x_3 \geq 0$, $x_4 \geq 0$
15. max. $Z = .60x_1 + .50x_2$; s.t. $.10x_1 \leq 30$, $.15x_2 \leq 30$, $.04x_1 + .04x_2 \leq 16$, $.010x_1 + .024x_2 \leq 6$, $x_1 \geq 0$, $x_2 \geq 0$
17. min. $Z = 10x_1 + 16x_2 + 7x_3$; s.t. $x_1 \geq 100$, $x_2 \geq 70$, $x_3 \geq 175$, $35x_1 + 20x_2 + 12x_3 \geq 3,500$, $x_1 \geq 0$, $x_2 \geq 0$, $x_3 \geq 0$
19. max. $Z = 2x_1 + 4x_2 + 3x_3 + 7x_4$; s.t. $x_2 + x_4 \leq 300$, $6x_1 + 15x_2 \leq 1,200$, $5x_3 + 12x_4 \leq 2,400$, $x_1 \geq 0$, $x_2 \geq 0$, $x_3 \geq 0$, $x_4 \geq 0$
21. max. $Z = 35x_1 + 20x_2 + 58x_3$; s.t. $14x_1 + 12x_2 + 35x_3 \leq 35,000$, $6x_1 + 3x_2 + 12x_3 \leq 20,000$, $x_1 \geq 0$, $x_2 \geq 0$, $x_3 \geq 0$
23. min. $Z = 15,000x_1 + 4,000x_2 + 6,000x_3$; s.t. $x_3/x_2 \geq 2/1$, $25,000x_1 + 10,000x_2 + 15,000x_3 \geq 100,000$, $15,000x_1 + 3,000x_2 + 12,000x_3/10,000x_1 + 7,000x_2 + 3,000x_3 \geq 2/1$, $15,000x_1 + 4,000x_2 + 9,000x_3/25,000x_1 + 10,000x_2 + 15,000x_3 \geq .30$, $x_2 \leq 7$, $x_1 \geq 0$, $x_2 \geq 0$, $x_3 \geq 0$
25. max. $Z = 3x_1 + 3.65x_2 + 2x_3 + 2.65x_4$; s.t. $x_1/(x_1 + x_2) \geq .30$, $x_2/(x_1 + x_2) \leq .40$, $x_3/(x_3 + x_4) \leq .60$, $x_3/(x_3 + x_4) \geq .10$, $x_1 + x_3 \leq 500$, $x_2 + x_4 \leq 700$, $x_1 \geq 0$, $x_2 \geq 0$, $x_3 \geq 0$, $x_4 \geq 0$
27. min. $Z = 40x_1 + 65x_2 + 70x_3 + 30x_4$; s.t. $x_1 + x_2 = 250$, $x_3 + x_4 = 400$, $x_1 + x_3 = 300$, $x_2 + x_4 = 350$, $x_1 \geq 0$, $x_2 \geq 0$, $x_3 \geq 0$, $x_4 \geq 0$

29. max. $Z = 175 (7x_1)$; s.t.
$8x_1 + 5x_2 + 6.5x_3 \leq 3,000$, $x_1 + x_2 + x_3 \leq$
120, $90(7x_1) \leq 10,000$, $7x_1 - 12x_2 = 0$,
$12x_2 - 10x_3 = 0$, $7x_1 - 10x_3 = 0$, $x_1 \geq 0$,
$x_2 \geq 0$, $x_3 \geq 0$

31. max. $Z = .085x_1 + .100x_2 + .065x_3 +$
$.130x_4$; s.t. $x_4/x_1 + x_2 + x_3 + x_4 \leq .20$,
$x_2 \leq x_1 + x_3 + x_4$, $x_2 + x_3/x_1 + x_2 + x_3 +$
$x_4 \geq .30$, $x_1/x_3 \leq 1/3$, $x_1 + x_2 + x_3 +$
$x_4 \leq 70,000$, $x_1 \geq 0$, $x_2 \geq 0$, $x_3 \geq 0$, $x_4 \geq 0$

33. (a) min. $Z = x_1 + x_2 + x_3 + x_4 + x_5 + x_6$;
s.t. $3x_1 + 2x_2 + 2x_3 + x_4 = 700$, $x_3 +$
$2x_4 + x_5' = 1,200$, $x_2 + x_5 + 2x_6 = 300$,
$x_i \geq 0$; (b) min. $Z = 4x_1 + x_2 + 2x_3 +$
$0x_4 + 6x_5 + 5x_6$; s.t. $3x_1 + 2x_2 + 2x_3 +$
$x_4 = 700$, $x_3 + 2x_4 + x_5 = 1,200$,
$x_2 + x_5 + 2x_6 = 300$, $x_i \geq 0$

35. max. $Z = 4x_1 + 8x_2 + 6x_3 + 7x_4 -$
$5y_1 - 6y_2 - 7y_3$; s.t. $s_0 = 2,000$, $x_1 \leq s_0$,
$s_1 = s_0 - x_1 + y_1$, $s_1 \leq 10,000$, $x_2 \leq s_1$,
$s_2 = s_1 - x_2 + y_2$, $s_2 \leq 10,000$, $x_3 \leq s_2$,
$s_3 = s_2 - x_3 + y_3$, $s_3 \leq 10,000$, $x_4 \leq s_3$,
$x_i \geq 0$, $y_i \geq 0$, $s_i \geq 0$

37. (a) max. $Z = 130x_{1a} + 150x_{1b} + 90x_{1c} +$
$275x_{2a} + 300x_{2b} + 100x_{2c} + 180x_{3a} +$
$225x_{3b} + 140x_{3c} + 200x_{4a} + 120x_{4b} + 160x_{4c}$;
s.t. $x_{1a} + x_{1b} + x_{1c} = 1$, $x_{2a} + x_{2b} + x_{2c} = 1$,
$x_{3a} + x_{3b} + x_{3c} = 1$, $x_{4a} + x_{4b} + x_{4c} = 1$,
$1 \leq x_{1a} + x_{2a} + x_{3a} + x_{4a} \leq 2$, $1 \leq x_{1b} +$
$x_{2b} + x_{3b} + x_{4b} \leq 2$, $1 \leq x_{1c} + x_{2c} + x_{3c} +$
$x_{4c} \leq 2$, $x_{ij} \geq 0$
(b) max. $Z = 130x_{1a} + 150x_{1b} + 90x_{1c} +$
$275x_{2a} + 300x_{2b} + 100x_{2c} + 180x_{3a} +$
$225x_{3b} + 140x_{3c} + 200x_{4a} + 120x_{4b} + 160x_{4c}$;
s.t. $x_{1a} + x_{1b} + x_{1c} \leq 1$, $x_{2a} + x_{2b} + x_{2c} \leq 1$,
$x_{3a} + x_{3b} + x_{3c} \leq 1$, $x_{4a} + x_{4b} + x_{4c} \leq 1$,
$x_{1a} + x_{2a} + x_{3a} + x_{4a} = 1$, $x_{1b} + x_{2b} +$
$x_{3b} + x_{4b} = 1$, $x_{1c} + x_{2c} + x_{3c} + x_{4c} = 1$,
$x_{ij} \geq 0$

39. max. $Z = 1.2x_1 + 1.3x_2$; s.t. $x_1 + x_2 \leq$
$95,000$, $.18x_1 + .3x_2 \leq 20,000$, $x_1 \geq 0$,
$x_2 \geq 0$

41. max. $Z = .85x_1 + .90x_2 - y_1 - y_2$; s.t.
$x_1 \leq 5,000 + 3y_1$, $x_2 \leq 4,000 + 5y_2$,
$.60x_1 + .85x_2 + y_1 + y_2 \leq 16,000$, $x_1 \geq$
$.3(x_1 + x_2)$, $x_1 \leq .6(x_1 + x_2)$, $x_1 \geq 0$,
$x_2 \geq 0$, $y_1 \geq 0$, $y_2 \geq 0$

43. min. $Z = 140,000x_b + 160,000x_1 +$
$.16y_1 + .16y_2$; s.t. $x_b + x_1 = 200$,
$140,000x_b + 80,000x_1 \leq 8,000,000 + y_1$,

$y_1 + .16y_1 \leq 24,000,000$, $80,000x_1 \leq$
$24,000,000 - y_1 - .16y_1 + y_2$, $y_2 +$
$.16y_2 \leq (24,000,000 - y_1 - .16y_1) -$
$80,000x_1 + 24,000,000$, $y_1 \leq 20,000,000$,
$y_2 \leq 20,000,000$, $x_b \geq 0$, $x_1 \geq 0$, $y_1 \geq 0$,
$y_2 \geq 0$

3

1. $x_1 = 5$, $x_2 = 0$, $Z = 40$
3. $x_1 = 0$, $x_2 = 8$, $Z = .24$
5. $x_1 = 4$, $x_2 = 2$, $Z = 22$
7. no labor left unused, 4.8 lb of wood left unused
9. 5 lb of flour left unused, no sugar left unused
11. $x_1 = 5.3$, $x_2 = 1$, $Z = 49.4$
13. $x_1 = 4$, $x_2 = 3$, $Z = 2,400$
15. $600
17. $x_1 = 15.8$, $x_2 = 20.5$, $Z = 1,610$
19. $x_1 = 8$, $x_2 = 3.2$, $Z = 65.6$
21. $x_1 = 6$, $x_2 = 1.5$, $Z = 31.5$
23. $x_1 = 0$, $x_2 = 12$, $Z = 240$
25. $x_1 = 6$, $x_2 = 0$, $Z = 24$
27. $x_1 = 3.2$, $x_2 = 6$, $Z = 37.6$
29. $x_1 = 2.4$, $x_2 = .8$, $Z = .22$
31. $x_1 = 5$, $x_2 = 5$, $Z = 8,500$
33. changes solution point to $x_1 = 5.3$,
$x_2 = 4.7$, $Z = 806$
35. the optimal solution point changes to
$x_1 = 26$, $x_2 = 14$, $Z = 14,600$
37. $x_1 = 4$, $x_2 = 3$, $Z = 57$
39. $x_1 = 300$, $x_2 = 100$, $Z = 230$
41. $x_1 = 333.3$, $x_2 = 166.6$, $Z = 1,666$

4

1. $x_2 = 8$, $Z = 80$
3. $x_1 = 5$, $s_2 = 8$, $Z = 40$
5. $x_1 = 6$, $x_2 = 3.2$, $s_2 = 4.8$, $Z = 2,720$
7. $x_1 = 4$, $x_2 = 3$, $s_3 = 1$, $Z = 2,400$
9. $x_1 = 10$, $x_2 = 10$, $s_1 = 20$, $Z = 2,500$
11. $x_1 = 4$, $x_2 = 3$, $s_3 = 1$, $Z = 24$
13. $x_3 = 8$, $s_2 = 6$, $Z = 96$
15. $x_2 = 20$, $x_3 = 3.5$, $x_4 = 11$, $s_3 = 1,216$,
$Z = 2,860$
17. $x_2 = 14$, $x_3 = 18$, $s_2 = 20$, $s_3 = 1$, $Z = 242$
19. $x_1 = 4$, $x_2 = 3$, $Z = 57$
21. $x_2 = 160$, $s_1 = 180$, $Z = 2,560$

23. $x_1 = 5,000$, $x_2 = 1,000$, $x_4 = 5,000$, $s_1 = 16,000$, $s_3 = 2,000$, $Z = 60,000$

25. $x_1 = 200$, $x_3 = 480$, $s_1 = 300$, $Z = 1,840$

27. $x_1 = 70,833.4$, $x_2 = 24,166.6$, $Z = 116,416.7$

5

1. $x_2 = 3$, $Z = 60$

3. $x_2 = 8$, $s_2 = 4$, $Z = .24$

5. $x_1 = 2.4$, $x_2 = .8$, $s_3 = 3.6$, $Z = .22$

7. $x_1 = 1,175$, $x_3 = 25$, $s_1 = 11,450$, $Z = 2,475$

9. $x_1 = 10$, $s_1 = 24$, $Z = .50$

11. $x_2 = 10$, $x_3 = 100$, $s_1 = 70$, $Z = 500$

13. $x_1 = 1$, $x_2 = 3$, $s_3 = 8$, $Z = 68$

15. max. $Z = 8x_1 + 2x_2 + 7x_3 + 0s_1 + 0s_2 + 0s_3 - MA_1 - MA_2 - MA_3$; s.t. $2x_1 + 6x_2 + x_3 + A_1 = 30$, $3x_2 + 4x_3 - s_1 + A_2 = 60$, $4x_1 + x_2 + 2x_3 + s_2 = 50$, $x_1 + 2x_2 - s_3 + A_3 = 20$, $x_1 \geq 0$, $x_2 \geq 0$, $x_3 \geq 0$

17. $x_1 = 6$, $x_2 = 12$, $s_3 = 1$, $s_4 = 0$, $Z = 960$

19. $x_1 = 4$, $x_2 = 1$, $s_1 = 4$, $s_4 = 6$, $Z = 18$

21. $x_1 = 4$, $x_2 = 4$, $s_1 = 2$, $Z = 60$

23. $x_1 = 4$, $x_2 = 2$, $s_2 = 14$, $Z = 22$

25. $x_1 = 4$, $x_2 = 3$, $s_2 = 2$, $Z = 36$

27. $x_1 = 4$, $x_2 = 16/3$, $x_3 = 4/3$, $Z = 52/3$

29. multiple optimal solutions: (1) $x_2 = 30$, $x_3 = 10$, $s_1 = 10$, $s_2 = 60$, $Z = 15,000$; (2) $x_1 = 20$, $x_2 = 20$, $s_1 = 20$, $s_2 = 20$, $Z = 15,000$

31. unbounded solution

33. $x_1 = 3$, $x_2 = 0$, $A_1 = 3$, infeasible

35. $x_1 = 2$, $x_2 = 3$, $Z = .17$

37. $x_1 = 200$, $x_3 = 480$, $s_1 = 300$, $Z = 1,840$

39. $x_1 = 27.5$, $x_2 = 20$, $s_2 = 1,200$, $Z = 2,775$

6

1. (a) min. $Z_d = 90y_1 + 60y_2$; s.t. $y_1 + 2y_2 \geq 6$, $4y_1 + 2y_2 \geq 10$, $y_1 \geq 0$, $y_2 \geq 0$; (b) $y_1 =$ marginal value of an additional lb of brass, $y_2 =$ marginal value of an additional hr of labor; (c) $y_1 = \$1.33$, $y_2 = \$2.33$

3. (a) min. $Z_d = 60y_1 + 40y_2$; s.t. $12y_1 + 4y_2 \geq 9$, $4y_1 + 8y_2 \geq 7$, $y_1 \geq 0$, $y_2 \geq 0$; (b) $y_1 =$ marginal value of an additional hr of process 1, $y_2 =$ marginal value of an additional hr of process 2; (c) s_1 column value of $\$.55$ is marginal value of process 1, s_2 column value of $\$.80$ is marginal

value of process 2; (d) value of process 1 = \$33, value of process 2 = \$24

5. (a) min. $Z_d = 19y_1 + 14y_2 + 20y_3$; s.t. $2y_1 + y_2 + y_3 \geq 70$, $y_1 + y_2 + 2y_3 \geq 80$, $y_1 \geq 0$, $y_2 \geq 0$, $y_3 \geq 0$; (b) $y_1 = \$20 =$ marginal value of an additional hr of production time, $y_2 = \$0 =$ marginal value of an additional lb of steel, $y_3 = \$30 =$ marginal value of an additional ft of wire; (c) value of production time = \$380, value of steel = \$0, value of wire = \$600

7. (a) min. $Z_d = 120y_1 + 160y_2 + 100y_3 + 40y_4$; s.t. $2y_1 + 4y_2 + 3y_3 + y_4 \geq 40$, $3y_1 + 3y_2 + 2y_3 + y_4 \geq 35$, $2y_1 + y_2 + 4y_3 + y_4 \geq 45$, $y_1 \geq 0$, $y_2 \geq 0$, $y_3 \geq 0$, $y_4 \geq 0$; (b) $y_1 = 0$, $y_2 = 0$, $y_3 = \$5 =$ marginal value of an hr of operation 3, $y_4 = \$25 =$ marginal value of a ft^2 of storage space; (c) no effect

9. $y_1 = 3/4$, $y_2 = 6/5$, $Z = 108$

11. min. $Z_d = 1,600y_1 + 400y_2 + 300y_3 + 150y_4 + 200y_5 + 100y_6$; s.t. $6y_1 + y_2 + y_3 + y_4 \geq 10$, $12y_1 + 3y_2 + y_3 + y_5 \geq 5$, $4y_1 + 2y_2 + y_3 + y_6 \geq 8$, $y_1 \geq 0$, $y_2 \geq 0$, $y_3 \geq 0$, $y_4 \geq 0$, $y_5 \geq 0$, $y_6 \geq 0$

13. max. $Z_d = 300y_1 + 600y_2 + 800y_3 + 10y_4 + 8y_5 + 10y_6 + 20y_7$; s.t. $10y_1 + y_4 \leq 1$, $12y_1 + 20y_3 + y_5 \leq 1$, $7y_1 + 50y_2 + y_6 \leq 1$, $8y_1 + 25y_2 + 30y_3 + y_7 \leq 1$, $y_1 \geq 0$, $y_2 \geq 0$, $y_3 \geq 0$, $y_4 \geq 0$, $y_5 \geq 0$, $y_6 \geq 0$, $y_7 \geq 0$

15. min. $Z_d = 6y_1 + 5y_2 + 10y_3 - 10y_4$; s.t. $y_1 - 2y_2 + 2y_3 - 2y_4 \geq 2$, $y_1 - y_2 + 6y_3 - 6y_4 \geq 2$, $-2y_1 + y_2 \geq -1$, $y_1 \geq 0$, $y_2 \geq 0$, $y_3 \geq 0$, $y_4 \geq 0$

17. min. $Z_d = 12y_1 + 20y_2 - 20y_3 - 8y_4$; s.t. $y_1 + 2y_2 - 2y_3 - y_4 \geq 1$, $y_1 + y_2 - y_3 - y_4 \geq 2$, $2y_1 + 5y_2 - 5y_3 + y_4 \geq 2$, $y_1 \geq 0$, $y_2 \geq 0$, $y_3 \geq 0$, $y_4 \geq 0$

19. (a) $5/2 < c_1 < 10$, $6 < c_2 < 24$; (b) $30 \leq q_1 \leq 120$, $45 \leq q_2 \leq 180$

21. (a) $7/2 < c_1 < 12$, $3 < c_2 < 18$; (b) $20 \leq q_1 \leq 120$, $20 \leq q_2 \leq 120$

23. (a) $40 < c_1 < 160$, $35 < c_2 < 140$; (b) $10 \leq q_1 \leq 22$, $q_2 \geq 13$, $19/2 \leq q_3 \leq 23$

25. (a) $35 < c_2 < 45$; (b) $25 \leq q_4 \leq 42.5$

27. (a) $c_1 < 16$, $c_2 < 4$, $c_3 > 6$; (b) $0 \leq q_1 \leq 30$, $q_2 \geq 24$

29. (a) $-7/2 < c_1 < 5$, $c_2 > 3$; (b) $q_1 \geq 25$, $q_2 \leq 65$, $-5 \leq q_3 \leq 35$

31. \$2.33, 180 hr

33. \$.55, 120 hr

35. yes

37. \$.01, 10.625 mg

39. (a) \$0, $q_2 \geq 90$; (b) \$2, $20 \leq q_3 \leq 80$; (c) either, $y_3 = y_4 = 2; (d) no; (e) \$6; (f) no

7

1. NW corner: 1A = 40, 1B = 20, 2B = 20, 2C = 10, 3C = 60, Z = 930; min. cell cost: 1A = 10, 1B = 40, 1C = 10, 2A = 30, 3C = 60, Z = 810; VAM: 1C = 60, 2A = 30, 3A = 10, 3B = 40, 3C = 10, Z = \$660

3. St. Louis—Chicago = 250, Richmond—Chicago = 50, Richmond—Atlanta = 350, Z = 24,000

5. (a) NW corner: 1—1 = 30, 1—2 = 40, 2—2 = 20, 2—3 = 20, 3—3 = 70, 3—4 = 30, Z = 1,710; min. cell cost: 1—3 = 70, 2—1 = 30, 2—3 = 10, 3—2 = 60, 3—3 = 10, 3—4 = 30, Z = 810; VAM: 1—3 = 70, 2—1 = 30, 2—3 = 10, 3—2 = 60, 3—3 = 10, 3—4 = 30, Z = 810; (b) VAM solution optimal

7. (a) unbalanced, demand > supply; (b) yes, only 6 occupied cells, place a dummy "0" in cell x_{4A} (as one possible choice); (c) yes, x_{3C}; (d) 13,700; (e) $x_{2B} = 0$

9. min. cell cost: A3 = 100, B1 = 5, B2 = 175, C1 = 130, C3 = 70, Z = 2,480; VAM: A3 = 100, B1 = 5, B2 = 175, C1 = 130, C3 = 70, Z = 2,480; no

11. $x_{11} = 70$, $x_{13} = 20$, $x_{22} = 10$, $x_{23} = 20$, $x_{32} = 100$, $x_{43} = 40$, Z = 1,240

13. (a) A1 = 30, A2 = 40, A3 = 60, B2 = 70, C1 = 50, C4 = 50, Z = 1,370; (b) A2 = 20, A3 = 60, A4 = 50, B2 = 70, C1 = 80, C2 = 20, Z = 1,290

15. (a) A3 = 90, B1 = 30, B3 = 20, C2 = 80, D1 = 40, D2 = 20, E1 = 50, Z = 1,590; (b) solution in (a) optimal; (c) yes, C1 has $k = 0$; alternative: A3 = 90, B1 = 30, B3 = 20, C1 = 40, C2 = 40, D2 = 60, E1 = 50, Z = 1,590

17. (a) T—NY = 130, T—C = 70, M—P = 170, M—C = 30, F—B = 150, F—Dummy = 50; (b) T—NY = 100, T—C = 100, M—NY = 30, M—P = 120, M—Dummy = 50, F—P = 50, F—B = 150, Z = 5,080; (c) no, no k values equal zero; (d) min. $Z = 9x_{TN} + 14x_{TP} + 12x_{TC} + 17x_{TB} + 11x_{MN} + 10x_{MP} + Mx_{MC} + 10x_{MB} + 12x_{FN} + 8x_{FP} + 15x_{FC} + 7x_{FB}$; s.t. $x_{TN} + x_{TP} + x_{TC} + x_{TB} \leq 200$, $x_{MN} + x_{MP} + x_{MC} + x_{MB} \leq 200$, $x_{FN} + x_{FP} + x_{FC} + x_{FB} \leq 200$, $x_{TN} + x_{MN} + x_{FN} = 130$, $x_{TP} + x_{MP} + x_{FP} = 170$, $x_{TC} + x_{MC} + x_{FC} = 100$, $x_{TB} + x_{MB} + x_{FB} = 150$, $x_{ij} \geq 0$

19. (a) 1—Dummy = 5, 2—Dummy = 25, 3B = 5, 3C = 15, 4A = 10, 4B = 15; (b) 1C = 5, 2C = 10, 2D = 15, 3B = 20, 3C = 0, 4A = 10, 4D = 15, Z = 195; (c) min. $Z = 7x_{1A} + 8x_{1B} + 5x_{1C} + 6x_{2A} + Mx_{2B} + 6x_{2C} + 10x_{3A} + 4x_{3B} + 5x_{3C} + 3x_{4A} + 9x_{4B} + Mx_{4C}$; s.t. $x_{1A} + x_{1B} + x_{1C} \leq 5$, $x_{2A} + x_{2B} + x_{2C} \leq 25$, $x_{3A} + x_{3B} + x_{3C} \leq 20$, $x_{4A} + x_{4B} + x_{4C} \leq 25$, $x_{1A} + x_{2A} + x_{3A} + x_{4A} = 10$, $x_{1B} + x_{2B} + x_{3B} + x_{4B} = 20$, $x_{1C} + x_{2C} + x_{3C} + x_{4C} = 15$, $x_{ij} \geq 0$

21. 1A = 70, 2B = 25, 2C = 90, 3A = 10, 3B = 25, 3D = 25, Z = 13,200

23. (a) 1B = 70, 1D = 350, 2A = 520, 2C = 90, 3C = 310, 3D = 30, Dummy—B = 180, Z = 22,470; (b) 1B = 250, 1D = 170, 2A = 520, 2C = 90, 3C = 130, 3D = 210, Dummy—C = 180, Z = 21,930

25. operator 1—press, operator 2—lathe, operator 3—grinder, 70 min

27. (a) 1—B, 2—D, 3—C, 4—A, \$32; (b) min. $Z = 12x_{1A} + 11x_{1B} + 8x_{1C} + 14x_{1D} + 10x_{2A} + 9x_{2B} + 10x_{2C} + 8x_{2D} + 14x_{3A} + Mx_{3B} + 7x_{3C} + 11x_{3D} + 6x_{4A} + 8x_{4B} + 10x_{4C} + 9x_{4D}$; s.t. $x_{1A} + x_{1B} + x_{1C} + x_{1D} = 1$, $x_{2A} + x_{2B} + x_{2C} + x_{2D} = 1$, $x_{3A} + x_{3B} + x_{3C} + x_{3D} = 1$, $x_{4A} + x_{4B} + x_{4C} + x_{4D} = 1$, $x_{1A} + x_{2A} + x_{3A} + x_{4A} = 1$, $x_{1B} + x_{2B} + x_{3B} + x_{4B} = 1$, $x_{1C} + x_{2C} + x_{3C} + x_{4C} = 1$, $x_{1D} + x_{2D} + x_{3D} + x_{4D} = 1$, $x_{ij} \geq 0$

29. 1—B, 2—E, 3—A, 4—C, 5—D, 6—F, Z = \$36; alternative solution: 1—E, 2—A, 3—B, 4—C, 5—D, 6—F, Z = \$36

31. 1—C, 2—F, 3—E, 4—A, 5—D, 6—B, 85 defects

33. (a) transportation method, all demands = 2; (b) $1C = 1$, $2A = 1$, $3C = 1$, $4A = 1$, $5B = 1$, $6B = 1$, total mileage = 150
35. 1—Dummy, 2—lamps, 3—sporting goods, 4—linen, $Z = 660$

8

1. (a) $x_1 = 3$, $x_2 = 0$, $Z = 15$; (b) node 1: $x_1 = 3.33$, $x_2 = 0$; node 2: $x_1 = 3$, $x_2 = 2.5$; node 3: infeasible; node 4: $x_1 = 3$, $x_2 = 0$; node 5: $x_1 = 2$, $x_2 = 1$
3. $x_1 = 10$, $x_2 = 24$, $Z = 1,460$
5. (a) $x_1 = 6$, $x_2 = 1$, $Z = 310$; (b) node 1: $x_1 = 6.25$, $x_2 = 0$; node 2: $x_1 = 6$, $x_2 = 1$; node 3: infeasible
7. $x_1 = 7$, $x_2 = 2$, $Z = 2,900$
9. $x_1 = 5$, $x_2 = 4.5$, $Z = 6,700$
11. $x_1 = 0$, $x_2 = 4$, $x_3 = 1.33$, $Z = 29.32$
13. max. $Z = x_1 + .4x_2 + 1.2x_3$; s.t. $9x_1 + 5x_2 + 10x_3 \le 15$, $30x_1 + 10x_2 + 20x_3 \le 50$, $x_1 + x_2 \le 1$, $x_1, x_2, x_3 = 0$ or 1; $x_1 = 0$, $x_2 = 1$, $x_3 = 1$, $Z = 1.6$
15. (a) max. $Z = 85{,}000x_1 + 60{,}000x_2 - 18{,}000y_1$; s.t. $x_1 + x_2 \le 10$, $10{,}000x_1 + 7{,}000x_2 \le 72{,}000$, $x_1 - 10{,}000y_1 \le 0$, $x_1 \ge 0$, $x_2 \ge 0$, $y_1 \ge 0$; (b) $x_1 = 0$, $x_2 = 10$, $Z = 600{,}000$
17. (a) min. $Z = x_1 + x_2 + x_3 + x_4 + x_5 + x_6$; s.t. $x_6 + x_1 \ge 90$, $x_1 + x_2 \ge 215$, $x_2 + x_3 > 250$, $x_3 + x_4 \ge 65$, $x_4 + x_5 > 300$, $x_5 + x_6 \ge 125$, $x_{ij} \ge 0$; (b) $x_1 = 90$, $x_2 = 185$, $x_3 = 65$, $x_5 = 300$, $Z = 640$

9

1. min. $P_1d_1^-$, $P_2d_2^-$, $P_3d_1^+$, $P_4d_3^+$; s.t. $5x_1 + 2x_2 + 4x_3 + d_1^- - d_1^+ = 240$, $3x_1 + 5x_2 + 2x_3 + d_2^- - d_2^+ = 500$, $4x_1 + 6x_2 + 3x_3 + d_3^- - d_3^+ = 400$
3. min. $P_1d_1^-$, $P_2d_2^-$, $P_3d_3^+$, $3P_4d_5^- + 6P_4d_6^- + P_4d_7^- + 2P_4d_8^-$, $P_5d_4^+$; s.t. $80{,}000x_1 + 24{,}000x_2 + 15{,}000x_3 + 40{,}000x_4 + d_1^- = 600{,}000$, $1{,}500x_1 + 3{,}000x_2 + 500x_3 + 1{,}000x_4 + d_2^- - d_2^+ = 20{,}000$, $4x_1 + 8x_2 + 3x_3 + 5x_4 + d_3^- - d_3^+ = 50$, $d_3^+ + d_4^- - d_4^+ = 10$, $x_1 + d_5^- - d_5^+ = 7$, $x_2 + d_6^- - d_6^+ = 10$, $x_3 + d_7^- - d_7^+ = 8$, $x_4 + d_8^- - d_8^+ = 12$

5. min. $P_1d_2^+$, $P_2d_7^+$, $4P_3d_4^- + 2P_3d_5^- + P_3d_6^-$, $P_4d_1^-$, $P_5d_3^-$; s.t. $x_1 + x_2 + x_3 + d_1^- = 2{,}000$, $800x_1 + 1{,}500x_2 + 500x_3 + d_2^- - d_2^+ = 20{,}000$, $10x_1 + 12x_2 + 18x_3 + d_3^- - d_3^+ = 800$, $x_1 + d_4^- - d_4^+ = 800$, $x_2 + d_5^- - d_5^+ = 900$, $x_3 + d_6^- - d_6^+ = 1{,}100$, $d_3^+ + d_7^- - d_7^+ = 100$
7. (a) 3; (b) min. $P_1d_2^-$, $P_2d_1^+$, $P_3d_3^+$; (c) $x_1 = 88$, $d_1^+ = 40$, $d_3^+ = 48$; (d) yes, all priority one goals have been achieved and any further achievement of priorities two and three would sacrifice priority one; (e) priority two and three goals have not been achieved
9. (a) $x_1 = 500$, $x_2 = 300$, $d_3^- = 500$
11. $x_1 = 30$, $x_2 = 80$, $d_3^- = 90$, $d_4^- = 50$
13. $x_1 = 3$, $x_2 = 6$, $d_1^- = 1$, $d_3^+ = 3$
15. $x_1 = 40$, $x_2 = 50$, $d_1^+ = 140$, $d_4^+ = 120$
17. (a) min. $P_1d_5^+$, $P_2d_2^-$, $5P_3d_3^- + 4P_3d_4^-$, $P_4d_1^-$; s.t. $5x_1 + 8x_2 + d_1 - d_1^1 = 4{,}800$, $.20x_1 + .25x_2 + d_2^- - d_2^+ = 300$, $x_1 + d_3^- = 500$, $x_2 + d_4^- = 400$, $d_1^+ + d_5^- - d_5^+ = 480$, (b) $x_1 = 431.4$, $x_2 = 135.4$, $d_1^- = 480$, $d_2^+ = 19.2$, $d_4^- = 11.6$
19. min. $P_1d_1^-$, $P_2d_2^+$, $P_3d_3^-$, $P_4d_4^-$; s.t. $x_1 + d_1^- - d_1^+ = 30$, $20x_1 + 40x_2 + 150x_3 + d_2^- - d_2^+ = 1{,}200$, $x_2 + x_3 + d_3^- - d_3^+ = 20$, $x_1 + d_4^- - d_4^+ = 6$

10

1. See p. 339.
3. (a) .23; (b) .08; (c) .25; (d) .02
5. (a) 0–19, .066; 20–29, .233; 30–39, .266; 40–49, .266; 50+, .166; (b) yes, only one of the events can take place each winter
7. $P(r \ge 5) = .0433$, $P(r < 5) = .9567$
9. $P(r = 4) = .2001$
11. .47
13. (a and b) $P(PN) = .225$, $P(FN) = .025$, $P(PS) = .34$, $P(FS) = .06$, $P(PC) = .332$, $P(FC) = .018$; (c) $P(\text{Fail}) = .103$
15. .177
17. $E(\text{grade}) = 2.2$, $\sigma^2 = 1.16$
19. $E(A) = 220{,}000$, $E(B) = 100{,}000$, select A
21. $8
23. $P(x \ge 400) = .8944$
25. $P(45 \le x \le 55) = .5934$

27. $P(x \geq 19) = .1056$
29. 256.8

11

1. (a) lease land; (b) savings certificate
3. (a) bellhop; (b) management; (c) bellhop
5. (a) course III; (b) course I
7. (a) product 3; (b) product 3
9. (a) stocks; (b) bonds; (c) real estate; (d) stocks; (e) stocks
11. (a) Alabama vs. Auburn; (b) Alabama vs. Auburn; (c) Army vs. Navy
13. $15,300
15. (a) sun visors; (b) sun visors
17. (a) widget; (b) widget; (c) EVPI = $6,000
19. $P(\text{good}) = .667$, $P(\text{bad}) = .333$
21. Marks, EVPI = $75,000
23. (b) 16 cases; (c) 16 cases; (d) EVPI = $5.80
25. (b) 26 dozen; (c) EOL(26) = $3.10; (d) EVPI = $3.10
27. select A
29. select A
31. if report favorable purchase lathe, if report unfavorable purchase grinder; EV = $16,480; EVSI = $5,280
33. if analyst predicts a shortage, they should stock compacts; if analyst predicts a surplus, they should stock full sized cars; EV = $342,094; EVSI = $102,094
35. the couple are risk averters, so the utility of savings bonds is greater for them
37. defense, welfare, medicare are three examples

12

1. (a) I—strategy 1, II—strategy B; (b) pure strategy
3. no dominant strategies in problem 2, but in problem 1 strategy 1 dominates 2
5. blue—strategy 1, red—strategy C, 1,700 troops lost
7. (a) player—strategy 1, owner—strategy C; (b) mixed, no equilibrium point
9. no pure strategy; EG(Truman) = 6.5, EL(Washington) = 6.5
11. (a) player I—strategy 1, player II—strategy C, no equilibrium point; (b) 1A → 1C → 3C → 3A; (c) player I—

strategies 1 and 3, player II—strategies A and C; (d) EG(I) = 36.7, EL(II) = 36.7
13. EG(I) = 57.5 = EL(II)
15. EG(Tech) = 68.4 points = EL(State)
17. min. $Z = x_1 + x_2$; s.t. $15x_1 + 7x_2 \geq 1$, $9x_1 + 20x_2 \geq 1$, $11x_1 + 12x_2 \geq 1$, $x_1 \geq 0$, $x_2 \geq 0$
19. min. $Z = x_1 + x_2$; s.t. $20x_1 + 15x_2 \geq 1$, $7x_1 + 21x_2 \geq 1$, $9x_1 + 16x_2 \geq 1$, $x_1 \geq 0$, $x_2 \geq 0$; $x_1 = .006$, $x_2 = .059$, $s_2 = .276$, $Z = .065$; EG(I) = 15.4 = EL(II)

13

1. starting state A: $P(A) = .55$, $P(B) = .45$; starting state B: $P(A) = .54$, $P(B) = .46$
3. $P(\text{Petroco}) = .14$, $P(\text{National}) = .54$, $P(\text{Gascorp}) = .32$
5. .417
7. [.36   .64]
9. [.583   .417]
11. $[t_t \quad d_t] = [.563 \quad .437]$
13. See p. 465.
15. (a) $[m \quad w] = [.642 \quad .358]$; (b) movie = 770, western = 430; (c) movie
17. yes
19. See p. 471.
21. $[p \quad b] = [\$268,800 \quad \$151,200]$
23. (a) $[P \quad C \quad G] = [.422 \quad .220 \quad .358]$; (b) Plant Plus gains 798 customers, Crop Extra loses 2,020 customers, Gro-fast gains 1,222 customers
25. (a) [1772   3906   4322]; (b) $[E \quad A \quad B] = [1670 \quad 3350 \quad 4980]$
27. $[P_1 \quad P_2 \quad P_3 \quad P_4] = [.2 \quad .4 \quad .2 \quad .2]$; EC = $280 per day

14

1. school registration, grocery store, bank, ball game, theater, garage, intersection, airport, doctor's office, post office
3. (a) .286; (b) 2.5; (c) 1.79; (d) 3 minutes; (e) .714
5. $W_q = 24.6$ minutes, $P_w = .833$
7. $L_q = 3.2$, $P_w = .80$, $1 - P_w = .20$
9. $W_q = 40$ minutes; the cars will not have to wait
11. yes, install the second window

13. (a) $L_q = 9.09$, $W = 24$ minutes, $W_q = 21.6$ minutes; (b) $W = 4$ minutes, the state should install scales
15. the new counter created 2 queues, not 2 servers
17. $L = 1.19$, $L_q = .26$, $W = 2.55$ minutes, $W_q = .56$ minute
19. $L = 5.44$, $L_q = 3.77$, $W = 3.26$ minutes, $W_q = 2.26$ minutes
21. no
23. 3 salespeople
25. 1.14 hours
27. (a) $L = 6.0$, $L_q = 3.5$, $W = 72$ minutes, $W_q = 42$ minutes; (b) implement improved system with savings = $3,600; (c) alternative 1, add a fourth dock

---

15

1. (a) 56; (b) $\mu = 2.8$, EV = 2.65
3. (a and b) $\mu \cong 3.48$, EV = 3.65, the results differ because not enough simulations were done in part a; (c) approximately 21 calls; no; repeat simulations to get enough observations
5. (a and b) $\mu \cong 2.95$
7. (a) $\mu = \$25.10$
9. (a) average time between arrivals = 4.3 days, average waiting time $\cong 6.25$ days, average number of tankers waiting $\cong 1.16$; (b) system has not reached steady state
11. See p. 542.
13. total yardage $\cong 155$ yards, the sportswriter will predict Tech will win
15. circling time, number of air traffic controllers, landing time, distance from runway to terminal, unloading time, refueling and maintenance, loading, terminal traffic

---

16

1. See p. 566.
3. (a) 20, 25, 30.3, 35.3, 35.7, 41, 48, 43; (b) 26.8, 28.2, 32.8, 39.4, 42, 40.4
5. (a) 6, 5.3, 5.7, 7.3, 10, 12.7, 14, 13.3, 13.3, 14.7; (b) 6, 6.8, 7.8, 10, 12, 12.4, 13.6, 14.8; (c) approximately the same

---

7. (a) 116, 121.3, 118, 143.7, 138.3, 141.7, 135, 156.7, 143.3, 136.7; (b) 121.8, 134.8, 125.8, 137.2, 143, 149, 137, 142; (c) 114, 116.5, 125.8, 151.8, 132.5, 138.3, 142.5, 160, 136.7, 130
9. $\alpha = .10$: 40, 39, 39.6, 41.6, 43; $\alpha = .30$: 40, 37, 39.4, 45.6, 48.4
11. (a) 800, 792.5, 776.3, 748.6, 738.3, 733.4, 733.1, 740.8, 786.7, 806; (b) 785.8, 755.6, 705.1, 689.9, 685.4, 689.6, 708.6, 799, 834.5
13. 8, 8.4, 8.3, 8.3, 9, 9.2, 9.3, 9.5
15. 130.7, 115, 120.3, 134.5, 160.8, 140.5, 152.4, 159.9, 175.6, 151.3, 145.9
17. problems 5, MAD = 3.6; problem 12, MAD = 3.72; problem 16, MAD = 3.13; the adjusted exponential smoothed forecast (#16) is most accurate
19. simple, MAD = 155.4; adjusted, MAD = 163.6; simple is most appropriate
21. $y = 9,205.9 + 2,075.3x$
23. (a) $y = 54.8 + 2.77x$; (c) \$90,810; (d) sales cannot increase infinitely
25. $r^2 = .79$, yes

17

1. $Q = 2,738.6$, TC = \$1,095.44
3. (a) 1,633; (b) \$1,224.74; (c) 3.06; (d) 119.3
5. $Q = 10,000$, TC = \$3,500, number of orders = 3.5, time between orders = 104.3 days
7. (a) 45,286; (b) \$13,748; (c) 9,863
9. (a) 774.6; (b) \$619.68; (c) 43.84
11. 575.34 yards
13. $Q = 2,702.66$, TC = \$1,036.02
15. (a) 60,000; (b) \$12,000; (c) 15,000
17. $Q = 2,211$, TC = \$7,428
19. (a) $Q = 1,200$; (b) TC = \$2,880; (c) $R = 300$
21. (a) $Q = 1,174.7$, TC = \$2,936.80; (b) $D/Q = 6.4$, days between runs = 57 days, length of run = 47.7 days
23. $Q = 3,240.4$, TC = \$4,629.11
25. (a) 333.5; (b) 142.9; (c) \$8,575.41
27. $Q = 103,683.5$, TC = \$4,973.50, allow shortages
29. $Q = 17,544$, $S = 4,616.84$, TC = \$3,231.84
31. $Q = 536.66$, $S = 178.88$, monthly TC = \$4,293.25, annual TC = \$51,519.01

33. without discount = \$45,490, with discount = \$38,875; take discount
35. without discount = \$4,619.68, with discount = \$4,680; do not take discount
37. price is a constant with no effect on inventory costs unless one of the model parameters is a function of price, as in quantity discount model

18

1. safety stock = 100, reorder point = 400, \$300
3. safety stock = 21, reorder point = 150, \$12.75
5. safety stock = 12, reorder point = 35, \$8,400
7. max. inventory level = 700, Q = 600, reorder point = 400, S_s = 100
9. 3,984 yards
11. 9,920 lb
13. zero
15. 7 barrels
17. 16 cases
19. 5 tons
21. average demand during lead time $\cong$ 44.5
23. average profit $\cong$ \$290; from problem 15, $E(7)$ = \$300
25. average cost $\cong$ \$22.50; to optimize, test various levels of Q and locate lowest cost combination of Q and lead time

19

1. 1—3 = 5, 1—3—2 = 8, 1—3—5 = 12, 1—4 = 9
3. 1—2 = 21, 1—2—5 = 46, 1—3 = 17, 1—3—4 = 29, 1—3—4—6 = 39, 1—3—4—7 = 38
5. 1—2 = 85, 1—3 = 53, 1—4 = 88, 1—3—5 = 114, 1—3—7 = 170, 1—3—7—6 = 194
7. 1—2 = 25, 1—2—3 = 60, 1—2—4 = 43, 1—5 = 48, 1—6 = 50, 1—7 = 32, 1—7—8 = 72
9. 1—2 = 7, 1—3 = 10, 1—4 = 8, 1—3—5 = 13, 1—3—5—8 = 21, 1—4—6 = 13, 1—4—6—9 = 20, 1—4—7 = 16
11. 1—7—6—10—12 = 18

13. 1—2—3—5—4—6 = 84
15. 1—2—5—4—3 and 5—7—6; 25 miles
17. 1—3—4—6—7 and 3—2 and 6—5; 265 yards
19. 1—4—2 and 4—6—3 and 6—7—5 and 7—8; 1,160 yards
21. 1—2—5—6—8—9 and 2—4—7 and 4—3; 22 miles
23. 1—2 = 6, 1—4 = 5, 1—3 = 5, 2—5 = 6, 2—4 = 0, 3—4 = 0, 3—6 = 5, 4—5 = 0, 4—6 = 5, 5—6 = 6; maximum flow = 16
25. 1—2 = 15, 1—4 = 20, 1—3 = 12, 2—5 = 11, 2—4 = 4, 3—4 = 3, 3—6 = 9, 4—6 = 27, 5—6 = 11; maximum flow = 47
27. 1—2 = 7, 1—4 = 7, 1—3 = 4, 2—6 = 6, 2—4 = 1, 3—4 = 3, 3—5 = 1, 4—6 = 0, 4—8 = 4, 4—7 = 7, 5—7 = 1, 6—8 = 6, 7—8 = 8; maximum = 18 flights
29. 1—2 = 4, 1—3 = 4, 1—4 = 4, 2—3 = 0, 2—5 = 4, 3—4 = 0, 3—5 = 2, 3—6 = 2, 4—6 = 4, 5—6 = 0, 5—7 = 6, 6—8 = 6, 7—8 = 0, 7—9 = 6, 8—9 = 6; 12,000 cars

20

1. 1—2—4 = 8, 1—3—4 = 10*
3. 1—2—4—6 = 14, 1—2—4—5—6 = 23*, 1—2—5—6 = 13, 1—3—5—6 = 22, 1—3—6 = 12
5. node 1: ET = 0, LT = 0; node 2: ET = 7, LT = 9; node 3: ET = 10, LT = 10; node 4: ET = 15, LT = 15; node 5: ET = 18, LT = 18; node 6: ET = 20, LT = 20; slack: s_{12} = 2, s_{13} = 0, s_{24} = 2, s_{34} = 0, s_{35} = 4, s_{45} = 0, s_{56} = 0. Critical path activities have no slack
7. node 1: ET = 0, LT = 0; node 2: ET = 10, LT = 10; node 3: ET = 7, LT = 12; node 4: ET = 14, LT = 18; node 5: ET = 19, LT = 25; node 6: ET = 25, LT = 25; node 7: ET = 34, LT = 34; slack: s_{12} = 0, s_{13} = 5, s_{24} = 4, s_{26} = 0, s_{34} = 5, s_{35} = 6, s_{46} = 4, s_{56} = 6, s_{67} = 0. Critical path = 1—2—6—7
9. node 1: ET = 0, LT = 0; node 2: ET = 8, LT = 12; node 3: ET = 12, LT = 12; node 4: ET = 3, LT = 12; node 5: ET = 5, LT = 21; node 6: ET = 21, LT = 21; node 7: ET = 33, LT = 52; node 8:

ET = 28, LT = 53; node 9: ET = 51, LT = 53; node 10: ET = 42, LT = 42; node 11: ET = 58, LT = 58; node 12: ET = 53, LT = 72; node 13: ET = 63, LT = 75; node 14: ET = 75, LT = 75; node 15: ET = 78, LT = 78; slack: $s_{12} = 4$, $s_{13} = 0$, $s_{14} = 6$, $s_{23} = 4$, $s_{36} = 0$, $s_{43} = 9$, $s_{45} = 10$, $s_{46} = 15$, $s_{56} = 16$, $s_{67} = 19$, $s_{68} = 25$, $s_{69} = 2$, $s_{6,10} = 0$, $s_{7,12} = 19$, $s_{9,11} = 2$, $s_{10,11} = 0$, $s_{11,13} = 12$, $s_{11,14} = 0$, $s_{12,15} = 19$, $s_{13,14} = 12$, $s_{14,15} = 0$. Critical path = 1—3—6—10—11—14—15 = 78

11. 1—2 = (9, 4), 1—3 = (10, 1), 2—3 = (5, 4/9), 2—4 = (3, 4/9), 3—4 = (6, 4/9), 3—5 = (3, 0), 4—5 = (4, 1/9). Critical path = 1—2—3—4—5 = 24 weeks

13. (a) 1—2 = 8, 1—3 = 10.17, 1—4 = 9.33, 2—5 = 6, 2—6 = 5, 3—5 = 7.5, 4—5 = 0, 4—7 = 7.67, 5—8 = 15.17, 5—7 = 12.33, 7—8 = 6.83, 6—9 = 18.67, 8—9 = 9.17; (b) ET—1 = 0, ET—2 = 8, ET—3 = 10.17, ET—4 = 9.33, ET—5 = 17.67, ET—6 = 13, ET—7 = 30, ET—8 = 36.83, ET—9 = 46; (c) LT—1 = 0, LT—2 = 11.67, LT—3 = 10.17, LT—4 = 17.67, LT—5 = 17.67, LT—6 = 34, LT—7 = 30, LT—8 = 36.83, LT—9 = 46; (d) $s_{12} = 3.67$, $s_{13} = 0$, $s_{14} = 8.34$, $s_{26} = 21$, $s_{25} = 3.67$, $s_{35} = 0$, $s_{45} = 8.34$, $s_{47} = 13$, $s_{57} = 0$, $s_{58} = 3.99$, $s_{69} = 21$, $s_{78} = 0$, $s_{89} = 0$; (e) 1—3—5—7—8—9; (f) duration = 46 months, ν_p = 25 months

15. (a) 1—2 = 3, 2—4 = 4, 2—3 = 6.33, 2—5 = 5, 3—4 = 0, 3—6 = 4.33, 4—7 = 2.33, 6—7 = 2, 5—6 = 1, 5—7 = 8, 5—8 = 9, 7—8 = 4, 8—9 = 3, 8—10 = 2, 9—10 = 0, 10—11 = 1; (b) node 1 (0, 0); node 2 (3, 3); node 3 (9.33, 9.67); node 4 (9.33, 13.67); node 5 (8, 8); node 6 (13.33, 14); node 7 (16, 16); node 8 (20, 20); node 9 (23, 23); node 10 (23, 23); node 11 (24, 24); (c) $s_{12} = 0$, $s_{24} = 6.67$, $s_{23} = .34$, $s_{25} = 0$, $s_{34} = 4.34$, $s_{36} = .34$, $s_{47} = 4.34$, $s_{56} = 5$, $s_{57} = 0$, $s_{58} = 3$, $s_{67} = .67$, $s_{78} = 0$, $s_{89} = 0$, $s_{8,10} = 1$, $s_{9,10} = 0$, $s_{10,11} = 0$; (d) 1—2—5—7—8—9—10—11; (e) 24 months, ν_p = 6.99

17. (a) 1—2 = 4.17, 1—3 = 5.33, 2—3 = 2.17, 2—4 = 5.5, 2—5 = 3.5, 5—6 = 4.17, 5—7 = 3, 4—9 = 3, 6—9 = 3.33,

7—9 = 2, 3—9 = 6.33, 3—8 = 5.5, 8—9 = 0; (b) node 1 (0, 0); node 2 (4.17, 4.17); node 3 (6.34, 8.84); node 4 (9.67, 12.17); node 5 (7.67, 7.67); node 6 (11.84, 11.84); node 7 (10.67, 13.17); node 8 (11.84, 15.17); node 9 (15.17, 15.17); (c) 1—2—5—6—9; (d) 15.17 days, ν_p = 3.19 days; (e) .9429

19. .2119

21. (a and b) a (12, $40); b (4, $50); c (7, $70); d (4, $80); e (6, $30); (c) 20 weeks. Crash 1—2, 5 weeks; 1—2 and 3—4, 1 week; 1—2, 1—4 and 3—4, 4 weeks; (d) $3,950, $4,700; (e) min. $Z = x_4$; s.t. $x_2 - x_1 \geq 20$, $x_3 - x_1 \geq 14$, $x_4 - x_1 \geq 24$, $x_4 - x_2 \geq 10$, $x_4 - x_3 \geq 11$, $x_i \geq 0$, $x_j \geq 0$; (f) min. $Z = 40y_{12} + 50y_{14} + 70y_{13} + 80y_{24} + 30y_{34}$; s.t. $y_{12} \leq 12$, $y_{14} \leq 4$, $y_{13} \leq 7$, $y_{24} \leq 4$, $y_{34} \leq 6$, $x_1 + 20 - y_{12} \leq x_2$, $x_1 + 14 - y_{13} \leq x_3$, $x_1 + 24 - y_{14} \leq x_4$, $x_2 + 10 - y_{24} \leq x_4$, $x_3 + 11 - y_{34} \leq x_4$, $x_4 \leq 20$, $x_i > 0$, $x_j > 0$, $y_{ij} > 0$

23. min. $Z = x_6$; s.t. $x_2 - x_1 \geq 7$, $x_3 - x_1 \geq 10$, $x_4 - x_2 \geq 6$, $x_4 - x_3 \geq 5$, $x_5 - x_3 \geq 4$, $x_5 - x_4 \geq 3$, $x_6 - x_5 \geq 2$, $x_i \geq 0$, $x_j \geq 0$

25. (a) min. $Z = x_5$; s.t. $x_2 - x_1 \geq 9$, $x_3 - x_1 \geq 10$, $x_3 - x_2 \geq 5$, $x_4 - x_2 \geq 3$, $x_4 - x_3 \geq 6$, $x_5 - x_3 \geq 3$, $x_5 - x_4 \geq 4$, $x_i \geq 0$, $x_j \geq 0$; (b) min. $Z = 100y_{12} + 50y_{13} + 200y_{23} + 100y_{24} + 75y_{34} + 0y_{35} + 200y_{45}$; s.t. $y_{12} \leq 3$, $y_{13} \leq 3$, $y_{23} \leq 2$, $y_{24} \leq 2$, $y_{34} \leq 2$, $y_{35} \leq 0$, $y_{45} \leq 1$, $x_1 + 8 - y_{12} \leq x_2$, $x_1 + 10 - y_{13} \leq x_3$, $x_2 + 5 - y_{23} \leq x_3$, $x_2 + 3 - y_{24} \leq x_4$, $x_3 + 6 - y_{34} \leq x_4$, $x_3 + 3 - y_{35} \leq x_5$, $x_4 + 4 - y_{45} \leq x_5$, $x_5 \leq 15$, $x_i \geq 0$, $x_j \geq 0$, $y_{ij} \geq 0$

21

1. (a) max. $R_1 + R_2$; s.t. $D_1 + D_2 \leq 3$. Solve in stages, where east is stage 1 and west is stage 2; (b) east—0, west—3

3. 5 mirrors, no knives

5. A—2, B—0, C—1

7. there are multiple optimal solutions: (1) Akron—0, Baltimore—1, Chicago—3; (2) Akron—2, Baltimore—1, Chicago—1

9. A—1, B—4, C—1

11. North—2, South—3, East—0, West—0

13. Lincoln—2, Dubuque—2, Terre Haute—1

15. January = 5, February = 5, March = 0, April = 4; TC = $454
17. 1—4—5—9—10; 15 hours

22

1. TC = $27,500, TR = $54,000, Z = $26,500
3. TC = $29,100, TR = $23,400, Z = −$5,700
5. 3,750 tires
7. 100,000 lb
9. break-even point at 100,000 lb
11. $93,750
13. 46.9%
15. 83.3%
17. reduces break-even volume to 55,555.5 lb
19. increase break-even volume to 102,631.5 lb
21. (a) .7486; (b) .05
23. (a) break-even probability = .7881; produce new fertilizer; (b) higher probability of breaking even with new fertilizer; two fertilizers have similar average profits; thus, new fertilizer should be selected
25. $25.39
27. $p = \$186.67$, $Z = \$18,313.33$

29. $p = \$1.68$, $v = 7.481$ yards, $Z = \$1,949.72$
31. $v = 316.67$, $Z = \$508.34$

23

1. See p. 809.
3. $p = \$35.16$, $Z = \$10,257.57$
5. $x_1 = 10$, $x_2 = 45$, $Z = \$212.50$
7. $x_1 = 12.06$, $x_2 = 10.35$, $Z = \$80.73$
9. $x_1 = 121.5$, $x_2 = 157$, $Z = \$2,064.28$
11. $\lambda = .27$; we would pay $.27 for one additional hour of labor

24

1. See p. 824.
3. See p. 825.
5. See p. 828.
7. See p. 829.
9. See p. 830.
11. See p. 832.
13. See pp. 839 and 840.
15. See p. 841.
17. See p. 843.

Glossary

a

absorbing state   a state in a Markov transition matrix from which the system cannot move once the state has been achieved (also known as a trapping state)

activities   in a CPM/PERT project network, the branches reflecting project operations

activity slack   in a CPM/PERT network, the amount of time that the start of an activity can be delayed without exceeding the critical path project time

adjusted exponential smoothing   the exponential smoothing forecasting technique adjusted for trend changes and seasonal patterns

analytical   containing or pertaining to mathematical analysis using formulas or equations

a priori probability   one of the two types of objective probabilities. Given a set of outcomes for an activity, it is the ratio of the number of desired outcomes to the total number of outcomes

arrival rate   the number of arrivals at a service facility

(within a queuing system) during a specified period of time

artificial variable   a variable that is added to an − or ≥ constraint so that initial solutions in a linear programming problem can be obtained at the origin

assignment model   a type of linear programming model similar to a transportation model, except that the supply at each source is limited to one unit and the demand at each destination is limited to one unit

b

back order   a customer order that cannot be filled from existing inventory but will be filled when inventory is replenished

backward pass   a means of determining the latest event times in a CPM/PERT network

balanced transportation model   a model in which supply equals demand

BASIC   a computer programming language

basic feasible solution   any solution in linear

programming that satisfies the model constraints

basic variables   in a linear programming problem, variables that have values (other than zero) at a basic feasible solution point

Bayes's law   a method for altering marginal probabilities, given additional information. The altered probabilities are referred to as revised or posterior probabilities.

Bernoulli process   a probability experiment that has the following properties: (1) each trial has two outcomes, (2) the probabilities remain constant, (3) the outcomes are independent, and (4) the number of trials is discrete

beta distribution   a probability distribution used in network analysis for determining activity times

binomial distribution   a probability distribution for experiments for which the Bernoulli properties hold

branch   in a network diagram, a line that represents the flow of items from one point (i.e., node) to another

branch and bound method a solution approach whereby a total set of feasible solutions is partitioned into smaller subsets, which are then evaluated systematically. This technique is used extensively to solve integer programming problems.

break-even analysis the determination of the number of units that must be produced and sold to equate total revenue with total cost

break-even point the volume of units that equates total revenue with total cost

c

calculus a branch of mathematics concerned with the rate of change of functions. The two basic forms of calculus are differential calculus and integral calculus.

calling population the source of customers to a waiting line

carrying cost the cost incurred by a business for holding items in inventory

cathode ray tube (CRT) the technical name for a computer terminal, video display unit, or video monitor that looks and acts like a television

classical optimization the use of calculus to find optimal values for variables

classical probability an a priori probability

closed path in a transportation tableau, a path along which transported items can be reallocated

coefficient of determination a measure of the strength of the relationship of the variables in a regression equation

coefficient of optimism a measure of a decision maker's optimism

collectively exhaustive events all of the possible events of an experiment

computer package a prewritten computer program or code

computer program a set of instructions that tell a computer what operations to perform

concave curve a curve shaped like an inverted bowl

conditional probability the probability that one event will occur, given that another event has already occurred

constrained optimization model a model with a single objective function and one or more constraints

constraint a mathematical relationship that represents limited resources or minimum levels of activity in a mathematical programming model

continuous distribution a probability distribution in which the random variables can equal an infinite number of values within an interval

convex curve a curve shaped like an upright bowl

critical path the longest path through a CPM/PERT network. It indicates the minimum time in which a project can be completed.

critical path method (CPM) a network technique that uses deterministic activity times for project planning and scheduling

cumulative probability distribution a probability distribution in which the probability of an event is added to the sum of the probabilities of the previously listed events

cycle movement up or down during a trend in a forecast

d

data pieces of information

data base an organized collection of numerical information

decision analysis the analysis of decision situations in which certainty cannot be assumed

decision support system (DSS) a computer-based information system that has the capability of interacting with a manager to assist and support decision making

decision tree a graphical diagram for analyzing a decision situation

decision variable a variable whose value represents a potential decision on the part of the manager

degeneracy (in a simplex tableau) a series of loops in the simplex solution to a linear programming problem, created by a tie for the pivot row, that prevents the solution from improving in subsequent simplex iterations

degeneracy (in a transportation tableau) when a transportation tableau does not have the required $m + n - 1$ cell allocations

dependent events events for which the probability of one event is affected by the probability of occurrence of other events

derivative in calculus, a transformed form of a mathematical function that defines the slope of the function

deterministic characterized by the assumption that there is no uncertainty

deviational variables in a goal programming model constraint, variables that reflect the possible deviation from a goal level

differential the derivative of a function

directed branch a branch in a network in which flow is possible in only one direction

discrete distribution a probability distribution that consists of values for the random variable that are countable and usually integer

dominant strategy a strategy used by a player in a game that has consistently better outcomes than another strategy (or strategies)

dual an alternative form of a linear programming model that contains useful information regarding the value of resources, which form the constraints of the model

dual constraints the constraints of the dual of a linear programming model.

There is a dual constraint corresponding to each variable in the primal model.

dual variables the variables of the dual of a linear programming model. There is a dual variable corresponding to each constraint in the primal model.

dummy activity a branch in a CPM/PERT network that reflects a precedence relationship but does not represent any passage of time

dynamic programming a solution approach in which problems are solved in stages

dynamic programming state the possible resource levels available at each stage of a dynamic programming problem

e

earliest event time in a CPM/PERT network, the earliest time at which an event can be started without exceeding the critical path project time

economic forecast a prediction of the state of the economy in the future

economic order quantity (EOQ) the optimal order size that corresponds to total minimum inventory cost

efficiency of sample information an indicator of how close to perfection sample information is. It is computed by dividing the expected value of sample information by the expected value of perfect information.

empirical consisting of (or based on) data or information gained from experiment and observation

equal likelihood criterion a decision-making method in which all states of nature are weighted equally

equilibrium point the outcome of a game that results from a pure strategy

event the possible result of a probability experiment

events in a CPM/PERT project network, the nodes that reflect the beginning and termination of activities

expected monetary value the expected (average) monetary outcome of a decision, computed by multiplying the outcomes by their probabilities of occurrence and summing these products

expected opportunity loss the expected cost of the loss of opportunity resulting from an incorrect decision by the decision maker

expected value an *average* value computed by multiplying each value of a random variable by its probability of occurrence

expected value of perfect information (EVPI) the value of information expressed as the amount of money that a decision maker would be willing to pay to make a better decision

expected value of sample information the difference between the expected value of a decision situation with and without additional information

experiment in probability, a particular action, such as tossing a coin

exponential distribution a probability distribution often used to define the service times in a queuing system

exponential smoothing a time series forecasting method similar to a moving average in which more recent data are weighted more heavily than past data

extreme points the maximum and minimum points on a curve (also known as relative extreme points); in a linear programming problem, a protrusion in the feasible solution space

f

factorial for a value of n, the factorial is $n! = n(n-1)(n-2)\cdots(2)(1)$

feasible solution a solution that does not violate any of the restrictions or constraints in a model

feedback decision results that are fed back into a management information system to be used as data

fixed costs costs that are independent of the volume of units produced

forecast a prediction of what will occur in the future

forecast reliability a measure of how closely a forecast reflects reality

forecast time frame how far in the future the forecast projects

forward pass a method for determining earliest event times in a CPM/PERT network

frequency distribution the organization of events into classes, which shows the frequency with which the events occur

functional relationship an equation that relates a dependent variable to one or more independent variables

fundamental matrix a matrix used in Markov analysis. It indicates the expected number of times a system will be in any nonabsorbing state before it is absorbed.

g

game players the competing decision makers in a game situation

game strategy a plan of action to be followed by a player

game theory an area of management science encompassing decision situations in which one or more decision makers compete for the best outcome

global maximum the absolute maximum extreme point on a curve

global minimum the absolute minimum extreme point on a curve

goal constraint a constraint in a goal programming model that contains deviational variables

goal programming a linear programming technique that considers more than one objective in the model

goals the alternative objectives in a goal programming model

gradient search methods computerized approaches for solving complex nonlinear programming problems

h

hard copy computer output printed on paper

hardware the computer machine and ancillary equipment

Hurwicz criterion a method for making a decision in a decision analysis problem. The decision is a compromise between total optimism and total pessimism.

i

identity matrix a matrix containing ones along the diagonal and zeros elsewhere in the matrix

implementation the use of model results

implicit enumeration a method for solving integer programming problems in which obviously infeasible solutions are eliminated and the remaining solutions are systematically evaluated to see which one is best

independent events events for which the probability of occurrence of one event does not affect the probability of occurrence of the other events

inequality a mathematical relationship that contains a $\geq$ or $\leq$ sign

infeasible problem a linear programming problem with no feasible solution area and thus no solution

information flow the flow of information from one point to another in an organization's management information system

instantaneous receipt the assumption that once inventory level reaches zero, an order is received after the passage of an infinitely small amount of time

integer programming a form of linear programming that generates only integer solution values for the model variables

interactive computer program a program that collects input data from a manager by asking questions

inventory analysis the analysis of the problems of inventory planning and control, with the objective of minimizing inventory-related costs

---

j

joint probability the probability of several events' occurring jointly in an experiment

---

k

knapsack problem a dynamic programming problem concerned with how many of each of several different kinds of items should be placed in a knapsack to maximize the return from the items

---

l

Lagrange multiplier a value, λ, that reflects the approximate change in the objective function resulting from a unit change in the right-hand-side quantity of a constraint equation

Lagrange multipliers method a solution approach for nonlinear programming problems in which the constraints, as multiples of a constant, are subtracted from the objective function

Lagrangian function the transformed objective function in a nonlinear programming problem being solved with Lagrange multipliers

LaPlace criterion a decision-making method in which all states of nature are weighted equally (more commonly known as the equal likelihood criterion)

latest event time in a CPM/PERT network, the latest time at which an event can be started without exceeding the critical path project time

LINDO (Linear Interactive and Discrete Optimizer) a computer software package for solving linear programming problems

linear programming a management science technique used to determine the optimal way to achieve an objective, subject to restrictions, in cases where all the mathematical relationships are linear

linear (simple) regression a form of regression that reflects the relationship of two variables

long-range forecast a forecast that typically encompasses a period of time longer than one or two years

---

m

mainframe a large stationary computer to which remote terminals are connected via cable or dedicated telephone lines, capable of solving complex problems

management information system (MIS) a system for accumulating, organizing, and distributing information in an organization

management science the application of mathematical techniques and scientific principles to management problems in order to help managers make better decisions

Markov analysis a probabilistic technique applicable to systems that exhibit probabilistic movement from one state of the system to another over a period of time

materials requirement planning (MRP) a computer-based production and inventory planning system for products consisting of several component parts

maximal flow problem a network problem in which the objective is to maximize the total amount of flow from a source to a destination

maximax criterion a method for making a decision in a decision analysis problem. The decision will result in the maximum of the maximum payoffs.

maximin criterion a method for making a decision in a decision analysis problem. The decision will result in the maximum of the minimum payoffs.

maximization problem a linear programming problem in which an objective, such as profit, is maximized

mean absolute deviation (MAD) a measure of the difference between a forecast and what actually occurs

medium-range forecast a forecast that encompasses anywhere from one month to a year

minimal spanning tree problem a network problem in which the objective is to connect all the nodes so that the total branch lengths are minimized

minimax regret criterion a method for making a decision in a decision analysis problem. The decision will minimize the maximum regret.

minimization problem a linear programming problem in which an objective, such as cost, is minimized

minimum cell cost method a method for determining the initial solution to a transportation model

mixed constraint problem a linear programming problem with a mixture of $\leq$, $=$, and $\geq$ constraints

mixed integer model an integer linear programming model that can generate a solution with both integer and noninteger values

mixed strategy game a game in which the players adopt a mixture of strategies

model an abstract (mathematical) representation of a problem

modified distribution

method (MODI) a method for solving a transportation model that is a modified version of the stepping-stone method

Monte Carlo process a technique used in simulation for selecting numbers randomly from a probability distribution

most likely time one of three time estimates used in a beta distribution to determine an activity time. It is the time that would occur most frequently if the activity were repeated many times.

moving average a time series forecasting method that involves dividing values of a forecast variable by a sequence of time periods

multiple optimum solutions alternative solutions to a linear programming problem, all of which achieve the same objective function value

multiple regression a form of regression that reflects the relationship among more than two variables

multiple-server queuing system a system in which a single waiting line feeds into two or more servers in parallel

mutually exclusive events in a probability experiment, events that can occur only one at a time

---

n

necessary condition a mathematical condition that must exist for a point on a curve to be a global maximum or minimum

network an arrangement of paths connected at various points (drawn as a diagram), through which an item (or items) moves from one point to another

network flow models a model that represents the flow of items through a system

node in a network diagram, a point that represents a junction or intersection. It is represented by a circle.

nonbasic variables the variables that equal zero at a basic feasible solution point in a linear programming problem

noninstantaneous receipt the gradual receipt of inventory over time

nonlinear programming a form of mathematical programming in which the objective function or constraints (or both) are nonlinear functions

normal distribution a continuous probability distribution that has the shape of a bell

northwest corner method a method for determining the initial solution to a transportation model

n-person game a game in which more than two decision makers compete

---

o

objective function a mathematical relationship that represents the objective of a problem solution

objective probability the relative frequency with which a specific outcome in an experiment has been observed to occur in the long run

opportunity cost table a table derived in the solution to an assignment problem

optimal solution the one best solution to a problem

optimistic time one of three time estimates used in a beta distribution to determine an activity time. It is the shortest possible time it would take to complete an activity if everything went right.

order cycle the time period during which a maximum inventory level is depleted and a new order is received to bring inventory back to its maximum level

ordering cost the cost a business incurs when it makes an order to replenish its inventory

p

parameter a constant value that is generally a coefficient of a variable in a mathematical equation

payoff table a table used to show the payoffs that can result from decisions under various states of nature

penalty cost the penalty (or regret) suffered by the decision maker when a wrong decision is made

permanent set in a shortest route network problem, a set of nodes to which the shortest route from the start node has been determined

pessimistic time one of three time estimates used in a beta distribution to determine an activity time. It

is the longest possible time it would take to complete an activity if everything went wrong.

pivot column the column in a simplex tableau that corresponds to the entering nonbasic variable

pivot row the row in a simplex tableau that corresponds to the leaving basic variable

Poisson distribution a probability distribution that describes the occurrence of a relatively rare event in a fixed period of time; often used to define arrivals at a service facility in a queuing system

political/social forecast a prediction of political and social changes that may occur in the future

postoptimality analysis the analysis of an optimal simplex solution in order to gain additional information. Duality and sensitivity analysis are forms of postoptimality analysis.

precedence relationship the relationship exhibited by events that must occur in sequence. Such events can be represented by a CPM/PERT network.

primal the original form of a linear programming model

priority the importance of a goal relative to other goals in a goal programming model

probabilistic techniques management science techniques that take into account uncertain information and give probabilistic solutions

probability distribution a distribution showing the probability of occurrence of all events in an experiment

probability tree a diagram showing the probabilities of the various outcomes of an experiment

production lot size model an inventory model for a business that produces its own inventory at a gradual rate (also known as the noninstantaneous receipt model)

prohibited route in a transportation model, a route (i.e., variable) to which no allocation can be made

project crashing a method for reducing the duration of a CPM/PERT project network by reducing one or more critical path activities and incurring a cost

project evaluation and review technique (PERT) a network technique, designed for project planning and scheduling, that uses probabilistic activity times

pseudorandom numbers random numbers generated by a mathematical process rather than by a physical process

pure strategy game a game in which each player adopts a single strategy as the optimal strategy

q

quantity discount model an inventory model in which a discount is received for large orders

queue a waiting line

queue discipline the order in which customers waiting in line are served

queuing analysis the probabilistic analysis of waiting lines

---

r

random numbers numbers that are equally likely to be drawn from a large population of numbers

random number table a table containing random numbers derived from some artificial process, such as a computer program

random variable a variable that can be assigned numerical values reflecting the outcomes of an event. Since these values occur in no particular order, they are said to be random.

recursive return function the return from stage n of a dynamic programming problem plus the *previous* returns at previous stages

regression a statistical technique for measuring the relationship of one variable to one or more other variables. This method is used extensively in forecasting.

regression equation an equation derived from historical data that is used to forecast

regret a value representing the regret the decision maker suffers when a wrong decision is made

relative frequency probability another name for an objective (a posteriori) probability. It represents the relative frequency with which a specific outcome

has been observed to occur in the long run.

relaxed solution a solution to an integer programming model in which the integer restrictions are relaxed

remote terminal a piece of computer equipment similar to a typewriter that is connected to the computer by telephone lines and can be used to operate a computer from a distance

reorder lead time the time between the placement of an order and its receipt into inventory

reorder point the inventory level at which an order is placed

revised simplex method an alternative version of the standard simplex method frequently used in linear programming computer packages

rim requirements the supply and demand values along the outer row and column of a transportation tableau

risk averter a person who avoids taking risks

risk taker a person who takes risks in the hope of achieving a large return

row operations an algebraic method for solving simultaneous linear equations

---

s

safety stock a buffer of extra inventory used as protection against a stockout (i.e., running out of inventory)

satisfactory solution in a goal programming model, a solution that satisfies the

goals in the best way possible

scatter diagram a diagram used in forecasting that shows historical data points

scientific method a method for solving problems that includes the following steps: (1) observation, (2) problem definition, (3) model construction, (4) model solution, and (5) implementation

search techniques methods for searching through the solutions generated by a simulation model to find the best one

seasonal pattern in a forecast, a movement that occurs periodically and is repetitive

seed value a number selected arbitrarily from a range of numbers to begin a stream of random numbers generated by a computerized random number generator

sensitivity analysis the analysis of changes in the parameters of a linear programming problem

sequential decision tree a decision tree that analyzes a series of sequential decisions

service level the percentage of orders a business is able to fill from inventory in stock during the reorder period

service rate the average number of customers that can be served from a queue in a specified period of time

shadow price the price one would be willing to pay to obtain one more unit of a resource in a linear programming problem

shared slack in a CPM/PERT network, slack that is shared among several adjacent activities

shortest route problem a network problem in which the objective is to determine the shortest distance between an originating point and several destination points

short-range forecast a forecast of the immediate future that is concerned with daily operations

simple regression a form of regression that reflects the relationship of two variables

simplex method a tabular approach to solving linear programming problems

simplex tableau the table in which the steps of the simplex method are conducted. Each tableau represents a solution.

simulated time the representation of real time in a simulation model

simulation the replication of a real system with a mathematical model that can be analyzed with a computer

simulation language a computer programming language developed specifically for performing simulation

single-server waiting line a waiting line that contains only one service facility at which customers can be served

slack variable a variable representing unused resources that is added to a ≤ inequality constraint to make the constraint an equation

slope the rate of change in a linear mathematical function

smoothing constant a weighting factor used in the exponential smoothing forecasting technique

software the mathematical and written codes that instruct a computer how to perform mathematical operations

stagecoach problem a network routing problem in which the shortest route between two places can be determined using dynamic programming or network flow models

stages the smaller subproblems of a dynamic programming problem

standard deviation a measure of dispersion around the mean of a probability distribution

standard form of a linear programming model a maximization model with all ≤ constraints or a minimization model with all ≥ constraints

states of nature in a decision situation, the possible events that may occur in the future

steady state a constant value, achieved by a system after an extended period of time

steady-state probability a constant probability that a system will end up in a particular state after a large number of transition periods

stepping-stone method a method for solving a transportation model

stockout running out of inventory

subjective probability a probability that is based on personal experience, knowledge of a situation, or intuition rather than on a priori or a posteriori evidence

substitution method a method for solving nonlinear programming problems that contain only one equality constraint. The constraint is solved for one variable in terms of another and is substituted into the objective function.

surplus variable a surplus variable that reflects the excess above a minimum resource requirement level. It is subtracted from a ≥ inequality constraint in a linear programming problem.

system a set or arrangement of related items that forms an organic whole

---

†

---

technological forecast a prediction of what types of technology may be available in the future

terminal a video display unit, similar to a television, that is attached to a computer so that users can provide input to the computer and receive output from it

time series methods statistical forecasting techniques that are based solely on historical data accumulated over a period of time

total revenue volume of units produced multiplied by price per unit

transient state   a state in a Markov transition matrix that will never be returned to once the system has moved out of it

transition function   a mathematical relationship that relates the stages of a dynamic programming problem

transition matrix   a matrix containing the transition probabilities for the states of a Markov system

transition probability   a probability that describes the transition from one Markov state to another in one time period

transportation model   a type of linear programming problem in which a product is to be transported from a number of sources to a number of destinations at the minimum cost

transportation tableau   the table in which the solution of a transportation model is determined

trend   a long-term movement of an item being forecast

two-person game   a game in which two decision makers compete

U

unbalanced transportation model   a transportation model in which supply exceeds demand or demand exceeds supply

unbounded problem   a linear programming problem in which there is no completely closed-in feasible solution area and therefore the objective function can increase infinitely

unconstrained optimization model   a model with a single objective function and no constraints

undirected branch   a branch in a network that allows flow in both directions

utiles   the units in which utility is measured

utility   a numerical measure of the satisfaction a person derives from money

utilization factor   the probability that a server in a queuing system will be busy

V

validation   the process of making sure model solution results are correct (valid)

value of the game   the value of one player's gain and another's loss in a game situation

variable   within a model, a mathematical symbol that can take on different values

variable costs   costs that are determined on a per-unit basis

variance   a measure of how much the values in a probability distribution vary from the mean

Venn diagram   a pictorial representation of mutually exclusive or nonmutually exclusive events

Vogel's approximation method (VAM)   a method that uses opportunity costs to determine the initial solution to a transportation model

W

weighted moving average   a time series forecasting method in which the most recent data are weighted

what-if? analysis   a form of interactive decision analysis in which a computer is asked to determine the results of making various changes in a model

Z

zero-one integer model   an integer programming model that can have solution values of only 0 or 1

zero-sum game   a game in which the sum of the players' gains and losses equals zero

Index

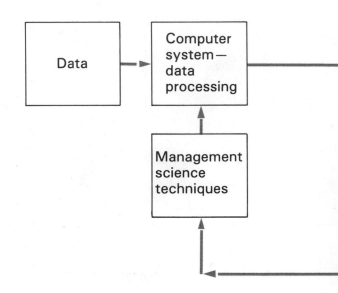